WOODPECKERS

A GUIDE TO THE WOODPECKERS
OF THE WORLD

WOODPECKERS

A GUIDE TO THE WOODPECKERS
OF THE WORLD

HANS WINKLER

DAVID A. CHRISTIE

AND

DAVID NURNEY

Houghton Mifflin Company

Boston New York

1995

Copyright © 1995 by Hans Winkler, David A. Christie, and
David Nurney

Library of Congress Cataloging-in-Publication data is available.

ISBN 0-395-72043-5

Printed in Great Britain
10 9 8 7 6 5 4 3 2 1

CONTENTS

African Piculet	*Sasia africana*	190	**2**
Rufous Piculet	*Sasia abnormis*	191	**2**
White-browed Piculet	*Sasia ochracea*	192	**2**
Antillean Piculet	*Nesoctites micromegas*	193	**8**
White Woodpecker	*Melanerpes candidus*	194	**9**
Lewis's Woodpecker	*Melanerpes lewis*	195	**9**
Guadeloupe Woodpecker	*Melanerpes herminieri*	196	**9**
Puerto Rican Woodpecker	*Melanerpes portoricensis*	197	**9**
Red-headed Woodpecker	*Melanerpes erythrocephalus*	198	**10**
Acorn Woodpecker	*Melanerpes formicivorus*	200	**10**
Black-cheeked Woodpecker	*Melanerpes pucherani*	202	**11**
Golden-naped Woodpecker	*Melanerpes chrysauchen*	203	**11**
Yellow-tufted Woodpecker	*Melanerpes cruentatus*	204	**11**
Yellow-fronted Woodpecker	*Melanerpes flavifrons*	205	**11**
White-fronted Woodpecker	*Melanerpes cactorum*	206	**12**
Hispaniolan Woodpecker	*Melanerpes striatus*	207	**12**
Jamaican Woodpecker	*Melanerpes radiolatus*	208	**12**
Golden-cheeked Woodpecker	*Melanerpes chrysogenys*	209	**12**
Grey-breasted Woodpecker	*Melanerpes hypopolius*	209	**12**
Yucatan Woodpecker	*Melanerpes pygmaeus*	210	**13**
Red-crowned Woodpecker	*Melanerpes rubricapillus*	211	**13**
Gila Woodpecker	*Melanerpes uropygialis*	212	**14**
Red-bellied Woodpecker	*Melanerpes carolinus*	214	**14**
West Indian Woodpecker	*Melanerpes superciliaris*	215	**14**
Golden-fronted Woodpecker	*Melanerpes aurifrons*	216	**15**
Hoffmann's Woodpecker	*Melanerpes hoffmannii*	219	**15**
Yellow-bellied Sapsucker	*Sphyrapicus varius*	220	**16**
Red-naped Sapsucker	*Sphyrapicus nuchalis*	222	**16**
Red-breasted Sapsucker	*Sphyrapicus ruber*	223	**16**
Williamson's Sapsucker	*Sphyrapicus thyroideus*	224	**16**
Cuban Green Woodpecker	*Xiphidiopicus percussus*	225	**16**
Fine-spotted Woodpecker	*Campethera punctuligera*	226	**17**
Nubian Woodpecker	*Campethera nubica*	227	**17**
Bennett's Woodpecker	*Campethera bennettii*	228	**17**
Reichenow's Woodpecker	*Campethera scriptoricauda*	229	**17**
Golden-tailed Woodpecker	*Campethera abingoni*	230	**18**
Mombasa Woodpecker	*Campethera mombassica*	231	**18**
Knysna Woodpecker	*Campethera notata*	232	**18**
Little Green Woodpecker	*Campethera maculosa*	233	**19**
Green-backed Woodpecker	*Campethera cailliautii*	233	**19**
Tullberg's Woodpecker	*Campethera tullbergi*	234	**20**
Buff-spotted Woodpecker	*Campethera nivosa*	235	**20**
Brown-eared Woodpecker	*Campethera caroli*	236	**20**
Ground Woodpecker	*Geocolaptes olivaceus*	237	**17**
Little Grey Woodpecker	*Dendropicos elachus*	238	**21**
Speckle-breasted Woodpecker	*Dendropicos poecilolaemus*	239	**21**
Abyssinian Woodpecker	*Dendropicos abyssinicus*	240	**21**

This work is dedicated to the world's dwindling forests,
and to our wives for their support of our efforts to conserve nature

INTRODUCTION

Woodpeckers, piculets and wrynecks represent a distinct group of birds characterised by a unique combination of various highly derived features. Their peculiar habits and the attractive coloration of many of their species make woodpeckers rather well-known and popular birds. Except in the Australasian region, where they are totally absent, they inhabit virtually all forests and woodlands of the tropics, subtropics and temperate zones. Some species even manage to thrive in savannas, desert scrub and mountain grasslands. The life of most species is based on digging holes in dead or live wood, in which these birds roost and breed, and on gleaning prey from trees, probing into crevices, prying off bark, or excavating for wood-boring insect larvae. Some feed on the sap which oozes from specially excavated holes, rob anthills, store food, or use anvils for pounding large prey items, opening nuts or extracting the seeds from cones. Most of these activities leave traces which can be identified by the observant naturalist, and some may run counter to man's own interests or even constitute a nuisance.

Woodpeckers as a whole have already been treated in keystone monographs. The first of these, written over 130 years ago, was the book by Malherbe (1861); the second the grand monograph by Lester L. Short (1982), who gave an excellent treatment of the group, with an emphasis on taxonomic problems, and with an unprecedented detailed description of the acoustical signals. A guide in Italian by Frugis *et al.* (1988) largely followed Short's treatment of the group. The present book is designed as a comprehensive guide and handbook to this fascinating family of birds. Not only should it enable birdwatchers to identify woodpeckers by coloration and voice, but it also provides scientifically accurate treatments of their habits.

ACKNOWLEDGEMENTS

An endeavour such as this is, as so many authors so frequently state, quite impossible without the direct and indirect help of many others. HW would like to mention all the people at the KLIVV who had to suffer his 'inaccessible demeanour'. Many of them, however, also contributed rather actively to this work. Particularly deserving of mention is Mrs B. Räuschl, who tracked down papers and books in a professional manner and responded to whimsical requests with prompt delivery.

In gathering material for this book, we have not only relied on our own studies and observations but have also been fortunate enough to have received information and assistance from a number of others. Word about our work on this book soon went around, and we received valuable contributions from many ornithologists. We are very grateful to the following individuals and institutions for their willingness to provide additional information and help.

P. Salaman provided us with his exciting findings on Colombian woodpeckers, the enthusiastic members of the Cambridge-based students project 'Canopy '92' on Paraguayan birds informed us about their observations, and so on. A. Gamauf and her colleagues contributed important field notes which were collected in the Philippines on a research project on raptors led by HW and supported by the Austrian Fonds zur Förderung der Wissenschaftlichen Forschung. H. Hoi informed us about the role of Great Spotted Woodpeckers as predators of Penduline Tit nests. Dr Pascal Villard helped to clarify issues of the ecology of some North American woodpeckers. J. Lowen and R.P. Clay provided valuable information on woodpeckers of Paraguay, particularly the Helmeted Woodpecker. E. H. Miller contributed greatly by making available his data on *Sphyrapicus nuchalis*. Some new information from Lou Jost and Paul Coopmans on *Celeus spectabilis* was kindly forwarded to us by Nigel Redman. First-hand data on Cuban Green Woodpecker and tape recordings of the Cuban species were very kindly given to us by A.D. Mitchell, I.S. Williams and T. Dolan, whose field research in that country is continuing and merits support. Tim and Carol Inskipp willingly provided extremely valuable information on the distribution of woodpeckers in India, in the form of preliminary maps from their forthcoming book on the birds of that subcontinent; we thank them warmly.

Birdlife International (formerly ICBP), in particular David Wege and Mike Crosby, kindly provided much useful (and up-to-date) information on several species, including especially those whose populations are little known, threatened or endangered, and made available advance proofs of the most recent list of threatened species (Collar *et al.* 1994, *Birds to Watch 2: the world list of threatened birds*). The important work done by Birdlife International is greatly appreciated and deserves full support.

Craig Robson devoted much time to reading the accounts of the South-east Asian species and made extensive comments, based on first-hand information, which significantly improved these texts; he also supplied us with very useful additional tape recordings of vocalisations/drumming of a number of South-east Asian species.

We thank Steve Howell and Sophie Webb for allowing us to refer to page proofs of their new treatise *The Birds of Mexico*, and also the publishers (Oxford University Press) for agreeing to forward the relevant pages to us. Hadoram Shirihai kindly allowed a sight of the woodpecker texts from his forthcoming *The Birds of Israel*, and Jochen Martens did the same for his forthcoming work on Himalayan birds.

Great support came from the Natural History Museum at Tring, England, on whose collection most of the paintings are based. HW also would like to acknowledge the help of the staff at the American Museum of Natural History, New York, and of the Naturhistorisches Museum in Vienna.

For much help with the literature and providing copies of reference material, DC is very grateful to Linda Birch of the Alexander Library at the EGI, University of Oxford, and to Ian Dawson, Librarian at the Royal Society for the Protection of Birds (RSPB).

DC wishes also to thank the following for their kindness: Bill Cole, for his assistance in the field and his superb driving in Thailand; Mike ('Canadian Mike'), for his help, guidance and hospitality in Thailand (sadly, Mike died suddenly in his sleep in 1993); also in Thailand, Ipol (of the Karen tribe) for helpful discussion and guidance, and for his genuine friendship; and Clive Pinder, for providing useful preliminary information and literature during preparations for travelling to South-east Asia. DC also thanks Dr J.T.R. Sharrock, Managing Editor of *British Birds* magazine, for demonstrating patience and understanding when final stages of work on woodpeckers meant that several other jobs had to be put off for a while!

For their help in various ways, DN also extends his gratitude to: Peter Colston (Natural History Museum, Tring), Ian Lewington, Tika Ram Giri, Roy and Moira Hargreaves, Forget-me-not Art Supplies, Martin Williams, Paul Holt, Tim Loseby, Vireo, David Cottridge.

We are all very grateful to Nigel Redman, for his encouragement and very helpful suggestions on many aspects, and for editing the final text; to Christopher Helm of Pica Press, for demonstrating much patience and understanding, as well as his belief in the entire project; and to Marc Dando and Julie Reynolds (Fluke Art), who skilfully dealt with the technical sides of production and offered their expert and most helpful advice.

It should not be forgotten that a work such as this one is also born from the years of help, discussion and encouragement of many other people. HW wishes particularly to mention L. L. Short, whose exceptional effort in the study of woodpeckers resulted in a great many papers and in a milestone book, a superb monograph on the Picidae, which has served as an indispensable base reference and source of inspiration, and is a model of accurate research in field and museum; his interest in HW's work and his friendship and support should be duly acknowledged. Financial support of much of HW's work on woodpeckers came from the Frank M. Chapman Fund of The American Museum of Natural History.

But the most important personal support for HW came from his wife Christiane. She helped with patience and encouragement, and proved twofold that there are other things to produce in life, besides bird books. Similarly, DC's wife Carmelia put up with a lot of strange behaviour from her husband, whose admiration for her tolerance (and her skills in the field) reached new heights. DN also owes a great debt to his wife Jackie for her constant support and encouragement throughout.

STYLE AND LAYOUT OF THE BOOK

The content of this book is broadly similar to that of other works on specific groups of birds. There is as much emphasis on identification as on accounts of general biology and ecology of the species. Many species inhabiting the tropical regions are poorly known and hence the coverage of general aspects of ecology, behaviour and reproduction varies greatly from species to species. Some species have been extremely well studied in recent years and the literature on these alone comprises a great number of scientific papers, notes and reports. To deal with the large amount of literature, we have tried to refer to regional guides, handbooks, monographs and some key papers wherever possible.

Before dealing with the species individually, we give an overview of the biology of woodpeckers, with an emphasis on the particular, highly specialised features of this group. Space does not allow for a detailed treatment at the technical level, but the interested reader will find plenty of references to the scientific literature to broaden his or her knowledge.

The greater part of the book is taken up by the plates and species accounts. The taxonomy we have followed is largely the one given by Sibley & Monroe (1990). While we recognise that Sibley & Monroe's treatment is by no means universally accepted, it is worth pointing out that, where the woodpeckers are concerned, it does not raise too many controversial questions. At this point, however, the reader is referred to the section below on taxonomy, in which we present a more detailed and critical overview of taxonomic problems.

SPECIES NUMBERS

Each species of woodpecker in this book has been given a number. It should be emphasised that these numbers have no taxonomic significance. They are used simply as a convenient means of reference, enabling the reader to turn quickly to a species whenever it is referred to within the text of another species, as, for example, when comparisons are made of appearance, voice, behaviour and so on. In addition, it also facilitates the labelling of the plates and their captions.

PLATES

The plates show not only the nominate form but in many cases other races as well. Some of the geographical differences are less pronounced than differences between adult and immature plumages. We would, of course, have liked to depict both of the latter, but this would have increased the number of plates considerably. Immature plumages are in most cases easy to describe and are worn during a relatively short period. Only in cases where juvenile plumage is very distinct is it shown on a plate. Woodpeckers do, on the other hand, represent a remarkable example of geographical variation, and provide an opportunity for this aspect of biodiversity, namely the diversity within species, to be beautifully demonstrated. To the birder and the conservationist alike, it should thus be made clear that our efforts to preserve the diversity of life on our planet must not stop at species boundaries. The plates may therefore be seen as a contribution towards enhancing awareness of this aspect of biology. The plates are arranged largely in taxonomic sequence. In some cases we have departed from a purely taxonomic arrangement in order to show similar forms together and, in a few instances, to group together those species which are likely to be encountered in the same region.

The captions opposite the plates give, for each species, a short summary of the range and habitat, list some diagnostic features, and in addition contain hints for the identification of juveniles. They also indicate the page on which each species account and map may be found.

SPECIES ACCOUNTS

In the species accounts we give information on field identification and present detailed descriptions of the appearance of all the species, and also treat their geographical variation. In other sections we emphasise ecology and related behaviour and particular aspects of reproduction.

Identification

Here we present the key features for field identification, including mean length of the bird as a rough indication of its size, and refer to similar species when necessary. When identifying woodpeckers, exact head markings are diagnostic for most species, but these are often difficult to see properly, and the shape/extent of bars and other markings on the head can depend on the bird's posture. It is not always easy to see the underpart colour/markings on a woodpecker, especially when it is clinging to a tree, while the plumage of head, breast and sometimes the entire underparts can be stained/sullied by contact with trunk, branches and vegetation (e.g. ground material in ground-feeding woodpeckers). The pattern of markings can also change with wear and appear different (e.g. bars/spots can disappear and bright ground colours can become much duller or even appear to change colour, e.g. red can become brown). In addition, effects of light can cause red on back and wings to appear yellow or olive (see flamebacks). All this needs to be taken into account when identifying a woodpecker, and it should also be remembered that almost all species (even monotypic ones) exhibit great individual variation.

Distribution

A general outline of the geographical range of the species is given, with an indication of its status where this is known (or meaningful). The accompanying maps are intended to give a condensed overview of each species' distribution. They have been compiled from various sources and are inevitably of somewhat limited accuracy, especially for those species which are only poorly known; they should, nevertheless, be seen as a good guide to where a species may be found. We have used equal-area projections which display latitudes as parallels to aid in the understanding of zoogeographic relations. Only a few species show significant seasonal movements: in such cases, breeding quarters are shown as a dark tint, and areas which are visited in the non-breeding season only are in a paler tint; a solid tone indicates all the remaining areas in which breeding and non-breeding ranges overlap. Thus, the ranges of resident species are depicted solely by a solid tone.

Movements

Movements are treated where appropriate, and in this section information on wintering grounds and seasonal aspects of migration is given.

Habitat

Since habitat is a very important aspect for field identification and also for appreciating details of distribution, we treat it in detail in a prominent place in the text.

Description

In the description, a detailed treatment of the plumage and the bare parts is presented, which is sufficient to identify a woodpecker in the hand and which also serves to provide additional information for use in the field. In polymorphic species, that is species with clear geographical variation, this description refers to one particular subspecies. In this section, particulars on sexual differences and on juvenile plumage are also mentioned. Note that woodpeckers with 'barred' wings more often than not have, in fact, large spots/half-bars on one or both webs of the remiges (separated by unmarked shaft area), so that 'bars' are actually rows of spots. In worn plumage (end of breeding season), brighter colours usually become duller as different-coloured feather bases become more visible, and certain markings (streaks etc.) sometimes become more sharply defined.

Geographical variation

Geographical variation in woodpeckers is often well pronounced and therefore merits special consideration. In the recognition of subspecies we largely follow Short (1982). In the main, deviations from the form described in full are pointed out, together with differences among subspecies. The geographical range of each subspecies is briefly summarised. (It is important to realise that not only species but also subspecies vary individually, in some instances quite markedly; the delimitations of such taxa are therefore extraordinarily difficult to define, and intermediates are very common.)

Measurements

Generally given as approximate ranges in millimetres. Usually, the subspecies to which measurements refer are indicated. Most are taken from the literature, and they should be seen as an initial guide and as basic data on proportions, and for comparisons among species and subspecies. The wing length is the flattened wing chord; tail length is from the base of the central feathers to the tip of the tail; the bill length is given as the length of the exposed culmen to the tip of the bill, unless stated otherwise (in this measurement authors often do not state the method they used clearly, and some caution is needed when making species comparisons); finally, the tarsus is given as the distance between the joint at the proximal end of the tarsus to the joint of the middle toe. Weights are in grams, and are also from various sources, most of the data being taken from Dunning (1992) and Short (1982).

Voice

Woodpeckers often have very distinct vocalisations and instrumental signals. We give condensed summaries of the calls as they have been described in the literature, and from our own field notes and those of other observers. Emphasis is put on field identification where possible. Written transcriptions of one and the same call often differ greatly among observers, sometimes so much so that it is impossible to be sure whether they refer to one call or to two different calls; caution is therefore advised in interpreting the descriptions. We have not included sonagrams or exact time and frequency measurements; the interested reader is referred to the many papers by Short, the account on *Picoides* by Winkler & Short (1978), and the monograph by Short (1982).

Habits

In the section on habits, we begin with those aspects of a woodpecker that an observer is most likely to note when encountering a species for the first time. These are sociability (i.e. whether it lives in pairs or in groups), including its inclination to join mixed-species flocks, how bold or shy a species is, and how conspicuous its overall attitude and coloration may appear to the observer. We then proceed with information on habitat use, foraging techniques, and the way in which the bird moves. Displays are also mentioned (for most woodpecker species displays are rather similar, and the reader should consult the section below on general biology), followed by territorial behaviour and interspecific relations. In social species, part of the social behaviour is treated also in the section on habits (however, since social behaviour is closely interwoven with reproduction many further details are given under *Breeding*).

Food

This section briefly outlines the major foods taken. The diet of a number of species is rather poorly known, or is known only very broadly (e.g. 'ants'), and this aspect is, as many others, deserving of further study.

Breeding

Courtship activities of woodpeckers may commence well before the nesting season proper. We have tried to refer to the breeding season (as the time in which nests can be found) as well as information available has allowed. Description of nest sites complements or adds to the information given in the habitat description and the description of habitat use. Very brief summaries of the breeding cycle, including clutch size and the role of the sexes, should provide a first insight into the reproductive biology of a species.

References

References point to the sources used for compiling the account for a species and should assist the reader in finding other relevant literature. To avoid redundancy, books with a wide scope, particularly Short's (1982) monumental work, are not cited. The references are given in full at the end of this book, but it should be noted that they certainly do not together represent a complete bibliography of books and papers on woodpeckers. One has to bear in mind that, even on species which have not been that well studied, many papers have been published; for instance, a recent bibliography of the White-backed Woodpecker alone contains about 200 entries. Nevertheless, the references provided should enable anybody to gain an appreciation of the literature for any one aspect of woodpecker biology.

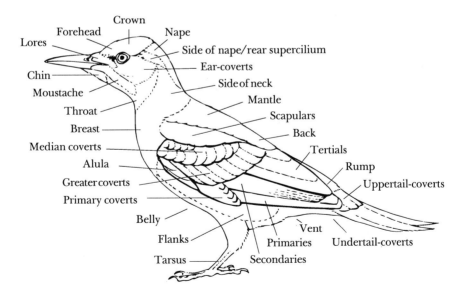

Topography of a typical woodpecker.

RELATIONSHIPS AND TAXONOMY

With the possible exception of the wrynecks, woodpeckers as a whole, including the tiny piculets, are easily recognisable as such. Their features are, in their particular combination, so unique among birds (Diamond 1990) that there seems to be no doubt that woodpeckers as we know them form one well-defined group.

Taxonomists have traditionally placed the wrynecks, the piculets and the true woodpeckers in one family, the Picidae. This family belongs to the order of woodpecker relatives known as the Piciformes, in which various other distinct families are united. There is, however, some debate over whether this order really is as uniform as it has long been considered. Before touching upon these matters briefly, let us look at the other birds which are the supposed relatives of the woodpeckers. These are the jacamars (Galbulidae), the puffbirds (Bucconidae), the honeyguides (Indicatoridae), the barbets (Capitonidae) and the toucans (Ramphastidae). These families are grouped together on account of certain characteristics of the deep plantar tendons of the feet (which are arranged such that one only moves toe 3, whereas the other toes are bent by a common tendon), and by other features of the breast bone, the palate and various others. European ornithologists, among them E. Stresemann, emphasised that the jacamars and puffbirds should be separated as a suborder, which is supported by analyses of hindlimb musculature (Swierczewski & Raikow 1981) and skeletal characters (Simpson & Cracraft 1981) respectively.

Recent data using analyses of DNA, the carrier of genetic information, conform with this latter view, but altogether suggest a slightly different classification. By 'hybridising' the genetic material of species in pairwise comparisons, relative 'distances' can be obtained. Sibley & Ahlquist proposed a new arrangement and based their classification on these data. Certainly, with the new and much more efficient and reliable methods which use the sequences of the basic components of particular genes, this classification will change again. At any rate, to understand the implications of the new arrangement, one has to know that the first two families (jacamars and puffbirds) are restricted to the Neotropics, that the parasitic honeyguides are found in Africa and southern Asia and that the barbets inhabit the tropics of Asia, Africa and the Americas, whereas the toucans are strictly neotropical. What the new data now suggest is that the barbets of America are more closely related to the toucans than to the barbets of the Old World. Unfortunately, the New World barbets are not well known, so it is hard to tell whether these biochemical similarities correlate with morphology and behaviour as well.

This case demonstrates, among other things, the difficulty of any classification. We classify objects and organisms into categories to reduce and to grasp the incredible diversity around us. The practical purpose of such a classification is to capitalise on similarities, shared properties and correlations among features of the objects and organisms. Knowing that an object is a car, we can be rather confident that it will have a steering wheel and so forth, without having seen or driven that particular type and make of car. Put in very simple terms, many modern systematists believe that taxonomy should directly (and only) reflect the lineage of organisms. Others maintain that shared ancestry is but one of the relationships among organisms which should be mapped in the categories of systematics. In other words, some would like to emphasise the similarity among all 'barbets', while others, and theirs seems to be the prevalent view today, would like to recognise more that toucans and New World Barbets share common ancestors.

The pendulum between these views has swung back and forth ever since scientists have attempted to classify organisms. The problem stems from the fact that organisms are adapted to their environment and often come up with very similar solutions in different lineages. There are other bark-foraging birds which show great similarities to woodpeckers in some or many of their features. For instance, the creepers (Certhiidae) use virtually the same climbing technique as the woodpeckers. But there are also woodcreepers, nuthatches and many more which resemble woodpeckers in one way or another.

The assemblage of four (traditional) families (Indicatoridae, Picidae, Capitonidae, Ramphastidae) forms the Pici in the strict sense (Olson 1983; Short 1982). Among the Picidae, there are the true woodpeckers (Picinae) together with the wrynecks (Jynginae) and the piculets (Picumninae). The fossil record is scant and does not help to elucidate the phylogenetic relationships of the extant species (Olson 1985).

Sibley *et al.* (1988) put the woodpeckers in the following taxonomic and phylogenetic context:

Parvclass Picae
  Order Piciformes
      Infraorder Picides
                Family Indicatoridae, honeyguides
                Family Picidae, wrynecks and woodpeckers
      Infraorder Ramphastides
            Superfamily Megalaimoidea

Family Megalaimidae, Asian barbets
Superfamily Lybioidea
Family Lybiidae, African barbets
Superfamily Ramphastoidea
Family Ramphastidae
Subfamily Capitoninae, New World barbets
Subfamily Ramphastinae, toucans

This assemblage of birds is related to the Galbuliformes, which now contain the jacamars and puffbirds, and to the Bucerotiformes, the hornbills and ground-hornbills. Furthermore, Upupiformes, the hoopoes and woodhoopoes, Trogoniformes, the trogons, and finally the Coraciiformes, ancient perching birds comprising nine families, among them three families of kingfishers, the motmots, todies and three families of 'rollers', also count among the distant relatives. These birds share many characteristics with woodpeckers. All coraciiform birds, for instance, are hole-nesters, have unmarked white eggs, and their young hatch naked and blind.

The 'inner structure' of the family Picidae has remained largely untouched by Sibley and his co-workers. The last major revision of the family was undertaken by Short (1982). Generally, woodpeckers are adapted to cling to vertical substrates and to move easily over them. They possess a mostly hard, more or less straight bill and a highly specialised tongue. The skull also has many derived features. The legs are short and the toes exhibit a special arrangement, which will be discussed below together with the other characters. The outer primary is greatly reduced. The tail feathers, with the exception of the outermost ones, are used as a prop in the true woodpeckers, but not in the tiny piculets. Besides these structural characters, woodpeckers are distinct in their habit of nesting in holes and, in most cases, producing holes, also by their foraging habits and instrumental signals. The incubation period is short and the young hatch naked and blind.

Short arranged the subfamilies, tribes and genera of the Picidae in the following way:

PICIDAE	JYNGINAE	Jyngini	*Jynx*
	PICUMNINAE	Picumnini	*Picumnus*
			Sasia
		Nesoctitini	*Nesoctites*
	PICINAE	Melanerpini	*Melanerpes*
			Sphyrapicus
			Xiphidiopicus
		Campetherini	*Campethera*
			Geocolaptes
			Dendropicos
			Picoides
		Colaptini	*Veniliornis*
			Piculus
			Colaptes
			Celeus
		Campephilini	*Dryocopus*
			Campephilus
		Picini	*Picus*
			Dinopium
			Chrysocolaptes
			Gecinulus
			Sapheopipo
			Blythipicus
			Reinwardtipicus
		Meiglyptini	*Meiglyptes*
			Hemicircus
			Mulleripicus

7

Previous attempts to classify woodpeckers were largely based on museum material and on anatomical data, and authors tried various characters to classify woodpeckers. In practically all anatomical investigations the material was limited. Large genera were represented by only a few species, and therefore variation within and between taxa could not be properly evaluated. So, convergent evolution of certain traits which, for instance, represent adaptations for ground feeding is still not fully understood, and the taxonomic value of the respective characters needs careful study. Whether a woodpecker tends to use pecking and hammering as foraging modes, rather than probing and gleaning, affects not only those structures obviously related to these behaviours, but also many others. Woodpeckers and piculets, for example, exhibit a significant broadening of the first thoracic rib where the ventral and dorsal portions join. Other ribs are modified as well. Woodpeckers which peck frequently have wider first sternal ribs than other species (Kirby 1980).

Anatomists rather early on (see Burt 1930 for more details and references) divided the woodpeckers into two groups according to whether or not a certain muscle was present, and the same grouping is apparent with relation to the structure of the skull. These characters were thought to be of taxonomic value at the subfamily level. Accordingly, genera such as *Picoides* (in the sense used in this book) and *Sphyrapicus* would be grouped together on the one hand, and *Melanerpes* and *Colaptes* on the other. Goodge (1972) concludes from his anatomical studies that *Dryocopus* and *Mulleripicus* are not directly related to the ivory-bills, *Campephilus*, but that they derive from ground woodpeckers. In his view, the limits of the ground woodpeckers are represented by closely related *Colaptes* and *Picus*. He also concludes that *Dendropicos* and *Picoides* are closely related and that *Sphyrapicus* is related to *Melanerpes*.

Many other detailed studies have contributed to the evidence used by Short to design his taxonomy of the woodpeckers, which is broadly documented in his 1982 book. One feature of this system is that Short acted as a 'lumper'. Lumping has the advantage that one is more likely to end up with clearly discernible groups. The arguments against such a practice are scientific and psychological. Lumping does obscure phylogenetic branching even more than traditional taxonomy does. To many who are not familiar with the whole group in question, lumping seems to combine forms which may in one geographical area look rather distinct: for instance, for the North American birder the former genera *Melanerpes* and *Centurus* look rather distinct, the first appearing boldly patterned and the others with ladder backs and less conspicuous. The difficulty arises when one has to draw the line between these two groups considering all the extant forms. Try it yourself by leafing through plates 9-15! Many feel uneasy about the fact that the former genus *Dendrocopos* has been 'moved to' *Picoides*, which before that contained only two species, namely the Three-toed and the Black-backed Woodpeckers. Of course, the opposite is true: the latter species were moved to *Dendrocopos* because the loss of one toe is judged to be of minor significance, and because there are indisputable close connections with the Hairy Woodpecker and its allies. By the strict laws of nomenclatural priority, the former genus *Dendrocopos* had to change its name, hence the aforementioned objections arose. *Picoides*, as it stands now, is one of the largest bird genera and attempts have been made to split it up into smaller units. Ouellet (1977), for instance, proposed separating all American species as *Picoides* and the rest as *Dendrocopos*. The problem here, as in other cases, comes with drawing the line. Clearly, the American species form a closely knit group which probably is also monophyletic, but, if they are split off, other species complexes within the genus have to be similarly recognised, giving rise to many obvious problems. Ouellet also separates *Picoides obsoletus* as *Dendropicos obsoletus*. Again, there are good reasons, for instance the coloration of the shafts, for retaining this species in *Picoides*. Sibley & Monroe (1990) follow largely the classification proposed by Short, but split his *Picoides* in the way suggested by Ouellet.

We follow Sibley & Monroe's arrangement, with the only exception that we retain *Picoides sensu* Short. Their system is certainly not perfect and it contains many inconsistencies. One such obvious inconsistency is that many forms are now treated as species, for instance in the genus *Piculus*, which are barely separable from the most closely related forms, while, on the other hand, the species *Chrysocolaptes lucidus* comprises many very distinct forms some of which may be shown by future research to be full species.

Both sources frequently use the concept of superspecies, the names of which are indicated in square brackets between genus and species names. Sibley & Monroe deviate from Short (1982) in the following cases.

The Orinoco Piculet *Picumnus [lafresnayi] pumilus* was considered by Short as a subspecies of Lafresnaye's Piculet *Picumnus lafresnayi*; data which suggest sympatry of these forms in Colombia (Hilty & Brown 1984) are the basis for separating the Orinoco Piculet.

The White-barred Piculet, *Picumnus cirratus*, is now split into three species, White-barred Piculet *Picumnus [cirratus] cirratus*, Ocellated Piculet *Picumnus [cirratus] dorbygnianus* (misspelt *dorbygianus* by Sibley & Monroe), and Ochre-collared Piculet *Picumnus [cirratus] temminckii*. *P. cirratus* and *P. temminckii* are known to hybridise. The whole systematics of the piculets will remain a problem for quite a while until more information on ecology and behaviour has been collected (the difficulties of studying piculets in the field are well known). As Short stated, all these forms together may turn out to be one single species in which *P. albosquamatus*, *P. pygmaeus* and *P. varzeae* are included as well.

The superspecies *Melanerpes [cruentatus]* is divided by Sibley & Monroe into *M. [pucherani]*, which includes the Black-cheeked Woodpecker *M. pucherani* and the Golden-naped Woodpecker *M. chrysauchen*, and *M. [cruentatus]*, combining the Yellow-tufted Woodpecker *M. cruentatus* and the Yellow-fronted Woodpecker *M. flavifrons*. They remark that these species-pairs are more closely related within themselves than each is to the other pair, without giving details for this statement.

The Yucatan Woodpecker *Melanerpes [rubricapillus] pygmaeus* is considered a subspecies of *M. rubricapillus* by Short on the grounds that the face pattern is rather variable in this group and should not, therefore, be recognised as a valid character for defining species limits in view of the close similarities shown by these forms.

Short recognised a large superspecies *Melanerpes [carolinus]* in which he placed the Gila Woodpecker *M. uropygialis*, retained by Sibley & Monroe as a full species outside this superspecies. Sibley & Monroe leave only the Red-bellied Woodpecker *M. carolinus* and the West Indian Woodpecker *M. superciliaris* in this superspecies. The Golden-fronted Woodpecker *M. aurifrons* and Hoffmann's Woodpecker *M. hoffmannii* are now placed in *M. [aurifrons]* and not in *M. [carolinus]*.

Reichenow's Woodpecker *Campethera [nubica] scriptoricauda* was considered a subspecies of *C. [nubica] bennettii* by Short (1982, 1988) because there are no distinct features, including voice, which would justify separation. The very distinct Mombasa Woodpecker *Campethera [notata] mombassica* is now considered a full species (see also Short 1988, 1990), but has formerly been placed in *C. abingoni*.

Sibley & Monroe rank the former Gaboon Woodpecker, *Dendropicos gabonensis*, as a superspecies comprising *D. [gabonensis] gabonensis* and the Melancholy Woodpecker *D. [gabonensis] lugubris*, but Short (1982, 1988) keeps both forms united because they seem to intergrade through the rather stable intermediate subspecies *D. g. reichenowi*.

There is some discussion in the literature on the separation of the Grey-headed Woodpecker *Dendropicos [goertae] spodocephalus* from the Grey Woodpecker *Dendropicos [goertae] goertae*. Short (1982) had both forms united, whereas Sibley & Monroe followed Prigogine & Louette (1983) in separating them. Short (1988) dismissed their arguments for this split and retains the Grey-headed Woodpecker in *D. [goertae] goertae*.

Short (1982, 1988) gives many good reasons why he considers the African Brown-backed Woodpecker *Picoides obsoletus* to be a relative of the Asian *Picoides moluccensis* group of woodpeckers, rather than of the *Dendropicos*. He stresses that the brown and black colours of this species are frequently found in *Picoides*, but not in *Dendropicos* group. Species of the latter genus are commonly characterised by having yellow shafts, while the Brown-backed Woodpecker lacks all yellow in its plumage. We follow Short's judgement, but leave this species in the sequence presented by Sibley & Monroe.

The systematics of the small Asian *Picoides* forms seem traditionally to be highly confused, and it is sometimes very hard to discover to which species earlier authors had been referring in their reports. The reason for this is that *nanus* and its synonymous designations (e.g. *hardwickii*) were either kept as separate species, or alternatively included in *moluccensis* or in *canicapillus*, respectively. Greenway (1943) clarified many issues, as did Voous (1947), who tentatively kept *nanus* separate. In our opinion, the best treatment of this group, so far, is that by Short (1982). Sibley & Monroe based their separation of *Picoides nanus*, the Brown-capped Woodpecker, from *P. moluccensis*, the Sunda Woodpecker, on the information given in Short (1982). Since this is rather poor evidence, we do not follow them and prefer instead to treat *nanus* as a subspecies of *moluccensis*, as did Short.

The Grey-capped Woodpecker *Picoides canicapillus* and the Pygmy Woodpecker *P. kizuki* were considered by Short to form a superspecies, *P. [kizuki]*.

Sibley & Monroe placed *Picoides lignarius*, Striped Woodpecker, and *Picoides mixtus*, Checkered Woodpecker, in the superspecies *[lignarius]*, presumably because of name priority, whereas Short named the same superspecies *[mixtus]*.

Short (1971b, 1982) considered *Picoides borealis* a member of the *scalaris-nuttallii-pubescens* complex. Voice and ecology (dependence on pines) suggest to us (see also Jackson 1994) closer relationships with *villosus-stricklandi-albolarvatus* .

The Choco Woodpecker *Veniliornis [affinis] chocoensis* has been given the status of an allospecies by Sibley & Monroe, following some not clearly specified information given to them by R. Ridgely. They concede that this form may represent a subspecies either of the Golden-collared Woodpecker *V. [affinis] cassini* or of the Red-stained Woodpecker *V. [affinis] affinis*; Short (see particularly Short 1974b) treats it as a subspecies of the latter.

Woodpeckers of the genus *Piculus* also pose many taxonomic problems which have not been sorted out comprehensively. As the recent discovery of a new form in Colombia shows, there is still a lack of basic information in many cases, not to mention an ignorance of important details of ecology and behaviour. Short included the White-throated Woodpecker *Piculus [leucolaemus] leucolaemus*, the Stripe-cheeked

Woodpecker *P. [leucolaemus] callopterus*, the Rufous-winged Woodpecker *P. [leucolaemus] simplex* and the Lita Woodpecker *P. [leucolaemus] litae* in one single species, *P. leucolaemus*. Meanwhile, there is good evidence for separating *simplex* and *callopterus*, but whether the Lita Woodpecker can be retained as a full species remains doubtful until more is known about these woodpeckers. The *Piculus rubiginosus* complex also requires more study; in particular, its vocalisations and displays need more extensive documentation, with special emphasis on variation within and among subspecies.

Sibley & Monroe maintain the Gilded Flicker *Colaptes [auratus] chrysoides* as a species, while Short lumped it with the other forms of the polytypic Northern Flicker *C. auratus*.

The Andaman Woodpecker *Dryocopus [javensis] hodgei*, formerly treated as a subspecies of the widespread White-bellied Woodpecker *Dryocopus javensis*, has been separated from the latter by Sibley & Monroe as an allospecies on no specified grounds. Long isolation of this form may justify this, and the calls are very distinct and different from those of the mainland form (B. King, pers. comm.). Whether this and the differences in coloration alone are sufficient to separate the Andaman Woodpecker from its highly variable ally requires careful analysis.

The specific name of *Picus miniaceus*, Banded Woodpecker, is spelt '*mineaceus*' in Sibley & Monroe. The little-known Streak-breasted Woodpecker *Picus [vittatus] viridanus* and the Laced Woodpecker *P. [vittatus] vittatus* were treated as a single species by Short. Sibley & Monroe, however, stress that the two forms meet without intergradation, although this may be open to question.

The Pale-headed Woodpecker *Gecinulus [grantia] grantia* and the Bamboo Woodpecker *Gecinulus [grantia] viridis* were both placed in a single species, *G. grantia* by Short. Since there seem to be no signs of intergradation where these two forms meet, Sibley & Monroe regard them as allospecies.

SUBFAMILIES, TRIBES AND GENERA

In the following, we discuss briefly the tribes and genera of woodpeckers as recognised by Short (1982).

Jynginae

There is only a single genus, *Jynx*, with 2 species, in this subfamily, which probably represents an old lineage of woodpecker-type birds, without being ancestral to the true woodpecker; instead, they must have evolved separately. Both species are cryptically coloured, with brown, grey and black predominating. The sexes are alike. The feathers are soft, including the tail feathers, which are long and rounded. Nostrils open and only partly covered by feathering. Bill short, slightly curved and pointed. Tongue slightly pointed at the tip, which otherwise is smooth and without any barbs. These birds have a rather passerine method of locomotion and perching, with a zygodactyl, four-toed perching foot. They breed in natural cavities and old woodpecker holes, but do not excavate their own nests.

Picumninae

Tiny woodpeckers with short and slightly pointed tail feathers, which are not, however, used as a prop. The plumage is soft, and brown colours with black markings predominate. Sexual differences relate to the forehead/crown, which is more or less densely spotted and streaked with orange or red in males and with white in most females. Nostrils covered by feathers. Bill pointed, slightly curved on the culmen and laterally compressed. Tongue long, with rounded tip and fine bristles. Habits rather woodpecker-like, except that the tail is not used as a brace. These tiny birds excavate their own holes, and at least some species use drumming as a means of communication.

Tribe Picumnini: Two genera. The 26 species of the larger genus, *Picumnus*, exhibit three white tail stripes, a central one and two lateral ones which converge towards the tip of the tail. Feet with four toes and zygodactyl. One species occurs in South Asia, all the other species being neotropical. The 3 species of the genus *Sasia* are distinguished by a bare area around the eye, lack of white tail stripes, very round cross-section of the upper mandible, and by zygodactyl feet with a greatly reduced (*africana*) or absent first toe. Two Asian and one African species.

Tribe Nesoctitini: One genus, *Nesoctites*, with a single, relatively large species, which is restricted to the West Indies. Bill long, slightly curved and pointed. Behaviour reminiscent more of a barbet than of a woodpecker.

Picinae

The true woodpeckers. Tail feathers strong and, apart from the outer ones, pointed and with stiff barbs; central tail feathers with especially strong shafts and vanes, which in arboreal species are clearly curved forwards at the tip. Bill usually straight, with pointed or chisel-like tip. Nostrils covered with feathers. Tongue long, with barbed tip, latter showing great diversity among species. Breed in holes which are excavated in wood; some species dig holes into the ground. Total of 182 species in 23 genera: most diverse in Asia and South America, widespread in the Holarctic region, and represented in Africa by rather small species only.

Tribe Melanerpini: This tribe comprises 3 genera restricted to the New World, with the largest of these, *Melanerpes*, containing 22 species. Most species boldly patterned in black and white with red and yellow. Sexual differences well marked to absent, some species also showing significant mensural and ecological sexual differences. Bill long, usually pointed and slightly to strongly curved. Most species fly well, and many are island endemics. Many are partial to fruits, nuts, and sapsucking. Most species conspicuous and very active vocally. The genus *Melanerpes* contains many highly social species, of which, however, only one, the Acorn Woodpecker, has been studied to any great extent. The 4 species of North American sapsuckers, *Sphyrapicus*, are also placed within this tribe because of many anatomical, behavioural and ecological similarities. They show similar principles in colour patterns as the preceding genus, and the juvenile plumage may also be distinct. Sexual dimorphism well expressed or absent. All species more or less migratory. Sapsucking habits well developed. Cuba and its nearby islands are the confines of the genus *Xiphidiopicus*, with one peculiar green species which exhibits general melanerpine characteristics.

Tribe Campetherini: This is a well-defined group of very small to medium-sized woodpeckers with a usually straight bill with pointed or chisel-like tip. Feet show the typical arrangement of arboreal woodpeckers, with mostly four toes (but reduced to three in two species). This group contains 4 genera totalling 60 species, which occur in Asia, Europe, Africa and the Americas. The African genus *Campethera* contains 12 species, which show a greenish coloration of the back and are also characterised by yellow shafts of the flight feathers. Sexual differences in coloration involve moustachial (malar) stripes and/or crown colour. In some species males possess red malar stripes; the crown of the males is red with more or less black streaking. Females lack red moustache, which instead is black (or greenish-black) or spotted black and white; crown with less or no red, often with white spots. Features related to arboreal feeding are moderately expressed: the bill is curved, mostly pointed or with only slightly developed chisel-tip; the hallux, the first toe, is rather short. One species nests in the nests of social insects. Also wholly African are the 14 species of the genus *Dendropicos*, which also often show some greenish coloration and in which most species possess yellow in the shafts of the flight feathers. Some species have yellow to gold, or red, rump or abdomen. Moustache, if present, not red in males. Males with red in crown or nape; no red in females, and only one species shows white spots in the frontal region. Rather arboreal, with strong claws, slightly or moderately curved bill, and short first toe. Another purely African genus, *Geocolaptes*, contains just one species showing many features related to ground foraging; tail feathers moderately stiff, bill long and curved. Colours are dull, flight feathers with yellow shafts. Most closely related to *Campethera*. Entirely terrestrial in its habits, and social. Closely related to *Dendropicos*, the 33 species of pied woodpeckers, *Picoides*, are mainly spread over Eurasia and the Americas. Their plumage is patterned in black, sometimes brown, and white and sexual badges of the males are on the crown and the nape, mostly centrally, but in some species these markings are confined to a small stripe or patch on the sides of the nape or crown. No red or yellow on the rump, which may be white in some species; only two species show yellow in the shafts of the flight feathers. Bill straight, chisel-tipped, with strong ridges which also protect the nostrils; tail stiff and curved ventrally. First toe variable in length, usually short, and absent in two species.

Tribe Colaptini: The Colaptini are an almost exclusively American lineage, most closely related to the African *Campetherini*. This tribe comprises 4 distinct genera, one of which (*Celeus*) is rather different and possibly merits higher taxonomic rank. The genus *Veniliornis*, containing 13 Central and South American species, shows many similarities with the campetherine lineage, particularly with the pied woodpeckers. There is also the possibility of convergent evolution, since this genus contains rather arboreal species. They have green and often more or less red upperparts, which distinguishes them from the pied woodpeckers. The bill is well adapted for woodwork, strong and straight, with ridges which also protect the nostrils. *Piculus*, with 10 Central and South American species, is intermediate between the preceding genus and the flickers. Its members show rather arboreal habits and morphological features, yet the bill is slightly curved and pointed or only slightly chisel-shaped at the tip. The tail is also only moderately stiff. Green to bronze colours prevail, and shafts are yellowish to brown. The flickers, combined in the genus *Colaptes*, comprise 9 species, of which the so-called 'forest flickers' resemble species of the preceding genus. The other species are (highly) terrestrial, with a long to very long, curved and pointed bill. Nostrils in one species (*C. fernandinae*) exposed and not covered by feathers. The tail is long, but not especially stiff and curved as in arboreal woodpeckers. The feet are large, with well-developed claws and relatively long hallux. The structure of the skull lacks the typical expression of features related to pounding. Shaft colours are yellow to orange. Conspicuous visual and vocal displays, with some little-investigated social and group behaviour in the ground-dwelling species. Sexual badges are restricted to the malar region. The 11 species of the genus *Celeus* are rather distinct and probably most closely related to *Piculus*. However, *Picus miniaceus* of the Picini tribe also shows close resemblances to *Celeus*, and one could speculate that the Asian Rufous Woodpecker *Celeus brachyurus* is merely a highly convergent offshoot of the *Picus* stock (see below). The main colours of *Celeus* are brown, black and cream, they show a greater or lesser degree of barring, and a crest is more or less well developed. The bill is not long, in most cases is curved, and the nostrils are not covered by feathers. The feet also show that these woodpeckers are not specialised trunk-climbers and pounders; the fourth toe is shorter than or equal to the front toes in length; the first toe is short. The sole Asian species (all others are neotropical) has the fourth toe reduced most. Sexual badges are mainly in the region between bill, eye and chin, and in one species also the sides of the crest; in all cases, the male is distinguished by red in these areas. A particularly large oil-gland is present in this genus. Some species nest in the arboreal nests of social insects.

Tribe Campephilini: This tribe holds 2 genera, distributed over Eurasia and the Americas. The 18 species are large, and are boldly coloured with black and white and a greater or lesser amount of red. Many species possess crests, some spectacular. The species of this group are highly specialised for excavating wood and, generally, are birds that forage on the trunks of large trees; bark-scaling is a very common feeding technique. The genus *Dryocopus* contains altogether 7 species, of which two are widely spread over the northern hemisphere, the rest being south-temperate, subtropical to tropical species which almost completely overlap with the 11 species of the genus *Campephilus*. Among the former is *D. magellanicus*, which is often seen as a good intermediate between *Dryocopus* and *Celeus* (and hence between Campephilini and Colaptini). It has a slightly curved bill, exposed nostrils and a narrow and pointed bill, whereas the other species of the genus *Dryocopus*, the 'logcocks', have a straight bill with well-developed chisel-tip and nostrils covered by feathers. The tail feathers are long, curved forwards ventrally, and the central pair has strong and pointed tips. The front toes and the fourth toe are of about the same length, the hallux about half their length. Visual sexual markings affect the crown and the malar region; most species have a well-developed crest. The large woodpeckers of the genus *Campephilus* are all crested; sexual badges encompass mainly the crown and crest coloration and the malar region, but also other parts of the head. The chisel-tipped bill is long and straight, the nostrils are well protected and covered by feathers. The tail is long and stiff, and curved forwards towards the tip, which is strong and pointed. All toes are long, the fourth significantly longer than the front toes.

Tribe Picini: The Picini represent a great Eurasian radiation of woodpeckers. The 7 genera are diverse, and some similarities in plumage and behaviour suggest that this group shares common ancestry with the Colaptini, particularly with *Celeus*. Convergence in the features involved may be considerable, however, and, as in other cases of woodpecker systematics, a combination of traditional methods with the techniques of molecular biology will certainly help towards a better understanding of all these relationships. Within the tribe there are two genera which contain only one species. The first is *Reinwardtipicus*, which shows some overall similarities to *Chrysocolaptes*, but morphologically and behaviourally seems to be closer to *Blythipicus*. The latter contains two species which are brown to reddish-brown in colour and more or less barred on the back, this coloration being most likely an adaptation to their gloomy habitat. Their long bill is straight and chisel-tipped, with the nostrils feathered and widely spaced. The tail is short and with stiff central feathers, which also are curved forwards at the tip. The fourth toe is a trifle longer than the front toes, and the first toe is short. The rather inconspicuous sexual markings affect the sides of the nape. Similar features and habits characterise the other monotypic genus *Sapheopipo*, the Okinawa Woodpecker, occurring only on the island of that name in the Ryukyu chain of the NW Pacific. The latter's bill, however, is to a small extent curved, though also chisel-tipped and with the nostrils covered by feathers, and the tail is longer and softer. The fourth toe is rather long. Males have crown and forehead feathers tipped red, and the sides of the nape are red as well. As an aside, just how problematic woodpecker classification used to be, and still is, may be illustrated with this genus: Goodwin (1968), basing his theory on overall appearance and coloration of museum specimens, made the point, not totally unconvincingly, that this peculiar species is a direct descendant of the White-backed Woodpecker (*Picoides leucotos*, Campetherini). The largest genus of the tribe, *Picus*, includes 14 species. They wear partly or mainly green plumage, they are often barred below, sometimes crested, and are distinguished by more or less ground-feeding habits with a diet of ants and the corresponding adaptations. Accordingly, the bill is straight to slightly curved and more or less pointed. The tail is long and stiff. The fourth toe is of about the same length as the front toes; the first toe is about half their size. Sexual coloration is dimorphic and affects crown and/or the moustachial stripe. The Banded Woodpecker *P. miniaceus* shows many similarities with *Celeus*. Green colour, sexual markings on the crown, and a small crest are also the characteristics of the two *Gecinulus* species, which are partial to bamboo. Their short bill is slightly curved, but the chisel-tip and rather broad base and the feather-covered nostrils hint at the importance of pecking. The tail is soft and broad, which presumably makes it better suited for bamboo-climbing. These woodpeckers possess three toes, about equal in length. The two remaining wholly South Asian genera, *Dinopium* (4 species) and *Chrysocolaptes* (2 species), contain an array of species and subspecies which show many parallels in coloration, which will be discussed separately below (see Plumage and Moult). They are clad in green, red, golden to yellow, black and white plumage, and all are crested. The bill in *Dinopium* is short to moderately long, curved, with nostrils not far apart and only partly covered by feathers; the tip is pointed to slightly chisel-tipped. The bill is long in *Chrysocolaptes*, straight, strongly built, and chisel-tipped; the nostrils are farther apart, form slits, and are fully covered with feathers. The tail is fairly soft, long and somewhat curved in *Dinopium*; it is much stronger, particularly in the central feathers with their stiffened and pointed tips, in *Chrysocolaptes*. The fourth toe is slightly shorter than the front toes in *Dinopium*, and long and more forward-directed in *Chrysocolaptes*; the first is short to very short and rudimentary (and completely absent in two species) in *Dinopium*, but moderately long in *Chrysocolaptes*. Sexual badges are worn on the crown in both groups, and in *Dinopium* also in the moustachial area. The latter region is also differently patterned in the two genera, with the black stripes in different positions.

Tribe Meiglyptini: The Meiglyptini represent an old Asian stock of rather aberrant woodpeckers, which at first glance have little in common. The 3 genera represent 8 very small to very large species. The characters they share are a thin, long neck, a bulky body and a relatively small head. Fine spots on the head and a contrasting white crown are found in some of their species and in no other woodpeckers. The name-giving genus *Meiglyptes* consists of three small brown, black and white species. The relatively small head is adorned by a crest; sexual badges are restricted to a moustachial stripe or patch, which is red in males and absent in females. The short bill is curved and pointed; the nostrils are only partly covered by feathers. The tail does not show the typical woodpecker features and is rather short, while the feet with the fourth toe about as long as the front toes do not deviate from the general woodpecker pattern. The genus *Hemicircus* contains two rather small species, which are predominantly black and white and are crested. The males of one species (*H. concretus*) have much red in the crest, whereas the females show at best only traces of cinnamon or red. The sexual dimorphism of the other species is unique among woodpeckers in that the male has a black face, crown and crest, while the female's forehead and frontal part of the crown are white. The bill is of medium length, rather straight, chisel-tipped and the nostrils widely spaced, indicating strong pecking habits. The tail is short, as in the preceding genus, but does show some stiffening and is slightly bent forwards near the tip. The fourth toe is longer than the front toes and the first is about half its length. In the plumage on the back of these woodpeckers a peculiar resin-like substance is found (Bock & Short 1971), the origin of which is still obscure since no glands or other sources have yet been identified (Menon 1985). The 3 species of *Mulleripicus* are medium-sized to large and have a conspicuously thin and long neck with a rather small head. The general colour is grey to black, and head and neck are finely spotted white. Females lack any red, whereas males have either a red malar or red 'face' (malar, forehead, orbital area). The bill does not show extreme features related to excavating, being long, slightly curved and only slightly chisel-tipped; nostrils fully covered. The long tail is bent forwards towards the tip and stiff. The fourth toe is shorter than or as long as the front toes, and the hallux is about half its length. The size of these species persuaded some authors to place this genus close to *Dryocopus*, but structure and behaviour of *Mulleripicus* do not warrant such a view.

DISTRIBUTION

Woodpeckers are found in most woodlands around the world and have also conquered treeless grasslands, while one species (the Andean Flicker) lives in the high Andes above the timber line. In Eurasia, these birds are found in the forests and woodlands from the tundra to tropical rain forests. They inhabit the mountains, savannas, woodlands and forests of Africa, though they are, not surprisingly, absent from the Sahara. One species, the Arabian Woodpecker *Picoides dorae*, has, however, survived on the Arabian peninsula. In the New World, woodpeckers are widespread from Alaska to Tierra del Fuego, and are found there in all kinds of forests and woodlands, in high mountains and in arid areas. Although they have largely failed to settle on oceanic islands, some species have found their ways to islands. They occur in Sri Lanka, the Andamans, the Greater and Lesser Sundas, the Philippines, Taiwan, Japan and the Ryukyu Islands, and they are also found in the Bahamas and West Indies. They are represented in Britain, but not in Ireland, and are found in the Canaries and on some Mediterranean islands. Woodpeckers have failed to settle only in Antarctica, Madagascar, Australasia, and the Pacific and other remote islands.

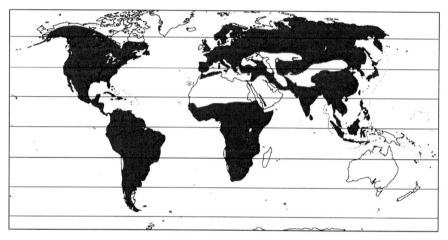

Approximate world distribution of the family Picidae.
The family is widespread and the ranges of its 214 members cover a wide range of habitats and altitudes. Note in particular, however, the lack of representatives in the Australasian region and in extreme desert areas, and an absence from many islands (including Madagascar).

The Oriental (or Indomalayan) region is the zoogeographical region which is richest in different lineages of woodpeckers, with species of 6 tribes found there. Most of its 48 species are restricted to this region, although the Grey-faced Woodpecker *Picus canus* also has a particularly large range in the Palearctic. The Picini are represented by 12 species, the Campetherini are represented by a diverse radiation of *Picoides* woodpeckers, the Campephilini have one widely distributed and one insular species there, and the Meiglyptini are confined to this region. Among the predominantly South American Picumnini, there are three species which are found in the Orient. Finally, the almost exclusively American Colaptini are represented by a single species.

At least 27 species are present in the Palearctic region, but several of these are Oriental species which only marginally reach the Palearctic. Six true woodpeckers (plus the migratory Eurasian Wryneck *Jynx torquilla*) occur across the northern parts of continental Eurasia, including Japan. One species, the Three-toed Woodpecker *Picoides tridactylus*, is shared with the Nearctic which has 24 species in total. The Neotropics, the treasury of our planet's birdlife, is the most important area of woodpecker radiation in terms of the number of species: 76 true woodpeckers and 26 piculets have evolved in the Neotropics.

The Afrotropical (or Ethiopian) region, which largely encompasses the African continent south of the Sahara, has developed a moderately species-rich woodpecker fauna (31 species) in which large species are completely absent, and which is based virtually exclusively on the radiation of the Campetherini (Short 1970). The only exceptions are *Sasia africana*, which belongs to the Picumnini, and the wrynecks (one resident, one winter visitor). One reason for the limited radiation of woodpeckers on this continent may be rooted in the competition with numerous species of barbets (Short 1970d). The northern mountains, from Morocco to

Tunisia, are part of the Palearctic, and it is in this part of Africa that the Picini, as an Oriental-Palearctic group, are represented, with one species, the Eurasian Green Woodpecker *Picus viridis* (of the distinctive race *vaillantii*); here, too, Eurasian Wryneck *Jynx torquilla*, Great Spotted Woodpecker *Picoides major* and Lesser Spotted Woodpecker *P. minor* breed.

The ranges of woodpeckers are often small and generally vary widely. Woodpeckers are poor dispersers, and only a few species are migratory. Once settled, adults move little and stay in one area for all their life. Often extremely localised resources enhance site-fidelity. Hence, there is relatively little gene flow and many subspecies have developed. Special habitat requirements may also help to confine a given species to a certain area. On the generic level, the genus *Picoides* is the most cosmopolitan. Some of its species have vast ranges in the Palearctic, and the Three-toed Woodpecker has conquered huge expanses in the northern hemisphere. Tropical species often have rather small ranges. In particular, South America is rich in localised species. In the tropics, many closely related species replace each other and occur in adjacent geographical areas. The little-known neotropical piculets are a good case in point, since no more than two species occur sympatrically anywhere (whereas up to four species of *Picoides* may live together in certain Central European habitats). The highest number of sympatric species seems to be found in Malaysian forests (Short 1978), although thorough surveys may show that this is matched by some South American habitats.

Woodpeckers are certainly an old group of birds. Nevertheless, the paleontological record is poor, and the oldest woodpeckers in the fossil record date from the middle Miocene of New Mexico (Olson 1985). They have probably evolved from the same stock as the barbets have. Present evidence seems to indicate a New World origin of the family. The evolution of African woodpeckers is rather difficult to understand, and the extant species are perhaps only the scant remnants of a once diverse woodpecker fauna. Some Asian groups could have come from the Americas. The Picini could be regarded as an offshoot of an early invasion of *Celeus*, and the Campephilini sent a representative as well, which gave rise to two now widespread Eurasian *Dryocopus* species (and one insular form, see above). *Picoides* may have come from an African stock, but its main radiation seems to have occurred in Asia, with a second radiation in North America after this continent had been reached. From this group, only the Three-toed Woodpecker managed to reinvade the Old World. Clearly, these scenarios are rather preliminary and a sensible history of the woodpeckers certainly has to be based on a classification which includes more information than presently available.

MORPHOLOGY AND MECHANICS

Their arboreal and pecking habits are reflected in the distinctive shape of the woodpeckers and render them instantly recognisable to the observer. Practically all aspects of their morphology and anatomy are influenced in some way or other by their unique life style. Here, we shall discuss only the more prominent aspects of structural adaptations and how they relate to the mechanics of climbing and pounding. For more details, the reader is referred to the literature mentioned.

The feet of woodpeckers are modified from the yoke-toed, zygodactyl, foot found in cuckoos, trogons, parrots and in toucans and barbets (see Bock 1959 for fuller details). This type of toe arrangement is particularly suited to grasping, and, in the modified, ectropodactyl, form found in woodpeckers, to climbing vertical surfaces. The ancestral zygodactyl condition is still found in the tiny piculets and also in the wrynecks and the flickers, which often forage on the ground and frequently perch crosswise on a branch, but can also climb on vertical substrates in the way we are used to observing other woodpeckers do.

Woodpecker feet.
Left to right:
Picoides (Great Spotted Woodpecker),
Picumnus (Olivaceous Piculet),
Campephilus (Crimson-crested Woodpecker).
Note that drawings are not to scale.

Piculets use their feet to grasp the surface; the tail is not used as a prop. In the genus *Sasia* only three toes are found, the first being absent. In the zygodactyl arrangement two toes are in front, namely toes 2 and 3, and two behind, the first toe and the more outward directed fourth. From the more general zygodactyl condition, two lines of specialisation for vertical climbing and clinging have emerged. One line, in which the hallux (first toe, the 'thumb') becomes less and less important and is vestigial or even lost in some cases (Three-toed and Black-backed Woodpeckers; *Dinopium* species; *Gecinulus*), is represented by small to medium-sized woodpeckers. There is some variation with general habits, more arboreal and woodpecking species tending to have longer fourth toes.

The large and powerful woodpeckers (*Dryocopus, Campephilus*) typify a different development. Their hallux is long and functional. In climbing, the legs have to bear the gravitational forces which pull the woodpecker down and away from the surface, and hence they tend to be stretched. When on the ground or perched on a horizontal surface, gravitation 'folds' the legs. In small species these forces end up solely on the toes, which are large in relation to the size of the woodpecker. The very large species of the genus *Campephilus*, however, cling on a trunk in a peculiar fashion. The legs are directed much more sideways than in other woodpeckers, as though the bird is trying to hug the tree. Since all toes are directed more or less forwards, the tarsus touches the surface, something which is prevented in other woodpeckers by the hallux and the general position of the feet under the body and the direction of the pulling forces. The role of the hallux (and the outer toe) is taken over by a callus at the 'heel', the proximal end of the tarsus, which is pressed against the trunk (Bock & Miller 1959, and own observations on Red-necked Woodpecker *C. rubricollis*). So, the morphology of the feet is dictated by life style (perching, ground foraging, vertical climbing) and by body size. Tiny woodpeckers can negotiate gravity and the forces generated during pecking and hammering with the feet alone. Small to medium-sized species use three toes and the tail for clinging; large woodpeckers need all four toes, plus the support of the tarsus, and the tail.

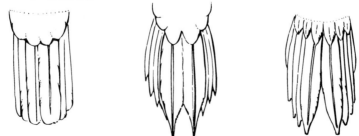

Woodpecker tails.
Left to right: *Picumnus, Melanerpes, Campephilus*. Note that drawings are not to scale.

From the above, it becomes clear that the woodpecker tail has to be modified for climbing and clinging. First, the pygostyle bone and the tail vertebrae are enlarged, because the large muscles need enough space for insertion. The tail is more or less stiff, the central feathers especially having very stiff shafts in specialised climbers. These shafts are strengthened by longitudinal ridges. The barbs are curved and thus the vanes are concave, so that their tip makes firm contact with the substrate. The central feathers have pointed tips. The tail is also curved ventrally at the tip. Woodpeckers possess six pairs of tail feathers (rectrices), the outermost of which is greatly reduced and probably functionless.

Feet and tail act together when a woodpecker clings to a vertical surface (Winkler & Bock 1976). In principle, the feet counteract the gravitational forces. The tail keeps the body of the woodpecker away from the tree surface and also helps to overcome gravitation. Because the centre of gravity is not in line with these three points of support, the woodpecker would tumble head over back were it not for the feet, which also counteract the resulting horizontal forces that would pull the woodpecker away from the trunk. The tail is, as mentioned, in charge of the opposite force.

Woodpeckers hop up a tree bipedally, and there is a continuum from hopping on horizontal surfaces to moving on vertical ones (Spring 1965; Winkler 1972b). On a vertical surface, the hop consists of a power stroke and a floating phase (Norberg 1986). At the start of such an upward hop, the woodpecker pushes itself up along the surface, with the front part of the body and the head (the bill points in the direction of the movement) close to the surface, and at the last moment the tail is lifted. At the climax of this movement the grip of the feet is relaxed, the tail is parallel to the surface, and for a split second the woodpecker floats in the air without any contact with the substrate. Then the feet are brought forward in a rapid movement, they catch hold, and the tail is also braced against the climbing surface again. Of course, all the forces generated during the initial acceleration have to be borne by the feet, and, unlike when at rest, the load also affects the now more or less backward-directed toes. It remains to be mentioned that the three entirely terrestrial species, Ground Woodpecker *Geocolaptes olivaceus*, Andean Flicker *Colaptes rupicola* and Campo Flicker *C. campestris*, use walking as a means of locomotion (Short 1971a).

Many morphological specialisations relate to wood-pecking. Other birds, including the related barbets, but also nuthatches, tits and so forth, also perform some strong pecking or even excavating, while others again (e.g. parrots, shrike-tits) manage to carve out wood by tearing and biting. Woodpeckers, however, use their bill as a chisel. The bones of the bill are strong and they are covered by hard ramphotheca. The tip of the bill forms a more or less chisel-like cutting edge.

Probably one of the most frequent questions asked about woodpeckers by laypersons and scientists alike is: why do woodpeckers not get a headache? This question, of course, alludes to their pecking. The answer certainly is not simple, and before we try to resolve some of the issues it is helpful to outline briefly exactly what happens when a woodpecker pounds against more or less hard wood with its bill (Winkler 1972b; Spring 1965). A stroke begins with the head being drawn back to the fullest extent; it is then shot forwards towards the surface in a straight trajectory, the eyes close a wink before impact, and the bill hits the substrate with considerable speed (600-700cm/s). This impact results in deceleration, measured in Pileated Woodpeckers at about 600-1500g. There are many reasons why repeated pecking does not cause any obvious injuries. First, the brain of woodpeckers is proportionately small, at least compared with the human brain (though not with that of similarly sized birds), and therefore mass-to-surface ratio is low, which means that the impact forces are distributed over a relatively greater area (this fact alone makes woodpeckers fifty to one hundred times less vulnerable than man). The straight trajectory reduces hazardous rotational and shearing forces (May *et al.* 1979). In addition, woodpeckers, as birds in general, possess little cerebrospinal fluid which would transmit dangerous shock waves. As Bock (1964, 1966) in particular has stressed, impact forces are transmitted below the braincase, which is situated above the line from bill tip to quadrate bone. Furthermore, certain muscles when contracted before the impact, attached at the rear end of the mandible, can act as shock-absorbers (Bock 1964, 1966). The tongue muscles almost certainly cannot fulfil such a function as May *et al.* (1976) surmised. Despite all these detailed facts which are already known, a comprehensive comparative study that also takes into account the function of the neck and the parallel swinging movements of the rest of the body is still lacking. Such a study should also resolve another, at first glance rather academic question, namely, whether or not the bill is open upon impact. If the aforementioned muscle is to act in the way proposed, then the upper mandible should be slightly lifted, as this is the usual function of these muscles. Consequently, the impact would force the bill open even more. To prevent this, woodpeckers possess a stop or locking device formed by folding the frontal bone over the maxilla. This structure is less developed in probing and gleaning species, in which, incidentally, the brain is also closer to the line of the pecking forces; it is absent in those species which lead a terrestrial life. Our own observations suggest that the bill indeed is (always?) used as a pincer or grab driven into the wood, rather than as a single solid chisel.

When the woodpecker actually excavates firm wood, it completes a blow with forceful tearing movements in which the head is turned around the axis of the bill, which takes a firm grip on a chip which ultimately is

17

ripped off the substrate by these actions. The cutting edges at the bill tip are self-sharpening through an exquisite arrangement of the cells growing the hard horny substance (Lüdicke 1933).

Not all woodpeckers are equally specialised for wood-pecking, and skulls and bills differ accordingly (Burt 1930). The bills of the more wood-pecking species are straight along the culmen, broad at the base and chisel-tipped; the braincase is larger and more sturdily built, and the frontal bones are more folded under at the insertion of the bill. These differences can be detected also in closely related species; compared with Syrian Woodpecker *Picoides syriacus*, the strongly built Great Spotted Woodpecker *P. major* has not only a wider and shorter bill, but also a broader forehead (by 3.5mm, a difference which can be measured even on the living bird). In most woodpeckers the nostrils are covered by feathers (notable exceptions are the wrynecks and *Celeus*), which is probably to protect them from pieces of debris during wood-working. The bills of strongly wood-pecking species bear longitudinal ridges as further reinforcement. Lateral ridges protect the nostrils, which are reduced to slits and spaced far apart.

There is another activity of woodpeckers which is rather similar to wood-pecking and is, in fact, often hard to distinguish from such actions, namely drumming (cartoon-woodpeckers clearly do not know the difference!). This is a salient feature of the behaviour of many woodpeckers, and its behavioural significance will be discussed below. The mechanics of drumming are different in that the main movements are carried out by the head-and-neck system. There have been many attempts to explain the fast rhythm and the time course of the individual strokes in a roll. The most recent model, by Kaiser (1990), leads to some interesting conclusions. Mass of the head, length of the neck muscles, their distance from the centre of the spine, and the length of the neck section all enter into his equation. All model computations showed that the downstroke is as long as or shorter by 40% than the upstroke and that there are some apparent ecological correlates. In typical wood-pecking species the rhythm accelerates, whereas gleaners slow down towards the end or the rhythm and amplitude of their rolls remain uniform. These are, of course, only general trends and these findings should be corroborated with a larger sample of material.

The distinct foraging modes of woodpeckers are inconceivable without the versatile action of the tongue. This also is a highly modified organ in woodpeckers (Leiber 1907; Scharnke 1931; Steinbacher 1934, 1957) and its function is assisted by a pair of sublingual salivary glands, which secrete a sticky fluid. It is very long, can be extended far beyond the tip of the bill, and is also capable of lateral movements. All this is achieved through the greatly elongated hyoid horns, which are sheathed by muscles. They meet at the tip of the tongue and run along the base of the skull and up over its rear, where they meet again. Depending on the length of the tongue, the horns end between the eyes, reach further down to the frontal bone, or extend even further into the (right) cavity of the upper mandible in some species or they curl around the right eye. Thus, for instance, the tongue is wound up around the right eye in the Heart-spotted and Grey-and-buff Woodpeckers *Hemicircus canente* and *H. concretus* and in the Hairy Woodpecker *Picoides villosus*, and ends in the bill in the flamebacks, in the Orange-backed Woodpecker *Reinwardtipicus validus* and in *Picus*. The tip of the tongue also exhibits great diversity among woodpeckers. Variation relates mainly to the pointedness of the tip and to the number, stiffness and arrangement of barbs. Woodpeckers which obtain their prey from crevices and surfaces tend to have longer tongues. Those species which go for insect larvae deep inside timber are vigorous hammerers and usually have shorter tongues; as powerful a hammerer as the Black Woodpecker *Dryocopus martius* has a relatively short tongue. On long tongues bristles are concentrated at the tip, whereas the shorter tongues of excavators and of some species which habitually drink sap are tufted

A: At rest or nearly so, retractor muscle (cross-hatched) of hyoid horns inserts well forwards.

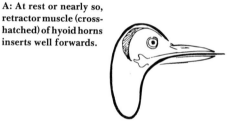

B: When retractor muscle contracts and draws hyoid horns forwards, the loop of the tongue is raised and the tongue is shot far beyond bill tip.

C: When fully retracted, horns end at or in front of eyes, in cavity of upper mandible or (as here) even wound up around the eye.

Tongue mechanism of a woodpecker.

like a brush. These differences are apparent even among close relatives: thus, the more probing and gleaning Syrian Woodpecker has a longer tongue than the Great Spotted Woodpecker, and with five or six barbs fewer (6-9) at its tip. The salivary glands also exhibit great variation. They may be short, ending below the ear or close to the quadrate bone, or they may, as in the Grey-crowned Woodpecker *Piculus auricularis*, reach much farther, to the back of the skull. Their glue-like fluid covers the tip of the tongue, which is thereby transformed into a versatile

and efficient foraging device. Woodpeckers either spear grubs concealed in recesses or lick up scores of swarming ants or termites.

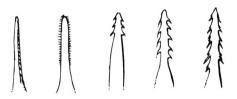

Tongue tips of woodpeckers to show range of variation.
Left to right:
smooth (wrynecks);
brush-like (e.g. White/Acorn Woodpeckers, Yellow-bellied Sapsucker);
2-3 barbs (e.g. Green-barred Woodpecker);
4-6 barbs (e.g. Little, Blond-crested and Lineated Woodpeckers);
grouped barbs of different sizes (e.g. Golden-fronted Woodpecker, *Campephilus* spp.)

Collectors often mention how tough the skin of woodpeckers is (e.g. Wetmore 1968; Short 1982). This feature, which they share, incidentally, with the honeyguides, may be an adaptation both to their habits, through which they constantly come into close contact with rough surfaces, and to their frequent interactions with stinging and biting prey, such as ants.

PLUMAGE AND MOULT

Some species are polychromatic. That means that in one population various types of coloration occur. Take as an example the *Dryocopus* woodpeckers of South America. There, the Black-bodied Woodpecker *D. schulzi* may have the scapular stripe white, but there are some individuals which lack this pattern. These forms occur close to another species of the same genus, the Lineated Woodpecker *D. lineatus*, which is represented there by the subspecies *erythrops*, and in this subspecies we find a similar polychromatism. The significance of this variation is not at all clear, but may be related to the problems discussed next.

Cody (1969) studied the plumage patterns of sympatric birds and, among other things, suggested that parallel variation among woodpeckers that are not directly related may be an adaptation to interspecific competition. His examples relate to the plumages of the flamebacks, genera *Chrysocolaptes* and *Dinopium*, which show parallel variation wherever they occur sympatrically. Other cases he discusses in the same context are the pairings *Meiglyptes-Hemicircus* and *Celeus brachyurus-Blythipicus*. The large *Dryocopus* ('logcocks') and *Campephilus* (ivory-bills) species, which are structurally well separated and yet often strikingly similar are another example. The question in such cases is, of course, whether plumage or structure reflect phylogenetic relationships more closely (Bock 1963; Cody 1969). Another speculative explanation, with a slightly different emphasis, invokes aggressive mimicry (Winkler *et al.* 1994). If that were the case, one species of such a pair of mimics should be fierce and the other one timid. The mimicry of the latter would protect it from interference by the former because the would-be attacker does not dare to attack an opponent which seems to be its match. Unfortunately, we lack sufficient information on actual interspecific aggression and on the outcome of struggles to test these hypotheses thoroughly.

Convergence in plumage may also reflect adaptation to common habitat characteristics. Many woodpeckers are brightly coloured. Ground woodpeckers, however, are generally less brightly coloured; their head is not strongly marked and brown, grey, or green colours prevail, and frequently these birds are barred and have pale, white or brightly yellowish rumps. Goodwin (1968), who discussed woodpecker coloration in a similar context, also believes that 'laddered' or lavishly mottled backs are more cryptic and are associated with open woodland. Resolution of all these question must await carefully planned comparative analyses which have to be based on a phylogeny which is founded on characters other than those being analysed.

Most woodpeckers are clearly sexually dimorphic and (the males) wear sexual badges. A great variety exists, however. In almost all cases, it is the male that has (more) red, in some cases yellow, somewhere on the head. Experiments (Noble 1936, on flickers; own experiments on *Picoides*) have shown that these badges are recognised by the woodpeckers. Hagan & Reed (1988) showed how strongly badges influence the social life of Red-cockaded Woodpeckers *P. borealis*. They found that in this practically monomorphic species the presence of red colour bands on males, and only on males, has a detrimental consequence for the number of young which such a male can fledge; other colours do not have such an effect. The reason for this may be that red colours lead to more frequent or more fierce agonistic interactions with this male. There are some other species which show only indistinct sexual markings. The males of some (sub)species of the small woodpeckers of the *Picoides canicapillus-moluccensis-temminckii-maculatus-kizuki* complex are only weakly marked. The sexual markings of flickers are also not very conspicuous; sometimes the male does not show red and is distinguished only by a black moustache. In the Heart-spotted Woodpecker *Hemicircus canente*, neither sex shows red or yellow: the female has the forehead and crown white, while in the male the forehead and crown are black with fine white spotting. Species in which both sexes are brightly coloured red on the head and in which there are no or very small sexual differences are Lewis's Woodpecker *Melanerpes lewis*, the Puerto Rican Woodpecker *M. portoricensis*, the Red-headed Woodpecker *M. erythrocephalus*, the Red-breasted and Red-naped Sapsuckers *Sphyrapicus ruber* and *S. nuchalis*, and the Middle Spotted Woodpecker *Picoides medius*. There is no doubt that this variation is not random and that it is associated with the social organisation of the various species and the role of the sexes and of aggression. A comprehensive treatment is not, however, presently available.

The coloration of young woodpeckers has given rise to many speculations, too. Most often it has been discussed under the notion of retained 'primitive' or 'advanced' characters (see Goodwin 1968; Kipp 1956; Verheyen 1957). Again, there is great diversity, an explanation of which will be made possible only with a clear understanding of the life histories of the species involved, including their interspecific interactions. There are species in which the juveniles show more red on the head than the adults. This condition is found in the Great Spotted Woodpecker and its allies, among them the Syrian Woodpecker, the immature of which possesses a more or less conspicuous red breast band in addition. In these species the crown is red, while the sexual badge of the adults is worn at the nape. A similar condition is found in the Maroon Woodpecker *Blythipicus rubiginosus*. In *Campethera* the reverse pattern is found: the juvenile male has the badge only on the hindcrown or nape, while the adult male has the entire crown red or yellow. There are some other cases in which the position of the juvenile marking differs from that of the adult: for instance, in the Red-cockaded Woodpecker, immatures have a red patch in the centre of the crown. In some species, the juvenile coloration agrees more or less with the adult one (e.g. many Colaptini, some Melanerpini, Picini and *Dryocopus*). Without going into further details, it should have become manifest that there are many interesting patterns which await explanation. Relevant studies may prove not so easy, because the sexing of juveniles by collectors was often based on some preconception on sexual differences rather than on anatomical confirmation.

It is not surprising that even the moult of woodpeckers shows some peculiarities which are clearly related to their unique life style (Stresemann & Stresemann 1966). After they have left the nest, piculets (*Picumnus*) moult the feathers of the crown only; *Sasia* moults the feathers of the underside as well. Both genera accomplish their first complete moult after they have bred for the first time. Young woodpeckers and wrynecks (Picinae, Jynginae) replace the primaries, the tail feathers and the rest of the plumage with the exception of the secondaries. Primaries and also the tail may differ considerably between juveniles and adults. The outer primary of juveniles is longer and wider, and the tail is shorter and differently graduated because the feathers adjacent to the central pair remain shorter. Juvenile moult commences with the replacement of the inner (1st) primary, and only when the 6th or 7th primary has been shed does the moult of the contour feathers commence. In some species, moult already begins in the nest and the first primaries are dropped before they have ever been used. In such species, the two innermost primaries remain small and thin. Young Three-toed Woodpeckers replace the five to seven inner primaries before they leave the nest. There is a tendency for tropical species to have the innermost primary only somewhat reduced, whereas northern species show stronger reduction. This is probably adaptive, because the latter have to finish the moult in the short summer season of cool-temperate areas in order to disperse and/or migrate. Tropical species lead a more sedentary life and their moult is spread over a long period. These differences can be detected in intrageneric comparisons. The tropical Laced Woodpecker *Picus vittatus* has only the innermost primary reduced, whereas in temperate Eurasian Green Woodpeckers *P. viridis* and Grey-faced Woodpeckers *P. canus* the two innermost feathers are greatly reduced. As already mentioned, the strongest reduction is found in the Three-toed Woodpecker; the congeneric Great Spotted Woodpecker shows less reduction, which is even less marked in the closely related, generally more southern Syrian Woodpecker. In *Colaptes*, there are two moult centres in the secondaries: after three or four feathers have been moulted in the first (beginning around the 8th secondary), moult starts at the 1st secondary, continuing inwards. Wing moult of the Andean Flicker is very variable and protracted, thus interfering little with flight (and presumably conditioned by the species' habitat and migration). Adult moult is tied in with the breeding cycle and occurs after the nesting season.

There are some deviations from the usual pattern of wing moult. Migratory Red-headed Woodpeckers suspend wing moult immediately after it has begun, and continue it upon arrival on the wintering grounds. Related Lewis's Woodpeckers complete the moult of the wings and tail early, but complete the body moult in late autumn or early winter. Similarly, sapsuckers complete their juvenile moult as late as February.

Woodpeckers with a stiff tail replace the central pair of rectrices last. The moult begins at the second-innermost feathers (which therefore stay short in juveniles to begin with) and continues outwards. The tail moult in wrynecks, and also in some true woodpeckers (notably in some Picini), proceeds from the outer feathers to the centre. The tail moult in the Picumninae seems to follow no regular pattern.

FOOD AND FORAGING

Woodpeckers regularly feed on insects and other arthropods, particularly spiders, and on various types of plant material. The composition of the diet varies from species to species and is also dependent on what the environment offers. Very frequently there are marked seasonal differences, as for instance in the northern populations of the Great Spotted Woodpecker, which change from a predominantly insect diet in summer to pine or spruce seeds in winter (Pynnönen 1943) and supplement their diet with tree sap in spring (Turcek 1954). Similar drastic seasonal changes are observed in the sapsuckers, which for much of the time rely on the sap of trees (see below), and in other melanerpines, e.g. Lewis's Woodpecker, Acorn Woodpecker *Melanerpes formicivorus* and Red-bellied Woodpecker *M. carolinus*.

Many species rely to a great extent on ants and termites. Among them are largely terrestrial woodpeckers and the wrynecks. These species plunder nests of terrestrial ants (e.g. many species of *Lasius*) in an often regular fashion, and they seem to have a good knowledge of the whereabouts of their prey. Other species, e.g. the large *Dryocopus* woodpeckers, go for the dens of large ants living within trees (e.g. *Camponotus* ants, which gnaw their tunnels and nest chambers into the trunks of living pines and spruce) and neotropical woodpeckers, e.g. Lineated Woodpecker, find ants of the genus *Azteca* in hollow parts of *Cecropia* trees. Woodpeckers such as the Cinnamon Woodpecker *Celeus loricatus* even locate those ants which live symbiotically in 'ant-plants', and many exploit these and other plant galls, and also figs (e.g. Arabian Woodpecker), and eat their insect inhabitants. Tree-dwelling ants, especially those of the genus *Crematogaster*, are also frequently preyed upon by woodpeckers. Many of their species build large nests, about the size of a football; highly specialised woodpeckers of the genus *Celeus* (e.g. the Rufous Woodpecker *C. brachyurus*) or *Campethera* not only feed on them (and on arboreal termites), but also dig their holes in these nests (see below).

Another important prey for many species of highly specialised woodpeckers is the larvae of wood-boring insects, predominantly beetles (Cerambycidae, Buprestidae), and larvae living directly under the bark (Scolytidae). Although difficult to procure, this prey is also fed to the young by some species (e.g. White-backed Woodpecker *Picoides leucotos*).

Woodpeckers occasionally also prey on the nests of other birds. Among them (see also species accounts) are *Picus, Melanerpes* and *Picoides* species, of which the Great Spotted Woodpecker is notorious for taking eggs and nestlings. On rare occasions they will snatch a scorpion or a lizard and have also been observed to open mussels (Huber 1965).

Many species of woodpecker more or less rely on plant material. Fruits and berries are taken by many species. Nuts and the stones of fleshy fruits are frequently eaten by pied woodpeckers, and the most frugivorous group, the genus *Melanerpes*, not only depends heavily on fruit-eating but many species eat nuts and, above all, acorns. The eating of coniferous seeds and the harvesting of acorns have led to the evolution of fascinating skills, which will be discussed below. Another highly derived habit is sap-sucking. This occurs among many pied woodpeckers, it is also found in *Melanerpes* and it is the main energy source for the sapsuckers (*Sphyrapicus*) and others, but no species of the Afrotropical region seems to utilise the sap of trees. Woodpeckers also take nectar, the fruit-eating and sap-sucking melanerpine species (which can be attracted by the provision of sugar-water) again being prominent, along with the smaller pied woodpeckers.

The Red-cockaded Woodpecker has been observed collecting bones from raptor pellets as a source of calcium prior to egg-laying (Repasky *et al.* 1991).

The diet of woodpeckers has been investigated mainly through analyses of stomach contents, observations at the nest, and direct observations of prey capture or seed- or fruit-eating. Woodpecker droppings are well suited for quantitative investigations, too. They can be obtained either by observing defecation directly (this can sometimes be provoked by flushing the bird from its foraging site) or by collecting the faeces at those sites which are habitually visited prior to roosting, at regular feeding stations (e.g. ant nests) or at the roost. The faeces are typically hook-shaped.

Woodpeckers frequently drink (see e.g. Blume & Jeide 1965). They get their water mostly from small puddles in tree forks and similar arboreal structures, but they will also descend to the ground to drink.

Woodpeckers utilise many enigmatic foraging techniques. Since woodpeckers are easy to observe, generally, and since they employ a range of techniques, they have often been the subject of detailed quantitative field studies. These are summarised in the various species accounts. The following provides a brief outline of the foraging modes at the disposal of woodpeckers. There are, in principle, two ways of approaching foraging: one is by describing the action, and the other by looking at the result. We begin with the former.

The various behaviours observed when woodpeckers forage have been given many different, often confusing, labels. For instance, 'tapping' has been used to describe various foraging methods, as well as for the various types of instrumental communication. Because of the use of different categories, many quantitative studies on woodpecker foraging are difficult to compare. We discuss here the more important aspects of woodpecker foraging behaviour based on the suggestions made by Remsen & Robinson (1990).

The most common surface manoeuvre of all woodpeckers is *gleaning*, during which the bird clings to or sits on a substrate (perch) and grabs a nearby food item without much in the way of acrobatics. Woodpeckers may also *reach* for more distant food. Most studies, however, do not distinguish this activity from the former category, but there are some species, e.g. melanerpines, that are particularly skilled in reaching under a perch and there are differences in how far a woodpecker will reach sideways on a trunk. Generally, it seems, those which do a lot of wood-work are poor reachers. Many woodpecker species, particularly small ones, *hang* upside-down to get at certain food items. A distinction should, however, be made as to whether a woodpecker runs along the underside of a branch (e.g. Middle Spotted Woodpecker, Arabian Woodpecker) or clings (crosswise) in a more tit-like fashion (Great Spotted Woodpecker, Lesser Spotted Woodpecker, Buff-rumped Woodpecker *Meiglyptes tristis*).

The typical woodpecker manoeuvres, however, are those in which the substrate is somehow penetrated or manipulated. During *probing*, the bill is inserted into crevices or holes in bark or exposed wood, in epiphytes and vine tangles, in the ground, in mud (e.g. in mangroves), in fruits and in flowers. Highly characteristic of woodpecker gleaning and probing (and that of hummingbirds) is the use of the sticky and barbed tongue, which increases the range of action far beyond the bill tip. It is flicked out to glue small insects, especially ants, and its barbed tip allows the woodpecker to spear grubs and other prey hidden deep in the substrate. When woodpeckers *peck*, they drive the bill into the substrate (bark, wood, soil) to remove parts of it. Pecking is used mainly to excavate, but also to remove large pieces of bark, often with lateral blows. Remsen & Robinson invented the category *chiselling* for oblique blows, claiming that this is associated more with chisel-tipped bills. Certainly, in woodpeckers, too (their examples comprise mainly ovenbirds and woodhewers), the bill is not always pounded perpendicularly into the substrate and it may also be used as a lever to *pry* off wood or bark. It may be useful to distinguish the impact angle in comparative studies in order to understand bill structure fully. In the species accounts we generally do not make such fine distinctions, simply because appropriate information is largely lacking. Pecking is often also referred to as tapping. With Remsen & Robinson, we would recommend using the term *tapping* for the seemingly exploratory blows woodpeckers deliver at the substrate, presumably to obtain information on its quality, and to refer to communication taps as signal-tapping, which some species produce at the hole. Continuous series of pecks are termed *hammering*, a technique almost exclusively restricted to woodpeckers (some ovenbirds, e.g. *Xenops*, and some tits hammer, too).

Woodpeckers, particularly when feeding on the ground, *sweep* or brush aside loose litter with sideways motions of the bill, a behaviour termed *flaking* by Remsen & Robinson. Often, parts of the substrate are grasped with the bill and torn or ripped off; this *pulling* occurs mainly when removing bark, but, as has been described above, it may also be an intrinsic part of pecking. Some woodpeckers (e.g. Red-cockaded Woodpecker, Strickland's Woodpecker *Picoides stricklandi*) also *scratch* with their feet to dislodge bark.

Many species of woodpecker *sally* occasionally, and for many melanerpine species (e.g. Acorn Woodpecker) this is one of the most important ways of catching insect food. Some species (e.g. Great Spotted Woodpecker) occasionally *hover* briefly to grab food at the tip of a twig. Only a few species (Golden-naped Woodpecker *Melanerpes chrysauchen*, Lewis's Woodpecker) attack aerial insects in continuous flight without returning to a perch after each attack; this behaviour has been called *screening* by Remsen & Robinson.

This classification may help to describe the foraging actions of woodpeckers and may also assist in understanding the corresponding morphological structures. These actions and combinations of them may lead to rather different results. Together with locomotion, they form the great diversity of woodpecker foraging styles. Pecking, hammering, chiselling and prying can have rather different results. Removal of bark has already been mentioned, and many woodpeckers, notably the campephiline species, but many others as well, employ various techniques to this end. After bark has been removed, some species (e.g. White-backed Woodpecker, Black Woodpecker) chisel horizontal rows in the exposed wood to uncover the burrows of bark beetles. Others (e.g. Hairy Woodpecker) drill holes of small diameter into the wood or bark, while yet others produce small elongate pits, culminating in the huge pits produced by the campephiline species when hunting ants (*Dryocopus*) or grubs (*Campephilus*). Some distinctly chisel-billed species (e.g. White-backed Woodpecker, Maroon Woodpecker) prefer soft wood for their work. They may be able literally to root into the substrate. The tiny piculets hammer small holes to gain access to the ants burrowing in small twigs. Some of the most complex bird behaviours, however, in their most highly developed form, are linked with the harvesting, manipulation and storage of sap, seeds and nuts (acorns).

Woodpeckers probably find their prey, concealed in timber, initially by some optical give-away signs. With some probing taps they are able to locate a hole. In field experiments they readily learn to find food (sunflower seeds) in holes covered with tape (Lima 1983, 1984). There is speculation that prey may be located by the sound it makes, but hard experimental evidence for this does not exist.

Many species of woodpecker, predominantly in the Old World, ring the bark of living trees with series of regularly spaced holes so as to obtain the sugary sap (Abdulali 1968; Gibbs 1983; Klima 1959; MacRoberts 1970; Miech 1986; Osmaston 1916; Ruge 1970b, 1973; Tate 1973; Turcek 1954; Zusi & Marshall 1970). The holes are just deep enough to reach the sap-transporting vessels of the tree. Secretions of the tree may appear within seconds after the woodpecker has penetrated the bark with several blows. The sap is then licked up by the woodpecker. Other bird species, including other woodpeckers, as well as squirrels, mice, dormice, deer and insects, take advantage of this food source. Ants which collect at the pits are also readily taken by the woodpeckers (Miech 1986). For North American sapsuckers this behaviour provides regular nutrition. For most other species, with the possible exception of the Acorn Woodpecker, Great Spotted and Middle Spotted Woodpeckers, Rufous-bellied Woodpecker *Picoides hyperythrus*, Arabian Woodpecker and Three-toed Woodpecker (see also species accounts), sap-sucking is a rather irregular habit.

With pecking and the ability to work on hard wood assured, yet another skill evolved. Practically all woodpeckers that take prey which they cannot mandibulate sufficiently for ingestion carry such items, including pieces of bark (in captivity, splinters are treated likewise), to a fork, crevice or similar structure which allows the item to be held firm. Here, beetles may be smashed, galls opened, the stones of cherries are removed, apricot stones with their edible contents are prepared, and so forth. The use of such 'anvils' is not unique among birds, since, for instance, kingfishers and thrushes smash snails on stones, but it is most highly developed in those woodpeckers which totally rely on anvils for obtaining pine and spruce seeds. The best-studied species in this respect is the Great Spotted Woodpecker (Fritsch 1952; Meijering 1967; see also Winkler 1968 and Pflumm 1979). There are various types of anvils, the most primitive ones being those used by most species, as described above. In many cases, such a structure is used only once, opportunistically, although some woodpeckers may use one site repeatedly. A still more advanced form of this behaviour is represented by the use of anvils of varying sizes according to the object to be worked. In the most highly developed form of anvil use, the anvil is created by the woodpecker itself for that purpose. Anvils which are used repeatedly have to be emptied before re-use; for this, the woodpecker places the new object between breast and substrate, removes the old object (pine cone, for instance), and finally fixes the new object for processing with a few blows. The latter behaviour occurs apparently in very advanced species. So far, the Great Spotted Woodpecker is the only species in which it seems to be a regular part of anvil use; it has not been observed in Middle Spotted or Syrian Woodpeckers (Meijering 1967; Winkler 1967). Hundreds (up to 5000) of cones may lie under a heavily used anvil. Anvil use in its most highly evolved form has all the characteristics of genuine tool-using. Another kind of tool use has been observed in a Gila Woodpecker *Melanerpes uropygialis*, which dipped pieces of bark or seeds into syrup (honey) provided at a feeder to feed its fledglings (Antevs 1948).

Storing of food is often not clearly separable from anvil use, especially if the anvil is not cleaned for re-use. Food or other objects are wedged into a crack in the bark, mandibulated, left, visited again, and maybe even transported to another place. Moving objects among different anvils is a rather common component of anvil use. Especially if anvils are primitive (i.e. when cracks and other suitable structures are used opportunistically), it is hard to draw a line between caching and anvil use if food pieces are left. Syrian Woodpeckers may thus fill long cracks with (opened) stones of plums or with apricots. Reports of caching by various species (e.g. Conner & Kroll 1979; Martin & Kroll 1975) have to be critically examined.

There is no doubt that the thousands of funnel-shaped holes produced by Acorn Woodpeckers are there to store acorns. The stores of Lewis's Woodpecker and other *Melanerpes* serve the same purpose (see species accounts). Details of behaviour and the variation found in anvil use leave no doubt that it is closely related to food-storing, which is its derivative (Fritsch 1952).

There are many overt and subtle differences in the way woodpeckers move while foraging. General theory holds that the most economic way for a bird which moves like a woodpecker would be to hop upwards and to fly downwards (Norberg 1981). Of course, there are many deviations from this general pattern, which, however, has not been systematically investigated in broad comparative studies. It applies more or less well to woodpeckers, woodhewers and creepers, but less so to nuthatches (Matthysen 1990). Gleaners are agile, move a lot sidewards and back again on large trunks, and frequently move downwards, and smaller species, e.g. Middle Spotted Woodpecker or Arabian Woodpecker, move deftly along the underside of limbs. Clinging to terminal twigs needs a strong grasp and therefore occurs mainly in small or rather strong species. As the accounts of many species show, there are many different forms of patch use. A woodpecker may spend a long time at one spot to excavate, may hardly stop at all while gleaning, or may just briefly pause to work on a single site. There also seem to be differences in the likelihood that a woodpecker may return to the same site. For gleaners, renewal times of the prey are short and re-use of the same site poses little problem. For birds which feed on solitary burrow-dwelling items, it usually pays not to return. Downy Woodpeckers *Picoides pubescens* studied by Lima (1984) returned to the same spot in only two out of more than 1200 cases.

Woodpeckers may use the wings to change their position even within the same tree, or they may do so only reluctantly. They may change feeding sites by flying just to the neighbouring tree or by moving great distances. The flight of woodpeckers is generally dipping or undulating. The large-winged melanerpine species tend to have a straight flight pattern (in the case of Lewis's Woodpecker, the flight is crow-like), and a straight flight is also found in the very large species. The flapping phase of the flight is often clearly audible. In many species, deep undulations and a loud wing noise are associated with some kind of (territorial) announcement.

24

Woodpeckers searching for the source of an acoustical signal (e.g. tape playback) also perform deep swoops near the source and fly back and forth as though zeroing in on it. Woodpeckers suddenly changing the direction of their flight also produce a conspicuous noise. Whether this is just the by-product of the flight manoeuvre which may take place when the bird sees an intruder or spots possible danger or whether it has become a signal in its own right, at least in some species, requires clarification.

ECOLOGICAL SEXUAL DIMORPHISM

Woodpeckers in general do not exhibit spectacular sexual dimorphism. Yet many instances exist in which various workers have shown that the sexes differ in their ecology. Differences in territory use are common, and many observers have noted that male and female use different parts of the territory when feeding nestlings. Besides this general phenomenon, there are other differences in morphology and foraging behaviour.

In a much-discussed study, Selander (1966) analysed the sexual dimorphism of two *Melanerpes* species, the insular Hispaniolan Woodpecker *M. striatus* and the mainland Golden-fronted Woodpecker *M. aurifrons*. The former, endemic to the West Indies, shows greater sexual dimorphism, with about 21% difference in bill length, than continental congeners (less than 10%). Other insular melanerpine species (35, 36, 59) also show a sexual difference of 15-19%. Although both sexes employ the same range of foraging modes and visit the same types of feeding sites, they do differ in the emphasis they devote to certain techniques. Males probe more often than females and there are also slight differences in foraging location (see species account for details). The explanation Selander offered was that the dimorphism expanded the feeding niche of the species. The divergence was believed to be the result of intense competition between the sexes, having not been constrained by the competition from other woodpeckers.

A little earlier, Kilham (1965) had found that female and male Hairy Woodpeckers also differ in their foraging and habitat use. Many other workers (see species accounts) have meanwhile documented sexual differences not only in the above-mentioned melanerpine species, but also in White-backed Woodpecker, Great Spotted Woodpecker, Downy Woodpecker, Red-cockaded Woodpecker, Strickland's Woodpecker, White-headed Woodpecker *Picoides albolarvatus*, Three-toed Woodpecker and others.

Sexual niche segregation is often maintained by intraspecific aggression. In the well-studied Downy Woodpecker, the male keeps the female away from the crown by frequent attacks (e.g. Matthysen *et al.* 1991). The reason why the male stays in the crown may also be related to signalling behaviour. As our own observations on this and other species have shown, males give long-distance calls more frequently and mainly at higher levels of the habitat. This alone would favour foraging in these strata.

HABITAT

It would consume too much space if we were to list all the many habitats in which woodpeckers are found. They will be expounded in the species accounts. Woodpeckers occur in practically all types of forest and woodland. There are few exceptions. Some very wet subalpine forests seem not to be occupied by woodpeckers. Diesselhorst (1968), for instance, noted that they are absent from certain Himalayan forests. Some species are restricted to primary forests; many others, however, favour secondary growth and have accordingly extended their range with deforestation. Again, the reader is referred to the species accounts.

Fire is an important agent for quite a few species. Those woodpeckers in particular which occupy coniferous forests take advantage of trees which have been killed by fire and become infested by insect pests. Among the species which go for such trees are both Three-toed and Black-backed Woodpeckers, Hairy Woodpecker, and even the (extinct) Ivory-billed Woodpecker *Campephilus principalis,* and Tullberg's Woodpecker and Fire-bellied Woodpecker in Africa. Red-cockaded Woodpeckers profit from fires because they keep the hardwood midstorey in check and maintain the specific characteristics of the open pine woodland which this endangered species needs.

Foraging sites vary with general lifestyle of a species, with season and with the food supply and demand. Many quantitative studies have revealed the variety found in this respect among woodpeckers. As with foraging techniques, the data have to be collected according to some standard to be useful in broad comparisons. Remsen & Robinson (1990) provide a fine discussion of this point. Most researchers have noted whether a woodpecker forages on dead or live trees, on the ground, in bushes, in reeds, on stalks of herbaceous plants, on rocks or on buildings.

In most studies, the diameter of the limb or trunk has been noted as well. In most cases the absolute dimensions are given, which is very useful if niche differences in woodpeckers occurring in the same habitat are to be analysed (e.g. Austin 1976; Aulén & Lundberg 1991; Block 1991; Gamboa & Brown 1976; Pierce & Grubb 1981). For an understanding of structural adaptations and behaviour, relative dimensions may be as useful. In this case, 'thin' would refer to a limb smaller in diameter than the woodpecker's body, 'medium' would be about the dimension of the woodpecker, and 'thick' to 'very thick' are those limbs and trunks on which the woodpecker clings more or less as on a flat surface (e.g. Winkler 1973, 1979; Winkler & Leisler 1985). Generally there is a trend that larger woodpeckers use larger branch sizes, but this is not a straight rule as sometimes surmised (Fretwell 1978). Besides the diameter, the surface type and the angle (vertical, diagonal, horizontal, overhanging) should be recorded as well. Many observers also give information on foraging heights. Many give this in absolute terms, again for reasons associated with the study of competition; others prefer to give foraging height in relative terms. Porter *et al.* (1985) recommend recognition of not too many categories, and suggest using 'branches', 'lower trunk', 'mid-trunk' and 'upper trunk' and subdividing tree heights into thirds to obtain the three trunk categories. Although this is certainly practicable in open pine-oak forests, we would suggest using trunk, defined as the trunk not bearing branches, trunk within the crown, and crown. Possible further subdivisions are outer and inner crown and recognition of the base of a tree as a category in its own right.

BEHAVIOUR

With all the excitement associated with new hypotheses about the function of behaviour, many may have forgotten that we have to deal with a wide spectrum of behaviour among the many species found on this earth. A monograph such as this may bring back the feeling for this diversity, and should also remind the reader of how little we actually know about it. If we learn to appreciate the variation of behaviour within one well-defined group of organisms, we may also become aware of how small a portion of the total variability we are truly able to explain with our current theories.

DISPLAYS

Most displays are rather similar among woodpeckers. They are mostly variants of bobbing or swinging head and body movements and bill-pointing. When *bill-pointing*, woodpeckers extend the bill, head and neck along the body axis. This pose is held rigidly and the bill is directed at an opponent. *Bobbing* movements are mostly in a plane perpendicular to the substrate, with the bill describing arcs downwards parallel to the surface and upwards to a more or less perpendicular position. These movements may be combined with lateral movements into *swinging* displays. They may occur in any situation which connotes an approach/retreat conflict, most commonly in agonistic encounters, but may also be given by wary birds approaching, for instance, a feeder. In social encounters these bobbing and swinging displays are usually accompanied by vocalisations, and sound and visual displays are often closely coupled (*contra* Malacarne *et al.* 1991). Since these displays are short-distance signals, asynchrony of visual and acoustical signals (Wickler 1978) does not matter.

Woodpeckers also show various flight manoeuvres. These consist either of a noisy wing burr, an exaggerated bouncing, or sudden, noisy twists in the flight path.

The most spectacular aerial display, described mainly for *Picoides* species, consists of a shallow flutter, with the tail raised above the horizontal. The displaying birds, usually (or always?) males, flutter-glide in most cases away from some site of interaction (female, neighbours, or both), and this behaviour seems also to be part of hole demonstration. The display is accompanied by calls belonging to the *quee*-type of calls described below. Gliding, fluttering and other exaggerated flight manoeuvres are often part of agonistic encounters. Published descriptions are mostly not detailed enough to ascertain whether the behaviours subsumed under *flutter-aerial-displays* (Short 1971b) really refer to one and the same display. At any rate, this behaviour is clearly associated with sexual activities, not necessarily meaning that it does not contain agonistic components. Careful studies of the contexts in which it is exhibited are most desirable.

Agonistic behaviour includes supplanting another bird by flying or hitching along the substrate to the place of the former, which eventually retreats. Chases on foot and on the wing are the next step in an escalation which may culminate in fierce attacks.

Serious fights are in the style of a 'war of attrition', mostly silent or accompanied by very low calls only. Very often these struggles are staged in the lower strata and involve pursuits on the wing and short infights. The typical displacement activities of woodpeckers are pecking and flaking off pieces of bark. Such behaviour is common in agonistic situations, at the staging post before roosting and at any disturbance, especially near or at the roost or nest.

ACOUSTICAL SIGNALS

Calls of woodpeckers are varied and are often tied to specific contexts. In a detailed study of the signals of *Picoides* species (Winkler & Short 1978), a complete enumeration of call categories is presented along with suggestions on how to record the behavioural context. In principle, similar categories and variations thereof can be found in other woodpeckers as well. Since in most cases the repertoires of woodpeckers are poorly documented, a comprehensive review is not feasible. The following types of calls are, however, found in all species:

1) A call used at low to great excitement, which reveals the location of an individual if sufficiently loud (may intergrade in function with the next type); these calls are given at high rates by excited and particularly alarmed birds (nesting season).
2) Long-distance calls are used for keeping contact among the members of a pair and are also part of territorial assertion. Shorter versions are given also by fledged young. Less specialised forms consist of series of more or less similar notes, and more derived forms consist of one or more introductory notes (often of type 1) followed by rhythmic series of characteristic notes. In *Dryocopus*, so it seems, two different calls serve long-distance communication: one given in flight, the other when perched. Pair

members which keep in vocal contact may respond immediately with this call when they receive the partner's signal.

3) Calls which are restricted to the breeding season, which are loud, often squeaky and long. They are given in often long series and may be associated with the flutter-aerial-display. These *quee*-type calls are most similar in function to the song of other birds, and become very important and conspicuous in those species which drum little.

4) Calls in agonistic situations, which in many species may be rendered as *wicka*-calls. They are uttered in synchrony with swinging or bowing displays and may be varied in intensity, emphasis and overall structure.

5) Low intimate calls, which can be heard at close distance only; typically, partners utter them prior to copulation and during changeovers at the nest.

6) Nestling calls comprise at least three types, the most conspicuous of which is a more or less constant twitter or buzz, which peaks when a feeding adult approaches and enters the hole.

7) Woodpeckers scream when captured or when hard pressed in escalating fights.

COURTSHIP AND COPULATION

Females often initiate copulations. A pattern typical of many, if not all, woodpeckers is that the male is near or at the hole, mostly excavating, and the female will fly to the hole and then fly to the copulation branch to adopt her soliciting crouch. In any event, woodpeckers often copulate near the nest, when the latter is nearly completed. Copulations by woodpeckers take place on more or less horizontal limbs. The female may perch lengthwise or crosswise on the branch. The usual pattern is that the female crouches down and the male mounts her, which in some species is associated with fluttering or hovering above the female. Copulations last for 6 to 16 seconds, and the male descends gradually (to the left). The male usually flies off. Both birds commonly preen afterwards. Copulations are accompanied by calls low in both pitch and loudness and often introduced by some activity at the hole, notably (mutual) tapping.

Copulations or pseudocopulations may take place weeks before egg-laying. Copulations are often associated with disputes with intruders, usually immediately after a clash has occurred (Ligon 1970; own observations). Early copulations have been traditionally explained as part of pair-bond formation, the onset of sexual activity, but must also be explained within the framework of the theory of sperm competition (Birkhead & Møller 1992).

An interesting aspect is the reversed mounting which is part of the copulatory behaviour of some *Melanerpes* species (Red-bellied, Lewis's). The female begins the sequence and mounts the male, who then performs the copulatory act proper. This reversed mounting may be an exaggerated form of soliciting by the female. Mounting of the male by the female after copulation has been observed in Middle Spotted Woodpeckers (Günther 1993).

COMFORT ACTIVITIES

Woodpeckers possess about the same repertoire of comfort movements as described for other birds; small differences occur only when a woodpecker has to perform while clinging to a vertical surface (Blume 1965; Gebauer 1982; Kilham 1959d; Lawrence 1967; Stickel 1965; Winkler 1972b). They scratch their head, neck and bill by moving the feet over as well as under the wing. Whether this follows a systematic pattern is not clear. Kilham, in observations of six American species of woodpecker, never saw any scratch with wing lowered. On the other hand, observers working with Great Spotted and Syrian Woodpeckers agree that both forms of scratching occur. Woodpeckers frequently rub their face on bark, a behaviour also known for toucans (Clayton & Cotgreave 1994). The feathers are preened with the bill, which requires some acrobatic action if the bird is clinging to a vertical surface and the lower breast or the belly have to be reached. The bill is also used to groom the toes. Fatty oil from the uropygial gland is distributed over the plumage with sweeping bill movements. The bill is cleaned by being wiped on twigs and bark. Woodpeckers also shake their body along the longitudinal axis and shake their wings. Leg/wing-stretching is particularly difficult for birds clinging to a vertical surface, as they have to release the grip of one foot for a while; thus, the leg is sometimes only minimally stretched or is not stretched at all (Blume 1965; Kilham 1959; Lawrence 1967). By contrast, the double wing-neck stretch largely conforms with the usual avian pattern.

Resting, dozing and sleeping woodpeckers fluff up their plumage, giving them a more round-headed appearance. The neck is also more retracted, which, together with the slack feathers, renders them 'neckless'. It remains to be mentioned that woodpeckers also show gaping and retching movements, commonly referred to as 'yawning'. Sunning (sunbathing) occurs in full sunlight; the feathers of the head and body are fully erected while cheeks and wings are fully exposed to the sun's rays, and the tail is fanned. Woodpeckers occasionally bathe; again, there are no specialised features in this behaviour which would merit detailed description at this point. Dusting (dustbathing), however, is known for only a few species, the Green-barred Woodpecker, the Northern Flicker *Colaptes auratus*, the Campo Flicker and the Black Woodpecker (Glutz & Bauer 1980; Short 1972a; Sick 1993; Skutch 1985).

Several species (Eurasian Wryneck, Red-headed Woodpecker, Red-bellied Woodpecker, Yellow-bellied Sapsucker *Sphyrapicus varius*, Northern Flicker, Scaly-breasted Woodpecker *Celeus grammicus* and Eurasian Green Woodpecker) exhibit passive as well as active anting (King 1974; O'Brien *fide* Short 1982; Skutch 1985; Stanford & Allsop 1949; Stone 1954). The function of this behaviour is not clear. It may be a method of countering ectoparasites, or it may also be a way of ridding ants of their acid and thus be part of foraging behaviour (Judson & Bennett 1992; Sauer 1957).

INTELLIGENCE

The complex foraging and feeding behaviour of woodpeckers, particularly food preparation in anvils and other forms of tool use, storage and utilisation of strongly localised food sources, certainly requires high cognitive skills. Particular studies are, however, scant and restricted to Great Spotted Woodpeckers (Chauvin-Muckensturm 1980; Chauvin 1987). Indirect evidence comes from studies of brain development. Great Spotted Woodpeckers, at least, score almost as high as parrots and corvids in the development of their forebrain (Portmann 1962).

INTERSPECIFIC INTERACTIONS

Woodpeckers are frequently involved in interactions with other bird species, including other woodpeckers, for two main reasons: because they compete with other birds of the bark-foraging guild for food and foraging sites, and because their holes attract many would-be occupants (see below).

The greatest diversity of sympatric woodpeckers probably occurs in Malayan forests (Short 1978). There, 14 species share the same forest; and the truly wood-pecking species differ greatly in size, species of similar size are rather different in habits, and congeners differ in size, morphology and habits to a sufficient degree. Practically all studies on woodpecker foraging have shown that woodpeckers differ in their habitat requirements and foraging habits both from each other and from other members of the guild (e.g. Gamboa & Brown 1976; László 1988; Otvos 1967; Pierce & Grubb 1981; Williams & Batzli 1979a,b; Winkler 1973). Woodpeckers often come in close contact with other woodpeckers, and may hence interact either during foraging or at holes. Some possible consequences of such interactions have already been discussed under the aspect of coloration. Many interactions may relate to drumming behaviour. These signals are fairly species-specific even to the human ear, but woodpeckers may react rather indiscriminately.

Many species join mixed-species flocks or are themselves joined by other birds, sometimes even other woodpeckers. Gleaning species tend to move quickly, skipping several trees when moving, and do not stay at a single site for long. Such species have a much easier time when joining mixed-species flocks. The main reason for associating with other species seems to be increased foraging efficiency owing to reduced need for vigilance (Sullivan 1984a). Woodpeckers also respond to the alarm calls of the species with which they forage (Sullivan 1985a) and resume foraging after a threat faster when others give contact calls (Sullivan 1984b). Tits and nuthatches, and others, not only take advantage of the removal of bark or similar foraging activities, but also may get a 'free' scrap of food if a woodpecker works on a large seed or nut. The peculiar feeding associations of the more arboreal and solitary Green-barred Woodpecker *Colaptes melanochlorus* and the wary and group-living terrestrial Campo Flicker at anthills are probably a combination of both enhanced safety (Short 1969) and foraging opportunities for the former.

Sap wells and seed stores attract commensals as robbers as well, but only stores are defended with vigour (see species accounts).

Woodpecker holes have become central to the survival of many other species of bird, mammals and other animals, even insects. Non-excavating cavity-nesters among birds are often serious competitors for wood-pecker nest sites and often force the woodpeckers to leave a nest and start a new one. Starlings, tityras, and some woodcreepers, to name some especially persistent usurpers, are notorious for their constant threat to woodpecker nests and roosts. Because of their action as hole-constructors in many habitats, and because of their important role in the food chain and foraging actions, woodpeckers are truly keystone species in numerous terrestrial ecosystems.

African woodpeckers suffer from their brood-parasitising relatives, the honeyguides (Indicatoridae).

REPRODUCTION AND SOCIALITY

HOLES AND NESTS

The ability to construct holes as nest sites is one of the key features of woodpeckers. Cavities provide almost perfect shelters for spending the night, as well as for rearing the offspring.

Holes are constructed, therefore, not only prior to nesting but also, for instance, after dispersal so as to provide a safe retreat. The seasonal distribution of hole-excavation activities is poorly documented, but the general pattern seems to be that major excavation work is carried out in the context of nest construction, with a second flurry of hole excavation after young have dispersed (typically in late summer and autumn in temperate climates). The demands on roost sites are less stringent than those on nest sites, and old cavities, nestboxes and other suitable structures are readily accepted for roosting. Most individuals have alternative roost sites at their disposal if disturbed at the main roost. Working on a hole is probably always part of the breeding cycle of most true woodpeckers. Even so, the actual nest may well be another, previously constructed, hole.

Woodpeckers can construct a new hole in one sustained effort, which may take roughly two weeks. This, of course, varies from species to species, and well-documented cases are referred to in the species accounts. Frequently, a particular site is abandoned at some stage of the construction; very often only short 'entrances' are produced. Hole construction begins with a circular funnel, and continues with a cylindrical hole which later forms the entrance. This tunnel often cuts through live and hard wood. The next step is the construction of the chamber, which is usually pear-shaped or in some cases (mainly in small woodpeckers and in piculets) rather cylindrical, following closely the structures of the trunk or limb. In most cases, even those in which the initial tunnel was carved into hard wood, the chamber is dug into soft wood. Many trees provide a hard outer 'shell' and a soft 'heart'. Fungal activities, for instance, cause heartrot. Often, a broken or cut branch is the source of decay which continues to the main trunk or limb. Many holes are therefore sited immediately below such an injury. Tree fungi (e.g. *Fomes*) are also associated with soft heartwood and woodpeckers select such spots, the umbrella of the body of the fungus sheltering the hole entrance. How important this combination of hard outer shell and soft heart is for many woodpeckers can hardly be overstressed. Indeed, most attempts at hole construction are probably abandoned if the woodpecker does not hit appropriate soft wood. It remains an interesting question whether such initial funnels and cylinders may themselves be the starting point for local decay and thus become suitable hole sites some time later. Practical application of these facts is the provision of artificial snags which consist of hard cylinders filled with styrofoam or polystyrene cylinders (Peterson & Grubb 1983).

The nest chamber is made by forceful pecking and tearing-off of pieces of substrate. Hammering is usually more rhythmic than when foraging, and this can help the experienced observer to detect hole sites. Initially, all work is done from outside; in the later stages, only the tail of the working woodpecker may be seen sticking out, jerking in rhythm with the pecks. In the final stage of construction, a bout of work typically commences with the woodpecker entering the hole and collecting chips. Beakfuls of these chips are then removed from the hole, the woodpecker sticking its head out of the entrance and tossing them away with energetic lateral flings. Although the chips may be spread over a wide area, particularly if the hole is high up or if weather conditions are windy, they are useful signs of construction activities for the careful observer and a very good way of detecting nest sites at an early stage. After chips have been removed, which can take some time and is often the only activity at the nest immediately before egg-laying, some excavation work may follow. Chip-tossing and some occasional pecks may still be recorded during incubation. The floor of the nest remains covered by chips, and these may later become soaked with faeces and form clods, which are then removed by the parents. This seems particularly prevalent among sapsuckers, which have rather liquid faeces with thin or possibly no faecal sacs (Kilham 1962).

Holes are often at the periphery of a home range and face a more open section of the habitat. Protection of the entrance is assured by orientation of the entrance. Of the many studies on hole-entrance orientation, one on artificial snags (Peterson & Grubb 1983) revealed that entrances of holes made in summer were randomly oriented, while those of holes made in winter faced away from the dominant wind direction. Hole-entrance diameter depends primarily on the species' body size, but also, to some extent, on temperature. The colder the outside temperature, the narrower the entrance and the deeper the chamber (Peterson & Grubb 1983).

Many species construct their holes on the underside of a sloping limb. Some holes are found even in virtually horizontal branches with the entrance facing vertically downwards. Species which construct their holes in rotten stubs often weaken these stubs considerably and lose their hole because the wood breaks at the site of the hole owing to wind stress (e.g. White-backed Woodpecker).

Woodpeckers which dig their holes into live pine wood can make the chamber only in heartwood, where it cannot be filled by resin. Similar problems are encountered by those species which excavate live cacti; they have to wait until the sap dries up before the hole can be used. It is not only in trees, bushes, palms and cacti that woodpeckers make their cavities, for some species carve out the nests of social insects (Hindwood 1959) and yet others dig their nests into the ground (Short 1971a). The football-sized nests of *Crematogaster* ants are used by the Rufous Woodpecker as its main nest site. Some of the latter's South American relatives, the Pale-crested Woodpecker *Celeus lugubris* and the Golden-green Woodpecker *Piculus chrysochloros*, frequently utilise the nests of social insects as well. Cuban Green Woodpeckers *Xiphidiopicus percussus* also occasionally use the nests of arboreal termites. Buff-spotted Woodpeckers *Campethera nivosa* use ant nests, as well as those of termites, and Campo Flickers also may use arboreal-termite nests. This kind of behaviour is not restricted to woodpeckers: they share it with parrots, trogons, kingfishers, jacamars and puffbirds.

One final note. Because holes play such an important role in the life of a woodpecker, closeness to a hole, entering it and other hole-directed behaviour should not necessarily be taken as a sign of actual nesting, not even if a bird is actually excavating. This caveat should be heeded especially in the case of (tropical) species whose nesting season is spread over several months, or is not known at all.

EGGS TO FLEDGING

Woodpecker eggs invariably are white. There are some differences in shape, some eggs being more spherical and others more elongate, and some species' eggs seem to have rather thin shells. In some cases the eggs become stained with resin, or by the substances present in the ant nests in which some woodpecker species breed. Eggs are usually laid daily until the clutch is complete.

Some experiments have shown that woodpeckers are indeterminate layers. In other words, the number of eggs laid is essentially controlled by clutch size and not by the number of eggs already laid. Thus, removing a new egg will cause the female to continue laying. With this kind of manipulation, as many as 71 eggs have been obtained from a single female Northern Flicker, 28 from a Red-headed Woodpecker (Bent 1939), and 62 eggs from a wryneck (Davis 1955).

Compared with other, non-excavating, hole nesters, woodpeckers have relatively small clutches. Even within the woodpeckers, species with a high propensity for nesting in old holes tend to have larger clutches. Recent hypotheses relate this to the fact that excavating species are usually not limited by nest sites and therefore need less reproductive effort (Martin 1993). On top of that, there is some latitudinal variation in clutch size in temperate species. Clutch size tends to increase with seasonality of the habitat, that is with the difference between winter and summer productivity (Koenig 1986).

Short bouts of nest attendance may even be observed before an egg is laid. Incubation proper, however, generally starts upon completion of the clutch or one or two days before that. Breeding in holes has some consequences for the development of the young. Woodpeckers have rather short incubation periods, but the chicks remain in the nest for a relatively long time. The two periods combined are similar in length to the total duration of chick development in other altricial birds of equivalent size. A possible explanation for the high fledging/incubation ratio of 2.09, compared with about 1.23 in other altricial birds, and the low embryonic metabolism (Berger *et al.* 1994) may be explained by the problems of gas exchange in the nest chamber (Yom-Tov & Ar 1993).

Both sexes have well-developed brood patches. Helpers of Red-cockaded Woodpeckers also develop brood patches, albeit smaller ones (see account for this species).

Nest success, computed as relative number of clutches which produce at least one young, is high among woodpeckers, typically from more than 70% to 100%, and relates to the fact that they excavate their own nests (Martin & Li 1992).

ROLES OF THE SEXES

The key feature of the social and sexual behaviour of woodpeckers is the relatively high contribution of males to nest-hole construction and brood care. In some species at least (Black-rumped Flameback *Dinopium benghalense*, Olive-backed Woodpecker *D. rafflesii*), males also feed the female during courtship. As a rule, the male stays with the eggs and young during the night. In the daytime, both parents are required to incubate and raise the young.

From these facts, one can also conclude that the consequences of sexual selection concern the evolution not only of male but also of female characteristics. For instance, sexual dimorphism in coloration is in almost all cases clearly developed. Nevertheless, it is never extremely pronounced, and in many species both sexes are brightly coloured. Intraspecific encounters often involve intense, albeit ordinarily not very conspicuous, prolonged female-female struggles.

Even in interspecific encounters, the sexes may interact sex for sex and attack only intruders of their own sex in territorial clashes (exceptions are Red-cockaded Woodpecker: Ligon 1970; and Golden-fronted Woodpecker: Selander & Giller 1959, Lawrence 1967). Own (HW) experiments with Syrian Woodpeckers also showed that dummies placed near the nest during the incubation period are attacked sex for sex, though males reacted more specifically than females. This behaviour may be explained by the different 'interests' of the sexes. Males primarily have to cope with sperm competition, to which they respond with sex-specific aggression and immediate copulation after or even during disputes with other male woodpeckers. Females have to avoid loss of fertilisations because the male copulates with other females (Birkhead & Møller 1992), hence male-directed aggression, and they may have to put up with foreign eggs being dumped in their nests. The latter problem regularly occurs in the communally breeding Acorn Woodpecker, in which two females of a group may share the same nest, and in which severe female-female competition has been clearly documented (see account for this species). For other species, corresponding evidence is scant and often indirect. Skutch (1985) mentions a large clutch (8 eggs) in a Yellow-bellied Sapsucker nest, where one male was associated with two females who both took part also in raising the brood. Bent (1939) reports on large clutches in Northern Flickers, and Grimes (1976) includes the Cardinal Woodpecker *Dendropicos fuscescens* among those African bird species in which exceptionally large clutches suggest that two females had produced the clutch. In passing, it should be mentioned that such sex-specific aggression also arises interspecifically. In the nestling period aggression ceases completely, which would agree with the predictions of the former hypothesis, and which must also be seen in the context of the opposing needs of brood care. The hormonal control of these behavioural changes apparently has not yet been studied in woodpeckers. The pertinent behaviour of sexually (near-) monomorphic species is insufficiently known, except in the case of the social Red-cockaded Woodpecker; this species is virtually monomorphic, and both members of the established pair attack single intruders, an understandable default action when the sex of the intruder is practically unknown.

As already mentioned, male parental effort is generally higher, or at least as high, as the effort by females. Only in multi-brooded species, i.e. many melanerpine woodpeckers, may the female take over most of the chores at the end of the nestling period. This is possibly in order to free the male for the preparation of the next nest cavity, so that the next brood can be started quickly. An analogous situation prevails in anatids (ducks, geese, swans), where generally only females incubate; only in the Black Swan *Cygnus atratus* do males participate, thereby helping females to produce clutches at shorter intervals (Brugger & Taborsky 1994).

Since the male takes a large share in hole construction and in the parental tasks, there is, in principle, a selective bias towards polyandrous mating systems and courtship-role reversal (Gwynne 1991). Because woodpeckers are indeterminate layers (see above), egg production would be no constraint for such a development. As both parents are needed to feed the young, however, multiple-nest polyandry is almost impossible (but see West Indian Woodpecker). One important constraint on the evolution of more diverse mating patterns is the nocturnal incubation and brooding by males (a feature also of the reproductive behaviour of non-parasitic cuckoos). This behaviour seems to be very conservative and it prevents the evolution of multi-nest polygyny, otherwise a rather common feature of avian reproductive systems, because the male's nocturnal contribution cannot be shared by two females at two different nests. The effort of the female is equally important, which precludes multi-nest polyandry. A single woodpecker cannot on its own raise a brood from beginning to end. Foraging is often very specialised and needs much time. Only if the nestlings no longer require brooding can one partner rear them to fledging, though without being able to compensate fully for the loss of its mate. So, woodpeckers are essentially monogamous. Even in the co-operatively breeding Red-cockaded Woodpecker helpers do not fertilise the eggs that produce the brood which they help to raise. Rare extra-pair fertilisations stem from males that do not belong to the group (Haig *et al.* 1993, 1994). The only way open to woodpeckers to more complex breeding systems is, so it seems, colonies, brood care by additional helpers, and polygamous systems in which the females attend to a single nest.

GROUP LIVING

Many tropical and subtropical species exhibit some kind of group living. Numerous others may be more social than usually believed, but careful long-term studies are lacking. So, for instance, the accounts on the behaviour of many species include comments about their being met with in family groups. How long the young stay with their parents is unknown in most cases. One could speculate that some of these species may have helpers at the nest frequently, as this kind of social structure appears on rare occasions in temperate populations (e.g. Grey-faced Woodpecker *Picus canus*: Südbeck & Meinecke 1992; Middle Spotted Woodpecker: Pasinelli 1993).

The so-called habitat-saturation model is the most likely explanation for the evolution of co-operative breeding in woodpeckers. This model assumes that conditions for dispersal are limited and therefore that chances for successful dispersal, that is finding an opportunity to breed, are low. One reason why dispersal is risky is the special resources which are critical for survival and reproduction. Among them are suitable breeding sites, specialised food sources (fruiting trees, mast, anthills) and large food stores. If these resources are hard to find or need great investment prior to exploitation (store construction, hole construction, learning of feeding sites), or are already occupied by other woodpeckers, successful establishment after dispersal becomes exceedingly difficult. Although woodpeckers can produce holes on their own, this is by no means an activity without costs and without constraints. Appropriate nest sites may be limited because suitable dead wood cannot be found, or hole-building may take a very long time if the wood is hard and requirements are very specific. This is the case in Red-cockaded Woodpeckers, which have great difficulty in establishing new roost and nest sites. Walters *et al.* (1992b) have shown that preparing initial artificial hole sites will greatly enhance the chance that a new hole cluster will be founded.

Kin selection (based on fitness gains obtained by actions which increase survival/reproductive success of relatives) as a driving agent for woodpecker sociality, or for better co-operative breeding, can almost certainly be ruled out for the Red-cockaded Woodpecker. For one thing, there is a negative correlation between the efficacy of helping and the relatedness between helpers and the brood they care for (Lennartz *et al.* 1987). Secondly, analyses of extensive demographic data show that staying and helping is as successful a strategy as dispersing and finding new breeding opportunities, even without invoking kin selection (Walters *et al.* 1992). This species, as probably other co-operatively breeding woodpeckers, has evolved some morphological and behavioural features which are probably responses to group living. Red-cockaded Woodpeckers are much more vocal than any of their congeners, and those vocalisations which are especially frequent in this species (the various twitters they utter) are certainly homologous to the less variable calls heard from other species only now and then, and only during more or less agonistic encounters (Winkler & Short 1978). In this species, as already discussed, badges which may elicit aggression are tiny and concealable. Both these features, and probably some others, reduce the costs of staying with the parents. So, once evolved under strong selective pressures, and after the evolution of respective social behaviour, particularly communication, group living is conservative in that less strong selective forces are needed to maintain it. A possible case in point is the Acorn Woodpecker. For this species, the localised resource provided by the granaries, which are the work of many woodpeckers over many years, may have been an important driving force for reduced dispersal and consequently group living. Yet these woodpeckers also form groups in areas where no (or only little) food-caching is found, and so, once sociality has evolved, there may be various benefits in staying together (Stacey & Ligon 1987). We know a great deal about the population biology of Acorn and Red-cockaded Woodpeckers, but insufficient (and surprisingly little) about their communication and agonistic behaviour to elaborate more on these ideas. The melanerpine woodpeckers in particular would be an ideal subject for comparative studies of the evolution of group living and co-operative breeding. Such studies would also need to evaluate the role of fruits and other plant material which may foster living in groups by the fact that they are clustered, therefore requiring joint effort on the part of the birds to find fruiting trees on the one hand and provide enough food for a large number of birds on the other. Indeed, reports of the way chattering groups of White Woodpeckers *Melanerpes candidus* drop into a fruiting tree are reminiscent more of parrots than of typical woodpeckers. Resources that are elusive and hard to procure, such as the large larvae of wood-boring beetles, certainly preclude similar behaviour.

Group living has also evolved among ground-dwelling woodpeckers (Short 1971e). The critical resource here seems to be proper nest sites. The Andean and, to a lesser extent, the Campo Flicker form loose colonies. Cases of incipient coloniality have also been described for the Northern Flicker, in which staggering of nesting times allows for close proximity of nests because of reduced aggression during incubation and brood care (Kilham 1973a). Another reason may be that ground woodpeckers are more vulnerable to predation and they 'close ranks' because of this. Ground woodpeckers seem to have evolved independently in Africa within the Campetherini and in South America within the Colaptini. These species form loose colonies the social structure of which is insufficiently known. As discussed under the section on foraging behaviour, woodpeckers, especially those which feed on ants, possess an excellent knowledge of the whereabouts of anthills in their home range. Such knowledge may also be an important resource shared by a group. The nice observations by Oatley *et al.* (1989) on the African Ground Woodpecker clearly hint at such a possibility. Unfortunately, we lack detailed studies of group living and demography comparable with those carried out on the two group-living North American species. As pointed out above, reduction of aggressive badges and other changes in behaviour help to maintain sociality. In terrestrial woodpeckers, a clear tendency towards more camouflaged plumage exists (Goodwin 1968). Brownish colours prevail, and there is even intraspecific co-variation between terrestrial habits and coloration in the Green-barred Woodpecker and the Northern Flicker (Short 1971e). Moreover, sexual (particularly red) badges are reduced in ground woodpeckers. If this has been primarily part of the changes towards more protective coloration, then it also may have fostered evolution of sociality.

High male investment is an important prerequisite for polyandrous mating systems (see above). In fact, breeding groups of *Melanerpes* are basically polyandrous. If there are additional females in such groups, they seem to do worse, or at least not better, than single females with several males (see especially the species account on the Acorn Woodpecker).

Our present understanding of woodpecker group living is based mainly on the extensive studies on two North American species, the Red-cockaded and Acorn Woodpeckers, both of which are co-operative breeders. In these better-studied species, female-female competition seems to be more intense than male-male competition. In both cases, this is connected with the fact that females disperse more readily and have to intrude into a new group and to compete with resident females for breeding opportunities (see also accounts for these species). In the Red-cockaded Woodpecker, females leave their breeding unit, possibly because they are forced out by older helpers, because a son inherits the territory, or through competition from female intruders.

The Acorn Woodpecker, and presumably some of its closer relatives, belongs to those species of birds which, like Purple Swamphen *Porphyrio porphyrio*, Common Moorhen *Gallinula chloropus*, anis *Crotophaga* and some corvids, breed co-operatively and in which two or more females may lay eggs in a single nest (Mumme *et al.* 1988).

A possible first step towards sociality in some cases, besides reduced juvenile dispersal, is communal roosting. In most woodpecker species (even in the social Red-cockaded Woodpeckers, in general), the birds possess individual roosts and only the male stays with the nestlings during the breeding season. In quite a few *Melanerpes* species (38, 40, 41, 42, 49, 54 and possibly 47), the Olive Woodpecker *Dendropicos griseocephalus*, the Blood-coloured Woodpecker *Veniliornis sanguineus* and some piculets (6, 11, 26), however, the pair sleeps together in one hole and/or the parents share the roost with the young more or less regularly. In the latter case, often only one fledgling is produced. The young may stay with the adults until they begin the next reproductive cycle. This also points towards a constraint on dispersal and hole production.

WOODPECKERS AND MAN

Broadly speaking, woodpeckers are popular birds, at least in the northern hemisphere. Their relationships with man are often amicable, but not free of some misunderstandings. Only cartoon-woodpeckers, for instance, combine the fast rhythm of drumming with the powerful and deliberate blows of wood-pecking to produce a destructive staccato sound. Yet woodpeckers do become a nuisance in certain areas for various reasons.

Many fruit-eating melanerpine species seem to be accused of damaging commercial crops. The opening of cacao pods by certain species also causes some concern, although it is not clear whether the seeds or insect larvae are the target of the woodpecker's activity. The habit of many species of excavating roosting or nesting holes in utility poles causes some corresponding damage, particularly if the poles break at the holes under wind stress. Clearly related to hole construction is the damage done by woodpeckers (mainly Great Spotted Woodpecker) to the styrofoam insulation of European houses. This insulation consists of a thin outer layer (a mixture of sand and artificial resin) and thick styrofoam into which woodpeckers excavate holes at house corners and under eaves. The hollow sound of the insulation probably triggers this behaviour. Log cabins, wooden houses, wooden shutters and the like are also subject to woodpecker damage locally. The endangered subspecies *owstoni* of the White-backed Woodpecker is not well esteemed among Japanese mushroom-growers, because it destroys the mushroom bed logs in its search for wood-boring beetle larvae (Ishida 1990a). And, if Syrian (!) Woodpeckers sabotage Israeli irrigation pipes, woodpeckers may even hit the front page of the *New York Times*. This kind of damage to polyethylene pipes near favoured foraging sites is economically more important than this woodpecker's predilection for almonds, pecans, walnuts and pistachios, for which they are also killed in great numbers (Moran 1977).

Woodpeckers do, however, suffer much more from man. Besides direct persecution, habitat loss is certainly the main reason for the decline in woodpecker populations. Provision of appropriate nesting sites is one very important management goal for many species. Nestboxes do not work well for woodpeckers, and managing artificial (Peterson & Grubb 1983) and, much better, natural snags is more promising.

General habitat loss, however, is the most important cause of woodpeckers becoming endangered or extinct. This is particularly true of island species (e.g. Okinawa Woodpecker *Sapheopipo noguchii*, Cuban woodpeckers), woodpeckers of restricted range or at the periphery of their range (e.g. Middle Spotted Woodpecker), and for those which need large unspoiled areas (ivory-bills). If populations are too small or isolated, they may become extinct even if the habitat does not undergo any further change (e.g. Pettersson 1985, for the Middle Spotted Woodpecker in Sweden).

Quite a few species benefit from the deterioration of forests. These are woodpeckers which prefer disturbed or open habitats (e.g. some melanerpine species). Some species adapt to living near human habitations and expand their breeding habitats accordingly (e.g. Pygmy Woodpecker *Picoides kizuki*). Black Woodpeckers seem to have recolonised Europe after a long period of deforestation and retreat (Glutz & Bauer 1980).

Direct persecution may have finally pushed the big ivory-bills over the brink, but generally it has not been the cause of local or global threat to any species of woodpecker. Disturbance through research activities has been ruled out as a cause of low reproductive success in vanishing Swedish Middle Spotted Woodpeckers (Pettersson 1985), but it may become a serious problem in the case of the Red-cockaded Woodpecker (J. Jackson, pers. comm.).

PLATES
1-64
&
SYSTEMATIC
SECTION

PLATE 1

1 Eurasian Wryneck *Jynx torquilla* Text and map page 167

N and C Palearctic, extending south to Himalayas, winters C Africa and S Asia: open forests, clearings, light woodland and edge, on passage also open treeless habitats.

Small, long-tailed and with terrestrial habits. Complex plumage pattern. Sexes alike. Juvenile similar to adult.

>   **Adult** (nominate; Eurasia) Greyish, mottled brown and buff, with dark diamond-shaped patch on mantle, barred tail; barred throat and upper breast. S European populations darker, more heavily marked below; N African birds pale-throated; Himalayan breeders heavily barred below.

2 Rufous-necked Wryneck *Jynx ruficollis* Text and map page 169

Sub-Saharan Africa in disjunct populations south to Cape: light woodland, semi-open areas, plantations and gardens.

Resembles Eurasian Wryneck, but rufous on breast diagnostic (extent varies according to wear); more streaked (less barred) below than Eurasian Wryneck, whose range partly overlaps in winter. Sexes alike. Juvenile resembles adult.

>   **2a** **Adult** (nominate; southern parts of range) Dark rufous-chestnut chin and throat; flanks barred and streaked.
>
>   **2b** **Adult** (*aequatorialis*; Ethiopia) Rufous of throat extends to lower breast, with rufous-buff from lower flanks to undertail-coverts; ventral streaking far less prominent; may show some barring on throat.
>
>   **2c** **Adult** (*pulchricollis*; SE Nigeria to S Sudan and NW Uganda) Chestnut on lower belly to undertail-coverts. Individual depicted shows throat more completely barred, resembling '*thorbeckei*' of Cameroon.
>
>   **2d** **Adult** (*pulchricollis*) Upperparts rufous-tinged; throat to breast darker, more chestnut, with stronger black and white barring on throat sides.

PLATE 2

30   Rufous Piculet *Sasia abnormis*   Text and map page 191

SE Asia, from Burma south to Greater Sundas: secondary forest, swamp forest and primary forest, especially with bamboo.

Tiny, with almost tailless appearance. Green above, with rufous face and underparts; red orbital ring and pale lower mandible; lacks white eye-stripe of White-browed Piculet. Juveniles greyer below.

    30a   **Adult male** Yellow forehead.

    30b   **Adult female** Forehead rufous.

---

29   African Piculet *Sasia africana*   Text and map page 190

Africa, from S Cameroon and NW Angola east to SW Uganda: secondary forest.

The only African piculet; very small and dark, with very short tail. Dark green above and dark grey below, with white behind eye and on rear ear-coverts; red legs and orbital ring.

    29a   **Adult male** Rufous forehead.

    29b   **Adult female** Forehead concolorous with crown.

    29c   **Juvenile** Red feather tips to head and underparts; grey/buff mixed in upperparts.

---

31   White-browed Piculet *Sasia ochracea*   Text and map page 192

S Asia, from N India to S China and Indochina: evergreen and mixed forest, preferring bamboo forest.

Very like Rufous Piculet, but with white stripe behind eye and some/much rufous in upperparts; forehead and central forecrown rufous; fairly prominent orbital ring and all-dark bill. Juvenile greener above and greyer below.

    31a   **Adult male** (nominate; India to Indochina) Yellow centre to rufous forehead. Reddish orbital ring.

    31b   **Adult female** (nominate) Forehead entirely rufous.

    31c   **Adult male** (*reichenowi*; S Burma and adjacent Thailand) Prominent blackish ring around eye.

---

3   Speckled Piculet *Picumnus innominatus*   Text and map page 170

NE Afghanistan and India to E China, and south to Sumatra: deciduous/mixed forest, montane forest, secondary growth, especially with bamboo.

Distinctive: tiny, olive-green above, bold black spots below, and black and white face stripes. Juvenile resembles a dull female.

    3a   **Adult male** (nominate; Afghanistan to Assam) Rufous forehead barred black.

    3b   **Adult female** (nominate) Forehead concolorous with crown.

    3c   **Adult male** (*chinensis*; China) Reduced orange/yellow on forehead. Crown to upper mantle cinnamon-brown, face stripes tinged brown; spots below somewhat heavier.

    3d   **Adult female** (*chinensis*) Forehead concolorous with crown.

30b

30a

29a

29b

29c

31c

31b

31a

3a

3b

3d

3c

PLATE 3

4   **Bar-breasted Piculet** *Picumnus aurifrons*   **Text and map page 171**

South America: lowland tropical forest.

Minute. Greenish-yellowish above with pale yellowish underparts; barred on breast and striped on belly. Back most heavily barred in *transfasciatus* (Tapajós east to Tocantins river). Black cap spotted white, but broadly streaked/spotted yellow (red or orange in some races) on males. Wings more or less broadly edged with greenish yellow. Juvenile duller and browner above; crown browner, streaked (not spotted) whitish.

4a   **Adult male** (nominate; Mato Grosso to Madeira river and east to Tapajós river) Forehead tipped yellow. May rarely show traces of barring on back.

4b   **Adult male** (*borbae*; lower Tapajós west to lower Madeira river) Forehead tipped orange or red. Tertial edges and belly brighter.

5   **Orinoco Piculet** *Picumnus pumilus*   **Text and map page 172**

N South America: tropical forest.

Tiny. Greenish above, with paler yellowish feather edges, and shallowly barred dark and pale below. Traces of barring above. Forehead to hindneck dark brown, spotted with white or brownish-white. Edges to wing feathers inconspicuous. Male with yellow forehead spots. Juvenile duller, with crown tipped buff.

Adult female No yellow in forehead.

6   **Lafresnaye's Piculet** *Picumnus lafresnayi*   **Text and map page 173**

N South America: forests up to 1400m.

Tiny. Greenish above, with fairly obvious paler barring or virtually unbarred, and pale below with blackish barring. Dark crown spotted with white. Juvenile duller, crown tipped buff.

6a   **Adult male** (*punctifrons*; E Peru) Forehead spotted yellow/orange. Faint barring on back.

6b   **Adult male** (nominate; Ecuador, SE Colombia to N Peru) Forehead spotted red. Back with pale bars.

6c   **Adult female** (nominate) Forehead spotted white.

7   **Golden-spangled Piculet** *Picumnus exilis*   **Text and map page 174**

NE South America: lowland forests and tepuis, savannas, edge.

Tiny. Upperparts variable, from dull olive to brighter yellow-brown or greenish, with black feather centres or bar-like markings. Underparts whitish to pale yellow-white, barred blackish. More or less distinct white stripe behind eye. Forehead to hindneck black. Females have entire top of head white-spotted. Juvenile duller and less contrastingly coloured; olive to olive-grey crown, streaked whitish.

7a   **Adult male** (*undulatus*; E Colombia, SE Venezuela, W Guyana and NE Brazil) Forehead and forecrown extensively tipped red (often forming patch). Strongly barred below.

7b   **Adult male** (*buffoni*; E Guyana east to Amapá in NE Brazil) Forehead and forecrown tipped red. Distinctive black-bordered white spots on upperparts; fine bars below, breaking into spots on abdomen.

PLATE 4

11   Guianan Piculet *Picumnus minutissimus*   Text and map page 177

NE South America: lowland to montane forests, plantations, mangrove.

Tiny. Dark brownish above, pale below, with belly brownish; dark edges of feathers give scaly, not barred, impression overall. Head mainly black with white spotting. Juvenile with unspotted crown; duller and less contrastingly coloured below.

11a   Adult male Bright red cap.

11b   Adult female Crown black, finely spotted white.

10   White-bellied Piculet *Picumnus spilogaster*   Text and map page 176

N South America: lowland forest, edges, thickets.

Tiny. Brownish above, unbarred or with indistinct pale bars; white below with black bars on chin and breast and with spots on belly and flanks, or entirely unmarked. Dark ear-coverts are vermiculated. Female has forehead to hindneck black with white spots. Juvenile with blackish unspotted crown, nape spotted; buffier below, more barred above and below.

10a   Adult male (nominate; Guianas and N Brazil) Red patch on forehead and crown.

10b   Adult tail (nominate).

10c   Adult tail (*orinocensis*, E Venezuela) Slightly more white in tail. This race is unmarked below, sometimes with slightly marked flanks.

9   Scaled Piculet *Picumnus squamulatus*   Text and map page 175

N South America: undergrowth of lowland to montane forests and woodlands.

Tiny. Brownish, somewhat scaly above, pale below with dark edges to feathers enhancing general scaly impression; wing with contrasting pale edges. Forehead, crown and hindneck black, spotted white on hindneck; brown ear-coverts unmarked and bordered above by white. Juvenile with darker, more strongly marked back and irregularly marked underparts; crown brown-blackish with dull marks.

9a   Adult male (nominate; Colombia) Forehead and crown with fine orange-red spots. Dark, heavily scaled below.

9b   Adult female (nominate) Crown with fine white spots.

9c   Adult male (*rohli*; N Venezuela, adjacent Colombia) Spots on forehead and crown yellow-orange. Finer and browner, variable bars below.

8   Ecuadorian Piculet *Picumnus sclateri*   Text and map page 175

NW South America: dry woodland and scrub below 2000m.

Tiny. Greyish to grey-brown above without any green tinge, very pale below. White-spotted black cap; face and breast barred dark, contrasting with streaks on belly. Strength of marks on underparts subject to racial variation. Adult female with entire crown and forehead finely spotted white. Juvenile less contrastingly marked; crown blackish, tipped pale.

Adult male (*parvistriatus*, W Ecuador) Forehead spotted with yellow.

11b

11a

10a

9b

10b

10c

9a

8

9c

PLATE 5

12 Spotted Piculet *Picumnus pygmaeus*   Text and map page 178

E South America, Brazil: dry, open woodland (caatinga) up to 750m.

Tiny. Brown, spotted white above and below; nasal tufts white. Female has head black with white spots. Juvenile duller, spots more bar-like below, crown weakly streaked.

Adult male Forehead and forecrown broadly tipped red.

---

14 Varzea Piculet *Picumnus varzeae*   Text and map page 179

NC South America, Brazil: seasonally flooded forest.

Tiny. Dull blackish-brown, unmarked above (tinged greenish), bar-spotted white below. Female with black crown, spotted white. Juvenile weakly spotted and more barred below, crown streaked.

Adult male Forehead and forecrown broadly tipped red.

---

28 Chestnut Piculet *Picumnus cinnamomeus*   Text and map page 190

N South America: coastal forests.

Tiny. Rusty-chestnut all over with no spots or dark marks; wings brown, edged buffy to rufous; nasal tufts and forehead white to cinnamon. Female with black crown, spotted throughout (NE Venezuela, E Colombia) or on forecrown (NW Venezuela) or nape only (Colombia). Juvenile insufficiently known.

Adult male (nominate) Black crown with white spots, spotted orange-yellow on centre.

---

20 Rufous-breasted Piculet *Picumnus rufiventris*   Text and map page 184

W South America: forest edge, secondary growth, lowlands.

Relatively large piculet with dark greenish, unmarked back; neck and underparts rufous-chestnut, unmarked. Male with black crown, tipped red and white (extent varies racially), female crown black with white spots. Juvenile with grey across breast, flanks weakly barred grey, crown olive-grey, tipped cinnamon-buff.

20a Adult male (nominate; Colombia) Mid crown spotted red. Back green, rufous hindneck band.

20b Adult female (*brunneifrons*, Bolivia) Crown spotted white. Back green with rufous hue.

---

13 Speckle-chested Piculet *Picumnus steindachneri*   Text and map page 178

W South America, Peru: humid montane forest, 900-2500m.

Tiny. Grey-brown above with obscure pale fringes and bold pale wing edgings; breast black with white spots, belly white with black bars. Female has black crown with fine white spots. Juvenile apparently unknown.

Adult male Crown broadly tipped red.

PLATE 6

15 White-barred Piculet *Picumnus cirratus*   Text and map page 180

South America: (dry) forests and woodland.

Tiny. Plumage highly variable, generally brownish to brownish-grey above, with only very indistinct barring (or none at all), and pale below with heavy black barring (not scalloped or spotted; some southern populations are less heavily barred below, or show open V-shaped markings). Mostly unmarked or faintly streaked brown ear-coverts. Crown often appears slightly crested. Immatures tend to lack white spots on crown. Juvenile duller and darker, more barred below. Identification complicated by hybridisation with other piculets, including Varzea (14, Plate 5), Ocellated (16), Ochre-collared (17) and White-wedged (18, Plate 7).

> **15a** **Adult male** (nominate; Brazil) Forehead and crown broadly tipped red. Finely barred below, throat scaly.
>
> **15b** **Adult female** (nominate) Fine white spots on crown.
>
> **15c** **Adult male** (*tucumanus*, N Argentina) Forehead with red patch. Faintly barred above, throat scaly; white crown spots often reduced.
>
> **15d** **Adult female** (*thamnophiloides*, NW Argentina) Crown spotted white. Underparts with wavy or wedged bars, throat with (few) fine marks.

17 Ochre-collared Piculet *Picumnus temminckii*   Text and map page 182

S South America: forest edge and scrub.

Tiny. Broad cinnamon-buff collar across hindneck and neck sides, combined with (usually bold) pale spot or line behind eye, diagnostic. Uniform brown above, with pale wing edgings, and prominently barred pale and dark below, with strong buff tone to flanks. Interbreeds commonly with nominate race of White-barred Piculet (15), producing many intermediate individuals. Female with black crown and sparse fine white spots. Juvenile duller and darker, more barred below.

> **Adult male** Red patch on forecrown.

16 Ocellated Piculet *Picumnus dorbygnianus*   Text and map page 181

W South America (E Andean slopes): humid montane forests at 900-2500m.

Tiny. Relatively pale-looking, greyish above with narrow barring, and whitish below with dark feather edges and shaft streaks or mainly dark-streaked; may show indication of a paler collar. Female with black crown, spotted white. Juvenile duller and darker, more barred below. Interbreeds with nominate race of White-wedged Piculet (18, Plate 7) in C Bolivia and with race *thamnophiloides* of White-barred Piculet (15) in S Bolivia.

> **Adult male** (nominate; Bolivia) Forehead tipped red.

15b

15a

15c

15d

17

16

PLATE 7

18 White-wedged Piculet *Picumnus albosquamatus*   **Text and map page 182**

South America: savanna woodland, gallery forest.

Tiny. Brown, with wedge-shaped marks below; can give impression of having a pale hindneck collar; may show small black-bordered white spots on upperparts. Rather variable individually, and races intergrade to some extent. Female with black crown, spotted white. Juvenile less contrasting, more bar-like marks, and with brownish-black crown, faintly marked on nape.

> **18a** **Adult male** (nominate; Bolivia) Forehead and forecrown broadly tipped red. Brownish above, with distinct pale wing edgings, and shows scaly pattern to neck sides and throat; below, has narrow dark borders to pale breast feathers, with flanks either almost unmarked or with subterminal black wedge marks.
>
> **18b** **Adult male** (*guttifer*; SE S America) Forehead and forecrown broadly tipped red. Dark brownish above, with contrasting dark ear-coverts, inconspicuous pale wing edgings (tertial edges brighter), pale spots on wing coverts; much black on throat and breast, and flanks generally show large black wedge-shaped markings.

19 Rusty-necked Piculet *Picumnus fuscus*   **Text and map page 183**

C South America: lowland riverine forest.

Tiny. Brownish to brownish-green upperparts and buffish underparts, buff extending as a broad collar over hindneck; may show very faint hint of barring below, mainly on flanks. Plain buff-brown ear-coverts. Female with unmarked black forehead and crown. Juvenile apparently unknown.

> **Adult male** Central crown and hindcrown tipped orange-red.

22 Ochraceous Piculet *Picumnus limae*   **Text and map page 185**

E South America: dry woodland and shrubs.

Tiny. Plain brown above and unmarked pale buffish-white below, with contrasting darker ear-coverts. Female with black crown, spotted white. Juvenile insufficiently known.

> **Adult male** Red forehead and crown and white-spotted black hindcrown and hindneck.

21 Tawny Piculet *Picumnus fulvescens*   **Text and map page 184**

E South America (NE Brazil): humid forest, woodland, plantations.

Tiny. Uniform rich fulvous-brown below, breast with faint pale streaks, brownish above; dark brown ear-coverts contrast somewhat with rest of face. Male presumably has some red on forehead/crown. Juvenile apparently unknown.

> **Adult female** Black forehead and crown spotted with white.

23 Mottled Piculet *Picumnus nebulosus*   **Text and map page 186**

SE South America: forest, edge, savannas.

Tiny. Brownish above; rusty-brown breast and flanks heavily marked black. Chin and throat barred, much white around lores and behind eye. Female with black crown, spotted white. Juvenile duller, with streaked crown.

> **Adult male** Forehead and forecrown broadly tipped red.

25 Fine-barred Piculet *Picumnus subtilis*   **Text and map page 187**

W South America (SE Peru): humid tropical forest.

Tiny. Yellowish-green and vaguely barred above, dull pale greyish to greyish-yellow below with indistinct fine dark vermiculations; breast somewhat darker. Female with black crown, spotted white. Juvenile greyer, more strongly barred, crown blackish and streaked. May hybridise with Plain-breasted Piculet (24, Plate 8), which differs in head pattern.

> **Adult male** Orange-red tips to crown.

PLATE 8

26   Olivaceous Piculet *Picumnus olivaceus* **Text and map page 188**

Central America and NW South America: undergrowth, secondary growth, mangrove.

Tiny. Olive above, with pale wing edgings and dark ear-covert patch, and paler olive to brownish below, with yellower, brown-streaked belly and flanks. Juvenile greyer, less green, crown blackish with large pale, indistinct spots.

> **26a   Adult male** (*flavotinctus*, Costa Rica, E Panama) Crown streaked yellowish-orange, nape finely spotted white.
> **26b   Adult female** (*flavotinctus*) Crown and nape black with fine white dots.
> **26c   Adult male** (nominate; Colombia) Crown spotted orange-red.

24   Plain-breasted Piculet *Picumnus castelnau* **Text and map page 186**

W South America (E Andean slopes): forest and second growth near water.

Tiny. Greyish-olive upperparts contrast with plain dull whitish underparts; hindneck and ear-coverts vermiculated pale, with white line behind eye. Crown black, nape finely barred pale. May hybridise with similar Fine-barred Piculet (25, plate 7), which differs in head pattern. Juvenile as female but duller, more barred.

> **24a   Adult male** Red feather tips in crown centre.
> **24b   Adult female** Crown black with no spots.

32   Antillean Piculet *Nesoctites micromegas* **Text and map page 193**

West Indies (Hispaniola): forest, second growth.

Small. Unmistakable, with olive-green upperparts, dark-streaked pale underparts, barred ear-coverts and a yellow crown. Juvenile duller, with crown dull yellow (crown briefly bare).

> **32a   Adult male** (nominate; Hispaniola) Red central patch on nape/hindcrown.
> **32b   Adult female** (nominate) No red on head.

27   Greyish Piculet *Picumnus granadensis* **Text and map page 189**

N South America (Colombia):

Tiny. Brownish above and whitish to pale grey below (slightly streaked on some), with chestnut, unmarked ear-coverts and scaly throat pattern; faint pale wing edgings. Juvenile duller and darker, more streaked below.

> **27a   Adult male** (nominate) Yellow-spotted black forehead and crown, and white-spotted black nape.
> **27b   Adult female** (nominate) Crown spotted white.

26b

26a

26c

24b

24a

32b

32a

27b

27a

PLATE 9

33   White Woodpecker *Melanerpes candidus*   **Text and map page 194**

South America: open wooded areas, cultivation; gregarious.

Back and wings black; rump and uppertail-coverts, head and underparts white. Prominent yellow ring around eye. Belly yellow in centre. Juvenile with yellow nape, blackish-brown above.

33a   Adult male Small area of yellow on hindneck.

33b   Adult female Without yellow on neck; black head stripe usually duller, more obscure.

---

34   Lewis's Woodpecker *Melanerpes lewis*   **Text and map page 195**

W North America: open woodland; gregarious.

Dark greenish above, silvery-pink below; appears very dark and crow-like in flight.

34a   Adult Deep crimson face, silvery hindneck band; sexes alike.

34b   Juvenile Less glossy, face brownish, streaked and barred below.

---

35   Guadeloupe Woodpecker *Melanerpes herminieri*   **Text and map page 196**

West Indies (Guadeloupe): forests and cultivation.

Unmistakable, the only woodpecker in the area. Glossy black on head, upperparts and wings; black with dull red hue below. Juvenile duller, red tinge to underparts more orange.

Adult Sexes alike.

---

36   Puerto Rican Woodpecker *Melanerpes portoricensis*   **Text and map page 197**

West Indies (Puerto Rico): forests, plantations.

Black above, forehead and rump white; brownish below. Face and breast red. Juvenile less red (more orange hue), some crown feathers tipped red on males.

36a   Adult male Red below reaches belly, centre of breast with some black.

36b   Adult female Malar area and throat mainly brown, with red more restricted to midline (but rarely, as here, with more red); red on belly more yellowish; forehead more extensively pale.

33a

33b

34a

34b

35

36a

36b

PLATE 10

38 **Acorn Woodpecker** *Melanerpes formicivorus* **Text and map page 200**

W North America to NW South America: open woodland with oaks; gregarious.

Glossy black, with red on crown, white on face and underparts, black breast band; small white wing patch; pale eyes. White rump and wing patches conspicuous in flight. Juvenile less glossy black, throat paler, undertail-coverts heavily streaked, orange spot in crown, brown eyes.

> **38a** **Adult male** (*bairdii*; W USA) Entire crown red. Throat moderately yellow; relatively little streaked below.
>
> **38b** **Adult female** (*bairdii*) Forecrown glossy black, hindcrown red.
>
> **38c** **Adult male** (nominate; S USA, Mexico) Entire crown red. Throat weakly yellow; moderately streaked below; white streaks in black of breast.
>
> **38d** **Adult female** (nominate) Forecrown glossy black, hindcrown red.
>
> **38e** **Adult male** (*flavigula*; Colombia) Forecrown glossy black, hindcrown red. Throat bright yellow, heavily streaked below; rump feathers tipped black.
>
> **38f** **Adult female** (*flavigula*) No red on head.

---

37 **Red-headed Woodpecker** *Melanerpes erythrocephalus* **Text and map page 198**

E North America: open deciduous woodland.

White rump, large white wing patches and white underparts. Prominently black and white in flight. Juvenile brown and white, but still shows large white areas above.

> **37a** **Adult** Unmistakable: red head, neck and throat. Sexes alike.
>
> **37b** **Juvenile** Largely patterned like adult, but brownish, head and neck uniformly brownish-black. Some dark bars in white wing patch.

38a

38c

38b

38d

38e

37a

37b

38f

PLATE 11

39 Black-cheeked Woodpecker *Melanerpes pucherani*   Text and map page 202

Central America, NW South America: forest, edge, plantations.

Black above, narrowly barred white, rump white, and wings black, spotted and barred white; pale below, heavily barred, with belly red in centre. Forehead and cheeks pale, ear-coverts and rear neck sides black, and a small pale streak behind eye. Juvenile duller and browner, belly paler red, crown and nape with some orange-red (crown often barred on female).

> **39a   Adult male** Crown and nape entirely red.
>
> **39b   Adult female** Pale forecrown, black central crown and large red nape patch.

---

40 Golden-naped Woodpecker *Melanerpes chrysauchen*   Text and map page 203

Central America, NW South America: forest, clearings, cultivation.

Black above with white panel from mantle to rump, black wings almost unbarred, entire hindneck bright yellow. Juvenile with reduced red below, duller.

> **40a   Adult male** (nominate; W Panama, Costa Rica) Central crown red.
>
> **40b   Adult female** (nominate) No red on head, but with black crown band.
>
> **40c   Adult male** (*pulcher*, Colombia) Mid crown to upper nape red. White back barred black.
>
> **40d   Adult female** (*pulcher*) Black across central crown, red hindcrown.

---

41 Yellow-tufted Woodpecker *Melanerpes cruentatus*   Text and map page 204

South America: forests, edge, clearings.

Upperparts, head and breast glossy black; belly red centrally, flanks broadly barred black; uppertail-coverts and rump white. Ring of bare whitish skin around eye. Juvenile with red cap, browner.

> **41a   Adult male** ('black-headed' morph; Brazil) Red crown patch.
>
> **41b   Adult female** ('black-headed' morph; Brazil) No red on head.
>
> **41c   Adult male** ('yellow-tufted' morph; Bolivia) Red crown patch. White to yellow stripe over eye, orange-yellow and white patch on nape.
>
> **41d   Adult female** ('yellow-tufted' morph; Bolivia) No red on head.

---

42 Yellow-fronted Woodpecker *Melanerpes flavifrons*   Text and map page 205

E South America: forest and woodland.

Upperparts and wings blue-black, white rump and broad white mantle streaks; grey below, breast bordered by red which extends down belly, pale flanks barred dark. Face black with bright yellow forehead and throat, pale eye ring. Juvenile with red below restricted and more yellowish; some red on crown.

> **42a   Adult male** Red crown, nape and hindneck.
>
> **42b   Adult female** No red on head.

PLATE 12

45   Jamaican Woodpecker *Melanerpes radiolatus*   **Text and map page 208**

West Indies (Jamaica): forest, plantations.

Back and wings black, finely barred white; dark below, with red patch on belly. Forehead and face whitish. Juvenile duller.

    45a   Adult male Entire crown, nape and hindneck red.

    45b   Adult female Grey crown; red nape and hindneck; more yellow than red on belly.

---

46   Golden-cheeked Woodpecker *Melanerpes chrysogenys*   **Text and map page 209**

Central America (Mexico): dry forest and woodland.

Barred black and white above; brownish below, with inconspicuous yellow belly patch and indistinct barring on lower flanks. Cheeks and ear-coverts golden, black marks over and broadly around eye, and bright yellow hindneck. Juvenile duller, paler below; some red in crown.

    46a   Adult male (nominate; W Mexico) Red crown and yellow to orange nape.

    46b   Adult female (nominate) Crown grey, orange-red nape patch.

    46c   Tail Outer feathers fully barred white; restricted white centrally.

---

47   Grey-breasted Woodpecker *Melanerpes hypopolius*   **Text and map page 209**

Central America (Mexico): cactus desert; gregarious.

Barred black and white above and on wings, plain grey-brown below. Forehead and throat white, with a small area of black around eye and a few red feathers beneath it. Juvenile duller, with red crown patch.

    47a   Adult male Red crown patch.

    47b   Adult female No red on crown.

    47c   Tail White central area with black bars; outer vanes with few white spots.

---

44   Hispaniolan Woodpecker *Melanerpes striatus*   **Text and map page 207**

West Indies (Hispaniola): woodland, cultivation, parks; gregarious.

Barred black and yellowish above, plain dark buff below. Rump yellowish, uppertail-coverts tipped red. Lower hindneck black and white. Juvenile browner, more barred below; crown with black patch, tipped white and red.

    44a   Adult male Crown red on black, nape red.

    44b   Adult female Smaller than male. Crown black with some fine white spots at edge, nape red.

---

43   White-fronted Woodpecker *Melanerpes cactorum*   **Text and map page 206**

C South America: woodland, arid scrub.

Very small. Largely black and white above, more or less plain pale buffish below. Head black, forehead, hindneck and face white; throat white or yellow. Juvenile browner, more barred below, with orange patch in crown.

    43a   Adult (yellow-throated morph).

    43b   Adult male Very small patch of red in crown.

    43c   Adult (white-throated morph).

45a

45b

46a

46c

46b

47a

47b

47c

44a

43a

43b

43c

44b

PLATE 13

49 Red-crowned Woodpecker *Melanerpes rubricapillus*   **Text and map page 211**

Central America, N South America: forest edge, woodlands, mangroves, gardens.

Barred black and white above, with white rump; grey-brown below (variable, top row of birds intended to show this variation), centre of belly red. Juvenile duller, red on belly pale, forehead brown.

> **49a** **Adult male** (nominate; Central America to NW South America) Crown and nape red.
>
> **49b** **Adult female** (nominate) Crown pale, nape (paler) red.
>
> **49c** **Tail** (nominate) Black or brownish-black with white spots on outer vanes.
>
> **49d** **Adult male** ('*terricolor*'; Venezuela) Crown and nape red. Dark below.
>
> **49e** **Tail** ('*terricolor*') Central feathers barred white on outer webs.
>
> **49f** **Adult male** (individual from N Venezuala resembling *paraguanae*) Hindcrown/nape buff-brown, belly patch more golden-yellow (less orange/red).
>
> **49g** **Tail** (of 49f) Much white in centre, outer feathers unspotted.

48 Yucatan Woodpecker *Melanerpes pygmaeus*   **Text and map page 210**

Yucatan and Honduras: forests, second growth, coastal scrub.

Usually extensive golden-yellow coloration in face. Juvenile duller, head pattern more diffuse, belly patch paler.

> **48a** **Adult male** Crown and nape red.
>
> **48b** **Adult female** Red restricted to nape.
>
> **48c** **Tail** White spots on outer feathers.
>
> **48d** **Adult male** (*tysoni*; Guanaja Island) Red of crown broken at rear; large bill.
>
> **48e** **Tail** (*tysoni*) Much white/whitish on central feathers, outers unmarked.

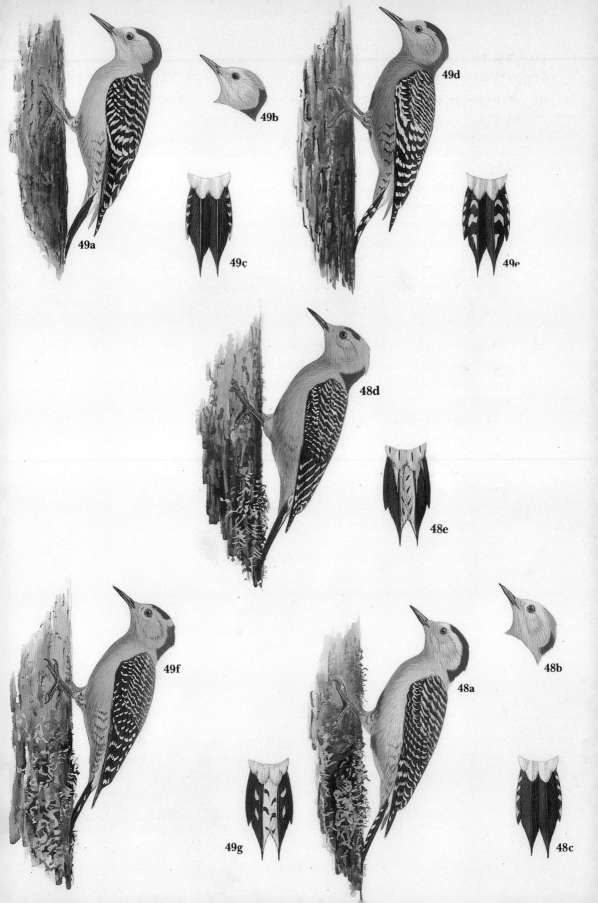

49a

49b

49c

49d

49e

48d

48e

49f

49g

48a

48b

48c

PLATE 14

50 Gila Woodpecker *Melanerpes uropygialis* Text and map page 212

SW North America: cactus desert.

Barred black and white above and on wings, greyish to light brown on head and underparts, belly patch yellow. White wing patch in flight. Juvenile duller, paler yellow on belly; sexes as adults.

- **50a Adult male** (nominate; Arizona) Small patch of red in centre of crown.
- **50b Adult female** (nominate) No red in crown.
- **50c Tail** Black, barred white in centre and at sides.

51 Red-bellied Woodpecker *Melanerpes carolinus* Text and map page 214

E North America: woodlands, suburbs, parks.

Barred black and white above, including wings, rump whitish; greyish below, belly patch orange-red. Nasal tufts/forehead pinkish to red, nape and hindneck usually red, sometimes orange-yellowish. White patch in wing. Juvenile blacker above, crown with some black, darker below with less prominent belly patch and more barring.

- **51a Adult male** Crown, nape and hindneck red, forehead red or with some grey.
- **51b Adult female** Crown without red or red restricted to centre.
- **51c Tail** White patch in centre, outer vanes and tips of outer feathers spotted white.

52 West Indian Woodpecker *Melanerpes superciliaris* Text and map page 215

N West Indies: forest edge, woodland, mangrove, cultivation.

Barred black and white to yellowish-reddish above and on wings; pale below, with red patch on belly. Often some black around/above eye. White wing patch in flight. Juvenile less contrastingly coloured, red on crown (mixed with black on females).

- **52a Adult male** (nominate; Cuba) Nasal tufts, crown and nape to hindneck red.
- **52b Adult female** (nominate) Hindcrown black, mixed with buff, joining black area around eye.
- **52c Tail** (nominate) Black, strongly marked white in centre and on outer feathers.
- **52d Adult male** (*blakei*; Abaco) Crown, nape and hindneck red. More black on back.
- **52e Adult female** (*blakei*) Crown largely black.
- **52f Tail** (*blakei*) Black, marked white in centre and on outer feathers.
- **52g Adult male** (*caymanensis*; Grand Cayman) Nasal tufts pale red, reduced or no black around eye; buff on back, with black bars.
- **52h Adult female** (*caymanensis*) No black on crown.
- **52i Tail** (*caymanensis*) Black, barred white in centre and on outer feathers.

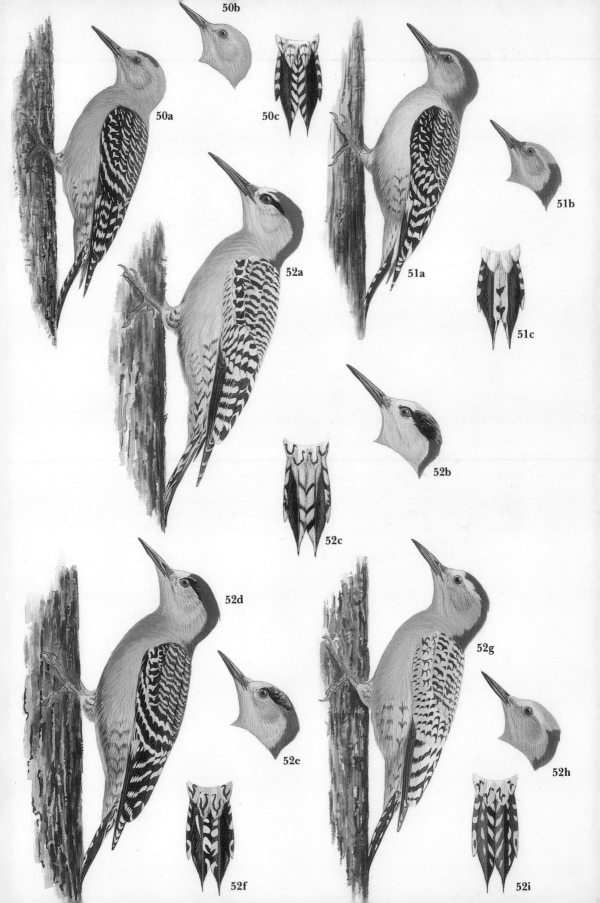

50a

50b

50c

51a

51b

51c

52a

52b

52c

52d

52e

52f

52g

52h

52i

PLATE 15

53   Golden-fronted Woodpecker *Melanerpes aurifrons*   Text and map page 216

S North America, Central America: dry forest, woodland, cultivation.

Barred black and white above; brown to pale buff below. Belly patch and nasal tufts yellow to red. Rump and uppertail-coverts whitish, often marked black. Juvenile vaguely streaked below, paler red on belly, more black above, some black in crown, with small or no orange-red crown patch.

- **53a**   **Adult male** (*dubius*; Yucatan) Nasal tufts red, crown and nape red. Narrow white bars on back; belly patch red with golden tinge.
- **53b**   **Adult female** (*dubius*) Crown pale, nape and nasal tufts red.
- **53c**   **Tail** (*dubius*) Mainly black, outer vanes spotted white.
- **53d**   **Adult male** (nominate; Texas) Red patch on crown, yellow nasal tufts, yellow-golden nape. Black and white bars on back about equally wide; belly patch yellowish.
- **53e**   **Adult female** (nominate) No red on crown; nape yellow.
- **53f**   **Tail** (nominate) Black, with white bars on outer vanes.
- **53g**   **Adult male** (*santacruzi*; El Salvador, Chiapas to Nicaragua) Crown red, golden nasal tufts; nape red, tinged golden at rear. Back with narrow white to brownish-white bars; belly patch with red tinge.
- **53h**   **Adult female** (*santacruzi*) No red on crown.
- **53i**   **Tail** (*santacruzi*) Relatively short; white spots on centre and on outer vanes.
- **53j**   **Adult male** (*polygrammus*; SW Oaxaca, W Chiapas) Crown red, nape and nasal tufts golden-yellow. Narrow white bars on back; belly golden-yellow.
- **53k**   **Adult female** (*polygrammus*) No red in crown.
- **53l**   **Tail** (*polygrammus*) Strongly barred on outer vanes, white bars in centre.

54   Hoffmann's Woodpecker *Melanerpes hoffmannii*   Text and map page 219

Central America: light woodland, gardens.

Back barred black and white; buff-white below, belly patch yellow-orange. Nape yellow. Juvenile duller, darker, more olive below belly patch paler. (See also 49 on Plate 13).

- **54a**   **Adult male** Forecrown red, hindcrown and nape yellow.
- **54b**   **Adult female** Crown grey, nape yellow.
- **54c**   **Tail** Black, with narrow white bars on outer vane, mainly white on inner vanes of central feathers.

53a

53b

53c

53d

53e

53f

53g

53h

53i

53j

53k

53l

54a

54b

54c

PLATE 16

55 Yellow-bellied Sapsucker *Sphyrapicus varius* **Text and map page 220**

North and Central America, West Indies: forest, woodland, orchards.

Appears black and white, with white wing patch, black upper breast, striped black and white on face; hindcrown/nape black.

55a Adult male Crown red; red on throat does not cross black malar.

55b Adult female Throat white; crown red, variably mixed with black, or entirely black.

55c First-winter Less white above; head brown with buffy streaks, breast brown, belly whitish in centre, barred on sides. Crown (incompletely) red; black (and red) on breast appears late in season.

56 Red-naped Sapsucker *Sphyrapicus nuchalis* **Text and map page 222**

W North America: montane (mixed) coniferous forest.

Appears black and white (white reduced on back), with white wing patch, black upper breast, striped black and white on face; red band on hindcrown/nape. Juvenile as in preceding species, but blacker above and darker below; red on head appears earlier.

56a Adult male Crown red; red on throat reaches white below eye.

56b Adult female As male, but most show partly white throat.

57 Red-breasted Sapsucker *Sphyrapicus ruber* **Text and map page 223**

W North America: coniferous and mixed forests.

Entire head red. Black above with white bars on back, and white wing patch. Sexes alike.

57a Adult (*daggetti*; California) White bars on back; white and black markings on face. Long white moustache (extending down neck side), as shown on plate, may indicate hybridisation with Red-naped Sapsucker.

57b Adult (nominate; Oregon, coasts) Pale spots on back, restricted white and black markings. Red coloration darker and extends further down breast.

57c Juvenile Dark, with white line from nasal tufts; *daggetti* paler.

58 Williamson's Sapsucker *Sphyrapicus thyroideus* **Text and map page 224**

W North America: montane coniferous forest.

Male unmistakable. Female very different, heavily barred and lacking white wing patch of other sapsuckers.

58a Adult male Black above, wings with prominent white patch; belly yellow. Head black, with white malar and stripe over eye, throat red.

58b Juvenile male As adult, but duller and throat with white patch (female like adult female, but duller).

58c Adult female Barred brown and buff; head brown, brown concentrated on breast, forming a patch; belly pale yellow.

59 Cuban Green Woodpecker *Xiphidiopicus percussus* **Text and map page 225**

West Indies (Cuba and adjacent islands): forest and woodland.

Green above, wings barred white on primaries; yellow below with dark streaks, and barred flanks. Face black and white; throat black and red, nape and hindcrown red with small crest. Juvenile generally more barred, throat less red; forecrown black mixed with red.

59a Adult male (nominate; Cuba) Crown red on black.

59b Adult female (nominate) Anterior crown black with white streaks; more barred below.

55a

55b

55c

56a

56b

57a

57b

57c

58a

58b

58c

59a

59b

PLATE 17

60 Fine-spotted Woodpecker *Campethera punctuligera*   **Text and map page 226**

W and C Africa: wooded savannas and acacia grassland.

Small. Yellow-green above; pale below, with delicate 'pinhead' spotting (mostly on breast); pale-faced. Juvenile as female, but darker and more barred above, buffish below, with unstreaked black forecrown and more obvious eye-stripe and moustache.

   60a **Adult male** (nominate; range of species except Sudan and NE Zaïre) Fully red crown
             to nape and red moustache.
   60b **Adult female** (nominate) Crown black with white streaks; red nape; no red moustache.

61 Nubian Woodpecker *Campethera nubica*   **Text and map page 227**

E Africa: open woodland and scrub, particularly acacia, up to 2300m; noisy.

Small. Combination of distinctly brownish-toned upperparts with irregular pale barring, barred tail and large spots on underparts should prevent confusion with other *Campethera* species (but see Reichenow's, below). Juvenile darker and more heavily marked, with black crown.

   61a **Adult male** (nominate; range of species except S Somalia) Red crown and nape, white
             supercilium, red moustache. Kenyan individual shown.
   61b **Adult female** (nominate) White-spotted black crown, red nape, black moustache.
   61c **Adult male** (nominate; Ethiopia) Darker, with heavier spotting.
   61d **Adult female** (nominate; Ethiopia).

62 Bennett's Woodpecker *Campethera bennettii*   **Text and map page 228**

Southern Africa: open woodland (especially *Brachystegia*) and acacia scrub in savanna areas; often on ground.

Small. Barred brown, yellow and white above, heavily spotted or rather plain below; wings strongly barred. Male has unmarked pale ear-coverts; female differs from all similar woodpeckers in region in having dark throat and ear-coverts. Juvenile darker and more spotted (less barred) above, coarsely spotted below, with white-spotted black crown. Overlaps in range with Golden-tailed (64, Plate 18), but habitats differ; compare also Nubian (61) and Fine-spotted (60) and very similar Reichenow's (63).

   62a **Adult male** (nominate; range of species except S Angola to Botswana) Red from
             forehead to nape, red moustache, white ear-coverts.
   62b **Adult female** (nominate) Red nape, dark brown chin and throat, dark brown ear-coverts.
   62c **Adult male** (*capricorni*; SW part of range) Paler above; stronger yellow below,
             with very sparse (or no) spots.
   62d **Adult female** (*capricorni*) Throat and ear-coverts blacker than in nominate female, but
             lores pale.

63 Reichenow's Woodpecker *Campethera scriptoricauda*   **Text and map page 229**

E Africa: open woodland, savanna and thorn scrub.

Extremely similar to nominate Bennett's (62), but shorter-winged, with dark band behind eye and chin and throat spotted with black; spots below perhaps larger and more rounded. Extensively pale lower mandible. More regularly barred above than Nubian (61), with less contrasting tail bars and paler face. Juvenile darker and more spotted above, crown black with white spots.

   63a **Adult male** Red forehead to nape and red moustache; dark-streaked ear-coverts.
   63b **Adult female** Crown largely black, nape red; dark-streaked moustache, dark ear-coverts.

72 Ground Woodpecker *Geocolaptes olivaceus*   **Text and map page 237**

South Africa: open rocky terrain, mountain slopes and barren areas, to about 2100m, down to sea level in southwest (e.g. at roadsides); totally terrestrial, gregarious.

Small, but Africa's largest woodpecker. Unmistakable: brownish to greenish above, with grey head, red rump, and barred wings and tail; pinkish-red below, barred flanks. Long curved bill. Juvenile duller, underparts paler.

   72a **Adult male** (nominate; C and W Cape Province) Red moustache visible at close range.
   72b **Adult female** (nominate) Lacks red in moustache.
   72c **Adult male** (*prometheus*; rest of species' range) Paler than nominate.

60a

60b

61a

61b

61c

61d

62a

62b

62c

62d

63a

63b

72b

72a

72c

PLATE 18

64 Golden-tailed Woodpecker *Campethera abingoni*   **Text and map page 230**

W, C and southern Africa: dense parts of forests and woodland, often near rivers in more open regions, in south, also thorn savanna, dry woodland and coastal forests.

Small. Yellow-green to grey-green or olive-brown above, barred pale yellowish, and whitish below with broad blackish streaks (may appear blotchy on breast); normally shows white supercilium and pale line below eye. Male mostly red on crown and moustache; female and more streaked juvenile have forehead, crown and moustache patterned black and white. Combination of barred greenish upperparts and streaked underparts generally separates it from most other woodpeckers within its range. Bennett's, Reichenow's and Nubian (Plate 17) are browner and more heavily barred above and spotted (not streaked) below, and female Bennett's has brown ear-coverts and throat; Fine-spotted (60, Plate 17) has paler face and underparts with delicate speckles; Mombasa Woodpecker (65) is very like Golden-tailed, but has brighter upperparts with small yellow spots (not bars).

> **64a Adult male** (*anderssoni*; SW Africa) Red crown and moustache. Grey-tinged above, heavily marked below (breast blackish).
>
> **64b Adult female** (*anderssoni*) White-spotted black crown, red nape; moustache barred black and white.
>
> **64c Adult male** (*kavirondensis*; E Rwanda to SW Kenya) Red crown and moustache. Ear-coverts streaked; paler below, with narrower streaks.
>
> **64d Adult female** (*kavirondensis*) White-spotted black crown and moustache.
>
> **64e Adult male** (*chrysura*; Senegambia to W Uganda) Smaller and greener, more streaked than barred above; streaked ear-coverts.
>
> **64f Adult female** (*chrysura*) White-spotted crown and moustache.

---

65 Mombasa Woodpecker *Campethera mombassica*   **Text and map page 231**

E Africa: forest and woodland.

Small. Differs from Golden-tailed (64) in bright golden-green upperparts with small whitish spots (not bars), paler throat, and olive-green (not blackish) bases to crown feathers; voice also differs (and rarely, if ever, drums). Juvenile much as adult female but duller, more spotted above, more heavily marked below.

> **65a Adult male** Crown red with olive feather bases; short red and black moustache.
>
> **65b Adult female** Crown olive-green with pale spots, moustache dark-streaked olive.

---

66 Knysna Woodpecker *Campethera notata*   **Text and map page 232**

Southern South Africa: coastal evergreen forest, thickets and scrub, occasionally gardens.

Small. Green above with fine spots; pale below, with prominent large dark spots (extending to neck sides). Appears relatively dark, especially when worn. Juvenile much as adult female, but less spotted and less yellow above, more heavily marked below.

> **66a Adult male** Crown red with dark olive bases; spotted red moustache (sometimes obscure).
>
> **66b Adult female** Crown olive-brown with pale spots, dark moustache.

64a

64b

64c

64d

64e

64f

65a

65b

66a

66b

PLATE 19

67 Little Green Woodpecker *Campethera maculosa*   Text and map page 233

W Africa: lowland forest edge and clearings with secondary growth.

Small and small-headed, with short bill. Bronzy-green above, with black tail; fully barred below, with yellow underwing; lacks moustache. Juvenile greener, pale-streaked above, paler and irregularly barred below. Differs from race *permista* of Green-backed (68e, f) in having bronze/yellowish tinge to upperparts, blacker tail, less obvious red on head (male) and unmarked underwing-coverts (of little use in the field); female lacks red nape of female Green-backed.

> **67a   Adult male** Red on nape, with suggestion of reddish crown.
>
> **67b   Adult female** Crown and nape buff-spotted olive.

68 Green-backed Woodpecker *Campethera cailliautii*   Text and map page 233

W, C and E Africa: forest edge and clearings, secondary growth, riparian and *Brachystegia* woodland, palm groves and thorn scrub; loud calls.

Small and small-headed, with short bill. Variable, green above (unmarked, spotted or barred) and pale below (spotted, semi-barred or, on western *permista*, heavily barred); yellow undertail and barred yellow underwing. Males have red forehead to nape; females have red only on nape. Juvenile less yellow-tinged above, with red on nape. In extreme west, race *permista* overlaps with highly similar Little Green Woodpecker (see above). Eastern races (barred/spotted above and spotted below) differ from similar-sized Cardinal Woodpecker (76, Plate 21) in greener, less black and white appearance, lack of dark moustache, and spotted (not streaked) underparts.

> **68a   Adult male** (nominate; coastal S Somalia to NE Tanzania) More spotted and less barred above.
>
> **68b   Adult female** (nominate) As male, but crown dark with pale spots.
>
> **68c   Adult male** (*nyansae;* Ethiopia, SW Kenya to Zambia and west to Angola) Greener, less yellow, above with narrow streaks rather than spots; heavily spotted below (almost barred).
>
> **68d   Adult male** (*loveridgei;* C Tanzania to Mozambique and west to E Zimbabwe) Yellow-green above with pale bar-like spotting; buff-tinged below, with dark spots becoming smaller on belly, and barred flanks.
>
> **68e   Adult male** (*permista;* E Ghana to SW Sudan, SW Uganda and NW Angola) Distinctive; plain green above and fully barred dark below.
>
> **68f   Adult female** (*permista*) Lacks red on crown.

67a

67b

68a

68b

68c

68f

68d

68e

PLATE 20

69 Tullberg's Woodpecker *Campethera tullbergi* Text and map page 234

WC and EC Africa: moist mountain forests, up to 3000m.

Small but rather distinctive; green-backed, with pale underparts finely barred (eastern races) or spotted (western race); no moustache. Males have red forehead to nape, females have red nape. Juveniles grey-tinged above, with heavier markings. Compare race *permista* of Green-backed (68e, f, Plate 19), which may possibly occur in similar areas.

> **69a** **Adult male** (*taeniolaema*; E Zaïre to W Kenya) Face and underparts green-tinged, with narrow dark barring.
>
> **69b** **Adult female** (*taeniolaema*) Forehead and crown black with white spots; usually has some reddish coloration on lower forehead (occasionally lacking, as here).
>
> **69c** **Adult male** (*hausburgi*; Kenya east of Rift Valley) Yellower above and below, with narrower barring.
>
> **69d** **Adult male** (nominate; Nigeria and Cameroon) Greener, less yellow, above; speckled face and breast and spotted yellow underparts; small area of red on carpal area (unique among woodpeckers).

71 Brown-eared Woodpecker *Campethera caroli* Text and map page 236

W and C Africa: lowland forest, secondary growth, plantations, occasionally gallery forest.

Small and rather dark. Dull greenish above, tinged bronze (more olive in west), with black tail; dark below with prominent pale spots; lacks moustache. Diagnostic brown ear-coverts bordered by long pale supercilium (but whole face may be stained green). Juvenile less bronzy, with pinky-brown ear-coverts, and more heavily patterned below.

> **71a** **Adult male** (nominate; range of species except W Africa) Dull red on hindcrown.
>
> **71b** **Adult female** (nominate) No red on head.

70 Buff-spotted Woodpecker *Campethera nivosa* Text and map page 235

W and C Africa: lowland forest, dense secondary growth.

Very small, with short bill. Unmarked bronze-green above, and dark olive or yellowish-olive below with pale spots/bars; crown dark olive; lacks moustache. Juvenile less bronzy above, and darker below. Compare Little Green (67, Plate 19) and race *permista* of Green-backed (68e, f, Plate 19).

> **70a** **Adult male** (nominate; Senegambia to W Zaïre and southwards) Nape red. Tinged bronze above.
>
> **70b** **Adult male** (*herberti*; Central African Republic east to Kenya and south to Zaïre) Smaller than nominate. Nape red. Lacks bronze tinge above, tail greener; yellower below, with pale bars broader.
>
> **70c** **Adult female** (*herberti*) Lacks male's red nape.

69a

69c

69b

71b

69d

71a

70a

70b

70c

PLATE 21

73 **Little Grey Woodpecker** *Dendropicos elachus*   Text and map page 238

Sub-Saharan Africa, from Senegambia to W Sudan: lightly wooded steppe and wadis in sahel and subdesert.

Very small. Barred grey-brown and white above; white below, lightly spotted brown. Looks pale, with poorly marked head (weak moustache). Red rump noticeable in flight. Juvenile duller.

73a **Adult male** Red hindcrown and nape.

73b **Adult female** Entire crown and nape brown.

75 **Abyssinian Woodpecker** *Dendropicos abyssinicus*   Text and map page 240

Ethiopian highlands: juniper woods, *Hagenia* forest, euphorbia, occasionally wooded savanna.

Small. Unmistakable within range: golden-yellow above, with barred wings and red rump, and pale and heavily streaked below; striped head pattern. Juvenile more greenish, less golden, above, more heavily marked below, both sexes with red on crown and black nape.

75a **Adult male** Red hindcrown and nape.

75b **Adult female** Crown and nape brown.

74 **Speckle-breasted Woodpecker** *Dendropicos poecilolaemus*   Text and map page 239

C Africa, from S Nigeria to W Kenya: forest edge and clearings, in west also upland savanna with forest.

Very small. Yellow-green above, wings spotted and barred; yellowish below, typically with scattered spots on breast (some show variable barring); small dark moustache, but facial markings rather poorly defined. Juvenile greyer, lacking yellow tones, with faint barring above and less marked underparts, both sexes having red on crown and black nape. Where sympatric with Cardinal Woodpecker, latter is obviously streaked below; Green-backed (68, Plate 19) is fully spotted below and spotted above, or (in west) entirely barred below, while Gaboon Woodpecker (78, Plate 22) has entire underparts heavily spotted/streaked.

74a **Adult male** Red hindcrown and nape.

74b **Adult female** Crown and nape all dark.

76 **Cardinal Woodpecker** *Dendropicos fuscescens*   Text and map page 240

Most of sub-Saharan Africa southwards to the Cape: widely varied habitats (if not too dense or too open), often forest edge and clearings, various woodland and scrub, and southern thornveld.

Generally Africa's commonest woodpecker. Very small. Variable, with a number of races. Upperparts vary from green and unbarred in northwest of range to barred blackish and white in south, browner and paler in northeast, and mostly more yellowish-green with variable barring in central part of range; rump usually yellower, wings and tail invariably barred. White to yellow below, heavily to rather lightly streaked, flanks usually with at least a trace of barring. Sides of head usually whitish and obscurely streaked, with variably prominent dark moustache. Juvenile duller and greyer, both sexes with red on central crown and black nape. In northwest and north-central part of range, Melancholy and Gaboon Woodpeckers (77 and 78, Plate 22) have stronger facial pattern, heavier markings below, and plain wings and tail, Speckle-breasted (74) has unbarred tail and very fine spots below (largely confined to breast), and Little Green (67, Plate 19) is barred below, has plain black tail and lacks moustache. Compare also Green-backed (68, Plate 19), whose range overlaps widely with Cardinal's.

76a **Adult male** (nominate; NC Namibia to W Natal) Forehead and forecrown brown, hindcrown and nape red. Barred above and heavily streaked below.

76b **Adult female** (nominate) Crown and nape black.

76c **Adult male** (*lafresnayi*; Senegambia to Nigeria) Red hindcrown and nape. Smaller. Back green with obscure barring; narrowly streaked below.

76d **Adult female** (*lafresnayi*) Lacks red on head.

76e **Adult male** (*lepidus*, E African highlands) Red hindcrown and nape. Back unbarred (but more barred in Kenyan highlands); pale and very finely streaked below.

76f **Adult female** (*lepidus*) Lacks red on head. May show more barring above than male.

73a

73b

75a

75b

74a

74b

76a

76b

76c

76d

76e

76f

PLATE 22

83 Elliot's Woodpecker *Dendropicos elliotii*   Text and map page 247

WC and C Africa: dense primary forest, also moist montane forest in northwest.

Small (but a relatively large woodpecker within its African range). Plain greenish above, with long unbarred tail, rather plain pale face and black forehead and forecrown; yellow to buffish below, streaked or (in west) unstreaked. Juvenile duller, with heavier streaking below, both sexes with red on crown.

83a   **Adult male** (*johnstoni*; highlands of Nigeria and Cameroon) Red hindcrown and nape. Underparts plain yellow.

83b   **Adult female** (*johnstoni*) Forehead to nape black.

83c   **Adult male** (nominate; Cameroon lowlands, south to Cabinda and east to Uganda) Red hindcrown and nape. Underparts darker, streaked.

77 Melancholy Woodpecker *Dendropicos lugubris*   Text and map page 242

W Africa: forest edge and secondary growth.

Small. Bronzy-green above, broadly and heavily streaked brown below (appears darkish). Distinctive head pattern, white with prominent dark ear-coverts and moustache. Juvenile duller, lacking bronze tinge, both sexes with red on hindcrown and black nape. Intergrades with Gaboon Woodpecker (78).

77a   **Adult male** (Sierra Leone) Red nape.

77b   **Adult female** Nape blackish.

77c   **Adult male** (S Nigeria) Intergrade between Melancholy and Gaboon Woodpeckers. Red on head more extensive, thinner moustache, more heavily streaked head and underparts (very like race *reichenowi* of Gaboon).

77d   **Adult female** (S Nigeria) Intergrade. Lacks red on head.

78 Gaboon Woodpecker *Dendropicos gabonensis*   Text and map page 243

C Africa: forest edge, secondary growth and edges of cultivation.

Small. Combination of unmarked green upperparts, including wings and tail, and yellowish, heavily streaked/spotted underparts distinguishes this from other small woodpeckers in its range; moustache indistinct or lacking. Juvenile duller and greener above, both sexes with red on hindcrown and black nape. Western race *reichenowi* intergrades with Melancholy Woodpecker.

78a   **Adult male** (nominate; range of species except S Nigeria to SW Cameroon) Red hindcrown and nape.

78b   **Adult female** (nominate) Forehead to nape dark brown.

83a

83c

83b

77a

77b

77c

78a

78b

77d

PLATE 23

80   Bearded Woodpecker *Dendropicos namaquus*   **Text and map page 244**

C, E and S Africa: more open broadleaf woodland, wooded savanna and acacia scrub.

With Ground Woodpecker (72, Plate 17), the largest African woodpecker. Very long, broad bill. Dark plumage, narrowly barred above and below; face white, with contrasting very broad black eye-stripe and moustache. Juvenile more diffusely barred, both sexes with crown mixed red, black and white.

80a   Adult male (nominate; range of species except northeast and south) Red hindcrown.

80b   Adult female (nominate) Lacks red on head.

80c   Adult male (*schoensis*, Ethiopia to N Kenya) Red hindcrown. Less barred below, with darker breast.

80d   Adult female (*schoensis*) Lacks red on head.

80e   Adult male (*coalescens*, S Africa, S Mozambique) Darker above with barring broken (more spot-like); less barred below than nominate.

---

79   Stierling's Woodpecker *Dendropicos stierlingi*   **Text and map page 244**

E Africa: *Brachystegia* woodland; rare.

Small. Easily distinguished from other woodpeckers in its range by combination of plain brown upperparts, wings and tail, barred and streaked underparts (scaly pattern), broad dark ear-covert patch and moustache, and small size. Juvenile duller, with irregular markings below, both sexes having red in crown centre. Has characteristic twisting flight.

79a   Adult male Red crown and nape.

79b   Adult female Forehead to nape brownish, vaguely streaked.

---

81   Fire-bellied Woodpecker *Dendropicos pyrrhogaster*   **Text and map page 246**

W Africa: lowland primary and secondary forest.

The largest forest woodpecker in its range. Long, broad bill. Mainly bronze-green above, with patterned flanks; combination of broad black and white head stripes, red rump, and red panel down underparts diagnostic. Juvenile duller, with less red below, both sexes with some red on crown.

81a   Adult male Red crown and nape.

81b   Adult female Forehead to nape black.

---

82   Golden-crowned Woodpecker *Dendropicos xantholophus*   **Text and map page 246**

C Africa: lowland forest and secondary growth; noisy.

One of Africa's biggest woodpeckers. Dark, with striking black and white head pattern. Dark brown above; dark olive below, with pale spots and bars. The only African woodpecker in which both sexes lack red in plumage. Juvenile duller, with more barring below, both sexes with yellow tips to hindcrown.

82a   Adult male Yellow crown

82b   Adult female Lacks yellow on head (may show a trace).

80a

80b

80c

80e

80d

79a

79b

81a

82a

81b

82b

PLATE 24

84   Grey Woodpecker *Dendropicos goertae*   Text and map page 248

W and C Africa: various woodlands, forest edge and savanna, in west also mangroves.

Small. Unbarred green or brownish-green above, with red rump and barred wings and tail; pale below, with orange to yellow belly patch and barred flanks; plain pale face. Juvenile duller, more barred below, with smaller, paler belly patch, both sexes with red in crown centre. Compare Grey-headed (85) and Olive Woodpeckers (86).

> **84a**   **Adult male** (nominate; most of species' range, excluding sahel zone and central isolates) Red crown and nape.
>
> **84b**   **Adult female** (nominate) Entire head grey.
>
> **84c**   **Adult male** (*koenigi*; sahel zone from E Mali to W Sudan) Much paler; white tips to wing-coverts; belly patch yellow and smaller (often lacking).

85   Grey-headed Woodpecker *Dendropicos spodocephalus*   Text and map page 249

E Africa: moist forest, forest edge and riverine forest.

Small. Yellow-green above, with red rump and barred outer tail; pale grey on face and underparts, with large red belly patch. Juvenile duller, lacking yellow tinge, slightly barred below and with smaller belly patch, both sexes having red in crown centre. Differs from very similar Grey Woodpecker (84) mainly in brighter upperparts, less barred wings and tail, and larger, red (not orange/yellow) belly patch. Race *abessinicus* of Grey-headed is intermediate between the two species.

> **85a**   **Adult male** (nominate; C and S Ethiopia) Red hindcrown and nape.
>
> **85b**   **Adult female** (nominate) Entire head grey.

86   Olive Woodpecker *Dendropicos griseocephalus*   Text and map page 250

Southern and EC Africa: montane forest, *Hagenia* forest, also riverine evergreen forest and (in south) coastal forest.

Small. Distinguished from all other African woodpeckers by plain olive plumage, with dark grey face, red rump and (some populations) red belly patch. Juvenile duller, somewhat barred below, with insignificant belly patch, both sexes with red and black in crown centre.

> **86a**   **Adult male** (*kilimensis*: Tanzanian highlands) Red hindcrown and nape (here in worn plumage, showing grey feather bases). Smaller than other two races; lacks red on belly.
>
> **86b**   **Adult female** (*kilimensis*) Head all grey.
>
> **86c**   **Adult male** (*ruwenzori*; range of species, excluding areas occupied by other two races) Red hindcrown and nape. Relatively bright; red belly patch often extensive; wings more barred.
>
> **86d**   **Adult female** (*ruwenzori*) Head all grey.
>
> **86e**   **Adult male** (nominate; eastern S Africa and Lebombo mountains) Red hindcrown and nape. Dark; small red belly patch (often lacking).
>
> **86f**   **Adult female** (nominate) Lacks red on head.

84a

84b

84c

85a

85b

86a

86b

86c

86d

86e

86f

PLATE 25

87 Brown-backed Woodpecker *Picoides obsoletus* Text and map page 251

Sub-Saharan Africa (the Gambia to Ethiopia and Tanzania): bush savanna, in scrub, edges of cultivation and *Combretum* woodland, also gardens and more open savanna.

Very small. Mostly brown/blackish and white, with plain back and strongly barred wings and tail; whitish below, variably dark-streaked; prominent white supercilium and moustache enclosing dark ear-coverts. Juvenile darker, greyer, usually with some barring below, both sexes with some red on hindcrown. Compare heavily worn (pale) individuals with unworn Little Grey Woodpecker (73, Plate 21).

  87a **Adult male** (nominate; W Africa to Uganda) Red hindcrown and nape.

  87b **Adult female** (nominate) Hindcrown and nape brown.

  87c **Adult male** (*ingens*; C Ethiopia to N Tanzania) Red hindcrown. Larger and darker than nominate.

  87d **Adult female** (*ingens*) Lacks red on head.

  87e **Adult male** (*crateri*; Tanzania, in Ngorongoro, Crater Highlands and Nou Forest) Red hindcrown and nape. Darkest race, almost black above; streaks below very broad and dark.

89 Philippine Woodpecker *Picoides maculatus* Text and map page 253

Philippines, including all main islands and Sulu archipelago, but not Palawan: secondary forest/cloud forest, edge, riverside woods and grassy clearings.

By far the smallest woodpecker in its range. Most races (except in Sulu) pale-barred dark above and on wings, and pale below with dark spots and streaks; black and white bands on head. Juvenile more heavily barred above, more obscurely marked below.

  89a **Adult male** (*fulvifasciatus*; Bohol, Leyte, Samar, Basilan and Mindanao) Small red patch on side of hindcrown. Ground colour above very dark, barring strongly tinged buff; underparts washed buff; much white on head, with buff nasal tufts.

  89b **Adult female** (*fulvifasciatus*) Side of nape lacks red.

  89c **Adult male** (*ramsayi*; Sulu Islands and Siassi) More red on nape than males of other races. Browner and unbarred above, back with white streaks; less marked below, but with brown and yellow breast band; long supercilium to hindneck.

  89d **Adult male** (nominate; Panay, Sibuyan, Cebu, Guimaros and Negros) Small red patch on rear crown side. Dark brown above; dark behind ear-coverts, supercilium short.

  89e **Adult female** (nominate) Lacks red crown patch.

  89f **Adult male** (*validirostris*; Luzon, Mindoro, Lubang, Marinduque and Catanduanes Islands) Red on rear crown side reduced to narrow line. Darker than nominate; white extends around rear ear-coverts.

  89g **Adult female** (*validirostris*) No red on side of crown.

88 Sulawesi Woodpecker *Picoides temminckii* Text and map page 252

Sulawesi: wooded areas and forests.

Very small and short-tailed. Unmistakable: the only woodpecker of its size in Sulawesi. Barred above and on wings, and streaked below; dark crown and ear-coverts. Juvenile as adult, but more brownish.

  88a **Adult male** Small red patch on side of nape (female lacks red).

  88b **Adult male** Many have white of cheeks extending to hindneck.

PLATE 26

90 Brown-capped Woodpecker *Picoides moluccensis*   Text and map page 254

Indian subcontinent to Greater and Lesser Sundas: secondary forest, open woodland, coastal scrub, mangroves, plantations and gardens.

Very small and generally dingy-looking. Barred above and on wings and tail, with brown to blackish crown and dark band through ear-coverts and down side of neck, and pale below; eastern races have prominent broad moustache and are streaked below. Juvenile less contrasting, but streaked below, males with orange-red nape patch. Grey-capped Woodpecker (91) bigger and darker, more contrastingly patterned, with less/no white on tail.

90a **Adult male** (*nanus*, N India and most of peninsula) Little streaking below; pale eyes, red orbital ring. Small red line on rear crown sides usually invisible (absent on female).

90b **Adult male** (*grandis*, Lesser Sundas) Larger; dark moustache; underparts dirty, with more streaking; dark eyes, no orbital ring.

90c **Adult male** (nominate: Malaya to Greater Sundas) Darker crown, prominent moustache; heavily streaked below; dark eyes, no orbital ring. Small red spot on nape side.

90d **Adult female** (nominate) Lacks red spot on side of nape.

90e **Adult male** (*gymnopthalmus*, Sri Lanka) Very small. Black and white above, with broader wingbars; unstreaked below; pale eyes, with red orbital ring. Small red spot on sides of rear crown.

90f **Adult female** (*gymnopthalmus*) Lacks red spot on side of crown.

---

91 Grey-capped Woodpecker *Picoides canicapillus*   Text and map page 255

S and E Asia: wide variety of not over-dense forests and woodlands, also scrub and gardens and (in mainland SE Asia) coastal vegetation.

Very small. Basically black and white, with streaked pale underparts; dark crown, dark band through ear-coverts and down side of neck, and obscure dark moustache; black tail usually with little white. Juvenile somewhat darker, with heavier streaking (and sometimes hint of barring) below, males with orange-red on nape.

91a **Adult male** (*doerriesi*, E Siberia to Korea) Largest race. Small red area on sides of rear crown. Very black and white, with white lower back and rump, white wing patch; little/no white in tail.

91b **Adult female** (*doerriesi*) No red on sides of crown.

91c **Adult male** (*kaleensis*, Taiwan, SE China to N Burma) Smaller. Small red spot on sides of crown. Less white in wings; barred back; heavily streaked below.

91d **Adult female** (*kaleensis*) No red on sides of crown.

91e **Adult male** (*semicoronatus*, E Nepal to W Assam) Red on sides of rear crown extends across nape. Lower forehead buff; barred white above and on sides of tail; yellowish below, streaked brown.

91f **Adult female** (*semicoronatus*) Nape and sides of crown wholly blackish-grey.

91g **Adult male** (*mitchelli*, N Pakistan to Nepal) As *semicoronatus*, but red restricted to narrow streak on side of crown; dark of ear-coverts often meets crown.

91h **Adult male** (*auritus*, S Thailand and Malaya) Similar to *mitchelli*, but with complete white supercilium. Central tail sometimes barred.

91i **Adult female** (*aurantiiventris*, Borneo) Smallest race, but relatively long-billed. More pronounced malar stripe. Belly generally with orange tone.

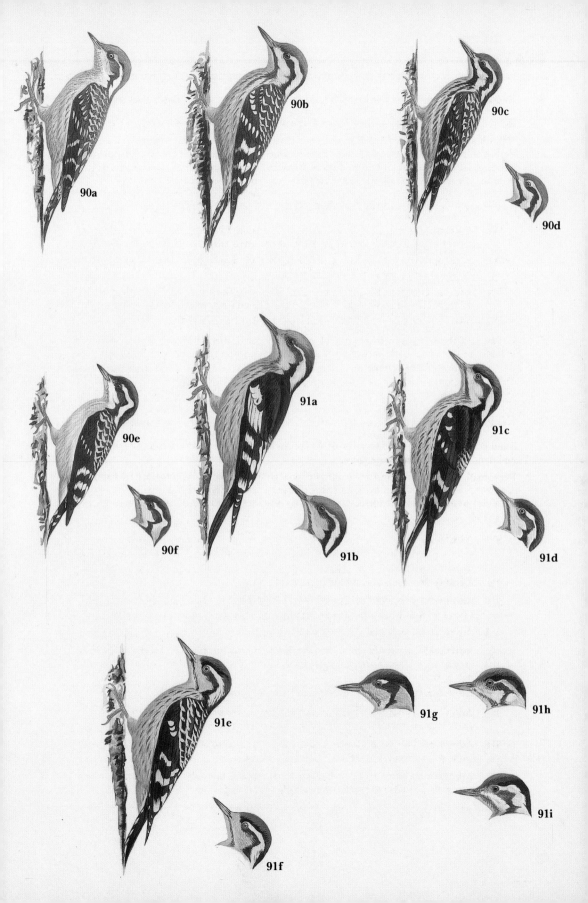

90a

90b

90c

90d

90e

90f

91a

91b

91c

91d

91e

91f

91g

91h

91i

PLATE 27

92 Pygmy Woodpecker *Picoides kizuki*   Text and map page 257

E Asia, including Japan: mixed and broadleaf woodland, edge, parks and gardens.

Very small. Brownish, grey/black and white, with barred back and wings; pale and variably streaked below, often with obscure breast band. Characteristic head pattern, with grey crown and brown ear-coverts, white above eye and on neck sides, white moustache and throat and brown/grey malar. Juvenile greyer, with streaked throat (male with red crown spot).

92a   **Adult male** (*ijimae*, Ussuriland to Sakhalin and Hokkaido) Small red patch on side of nape side (normally concealed). The largest and palest race.

92b   **Adult female** (*ijimae*) Lacks red on side of nape.

92c   **Adult male** (*seebohmi*, most of Korea, Quelpart Islands and Honshu) Shows less white above.

92d   **Adult female** (*seebohmi*) No red on side of nape.

92e   **Adult male** (nominate; NE China, Tsushima and Kyushu south to Iriomote) Smaller, with heavy flank streaking; less white on head and neck.

92f   **Adult female** (nominate) No red on side of nape.

93 Lesser Spotted Woodpecker *Picoides minor*   Text and map page 258

N and C Palearctic, south to NW Africa: open deciduous woodland, parks, gardens.

Very small and compact. Essentially black and white above, with barred back and wings; variably whitish to brown-buff below, usually with some streaking. Black moustache contrasts with pale ear-coverts and white patch on sides of neck. Juvenile duller, browner, with obscure streaking below, forecrown mottled reddish/pink.

93a   **Adult male** (nominate; N Europe east to Urals) Black-bordered red crown and pale forehead; underparts very pale, with reduced streaking.

93b   **Adult female** (nominate) Crown whitish, bordered with black.

93c   **Adult male** (*ledouci*; NW Africa) Red crown. Slightly longer- and darker-billed; darker below, with heavier flank streaking (variable).

93d   **Adult female** (*ledouci*) Crown and pale areas of head buffish-brown.

93e   **Adult male** (*comminutus*, Britain) Red crown. Darker below and on head, with a few dark streaks on flanks and breast.

93f   **Adult female** (*comminutus*) Lacks male's red crown.

93g   **Adult male** (*buturlini*; S Europe) Red crown. Darker and heavily streaked below.

93h   **Adult male** (*danfordi*; Greece and Turkey) Red crown. Even darker below than *buturlini*; black band behind ear-coverts (often reaches crown).

93i   **Adult female** (*danfordi*) Crown pale.

93j   **Adult male** (*morgani*; Iran) Red crown patch. Bill long and narrow. Black band from lower moustache to nape; flanks prominently streaked.

93k   **Adult female** (*morgani*) Crown wholly pale.

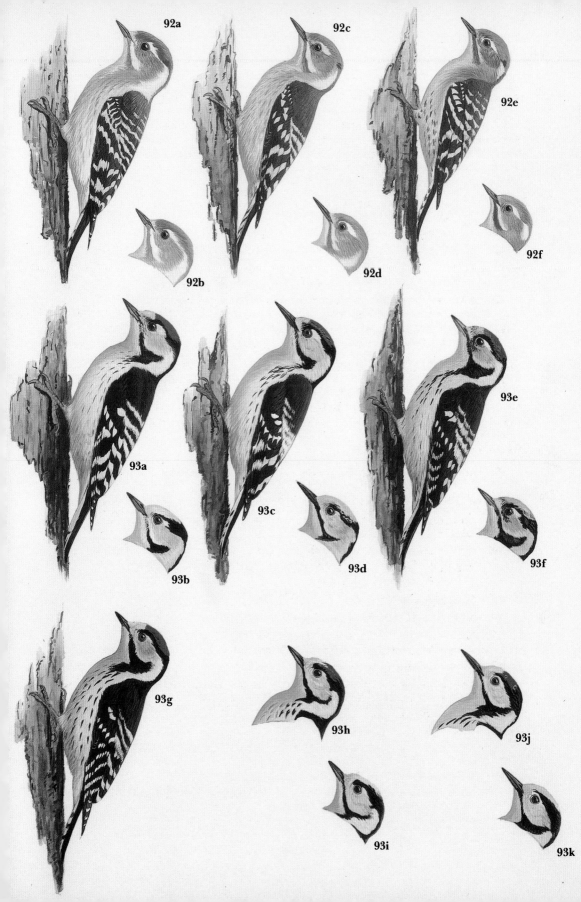

92a

92c

92b

92d

92e

92f

93a

93b

93c

93d

93e

93f

93g

93h

93i

93j

93k

PLATE 28

96 Stripe-breasted Woodpecker *Picoides atratus*   Text and map page 263

SE Asia: open woodland in hill evergreen forest, also forest edges and clearings.

Smallish and broad-bodied, with barred upperparts and conspicuously striped underparts; red vent; whitish face with contrasting black moustache; only outer tail barred white. Juvenile greyer, with broad but more obscure streaking below and orange vent.

  96a **Adult male** Red crown and nape.

  96b **Adult female** Crown and nape black.

97 Yellow-crowned Woodpecker *Picoides mahrattensis*   Text and map page 263

S Asia east to S Laos: arid open woodland, scrub, roadside trees, also cultivations and gardens.

Small. Black and white above, with mainly white rump, and barred wings and tail; strongly streaked below, with orange-red belly centre. Relatively dark face with obscure pale moustache; forehead and forecrown golden-yellow. Western race *pallescens* is paler overall. Juvenile duller and browner, with some orange-red on crown; diffusely streaked below, with pinker vent.

  97a **Adult male** (nominate; range of species except Pakistan/NW India) Yellow forecrown becoming red on hindcrown and nape.

  97b **Adult female** (nominate) Crown to nape brownish.

98 Arabian Woodpecker *Picoides dorae*   Text and map page 264

SW Arabian peninsula: open acacia woodland and wadis, also junipers and palms, often close to habitation. Unmistakable: the only woodpecker in Arabia.

Brownish to olive-grey, barred on wings and outer tail; paler below, red on belly. Juvenile greyer below, faintly streaked.

  98a **Adult male** Red on nape.

  98b **Adult female** Forehead to nape uniform brown/grey-brown.

94 Brown-fronted Woodpecker *Picoides auriceps*   Text and map page 260

S Asia (E Afghanistan to E Nepal): coniferous and montane dry deciduous forests, also park-like woodland and secondary growth, reaching 3100m in Nepal.

Small. Barred black and white above and heavily streaked below, with pinkish-red belly centre and vent; face white, with darker ear-coverts, black moustache and brown forehead. More barred (less scaly or 'marbled') above than Yellow-crowned (97), and only outer tail barred (in overlap areas, Brown-fronted generally found at higher elevations). Juvenile duller, with darker ear-coverts, greyer below with paler (pink) belly; crown pattern as adult female, with trace of red/orange-red in hindcrown.

  94a **Adult male** Yellow central crown and orange-red nape.

  94b **Adult female** Crown duller yellow/greener, as nape.

95 Fulvous-breasted Woodpecker *Picoides macei*   Text and map page 261

S and SE Asia: open forest and open wooded areas, gardens, also tall deciduous forest (Himalayas) and dry deciduous scrub (Pakistan).

Small. Strongly barred black and white above (white bars at least as wide as black ones), variably buff below with rather minimal streaking and red/pink lower belly and undertail-coverts; looks pale-faced with contrasting black moustache. Juvenile duller, with pink vent, and with some red in centre of crown.

  95a **Adult male** (*westermani*; Pakistan to W Nepal) Red forehead to nape. Tail barred only at sides.

  95b **Adult female** (*westermani*) Forehead to nape black.

  95c **Adult male** (*analis*, Java, Bali) Red crown, black nape. Paler and less streaked below, with vent pink (not red); tail fully barred.

  95d **Adult female** (*analis*) Forehead to nape all black.

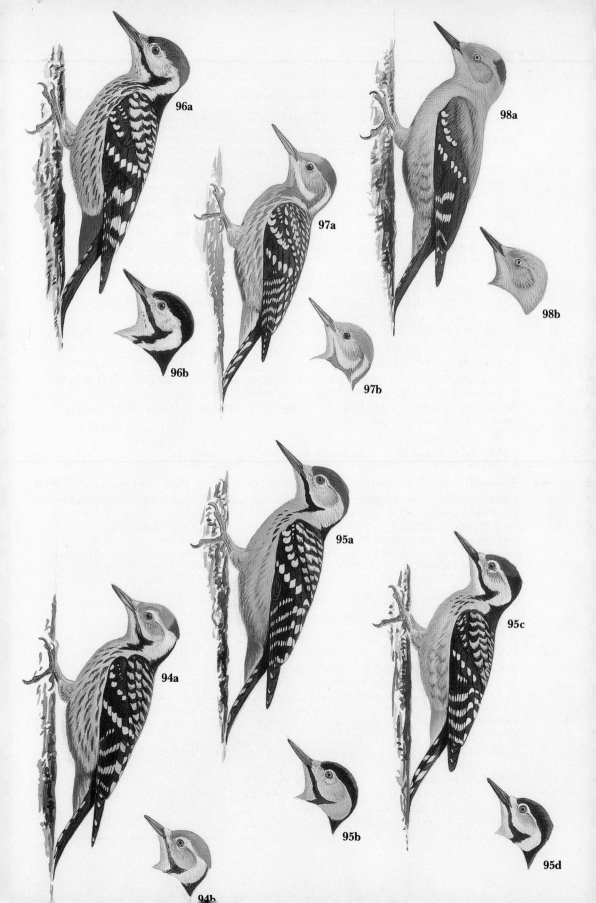

96a

96b

97a

97b

98a

98b

95a

95b

95c

95d

94a

94b

PLATE 29

100 Crimson-breasted Woodpecker *Picoides cathpharius*   Text and map page 267

S Asia east to C China and south to Indochina: mountain forests, generally on lower and middle slopes.

Small. Black above, with white wing patch, barred wings and tail; black moustache continuing onto breast, variable amount of red in centre of breast. Two racial groups, differing in underpart pattern and in male's head markings. Juvenile darker below and lacks all red on breast.

    100a **Adult male** (*pernyii*; China, from NW Yunnan to SW Kansu) Red nape patch (nape all black on female). Rather dark below, red on breast bordered by much solid black; red vent.

    100b **Adult male** (nominate; Nepal to N Assam) Red from nape to rear of ear-coverts and over hindneck. Heavily streaked below, breast with variable amount of red (sometimes little or none) bordered by only little black; vent orange-red or with small orange-red tips.

    100c **Adult female** (nominate) Rear of head all black.

101 Darjeeling Woodpecker *Picoides darjellensis*   Text and map page 268

S Asia east to China (S Sichuan) and south to N Burma, also N Vietnam: high-altitude woodland and forest.

Very like Crimson-breasted Woodpecker (100), but larger and longer-billed, with bright yellow on neck sides (male also with less red on nape), no red on breast, and black breast streaks never form solid patch. Juvenile duller, more barred below, with streaked throat; lacks yellow on neck (male with dull red crown). Often at higher elevations than Crimson-breasted.

    101a **Adult male** Red nape patch.

    101b **Adult female** Entire crown and nape black.

99 Rufous-bellied Woodpecker *Picoides hyperythrus*   Text and map page 266

S, SE and E Asia, northeast populations wintering S and SE China: high altitude forests.

Combination of barred upperparts, wings and outer tail, and chestnut to rufous/rusty-buff underparts (paler when worn) with red vent diagnostic; white face. Juvenile barred below, with vent pinker, face and throat patterned, and crown white-spotted black with reddish/orange tips; adult plumage develops towards first winter.

    99a   **Adult male** (*marshalli*; Pakistan/NW India) Considerable amount of red on head, reaching hindneck and neck sides. Deep chestnut below.

    99b   **Adult female** (*marshalli*) Forehead to hindneck black with prominent white spots.

    99c   **Adult male** (*subrufinus*; Manchuria and Ussuriland, winters S China) Much less red on head. Larger and paler.

    99d   **Adult female** (*subrufinus*) Crown black, heavily spotted white.

100a

100b

100c

101a

101b

99a

99b

99c

99d

PLATE 30

102 Middle Spotted Woodpecker *Picoides medius*   **Text and map page 269**

Europe, W Asia: mature forest, old orchards.

Red crown, not lined with black, face with relatively little black; back black; wings black, barred white, white wing patch; white below with streaks on sides of breast and on flanks, belly pinkish. Brownish moustache inconspicuous.

    102a **Adult male** (nominate; Europe, NW Anatolia) Crown red.

    102b **Adult female** (nominate) Crown red, golden at rear (often difficult to see in field).

    102c **Juvenile** Less contrastingly patterned, crown mottled blackish-grey.

    102d **Adult male** Showing raised crown feathers.

103 White-backed Woodpecker *Picoides leucotos*   **Text and map page 271**

N Eurasia: mature forests.

Back and wings barred black and white, no extensive white wing patch (but upper most bar may be wide); white below with pinkish belly, breast and flanks streaked black (almost forming a band on breast). Prominent black malar stripe. White back often inconspicuous, prominent in flight. Juvenile duller, browner above, pale areas dirtier, red of vent paler; both sexes with red and black crown, female with less red.

    103a **Adult male** (nominate; N Eurasia) Entire crown tipped red (bases grey), finely lined black (less obvious in field than shown on plate).

    103b **Adult female** (nominate) Crown black.

    103c **Adult male** (*fohkiensis*, Fukien, SE China) Dark; less black on breast and more white on back than *owstoni*; much black on neck side.

    103d **Adult male** (*lilfordi*; S Europe) White back barred black; darker and with less white in wings than nominate.

    103e **Adult male** (*subcirris*, Hokkaido) More black on neck and breast, less white above, paler below, than nominate; throat buffy, heavily bordered with black. (Bill usually stronger than indicated on plate.)

    103f **Adult male** (*namiyei*; S Honshu, Kyushu, Shikoku and Quelpart Islands) Darker than *subcirris*, back barred, reduced white in wing, darker red on belly.

    103g **Adult male** (*owstoni*; Amami Island, Japan) Relatively large; very dark, breast virtually black, face and throat pale buff; very little white in wing.

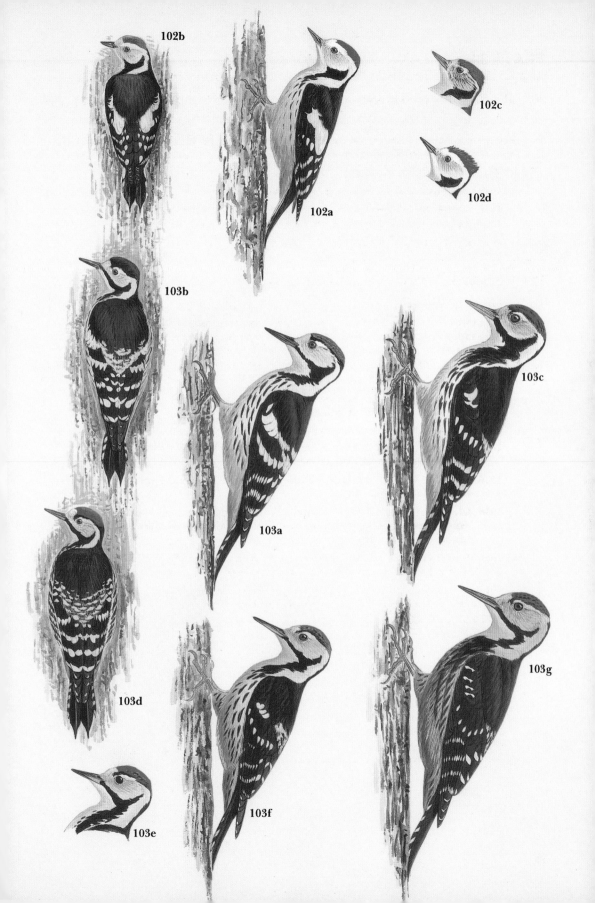

102b

102a

102c

102d

103b

103a

103c

103d

103e

103f

103g

PLATE 31

104 Great Spotted Woodpecker *Picoides major*　　　Text and map page 273

Eurasia, N Africa: forest, woodlands, parks, gardens.

White to light brown below, vent dark red; black facial 'Y' connected to black crown. Geographical variation within immense range shown with a few examples.

104a **Adult male** (nominate; N Europe) Red band on nape.

104b **Adult female** (nominate) No red on head.

104c **Adult female** (nominate) Black above, with black wings narrowly barred white, and prominent white wing patch. Tail black, with white outer vanes spotted black.

104d **Juvenile** Crown more or less red, lined with black at sides.

104e **Adult male** (*numidus*, N Tunisia, N Algeria) Prominent red and black band across breast.

104f **Adult male** (*harterti*, Sardinia, Corsica) Darker; reduced white on wings.

104g **Adult male** (*cabanisi*, N populations; E Asia) Buff below. Red on breast can be found on some individuals of the *cabanisi* group (and in fact in any population of the species).

104h **Adult male** (*cabanisi*, S populations; E Asia) Dark buff below (darker in south), sometimes red on breast.

106 White-winged Woodpecker *Picoides leucopterus*　　　Text and map page 278

SC Asia: dry woodland, cultivations, gardens.

Black above, with black wings showing much white; white below, vent dark red; black facial 'Y' connected to black crown. Tail black, with white outer vanes spotted black. Juvenile duller, browner above, with pink vent, tail and wings often with even more white; both sexes with some red on crown (not nape), less on female.

106a **Adult male** Red band on nape.

106b **Adult female** No red on head.

106c **Adult female** In rear view, shows large white area on wings, wide white bars on primaries.

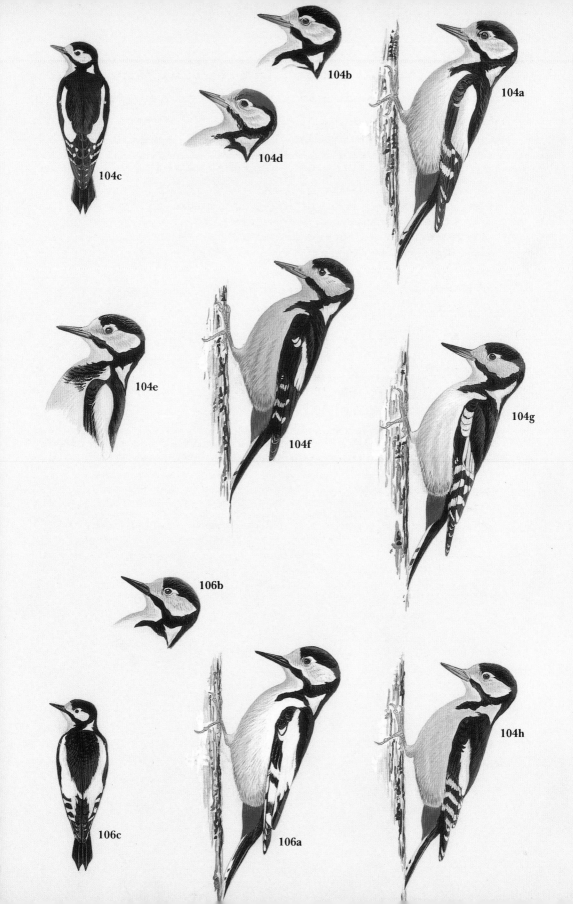

104c

104b

104d

104a

104e

104f

104g

106b

106c

106a

104h

PLATE 32

105 Syrian Woodpecker *Picoides syriacus*   Text and map page 276

SE Europe, SW Asia: open habitats, edge, gardens.

Black above, with white wing patch; primaries and secondaries barred white. Rather similar to Great Spotted (104, Plate 31), but easily distinguished by calls and some features of coloration: vent pale red, upper rear part of black facial 'Y' missing or small, less white in outer tail than Great Spotted. Bill longer and more slender than in most sympatric forms of Great Spotted.

  105a Adult male Red nape band, slightly wider than on Great Spotted Woodpecker.
  105b Adult female Crown and nape black.
  105c Juvenile Front part of crown red, lined with black. Has red breast band more or less well developed and without black feathers; vent pale reddish.

107 Sind Woodpecker *Picoides assimilis*   Text and map page 279

SW Asia: open habitats, thorn scrub, plantations.

Similar to Syrian, which it meets in Iran. Note differences in tail pattern. White wing patch; lower belly and undertail-coverts red. Juvenile browner above than adult, a shade more buffy below, red on underside pale; both sexes with red crown (does not reach nape), less on female.

  107a Adult male Red crown.
  107b Adult female Crown black.

108 Himalayan Woodpecker *Picoides himalayensis*   Text and map page 280

SC Asia: fairly dense mountain forests at about 1900-3200m.

Black moustache branches upwards behind ear-coverts; bill with black tip; white wing patch smaller than on Sind; breast with fulvous or grey wash, lower belly and undertail-coverts red; wingbars narrow, much white in outer tail feathers. Juvenile duller, with faint streaks and barring on sides (sometimes also breast), and pink vent; forecrown spotted white; crown orange-red, more so on males.

  108a Adult male (nominate; W Nepal, NW India) Red crown with some black streaks, lined black.
  108b Adult female (nominate) Crown black.

105c

105b

105a

107a

107b

107c

108b

108a

PLATE 33

111 Nuttall's Woodpecker *Picoides nuttallii* Text and map page 282

W North America: oak woodland, riparian woodland.

Contrastingly patterned black and white. Black with white bars and spots above, white below with spots and bars on breast sides and flanks; black moustache connected with large black patch behind eye; nasal tufts white, contrasting with black forehead. Outer tail white, spotted black. Juvenile duller and less white below, whiter above, crown with white marks and red patch in centre, nape black. Overlaps in range (and sometimes hybridises) with Ladder-backed in N Baja California, Mexico.

> **111a Adult male** Red on hindcrown and nape, often spotted white; black forehead and forecrown, streaked white.
>
> **111b Adult female** Crown and nape black, sometimes spotted white. Black on upper mantle.

112 Ladder-backed Woodpecker *Picoides scalaris* Text and map page 283

S North America: deserts, woodland, mangroves.

Black above with white to brownish bars and spots, pale below with spots and streaks on breast sides and on flanks; blackish moustache connected with black stripe behind eye; nasal tufts dark, gradually blending into crown. Tail black, equally barred white or almost white (particularly *eremicus*) on outer vanes. Juvenile more heavily streaked and barred, duller on belly, nape black, red patch in centre of crown.

> **112a Adult male** (*cactophilus*, USA, NC and C Mexico) Black crown tipped red, spotted white.
>
> **112b Adult female** (*cactophilus*) Crown black, sometimes spotted and streaked white. Upper mantle with white bars.

110 Checkered Woodpecker *Picoides mixtus* Text and map page 281

S South America: dry woodland, scrub.

Very small. Brown above and on wings with white marks and spots, pale below with brown spots and streaks on breast sides and on flanks; brown patch behind eye. Tail fully barred white. Juvenile darker above, more heavily streaked and barred below; red on crown (not on nape).

> **110a Adult male** (nominate; Parana river, Buenos Aires) Red to orange-red patch on nape, often restricted to sides only; crown streaked whitish.
>
> **110b Adult female** (nominate) No red on head, crown with few or no streaks.
>
> **110c Adult male** (*berlepschi*, S Argentina) Red to orange-red patch on nape, often restricted to sides only; forecrown streaked whitish. Bill longer than in nominate, larger patch behind ear, whiter ground colour below.
>
> **110d Adult female** (*berlepschi*) No red on nape.

109 Striped Woodpecker *Picoides lignarius* Text and map page 281

S South America: forest; dry highlands with cacti.

No apparent overlap in range with Checkered, from which it differs in generally darker coloration and longer wings, tail and bill, characters which do not allow field separation. Juvenile duller and browner, more heavily patterned below; both sexes with red crown, much less extensive on female.

> **109a Adult male** Red to orange-red patch on nape, usually complete; crown streaked white.
>
> **109b Adult male** With reduced red on nape. (Female similar but lacks red.)

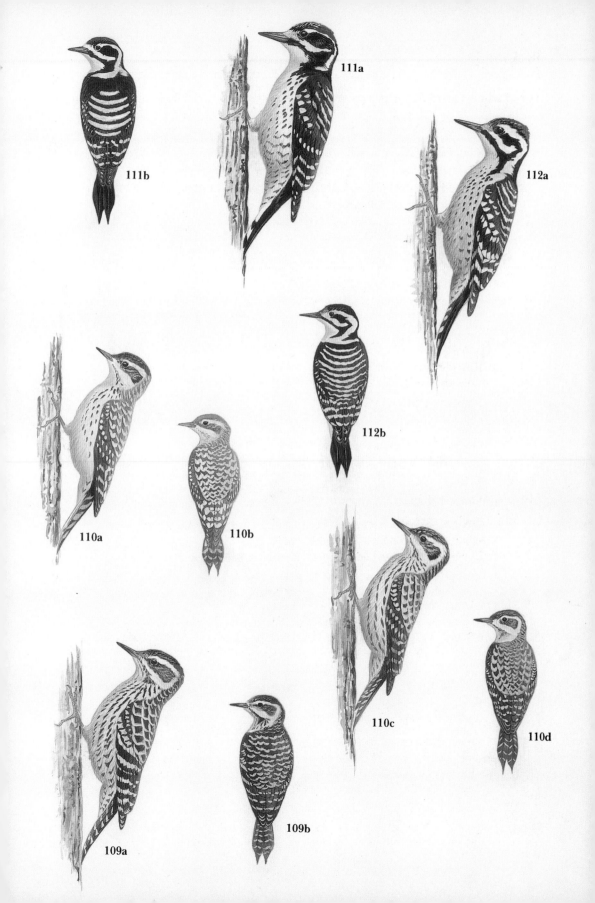

111b

111a

112a

110a

110b

112b

110c

110d

109a

109b

PLATE 34

114 Red-cockaded Woodpecker *Picoides borealis*   Text and map page 287

SE USA: pinewoods; gregarious.

Black above, barred white, white below with black spots on sides; forehead, crown and nape black, moustache black, no black behind eye. Tail black, outer vanes white with black spots. Juvenile browner, red in centre of crown (rather variable). Endangered through habitat loss.

114a Adult male Tiny red mark on side of nape (generally invisible in the field).

114b Adult female No red on head.

114c Adult female Only 'ladder-backed' species in its range.

117 White-headed Woodpecker *Picoides albolarvatus*   Text and map page 292

W North America: mountain coniferous forests.

Unmistakable: black, with white face and white wing patch. Juvenile browner, with larger wing patch broken by black; orange-red on centre of crown and hindcrown, red restricted to hindcrown on some females.

117a Adult male Red nape.

117b Adult female Nape black.

117c Adult male In flight, shows white patch at base of primaries.

115 Strickland's Woodpecker *Picoides stricklandi*   Text and map page 289

SW North America: pine and pine-oak woodland.

Brown to blackish-brown. Brown above, white with brown spots and streaks below; crown and nape dark brown; brown moustache, large brown ear patch. Juvenile with brown markings on underside larger, more streaking and barring; mid crown and hindcrown tipped dull orange-red, restricted to hindcrown on female.

115a Adult male (*arizonae*, Arizona to NW Mexico) Red hindcrown. Brown above.

115b Adult female (*arizonae*) No red on head.

115c Adult female (*arizonae*) Little or no white on back and wings.

115d Adult male (nominate; Mexico, SE section of range) Red band on nape. Dark areas blackish-brown.

115e Adult female (nominate) No red on head.

115f Adult female (nominate) Blackish-brown upperparts barred white.

114a

114b

114c

117a

117b

117c

115a

115b

115c

115d

115e

115f

PLATE 35

113 Downy Woodpecker *Picoides pubescens*   **Text and map page 285**

North America: forests, gardens.

Very small. Contrasting black and white plumage. Upperparts and wings black, with broad white band down back and with much or just a little white in wings; underparts very pale whitish to pale buffish or browny-grey, unmarked. Basic plumage pattern, including pale back, is very like that of Hairy Woodpecker (116); Downy best separated by its clearly smaller size and, especially, its much smaller and shorter bill, as well as its black-barred outer tail and lack of moustachial extension to breast sides.

> **113a Adult male** (*gairdneri*; British Columbia to NW California, coastal) Narrow red band across nape. Brownish-grey below, wing-coverts with few white spots.
>
> **113b Adult male** (*medianus*; NE North America) Larger. White below; wing-coverts broadly spotted white.
>
> **113c Adult female** (*medianus*) No red on head.
>
> **113d Juvenile male** (*medianus*) Red tips on crown (lacking on females). Browner, more streaked on back than adult.

116 Hairy Woodpecker *Picoides villosus*   **Text and map page 290**

North and Central America; forests, usually at high elevations, gardens.

Black above, centre of back white to brown (barred in some races); outer tail white, usually without marks. Bill long. Juvenile browner above, darker below, with some streaks/bars on underparts and on outer tail; orange-red patch on crown, reduced on female.

> **116a Adult male** (*sanctorum*; Central America) Narrow red patch on nape. Relatively small; dark.
>
> **116b Adult male** (*audubonii*; SE North America) Washed greyish-buff below.
>
> **116c Adult male** (nominate; NE North America) Relatively large and white.
>
> **116d Adult female** (nominate) No red on head.
>
> **116e Adult male** (*harrisi*; coastal NW North America) Brownish-grey on pale parts, reduced wing spotting.
>
> **116f Adult male** (*septentrionalis*; W North America) Relatively large; pale parts white.

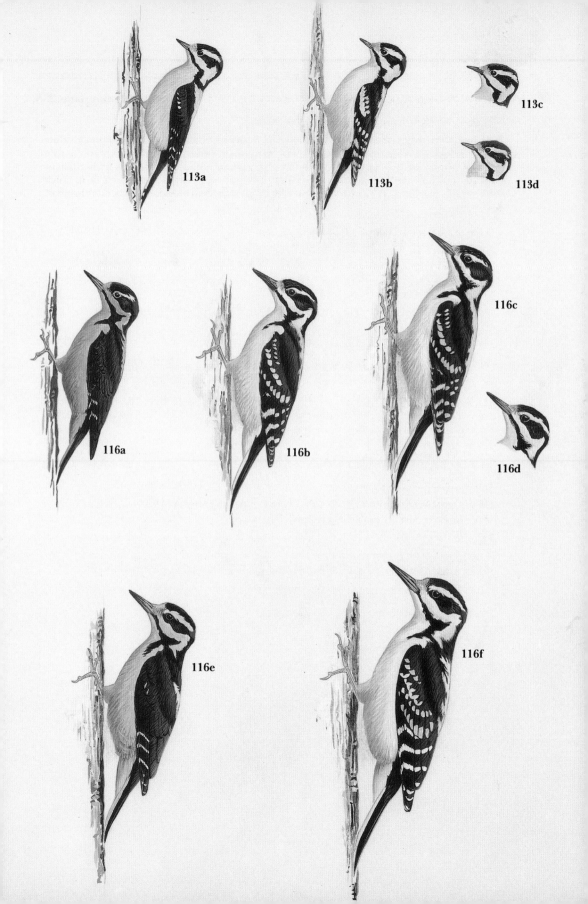

113a

113b

113c

113d

116a

116b

116c

116d

116e

116f

PLATE 36

118 Three-toed Woodpecker *Picoides tridactylus*   Text and map page 293

N Eurasia, North America: (mixed) coniferous forests.

Black and white; no red in any plumage. Black moustache in combination with black patch behind eye distinguishes it from other black-and-white woodpeckers within its Old World range. In New World, white on back distinguishes it from Black-backed (119); told from Hairy (116, Plate 35) by black and white back and black-marked underparts. Juvenile browner and duller, markings below more extensive; small yellow patch, variable in size (but smaller than adult male's), on forecrown.

    118a Adult male (nominate; N Eurasia) Yellow crown.

    118b Adult female (nominate) Crown black, spotted/streaked white.

    118c Adult male (*alpinus*, mountains of Eurasia) Darker than nominate, strongly barred below.

    118d Adult male (*albidior*, Kamchatka) Relatively small. Unmarked white below; outer tail entirely white.

    118e Adult male (*funebris*, Tibet) Very dark; below, black with fine pale bars.

    118f Adult male (*dorsalis*, Rocky Mountains of W North America) Dark head; outer tail white without bars.

    118g Adult male (*fasciatus*, NW North America, Alaska to Oregon) Narrow white stripes on head; strongly barred back.

    118h Adult male (*bacatus*, NE North America) Smallest race. White stripe over eye broken by black or absent; back with few white marks. (Female has only a few white spots on crown).

119 Black-backed Woodpecker *Picoides arcticus*   Text and map page 296

N North America: coniferous forests.

Black above, with no white marks on back; head black with little white; underparts white, barred black. Juvenile browner, with more white in wings; yellow to orange-yellow patch on crown (smaller than in adult male, reduced on female).

    119a Adult male Crown yellow.

    119b Adult female No yellow on black crown.

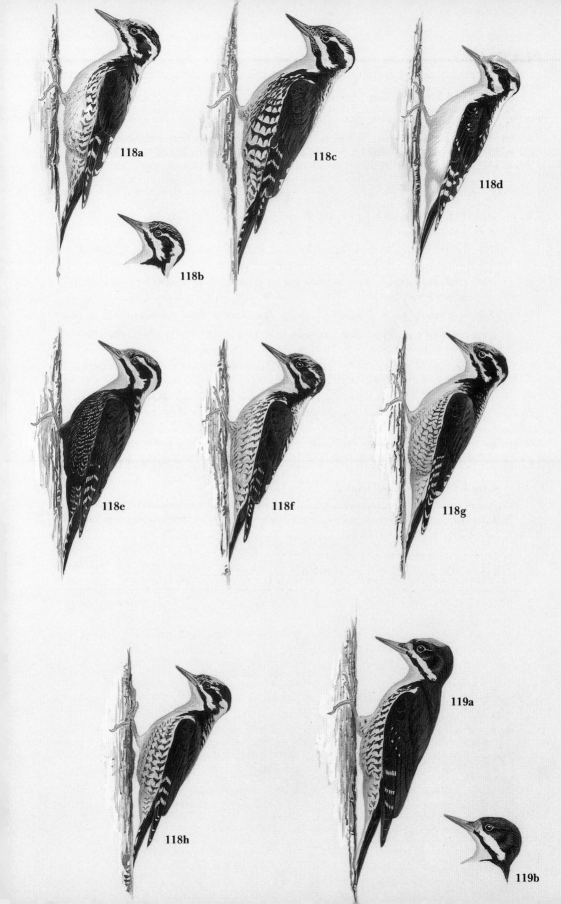

118a

118b

118c

118d

118e

118f

118g

118h

119a

119b

PLATE 37

121 Yellow-vented Woodpecker *Veniliornis dignus*   Text and map page 297

NW South America (to E Peru): humid forest at 700-2700m.
Back bronzy yellow-green; yellowish below, barred black on throat and breast. Broad white stripes above and below eye; hindneck red. Juvenile duller, greener above, some red in crown.

121a Adult male Crown black with much red.
121b Adult female Crown black with olive tinge.

120 Scarlet-backed Woodpecker *Veniliornis callonotus*   Text and map page 297

WC South America: dry forest, desert scrub.
Very small. Red above, white below, with few or no faint markings; ear-coverts streaked brown. Juvenile mottled olive above, buffier below, male with red tips to forecrown.

120a Adult male (*major*, S Ecuador, Peru) Black crown broadly tipped red. Dark patch behind eye, fine barring below.
120b Adult female (*major*) No red in black crown.
120c Adult male (nominate; Ecuador) Ear-coverts paler, little or no barring below.
120d Adult female (nominate) No red in black crown.

122 Bar-bellied Woodpecker *Veniliornis nigriceps*   Text and map page 298

W South America (Andes): humid montane forest at 2000-4000m.
Narrow white face stripes. Brownish-olive above, olive-brown to blackish below with narrow pale bars; may show red edges on nape (female) and back. Juvenile greener, duller, crown more or less red.

122a Adult male (*pectoralis*, S Ecuador, Peru) Crown red on black base, nape red.
122b Adult female (*pectoralis*) Crown blackish (no red on head).

125 Dot-fronted Woodpecker *Veniliornis frontalis*   Text and map page 301

SC South America: forest.
Yellow-green above, with pale spots on wing-coverts (no red marks); olive below, with fine pale buffy bars. Tail clearly barred. Ear-coverts distinctly streaked; thin white stripes over and under eye. Juvenile greyer above, red in crown not reaching nape (and reduced on female).

125a Adult male Dark grey crown broadly tipped red to nape.
125b Adult female Dark crown spotted with white, streaked on nape.

123 Smoky-brown Woodpecker *Veniliornis fumigatus*   Text and map page 299

Central America and W South America: tropical forest up to 4000m.
Uniformly brown; paler around eye. Juvenile duller, male sooty, crown red (reduced on females).

123a Adult male (*reichenbachi*; E Panama to E Ecuador) Crown red on grey-black base.
123b Adult female (*reichenbachi*) Crown blackish-brown, occasionally with fine white spots.

126 White-spotted Woodpecker *Veniliornis spilogaster*   Text and map page 302

South America: forest to open woodland.
Checkered olive-green and white throughout, tail fully barred; moustache and line over eye white. Juvenile more spotted rather than barred above.

126a Adult male Dark crown very finely streaked red (these marks are lost through wear).
126b Adult female Dark crown spotted white in unworn plumage.

124 Little Woodpecker *Veniliornis passerinus*   Text and map page 300

South America: forest edge, gallery forest, shrub, savanna.
Bronze to yellow-green above (red streaks/edges may be visible), wing-coverts with few pale spots; olive below, with fine pale buffy bars. White stripes on face thin or absent; no gold or red on sides of neck. Juvenile irregularly barred or scalloped on breast; red on crown does not reach nape (reduced on female).

124a Adult male (*olivinus*, S Bolivia, S Brazil, Paraguay, N Argentina) Mid crown to nape red. Facial stripes reduced or lacking.
124b Adult female (*olivinus*) Brown crown, more or less pale-spotted.
124c Adult male (*taenionotus*; E Brazil) Forehead and entire crown red. Wider pale bars below; thin whitish facial stripes.
124d Adult female (*taenionotus*) No red on crown.

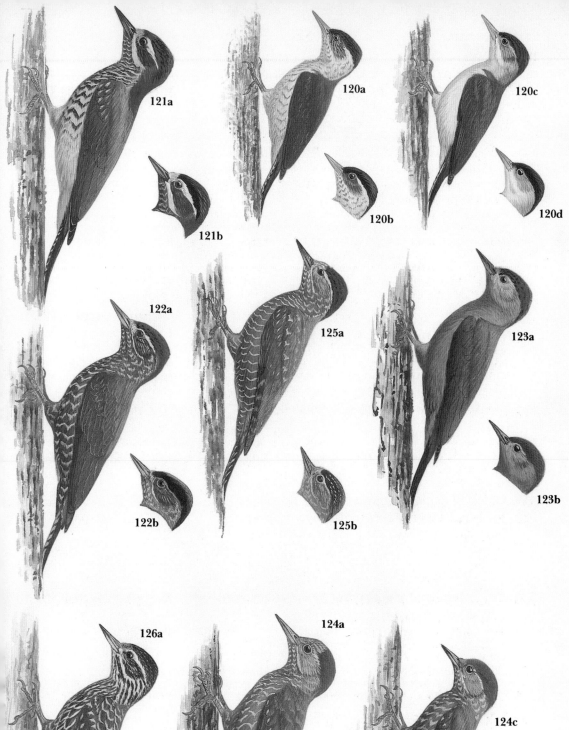

121a

120a

120c

121b

120b

120d

122a

125a

123a

122b

125b

123b

126a

124a

124c

126b

124b

124d

PLATE 38

127 Blood-coloured Woodpecker *Veniliornis sanguineus*   **Text and map page 303**

NE South America (Guianas): mangroves, swampy forest, plantations.
Dark red above, browner when worn; grey below with fine pale bars, becoming broader on belly.
Juvenile duller, spotted on wing-coverts.
>   **127a Adult male** Brown crown broadly tipped red (less red when worn).
>   **127b Adult female** Crown brown, with small white spots.

128 Red-rumped Woodpecker *Veniliornis kirkii*   **Text and map page 303**

Central America, N South America: forest.
Yellow-green above, with red rump; barred olive and white below. Ear-coverts streaked. Juvenile with
red in crown, restricted on female.
>   **128a Adult male** (*continentalis,* N and W Venezuela) Crown greyish-black, broadly tipped red.
>   **128b Adult female** (*continentalis*) Crown greyish-/greenish-black, faintly spotted at rear end.
>   **128c Adult male** (*monticola,* mountains of S Venezuela) Larger. Crown with red tips. Broad
>   blackish bars below.
>   **128d Adult female** (*monticola*) No red in dark crown.

131 Red-stained Woodpecker *Veniliornis affinis*   **Text and map page 306**

South America: forest.
Greenish to bronzy above, often washed with red, no red rump; wings with red spots. Barred olive-
black and pale below, with usually buff breast. Golden nape. Juvenile with strongly streaked ear-
coverts; red in crown, but less than in adult male (even more reduced on female).
>   **131a Adult male** (nominate; E Brazil) Crown blackish, boldly tipped red. Wings with very
>   small red spots.
>   **131b Adult male** (*hilaris,* E Ecuador to N Bolivia and W Brazil) Crown blackish, boldly
>   tipped red. Wings with prominent red spots; brighter upperparts.
>   **131c Adult female** (*hilaris*) Crown olive-brown with obscure pale streaks in centre and
>   golden streaks towards nape.

129 Choco Woodpecker *Veniliornis chocoensis*   **Text and map page 304**

NW South America (Pacific coast of Colombia): forest.
Golden-green above, faintly suffused red, rump barred; wing-coverts lack red spots, but have obscure
yellowish spots. Barred below. Nape and neck sides dull yellowish; ear-coverts buffy and not streaked,
but often with pale spots. Juvenile with streaked face; both sexes with red on crown, less on female.
>   **Adult male** Blackish crown broadly tipped red (female has no red on crown).

130 Golden-collared Woodpecker *Veniliornis cassini*   **Text and map page 305**

N South America: forest, clearings, shrub.
Yellowy-green above, with pale-spotted wing-coverts (no red); prominently barred black and whitish
below. Bright golden nape and neck sides. Tail obscurely barred, but usually with obvious white
notches on outer feathers. Juvenile greener above, nape yellow rather than golden; streaks rather than
spots on wing-coverts.
>   **130a Adult male** Dark crown broadly tipped red.
>   **130b Adult female** Dark crown without red. (Usually spotted gold-white towards nape.)

132 Yellow-eared Woodpecker *Veniliornis maculifrons*   **Text and map page 307**

E South America (E Brazil): secondary forest, parkland.
Yellow-green to bronzy-green above with no red, and with yellowish spots (not bars) on mantle; heavily
barred olive and whitish below. Ear-coverts olive, mottled whitish, thin white moustache and pale line
over eye. Juvenile duller and greener above, with yellowish bars on mantle and back, irregularly
barred below; forecrown reddish, nape patch less golden and smaller than adult's.
>   **132a Adult male** Crown brown, streaked whitish in front, becoming broadly tipped red
>   towards nape.
>   **132b Adult female** Crown dark olive, marked whitish, these marks becoming gold at rear.

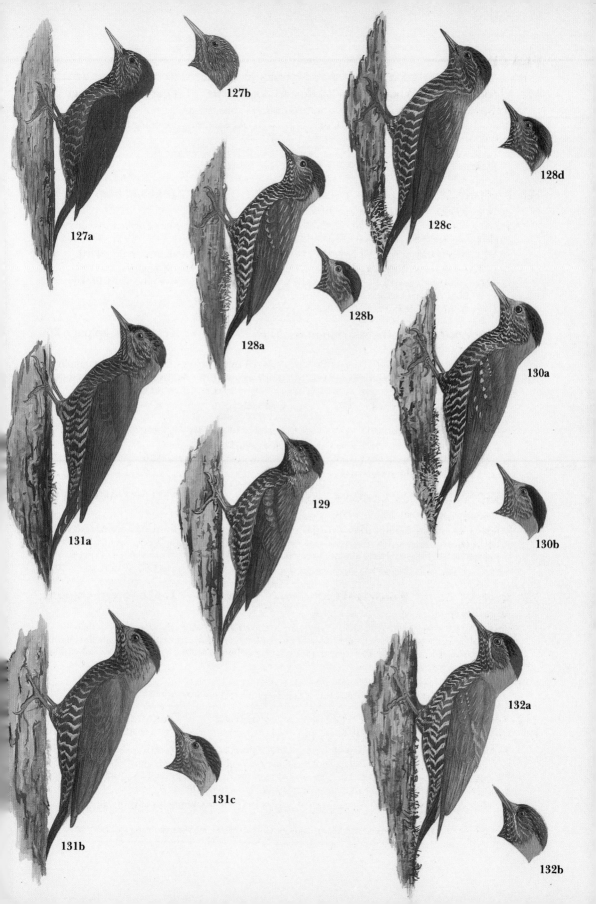

127a

127b

128a

128b

128c

128d

129

130a

130b

131a

131b

131c

132a

132b

PLATE 39

137 Yellow-throated Woodpecker *Piculus flavigula*   Text and map page 310

N and C South America: lowland forest.

Yellowish-green above, variably patterned whitish and olive below; ear-coverts yellow, throat variable. Juvenile greener, less yellow, above, and darker below; less yellow and golden on head, pale spots on throat.

> **137a Adult male** (*erythropis,* E Brazil) Red throat, including malar, and red forehead to nape (female has golden forecrown and throat, latter sometimes slightly marked red). Barred below.
>
> **137b Adult male** (nominate; N South America) Throat yellow, short red moustache; forehead to nape red. Green below with white feather centres.
>
> **137c Adult female** (nominate) Throat and moustache yellow; crown greenish, tipped yellow; nape red.
>
> **137d Adult male** (*magnus,* C South America) No red moustache; entire crown red.
>
> **137e Adult female** (*magnus*) Hindcrown red.
>
> **137f Adult male** (undescribed form, SW Colombia) Chin and throat black. Male with red crown and red moustache.
>
> **137g Adult female** (undescribed form, SW Colombia) Female with red hindcrown and red moustache.

136 White-throated Woodpecker *Piculus leucolaemus*   Text and map page 309

N South America east of Andes: forest.

Golden olive-green above; breast greenish with paler spots, belly whitish with bars. Ear-coverts olive, bordered by broad golden stripe below; chin and throat white. Juvenile duller and darker.

> **136a Adult male** Red forehead to nape, red moustache.
>
> **136b Adult female** Red on head restricted to nape; moustache green.

134 Stripe-cheeked Woodpecker *Piculus callopterus*   Text and map page 308

Central America (Panama): humid forest at 300-900m.

Yellowish bronzy-green above; breast greenish, belly barred. Ear-coverts, unspotted throat, and sides of neck greenish; whitish stripe across lower cheeks. Male with long, broad red moustache and red crown and nape; female with red nape. Juvenile duller and darker.

> **Adult female** Red restricted to hindcrown/nape.

133 Rufous-winged Woodpecker *Piculus simplex*   Text and map page 307

Central America: humid lowland forest.

Yellowish bronzy-green above; flight feathers with cinnamon-rufous spots, forming patch in flight. Breast greenish, belly barred. Ear-coverts, spotted throat, and sides of neck greenish. Juvenile duller and darker, ear-coverts bordered below with short narrow stripe.

> **133a Adult male** Moustachial region, lores and entire crown to hindneck red.
>
> **133b Adult female** Red on head restricted to nape.

135 Lita Woodpecker *Piculus litae*   Text and map page 309

W South America (W Andean slopes): forest at 800-1800m.

Greenish above, with much red and yellow on head, and strongly barred on belly. Upper lores and ear-coverts green to golden-green, bordered below by golden-yellow stripe; chin and upper throat whitish to green. Juvenile duller and darker, no red on head.

> **Adult male** Forehead to nape red, broad red moustache. (Female has red on head restricted to nape.)

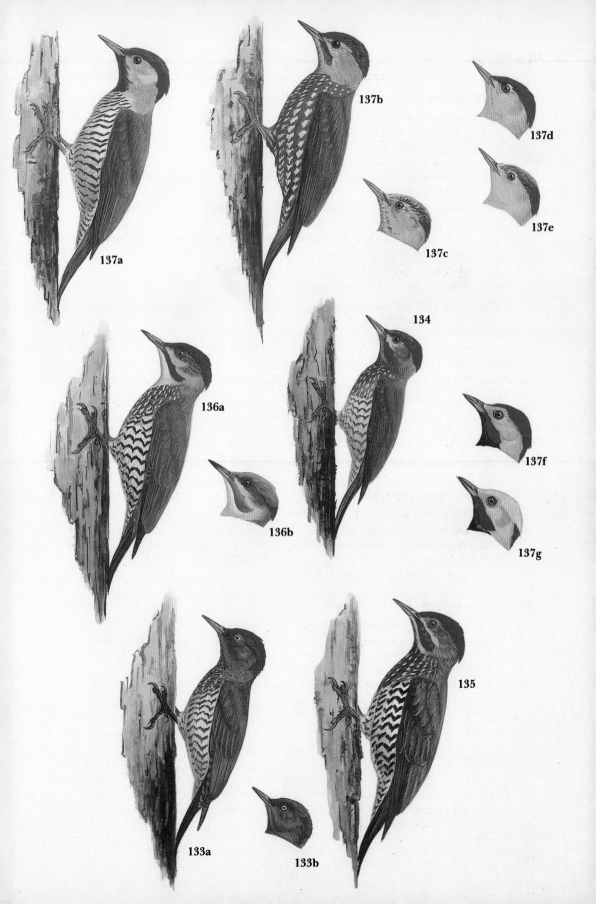

137a

137b

137c

137d

137e

137f

137g

136a

136b

134

133a

133b

135

PLATE 40

142 Crimson-mantled Woodpecker *Piculus rivolii* Text and map page 315

W South America (Andes): humid forest at 700-3700m.

Reddish above, with hindneck and sides of neck red; yellowish below with strongly marked breast; throat black. Juvenile duller (no red on breast), mottled above.

142a **Adult male** (nominate; EC Colombia, W Venezuela) Crown black, tipped red; moustache spotted red.

142b **Adult female** (nominate) Crown and moustachial region black.

142c **Adult male** (*atriceps*; SE Peru, N Bolivia) Forehead to crown black, moustache spotted red. Short-billed. Ear-coverts pale olive; less red above; breast feathers edged yellowish (with no red).

142d **Adult female** (*atriceps*) Black crown and moustache.

139 Yellow-browed Woodpecker *Piculus aurulentus* Text and map page 312

EC South America: forest.

Olive-green above, and with broad dark bars below. Dark olive band through eye bordered by yellowish stripe below and above; eyes dark. Juvenile duller, with coarser barring.

139a **Adult male** Entire top of head red, moustachial stripe red and green.

139b **Adult female** Red on head restricted to hindcrown, moustache red and green.

138 Golden-green Woodpecker *Piculus chrysochloros* Text and map page 311

SE Central America, South America: forests to savannas.

Highly variable. Olive-green to yellowish-green above, with evenly barred pale yellowish and dark underparts; underwings with cinnamon on inner webs. Dark olive band from lores to nape bordered below by narrower yellowish stripe; eyes white. Juvenile plumage softer.

138a **Adult male** (*polyzonus*, SE Brazil) Red forehead to nape, extensively red in moustachial stripe. Yellowish ground colour below.

138b **Adult female** (*polyzonus*) Top of head and moustache green.

138c **Adult male** (*capistratus*, C Colombia to NW Brazil) Red forehead to nape, red in green moustache confined to short stripe. Greener ground colour below than *polyzonus*; throat barred.

138d **Adult female** (*capistratus*) Top of head and moustache entirely green.

138e **Adult female** (*paraensis*, NE Brazil) Golden-buff on throat and crown. (Male has red crown and green moustachial stripe.)

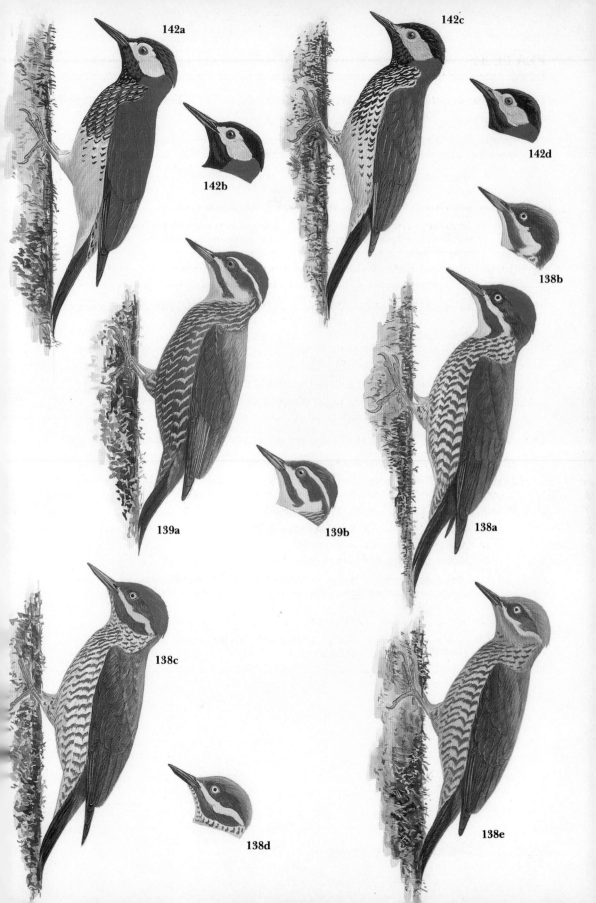

142a

142c

142b

142d

138b

139a

139b

138a

138c

138d

138e

PLATE 41

140 Grey-crowned Woodpecker *Piculus auricularis* Text and map page 312

Central America (W Mexico): evergreen forest, pine-oak woodland.

Greyish-green above, with indistinct pale bars; neck sides and underparts barred olive and greenish-white. Tail with yellow tinge. No red on nape. Juvenile insufficiently known.

> **Adult male** Red moustachial stripe, most also with some red on lores. (Female without red.)

141 Golden-olive Woodpecker *Piculus rubiginosus* Text and map page 313

Central America and South America: forests, mainly in mountainous terrain up to 3100m.

Green to bronze-green above, unbarred (except on rump); barred below. Wings edged red-bronze to green-bronze. Juvenile with softer plumage, may show black marks on lores.

141a Adult male (*aeruginosus*, E Mexico) Crown lined with red behind eye, forming red band across nape; red moustachial stripe. Back green.

141b Adult female (*aeruginosus*) Red on head restricted to nape.

141c Adult male (*yucatanensis*, Mexico to Panama) Red border of crown extends to sides of forehead, also reaching farther down on nape. Back more bronzy-olive.

141d Adult female (*yucatanensis*) No red moustache, less red on sides of crown.

141e Adult male (*gularis*, S Colombia) Crown and moustache red. Throat black, finely spotted white.

141f Adult female (*gularis*) Throat and moustachial region black, forecrown blackish.

141g Adult male (*buenavistae*, E Colombia, E Ecuador) Sides of crown and moustachial stripe red. Relatively large; reddish-bronzy back.

141h Adult female (*buenavistae*) Moustache black.

141i Adult male (*guianae*, E Venezuela, Guyana) Moderate red in crown, red moustache. Tinged bronze above.

141j Adult female (*guianae*) Moustache without red.

141k Adult male (*chrysogaster*, C Peru) Crown red, moustache red. Bronzy back, belly unbarred yellowish.

141l Adult male (*tucumanus*, S Bolivia to NW Argentina) Crown moderately red, moustache red. Thin bill; blackish barring below, ear-coverts tinged olive.

141m Adult female (*tucumanus*) No red moustache.

140

141a

141b

141c

141d

141e

141f

141g

141h

141i

141j

141k

141l

141m

PLATE 42

143 Black-necked Woodpecker *Colaptes atricollis* Text and map page 316

W South America: woodland, scrub.

Green to whitish-brown above, barred black; yellowish, barred black, below. Throat and upper breast black; centre of crown to hindcrown red. Juvenile duller, variably barred; crown entirely red (barred dark), black over lores, moustache black mixed with red.

143a Adult male (nominate; W Peru) Red in moustache, red of crown reaches forehead. Greenish above, fully barred below.

143b Adult female (nominate) Moustache black, no red in black forecrown.

143c Adult male (*peruvianus*, E Peru) Moustache with red, forecrown tipped red. Browner and whiter (with wider bars) above, fewer bars below.

143d Adult female (*peruvianus*) Moustache black.

144 Spot-breasted Woodpecker *Colaptes punctigula* Text and map page 317

N South America: forest, forest edge, cultivations.

Green above with black marks; yellowish below, spotted black. Forecrown black, hindcrown and nape red. Juvenile duller, less yellow and more green, with larger, irregular spots below; back greener.

144a Adult male (*guttatus*, Amazonia) Red moustache. Variable, usually well spotted below; breast often tinged olive.

144b Adult female (*guttatus*) Moustache black.

144c Adult male (*striatigularis*, Panama to WC Colombia) Red moustache (black on female). Reddish tinge on breast and rump.

145 Green-barred Woodpecker *Colaptes melanochloros* Text and map page 318

E and C South America: forest, open woodland, deserts.

Greenish above, barred black; pale below, with greenish/golden tinge on breast and black heart-shaped spots. Crown black, hindcrown and nape red. Juvenile duller, more strongly marked, bars wider, spots below more bar-like.

145a Adult male (*melanolaimus*, arid valleys of Bolivia) Moustache black with red tips. Partly terrestrial.

145b Adult female (*melanolaimus*) Moustache all black.

145c Adult male (*nattereri*, savannas and caatinga, Brazil, Bolivia) Moustache with red tips. Relatively small and short-billed. Greener above and more yellow below. Arboreal.

145d Adult female (*natterei*) Moustache all black.

143b

143d

143a

143c

144b

144a

144c

145b

145d

145a

145c

PLATE 43

147 Gilded Flicker *Colaptes chrysoides* Text and map page 321

W North and Central America: deserts.

Shafts, underwing and undertail yellow. Crown rusty-brown, throat grey; no red nape patch. Paler above than Northern Flicker (146), narrow bars on back. Juvenile with paler shafts, more broadly barred above.

147a Adult male (*mearnsi*; SW Arizona, SE California, Sonora) Moustache red.

147b Adult female (*mearnsi*) Moustachial stripe obscure.

147c Adult male (nominate; S Baja, California) Moustache red. Smaller and paler.

147d Adult female (nominate) Moustachial stripe obscure/lacking.

146 Northern Flicker *Colaptes auratus* Text and map page 319

North and Central America: forest, woodland, gardens.

Brown and barred above, white rump with no or strong barring/spotting; black patch across breast, prominently spotted belly. Juvenile with paler shafts; colours and markings variable, often grey-black patch over lores, males in particular often with red in forecrown and more commonly on hindcrown.

146a Adult male (*luteus*; N and NE North America) Moustache black. Shafts, underwing and undertail yellow; crown grey, throat brownish; nape with red patch.

146b Adult female (*luteus*) No moustache.

146c Adult male (*cafer*; NW North American coasts) Moustache red. Shafts, underwing and undertail pinkish; crown brown, throat grey; nape without red patch.

146d Adult female (*cafer*) Moustache brownish or grey.

146e Adult male (*gundlachi*; Grand Cayman) Moustache black. Shafts yellow; crown grey, throat pale grey; nape with red patch; greenish above, rump spotted. Highly arboreal.

146f Adult female (*gundlachi*) No moustache.

146g Adult male (*mexicanoides*; Central American highlands) Moustache red. Shafts orange-red; crown cinnamon, throat grey; no red nape patch; back brown and buff, barred black, white rump barred.

146h Adult female (*mexicanoides*) Moustache cinnamon (sometimes with fine dark streaks).

147a

147b

146b

146a

147c

147d

146d

146c

146e

146f

146h

146g

PLATE 44

148 Fernandina's Flicker *Colaptes fernandinae* — Text and map page 322

Cuba: dry woodland, pastures, palm groves; terrestrial.

Yellowish-white and strongly barred dark brown below and above; crown brown-cinnamon. Juvenile duller, with wider dark bars below, less barring above; crown deeper cinnamon.

148a Adult male Black moustache, sometimes with some red.

148b Adult female Moustache streaked, as throat.

149 Chilean Flicker *Colaptes pitius* — Text and map page 322

S South America: forest, scrub; terrestrial.

Heavily barred brown and whitish (browner, less barred, above when worn); grey-black crown, white rump; uppertail-coverts barred black and white. Juvenile with wider dark bars above, broad spots below, crown blacker.

149a Adult male Moustache finely dotted black and red (difficult to see in the field).

149b Adult female Moustache unmarked.

150 Andean Flicker *Colaptes rupicola* — Text and map page 323

W South America (Andes): puna at 2000-5000m; terrestrial, gregarious.

Barred brown and white above, spotted on breast below; very long bill; rump whitish. Crown slaty-grey, black at sides. Juvenile duller, with more dark markings below; sexes as adults, nape of males more frequently with some red.

150a Adult male (*cinereicapillus*, N Peru) Moustache grey-black, broadly tipped red at rear. Deep cinnamon on face and underparts, breast narrowly barred.

150b Adult female (*cinereicapillus*) Moustache without red. Bill shorter than male's.

150c Adult male (*puna*; C and S Peru) Dark moustache tipped red; lower nape often with some red. Breast spots large.

150d Adult female (*puna*) Indistinct moustache; lower nape often with some red. Bill shorter than on male.

150e Adult male (nominate; Bolivia, Chile, Argentina) Dark moustache tipped with red; occasionally some red in nape. Pale overall, mainly white below.

150f Adult female (nominate) Moustache without red. Bill shorter than male's.

151 Campo Flicker *Colaptes campestris* — Text and map page 324

C South America: grasslands, cultivation, lowlands; terrestrial, gregarious.

Golden patch on upper breast, extending to face and neck. Barred white, buffy and dark brown above; pale with dark bars below. Rump white, uppertail-coverts barred brown and white. Juvenile duller, gold of breast restricted; wider dark bars below, barred dark brown and light brown above.

151a Adult male (nominate; Brazil, C Paraguay) Moustache red and black. Chin and throat black.

151b Adult female (nominate) Moustache streaked black.

151c Adult male (*campestroides*, pampas of Argentina, S Brazil, S Paraguay) Moustache with red. Chin and throat white.

151d Adult female (*campestroides*) Moustache streaked black.

148b

148a

149b

149a

150a

150b

150c

150d

150e

150f

151a

151b

151c

151d

PLATE 45

154 Scaly-breasted Woodpecker *Celeus grammicus*   **Text and map page 328**

N South America: forest.

Rufous-chestnut to cinnamon overall, with head as dark as body. Barred black above and below; rump unbarred, cinnamon to greenish-yellow. Small to longish crest. Juvenile with wider dark bars above; head and throat with black marks, particularly at base of bill.

> **154a Adult male** (nominate; Venezuela south to NE Peru and W Brazil) Red on moustache (and often also under eye).
>
> **154b Adult female** (nominate) No red on head.
>
> **154c Adult male** (*latifasciatus*, SE Peru, N Bolivia, and upper Madeira river, Brazil) Very pale, with pale rump; mantle broadly barred.

156 Chestnut-coloured Woodpecker *Celeus castaneus*   **Text and map page 330**

Central America: forest

Generally more or less chestnut, with paler head and long crest. Barred black above and below, wings partially unbarred; rump somewhat paler than back, usually unbarred. Juvenile duller, often barred below eye and in moustachial region.

> **156a Adult male** Moustache, lores, cheeks, and sometimes over eye and around base of bill red.
>
> **156b Adult female** No red on head.

153 Cinnamon Woodpecker *Celeus loricatus*   **Text and map page 327**

S Central America, W South America: forest.

Head and upperparts rufous, weakly barred; cinnamon to pale buffish below, with black scallop markings; tail barred cinnamon-buff and black. Medium crest, variably streaked black. Juvenile less regularly marked below, male with reddish face.

> **153a Adult male** (*diversus*, Nicaragua to W Panama) Chin, throat and moustachial region red.
>
> **153b Adult female** (*diversus*) No red on head.

155 Waved Woodpecker *Celeus undatus*   **Text and map page 329**

NE South America: forest.

Rufous to cinnamon throughout, slightly paler on rump, and barred; head usually paler than body, tail usually strongly barred. Moderate crest; relatively dark bill. Adult female without red on head. Juvenile duller, rump less barred.

> **155a Adult male** (nominate; Guyana, Venezuela) Red moustache, red often extending under eye and to ear-coverts. Crest unbarred.
>
> **155b Adult male** (*multifasciatus*, Pará, Brazil) Red below eye and on moustache. Dark bill with pale lower mandible; crown streaked with black, paler back, streaked throat; tail unbarred.
>
> **155c Adult male** (nominate from Brazil, to show variation) Crest checker-barred; breast blackish.

154b

156b

153b

154a

156a

153a

154c

155c

155a

155b

PLATE 46

157 Chestnut Woodpecker *Celeus elegans*   Text and map page 331

N South America: forest.

Basic coloration brown, with paler flanks/belly (and underwings) and pale rump and uppertail-coverts; tail blackish-brown. No dark barring. Short to long crest. Juvenile usually mottled with black below; black around bill, lores, and occasionally on ear-coverts (sometimes with some red on forehead or sides of crown).

> **157a Adult male** (nominate; Surinam, French Guiana, NE Brazil) Red moustache. Long crest buff-cream to cinnamon buff; white spots on wing-coverts.
>
> **157b Adult female** (nominate) No red on head.
>
> **157c Adult male** (*leotaudi*; Trinidad) Red moustache. Relatively small, and paler; crown cinnamon to yellow-cinnamon.
>
> **157d Adult female** (*leotaudi*) No red on head.
>
> **157e Adult male** (*jumana*; SW Venezuela, Colombia, Brazil south of Amazon) Red moustache. Dark, with shorter (dark) crest, rump often rather dark; tertials rufous, no wing-covert spots.

159 Blond-crested Woodpecker *Celeus flavescens*   Text and map page 333

E South America: forest to dry shrub.

Whitish to cinnamon-buff head, long crest and rump. Variably barred black and creamy-white to cinnamon above. Juvenile duller, with more black marks on head.

> **159a Adult male** (*ochraceus*; E Brazil) Red moustache, red occasionally reaching under eye. Cinnamon-buff above, with variable black markings; underparts often with buffy-cinnamon feather edges, flanks with much cinnamon-buff.
>
> **159b Adult female** (*ochraceus*) Moustache black-streaked.
>
> **159c Adult male** (nominate; E Paraguay, SE Brazil) Red moustachial region. Narrow pale barring above; more uniform below.
>
> **159d Adult female** (nominate) Moustache black-streaked.

158 Pale-crested Woodpecker *Celeus lugubris*   Text and map page 332

C South America: dry forest and shrub.

Blond head, long crest and blond rump; nasal tufts and areas around eye often brown. Black wings barred rufous on tertials, dark mantle with narrow pale bars. Juvenile with black marks on head.

> **158a Adult male** Red moustache (some red may also appear on forehead, and above and below eye).
>
> **158b Adult female** Moustache scaled or barred brown.

157b

157d

157a

157c

159b

159a

157e

159d

159c

158b

158a

PLATE 47

162 Ringed Woodpecker *Celeus torquatus*   Text and map page 335

N South America: forest.

Variably barred black and rufous above, barred to unmarked light buff to rufous-cinnamon below; breast and lower throat black, variably extending to back. Head and moderate crest clearly paler than back. Juvenile more barred, black of breast reaching bill, with lores and area around eye also black.

> **162a Adult male** (nominate; E Venezuela, Guianas, Amazonian NE Brazil) Red moustache (traces of red may also appear on lores, forehead and on sides of crest). Unbarred below, minimal barring above; black of breast continues around upper mantle.
>
> **162b Adult female** (nominate) No red on head.
>
> **162c Adult male** (*occidentalis*; S Venezuela, E Peru, W and C Amazonian Brazil) Moustachial area red. Barred below and above.
>
> **162d Juvenile male** (*occidentalis*) Moustache tipped red.
>
> **162e Adult male** (*tinnunculus*; Bahia, Brazil) Red moustache. Heavily barred, pale head, outer tail black.
>
> **162f Adult female** (*tinnunculus*) No moustachial stripe.

161 Rufous-headed Woodpecker *Celeus spectabilis*   Text and map page 334

C South America: forest; rare, consult text.

Variably barred black and buffy-cream above and below (dark markings small in SE Peru and N Bolivia, very reduced in Brazil); black breast shield; rump and uppertail-coverts more or less unmarked buff to cinnamon-buff. Head and moderate to long crest rusty. Juvenile black around base of bill, more red in head.

> **161a Adult male** (nominate; E Ecuador, NE Peru) Red moustache; red also above eye, extending onto crest.
>
> **161b Adult female** (nominate) No red moustache; may have traces of red in crest.

160 Cream-coloured Woodpecker *Celeus flavus*   Text and map page 334

N South America: forest, woodland, mangroves, plantations.

Cream-coloured overall, apart from brown/rufous flight feathers and black tail; browner when worn, and plumage often discoloured. Easternmost population with brownish mantle and breast. Juvenile more buffy to cinnamon-buff.

> **160a Adult male** (nominate; northern part of range) Red moustache.
>
> **160b Adult female** (nominate) Moustache as rest of head.

162b

162a

162d

162c

162e

162f

161a

161b

160b

160a

PLATE 48

163 Helmeted Woodpecker *Dryocopus galeatus*   Text and map page 336

EC South America: forest.

Black above, with white neck stripe and whitish lower back, rump and uppertail-coverts; entirely barred below. Long red crest; face and throat buffish-cinnamon, finely marked dark. Juvenile browner, with less red in crown.

163a Adult male Red moustache (red sometimes extending over lower face).

163b Adult female No moustache, entire face finely barred black and cinnamon.

164 Pileated Woodpecker *Dryocopus pileatus*   Text and map page 337

North America: forest.

Very big and mainly black with some white, and red crown and crest; white patch at front of wing, rear border of which is black. Immature browner and duller, red more orange in tone.

164a Adult male Red moustache, forehead and forecrown.

164b Adult female Moustache, forehead and forecrown black.

165 Lineated Woodpecker *Dryocopus lineatus*   Text and map page 338

Central and South America: forest (edge), woodland.

Black above, with white neck stripe and with or without white scapular stripe; breast black/sooty, belly pale and more or less barred. Throat pale with black streaks; crown and crest red. Juvenile duller, black on breast usually more extensive; males may show yellow in crown.

165a Adult male (*scapularis*, W Mexico) Red moustache, forehead and forecrown. White cheek stripe greatly reduced or lacking.

165b Adult female (*scapularis*) Moustache, forehead and forecrown black.

165c Adult male (*erythrops*, SE and S Brazil, E Paraguay, NE Argentina) Red moustache, forehead and forecrown. White line below eye from lores to side of neck. (Some in N Argentina have much rufous on underparts.)

165d Adult female (*erythrops*) Moustache, forehead and forecrown black.

165e Adult male (*fuscipennis*, W Ecuador, NW Peru) Red moustache, forehead and forecrown. Browner; markings on belly irregular and obscure; wings and tail with pale shafts.

165f Adult female (*fuscipennis*) Moustache, forehead and forecrown black.

166 Black-bodied Woodpecker *Dryocopus schulzi*   Text and map page 340

SC South America: dry woodland.

Black with white neck stripe and red crest; throat grey-white, ear-coverts grey, lores with yellow patch. Juvenile browner, often with some lateral barring below and some white spots on forecrown.

166a Adult male (morph 1; more common in south of range) Red moustache, forehead and forecrown. Entire upperparts black.

166b Adult female Moustache and forehead black (forehead sometimes almost fully red).

166c Adult male (morph 2; more common in north of range) Moustache red. Wing with white scapular line.

163a

163b

164a

164b

165a

165b

165c

165d

166a

166b

165e

165f

166c

PLATE 49

167 White-bellied Woodpecker *Dryocopus javensis*   Text and map page 341

S and E Asia: forest.

Large. Mainly black, with red crest and white belly; rump black or white, variable white wing patch in flight. Bill dark. Juvenile duller, paler.

> **167a Adult male** (*confusus*, Luzon) Red moustache, forehead and crown. No or little white on rump; white marks on throat.
>
> **167b Adult female** (*confusus*) No red moustache; forehead and forecrown black.
>
> **167c Adult male** (*feddeni*, most of Thailand, Burma, Indochina) Red moustache, forehead and crown. White rump; bases of primaries white.
>
> **167d Adult female** (*feddeni*) No red moustache; forehead and forecrown black.
>
> **167e Adult male** (*hargitti*, Palawan) Red moustache, forehead and crown. Rump partly white, pale thighs, white-streaked throat.
>
> **167f Adult female** (*hargitti*) No red moustache; forehead and forecrown black.

169 Black Woodpecker *Dryocopus martius*   Text and map page 343

Eurasia: forest.

Large; entirely black, with pale bill, moustachial region black. Juvenile sootier, with paler throat.

> **169a Adult male** Entire crown red.
>
> **169b Adult female** Red band across nape.

168 Andaman Woodpecker *Dryocopus hodgei*   Text and map page 343

SE Asia (Andaman Islands): forest.

Large; entirely black, with red crest. Juvenile browner.

> **168a Adult male** Red moustache, forehead and forecrown.
>
> **168b Adult female** No red moustache; forehead and forecrown black.

167a

167b

167c

167d

169a

169b

168a

168b

167e

167f

PLATE 50

172 Red-necked Woodpecker *Campephilus rubricollis*   **Text and map page 347**

N South America: forest.

Large. Black above, dark rufous below; head and neck red, bill pale. Juvenile duller, face pattern more or less as adult female's.

172a Adult male Small black and white spot below ear.

172b Adult female Large white band from bill to below ear, bordered with black above and below; black chin.

172c Adult male In flight, shows dark rufous wing patch.

170 Powerful Woodpecker *Campephilus pollens*   **Text and map page 345**

NW South America: forest at 900-3600m.

Large. Black above, with lower back and rump white to dark-barred cinnamon; cinnamon with black bars below, with black breast. White cheek stripe continues down neck; short crest, black bill. Juvenile browner, with wider dark bars below; longer, fluffier crest.

170a Adult male (nominate; Venezuela to Ecuador) Red crown, nape and crest.

170b Adult female (nominate) No red on head.

170c Adult male (nominate) In flight, shows pale rump and white bars across flight feathers; white underwing-coverts.

171 Crimson-bellied Woodpecker *Campephilus haematogaster*   **Text and map page 346**

NW South America: (lowland) forest.

Large and hefty-looking. Back and wings black; rest of body red to dull red, showing dark barring when worn, with black and whitish face. Crown, small crest and hindneck red. Juvenile less barred and less red, browner above, crown with some blackish.

171a Adult male (*splendens*, Panama to W Ecuador) Crown and sides of neck red.

171b Adult female (*splendens*) Pale stripe down sides of neck.

171c Adult male In flight, shows whitish barring across flight feathers (pale underwing-coverts); rump dull red.

172c

172a

172b

171c

171b

170b

170c

170a

171a

PLATE 51

173 Robust Woodpecker *Campephilus robustus* Text and map page 348

EC South America: forest.

Large. Back to uppertail-coverts whitish, wings black; whitish, fully barred black, below. Head and neck red; pale bill. Juvenile duller, wings browner, undertail-coverts unbarred; head pattern approaches adult female's.

> **173a Adult male** Small black and white mark below ear.
>
> **173b Adult female** White line from bill to below ear, bordered with black above and to about halfway below; black chin.

175 Crimson-crested Woodpecker *Campephilus melanoleucos* Text and map page 349

Panama and South America: forest, woodland, savanna.

Large. Black above, with white neck stripe and white V on back; barred pale and black below, with black breast. Black and white marks on side of largely red, crested head; pale around base of bill. Juvenile browner above, darker below; red of head more pinkish, with pale supercilium.

> **175a Adult male** (nominate; east of Andes) Sides of head red, except for small white and black patch below ear; entire crown and crest red, lower forehead black.
>
> **175b Adult female** (nominate) Whitish area around bill extends into broad black-bordered white moustache, joining with white line on sides of neck; forehead to centre of longer crest black.
>
> **175c Adult male** (*malherbii*; Panama to Colombia) Head pattern much as nominate, but area around eye completely red. Bill brown-grey; ground colour below darker.
>
> **175d Adult female** (*malherbii*) Head pattern much as nominate female. Bill and underparts darker.

176 Guayaquil Woodpecker *Campephilus gayaquilensis* Text and map page 351

W South America: dry forest.

Large. White neck stripe and white V on black back, lower back to uppertail-coverts variably barred black and buff; whitish, barred brown, below. Head largely red. Juvenile less barred above, with white facial patch: female as adult female, but black around eye, including a black line behind eye and black from forehead to central crest; male as adult, but with additional white band on sides of head.

> **176a Adult male** Head, crown and crest red, with black and white patch below ear.
>
> **176b Adult female** Entire crown, crest, nape and ear-coverts red; white band from base of bill connecting with white neck stripe; chin black.

174 Pale-billed Woodpecker *Campephilus guatemalensis* Text and map page 348

Central America: forest, pastures, plantations.

Large. Black above, with white neck stripe and white V on back; barred pale and black below, with black breast. No black and white mark on side of largely red head. Juvenile browner, red more orange, bill darker.

> **174a Adult male** Entire head, crown and moderate crest red.
>
> **174b Adult female** Forehead, crown to centre of crest black; nasal tufts and chin red, throat black.

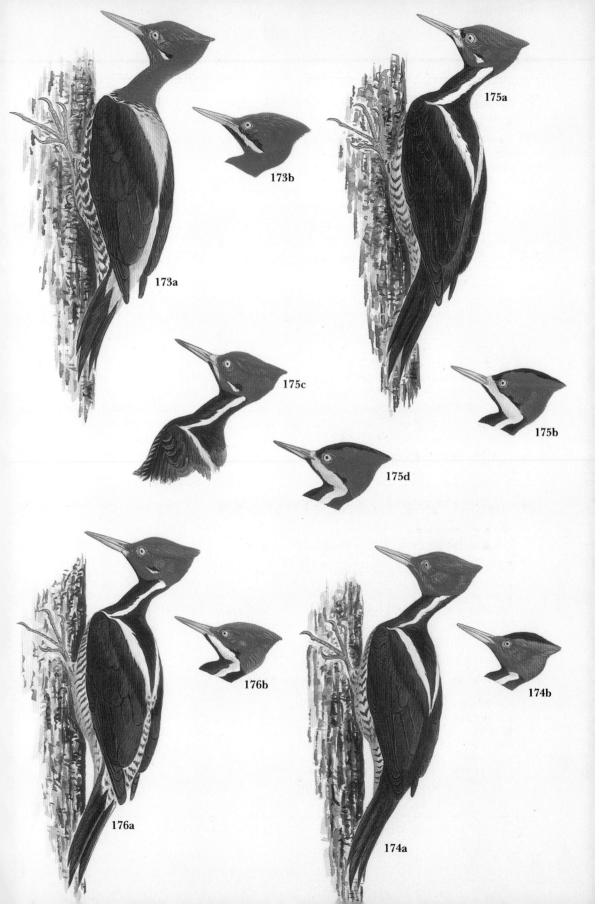

173a

173b

175a

175b

175c

175d

176a

176b

174a

174b

PLATE 52

177 Cream-backed Woodpecker *Campephilus leucopogon*   Text and map page 351

C South America: dry woodland.

Large. Cinnamon-white on mantle, black on lower back to tail; all black below. Head largely red. Wings with pale patch. Bill ivory. Juvenile a trifle browner, less red on head.

> **177a Adult male** Entire head and short crest red, apart from small black and white patch below ear.
>
> **177b Adult female** Forehead to centre of crown and long crest and area around eye black; black-bordered white line from bill to below ear, chin black.

178 Magellanic Woodpecker *Campephilus magellanicus*   Text and map page 352

S South America: temperate forest.

Very large. Black overall with more or less red on head; white wing patch. Bill grey-black. Juvenile as adult female but browner, with smaller crest.

> **178a Adult male** Entire head and curled crest red.
>
> **178b Adult female** Head and rather long, pointed crest black, but for red area around base of bill.

179 Imperial Woodpecker *Campephilus imperialis*   Text and map page 353

Central America (Mexico): pine forest; probably extinct.

Huge. Black, with large white patch on wing (not bordered black at rear) and white lines on mantle. Bill ivory-coloured. Juvenile browner, male with some red on head.

> **179a Adult male** Long red crest with black centre.
>
> **179b Adult female** No red on head, very long curled crest.

180 Ivory-billed Woodpecker *Campephilus principalis*   Text and map page 354

SE North America, Cuba: pine and swamp forest; most likely extinct.

Very large. Mainly black, with white lines on mantle, white stripes on sides of neck (do not reach bill), and large white wing patch (not bordered black at rear); underwing-coverts white, separated by black from white flight feathers. Juvenile browner, crest shorter and black, with males showing more or less red.

> **180a Adult male** (nominate; SE USA) Crest red, with black in centre.
>
> **180b Adult female** (nominate) No red on head.

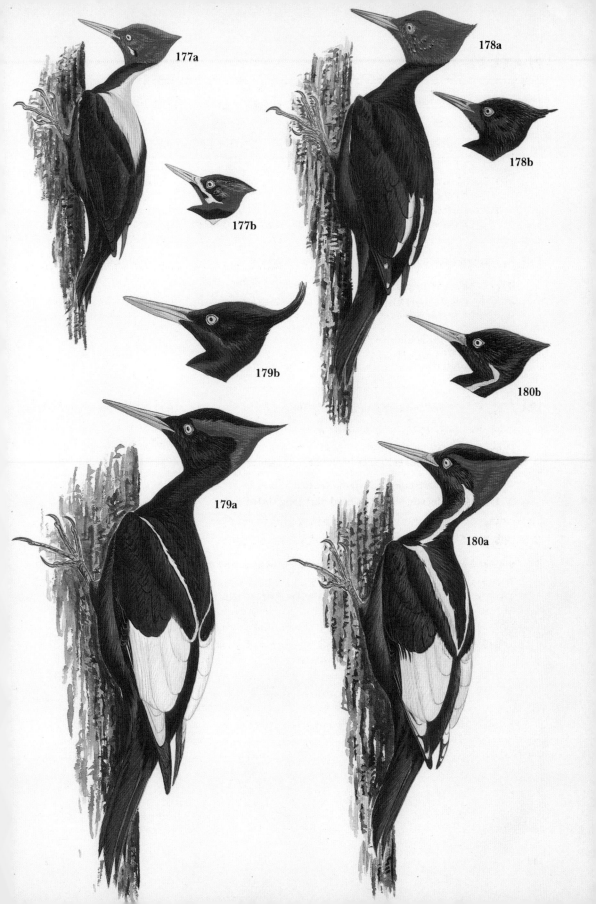

177a

177b

178a

178b

179b

180b

179a

180a

PLATE 53

181 Banded Woodpecker *Picus miniaceus*   Text and map page 355

Southern SE Asia: dense primary forest, also more open woods, gardens and mangroves.

Dull red crown and wings and yellowish-tipped crest; dull olive back, with paler barring (indistinct when worn); barred pale and dark below, with brownish breast. Juvenile duller, more obscurely barred.

> **181a Adult male** (nominate; Java) Reddish feather tips to face and throat (browner when worn); when fresh, mantle feathers tipped dull red.
>
> **181b Adult female** (nominate) Face and throat browner, with buffish speckles.

183 Crimson-winged Woodpecker *Picus puniceus*   Text and map page 357

Southern SE Asia: forest, edge and plantations, occasionally coastal scrub and gardens.

Much brighter than Banded Woodpecker (181), with green body, red wings, red crown and yellow crest; almost unbarred. Bluish area around eye. Juvenile duller and greyer, more patterned below, with less red on crown.

> **183a Adult male** (*observandus*; range of species except Java and Nias Island) Red moustache.
>
> **183b Adult female** (*observandus*) Sides of head all green.

182 Lesser Yellownape *Picus chlorolophus*   Text and map page 356

S and SE Asia: varied habitats, mainly forests, also more open woodland and scrub.

Highly variable, both individually and geographically, but always with prominent yellow crest and green/greenish upperparts (dull red in wings generally not visible when perched). Most have dark green breast and paler, dark-barred belly/flanks, but those in south and east generally all dark below with reduced (pale) barring; both sexes always have at least some red on crown, and usually pale face stripes. Juvenile duller, with more barring on breast, and less red on crown.

> **182a Adult male** (nominate; E Nepal to N Vietnam) Red moustache; forehead and rear crown bordered with red. The brightest race. Crest golden or orange; obviously barred below.
>
> **182b Adult female** (nominate) No red moustache, only small red patch on rear crown sides.
>
> **182c Adult male** ('*laotianus*'; Laos) Red of moustache reduced, more red on forehead/crown sides. Darker, with underparts greyer and bars more obscure; crest paler; less white on face.
>
> **182d Adult female** ('*laotianus*') Red on head confined to narrow red band on crown sides.
>
> **182e Adult male** (*rodgersi*; W Malaysia) Red moustache, red forehead and crown sides. Dark. Crest tinged golden; prominent pale cheek stripe.
>
> **182f Adult female** (*rodgersi*) Less red on crown, no red moustache.
>
> **182g Adult male** (*wellsi*; Sri Lanka) Red moustache, much red on hindcrown (covers much of crest) Small and dark, with belly/flank bars reduced; no white face stripes.
>
> **182h Adult female** (*wellsi*) No red moustache, face plain greenish.

181a

181b

183a

183b

182d

182a

182b

182c

182f

182e

182g

182h

PLATE 54

184 Greater Yellownape *Picus flavinucha*   **Text and map page 358**

S and SE Asia: forests, secondary growth, occasionally near edges or in clearings.

Dark green, usually paler or greyer below, with conspicuous erect/upcurved yellow crest and yellow hindneck (head appears triangular-shaped in side view); flight feathers barred rufous and black. Most have black and white throat pattern. Lacks obvious red in all plumages. Juvenile greyer below, crest less bright.

> **184a Adult male** (nominate; NW India to N Vietnam) Chin, moustache and upper throat bright yellow (chestnut on female). The brightest race, yellowish-green above.
>
> **184b Adult female** (*styani*; Hainan) Moustache dull chestnut (yellow on male). Darker overall; yellow hindneck paler.
>
> **184c Adult male** (*korinchi*; SW Sumatra) Chin and throat plain, with contrasting yellow moustache (chestnut on female). Breast extensively dark; wingbars duller.

185 Checker-throated Woodpecker *Picus mentalis*   **Text and map page 360**

Southern SE Asia: primary forest, overgrown clearings, occasionally mangrove edge.

Dark green, with reddish/rufous wings, chestnut neck sides and breast; yellow crest, throat black and white. Juvenile fully chestnut from breast downwards, with less chestnut in wings.

> **185a Adult male** (*humii*; range of species except Java) Chin and throat white, streaked/barred dark olive (female has chestnut of neck extending over moustache and often to chin). Bright chestnut-red in wings.
>
> **185b Adult male** (nominate; Java) Chin, throat and moustache blackish with white spotting (female has chestnut covering chin and throat). Larger and darker; chestnut of neck more extensive. Rare.

184a

184b

184c

185a

185b

PLATE 55

186 Streak-breasted Woodpecker *Picus viridanus* Text and map page 361

SE Asia: forests, coastal scrub, mangroves.

Bronzy-green above, with yellowish rump; entire underparts heavily marked with dark and light scalloping (appears markedly scaly). Variable black moustache. Juvenile duller, more diffusely patterned below.

> **186a Adult male** Forehead to nape red.
>
> **186b Adult female** Top of head entirely black.

187 Laced Woodpecker *Picus vittatus* Text and map page 362

SE Asia: open forests, scrub, plantations, gardens.

Green above, with yellow rump; throat and upper breast plain buff-yellow, lower underparts boldly streaked (scaly or scalloped). Sides of head bluish-grey, with pale moustachial stripe and supercilium, and prominent black malar stripe. Juvenile duller, more diffusely marked below, throat variably streaked.

> **187a Adult male** Forehead to nape red, bordered with black.
>
> **187b Adult female** Top of head entirely black.

188 Streak-throated Woodpecker *Picus xanthopygaeus* Text and map page 363

S and SE Asia: open forests, secondary growth, plantations.

Green above, with bright yellow rump; rather pale below, with heavy dark arrowhead markings. Thin white supercilium, moustache poorly defined. Pale eyes. Juvenile more variegated above, with broader markings below.

> **188a Adult male** Forehead to crown red, bordered with black.
>
> **188b Adult female** Top of head fully black, usually with greyish streaks.

189 Scaly-bellied Woodpecker *Picus squamatus* Text and map page 364

SC Asia: forests, orchards, scrub; often visits ground, noisy.

Large. Green above, with yellower rump; throat and breast olive, rest of underparts pale with heavy scale-like pattern; wings and tail barred. Face olive-grey, with white supercilium and black moustache; strong, pale bill. Western race *flavirostris* is much paler overall. Juvenile greyer, blotchy above, with black hindneck.

> **189a Adult male** (nominate; NE Afghanistan to Sikkim) Red forehead to nape, bordered with black.
>
> **189b Adult female** (nominate) Top of head black with pale streaks.

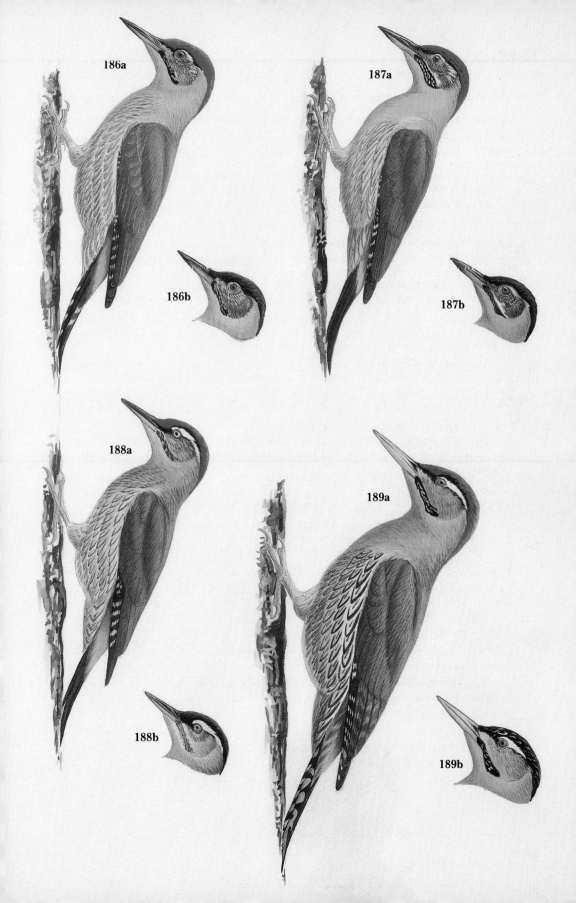

186a

186b

187a

187b

188a

188b

189a

189b

PLATE 56

191 Eurasian Green Woodpecker *Picus viridis*   Text and map page 366

Europe, W Asia, N Africa: semi-open habitats with wooded areas; often noisy (loud laughing call), spends much time on ground.

Relatively large, fairly unmistakable within its range: bright green/yellowish-green above, with brilliant yellow rump (striking in flight); greyer and paler below, flanks lightly barred (except in Iberia); red crown and nape, red/black moustache and (most races) much black around pale eye. Juvenile duller, strongly spotted/barred throughout, with much grey in red on head. N African race *vaillantii* (often treated as separate species) differs in several respects (see 191d,e, below).

> **191a Adult male** (*innominatus*, SW Iran) Red centre to moustache. Face and underparts very pale; black eye patch; small pale spots above.
>
> **191b Adult male** (*sharpei*, Pyrenees and Iberia) Red moustache. Black lores; supercilium and ear-coverts green-grey, thin white line above moustache; flanks virtually unbarred.
>
> **191c Adult female** (*sharpei*) Moustache all black, bordered by white. (Juveniles of both sexes less heavily patterned than in most races.)
>
> **191d Adult male** (*vaillantii*, N Africa) Red crown and nape. Moustache all black, bordered by white; ear-coverts and area around eye grey-green; pale below, flanks relatively well barred.
>
> **191e Adult female** (*vaillantii*) Red restricted to nape, with crown dark grey (red in all other races). (Juveniles of both sexes less barred and spotted than in other races.)
>
> **191f Adult male** (nominate; range of species excluding southern areas) Red centre to moustache. Brighter, yellower, above; large black eye patch, rear ear-coverts pale whitish-green
>
> **191g Adult female** (nominate) No red in moustache.

190 Japanese Woodpecker *Picus awokera*   Text and map page 365

Japan (Honshu southwards): open mixed forest, evergreen forest, parks and gardens.

Green above, tipped yellow on rump; breast greyish to buff-green, rest of underparts paler and heavily barred. Forehead and face grey to greenish, with black lores and red-centred black moustache. Juvenile duller overall, with grey tone above and coarser barring below (including breast).

> **190a Adult male** Red crown and nape; much red in centre of moustache.
>
> **190b Adult female** Crown grey, streaked/barred black in centre, small red nape patch; less red in moustache.

192 Red-collared Woodpecker *Picus rabieri*   Text and map page 368

SE Asia (Laos, Vietnam): forests.

Dark green above; somewhat paler green below, with lower underparts mottled/streaked. Diagnostic red collar from nape across breast. Juvenile duller, greyer below, red of collar mixed with orange/yellow.

> **192a Adult male** Red forehead and crown connecting with red collar and red moustache.
>
> **192b Adult female** Forehead and crown green or blackish-green, face with less red; collar sometimes obscure at front.

191a

191b

191c

191d

191e

191f

191g

190a

190b

192a

192b

PLATE 57

194 Grey-faced Woodpecker *Picus canus*

Text and map page 369

N Eurasia, S and SE Asia: varied wooded and forested habitats with some open areas, parks, orchards, gardens.

Variable. Most races green or greenish above, with bright yellow-green rump, paler below, and unbarred (except on wings and usually tail); face grey with thin black moustache, crown and nape black/grey. Distinctive Sumatran race *dedemi* has dull red body with bright red rump. Juvenile duller and greyer, initially with faint barring on belly. Compared with Eurasian Green (191, Plate 56), is smaller and duller (less yellow-toned), with different head pattern (less black and less red) and with less 'nose-heavy' appearance; unpatterned underparts and reduced red on head also distinguish it from similar species in SE Asia (Plate 55).

194a **Adult male** (*guerini*; E Yangtze river west to C Sichuan, China) Red forehead and forecrown. Crown to nape black with pale streaks.

194b **Adult female** (*guerini*) Forehead black.

194c **Adult female** (*robinsoni*; Malaya) Forehead to nape black, crown slightly streaked (forehead/forecrown red on male). Plumage very dark overall.

194d **Adult male** (nominate; Europe east to W Siberia) Forehead and forecrown red. Rest of head greyish; pale grey below.

194e **Adult female** (nominate) No red on head (rarely, a few scattered red tips on forehead); moustache often incomplete/fainter (so head plain-looking).

194f **Adult male** (*dedemi*; Sumatra) Red forehead and forecrown. Distinctive: small and very dark, mostly dark brown-red; red rump, crown and nape black; some grey and green mixed in underparts.

194g **Adult female** (*dedemi*) Forehead and forecrown black.

194h **Adult male** (*sanguiniceps*, W Nepal, NW India, Pakistan) Red forehead to mid crown. Crown to nape black; dull dark green above, dark green (less grey) below.

194i **Adult female** (*sanguiniceps*) No red on head.

193 Black-headed Woodpecker *Picus erythropygius*

Text and map page 368

SE Asia: (dry) forests, scrub; noisy, often gregarious.

Unmistakable: mainly black head with striking yellow throat, breast and neck diagnostic. Yellowish-green above, with bright red rump; flanks and belly whitish with brown or blackish bars. Juvenile less yellow-tinged above, throat paler, and breast more buff than yellow.

193a **Adult male** (*nigrigenis*; Burma and W Thailand) Red crown patch. Dark bill.

193b **Adult female** (*nigrigenis*) No red in crown.

193c **Adult male** A few individuals (of both races) have a thin whitish line from eye over ear-coverts.

193d **Adult male** (nominate; Indochina west into Thailand) Red crown patch (generally smaller than in *nigrigenis*). Pale bill.

193e **Adult female** (nominate) No red in crown.

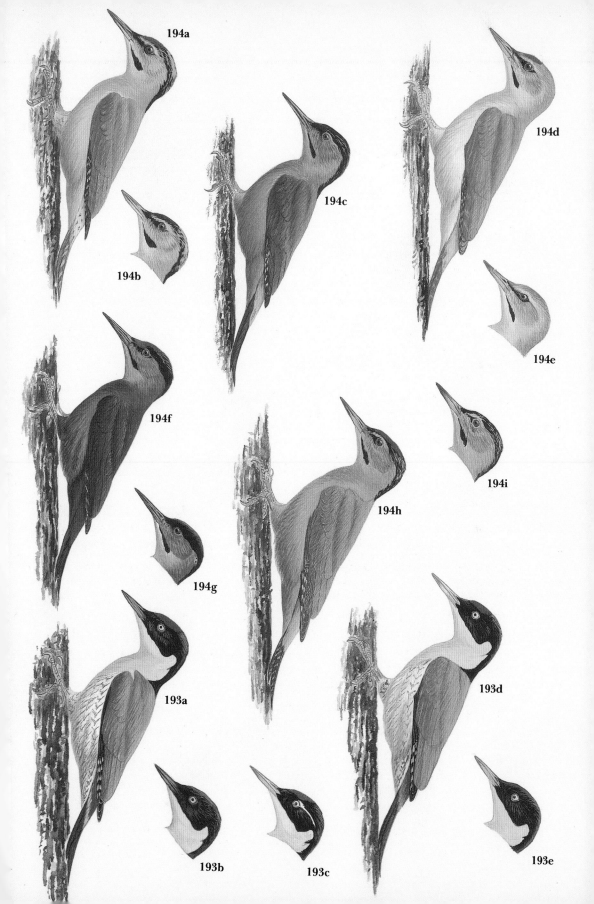

194a

194b

194c

194d

194e

194f

194g

194h

194i

193a

193b

193c

193d

193e

PLATE 58

198 Black-rumped Flameback *Dinopium benghalense* Text and map page 375

S Asia: various woodland, plantations, villages, towns; often quite tame.

Back and wings golden or golden-olive, mantle and rump black (Sri Lankan race *psarodes* all deep red above), wing-coverts usually with some white spots; pale below, with black markings. Face and neck black and white (black hindneck), chin and throat with much black; crested. Juvenile duller, greyer and more obscurely marked below, males with small red tips to crown (and sometimes white crown spots), females with little or no crown spotting.

> **198a Adult male** (*dilutum*; Pakistan) Red crown and crest with black bases (when worn, forehead and crown often largely black). Back and wings pale golden; whitish ground colour below.
>
> **198b Adult female** (*dilutum*) Crown white-spotted black, crest red.
>
> **198c Adult male** (*puncticolle*; C India south to N Sri Lanka) Red crown and crest with black bases. Back and wings more orange-yellow; creamy-buff ground colour below.
>
> **198d Adult female** (*puncticolle*) Crown white-spotted black, crest red.
>
> **198e Adult male** (*psarodes*; most of Sri Lanka) Red crown and crest with much black. Deep crimson-red above; more black on throat and underparts; black eye-stripe extends to hindneck.
>
> **198f Adult female** (*psarodes*) Crown black, spotted white, crest red.

196 Himalayan Flameback *Dinopium shorii* Text and map page 373

S Asia: forests.

Golden-olive above with strong red suffusion, bright red rump; throat and breast buffy-brown, belly and flanks whitish with dark scallop markings. Face and neck striped black and white (black hindneck and upper mantle), double moustachial line; bushy crest. Juvenile browner, with markings below more obscure, males with red on crest. Compare very similar Common Flameback (197), which overlaps in Burma.

> **196a Adult male** (nominate; range of species except Burma) Red crown and crest, black-edged reddish moustache.
>
> **196b Adult female** (nominate) Crown and crest black with white streaks, two thin black moustachial lines.

195 Olive-backed Woodpecker *Dinopium rafflesii* Text and map page 372

SE Asia: forests, mangroves.

Olive-green above and below (flanks spotted white), when fresh usually tinged bronze or yellow above and with yellowish, orange or crimson tips to rump (rump never truly crimson). Head and neck striped black and white (black hindneck and upper mantle), throat yellow to rusty; pointed crest. Juvenile duller and greyer, males with crown blackish/dark olive with red on crest.

> **195a Adult male** Red crown and crest.
>
> **195b Adult female** Crown and crest black (unspotted).

197 Common Flameback *Dinopium javanense* Text and map page 374

S and SE Asia (including Palawan, Philippines): open forests, mangroves, cultivation, gardens.

Golden to olive above, with bright red rump; white with black markings below. Face and neck generally black and white (black hindneck and upper mantle), with dark moustachial line; neat crest, short bill. Juvenile with breast more blackish-brown and spotted white, more obscurely barred below, males with red crest. Differs from Himalayan Flameback (196) in colour/pattern of throat and breast and in single black moustachial line; best told from superficially similar Greater Flameback (199, Plate 59) by smaller size, shorter, less powerful bill, neater crest, black hindneck/upper mantle, single moustachial line, usually darker eyes, and only three toes (Greater has four).

> **197a Adult male** (nominate; Malaysia, Sumatra, W Java, Borneo) Red crown and crest.
>
> **197b Adult female** (nominate) Crown and crest black, streaked white.
>
> **197c Adult male** (*everetti*; Palawan, Philippines) Red crown and crest, red invading face and moustache. Neck and breast tinged reddish-buff, supercilium very narrow; more barred below.
>
> **197d Adult female** (*everetti*) Crown black, unspotted, crest red.

198b

198a

198d

198f

198c

196b

198e

195b

196a

197d

195a

197b

197a

197c

PLATE 59

199 Greater Flameback *Chrysocolaptes lucidus* Text and map page 377

S and SE Asia: forests, woodland, edge, riparian vegetation, mangroves,

Extreme geographical variation. All races with lower back and rump crimson, and most with hindneck and upper mantle white or whitish (never totally black as in *Dinopium* species, Plate 58); wings and mantle golden-olive or dark red; moustache usually double-striped. Bill as long as head; eyes pale or bright in some races. Females have rounded spots (not streaks) in crown. Juvenile generally duller, with dark eyes, and with obscure spots and bars on back.

199a Adult male (*guttacristatus*, NW India east to Yunnan and Indochina) Red crown and crest. Mantle and wings golden-green; much black on breast; pale eyes.

199b Adult female (*guttacristatus*) Crown and crest black with whitish spots.

199c Adult male (*strictus*, E Java) Red crown and crest. Rump duller red, faintly barred; face and breast buff-tinged; eyes dark.

199d Adult female (*strictus*) Crown and crest golden-yellow, almost unmarked.

199e Adult male (*xanthocephalus*, Negros, Guimaras, Panay, Masbate and Ticao, Philippines) Red crown and crest. Highly distinctive: mantle and wings dark red; sides of head, neck and underparts golden-yellow; pale bill.

199f Adult female (*xanthocephalus*) Entire head, including crown and crest, yellow (crest often tinged orange).

199g Adult male (*erythrocephalus*, Balabac, Palawan and Calamians, Philippines) Entire head and crest red, with black ear spot and thin moustache. Mantle and wings golden-green with red admixed; neck striped black, belly/flanks barred; pale bill and legs.

199h Adult female (*erythrocephalus*) Head and crest dark reddish, with pale crown spotting. (Juvenile of both sexes similar to adult female.)

199i Adult male (*stricklandi*, Sri Lanka) Crown and crest dark red. Mantle and wings dark crimson; narrow white supercilium; bill and eyes very pale.

199j Adult female (*stricklandi*) Crown and crest black with white spots.

199k Adult male (nominate; Basilan and Zamboanga peninsula of W Mindanao, Philip pines) Red crown and crest. Mantle and wings dark red; face, neck and breast reddish-buff, strongly patterned black; underparts heavily marked black.

199l Adult female (nominate) Crown and crest dark olive-brown to reddish-black, spotted darkish.

199m Adult male (*haematribon*, Luzon, Polillo and Marinduque, Philippines) Crown and crest red, face whitish with heavy black spotting. Mantle and wings dark crimson, suffused olive; hindneck and upper mantle with much black; belly/flanks buffish, barred.

199n Adult female (*haematribon*) Crown and crest blackish, boldly spotted white, face dark.

199o Adult male (*rufopunctatus*, Bohol, Leyte and Samar, Philippines) Red crown and crest, dark-bordered reddish moustache; reddish-buff face, neck and breast. Mantle and wings dark red; belly strongly patterned. (Female has crown and crest dark brown, spotted reddish-buff.)

200 White-naped Woodpecker *Chrysocolaptes festivus* Text and map page 379

India and Sri Lanka: open woodland, scrub, cultivation.

Back black, wings golden-green; diagnostic large white triangle on mantle; white below with black streaks. Juvenile generally duller, with yellow crown and some orange-red on crest.

200a Adult male (nominate; Indian mainland) Red crown and crest.

200b Adult female (nominate) Crown and crest yellow.

199b

199d

199c

199a

200b

200a

199j

199h

199f

199i

199e

199g

199n

199l

199k

199o

199m

PLATE 60

201 Pale-headed Woodpecker *Gecinulus grantia*   Text and map page 380

S and SE Asia: evergreen and secondary forest, scrub (favours bamboo); rare in many parts.

Small and stocky, rather plain and dark, with short crest. Dull red above (more olive in east), dark olive below, with paler head and noticeably pale bill; wingbars fairly broad but rather indistinct. Juvenile duller, darker, with plain crown. Eastern populations more olive above, greyer below, with darker head. Appears to overlap little, if at all, in range with Bamboo Woodpecker (202).

  201a Adult male (nominate; Nepal to W Yunnan, China) Crimson and pink crown patch.

  201b Adult female (nominate) Crown greenish.

  201c Adult male (*viridanus*, SE China) Small, dull pink crown patch (absent on female). Bigger and darker; mainly olive above (red on greater coverts), browner/greyer below; duller head, wingbars more extensive.

203 Okinawa Woodpecker *Sapheopipo noguchii*   Text and map page 382

S Ryukyus, Japan (Yambaru mountains, N Okinawa): evergreen forest, edge and clearings; rare.

Very dark, long-tailed; inconspicuous. Deep red-brown, with paler face, throat and bill (in the field often appears uniformly dull brown). Juvenile duller and greyer, less red.

  203a Adult male Extensive red tips to crown and nape feathers.

  203b Adult female Crown and nape black.

202 Bamboo Woodpecker *Gecinulus viridis*   Text and map page 381

SE Asia: bamboo (including large stands in evergreen and deciduous forest).

Small and modest-looking, found almost exclusively in areas of bamboo. Very dark olive, upperparts with bronzy yellowish-green tinge; paler head and bill; buffish wingbars inconspicuous. Juvenile darker and browner.

  202a Adult male Bright red crown and small crest.

  202b Adult female Crown and crest yellow.

201a

201c

201b

203b

202b

203a

202a

PLATE 61

205 Bay Woodpecker *Blythipicus pyrrhotis*   Text and map page 383

S and SE Asia: dense growth in forests; often in pairs, low down or on ground.

Dark rufous above with prominent broad black barring, dark brown to rusty-brown below; head paler. Long, very broad-based, pale bill a useful field character (especially when birds foraging low down in dense undergrowth). Juvenile duller and darker below, more prominently barred, head pale-streaked; male with dull red nape.

> **205a Adult male** (*cameroni*; W Malaysia) Small red patch on side of neck. Very dark.
>
> **205b Adult female** (*cameroni*) No red on neck.
>
> **205c Adult male** (nominate; Nepal to W China) Large red patch on neck. Paler overall; variable, often with paler throat or moustache.
>
> **205d Adult female** (nominate) No red on neck.

204 Maroon Woodpecker *Blythipicus rubiginosus*   Text and map page 383

SE Asia: humid forests, second growth, bamboo.

Small. Very dark overall, distinctly maroon-chestnut above, and generally unbarred (except on flight feathers); long pale yellow bill. Juvenile tinged dull orange above, crown with some red.

> **204a Adult male** Variable patch of crimson on sides of nape and neck, crimson tips to hindcrown and moustachial region.
>
> **204b Adult female** No crimson on head (but often tinged dull red on hindcrown and nape).

152 Rufous Woodpecker *Celeus brachyurus*   Text and map page 326

S and SE Asia: open forests, secondary growth, scrub; associated with tree-ant nests.

Much individual variation: generally rufous to dark chestnut, usually heavily barred dark above (though some are almost blackish above, with rufous barring), unbarred or variably dark barred on flanks and lower belly. Head often paler, throat usually with streaks or scallop markings; short black bill. Juvenile much as adults.

> **152a Adult male** (*squamigularis*; S peninsular Thailand to Sumatra) Small red patch below eye. Brown head; flanks and belly barred.
>
> **152b Adult female** (*squamigularis*) No red below eye.
>
> **152c Adult male** (*jerdonii*; W India to Sri Lanka) Red patch below eye. More rufous, with paler head; unbarred below, throat scaly.
>
> **152d Adult female** (*jerdonii*) No red below eye.
>
> **152e Adult male** (*fokiensis*; S China, N Vietnam) Small red patch below eye. Sooty below, breast tinged greyish; throat broadly streaked black and pale.

205a

205b

205c

204a

204b

205d

152d

152b

152c

152a

152e

PLATE 62

209 Buff-necked Woodpecker *Meiglyptes tukki*   Text and map page 388

SE Asia: evergreen forest with dense undergrowth.

Small. Mostly dark brown, narrowly barred buff; upper breast black, appears dark below. Head plain; distinctive buffish patch on side of neck. Juvenile with pale bars broader and dark breast less obvious. Dark plumage, lack of pale rump and absence of obvious crest distinguish this from all other woodpeckers in its range.

> **209a Adult male** (nominate; continental mainland, Natuna Islands, N Borneo, Sumatra and most offshore islands) Red moustache.
>
> **209b Adult female** (nominate) No red in moustache.

208 Black-and-buff Woodpecker *Meiglyptes jugularis*   Text and map page 387

SE Asia: evergreen forest, edges, clearings (often in bamboo).

Small, short-tailed. Mostly black, with white hindneck, rump and also on scapulars and tertials. Face barred; prominent black crest. Juvenile duller, head more clearly barred. Differs from Heart-spotted Woodpecker (211, Plate 63) in white hindneck, black throat with pale marks, barred head, and narrow pale bars on flight feathers; tail longer (extends beyond wings when perched). Female Heart-spotted also has white forehead and forecrown.

> **208a Adult male** Red in moustache (inconspicuous).
>
> **208b Adult female** Moustache lacks red.

207 Buff-rumped Woodpecker *Meiglyptes tristis*   Text and map page 386

SE Asia: forests, second growth, edges, clearings.

Small, short-tailed. Heavily barred pale and black, with pale buffish-white rump; head and short crest (often raised) with very narrow bars. Usually shows buffish eye-ring and buffy area around base of bill. Juvenile duller, with barring broader and browner (can be almost all dark below).

> **207a Adult male** (*grammithorax*; range of species except Java) Dark red moustache (inconspicuous). Pale bars buffish.
>
> **207b Adult female** (*grammithorax*) No red moustache.
>
> **207c Adult male** (nominate; Java) Small red moustache. Pale bars above narrower and whiter; darker below, with more black (may also have some white on upper flanks).
>
> **207d Adult female** (nominate) No red moustache.

209b

208b

209a

208a

207d

207c

207b

207a

PLATE 63

211 Heart-spotted Woodpecker *Hemicircus canente*   **Text and map page 390**

S and SE Asia: moist forests, edge, secondary growth, plantations; very active.

Very small, 'dumpy', with strikingly short rounded tail; thin neck, large head with prominent crest. Black, white and greyish, with white rump, throat and wing patch, and with bold heart-shaped markings on tertials and wing-coverts. Compare Black-and-buff Woodpecker (208, Plate 62).

> **211a Adult male** Forehead to crest entirely black.
>
> **211b Adult female** Forehead and forecrown contrastingly white.
>
> **211c Juvenile** As adult female, but pale areas more buffy, less white, forehead often partly barred black; dark brownish to black below, white of throat partly obscured (isolating pale stripe down neck).

210 Grey-and-buff Woodpecker *Hemicircus concretus*   **Text and map page 389**

SE Asia: evergreen forests, edge, plantations, gardens.

Very small and compact, with slender neck, large head and markedly short, rounded tail. Mainly dark grey with pale rump, upperparts boldly edged and tipped pale (scaly), lower underparts barred. Hindneck and rump pale, thin white neck stripe; very long crest (often raised).

> **210a Adult male** (nominate; Java) Red crown and entire top of crest. Dark, with darker hindneck.
>
> **210b Adult female** (nominate) No red on head.
>
> **210c Juvenile** (nominate) Crown and crest cinnamon-rufous, crest with variable reddish in centre (on male); heavily barred (rufous) below.
>
> **210d Adult male** (*sordidus*, entire range except Java) Red crown and front of crest (red lacking on female). Paler overall, with whitish hindneck.

211c

211a

211b

210b

210c

210a

210d

PLATE 64

214 Great Slaty Woodpecker *Mulleripicus pulverulentus*   **Text and map page 392**

S and SE Asia: forests, clearings, open woodland, mangroves.

Very large (the biggest Old World woodpecker), with long neck, long tail and very long bill. Dark grey overall (especially nominate, southern race), slightly paler below, with darker wings and tail; head and neck with small white spots, throat pale yellow-buff. Juvenile tinged brown (especially above), more spotted below, with whiter throat; males may show some red in crown.

> **214a Adult male** (*harterti*; India to SW China and Indochina) Small red patch in moustachial region (often inconspicuous), lower throat tipped red.

> **214b Adult female** (*harterti*) No red in moustache or on lower throat.

206 Orange-backed Woodpecker *Reinwardtipicus validus*   **Text and map page 385**

SE Asia: moist forest, coastal vegetation, mature plantations, edge, clearings.

Medium-sized/rather large, with short tail. Distinctive: pale above with contrasting blackish wings (barred rufous) and tail, darkish below. Head with short crest, long bill. Marked sexual dimorphism. Juveniles of both sexes resemble adult female, young male usually with some red on crown (sometimes also orange on rump).

> **206a Adult male** (nominate; Java) Red crown to nape, orange face, broad pale band from hindneck to rump variably tinged orange (darkest on rump); brown foreneck and underbody with broad deep red feather tips creating largely red appearance, narrowly edged yellowish on flanks and belly.

> **206b Adult female** (nominate) Crown to nape dark brown, face grey-brown, hindneck to rump whitish; side of neck with slight rufous tinge; foreneck and below dull greyish-brown, obscurely barred.

213 Sooty Woodpecker *Mulleripicus funebris*   **Text and map page 391**

Philippines: forests.

Medium-sized. Unmistakable: entire plumage very dark or blackish, head and neck with very fine pale speckles (visible at close range); pale eyes, pale or darkish bill. Juvenile similar to adults, but more heavily spotted.

> **213a Adult male** (*mayri*; N Luzon) Dark red face extending to forecrown, ear-coverts and moustache.

> **213b Adult female** (*mayri*) No red on head.

> **213c Adult male** (*fuliginosus*; Samar, Leyte, Mindanao) Red on face confined to moustachial region (red absent on female). Bill shorter, deeper, paler (ivory-yellow); plumage generally slightly paler, slaty-grey.

212 Ashy Woodpecker *Mulleripicus fulvus*   **Text and map page 391**

Sulawesi, Indonesia: forest.

Large and long-tailed. Unmistakable within its small range. Plain slaty-brown above, including wings and tail, and uniformly buff below (often stained reddish/yellowish). Head and neck dark grey, with fine white speckles; eyes pale. Juvenile more spotted.

> **212a Adult male** (nominate; N Sulawesi) Dark red face

> **212b Adult female** (nominate) No red on face.

> **212c Adult male** (*wallacei*; S Sulawesi) Bright red of face extends over crown and ear-coverts (red lacking on female). Plumage slightly paler overall.

214a

214b

206a

206b

213b

212b

213a

212a

212c

213c

1   EURASIAN WRYNECK
Jynx torquilla   Plate   1

Other names: Northern Wryneck, Wryneck
Forms a superspecies with *ruficollis*.

IDENTIFICATION Length 16-17cm. Very small, with
short, pointed bill with curved culmen and very narrow
across nostrils. An aberrant, long-tailed woodpecker of the
Palearctic, migrating to Africa and south Asia. Although
may at first cause some bewilderment, its small size, complex plumage pattern (upperparts strongly reminiscent of
a nightjar *Caprimulgus*) and terrestrial habits, as well as its
snaking head movements, render it unmistakable when
seen well. Appears rather greyish overall, with brown and
buff mottling. Notable features are a dark patch on mantle
(can appear almost diamond-shaped), often extending to
central nape/crown, pale-edged scapulars, barred tail, and
barred throat and upper breast. Flight, when long tail is
obvious, is rather weak compared with that of other woodpeckers. Has distinctive territorial song, very like call of a
small falcon *Falco*.

Similar species The only real confusion species is Rufous-
necked Wryneck (2), which it may meet in non-breeding
season in a few parts of Africa, but Eurasian is immediately
distinguished by lack of rufous on breast/throat and by
more barred rather than streaked flanks. In poor or long-
range views, when perched on side of a bush, can at first
resemble a large passerine, especially Barred Warbler *Sylvia
nisoria*, but this impression soon dispelled with further
observation.

DISTRIBUTION Breeds across the Palaearctic between
35° and 64° latitude, from Europe, east over temperate and
boreal Asia to Japan. Disjunct breeding areas in W Asia and
N Africa.

MOVEMENTS A genuine migrant, which can cover a
distance of 600km in eight days. Migrates mainly at night.
European and W Asian populations winter in the savannas
and drier areas of W and C Africa. Eastern populations
winter in the Indian subcontinent and in SE Asia. Some
individuals of the nominate form winter in Mediterranean
countries and in SE Iran (not shown on map). Rounder-
winged Mediterranean and N African populations migrate
short distances or move altitudinally only. European breeders depart in late summer (breeding sites may be vacated as
early as July), and in autumn cross the Alps and then the
Iberian peninsula or the Balkans; some Scandinavian
wrynecks wander through Britain. More easterly

populations probably fly over Turkey and the Arabian
peninsula. Migrating Eurasian Wrynecks pass through C
Europe mid August to end of September, over Turkey and
C Anatolia by the end of September/beginning of October;
peak migration in the Caucasus is mid August. In the Far
East, migrants pass through Korea in September and again
in April and May; stragglers may appear in W Alaksa.
African winter quarters are reached in late August and
early September; winters in E Africa October-April. Winters from early September to end of April in northern India
and from October to April in Burma. Returns to C European breeding grounds at the beginning of April, in Russia
in late April to early May, and has arrived by mid May in
northern Europe.

HABITAT Inhabits open forests, clearings, woodland
with low undergrowth and other habitats with a fair
proportion of not too well-developed grass. Open riparian
forests and lighter parts of more closed mixed or deciduous
broadleaf forest and forest edge are its more common
habitats; copses, avenues, tree plantations, parks, orchards
and gardens are also important breeding sites, and it nests
locally in pure pine or larch stands as well. Moist vegetation
and higher mountains are avoided. Loss of certain habitats,
such as orchards and unimproved meadows, and increase
of coniferous forests at the expense of hardwoods, are
among the important causes of the species' decline in
Europe. Home range at the start of the breeding season is
large, shrinking considerably after pairing. Migrants may
be seen in treeless open habitats, including deserts. Wintering birds in E Africa are found in open woodlands, bushy
grassland and gardens; similar habitats are frequented in
Indian and SE Asian winter quarters, where it may be seen
in semi-desert scrub, open deciduous thickets, in the
canopy of forests and in cultivations. Occurs up to 1600m
in the Alps, breeds in the Himalayas between 1500 and
3300m, and is found up to 1800m in winter in SE Asia.

DESCRIPTION

J. t. torquilla **Adult** Sexes similar in plumage. Forehead to
hindneck pale grey, speckled darker, finely barred black
and rufous and with very small white feather tips (white
spots and black bars usually more distinct on crown).
Narrow creamy stripe from nostrils to below eye; thin,
indistinct, creamy supercilium above and behind eye,
bordered below by broad rufous-mottled black band from
eye backwards through upper ear-coverts and irregularly
down neck sides. Buffish or cinnamon-buff stripe from
sides of bill base to lower ear-coverts and neck sides, usually
finely barred dark. Chin white (sometimes continuing into
submoustachial stripe), becoming strongly buff or cinna-

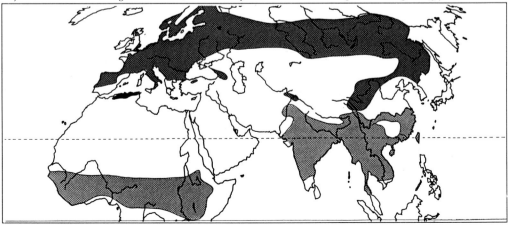

mon-buff on throat and upper breast, all narrowly barred/ vermiculated black, and often with incomplete malar stripe on lower throat sides. Feathers of central mantle black, edged rufous (outer feathers in this area edged white on outer webs), this pattern often continuing as irregular band through central hindneck to crown centre; mantle sides, inner scapulars and back to uppertail-coverts pale grey, finely speckled darker and sometimes with black/rufous/ whitish marks at feather tips, and with narrow dark shaft streaks (becoming arrowhead marks on rump); outer scapulars black, with large pale buffish spot at tip and at base. Uppertail similar to back or slightly darker, and with variable number of (usually 4-5) irregular thin black bars bordered proximally by greyish band and distally by buffish band (marginal bands often indistinct or lacking). Upperwing-coverts and tertials brown-buff, finely speck-led grey and rufous-buff, with thin black shaft streaks, black subterminal bars, and creamy spots at tips; primaries and secondaries dark brown, all with rufous-buff spot-bars. Underparts from breast white or whitish, variably suffused creamy or buff, and with narrow dark bars on breast becoming arrowhead marks on lower underparts (extent of markings variable, but belly usually unmarked). Undertail as uppertail, but paler. Underwing-coverts buff, barred black; flight feathers barred grey and white below. (In heavily worn plumage, appears somewhat greyer and more uniform above, with fewer/no white markings, and dark markings below are more pronounced.)

Juvenile Similar to adults, but upperparts duller and generally darker and more barred (less streaked), under-parts duller and more clearly barred, and tail bars fewer but more pronounced. In the hand, outer primary (retained until autumn of first calendar-year) at least twice as long as on adults.

Bare parts Bill dark horn-brown, often tinged green. Legs and feet brownish to grey-green, occasionally tinged yel-low/pink. Eyes brown or red-brown.

MEASUREMENTS Wing of male 76 (*mauretanica*) to 83-97 (nominate), of female 83-93; tail 60-71; bill 14-17; tarsus 18-21. Weight: highly variable; 22-54 on migration, 34-47 on breeding grounds (nominate).

GEOGRAPHICAL VARIATION Four races are recog-nised here, but note that considerable variation exists within nominate.

    J. t. torquilla (most of Eurasia, apart from some southernmost populations) Described above. Varies clinally and also rather randomly, with great indi-vidual variation. Within its vast range a number of other races have been described, but variation and overlap in characters are such that it seems better to include them within nominate *torquilla*. Those breed-ing between Urals and Yenisey ('*sarudnyi*') are paler and have fewer markings below, but some are much closer to European breeders; those further east and in China ('*chinensis*') are more barred, though some are close to '*sarudnyi*', and overlap also exists (especially in C Siberia) with western birds; Japanese population ('*japonica*') is also more barred and tends to have much more rufous in plumage, but again some individuals from western populations (including European) are identical to some Japanese ones.
    J. t. tschusii (Corsica, Sardinia, Italy and E Adriatic coast) Clearly darker overall than nominate, with dark stripe/patch on upperparts more prominent and with heavier markings below. Wings shorter, more rounded.
    J. t. mauretanica (NW Africa) As *tschusii* but slightly smaller, and paler below, especially on throat.

    J. t. himalayana (Kashmir region) Much more strongly barred below than other races, including on lower underparts.

VOICE May call even when on passage in autumn, but vocally most active during the breeding season. Most distinctive call consists of a slightly ascending series of 8-15, sometimes raucous *kwia kwia kwia...* notes, uttered by a single bird or by both members of a pair simultaneously. This call may sound rather similar to a falcon's (e.g. Hobby, *Falco subbuteo*) and is delivered at a rate of 5-6 calls per minute. Although serving as territorial announcement and for communication between the sexes, this call is also given far away from the nest site. Low, guttural *kroo* notes are heard during intimate contacts of the partners. When alarmed, utters long wavering series of *tak* notes. Screams when caught. Nestlings chirp with warbling and hissing notes from day 17 onwards; before that their sounds are more whizzing.

HABITS Territorial pairs are encountered in the breeding season, otherwise single birds or small family parties. Forages mainly on the ground, where prey is procured from crevices or from the surface. Anthills are opened up with the bill. Most prey is licked up with the sticky tongue. Hops when on the ground, tail slightly raised, and along horizontal or sloping branches in arboreal foraging. Al-most never climbs up vertical surfaces. Flight dipping, some wing-flicking may be seen upon landing. Wrynecks call from prominent perches whereby they raise their head. In agonistic situations, wrynecks display with feathers erect (most conspicuous on crown), head extended, and the bill directed forwards at the opponent; at the same time, the tail is spread, wings droop, and the head swings horizontally from side to side. During courtship calls, on an exposed perch or from the prospective nest hole, the head is stretched out. When partners meet, they display with head-swinging with ruffled head feathers. Mate-feeding is part of the courtship and may extend to the incubation period. Territorial activities take place in a large area upon arrival from the wintering grounds. Later, territories may shrink to a size of 0.4ha. When threatened, crouches to the substrate and takes advantage of the camouflage of the plumage. When cornered in the nest, wrynecks show their name-giving behaviour, which is interpreted as snake mimicry: the crown feathers are raised and with opened bill, head and neck are stretched out slowly. At the point of maximum extension the bird recoils suddenly and hisses. Caught birds stay silent and perform with stereotyped turning movements of the head. This behaviour is also shown by nestlings from day 13 onwards.

FOOD Ants, mainly larvae and pupae, predominate in the diet; in Europe, the genera *Lasius* and *Tetramorium* are especially important. Other insects (aphids, small beetles, caterpillars etc.) and spiders are less significant. Nestlings often are also provided with snails or (fragments of) their shells. Berries are taken occasionally. On the wintering grounds, ants (e.g. *Crematogaster, Camponotus, Pheidole*) again prevail.

BREEDING Both sexes are involved in nest-site selection. In optimal habitats breeding densities may be high, with nests only 40-50m, or even 20m, apart. The nest may be situated in old woodpecker holes (e.g. Great Spotted, Brown-fronted), other natural cavities (including aban-doned Common Kingfisher or Sand Martin nests, mole burrows), and nestboxes (also buildings, waterpumps and other odd sites), at height of 1-15m. Nest is cleaned out for several days, old nest (or nests), including eggs and chicks of competitors, thereby being removed. Occasionally the nest bottom is lined with grass or moss. Sometimes holes in soft wood are excavated at the bottom. Egg laying season begins in the second half of May in C Europe, and spans from May to June in Kashmir. Seven to 12, sometimes far fewer, eggs comprise a clutch; clutches of 18-23 eggs are the product of more than one female. Copulation occurs mainly during the egg-laying period, sometimes earlier. On average, chicks hatch after 11 (14) days of incubation, which is shared by both parents, and which commences after the last egg has been laid, but sometimes earlier. Both parents feed the nestlings and remove faeces. The young fledge after (19) 20-22 (27) days. A second clutch may be produced in June, rarely July, usually 9-11 days after the young of the previous brood have fledged, rarely even during fledging. The parents care for the fledged young for 10-14 days.

REFERENCES Ali & Ripley 1970; Bezzel 1985; Britton 1980; Cramp 1985; Dement'ev & Gladkov 1966; Ganguli 1975; Glutz von Blotzheim & Bauer 1980; Gore & Pyong-Oh 1971; Roberts 1991; Smythies 1953; Stanford & Mayr 1941; van den Berk 1990.

---

2 RUFOUS-NECKED WRYNECK
Jynx ruficollis   Plate 1

Other names: Rufous-breasted/Red-breasted Wryneck, Rufous-throated/Red-throated Wryneck, African Wryneck Forms a superspecies with *torquilla*.

IDENTIFICATION Length 19cm. Small, with short, pointed bill with curved culmen. A typical wryneck, with cryptically patterned plumage and ground-feeding habits. Rufous on breast, and sometimes also on throat, varies in extent, but always diagnostic.

Similar species Unmistakable in most of its African range. The slightly smaller Eurasian Wryneck (1) is a non-breeding visitor to C Africa, overlapping with Rufous-necked only in some northern parts of latter's range. In reasonable views, Rufous-necked is easily separated by its dark rufous on throat and/or breast and its more streaked (less barred) underparts. In the hand, Rufous-necked also has much longer outermost primary than adult Eurasian. See also under latter species.

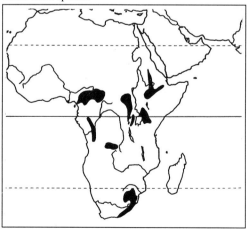

DISTRIBUTION An endemic resident of sub-Saharan wooded grassland and forest edge, breeding locally and in scattered populations. Occurs from SE Nigeria and C Cameroon to southernmost Chad and W Central African Republic; from SE Gabon south through Congo to NW

Angola; from S Sudan (and NE Zaïre?) to at least westernmost Uganda; in SW Uganda south through NE Rwanda and NW Tanzania, and E Uganda through C and SW Kenya to NC Tanzania; in the W and C Ethiopian highlands; in NE Angola, S Zaïre and adjacent NW Zambia; and in S Africa, from C Transvaal south to Orange Free State, Natal and eastern Cape Province. May also breed, at least occasionally, in other areas between these disjunct ones. Locally common but often irregular in occurrence, with populations fluctuating in numbers; often disappears from an area after apparent colonisation, only to reappear after lapse of several years.

MOVEMENTS Records outside known breeding areas may represent post-breeding dispersal or short-distance migration. At least partially migratory in southern parts of its range. Migrants pass through Natal in February and March. S African birds winter as far north as eastern Zaïre.

HABITAT Its principal habitats are woodlands, open areas with trees and forest edges. The species is widely dispersed over drier acacia veld and also open bush, particularly in wooded gorges on hillsides and along streams; also inhabits plantations, gardens, and stands of exotic trees in urban areas. Altitudinal range extends from 600 to 3000m (only occasionally below 1700m in Kenya) in E Africa, and to 1550m in southern Africa.

DESCRIPTION
J. r. ruficollis Adult Sexes similar in plumage, but male somewhat larger (averages 10% heavier). Lores and ear-coverts barred buffy-white and brown; moustachial and malar area whitish, vermiculated brown. Chin and throat to upper breast rufous-chestnut. Entire upperparts from forehead to uppertail-coverts, including scapulars, upperwing-coverts and tertials, grey-brown, feathers variably marked with black shaft streaks/half-bars and black subterminal spots and with white edges/tips (especially on coverts and tertials), and with irregular central black stripe from crown centre to mantle; crown sides, rump, uppertail-coverts, wing-coverts and tertials usually very finely barred/vermiculated. Uppertail similar to back, with more prominent white-margined black bars. Flight feathers dark brown, barred paler, bars usually with rufous or rusty tone (especially on primaries). Underparts below upper breast whitish, tinged buffy (strongest on lower belly and flanks), and with brown shaft streaks, becoming barred and streaked on lower flanks and barred on undertail-coverts. Undertail as uppertail. Underwing barred brown and pale rufous-buff.

Juvenile Upperparts darker than on adults, and with more indication of barring; rufous of throat and breast generally duller and less extensive, and, together with most of underparts, finely barred.

Bare parts Bill brownish-grey, darker towards tip. Legs and feet olive-green to brownish. Eyes brown.

MEASUREMENTS Wing 89-96; tail 66-74; bill 15-18; tarsus 18-21 (females on average 2-3% smaller in linear measurements). Weight: male 52-59, female 46-52.

GEOGRAPHICAL VARIATION Three races are recognised, all reasonably distinguishable in the field. Note, however, that amount of rufous and of barring on throat is somewhat variable throughout entire population, and is also influenced by degree of plumage wear.
  T. r. ruficollis (SE Gabon, SW and E Uganda, Kenya, and all breeding areas south of these) Described above. Shows very slight size increase clinally northwards. Some individual variation in greyness/brownness of upperparts and in darkness of throat colour, and in Kenya may occasionally show some barring on central throat.

J. r. aequatorialis (Ethiopia) Rufous below is more extensive, reaching to lower breast and often to flanks, and has extensive rufous-buff on lower flanks, lower belly and on to undertail-coverts; ventral streaking also sparser and far less prominent. Sometimes shows some barring on throat.

J. r. pulchricollis (SE Nigeria and Cameroon east to S Sudan and NW Uganda) Upperparts less grey-brown, more rufous-tinged, than in other races, and has throat to breast deeper-coloured, more chestnut, with stronger black and white barring on throat sides (at least), and chestnut on lower belly to undertail-coverts; flanks slightly tinged rusty (less marked than in *aequatorialis*). Cameroon population has throat more completely barred and was formerly separated as '*thorbeckei*', but in this feature overlap apparently occurs with eastern populations of *pulchricollis*.

VOICE The most frequent call, which serves as territorial advertisement, is a loud, high-pitched harsh (2) 9 (12) syllabled *kwik-kwik-kwik-kwik-kwik-kwik*, *kwee kwee kwee* or *week-week-week-week* and is mainly uttered by males; females call at a higher pitch, *ooit-ooit-ooit-ooit-ooit*. This call can be delivered 5-8 times a minute. Also a low-pitched guttural *peegh-peegh-peegh* in encounters, associated with visual displays. Before supplanting attacks or copulation long series of *krok-krok-krok-...* notes are produced which, in case of an incipient attack, builds up to a crescendo. When alarmed or before entering the roost, quiet *klik* calls are given. Shrieks when caught. Nestlings utter whispering, squeaky calls in first 6 days, later *tsch-tsch-tsch...* Rapid tapping has been noted in encounters between bursts of calling and displaying and may represent this species' tapping/drumming.

HABITS Mostly met singly, but pairs stay in vocal contact. Usually seen perched in the open on dead trees, often uttering its characteristic note. Relaxed birds sit crosswise, tail vertically down; when calling head is raised and neck is stretched. Forages primarily on the ground, less frequently on the base or trunk of a tree, on a larger branch, or in a larger bush. Ants are gleaned from the surface or obtained by excavating their nests. Hops when foraging, often flying up to an elevated perch briefly before foraging on the ground is continued. The flight is undulating. Displaying, calling birds in encounters point the bill forward, raise the tail vertically and exhibit lateral swinging motions. Also bob more vertically or approach each other with stiffly raised heads and tails without loud vocalisations prior to copulation. Large nestlings threaten by stretching the head slowly to the predator, bill half opened, then rapidly recoiling and simultaneously opening the bill widely and hissing suggesting a striking snake. Territories are advertised throughout the year from prominent positions. These activities (calling) culminate July-September in South Africa where pair bonds are formed August-September. Territory sizes vary between 8 and 24ha. Roosts in woodpecker or barbet holes, hollow trunks, other natural cavities, behind loose bark, or in dense leaf clusters.

FOOD Mainly ants and their pupae and eggs; the genera *Pheidole* and *Crematogaster* dominate. Nestling food also ants and occasionally winged termites.

BREEDING Breeds from late July to February in southern Africa, from January to June in eastern Africa and Ethiopia, and from February to July in the western parts of its range. Does not excavate its own nest, but uses disused nest of a barbet or woodpecker, or a natural crevice in a tree trunk or bough; has also been known to use artificial nestboxes, hollow fence poles and holes under the eaves of houses. Nests are found 0.5-9m above ground. May use the

same nest cavity in successive years. Occasionally the bottom of the hole is somewhat deepened by the wrynecks. Usually 3 or 4 eggs are laid, with exceptional clutches containing 1 to 6 eggs. Parasitic honeyguides may add another egg. Both sexes incubate, starting before clutch is complete, for 12-15 days. The nestling period of the, on average, 2.5 chicks lasts 25 or 26 days; both parents care for the chicks. Up to four breeding attempts in one season have been recorded, three of them successful at intervals of 14 to 24 days between fledging and laying the next clutch.

REFERENCES Britton 1980; Clancey 1964; Cyrus & Robson 1980; Maclean 1985; Newman 1989; Roberts *et al.* 1981; Short *et al.* 1990; Tarboton 1976.

---

3 SPECKLED PICULET
Picumnus innominatus   Plate 2

IDENTIFICATION Length 10cm. Tiny, with short, pointed bill slightly curved on culmen. Unmistakable within its range. Bright olive-green upperparts and pale underparts with bold black spotting highly distinctive, as also are black and white stripes on face and tail; male has rufous/yellow and black forehead. Common in mixed-species flocks, and often reveals its presence by loud persistent tapping while foraging.

Similar species Allopatric with Rufous Piculet (30) in most areas. Forages more with loud pecking than the latter.

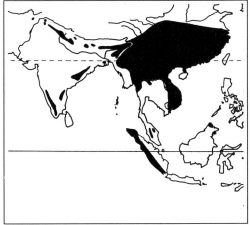

DISTRIBUTION Occurs in NE Afghanistan and N Pakistan (Punjab), and from Kashmir east to Sichuan and southern Jiangsu in C and E China, extending south in India to Andhra Pradesh and eastern Madhya Pradesh and in the east to NW Thailand, Indochina, Malaya and Sumatra, with records also from Borneo. An isolated population exists in the Western Ghats of SW India, from the Goa area southwards. Common or fairly common throughout much of its range, but uncommon in China and described as local and extremely rare in northwesternmost part of range, though probably frequently overlooked. Its status in Borneo is unclear; specimens exist apparently only from Sabah in the north, but its presence elsewhere would perhaps not be unexpected.

HABITAT Deciduous and mixed deciduous (oak) forest, evergreen tropical montane forests and open secondary growth, particularly where bamboo is present. Its habitats belong to the foothill or lower hill zone, but it may be found sporadically lower down near sea level. Lower limit is about

900m in Nepal and Malaysia, 650m in Vietnam and 100m in the Greater Sundas, where it can also reach sea level; upper extreme appears to be 1830m in Nepal and Sikkim, 2400m in NE India and c. 3000m in NW Himalayas.

DESCRIPTION

P. i. innominatus **Adult male** Forehead rufous to orange or yellow, barred/spotted black; crown to hindneck olive-green. Lores yellowish-white. Broad white supercilium (reaching to at least halfway down eye) and broad white band from lower lores meet on lower neck side, enclosing broad black band from lower rear eye backwards. Moustachial stripe black, with white fringes to feathers especially prominent at rear. Chin and throat dull white, tinged yellowish on lower throat, where usually a few black spots. Upperparts bright yellowish-green. Upperwing and its coverts brownish-black, edged and tipped greenish or yellow-green, edges broadest on outer webs of secondaries (forming pale panel). Uppertail black, inner webs of central feather pair white, outer two pairs with white subterminal patches. Underparts below throat white to pale yellowish-white (whitest when worn), spotted black, spots largest (and often heart-shaped) on sides and becoming more bar-like or arrowhead-shaped on flanks, with belly and centre of undertail-coverts usually unmarked. Underwing grey, tinged yellow and spotted black on coverts. Undertail as above, but paler.

Adult female As male, but has forehead concolorous with crown.

Juvenile Both sexes resemble adult female, but with plumage duller overall.

Bare parts Bill black or bluish-black, somewhat paler at base. Legs and feet blue-grey. Eyes brown. Orbital skin blue-grey.

GEOGRAPHICAL VARIATION Three races, one rather distinctive.

P. i. innominatus (northwest part of range, east to Assam) Described above.

P. i. malayorum (peninsular and NE India and SE Asia, including S Yunnan in China) Very like nominate, being barely smaller and only a little duller, but with darker, greyer crown and heavier spotting below.

P. i. chinensis (China) Slightly larger than above two races. Has crown to uppermost mantle cinnamon-brown and black facial markings distinctly brown-tinged; lores whiter and underpart markings somewhat heavier. Males have reduced orange/yellow on forehead.

MEASUREMENTS Wing 52-63 (55-61 *malayorum*, 59-63 *chinensis*); tail 29-36; bill 10-14; tarsus 10-11. Weight: 9-13.2.

VOICE An occasional sharp *tsick* or *tsit*. A high-pitched squeak, *sik-sik-sik*, given at regular intervals; also a *ti-ti-ti-ti-ti*, uttered (by males) presumably as advertising or territorial call. Also drums loudly, the beats being less rapid than, for instance, Himalayan Woodpecker's (108).

HABITS Tame but inconspicuous; often detected by the sound of its persistent pecking. Solitary or in pairs most of the time (families split up soon after nesting). Outside the breeding season, single individuals regularly accompany other small birds, e.g. tits, babblers, staying at the periphery of such mixed-species flocks. This is a bird of the under-growth, which forages on trunk and branches of small trees, big and small bushes, vines and bamboo. Although it may give impression of an active and agile forager, frequently hanging upside-down and moving along thin vertical twigs, it often concentrates on one spot for several minutes, pecking and hammering vigorously to open up

the substrate. During forceful pecks and hole excavation the tail may be pressed against the substrate. Also takes to hovering to get at prey not otherwise accessible. Its very long tongue suggests an important role in foraging. Also probes and pursues flushed prey and catches it on the wing. May perch crosswise or cling like a woodpecker, but without using its tail much for support. Flight undulating, as in a typical woodpecker. The little of what is known about displays suggests that, as with other piculets, the male circles the female around and around a branch.

FOOD Insects and their larvae, especially ants. Geometrid caterpillars. Spiders and their eggs, weevils, and longhorn beetles.

BREEDING Breeds January to May. Both sexes excavate the breeding hole. Nest or roosts are made in dead branches, which can be quite small, in bamboo, or even in palm fronds, at heights between 0.3 and 5m; hole entrance measures about 2.5cm across. Usual clutch contains (2)3-4 eggs. Both parents incubate, and the young hatch after 11 days. Both feed the nestlings until they fledge, after 11 days.

REFERENCES Ali 1962; Ali & Ripley 1970; Diesselhorst 1968; Inskipp & Inskipp 1991; King & Dickinson 1975; Lekagul & Round 1991; MacKinnon & Phillipps 1993; Medway & Wells 1976; Roberts 1991; Short 1973a; Smythies 1953; Stanford & Mayr 1941; Vaurie 1963.

---

4 BAR-BREASTED PICULET
Picumnus aurifrons   Plate 3

Other name: Gold(en)-fronted Piculet

IDENTIFICATION Length 7.5cm. Minute, with short, pointed bill barely curved on culmen. Generally greenish above (some races barred yellower), and with distinctively patterned pale yellowish underparts: barred on breast and striped on belly. Black cap is spotted white on females, but broadly streaked/spotted yellow on males (forehead of males red or orange in some races).

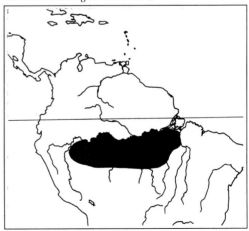

DISTRIBUTION Ranges from extreme SE Colombia and E Peru south to N Bolivia and the northern Mato Grosso, and east in Brazil to E Pará.

HABITAT Frequents humid tropical *terra firme*, and seasonally inundated forests (*várzea*), where found mainly at edge and clearings and in secondary growth. From lowlands up to 920m.

DESCRIPTION

P. a. aurifrons **Adult male** Forehead and crown to hindneck black, with broad but sparse yellow to yellow-gold streaks (latter most pronounced on forehead and nape). Lores buff. Cheeks and ear-coverts grey-brown, with blackish feather edges; whitish stripe behind eye. Lower neck side dull greyish-white. Chin and throat off-white to yellowish-white, with dark bars/arrowhead marks at throat sides. Upperparts olive-green to brownish-green, generally unmarked but occasionally with very faint traces of paler barring (more visible on rump); uppertail-coverts duller, grey-green, tipped whitish (when fresh). Upperwing-coverts and tertials much as upperparts or a little browner, edged and tipped paler greenish; primaries and secondaries brownish-black, edged greenish-yellow. Uppertail black, central feather pair with white or yellowish-white inner webs (normally extending slightly onto outer webs) and outer two pairs with white/whitish subterminal patch. Underparts pale yellowish-white, barred brown on breast (markings becoming more arrowhead-shaped on breast sides and upper belly) and broadly streaked brown on belly and flanks. Underwing as upperwing but paler, with yellowish coverts. Undertail as above, but paler.

Adult female Differs from male in having white spots on crown and hindneck and smaller white spots on forehead (latter often stained buffy).

Juvenile Duller and browner above than adults, and with crown browner and pale-streaked (not spotted); markings below more diffuse and/or incomplete, with belly streaks extending up onto lower breast. Males soon acquire some yellow feathering in forehead.

Bare parts Bill grey to blue-grey, with darker tip. Legs and feet grey to greenish-grey or blue-grey. Eyes brown. Orbital skin grey or blue-grey.

GEOGRAPHICAL VARIATION Seven races are recognised here.

> ***P. a. aurifrons*** (Mato Grosso to Madeira river and east to Tapajós river) Described above.
> ***P. a. transfasciatus*** (Tapajós east to Tocantins river) Upperparts heavily barred; breast bars blacker.
> ***P. a. borbae*** (lower Tapajós west to lower Madeira river) Differs from nominate in having yellower tertial edges and belly and much stronger and blacker breast barring; forehead streaks of male more orange (or red).
> ***P. a. wallacii*** (west of lower Madeira to Purus river) Obscurely barred above; underparts very pale, less yellow, with breast bars much fainter and incomplete and belly more spotted than streaked.
> ***P. a. purusianus*** (upper Purus river) As nominate, but darker above and more heavily black-barred on breast.
> ***P. a. flavifrons*** (Solimões river westwards into Peru) As *purusianus*, but upperparts faintly barred, breast barring less heavy and belly strongly spotted (not streaked).
> ***P. a. juruanus*** (upper Juruá river west into Peru) As nominate generally, but with breast barring duller and weaker and with orange/red forehead streaks (as *borbae*).

MEASUREMENTS Wing 44-53; tail 23-26; bill 9.5-11.5; tarsus 11-11.8. Weight: 8-10.

VOICE Call resembles that of a hummingbird, *tsirrrit-tsit-tsit*.

HABITS Almost nothing is known; seems to prefer the upper tiers in its habitat.

FOOD Not known.

BREEDING Breeding season presumably June-November.

REFERENCES Parker *et al.* 1982; Sick 1993.

5   ORINOCO PICULET
Picumnus pumilus   Plate   3

Forms a superspecies with *lafresnayi*

IDENTIFICATION Length 9cm. Tiny, with short, pointed bill slightly curved on culmen. Greenish above, with paler yellowish feather edges, and barred dark and pale below. Forehead to hindneck are dark brown, spotted with white or brownish-white, males having forehead spots yellow.

Similar species Often treated as conspecific with Lafresnaye's Piculet (6), but the two apparently do not interbreed in area of slight overlap in E Colombia. Nominate Lafresnaye's is slightly bigger, generally has somewhat brighter upperparts with rather obvious barring and with brighter and broader edges to wing feathers, and is more broadly dark-barred below; in addition, it has paler ear-coverts, and male has red (not yellow) forehead spots.

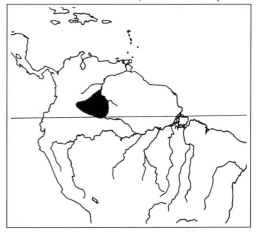

DISTRIBUTION Confined to small area of lower Uaupés river in extreme NW Brazil and adjacent areas of E Colombia and S Venezuela.

HABITAT From the few records available, it is supposed that this piculet lives at edge of gallery woodland and in thickets. Lowlands to 300m.

DESCRIPTION

Adult male Forehead to hindneck dark brown, with small yellow spots on forehead becoming whiter on crown and sometimes pale brownish and more streak-like on nape/hindneck. Lores pale buff. Ear-coverts blackish, variably spotted with white, and with white feather tips along upper edge. Neck side, moustachial region, chin and throat white/whitish, with dark subterminal bars to feathers. Upperparts brownish-green, with pale green edges and tips to feathers, paler and yellower on uppertail-coverts, and sometimes with indication of barring on rump. Upperwing-coverts and tertials as upperparts or somewhat browner, edged and tipped yellowish-green; primaries and secondaries brown, edged and tipped greenish. Uppertail black, central feather pair with white inner webs and outer three with white area inside tip. Underparts pale yellowish to buff-white, barred dark brown, bars becoming narrower in lower region and with belly centre usually unbarred. Underwing greyish-brown, with yellower and dark-barred coverts. Undertail as above, but paler.

Adult female As male, but with forehead spots white.

Juvenile Duller than adults, but with somewhat greener

upperparts; forehead and crown streaked/spotted buffish, and underpart markings more diffuse and less regular.

Bare parts Bill blackish, with paler, greyer, base. Legs and feet grey. Eyes brownish to grey-brown. Orbital skin grey to blue-grey.

GEOGRAPHICAL VARIATION None known.

MEASUREMENTS Wing c. 51; tail c. 20; bill c. 11; tarsus c. 10.2.

VOICE Not described.

HABITS Forages from lower levels up to the canopy, much in the fashion of other piculets.

FOOD Not known.

BREEDING A likely time to search for nests of this poorly known piculet is November-December.

REFERENCE Hilty & Brown 1984.

---

6 LAFRESNAYE'S PICULET
Picumnus lafresnayi   **Plate 3**

Forms a superspecies with *pumilus*.

IDENTIFICATION Length 9-10cm. Tiny, with short, pointed bill curved on culmen. Greenish above, with fairly obvious paler barring or virtually unbarred, and pale below with blackish barring. Dark crown is spotted with white, and males have red or yellow forehead spots (white on females).

Similar species Very like Orinoco Piculet (5), with which nominate race overlaps in E Colombia; the two are often treated as conspecific, but appear not to interbreed. See Orinoco for differences.

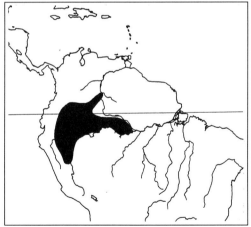

DISTRIBUTION Ranges from E Ecuador and E and NE Peru through SE Colombia to NW Brazil north of Amazon, eastwards to Rio Negro region (but excluding area of Uaupés river occupied by Orinoco Piculet).

HABITAT Lives in heavily forested and very humid country, preferring secondary growth, edge and clearings. Found at altitudes of up to 1200m (Ecuador) and to 1400m in E Peru.

DESCRIPTION
P. l. lafresnayi **Adult male** Forehead to hindneck dark olive-brown, forehead and forecrown with red spots and rear crown to hindneck spotted white. Lores pale buff. Whitish feather edges form pale stripe behind eye. Ear-coverts greyish-buff, streaked/spotted brown, and with dark upper and rear borders. Entire chin and throat buffish-white, with narrow black feather edges. Upperparts dark green or brownish-green, with paler yellow-green barring, becoming paler on uppertail-coverts. Upperwing and its coverts greenish-brown, browner on primaries and outer coverts, and edged and tipped greenish-yellow (yellow edges broadest on tertials, where often form half-bars). Uppertail blackish, central feather pair with broad white stripe on inner webs and outer three pairs with large area of white towards tip. Underparts below throat pale yellowish-tinged buffish-white, broadly barred blackish, bars broadest from lower breast to belly (including flanks) but occasionally broken in belly centre. Underwing brownish, with dark-barred yellowish-white coverts. Undertail as uppertail, but paler.

Adult female As male, but with forehead and forecrown spots white.

Juvenile Duller than adults overall, with greener upperparts and less evenly barred underparts. Both sexes have top of head, including forehead, streaked/spotted buffish.

Bare parts Bill black, with greyish base to lower mandible. Legs and feet grey. Eyes brownish to brown-grey. Orbital skin greyish.

GEOGRAPHICAL VARIATION Four races.
    P. l. lafresnayi (E Ecuador, SE Colombia and N Peru) Described above.
    P. l. punctifrons (E Peru) Barely smaller than nominate, but with slightly larger bill. Upperparts less heavily barred, or even unbarred, and dark bars below narrower; ear-coverts darker, blackish; usually has one or two dark spots in white of central tail. Forehead spots of male yellow/orange.
    P. l. taczanowskii (NE Peru, in region of Huambo, Inayabamba and Huanuco) Lacks barring above (or barring virtually invisible); underparts very pale, more or less white, with dark bars broader and blacker. Ground colour of crown blacker, and male's forehead spots yellow/orange.
    P. l. pusillus (NW Brazil in region of Rio Solimões to Rio Negro) Upperparts unbarred or faintly barred, and slightly tinged rufous; dark bars below are narrow, with belly centre more or less unbarred. Nape/hindneck spots often brown-tinged, and male's forehead spots yellow/orange.

MEASUREMENTS Wing 47-55; tail 24-27; bill 14; tarsus 10-12. Weight: 9-10.

VOICE Not described.

HABITS Virtually unknown. Presumably lives in the undergrowth. Gleaning is the only feeding technique on record. It has been observed that not only the pair but also an additional fully grown female roosts with the eggs.

FOOD Termites have been determined as food by direct observation.

BREEDING The few records available suggest nesting about July-November. The nest, about 3m up in shrub, contains 2 eggs. Both sexes, plus possibly a further bird, care for the brood; the nest is often left unattended.

REFERENCES Hilty & Brown 1984; Skutch 1948b.

7 GOLDEN-SPANGLED PICULET
Picumnus exilis   **Plate 3**

Other name: Black-dotted Piculet ('*P. nigropunctatus*' = *P. e. salvini*)

IDENTIFICATION Length 9-10cm. Tiny, with fairly short, pointed bill curved on culmen. Upperparts vary in basic colour from dull olive to brighter yellow-brown or greenish, with black feather centres or bar-like markings, while underparts are whitish to pale yellow-white, barred blackish; a white stripe behind the eye varies in prominence. Forehead to hindneck are black, males having quite extensive red feather tips to forehead and forecrown (often forming a patch) and with rear of head spotted white, while females have entire top of head white-spotted. In northeast part of range, race *buffoni* has distinctive black-bordered white spots on upperparts.

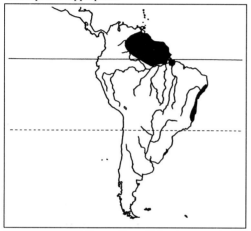

DISTRIBUTION Occurs from Delta Amacuro in NE Venezuela southwest to extreme eastern Colombia (E Guainía) and east through northernmost Brazil and the Guianas to Amapá, and in E Brazil in E Pará and Maranhão and from Pernambuco south along the coastal lowlands to Espírito Santo. Range extension may be promoted through human activities.

HABITAT Rain and cloud forests, second growth, disturbed forest, dense growth (with bamboo) along rivers, mangroves, also open woodland and savanna edge in the sandy belt, to 1900m in areas with tepuis. Race *salvini* (form '*nigropunctatus*') inhabits rain forest and second growth, down to sea level.

DESCRIPTION
P. e. buffoni **Adult male** Forehead to hindneck black, feathers of forehead and forecrown (often also crown sides) tipped red and those of mid crown to hindneck tipped white. Lores white, tinged buff. Area around rear half of eye and line running back to lower neck white. Cheeks and fore ear-coverts whitish with dark feather edges, becoming black-brown with a few (variable) white spots on rear ear-coverts. Lower neck side white, variably barred dark. Malar region, chin and throat pale yellowish-white, barred blackish. Upperparts dark olive-green, with large black-bordered white spots at feather tips. Upperwing-coverts as upperparts, greater coverts also narrowly edged white and with the black-edged white tips forming a broken wingbar; flight feathers brownish-green, edged white to pale greenish, edges broadest on tertials, which also have black submarginal lines. Uppertail dark

brown, central feather pair with broad white stripe on inner webs and outer three pairs with large white subterminal mark on outer webs. Underparts below throat pale yellowish-white, rather narrowly barred blackish, bars often breaking up into spots on (especially) belly. Underwing brown and white, with whitish coverts. Undertail much as uppertail, but paler.

Adult female As male, but top of head entirely spotted white (lacks red).

Juvenile Duller than adults, with olive or greyish crown streaked off-white; markings above and below more diffuse and irregular. Both sexes lack red on head.

Bare parts Upper mandible black; lower mandible silver, with black tip. Legs and feet greyish, with green or blue tinge. Eyes yellow to dark brown. Orbital skin greyish.

GEOGRAPHICAL VARIATION Seven races. Only the first shows white spots on upperparts, the others having blackish feather centres or crescentic markings.

P. e. buffoni (E Guyana east to Amapá in NE Brazil) Described above.
P. e. salvini (Delta Amacuro in NE Venezuela) A distinctive race, sometimes treated as '*P. nigropunctatus*' (which is now considered synonymous with *salvini*). Upperparts distinctly yellowish and with blackish markings bar-like; underparts pale yellowish-white, with markings more spot-like, or sometimes unmarked apart from some spots on breast.
P. e. undulatus (E Colombia, SE Venezuela, W Guyana and NE Brazil) Somewhat larger than above races. Olive-brown to yellowish-olive above, with large blackish feather centres (appears scaly); underparts more broadly dark-barred than in other races. Male has much red in crown, extending to nape.
P. e. clarus (eastern Bolívar in E Venezuela) Size much as *undulatus*. Resembles latter, but slightly yellower above and with narrower, broken barring below.
P. e. alegriae (coastal Maranhão in NE Brazil) Rather dull, more olive, above, and whiter below. Red on head of male more orange in tone.
P. e. pernambucensis (coastal Pernambuco and Alagoas in E Brazil) As nominate *exilis*, but with upperparts more olive, less yellow, and underparts more evenly barred.
P. e. exilis (Bahia to Espírito Santo) Ground colour of plumage in general more yellow-toned: upperparts more yellow-green and underparts pale yellowish. Barring below more spot-like on belly.

MEASUREMENTS Wing (females tend to be longer-winged) 46-54; tail 25-27; bill 10-11; tarsus 13. Weight: 8.5-10.

VOICE Described as *tsilit, tsirrrr*.

HABITS Forages inconspicuously alone or in pairs. Also accompanies mixed-species flocks. Pecks and hammers on small branches of the lower tiers at 1-5m. Moves about in manner similar to a tit, often hanging on thin twigs.

FOOD Ants are the only food on record.

BREEDING Breeding recorded December to March in Venezuela and Surinam. The nest is built in branches and stumps with soft wood.

REFERENCES Haverschmidt 1968; Meyer de Schauensee & Phelps 1978; Sick 1993; Tostain *et al.* 1992; Willard *et al.* 1991.

8 ECUADORIAN PICULET
Picumnus sclateri   Plate 4

IDENTIFICATION Length 8-9cm. Tiny, with shortish, pointed bill curved on culmen. A rather distinctive piculet, lacking green tones in plumage. Greyish to grey-brown above, with white-spotted black cap, males having forehead spotted with yellow; very pale below, with face and breast barred dark and belly streaked dark, strength of barring and streaking varying racially (from narrow and grey to broad and black).

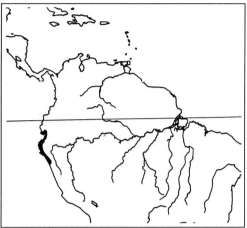

DISTRIBUTION Restricted to the western slope of the Andes, from Manabí and Guayas in W Ecuador south to northern Lambayeque in NW Peru.

HABITAT Occurs in the arid tropics in dry deciduous forests and in areas with cacti and low thorny scrub. From lowlands to almost 2000m.

DESCRIPTION
P. s. parvistriatus **Adult male** Forehead to hindneck black, feathers of central forehead to about mid crown narrowly tipped yellow and remainder tipped white. Lores white. Rest of head, including chin and throat, white, finely barred grey. Upperparts brownish-grey (in fresh plumage, usually with very faint pale and dark bars on mantle and rump), paler and brown-barred on uppertail-coverts. Upperwing and its coverts brownish to brown-grey, edged and tipped paler, edges broadest and whitest on tertials, and with whiter area at base of inner webs of flight feathers. Uppertail dark grey-brown, central feather pair with broad white stripe on inner webs and outer three pairs with much white inside tips. Underparts white, with narrow wavy greyish-black barring in upper region down to lower breast, and flanks and belly with rather narrow, often sparse greyish streaks. Underwing whitish, coverts sometimes faintly barred grey. Undertail much as uppertail.

Adult female As male, but top of head entirely spotted white (lacks yellow).

Juvenile As adults, but crown and forehead duller, more grey-brown, and with off-white streaks/spots (both sexes); markings below more diffuse and less regular.

Bare parts Bill black, with greyer base. Legs and feet grey. Eyes brown.

GEOGRAPHICAL VARIATION Three races.
    P. s. parvistriatus (W Ecuador, from Guayas to Manabí provinces) Described above.
    P. s. sclateri (SW Ecuador and adjacent northwestern-

most Peru) Much as *parvistriatus*, but barring and streaking below somewhat darker and heavier (broader), more or less intermediate between the other two races.
    P. s. porcullae (Peru, from C Piura to N Lambayeque) Chin and throat broadly barred black, breast very broadly barred black, and flanks and belly very broadly black-streaked.

MEASUREMENTS Wing 49-54; tail 25-31; bill 14-16; tarsus 12. Weight: 9-12.4.

VOICE Not known.

HABITS Behaviour, including voice, and ecology of this piculet have not been studied.

FOOD Not known.

BREEDING Nests from June (Peru) and July (Ecuador) to September.

REFERENCES Parker *et al.* 1982.

9 SCALED PICULET
Picumnus squamulatus   Plate 4

IDENTIFICATION Length 8-9cm. Tiny, with short, pointed bill curved on culmen. Brownish upperparts appear somewhat scaly (feathers edged black), while (usually prominent) dark edges to pale underpart feathers enhance this general impression; has contrasting pale edges to secondaries and especially on tertials. Head pattern is relatively distinctive: black cap, with forehead and crown spotted with red/yellow (male) or white (female) and hindneck spotted white, and brown ear-coverts bordered above by white.

Similar species The somewhat larger Guianan Piculet (11) is similarly scaly-looking above and below, but has belly deep buff or brownish and tends to have ear-coverts extensively spotted white (at least when fresh); also, red crown spots of male form large patch. The ranges of the two do not, however, overlap.

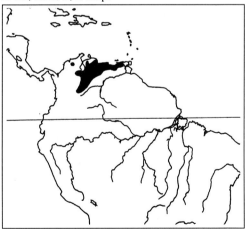

DISTRIBUTION Occurs from Santa Marta in N Colombia southwards through Norte de Santander east of Andes to Meta, and east through Venezuela north of the Orinoco to Sucre and Monagas.

HABITAT Gallery forest, second growth, deciduous woodland, open terrain and farmland with scattered trees, forest edge, xerophytic areas and pastures, up to 1900m.

175

DESCRIPTION

***P. s. rohli* Adult male** Forehead to mid crown black, feathers narrowly tipped orange-red (on some, feather tips yellow or orange); rear crown to hindneck and neck sides brownish-black, spotted white. Lores whitish. Ear-coverts dark brown, feathers at upper edge tipped white. Moustachial region, chin and throat white, with narrow grey-brown feather tips. Upperparts olive-brown, with paler feather centres (often forming rather diffuse yellowish spots towards tips) and narrow black borders, creating rather scaly effect. Upperwing-coverts brownish, lessers and medians edged and tipped black, greaters narrowly margined pale brownish; flight feathers brown, edged and tipped whitish to yellowish-brown, edges palest and broadest on secondaries and especially tertials. Uppertail brownish-black, central feather pair with broad white stripe on inner webs and outer two pairs with white stripe inside tip. Underparts white, faintly tinged brownish-yellow on belly, and with dark brown feather margins (of variable width, usually narrow) creating scaly pattern, dark feather edges becoming paler and narrower on belly and undertail-coverts. Underwing mainly brownish, with white coverts. Undertail much as uppertail.

Adult female As male, but lacks red/yellow tips on head.

Juvenile Somewhat darker above than adults, often with darker feather centres, and more diffusely and irregularly patterned below. Both sexes initially have pale brown bar-like spotting on crown, but males soon acquire red/yellow feather tips.

Bare parts Bill grey to dark grey, paler on lower mandible (which often has horn-coloured base), and with blackish or horn-coloured tip. Legs and feet generally olive-toned. Eyes brown.

GEOGRAPHICAL VARIATION Three races.

> ***P. s. rohli*** (N Venezuela, except northeast, and adjacent parts of Colombia south to about Boyacá) Described above.
> ***P. s. obsoletus*** (Sucre and Monagas in NE Venezuela) Plumage much yellower in tone, with yellow-green tinge above and on wings and yellowish-white ground colour below; scallop markings finer than in *rohli*, but both upperparts and underparts have small dark wedges or wedge-shaped streaks in feather centres. Male's crown feathers always red-tipped.
> ***P. s. squamulatus*** (Colombian part of species' range, apart from Santa Marta to Boyacá) Larger than above two races, and with heavier, darker markings. Crown feathers of male always red-tipped.

MEASUREMENTS Wing 48.6-55.4; tail 24.5-27.2; bill 11.8-12.4; tarsus 11.8-12.8. Weight: 7-12.

VOICE The commonly heard call is a rather high-pitched and squeaky *chi-chi-ch'e'e'chi*, becoming trill-like at the end.

HABITS Alone or in pairs, and inconspicuous. Forages in dense scrub, tangled undergrowth and small trees, examining the thin branches and twigs. Displays include wing-spreading and 'synchronised' movements; possibly the sewing-machine-like movements of other small woodpeckers facing each other.

FOOD Insects.

BREEDING Nesting records in Colombia from September to May, and from April to June in Venezuela.

REFERENCES Hilty & Brown 1984; Meyer de Schauensee & Phelps 1978.

---

10 WHITE-BELLIED PICULET
Picumnus spilogaster　　　Plate　4

Other names: Sundevall's Piculet, Pará Piculet (race *pallidus*)

IDENTIFICATION Length c. 9cm. Tiny, with short, pointed bill slightly curved on culmen. Brownish above, variably unbarred or indistinctly barred paler, and white below with variable black barring from chin to breast and with rather sparse black spots on belly and flanks; dark ear-coverts are vermiculated white. Females have forehead to hindneck black with white spots, while males have a red patch on forehead and crown. Like many S American piculets, a poorly known species.

Similar species Guianan Piculet (11), which overlaps in range, is superficially similar to White-bellied, though rather bigger and with paler eyes; it is more variegated above, with pale scallop markings, and has brownish-buff belly and flanks, while entire underparts are covered with dark scaly markings (breast scalloped, not barred). White-barred Piculet (15) is also partly sympatric and similar to White-bellied, but the races of White-barred involved have dark barring below extending over entire underparts and also show virtually unmarked brown ear-coverts.

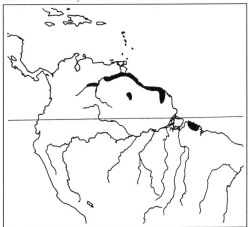

DISTRIBUTION Found from E Venezuela in Delta Amacuro and northern Bolívar, south to N Roraima in northernmost Brazil and eastwards through Guyana and northern parts of Surinam and French Guiana. A little-known isolated race (*pallidus*) has also been recorded from eastern Pará (near Belém) and adjacent Maranhão in NE Brazil.

HABITAT Rain, gallery and deciduous forests, clearings, forest edge, mangroves, open woodland and thickets, to 100m.

DESCRIPTION

***P. s. spilogaster* Adult male** Feathers of forehead and much of crown black with broad red tips, latter forming fairly solid patch; hindcrown to hindneck black, spotted white. Lores whitish. Ear-coverts vermiculated black and white. Neck sides white, finely barred black (bars sometimes lacking). Moustachial region, chin and throat white, barred blackish. Upperparts dull olive-brown, diffusely barred paler greyish (barring variable, sometimes lacking or may be more profuse). Upperwing-coverts olive-brown, narrowly edged paler; flight feathers brown, edged pale buffish, edges broadest and brightest on tertials. Uppertail dark brown, central feather pair with broad white stripe on inner webs and outer two pairs with white stripe inside tip on outer webs. Upper breast white, washed pale yellowish-buff, with fairly broad black bars (bars sometimes broken); lower breast to belly white, sparsely marked with broad, streak-like black spots, flanks occasionally somewhat barred (some individuals may have all these markings much reduced); undertail-coverts plain white. Underwing greyish-brown, with white coverts. Undertail much as uppertail.

Adult female As male, but lacks red on head, having entire crown spotted white.

Juvenile Differs from adults in both sexes having sooty-brown crown with buffish spots restricted to hindneck, and dirtier, more buffish underparts; generally shows more barring both above and below.

Bare parts Bill slate-grey, with black tip. Legs and feet greenish-grey. Eyes brown.

GEOGRAPHICAL VARIATION Three races.

    P. s. spilogaster (the Guianas and N Brazil) Described above. Population in N Brazil is somewhat intermediate between this race and the following, but generally closer to nominate.

    P. s. orinocensis (E Venezuela) Slightly smaller than nominate. Usually lacks spotting below, but may show trace of vermiculation on flanks; slightly more white in tail.

    P. s. pallidus (E Pará in NE Brazil) Known from only a few specimens. Size as *orinocensis*, but has proportionately shorter tail. Plumage much as nominate.

MEASUREMENTS Wing 51-58.4; tail 25.5-33.5; bill 12-14; tarsus 9. Weight: 13-14.

VOICE Not known.

HABITS Not known.

FOOD Not known.

BREEDING Probably September-November.

REFERENCES Meyer de Schauensee & Phelps 1978; Tostain *et al.* 1992.

---

11 GUIANAN PICULET
Picumnus minutissimus   Plate 4

Other name: Arrowhead Piculet

IDENTIFICATION Length c. 9-10cm. Tiny, with fairly short, stout, pointed bill curved on culmen. One of the better-known piculets. Dark brownish upperparts with darker feather centres and pale tips, together with dark-edged pale feathering of underparts, produces a scaly impression overall, set off by buffy-brown ground colour to belly; head is mainly black with white spotting, male also having a fairly solid bright red cap. Has pale yellow or darker red eyes.

Similar species White-bellied (10) and White-barred (15) Piculets both occur in the Guianas, but both lack the brownish belly coloration and scaly upperpart markings, White-bellied having black-barred breast and sparsely spotted belly and White-barred being completely barred black and white below.

DISTRIBUTION Restricted to the Guianan lowlands, from Guyana to French Guiana.

HABITAT Inhabits wide variety of habitats including secondary forests, mangroves, plantations, vegetation along rivers and lakes, up to montane forests.

DESCRIPTION
Adult male Forehead and crown black, with broad red

feather tips (forming red patch). Lores white. Superciliary area to nape and hindneck black, finely spotted white. Cheeks and ear-coverts dark brown, with feathers tipped/edged white. Rear neck side white, variably barred/spotted black (occasionally unmarked). Moustachial region, chin and throat white, narrowly barred black. Mantle, scapulars and back olive-brown, feathers variably patterned with blackish wedge-shaped centre, very narrow black bar at tip (when fresh) and pale or whitish subterminal spot or diffuse bar; rump plainer, with some obscure black barring, and uppertail-coverts sometimes barred pale and dark. Upperwing-coverts olive-brown, edged paler; flight feathers brown, inner webs narrowly edged white and outer webs edged buffish-white, latter edges broadest on secondaries and tertials. Uppertail brownish-black, central feather pair with broad white stripe along inner webs and outer two pairs with angular white stripe on outer webs. Breast white, becoming buff-tinged on lower breast and flanks and brownish-buff on belly and lower flanks, entire underparts with brownish-black feather fringes creating prominent scaly pattern (markings vary individually, however, some being less well marked than others, and a few also having dark shaft streaks in region of lower breast). Underwing greyish-brown, with coverts mottled brown and white. Undertail much as uppertail. (In worn plumage, upperparts appear much more uniform and ear-coverts may also appear plainer and less barred.)

Adult female Slightly shorter-billed than male, but averages slightly larger in wing and tail measurements. Lacks red on head, having crown all black with white spots.

Juvenile As adults, but with browner upperparts barred blackish and with crown dark brown and lacking spots; duller and less clearly patterned below.

Bare parts Bill dark greyish, with pale base to lower mandible. Legs and feet green-grey. Eyes variable, yellow to deep red or reddish-brown. Orbital skin greyish.

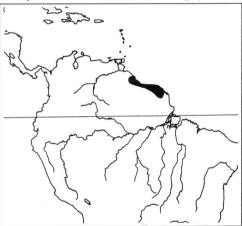

GEOGRAPHICAL VARIATION None recognised.

MEASUREMENTS Wing 51.6-57. Weight: 11-14.3 (16).

VOICE The most common call is represented by a thin series of about 14 notes, *it-it-it-it...*, or *kee kee kee*, and is reminiscent of Lesser Spotted Woodpecker (93). Attacks on other birds are accompanied by a loud twitter.

HABITS As other piculets, forages tit-like on small twigs. The pair, and until incubation of the next clutch also a third individual, presumably a young from the previous brood, roost together in the same hole. During nesting, attacks other birds, even bigger ones, in the vicinity of the nest.

FOOD Ants and small beetles (Bostrichidae).

BREEDING The breeding season starts in March and extends to December. The male takes on most of the excavation of the nest, which also serves as the common roost of the pair. Nest high up (e.g. 8 m) in a tree. Clutch comprises 2-3 eggs. Both sexes incubate (12-14 days), feed the young and remove the faeces. Fledging takes place after 28 days, and parents and young stay together for at least another two months.

REFERENCES Haverschmidt 1951, 1968; Snyder 1966; Tostain *et al.* 1992.

---

12 SPOTTED PICULET
Picumnus pygmaeus   Plate 5

IDENTIFICATION Length c. 10cm. Tiny, with short, pointed bill very slightly curved on culmen. Unmistakable. Has dark plumage spotted with white both above and below, apart from white-barred neck sides and throat and pale-edged brown wings; male has red forehead. May reveal its presence by its extremely high, squeaky voice.

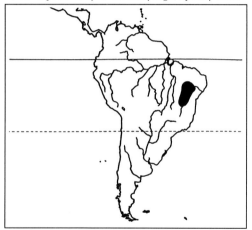

DISTRIBUTION Found only in NE Brazil, from Maranhão and Piauí south to Bahia and the São Francisco river into northernmost Minas Gerais.

HABITAT Dry and open woodland and dense shrubs (caatinga) up to 750m.

DESCRIPTION
Adult male Forehead and forecrown black, with broad red feather tips (forming patch); rest of crown and nape and hindneck black, spotted white. Nasal tufts and lores white, narrowly bordered black above. White crescent above eye. Cheeks and ear-coverts blackish-brown, variably spotted white. Moustachial region and neck sides black, broadly barred white. Chin and throat black with large white spots, or mainly white with black scaly markings. Upperparts dark brown, somewhat paler on rump, and with prominent white or whitish spots on mantle, scapulars and back. Upperwing-coverts dark brown, edged paler, and with white spot at or near tip; flight feathers dark brown, secondaries and tertials broadly edged and tipped pale buff or cinnamon-buff. Uppertail blackish, central feather pair with broad white stripe along inner webs and outer two pairs with white stripe inside tip. Underparts below throat variably rather dark brown to medium or light brown (often with rufous tinge), frequently paler on belly, and bearing

generally large white spots with contrasting black mark at base and tip of each spot, spots usually larger on flanks (belly may be virtually unmarked, or may appear more barred black and white). Underwing pale brownish, with whitish coverts. Undertail much as uppertail, but paler.

Adult female As male, but lacks red on head, having entire crown and forehead white-spotted black.

Juvenile Duller and more diffusely patterned than adults, with underpart markings tending towards bars. Both sexes have top of head brownish-black or sooty-black, with broadly streaked nape and plain or faintly streaked crown.

Bare parts Bill black, with blue-grey base. Legs and feet grey. Eyes deep brown.

GEOGRAPHICAL VARIATION Monotypic. As most S American piculets, this species shows great individual variation, but no clear geographical pattern emerges.

MEASUREMENTS Wing 49-55; tail 27-31; bill 11.1-13.0; tarsus 12.2-14.

VOICE A very high-pitched *tsirrrrr, tsi, tsi, tsi.*

HABITS Practically unknown.

FOOD Not known.

BREEDING Possibly (July) November-February.

REFERENCES Reiser 1929; Sick 1993.

---

13 SPECKLE-CHESTED PICULET
Picumnus steindachneri   Plate 5

IDENTIFICATION Length c. 10cm. Tiny, with short, almost straight, pointed bill. A relatively rare and virtually unknown piculet of Peruvian mountain forests. Fairly unmistakable if seen well. Dark grey above with obscure scaly pattern, wings with prominent pale edging, and with strikingly white-spotted black breast and black-barred white belly; head pattern similar to that of many other piculets, male having extensive red tips to crown feathers.

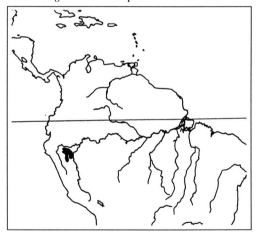

DISTRIBUTION Known only from the region of the Huallaga river and its tributaries in San Martín department of NE Peru.

HABITAT Humid tropical and subtropical montane forests with many epiphytes and tall second growth, roughly at elevations between 900 and 2500m.

DESCRIPTION Adult male Lowermost forehead and

lores white; rest of forehead and most of crown black, feathers broadly tipped red; remainder of crown and hindneck black, spotted white. Sides of head and neck plus moustachial region basically white with black barring, bars narrowest in moustachial area. Chin and throat white, with narrow black feather fringes forming scaly pattern. Upperparts grey-brown, feathers with normally obscure (though sometimes fairly prominent) paler greyish fringes with blackish inner border, producing vaguely scalloped pattern. Upperwing and its coverts brown, edged and tipped pale grey to off-white, edges broadest and more buffy on secondaries and, especially, tertials. Uppertail blackish, central feather pair with white stripe along inner webs and outer two pairs with white stripe inside tip. Breast black, with large drop-shaped white spots; belly to undertail-coverts white, broadly barred black. Underwing pale brown, with white coverts. Undertail much as uppertail, but paler.

Adult female As male, but with black forehead and crown spotted with white.

Juvenile Apparently unknown. Presumably differs from adults in much the same way as do juveniles of related species.

Bare parts Bill black, with base and all but tip of lower mandible blue-grey. Legs and feet grey. Eyes brown.

GEOGRAPHICAL VARIATION None known.

MEASUREMENTS Wing 53.7-57.5; tail 33; bill 13.5-14; tarsus 11.5-12. Weight: 9-11.

VOICE A high-pitched trill, lasting several seconds. Fledged young rather vociferous when begging for food.

HABITS Met with singly, in pairs or small family groups. Joins mixed-species flocks, with which these piculets move through the canopy and through second growth. Forages at the ends of thin twigs and on vines. Its hammering is loud and distinctive.

FOOD Not known.

BREEDING Totally unknown.

REFERENCES Parker & Parker 1982; Parker *et al.* 1982.

---

14 VARZEA PICULET
Picumnus varzeae   Plate 5

IDENTIFICATION Length c. 8-9cm. Tiny, with short, pointed bill slightly curved on culmen. Another extremely poorly known species, this one confined to a small region of the Amazon in N Brazil. Has plain dark upperparts, vermiculated face, and dark underparts with black-and-white spots forming rows or broken-bar pattern; male has red forehead and crown, with white-spotted hindneck, while female has top of head white-spotted black. This species interbreeds at least occasionally (and perhaps more commonly) with White-barred Piculet (15), and hybrids frequently show a more barred pattern below.

Similar species See White-barred Piculet.

DISTRIBUTION Restricted to a small area of the Amazon in Brazil, between the lower Madeira river in E Amazonas and Obidos in westernmost Pará, including the islands.

HABITAT Lowland, *várzea*, forest with dense under-growth.

DESCRIPTION
Adult male Forehead and crown black, all but lowermost forehead with broad red feather tips forming solid patch;

nape and hindneck black, spotted white. Lores speckled black and white. Sides of head and neck dark brown, obscurely vermiculated/spotted whitish. Chin and throat black-brown, finely spotted/barred white. Upperparts dark olive-brown to greenish-brown, unmarked or with a few faint black bars (latter normally invisible in the field). Upperwing and its coverts dark brown, narrowly edged and tipped paler, edges broader and brighter (more buff) on secondaries and tertials. Uppertail dark brown, central feather pair with white (sometimes brown-barred) stripe along inner webs and outer two pairs with narrow white stripe inside tip (outer stripe sometimes much reduced or even occasionally absent). Underparts below throat highly variable, both in colour and in markings: ground colour generally brown or greenish-brown, with rows of broadly white-tipped black feathers (but can appear more barred). Underwing pale brownish, barred white on coverts. Undertail much as uppertail, but paler.

Adult female Differs from male in having entire top of head black with white spots, lacking red.

Juvenile As adults, but with more barred appearance to underparts; both sexes have pale-streaked crown, without red.

Bare parts Bill black, with blue-grey base to upper mandible and dull yellowish base to lower mandible. Legs and feet grey. Eyes brown.

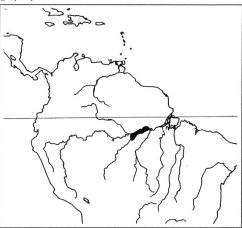

GEOGRAPHICAL VARIATION No populations show any characters warranting subspecific separation, but individual variation is widespread.

MEASUREMENTS Wing 50.9-55.5; tail 29-33; bill 13-14.

VOICE Not known.

FOOD Unknown.

BREEDING Unknown.

HABITS Information on life history completely lacking. Possible breeding season June-December.

---

15 WHITE-BARRED PICULET
Picumnus cirratus   Plate 6

Other name: Pilcomayo Piculet (southern forms)
Forms a superspecies with *dorbygnianus* and *temminckii*.

IDENTIFICATION Length c. 10cm. Tiny, with fairly
short, pointed bill slightly curved on culmen. One of the
better-known piculets and within its range the one most
likely to be encountered. Plumage highly variable, with a
number of races intergrading and interbreeding where
they meet. Generally, however, brownish to brownish-grey
above, with only very indistinct barring (or none at all), and
pale below with heavy black barring (some southern
populations are less heavily barred below, or show open V-
shaped markings). Head pattern is basically similar to that
of other *Picumnus* species, males having red on forehead
and (usually) crown; often appears slightly crested.
Immatures tend to lack white spots on crown. The variability of this species is further complicated by its hybridisation
with other piculets, including Varzea (14), Ocellated (16),
Ochre-collared (17) and White-wedged (18).

Similar species See above-mentioned species. White-barred
also occurs with Mottled Piculet (23) in SE Brazil, but latter
is dark-breasted and shows heavier black markings on
flanks.

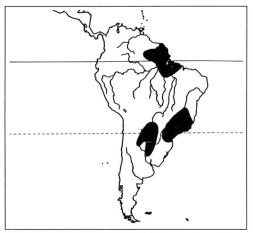

DISTRIBUTION Occurs in two discrete areas. In the
north, found discontinuously from Guyana and French
Guiana south to Marajó island in NE Brazil, then westwards
along the Amazon to the lower reaches of the Tapajós river
and Obidos. In the south, from Chuquisaca in SE Bolivia,
east to the southwestern Mato Grosso in SW Brazil and
south to Santa Fé and Entre Ríos in Argentina, including
most of Paraguay. The picture is complicated in SE Brazil,
where nominate race of White-barred interbreeds freely
with Ochre-collared Piculet (many apparent hybrids exist,
and assigning other individuals to species may be difficult),
but White-barred seems to be present north and east to
Minas Gerais and Espírito Santo. This species is fairly
common locally, although, as with other piculets, it is by no
means easy to observe.

HABITAT Frequents tall bushes and gallery forests of
savannas, open woodland, edges of woods and transitional
forests. In mountain ranges, found at up to 2100m.

DESCRIPTION
***P. c. cirratus* Adult male** Forehead and crown black, with
broad red feather tips often forming fairly solid patch;

nape and hindneck black, spotted white. Nasal tufts white
to buffish. Cheeks and ear-coverts dark buffish, faintly
barred blackish, and bordered above by white stripe behind
eye. Neck sides, moustachial area, chin and throat white to
pale buff, barred blackish. Upperparts dull brownish,
faintly barred. Upperwing-coverts brown, narrowly edged
buffish; flight feathers dark brown, secondaries and tertials
edged buffish-white. Uppertail dark brown, central feather
pair with white stripe along inner webs and outer two or
three pairs with diagonal white stripe inside tip. Underparts white, slightly tinged buff on belly and flanks, and
fully barred black (black bars narrower on belly). Underwing
pale brown, with paler or white coverts. Undertail much as
uppertail. (The above description refers to fairly 'typical'
individuals; note that considerable individual variation
exists, as well as many intergrades and hybrids between *P.
c. cirratus* and other races and species.)

Adult female As male, but lacks red tips to forehead and
crown feathers.

Juvenile Duller and somewhat darker in appearance than
adults, and with tendency towards more obvious barring
above and heavier barring below. Both sexes have dark
brown or sooty crown, generally unspotted, but with buffish
streaks on rear crown sides and nape/hindneck.

Bare parts Bill black, with distinctly paler base to lower
mandible. Legs and feet grey. Eyes chestnut-brown. Orbital skin blue-grey.

GEOGRAPHICAL VARIATION Complex, with several
intergrading races and with hybridisation with other species also occurring. Much further research is required, but
the difficulties of studying piculets in the field are well
known. Here we recognise six races, but this should be
regarded as a tentative arrangement.

P. c. cirratus (SE Brazil, from Minas Gerais and
Espírito Santo south to Paraná, and E Paraguay)
Described above. Intergrades with *pilcomayensis*; also
interbreeds with Ochre-collared Piculet (17) and with
race *guttifer* of White-wedged Piculet (18).
P. c. pilcomayensis (southern Santa Cruz and eastern
Tarija in SE Bolivia, south to Corrientes and Entre Ríos
in Argentina, and in W and E Paraguay) Typically,
much greyer above than nominate, and whiter below,
with bars much sparser and broken; male shows less
red on crown. Interbreeds with nominate *cirratus* and
with race *guttifer* of White-wedged Piculet (18).
P. c. tucumanus (northern Argentina, from W Salta
south to La Rioja) Rather greyish-brown above with
more distinct barring, throat and breast somewhat
buffy and more diffusely barred, and black bars below
more widely spaced; primaries tipped pale; male has
less red on head (confined to forehead), and white
crown spots may be much reduced, indistinct or rarely
even absent.
P. c. thamnophiloides (Chuquisaca in S Bolivia, south
along Andes to northern Salta in NW Argentina)
Often rather greyish above, but differs mainly in
underpart pattern: throat and upper breast white or
buffy-white with only a few dark markings, flanks
variably patterned with bars, arrowheads or Y-shaped
markings, and belly unmarked or with just a few dark
spots/bars. Male has somewhat narrower red tips to
forehead and crown feathers. Interbreeds with White-
wedged (18) and Ocellated Piculets (16).
P. c. confusus (Guyana and French Guiana) Brown
above with pale mantle bars, pale wing edgings very
narrow, darker ear-coverts lack white upper border,
and throat well barred; underparts fully barred, black
bars becoming very fine on belly.

P. c. macconnelli (eastern Amazon region of NE Brazil) Similar to *confusus* above, but unbarred, and deep brown ear-coverts sometimes show a few white spots; moustachial area, throat and breast heavily barred black (appearing more black than white), and belly and flanks evenly barred black and white. Interbreeds with Varzea Piculet.

MEASUREMENTS Wing 46-59; tail 33-39; bill 9.5-12; tarsus 12.4-13.3. Weight: 6.8-12.

VOICE A high descending or long and wavering *tsirrrr* seems to be the call for long-distance communication. Also *tsirit, tsick*. Drums a loud staccato sound on small dead stubs.

HABITS This tame piculet is seen singly and in pairs; sometimes with mixed-species flocks. Forages at low and middle heights, mainly in the undergrowth. Mostly seen at tips of branches and on twigs, often clinging to their underside; also gathers food from vines, small trees and bamboo. The main feeding technique is vigorous and audible hammering, by which small holes are excavated into the substrate. Flies considerable distances when finished at a particular foraging site. Moves like other piculets, sometimes downwards like a nuthatch. As with other small woodpeckers, in close and silent encounters opponents perform pecking attacks at each other without hitting.

FOOD Small insects, including ants. Perhaps also takes sap obtained by wounding the tip of a twig.

BREEDING Breeds late in the year, from October to March; July-December in the north. Nest is excavated by both sexes into slender stubs at all heights. The hole is long with a round entrance, and it extends almost to the cambium. Clutch size 2 eggs.

REFERENCES Hoy 1968; Olrog 1984; Short 1970a; Sick 1993.

16 OCELLATED PICULET
Picumnus dorbygnianus   Plate 6

Forms a superspecies with *cirratus* and *temminckii*.

IDENTIFICATION Length c. 10cm. Tiny, with fairly short, pointed bill barely curved on culmen. A little-known species of the eastern slopes of the Andes. A relatively pale-looking piculet, greyish above with narrow barring, and whitish below with dark feather edges and shaft streaks or mainly dark-streaked; may show indication of a paler collar, and has typical *Picumnus* head pattern. Interbreeds with nominate race of White-wedged Piculet (18) in C Bolivia and with race *thamnophiloides* of White-barred Piculet (15) in S Bolivia, making identification difficult.

DISTRIBUTION Occurs on the eastern Andean slopes, from E Peru south to Cochabamba and western Santa Cruz in Bolivia, and possibly into N Argentina. Apparently rare.

HABITAT Humid tropical and subtropical montane forests with many epiphytes (Peru), roughly at elevations between 900 and 2500m. Tall bushes of transitional forests (Argentina).

DESCRIPTION
P. d. dorbygnianus Adult male Forehead and forecrown feathers black, tipped red; hindcrown and nape black, spotted white. Lores and nasal tufts buffish-white. Cheeks and ear-coverts buff-brown, barred whitish, bordered above by white-tipped feathers in short stripe behind eye. Neck sides buffy-white with darker streaking. Moustachial area,

chin and throat whitish, faintly tinged buff, with a few dark feather edges/tips, throat sometimes appearing scaly. Hindneck pale greyish-brown; upperparts greyish-brown, feathers having pale tip and blackish subterminal bar. Upperwing-coverts grey-brown, narrowly edged paler; flight feathers dark brown, prominently edged and tipped buffish-white. Uppertail blackish, central feather pair with broad stripe along inner webs and outer two pairs with diagonal white stripe inside tip. Underparts below throat white, becoming buffy-white on belly, with breast and flank feathers narrowly edged blackish and with black shaft streaks (belly unmarked or with some faint, narrow bars). Underwing pale grey-brown, with whitish coverts. Undertail much as uppertail.

Adult female As male, but without red feather tips to forehead and crown.

Juvenile Duller than adults and slightly darker, with diffuse barring above and below. Both sexes have sooty crown, with off white streaks at rear and on nape.

Bare parts Bill black, with grey base. Legs and feet greyish. Eyes brown. Orbital skin greyish.

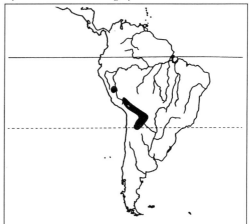

GEOGRAPHICAL VARIATION Two races.
    P. d. dorbygnianus (Bolivia) Described above.
    P. d. jelskii (Peru) Somewhat shorter-tailed than nominate. Underpart markings generally restricted to broad black shaft streaks on breast, becoming fine streaking on flanks (belly sometimes with a few dark spots). Male has broader red tips to crown feathers.

MEASUREMENTS Wing 56-59; tail 31-33; bill 14-15.6; tarsus 12.

VOICE Not known.

HABITS Probably very much as for preceding species.

FOOD Not known.

BREEDING Breeds probably before December.

REFERENCES Olrog 1984; Parker *et al.* 1982.

17 OCHRE-COLLARED PICULET
Picumnus temminckii   Plate 6

Forms a superspecies with *cirratus* and *dorbygnianus*.

IDENTIFICATION Length 9-10cm. Tiny, with short, pointed bill slightly curved on culmen. In good views, readily identified by diagnostic broad cinnamon-buff collar across hindneck and neck sides, combined with (usually bold) pale spot or line behind eye. Otherwise, fairly uniform brown above, with pale wing edgings, and prominently barred pale and dark below, with strong buff tone to flanks. Interbreeds commonly with nominate race of White-barred Piculet (15), producing many intermediate individuals.

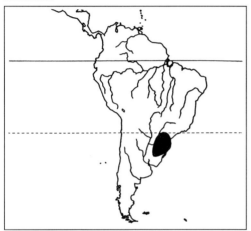

DISTRIBUTION Found from E Paraguay and Misiones in NW Argentina eastwards to Paraná, São Paulo and Rio Grande do Sul in SE Brazil.

HABITAT Tall scrub and *tacuarales* of humid forests, and forest edge.

DESCRIPTION
Adult male Lower forehead, nasal tufts and lores buffy-white; upper forehead and forecrown black, feathers tipped red; hindcrown and nape black, finely spotted white. Cheeks and ear-coverts rich dark buff-brown, bordered above by bright buffish-white or white line (or spot) behind eye. Hindneck and neck sides cinnamon-buff, often brighter at junction with nape. Moustachial area, chin and throat pale buffish-white, feathers narrowly tipped blackish (appearing scaly). Upperparts brown, unmarked or very faintly barred paler. Upperwing-coverts brown, edged buff; flight feathers dark brown, narrowly edged buff. Uppertail blackish, central feather pair with white stripe along inner webs and outer two pairs with diagonal white stripe inside tip. Underparts below throat whitish, becoming strongly buff on flanks and lower belly, all with bold but fairly narrow black bars. Underwing light brown, with whitish coverts. Undertail much as uppertail.
Adult female As male, but lacks red on crown and forehead.
Juvenile Darker and duller than adults, and with heavier but more diffuse barring. Both sexes have sooty crown and buff-streaked nape.
Bare parts Bill black, with greyish base. Legs and feet greyish. Eyes brown. Orbital skin greyish.

GEOGRAPHICAL VARIATION No races are recog-

nised, but species commonly hybridises with nominate White-barred Piculet, resulting in intergrading populations in SE Brazil.

MEASUREMENTS Wing of male 56; tail 30-33; bill 11-12.9; tarsus 12.5-14. Weight: 10-12.5.

VOICE The only vocalisation known is described as a high-pitched whistle, *tsirrrr, si-si-si.....* Drumming slower than that of Mottled Piculet (23).

HABITS Forages at low levels on slender stalks.

FOOD Not known.

BREEDING Nests presumably in October-March.

REFERENCES Belton 1984; Olrog 1984; Sick 1993.

18 WHITE-WEDGED PICULET
Picumnus albosquamatus   Plate 7

Other names: Guttate Piculet (race *guttifer*), Blackish Piculet ('*P. asterias*' = *P. a. guttifer*)

IDENTIFICATION Length 10-11cm. Tiny, with rather long, pointed bill only barely curved on culmen. Occurs in two distinct forms, typical individuals of which exhibit a number of plumage differences. Nominate southwestern race is brownish above, with distinct pale wing edgings, and shows a scaly pattern to neck sides and throat; below, has narrow dark borders to pale breast feathers (scalloped effect), with flanks either almost unmarked or with subterminal black wedge marks. Eastern race *guttifer* is bigger and darker, with contrasting dark ear-coverts, and has less obvious pale wing edgings; it has much more black on throat and breast, and the flanks generally show large black wedge-shaped markings. Both races have the characteristic *Picumnus* crown and nape pattern, and can give the impression of having a pale hindneck collar; both may also have small black-bordered white spots on the upperparts (sometimes rather obvious on *guttifer*), but these are often indistinct and can soon disappear with wear. The two races are, in addition, rather variable individually and also intergrade to some extent.

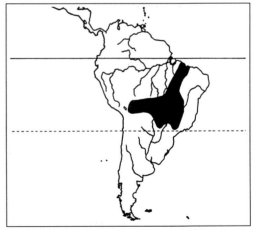

DISTRIBUTION Ranges from E Pará and Maranhaõ in eastern Brazil south to northern São Paulo, and through Mato Grosso to northern Santa Cruz and La Paz in N and E Bolivia.

HABITAT This piculet is a denizen of dense parts of

open, moderately dry savanna woodland (cerrado) and gallery forests. From lowlands to, locally, 2100m.

DESCRIPTION

P. a. albosquamatus **Adult male** Nasal tufts and lores buffish-white, bordered by black line across lower forehead; upper forehead and forecrown black, feathers broadly tipped red; hindcrown and crown sides to nape and upper hindneck black, finely spotted white. Lower hindneck, neck sides and side of head white, strongly tinged brown on hindneck and ear-coverts, all with black margins to feathers (producing scaly effect). Moustachial area, chin and throat white, with black borders to feathers. Upperparts warm brown to greyish-brown, often with variable black-bordered white spots at tips of some feathers when fresh (spots can rapidly wear away). Upperwing-coverts brown, broadly edged pale; flight feathers dark brown, secondaries and tertials with broad and prominent buffish-white edges to outer webs. Uppertail dark brown, central feather pair with broad white stripe along inner webs and outer two pairs with broad diagonal white stripe inside tip. Underparts below throat whitish, breast feathers with narrow black border (appearing typically scalloped), flank feathers with black wedge-shaped subterminal marks, and belly unmarked or slightly streaked (note, however, that markings vary: breast may show some broad shaft streaks, and lower underparts may be more heavily patterned). Underwing pale brown, with whitish coverts. Undertail much as uppertail.

Adult female As male, but without red on head, crown being spotted white.

Juvenile Duller and less contrastingly patterned than adults, and with more barred appearance. Both sexes have unmarked brownish crown and buff spots or broad streaks on nape.

Bare parts Bill blackish, with paler base to lower mandible. Legs and feet grey to green-grey. Eyes brown. Orbital skin greyish.

GEOGRAPHICAL VARIATION Two races, well defined but intergrading to some extent.

  P. a. albosquamatus (Bolivia and SW Mato Grosso in Brazil) Described above. Appears to intergrade with following race in western Mato Grosso.
  P. a. guttifer (range of species, apart from area occupied by nominate) Includes '*P. asterias*' and '*P. sagittatus*'. Larger than nominate, and generally darker in appearance. Ear-coverts dark brown, vaguely barred black; broader black borders to feathers of throat and breast (latter also with black shaft streaks), these areas sometimes appearing blackish with white spots, and lower underparts warm buff with broad black wedge marks on flank feathers (note that some less well-marked individuals may approach nominate in patterning of underparts); wing-coverts usually show pale spots at tips, and flight feathers prominently pale-edged only on tertials. Male has more extensive red tips to crown feathers.

MEASUREMENTS Wing 48.6-60.1; tail 32-37; bill 12.5-14. Weight: 9-11.

VOICE A descending *si-si-si....* is the only known vocalisation.

HABITS Largely unknown.

FOOD Not known.

BREEDING Apparently unknown.

REFERENCE Sick 1993.

19 RUSTY-NECKED PICULET
Picumnus fuscus Plate 7

Other name: Natterer's Piculet

IDENTIFICATION Length c. 10cm. Tiny, with short, more or less pointed bill slightly curved on culmen. A virtually unknown species with a very small range. Has brownish to brownish-green upperparts and buffish underparts, buff extending as a broad collar over hindneck; may show very faint hint of barring below, mainly on flanks. Distinctive head pattern: plain buff-brown ear-coverts, and black forehead and crown either unmarked (female) or with reddish tips to hindcrown feathers.

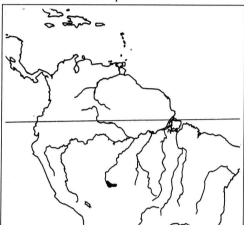

DISTRIBUTION A rare species, known only from the westernmost Mato Grosso in SW Brazil and adjacent Beni in Bolivia.

HABITAT Lowland riverine forest.

DESCRIPTION

Adult male Sides of lower forehead and nasal tufts/front of lores buffish; rest of forehead, rear lores and crown back to nape black, feathers of hindcrown and nape broadly tipped orange-red (may form a patch), and with pale tips forming broken stripe behind eye. Cheeks and ear-coverts buffish-brown, tinged with rufous. Hindneck and side of neck rusty-buff to buffy-brown. Moustachial region buff, usually with rather indistinct dark barring. Chin and throat buff-brown, occasionally with a trace of fine barring. Upperparts brown to brownish-green, often tinged rufous on scapulars. Upperwing and its coverts dark brown, coverts edged and tipped paler, secondaries and tertials edged yellowish-buff. Uppertail dark brown, central feather pair with broad white stripe along inner webs and outer two pairs with narrower diagonal white bar. Underparts below throat pale buffish, tinged cinnamon or light rusty on breast sides and flanks, becoming browner on undertail-coverts; often unmarked, but may show faint vestiges of barring on flanks and occasionally on breast and belly. Underwing pale brown, with rufous-buff coverts. Undertail much as uppertail.

Adult female As male, but without red feather tips on head.

Juvenile Apparently undescribed.

Bare parts Bill black, with paler base to lower mandible. Legs and feet greyish-brown. Eyes brown. Orbital skin greyish.

GEOGRAPHICAL VARIATION None known.

183

MEASUREMENTS Wing 49-53; tail 24-27; bill 12-12.4; tarsus 19.8.

VOICE Unknown.

HABITS Unknown.

FOOD Unknown.

BREEDING Unknown.

---

20 RUFOUS-BREASTED PICULET
Picumnus rufiventris   Plate 5

IDENTIFICATION Length 9-11cm. Tiny, with comparatively long, fairly straight and slightly chisel-tipped bill. Reasonably distinctive, having greenish upperparts, rufous hindneck, sides of neck and entire underparts, and white-spotted black cap, male with red-tipped feathers on crown.

Similar species Chestnut Piculet (28) is easily distinguished by its entire body, including upperparts, being rufous and by its pale creamy to pale tawny forehead, male also having yellow (not red) crown spots. The two appear not to overlap

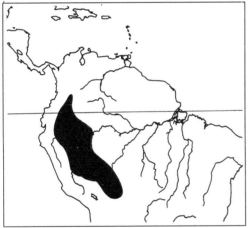

DISTRIBUTION Occurs from western Meta in C Colombia southwards along the eastern slope of the Andes through E Ecuador and E Peru (apparently extending into W Brazil) to Pando, Beni and Cochabamba in NW Bolivia.

HABITAT A piculet of humid forests which inhabits thick understorey of forest edge, second growth including overgrown clearings, and vegetation along watercourses, at low elevations of up to 400 (1000)m. Found also inside *terra firme* and *várzea* forests.

DESCRIPTION
P. r. rufiventris Adult male Forehead to nape black, spotted with white (most prominently on nape), apart from red-tipped feathers of central crown (red sometimes more extensive, reaching onto forehead). Lores and nasal tufts white, variably tipped black. Rest of head and hindneck rufous to cinnamon-rufous, sometimes somewhat darker on ear-coverts (which may also show some dark streaking or barring). Upperparts dark green, usually with faint rufous tinge on scapulars and, particularly, rump. Upperwing and its coverts dark brown, edged and tipped greenish on coverts, with secondaries and tertials edged cinnamon on inner webs and edged rusty on outer webs

and at tips. Uppertail dark brown, central feather pair with pale cinnamon stripe along inner webs and outer two pairs with similarly coloured stripe on outer web. Rufous coloration of head extends entire underparts, which are unpatterned. Underwing brown, with rufous coverts. Undertail much as uppertail.

Adult female As male, but with entire top of head spotted white.

Juvenile Differs from adults in having grey tone to green of upperparts, grey breast and flanks (and sometimes grey-barred belly), and less obvious rufous area on hindneck. Both sexes have greyish or olive cap lacking spots, but frequently with buffish barring.

Bare parts Bill black, with slightly paler base to lower mandible. Legs and feet grey. Eyes brown. Orbital skin blue.

GEOGRAPHICAL VARIATION Three races, differing mainly in size and in depth of coloration, and also somewhat in markings.
　　P. r. rufiventris (Colombia and Ecuador) Described above. The smallest race.
　　P. r. grandis (E Peru) Noticeably bigger and heavier than nominate. Tends to show yellowish tone to green upperparts, and paler underparts; black of cap ends higher up on nape, and red crown spots of male reach further back on crown.
　　P. r. brunneifrons (Bolivia) Intermediate in size between above two races. Plumage similar to *grandis*, but darker overall, and with green of upperparts rather strongly suffused with rufous-chestnut (rufous often also pervades forehead).

MEASUREMENTS Wing of male 57-61.5, of female 58-61 (*brunneifrons*; general range 54-67); tail 28.5-35; bill 15-18.5; tarsus 13-16. Weight: 12-16.

VOICE Unknown.

HABITS Usually occurs singly or in pairs, and often in mixed-species parties. Forages in lower strata, 1-7m above ground.

FOOD Unknown.

BREEDING Breeding season January-March in Peru and Bolivia; probably later in Ecuador.

REFERENCES Hilty & Brown 1984; Parker *et al.* 1982.

---

21 TAWNY PICULET
Picumnus fulvescens   Plate 7

IDENTIFICATION Length c. 10cm. Tiny, with short, pointed bill slightly curved on culmen. Another almost unknown piculet, this one having a very small range in NE Brazil. Differs from all other piculets in its uniform rich fulvous-brown underparts (breast with faint pale streaks), but see race *saturatus* under Ochraceous Piculet (22). Has brownish upperparts and wings, and dark brown ear-coverts contrasting somewhat with rest of face. Female has black forehead to hindneck spotted with white; male is apparently undescribed, but presumably differs from female in having some red or reddish coloration on forehead/crown feathers.

DISTRIBUTION Recorded only from localities in the states of Pernambuco and Alagoas in NE Brazil. Scarce, and threatened by habitat destruction.

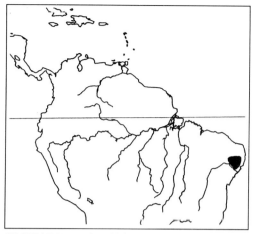

HABITAT Mature humid forests, wooded foothills and coffee plantations are the more humid habitats frequented by this piculet. Also occurs in open, moderately dry woodland. Lowlands up to 900m.

DESCRIPTION

Adult male Apparently unknown.

Adult female Forehead to hindneck black, spotted with white. Nasal tufts and lores white or buffish-white, this colour extending to tips of a few feathers beneath eye and in upper moustachial region. Ear-coverts dark brown, vaguely streaked paler. Neck sides rusty-buff. Chin and throat variably whitish to buff or buffy-brown. Upperparts brown to rufous-brown or tinged yellowish-brown, paler on uppertail-coverts, and unmarked. Upperwing and its coverts dark brown, narrowly edged and tipped paler. Uppertail brownish-black, central feather pair with broad white stripe along inner webs and outer two pairs with diagonal white stripe inside tip. Underparts below throat light yellowish-brown to rufous or rusty, with indistinct, narrow whitish shaft streaks on breast becoming broader and more cinnamon-toned (and even more obscure) on flanks and belly. Underwing pale brown, with yellowish-brown to rusty coverts. Undertail as uppertail, but paler.

Juvenile Apparently undescribed.

Bare parts Apparently undescribed. Presumably much as those of related species.

GEOGRAPHICAL VARIATION None known within small range (but see Ochraceous Piculet).

MEASUREMENTS Wing 51-53.

VOICE Call is a descending series, *driée driée driée....*

HABITS Unknown.

FOOD Unknown.

BREEDING Unknown.

REFERENCES Sick 1993; Stager 1961.

---

22 OCHRACEOUS PICULET
Picumnus limae   Plate 7

IDENTIFICATION Length 10cm. Tiny, with short, pointed bill curved on culmen. Almost unknown, but relatively distinctive. Plain brown above and unmarked pale buffish-white below, with contrasting darker ear-coverts; male has red forehead and crown and white-spotted black hindcrown and hindneck, female having top of head wholly black with clear white spots.

Similar species Unlikely to be confused with other piculets in its range (but see race *saturatus* under Geographical Variation).

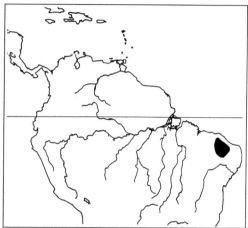

DISTRIBUTION Known to occur only in area from Ceará to Alagoas in E Brazil. Apparently rare, and threatened by clearance of habitat.

HABITAT Dry and open woodland and shrubs.

DESCRIPTION

Adult male Forehead and most of crown black, with broad red feather tips forming almost solid patch; sides of forehead and crown, plus hindcrown, nape and hindneck black, spotted white. Nasal tufts and lores white. Black line behind eye, bordered above by short white line. Ear-coverts pale rusty-brown. Moustachial area, neck side, chin and throat white, occasionally with some faint fine barring in chin/moustachial region. Upperparts plain greyish-brown, with yellowish-rusty cast. Upperwing and its coverts dark brown, edged and tipped pale or buffish. Uppertail dark brown, central feather pair with broad white/buffish-white stripe along inner webs and outer two pairs with diagonal white stripe inside tip. White of neck side and throat continues over entire underparts, becoming buff-tinged or pale yellowish in, especially, lower regions; underparts generally unmarked, but may show very faint hint of barring on belly and flanks. Underwing pale brown, with whitish coverts. Undertail much as uppertail.

Adult female As male, but with forehead and crown black with white spots.

Juvenile Insufficient information is available on plumage of juvenile.

Bare parts Bill blackish, with horn-coloured inner half of lower mandible. Legs and feet blue-grey. Eyes deep brown.

GEOGRAPHICAL VARIATION Some confusion exists over the position of the form *P. l. saturatus* described from Paraíba. This differs from typical individuals in being less grey above, and in having much darker, more rufous/

rusty-ochre, underparts with tendency towards whitish shaft streaks; hence, this form is very close to Tawny Piculet (21), and may possibly be a race of latter or even represent simply a variant of typical Tawny. All of these piculets, however, are so little known that much further research and field study are required before their true positions and relationships can be elucidated.

MEASUREMENTS Wing 50-53.

VOICE A high-pitched, hummingbird-like *sirr-sirr-sirr*.

HABITS Unknown.

FOOD Unknown.

BREEDING Unknown.

REFERENCES Sick 1993.

---

23 MOTTLED PICULET
Picumnus nebulosus   Plate 7

IDENTIFICATION Length 10-11cm. Tiny, with short, straight, slightly chisel-tipped bill. Has brownish upperparts, rusty-brown breast and heavily black-mottled flanks. Head pattern fairly distinctive: typical forehead to hindneck markings (male with red crown patch), barred chin and throat, and much white around lores and behind eye.

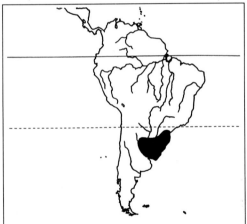

DISTRIBUTION Occurs in SE Brazil, from Paraná south to Rio Grande do Sul, in adjacent parts of Uruguay, and in Misiones and Corrientes in NE Argentina; probably also in easternmost Paraguay. Somewhat local and uncommon, but appears to be common in southern part of Brazilian range.

HABITAT Found in forests, forest edge and in savannas and semi-arid areas with bushes, to at least 900m.

DESCRIPTION
Adult male Forehead to nape black, feathers of upper forehead and crown tipped broadly red (often forming patch) and those of crown sides and nape tipped white (spotted). Lores and line above bill base (and often extending around upper fore edge of eye) white, occasionally with a few black tips. Cheeks and lower ear-coverts rather dark olive-brown, bordered above by large but irregular area of white. Neck side buffish olive-brown. Moustachial area, chin and throat white, barred black. Hindneck and upperparts warm olive-brown, tinged buff or rusty on back

and scapulars. Upperwing and its coverts dark brown to brown-black, broadly margined paler, margins broadest and brightest (pale buff) on tertials. Uppertail black, central feather pair with white stripe along inner webs and outer three pairs with white streak on outer webs. Breast rusty buffish-brown, becoming paler buff on belly, and usually with bright rich buff tone on flanks; markings somewhat variable, usually indistinct or lacking on breast, but with broad blackish streaks, spots or even U-shaped bars from lower breast to flanks. Underwing pale brownish, with rusty-buff coverts. Undertail as uppertail, but paler.
Adult female Lacks male's red, having top of head entirely white-spotted black.
Juvenile Duller than adults, both sexes also having dull brown crown streaked pale buffish.
Bare parts Bill black, with grey base to lower mandible. Legs and feet grey. Eyes brown. Orbital skin greyish.

GEOGRAPHICAL VARIATION None known.

MEASUREMENTS Wing 54-60; tail 34-37; bill 10.9-14.3. Weight: 11-12.

VOICE A humming *tsewrewt, si-si-si...* Also recorded are series of weak, single short squeaks uttered by a juvenile (contact with parent). Drums loudly on bamboo, the sound resembling that made by some frogs (*Strombus*); short pauses between bursts of 2-4 strokes.

HABITS Not well known. Forages at low levels on slender woody stems, particularly dead bamboo.

FOOD Unknown.

BREEDING Nests October to December.

REFERENCES Belton 1984; Gore & Gepp 1978; Olrog 1984; Sick 1993.

---

24 PLAIN-BREASTED PICULET
Picumnus castelnau   Plate 8

IDENTIFICATION Length 8-9cm. Tiny, with short, pointed bill curved on culmen. A virtually unknown piculet of western S America. Greyish-olive upperparts (may show faint hint of barring at very close range) contrast with plain dull whitish underparts; hindneck and ear-coverts vermiculated pale, with white line behind eye. Both sexes lack white spotting on black crown (though nape is finely barred pale), male having red feather tips in crown centre.
Similar species In E Peru, range of Plain-breasted overlaps with that of Fine-barred Piculet (25), and the two may possibly hybridise (at least occasionally). Confusion is possible in the field, given the usually poor views obtainable. Fine-barred differs in having white crown and hindneck spots and in male having crown feathers tipped orange-red (rather than red); it also appears somewhat yellower in tone above, more clearly (though still faintly) barred below, and has a somewhat longer tail.

DISTRIBUTION Found on the eastern slope of the Andes from E Ecuador across to SE Amazonas in Colombia, and south through eastern Peru to Pucallpa. Appears to be rare.

HABITAT Swamp and *várzea* forests and forest edge near water. Especially fond of well-developed second growth in which *Cecropia* and *Mimosa* dominate. In lowlands up to 900m.

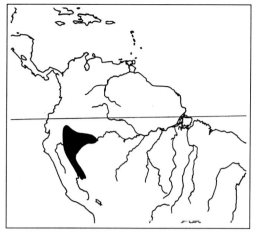

DESCRIPTION
Adult male Lower forehead, lores and nasal tufts buffish-white; upper forehead, crown and nape black, central area of crown with broad red feather tips and lower nape finely vermiculated whitish. Ear-coverts brown, vermiculated grey and whitish, bordered above by white stripe behind eye. Hindneck and neck sides olive-brown, barred/vermiculated buff-grey. Moustachial area, chin, throat and underparts pale yellowish-white, sometimes lightly barred on breast or abdomen, and moustache also sometimes faintly barred towards bill. Upperparts dark greyish-olive, sometimes indistinctly barred paler (dull yellowish). Upperwing-coverts as upperparts, edged and tipped slightly paler yellow-green; flight feathers dark brown, edged paler, with tertials more broadly margined brighter yellow. Underwing grey-brown, with white coverts. Uppertail dark brown, with white stripe on inner webs of central feather pair and on outer three pairs. Undertail much as uppertail.

Adult female As male, but with unmarked black crown.

Juvenile Both sexes resemble adult female, but duller and with stronger hint of barring above and very faint barring below.

Bare parts Apparently undescribed. Presumably much as in related species.

GEOGRAPHICAL VARIATION None known.

MEASUREMENTS Wing 48.5-53.7; tail 25; bill 13. Weight: 11-12.

VOICE A very high-pitched, thin trill, *TE'E'e'e'e'e'e'*, dropping in pitch and amplitude at the end.

HABITS Lives solitarily or in pairs, joining mixed-species flocks only rarely. This species' unhurried behaviour makes it inconspicuous most of the time, although the sound of its pecking often betrays it. Forages in the lower parts of the canopy and below.

FOOD Unknown.

BREEDING Nesting recorded in Colombia in June, generally probably May-July.

REFERENCES Hilty & Brown 1984; Parker *et al.* 1982; Remsen 1977.

---

25 FINE-BARRED PICULET
Picumnus subtilis   Plate 7

Other names: Marcapata Piculet, Stager's Piculet

IDENTIFICATION Length c. 10cm. Tiny, with short, pointed bill curved on culmen. A rare and virtually unknown Peruvian endemic, not described until 1968. Has yellowish-green upperparts, vaguely barred darker, and dull pale greyish to greyish-yellow underparts with indistinct fine dark vermiculations; breast somewhat darker, olive-tinged. Typical piculet head pattern, male with orange-red tips to crown feathers.

Similar species The partly sympatric Plain-breasted Piculet (24), also rare and little known, is most reliably distinguished by its somewhat different head pattern (both sexes); the two may hybridise occasionally.

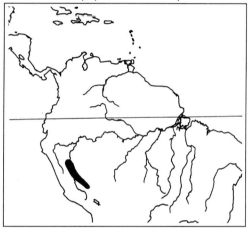

DISTRIBUTION Found only in E Peru, from the Ucayali river in Loreto south to Cuzco. Apparently rare.

HABITAT As Plain-breasted Piculet, a bird of humid tropical forests. Found from the lowlands to Andean foothills at 1000m.

DESCRIPTION
Adult male Forehead and crown feathers black, tipped orange-red (tips broadest/longest on crown); crown sides, nape and hindneck black, spotted white. Nasal tufts and lores pale buff-white. Ear-coverts brownish-olive, barred olive and whitish. Neck sides pale olive-buff, vermiculated darker. Moustachial area pale buffish, barred olive. Chin and throat pale greyish-buff, occasionally finely barred olive. Upperparts yellowish-green with obscure olive barring. Upperwing-coverts dark olive-brown, edged yellowish-green; flight feathers dark brown, narrowly margined yellowish-green, but outer webs of secondaries with broader pale edges (when fresh, forming panel on closed wing). Uppertail dark brown, central feather pair with broad white stripe along inner webs and outer two pairs with narrower white streak inside tip. Breast light olive-grey, becoming paler yellow/buffish-grey on belly and flanks, with fine olive barring/vermiculation (bars strongest on breast, usually indistinct or lacking on belly). Underwing pale brownish, with largely white coverts. Undertail much as uppertail.

Adult female Lacks male's orange-red on head, having black crown spotted white.

Juvenile Rather more heavily barred than adults, but underpart barring more diffuse. Both sexes have brownish-black or sooty-black crown, broadly streaked off-white to buff.

Bare parts Bill black, with blue-grey base to lower mandible. Legs and feet olive, tinged green. Eyes brown. Orbital skin greyish.

GEOGRAPHICAL VARIATION None known.

MEASUREMENTS Wing 48.9-55; tail 25-29; bill 12-14.5; tarsus 12-12.5. Weight: 10-11.

VOICE Unknown.

HABITS Unknown.

FOOD Unknown.

BREEDING Breeding season can tentatively be assumed to be April-July.

REFERENCES Parker *et al.* 1982; Stager 1968b.

26 OLIVACEOUS PICULET
Picumnus olivaceus   Plate 8

Forms a superspecies with *granadensis*.

IDENTIFICATION Length 8.5-10cm. Tiny, with short, pointed bill slightly curved on culmen. A mainly C American species, where the only piculet, and extending a little way into northwestern S America. Olive above, with distinct pale wing edgings and dark ear-covert patch, and paler olive to brownish below, with yellower, brown-streaked belly and flanks. Crown and nape of female are black with very small white dots, while males have crown spots varying from yellow to red.

Similar species Overlaps slightly with Greyish Piculet (27) in Colombia, the latter being told by its paler underparts, browner, less yellowish-olive, upperparts, usually less prominent pale wing edgings, and by the male having yellow (not red) crown spots.

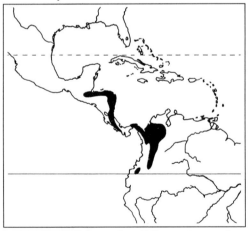

DISTRIBUTION Occurs from E Guatemala, east along the Caribbean slope through N Honduras and Nicaragua, in N and SW Costa Rica and through N and S Panama to N and W Colombia, southwards along the Cauca and Magdalena valleys and to the eastern slope of the Andes; also in the Perijá mountains and SW Táchira in NW Venezuela, and in W Ecuador. Uncommon to fairly common in much of C American range, but status elsewhere less clear.

HABITAT This piculet occurs in a wide variety of habitats in regions with humid rain and cloud forests (mature

stands apparently avoided), mangroves, drier forests, and cultivated lands, where can be found in dense forest edge with many creepers, in second growth and in shrubby clearings. Also in tall scrub, open woodland, shady plantations and gardens. Most frequent in lowlands and foothills, but may also reach higher elevations. In Mexico to 500m; in Panama (Pacific slope, Chiriquí) recorded at up to 1600m; in Venezuela, between 800 and 2300m in Táchira; and in adjacent Colombia to 1800m, rarely to 2500m.

DESCRIPTION

P. o. flavotinctus **Adult male** Forehead to nape black, feathers of upper forehead to central crown with narrow yellow to orange or orange-red tips and hindcrown to nape with very small white spots. Rear lores whitish. Cheeks and ear-coverts brown, tipped white in area below and behind eye. Neck sides brownish-olive. Moustachial area, chin and throat buff to yellowish-white, with narrow dark feather edges producing scaly pattern. Upperparts dark olive to olive-green or brownish-olive, unmarked. Upperwing-coverts dark olive-brown, very narrowly edged yellowish; flight feathers dark brown, edged yellow to yellow-green. Uppertail brown, central feather pair with pale buff/yellowish stripe along inner webs and outer two pairs with diagonal stripe of similar colour. Breast dull olive to pale olive-brown, becoming a paler buffish to dull yellowish on lower underparts, with fairly broad (occasionally finer, usually indistinct) brownish to dusky-olive streaks on belly and, especially, flanks. Underwing brownish-grey, with whitish coverts. Undertail much as uppertail.

Adult female Resembles male, but with tiny white spots covering entire upper forehead and crown (lacks orange).

Juvenile Duller and browner/greyer than adults, and sometimes somewhat paler below and more heavily streaked (occasionally barred/spotted) on belly and flanks. Both sexes have sooty-brown or olive-tinged crown, indistinctly streaked/spotted buff or greyish.

Bare parts Bill black, with greyish base to lower mandible. Legs and feet grey, often tinged blue or green. Eyes dark brown. Orbital skin grey to blue-grey or brownish.

GEOGRAPHICAL VARIATION Six races, differing mainly in tone of plumage and in colour of male's crown spots.

 P. o. flavotinctus (Costa Rica to easternmost Panama) Described above.

 P. o. dimotus (E Guatemala to Nicaragua) Similar to *flavotinctus*, but tends to be slightly greener (less brown) above and on breast and somewhat paler below. Male's crown spots normally more red.

 P. o. olivaceus (much of Colombian part of range) Relatively large. Upperparts tinged yellow, and breast more brownish. Male's crown spots usually bright red.

 P. o. harterti (SW Colombia and W Ecuador) Smaller than nominate *olivaceus*, and generally darker olive (less yellow). Male's crown spots more yellow or golden, less red.

 P. o. tachirensis (Andes in Táchira, Venezuela, and adjacent Norte de Santander, Colombia) About the size of nominate, but greener (less yellow) above and with more olive-grey breast. Male's crown spots vary from orange to yellow.

 P. o. eisenmanni (Perijá mountains in Venezuela/Colombia) Distinctly yellowish above, with more yellow in wings than in other races, and with pale yellowish-olive breast and yellow belly. Male's crown spots as in *tachirensis*.

MEASUREMENTS Wing 48-54; tail 23-30; bill 10.5-13; tarsus 11.5-15.4. Weight: 10-15.

VOICE Fine, rapid twitters or trills, soft and clear (at the hole by arriving partner) or shrill and insect-like (self-announcement), suggesting Yellow-faced Grassquit *Tiaris olivacea* or Worm-eating Warbler *Helmitheros vermivorus*. Also a sharp sibilant *sst, ssip-ssip* or *peep*, sometimes repeated (these calls are, for instance, given by fledglings as response to the trills of their parents). Nestlings utter a continuous buzz. Apparently does not drum.

HABITS Lives singly, in pairs or in family groups of 4-5 birds, and frequently joins mixed-species flocks. Not shy. Usually forages at lower and middle heights in undergrowth, open thickets and low tangles, but also seen to forage in treetops. These piculets apparently avoid trunks and large limbs of tall trees, instead climbing over thin branches, fine twigs and vines. They drill little holes by very rapid hammering into the substrate to get at nests, from which they extract the brood and glean the adults. In addition, they remove other types of insect from dead twigs and vines, peck in the stalks of large leaves (even when fallen and caught up in vines or branches), perforate them and extract grubs. Without using the tail for support, they creep up and down much as one would expect from a woodpecker, although many movements recall a nuthatch *Sitta* or a xenops *Xenops*, and even a typical songbird, when perched upright. Roosts are made at any season; roosts singly, in pairs or as a family group.

FOOD Ants (e.g. *Camponotus, Pseudomyrmex, Crematogaster*), termites and their brood comprise the main part of the diet, species which live in hollow twigs being particularly important. Also takes cockroach eggs and beetles.

BREEDING Breeding records extend from (December) January to May in Costa Rica and Panama, and from February to September in Colombia. Nest a shallow cavity with circular entrance barely 2.5 cm in diameter, carved by both sexes 0.9-2 (9)m up in slender stubs with very soft wood, or in rotting fence post if fence near thicket; this work takes about 1-4 weeks, but may be accomplished within 4-5 days. Clutch of 2 or 3 eggs. Both parents sleep in the nest before egg-laying and also during incubation, the male entering first to roost. Both incubate, though the male seems to do more. The chicks hatch after 14 days and are fed by both parents, this time the female's share appearing to be greater. The young leave the nest for the first time after 24-25 days, but are led back to the nest, where the whole family continues to sleep for 4-15 weeks. Young of the first brood remain and roost with the parents while a second brood is incubated, at least until hatching.

REFERENCES Hilty & Brown 1984; Howell & Webb in press; Meyer de Schauensee & Phelps 1978; Otvos 1967; Ridgely & Gwynne 1989; Skutch 1948b, 1969, 1985; Stiles & Skutch 1989; Wetmore 1968.

---

27 GREYISH PICULET
Picumnus granadensis   Plate 8

Forms a superspecies with *olivaceus*.

IDENTIFICATION Length c. 9-10cm. Tiny, with short, pointed bill curved on culmen. A virtually unknown Colombian endemic. Brownish above and whitish to pale grey below (slightly streaked on some), with chestnut ear-coverts and scaly throat pattern. Males have yellow-spotted black forehead and crown and white-spotted black nape, while females have top of head wholly spotted white.

Similar species Where range overlaps with that of closely related Olivaceous Piculet (26), latter is distinguished by its more olive-toned upperparts, its darker underparts, the white spotting on its ear-coverts, and by the male having red (not yellow) crown spots, the latter often forming a patch.

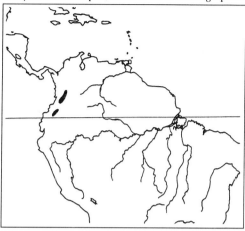

DISTRIBUTION Found only on the Andean slopes of Colombia, where it occurs in Antioquia and in the valleys and adjacent slopes of the Cauca, Dagua and Patía rivers.

HABITAT The Greyish Piculet, endemic in Colombia, occupies similar habitats to those of the preceding species, which it replaces geographically in the Cauca valley and adjacent valleys of the dry Pacific slope. It inhabits edges of dry to moderately humid forests, second growth, scrub and woodland at elevations from 800 to 2100m.

DESCRIPTION
P. g. granadensis **Adult male** Forehead back to upper hindneck black, finely tipped yellow on forehead and crown and tipped white from rear crown to hindneck. Lores white. Ear-coverts chestnut-brown, sometimes with a few white streaks. Neck sides grey-brown, this colour extending slightly onto upper breast sides. Cheeks, moustachial area, chin and throat off-white, with narrow blackish feather tips (latter often lacking on throat). Lower hindneck and upperparts greyish-brown, often tinged olive. Upperwing and its coverts dark brown, edged yellowish-green. Uppertail dark brown, central feather pair with broad white stripe along inner webs and outer two pairs with diagonal subterminal white stripe. Underparts below throat dull white, tinged greyish on breast sides, and sometimes with very fine greyish streaks on flanks. Underwing pale brownish, with coverts patterned grey and white. Undertail much as uppertail.

Adult female As male, but with crown spotted white (lacks yellow).

Juvenile Duller and darker than adults, with greyish underparts more clearly streaked. Both sexes have sooty-black crown streaked off-white.

Bare parts Bill blackish. Legs and feet grey, tinged blue or green. Eyes brown. Orbital skin grey-blue.

GEOGRAPHICAL VARIATION Two races are recognised.

>*P. g. granadensis* (central Cauca valley southwards) Described above.

>*P. g. antioquensis* (Antioquia) Greyer below than nominate, especially on throat and breast, and with more obvious grey streaking on belly and flanks.

MEASUREMENTS Wing 52.1-57.7. Weight: 12-13.

VOICE Calls infrequently, a high-pitched weak trill

which remains on one pitch.

HABITS This species' behaviour seems to be similar to that of its close relative the Olivaceous Piculet, but no details are known.

FOOD Unknown.

BREEDING So far as is known, the breeding period extends from January to about June.

REFERENCE Hilty & Brown 1984.

---

28 CHESTNUT PICULET
Picumnus cinnamomeus   Plate 5

IDENTIFICATION Length 9-10cm. Tiny, with short, stout, pointed bill slightly curved on culmen. A very distinctive piculet: entire plumage rufous or chestnut, apart from brown wings, pale-spotted black crown, large pale forehead patch, and typical pale tail stripes. Male has yellow spots on crown, and both sexes have a broad yellow ring around eye.

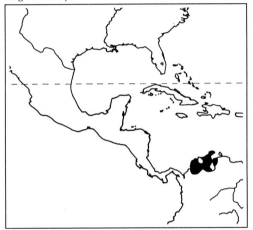

DISTRIBUTION Known only from NE Colombia and NW Venezuela, from Bolivar north to the coastal region and east to the eastern shores of Lake Maracaibo. Apparently rare, and very little known.

HABITAT Occurs in a wide range of habitats, being found in rain forest, humid coffee plantations, deciduous forest and open terrain with scattered trees, and in arid and semi-arid scrub, dry forest borders, and mangroves; fond of thickets, tangles and thorny woodland. Lives at elevations from sea level to 100m in Venezuela, and up to 300m in Colombia.

DESCRIPTION
P. c. cinnamomeus **Adult male** Forehead, lores and nasal tufts pale creamy-white; crown to nape black, feathers tipped yellow on crown (broadest at rear) and white on rear crown and nape. Rest of body plumage entirely deep rufous to rusty-brown, becoming a shade paler on rump and belly. Upperwing and its coverts dark brown, edged and tipped cinnamon or rufous. Uppertail brownish-black, central feather pair with broad pale cinnamon (occasionally buffy or whitish) stripe along inner webs and outer two pairs with stripe of similar colour on outer web. Underwing greyish-brown, with rufous coverts. Undertail much as uppertail.
Adult female As male, but lacks yellow on crown, having

white spots confined to rear crown and nape.

Juvenile Insufficient information. Presumably similar to adult female, but with duller plumage and possibly with streaked crown.

Bare parts Bill blackish. Legs and feet grey. Eyes brown. Orbital skin yellow.

GEOGRAPHICAL VARIATION Four races, showing slight differences in depth of colour and in head pattern.
> *P. c. cinnamomeus* (coastal Colombia and Magdalena river) Described above.
> *P. c. persaturatus* (Serranía de San Jerónimo in Bolivar, Colombia) Darker than nominate, more dark chestnut, with brighter wing edgings but more obscurely patterned tail. Females have crown fully spotted with white.
> *P. c. perijanus* (northern Lake Maracaibo, Venezuela) Darker than nominate, more chestnut (but less dark than *persaturatus*). Females with fully spotted crown.
> *P. c. venezuelensis* (southern and eastern shores of Lake Maracaibo) As dark as *persaturatus*, and with forehead more cinnamon-tawny in colour. Females have white crown spots restricted to forecrown.

MEASUREMENTS Wing (50.3) 55-58; tail 26-29; bill 13-15.

VOICE Unknown.

HABITS This species is met with singly, in pairs, and sometimes in small family groups; also known to join mixed-species groups. Very active, though not shy, and easier to spot than most other piculets as it tends to forage in dense thickets and thickly tangled vines. Forages in almost all strata.

FOOD Unknown.

BREEDING In Colombia, the breeding season seems to range from December to March.

REFERENCES Haffer 1961; Hilty & Brown 1984; Meyer de Schauensee & Phelps 1978.

---

29 AFRICAN PICULET
Sasia africana   Plate 2

IDENTIFICATION Length c. 9-10cm. Tiny, with short, pointed bill curved on culmen and broad and very rounded at base. Very small size combined with dark appearance and very short tail distinctive, but difficult to see as it continuously darts about rapidly low down in dense undergrowth. Mainly dark grey, with greenish upperparts and yellow edges to wings; has short white line behind eye and white arc at lower rear ear-coverts, as well as red/reddish legs and bare orbital ring. Male has chestnut forehead. Unlikely to be confused once seen well.

Similar species None - the only African Piculet.

DISTRIBUTION Ranges from S Cameroon south to N W Angola, and eastwards through SW Central African Republic and most of Zaïre (excluding northernmost parts and the south and southeast) to Bwamba Forest in SW Uganda. Locally abundant, as in parts of Gabon, and common in Bwamba, but generally uncommon; its habits, however, make it likely to be overlooked.

MOVEMENTS Essentially resident. Single isolated records from Ghana and possibly also Nigeria presumably represent abnormally long-distance dispersal.

HABITAT Reasonably common in secondary forest at 700m(?). Prefers old second growth to open primary forest.

DESCRIPTION

Adult male Forehead chestnut to rufous; crown to hindneck olive-green to greyish-olive. Lores and thin rear eye-stripe blackish, latter bordered above by short white line; short arc of white bordering lower rear ear-coverts. Rest of head rather dark grey, often streaked darker on ear-coverts. Chin and throat dark olive-grey. Entire upperparts dark green, tinged yellow, duller on uppertail-coverts. Upperwing-coverts, secondaries and tertials as upperparts or slightly darker, but with brighter yellow fringes; primaries brownish-black, whitish on inner webs, outer webs narrowly edged and tipped yellow. Uppertail (tail has 8 feathers) brownish-black, feathers edged olive/greenish. Entire underparts darkish grey, often somewhat paler on belly, and with variably slight to strong olive tinge. Underwing mostly whitish. Undertail much as uppertail.

Adult female As male but slightly longer-winged, and lacks chestnut on forehead (which is concolorous with crown).

Juvenile Differs from adults in having grey and buffy tones admixed in mantle and back, and rufous-tipped feathers on head (especially ear-coverts) and underparts (especially throat, belly and flanks). Male generally shows chestnut colour on forehead.

Bare parts Bill black, paler on lower mandible. Legs and feet reddish to purple-red. Eyes red; brown in juveniles. Bare orbital skin light red to pale purple-red or pinkish-purple.

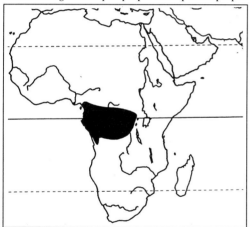

GEOGRAPHICAL VARIATION None. Monotypic.

MEASUREMENTS Wing of male 46-49, of female 47-53; tail of male 16-21, of female 17-21; tarsus of male 10.4-11.8, of female 10.9-11.4. Weight: 7.5-10.5.

VOICE A weak high trill, *ti-ti-ti-...*, is the only call on record.

HABITS Commonly seen in pairs or in threes; occasionally joins mixed flocks of forest birds. Hops and flies through the lower storeys of the vegetation, forages in bushes and also clings to the often slippery stems of larger herbaceous plants and grass. Despite their small size, these piculets hammer vigorously into the substrate and split it open to get at their prey. Constantly on the move, and a fast flier, this miniature woodpecker is difficult to observe and to follow.

FOOD The staple food consists of wood-boring beetle larvae; adult beetles and other insects are taken, too. Ants seem to play no role in the diet.

BREEDING The known laying dates span June-February. The nest is low down at 1-5m in a slender stub. Clutch usually of 2 eggs. Both parents take part in raising the brood.

REFERENCES Chapin 1939; Short 1988.

30 RUFOUS PICULET
Sasia abnormis **Plate 2**

IDENTIFICATION Length c. 9cm. Tiny, with relatively long, pointed bill curved on culmen and broad and rounded at base. Has only three toes. Almost tailless. Green above, with rufous face and underparts; male has a yellow forehead (rufous on female), and both sexes have a red orbital ring. Juveniles are greyer below.

Similar species In southernmost Burma and adjacent Thailand, where range overlaps with that of White-browed Piculet (31), distinguished from latter by having rufous superciliary area, lacking white stripe behind eye, and by red (not blackish) orbital ring and paler bill. Somewhat longer primary projection of White-browed is difficult to observe in the field, particularly in view of the restless behaviour and rapid movements of both species.

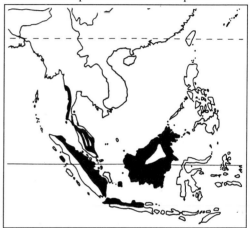

DISTRIBUTION Occurs from S Burma (Tenasserim) and peninsular Thailand, southwards through Malaya to Sumatra, including Nias and Belitung Islands, W and C Java and Borneo. Fairly common in Thailand and in Sumatra and Borneo, but said to be uncommon in Malaya (absent Singapore); difficult to observe, however, and probably overlooked. Its status in Burma requires investigation.

HABITAT Secondary forest with old decaying trees, swamp forests and to a lesser extent primary forest are the main habitats. Dense second growth, particularly bamboo groves, and other low and dense vegetation are preferred. Because of this predilection, Rufous Piculets are often found near water. It inhabits lowlands and hills up to 800m (Borneo, Sumatra) and even to 1300m (Malaya, Thailand).

DESCRIPTION

S. a. abnormis **Adult male** Forehead yellow, sometimes admixed with rufous; crown to hindneck yellowish-green. Rest of head and neck, including superciliary area and chin and throat, rufous to orange-rufous, generally darker on ear-coverts. Upperparts yellowish-green (as crown), with rump partly or wholly rufous, and with black uppertail-coverts. Upperwing-coverts, secondaries and tertials green, feathers edged yellow; primaries brown, inner webs edged rufous (outer webs sometimes edged dark rufous). Uppertail (tail has 10 feathers) black, feathers edged dull olive. Entire underparts rufous, usually washed yellow on flanks. Underwing whitish, with pale rufous/cinnamon primary patch. Undertail as uppertail.

Adult female Very slightly larger than male in bill, wing and tail measurements; forehead rufous, not yellow.

Juvenile Generally darker than adults, with variable amount of grey elements in plumage of upperparts and underparts, as well as in crown and forehead.

Bare parts Bill grey to brown on upper mandible, with yellow lower mandible. Legs and feet (three toes) dull yellow to orange. Eyes red to orange-rufous; brown in juveniles. Orbital skin dark red to purplish.

GEOGRAPHICAL VARIATION Two races, differing only in bill size.

 S. a. abnormis (entire range of species, except Nias Island) Described above.

 S. a. magnirostris (Nias Island) Differs from nominate only in having a longer and deeper bill.

MEASUREMENTS Wing 48-56; tail 21-28; bill 11.4-14.5; tarsus 12.7. Weight: 7.2-12.

VOICE Single, sharp *ssit*, *tic* or *tsit*, usually repeated several times. Also a rapid, insistent *kih-kih-kih-kih-kih* or *kik-ik-ik-ik-ik-ik*, high-pitched and loud. Drums loudly in rolls of 1.5-2 secs in duration.

HABITS Because of its fast movements, this tiny piculet, which is sometimes met with in parties of four or five, is hard to observe. Forages at low and middle levels, hardly over 5m above ground, on trunks, dead branches, vines, bamboo, shrubs and saplings. Its tiny size allows this woodpecker to feed even on grasses in the understorey. Foraging techniques include quiet, but persistent, pecking and gleaning. Ants in bamboo are reached by excavating small holes and are then obtained with the aid of the long tongue. Moves very rapidly through dense vegetation, and often flies greater distances from one spot to another rather than proceeding steadily from tree to tree. Often perches crosswise and moves upwards in short flights, thereby changing the direction in which it faces. Families stay together for a rather long time, and the three or four birds of a group move almost simultaneously.

FOOD Ants and their larvae; small barle beetles; soft insects and their larvae; spiders.

BREEDING Nestlings have been found in May and June in W Malaysia and in February in Borneo. Nest is built into dead branches and bamboo. Broods contain two chicks.

REFERENCES Lekagul & Round 1991; MacKinnon 1990; MacKinnon & Phillipps 1993; Medway & Wells 1976; Robinson 1928; Short 1973, 1978; Smythies 1981.

---

31   WHITE-BROWED PICULET
Sasia ochracea   Plate   2

Other names: Himalayan Rufous Piculet, Burmese Rufous Piculet

IDENTIFICATION Length c. 9-10cm. Tiny, with shortish, pointed bill curved on culmen, and broad and rounded at base. Has only three toes. With its rufous face and underparts, green/greenish upperparts and almost tailless appearance, bears an overall resemblance to Rufous Piculet (30), but has a white stripe from eye to side of nape and at least some (sometimes much) rufous in green of upperparts. Forehead and central forecrown are rufous, male also having a yellow centre to forehead, and both sexes have a reddish orbital ring (black in *reichenowi* of S Burma and SW Thailand). Juveniles are greener above and greyer below.

Similar species Race *reichenowi* overlaps in range with very similar Rufous Piculet in southernmost Burma and adja-

cent Thailand; in good views, readily told from latter by white 'eyebrow' bordering green of rear crown (green reaching to eye), darker bill and blackish orbital ring.

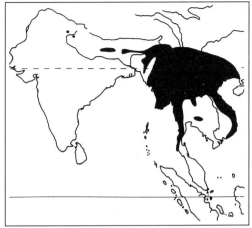

DISTRIBUTION Resident from N India (Gahrwal) and southern Nepal eastwards to Burma and S China (Yunnan, Guangxi), and south to Tenasserim, Burma, SW and peninsular Thailand and Indochina; probably present in Cambodia, but not yet recorded from there. Fairly common in Thailand and Burma and described as not uncommon elsewhere in range, but uncommon in Nepal and rare in China; as with other piculets, its unobtrusive behaviour no doubt leads to its being overlooked.

HABITAT Occurs in evergreen and mixed deciduous forest, but generally prefers bamboo forest; frequents mixed secondary scrub, and avoids open country. Its altitudinal range includes the plains and moderate elevations up to 1850m in SE Asia, and over 2100m in Nepal and Sikkim.

DESCRIPTION
S. o. ochracea **Adult male** Forehead to centre of forecrown rufous to orange-rufous, with bright golden-yellow patch in centre of forehead; rest of crown to hindneck olive-green, variably tinged rufous. White eye-stripe behind eye, extending to side of nape. Lores, cheeks, ear-coverts and sides of neck rufous to cinnamon-rufous, somewhat darker on ear-coverts and lores. Chin and throat similarly rufous. Upperparts green, with variable element of rufous, becoming mainly rufous on rump; uppertail-coverts blackish. Upperwing and its coverts brown, edged and tipped green to yellow-green (broadly so on coverts and tertials), primaries with buffish edge to inner webs. Uppertail (tail has 10 feathers) brownish-black, feathers narrowly edged greenish. Entire underparts deep rufous, sometimes with just a hint of yellowish on flanks and breast centre. Underwing mostly buffish-white. Undertail as above, but somewhat paler.

Adult female As male, but with forehead entirely rufous, lacking golden-yellow patch.

Juvenile Much as respective adult, but with upperparts greener, less rufous-tinged, and underparts with variably strong element of grey or green.

Bare parts Bill black on upper mandible, lower mandible with grey base and becoming generally paler towards tip. Legs and feet (three toes) orange, sometimes yellower. Eyes red. Orbital skin pinkish-red, often paler in female.

GEOGRAPHICAL VARIATION Three races.
 S. o. ochracea (N India east to Vietnam) Described

above. A rather variable race. Populations of S Assam east to at least Burma (formerly separated as '*querulivox*') tend to be paler in general plumage coloration, with more rufous in upperparts (mantle to rump sometimes entirely pale rufous), but similar individuals may be found scattered through other northeastern parts of the range.

S. o. reichenowi (= '*hasbroucki*'; S Burma and adjacent Thailand) Differs most obviously from nominate race in having bare orbital skin blackish (not pink-red), and often black-tipped feathers to lores; white rear eye-stripe may also be a trifle shorter.

S. o. kinneari (northernmost Vietnam and adjacent Yunnan to Guangxi in China) Similar to nominate, but darker overall.

MEASUREMENTS Wing 48-56; tail 22-24; bill 12-15.5; tarsus 14-15. Weight: 8.3-11.8.

VOICE A high-pitched, staccato trill, *ti-i-i-i-i*, given both in flight and when climbing or perched. Also single *tsick* notes. During close contact at courtship, series of weak squeaks are given. Drums loudly.

HABITS This diminutive woodpecker is not shy and may be met with singly, in pairs or, at times, in small groups of four or five. Joins mixed-species flocks. Moves rapidly through dense vegetation near the ground; climbs bamboo, particularly when fallen, stems of shrubs, and vines. May be seen foraging on the ground, too, with short tail cocked like a wren *Troglodytes*. Does not excavate for wood-dwelling larvae, although nuthatch-like pecking is heard frequently. It is not clear whether the short fluttering flights returning to the same perch, mentioned by Smythies (1953), refer to aerial hunting or to some kind of display. For instance, prior to copulation the male courts the female by flying above her, backs up to her position, drops lower, moves up rapidly again to a place above her and so on; this may be repeated several times, and is associated with calls.

FOOD Ants and their brood, spiders, and small bark-beetles.

BREEDING The breeding season extends from March to July. Nest is a tiny hole, excavated at low heights in dead bamboo or narrow tree stump, with entrance just below a node, or in a branch. Lays 2-4 eggs.

REFERENCES Ali 1962; Ali & Ripley 1970; Inskipp & Inskipp 1991; Lekagul & Round 1991; Robinson 1928; Smythies 1953; Stanford & Mayr 1941; Stresemann & Heinrich 1940.

---

32 ANTILLEAN PICULET
Nesoctites micromegas   Plate 8

IDENTIFICATION Length c. 14-16cm. Small, with short, pointed bill curved on culmen and narrow and flattened between nostrils. An unmistakable bird, confined to Hispaniola. Has olive-green upperparts, dark-streaked pale underparts, barred ear-coverts and a yellow crown, male also having red central patch on nape/hindcrown. A rather noisy species, pair members frequently calling to each other.

DISTRIBUTION Found only on Hispaniola, including the island of Gonâve off Haiti.

HABITAT Humid to dry primary and secondary forest, both in lowlands and in mountains, and mixed desert scrub and thorn forest in semi-arid regions; most numerous in

latter environment. Dense undergrowth is favoured. Also found in orchards and in cultivations, avoiding, however, open plantations and palm groves. Reaches pine-forest zone in the mountains, in which middle elevations around 500m are preferred, even though it may be found at least to 1750m.

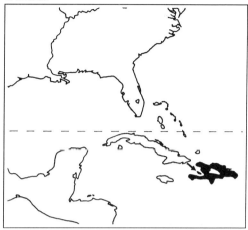

DESCRIPTION

N. m. micromegas Adult male Forehead, crown sides and hindneck yellowish-green; crown to nape lemon-yellow (extent variable), with patch of orange-red to dull red in centre of hindcrown/nape, latter sometimes with a few white spots. (Some individuals, of both sexes, have forehead and crown sides blackish.) Ear-coverts dull whitish, barred olive, becoming more uniform olive-grey on neck side. Lores and moustachial region white, spotted/barred greyish-olive. Chin and throat white, faintly tinged yellow, with a few small dark spots. Upperparts dull olive-green to yellow-green, faintly tinged rusty-bronze on mantle and scapulars. Upperwing-coverts and tertials as mantle, edged and tipped brighter and paler greenish; primaries and secondaries brown, edged yellowish-green. Uppertail brownish-olive, suffused bronze. Underparts below throat pale yellowish-white, sometimes deeper yellow (or even pale golden) on breast, all with variably broad dark streaks. Underwing greyish-olive. Undertail much as uppertail.

Adult female Somewhat larger than male, and without red on hindcrown.

Juvenile Duller overall than adults, both sexes having crown pattern as adult female but with yellow colour less bright; belly vaguely barred, rather than streaked. Juveniles may apparently lose crown feathers and become bare-crowned for a short period, but soon acquire adult feathers.

Bare parts Bill blackish. Legs and feet green-grey. Eyes brown to red-brown or red.

GEOGRAPHICAL VARIATION Two very similar races.
    N. m. micromegas (entire range apart from Gonâve Island) Described above.
    N. m. abbotti (Gonâve Island) Differs from nominate race in being paler, with greyer (less green) upperparts; both sexes show smaller area of yellow on crown, restricted more to crown centre.

MEASUREMENTS Wing 66-77; tail 37-44; bill 15-18; tarsus 17-18.5. Weight: 26-33.

VOICE Single mechanical *pit* and *pew* notes indicate various degrees of alarm and may also be associated with the most prominent vocalisation, which is a loud, rapid whistling *kuk-ki-ki-ki-ke-ku-kuk*. Woodpecker-like in quality, although very musical, this latter is a long-distance signal exchanged frequently between members of a pair and given also during territorial encounters. In close proximity to another piculet, short series of weak notes, *wiii*, are uttered. During fights, a continuous noisy chatter, *yeh-yeh-yeh-yeh*, is heard. Apparently does not drum.

HABITS Occurs singly or in pairs which keep loose contact. Difficult to observe because of its agility. Forages on vines, small branches and twigs, stalks of herbaceous plants, and leaf clusters, much less commonly on trunks. Although mainly flitting through the understorey below 8m it may move up to the crown, from where it departs to another feeding site. Often perches and moves in a passerine manner, zigzagging through entangled vegetation. This is more noticeable than with other piculets, which similarly do not use their soft tail as a brace when climbing. This impression is reinforced through its way of foraging, which recalls a vireo or tanager and comprises mainly gleaning. The occasional pecks are weak and often directed laterally. Probes on fruits and flowers, and in leaf or pine-needle clusters. Moves rapidly within the undergrowth and from one foraging site to the next, which may be some distance away. The flight also is not woodpecker-like, being fast and direct without distinct undulations. Displays with lateral jerks, with brief pauses at the culmination of each swing, head a little raised, the bill pointing slightly upwards. This piculet seems to be rather territorial and does not form groups.

FOOD Mainly insects, ants, small beetles, but other kinds of arthropods have been found, too. Also takes larger amounts of fruit.

BREEDING Holes low (below 5m) in stubs and fence posts. The clutch comprises 2-4 eggs and is produced in March-July. Since the female is significantly larger than the male, details of the reproductive behaviour promise to be interesting.

REFERENCES Bond 1985; Short 1974a; Wetmore & Swales 1931.

---

33 WHITE WOODPECKER
Melanerpes candidus   Plate 9

IDENTIFICATION Length c. 24cm. Small to medium-sized, with longish, slightly chisel-tipped bill curved on culmen and moderately broad across nostrils. A totally distinctive woodpecker: mainly white, with black mantle, wings and tail and a black stripe from eye and down neck side; the broad yellow ring around eye is often prominent in the field. Both sexes have a yellow patch on lower belly, and males also have a small area of yellow on hindneck.

DISTRIBUTION From lower Amazon south through Brazil to eastern Bolivia, Paraguay, western Uruguay and Argentina (La Rioja, Entre Ríos); also Peru, southern and coastal Surinam and French Guiana.

HABITAT Dry subtropical forest, woodland and open wooded areas, savannas with scattered trees, and dry scrub areas are the major habitats. Often found at forest edge and in cultivated areas, where it inhabits palm groves and orchards. From lowlands to locally about 2200m.

DESCRIPTION
Adult male Entire head white to creamy-white, occasionally slightly buff-tinged, apart from dusky to blackish loral line and narrow black stripe from lower rear corner behind eye that curves backwards and down neck side to mantle;

lower hindneck pale lemon-yellow. Mantle, scapulars, upper back, upperwing-coverts and tertials black, slightly glossed blue; lower back, rump and uppertail-coverts white. Flight feathers brownish-black. Uppertail brownish-black, with white of base extending beyond uppertail-coverts, and usually with a few white spots in distal part of outer feathers. Underparts white to creamy-white or pale buffish-white, with yellow patch of variable extent in centre of lower belly (occasionally reaching to feather tips of lower breast). Underwing grey-brown, with black coverts. Undertail as uppertail. (Note that white parts of plumage often become stained brownish, especially on underparts and around face.)

Adult female As male, but lacks yellow on hindneck; black head stripe often duller, more obscure.

Juvenile Much as adults, but dark areas browner and less glossy, white areas more buff-tinged, and yellow on belly duller. Young males have yellow extending from hindneck/nape to crown; females have broken band of yellow in nape area.

Bare parts Bill black, paler (even greenish or whitish) at base. Legs and feet olive to grey-green or brownish. Eyes white to pale bluish-white or yellow; grey in juveniles. Orbital skin a very broad ring of golden-yellow; possibly bluish in juveniles.

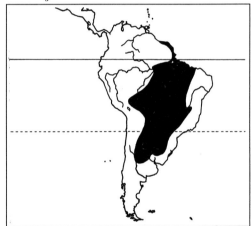

GEOGRAPHICAL VARIATION None. Monotypic.

MEASUREMENTS Wing 154-167; tail 99-109; bill 25-31. Weight: (68)98-136.

VOICE A very distinctive *kirr-kirr-kirr* or *cree-cree-cree-creek*, recalling a tern *Sterna*, is given in flight. The common call when perched may be rendered as *ghirreh* or *kreer*.

HABITS Usually seen in small groups. An arboreal woodpecker which forages with gleaning and pecking and which also takes fruits. Opens nests of wild bees and of wasps to take their brood and honey. Occasionally catches insects on the wing, and even observed feeding on meat hung up to dry. Often visits more open places, and to reach certain foraging sites long distances may be flown. Hence, individuals or small groups may be seen crossing open country in relatively straight (non-undulating) flapping flight, pausing to forage on any trees they happen across. In the breeding season, display flights can be observed. Other displays include bobbing and bowing similar to its closer relatives. Appears to be rather social, though details of social organisation are insufficiently known.

FOOD The favourite food is plant material, fruits, seeds and honey. Also takes insects. Seems to afflict commercial fruit plantations (e.g. oranges) locally.

BREEDING The nesting season spans September to November. Apparently able to use holes among rocks. The clutch of 3-4 eggs is incubated by both parents. Many more data are needed, especially concerning possible communal breeding.

REFERENCES Dubs 1992; Gore & Gepp 1978; Olrog 1984; Parker *et al.* 1982; Short 1970a, 1975; Sick 1993.

---

34 LEWIS'S WOODPECKER
Melanerpes lewis   Plate 9

IDENTIFICATION Length c. 26-29cm. Small to medium-sized, with longish, almost pointed bill slightly curved on culmen and fairly broad across nostrils. An unmistakable glossy greenish-black woodpecker with a deep crimson face, silvery breast and collar and silvery-pink belly. Juveniles lack the crimson and silvery colours on head, which is browner, and show some barring on underparts. A migratory species; in flight, appears very dark and crow-like, flying with slow beats in a straight line (not undulating). Often markedly gregarious, sometimes in large flocks in winter. Has distinctive 'flycatching' behaviour, hunting insects both from a perch and in circling flight.

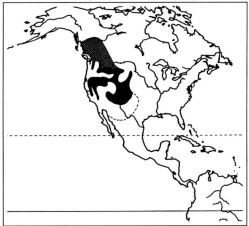

DISTRIBUTION Western N America along the coastal ranges from southern British Columbia south to Arizona and New Mexico. In the east reaches South Dakota, Wyoming and Colorado.

MOVEMENTS Because of the marked changes in the diet, Lewis's Woodpeckers have to move greater or lesser distances to wintering areas which provide acorns or nuts. Before arriving at the wintering grounds, nomadic flocks may exploit other habitats in the mountains or visit orchards. If suitable winter habitats are very close by, distances covered are small; some birds (about half of the population in SE Colorado) may even remain resident throughout the year. Populations of Idaho, Wyoming and Montana are forced to migrate longer distances. Winter range includes parts of Oregon, occasionally staying in British Columbia, in the north down to C Texas in the south; irregularly down to Mexico (from Baja California to N Chihuahua; rarely N Coahuila). Weather conditions and the distribution of acorn crops heavily influence winter distribution. Migration can be rather spectacular, with more than 2,000 birds passing a particular place in one hour (flocks are not organised). Arrives on the winter grounds in late September and the first half of October,

staying until late April. Autumn migration is more nomadic than that in spring, which therefore takes less time.

HABITAT The common feature of breeding habitats is their openness. Some dead trees with decayed wood are needed for nesting and as hawking perches, and rich food sources are also required. Open pine forests, especially ponderosa, constitute the most important natural habitat, others being logged or burned forests and open riparian woodland; some pairs nest in orchards. In areas of contact, Red-headed Woodpeckers (37) prefer riverine woodland and clearings, whereas Lewis's Woodpeckers are more likely on cultivated land and on edges. In winter, food supply is the most important aspect of habitat selection, and oak woodland and commercial orchards (almond, walnut, pecan) are therefore common winter settings; local supply of corn may also be important. Winter altitudinal range spans from sea level to 2000m.

DESCRIPTION
Adult Sexes alike in plumage. Head black, glossed green, with deep crimson-red (black-based) feathers on lower forehead, lores, around eye, and on moustachial region and cheeks; band of silvery-grey (black-based) feathers on rear neck sides usually forms narrow collar around hindneck and also continues broadly across entire breast. Chin and throat brownish-black. Entire upperparts, including upperwing and its coverts and uppertail, black, with strong green gloss, gloss normally somewhat more blue-green on flight feathers (secondaries occasionally with small white tips, and rarely outer tail narrowly edged white). Belly silvery-pink, becoming greenish-black on lower flanks and undertail-coverts. Underwing and undertail blackish-brown.

Juvenile Drabber and less glossy than adults, with head and neck browner, with no (or only very little) red on face and without silvery collar; underparts with dull red on belly, and variably barred whitish and brown. Has prolonged moult, acquiring adult plumage gradually, sometimes not fully until autumn/early winter (when family breaks up).

Bare parts Bill slaty-grey to blackish. Legs and feet bluish to blue-black. Eyes dark reddish-brown; brown in juveniles.

GEOGRAPHICAL VARIATION None. Monotypic.

MEASUREMENTS Wing 155-180; tail 83-102; bill 25.5-33; tarsus 23-26.5. Weight: 85-138.

VOICE Series of short, rather loud and harsh *churr* calls, usually three to eight times in quick succession, are common during the breeding season, uttered by males. They are about half as long as the equivalent calls of Red-headed Woodpecker. Throughout the year chatter-calls can be heard which comprise rapidly descending series of short squeaks; given most frequently in encounters of any kind, intra- or interspecifically. Males give single *yick* notes when alarmed; females utter double *yick-ick* notes in same situation. When approached by the parents, young render 'begging' calls. Drumming, infrequent and restricted to the courtship period, consists of a weak roll followed by three or four individual taps.

HABITS This is probably the most specialised of all woodpeckers in flycatching. Flights are initiated from prominent perches, from where much time is spent scanning the surroundings for prey. Prey is approached in a crow-like flight, and elaborate manoeuvres lead to the final capture; when possible, gliding is used in returning to the perch. Over 10% of flycatching is performed in continuous flights lasting several minutes, and in which several insects may be taken. Near scanning posts insects are also taken on the ground or in low brush, where the species shows considerable agility when moving among outer branches. When gleaning it progresses slowly, probes, taps lightly, chips off small pieces of bark, and most frequently searches visually for prey. In autumn, acorns (or nuts) are harvested, shelled and stored in natural crevices; cracks may occasionally be widened by the woodpecker, but it does not drill individual holes for each acorn. Nuts are shelled in several anvils. Stores are tended by moving acorns around, which inhibits fungal growth. If superabundant, insects, such as swarming carpenter ants (*Camponotus*), are also stored in cracks near the nest and fed to the young later. No feeding territories are maintained, but individual food caches are defended vigorously. Competition is most intense for the mast accumulated in the stores, with the Acorn Woodpecker (38) the main competitor. Other species involved commonly in direct interactions are flickers, Nuttall's Woodpecker (111), Red-headed Woodpeckers (rarely), titmice, and, in the breeding season, starlings. Males display in two ways, both in territorial disputes and in courtship. In the 'wing-out' display, the bird usually perches on a horizontal limb, with wings extended, head lowered, and the silvery feathers of the throat and upper breast fluffed up. The 'circle-flight', in which the male circles its nest tree in a smooth glide with wings extended and held at a high angle, ends at the nest entrance, where the *churr* call is uttered; the male possibly uses this display to show the female a prospective nest. In both displays, the pink feathers of the flanks and the belly are conspicuously exposed. Wing-spreading and other more aggressive displays, for instance postures with the bill straight and the body rather upright, are also used in interspecific disputes. Copulations may be initiated by the female with reversed mounting. Lewis's Woodpeckers are rather philopatric, and seem to pair monogamously for life. Young and adults stay together in migrating flocks. On arrival at the wintering grounds, when mast stores are established, flocks break up and probably all individuals try to found and defend their own stores.

FOOD In spring and summer feeds on insects, fruits and berries, and in winter on acorns and nuts obtained from stores laid up in autumn. Only when this latter type of crop is in ample supply, as in almond plantations or exceptionally in corn silos, may they do without stored mast. The nestlings are fed with insects and berries. The animal food includes various insects, grasshoppers, crickets, ants, beetles, mayflies and so on. Wild berries of various kinds and cherries are commonly taken fruits.

BREEDING Nests generally during May to July, with April and September the extreme limits. Populations in the south of the range or at low altitudes breed one to three weeks later than their northern or upland counterparts. Nests can be found 1.5-5.2m up in sycamores, conifers, oaks and other trees, and even in electricity poles; about three-quarters of nests are in dead stubs. The depth of the nest cavity ranges from 22.8 to 76.2cm; the entrance is 5-7.5cm. Unlike most woodpeckers, Lewis's only infrequently excavates completely new nest holes and may breed in the same nest in consecutive years, or males may select their winter roosts. If forced to establish a new nest, prefers to adapt natural hollows or flicker holes. The male defends the immediate nest vicinity from intruders. Clutch size ranges from 6 to 7 (4-9) eggs (average 5.88), increasing from south to north. Incubation takes about 14 days. The nestling period lasts from four to five weeks. Both parents seem to contribute equally to feeding and to brooding, but the male alone spends the night in the nest and possibly removes feacal sacs more often. After the young fledge, each parent

accompanies part of the brood. Both partial families stay in the vicinity of the nest for about ten days.

REFERENCES Bent 1939; Bock 1970; Bock *et al.* 1971; Hadow 1973; Howell & Webb in press; Smith 1941.

35 GUADELOUPE WOODPECKER
Melanerpes herminieri   Plate 9

IDENTIFICATION Length c. 24cm. Small, with long, somewhat pointed bill slightly curved on culmen and narrow across nostrils. The only woodpecker on Guadeloupe, and as such quite unmistakable. Has blue gloss to upperparts and dull red feather tips below, but normally appears all black in the field.

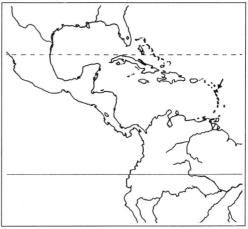

DISTRIBUTION Endemic to Guadeloupe, Lesser Antilles, West Indies, being more common on Basse Terre.

HABITAT Prefers humid forests, but also found near plantations with larger trees; less frequently found in drier hill forests. Ranges from sea level to about 900m, but most common on wooded hills from 100 to 700m.

DESCRIPTION
Adult Sexes alike in plumage, but females a little smaller and clearly shorter-billed. Head and upperparts, including entire wings and tail, black, with blue gloss; tail feathers and inner parts of primaries and secondaries more brownish-black and unglossed. Underparts sooty-black, with dull deep red tips to feathers from throat to belly; flanks and undertail-coverts blackish-brown.

Juvenile Very like adults, but duller, less glossy, and browner overall; underparts suffused dull orange-red.

Bare parts Bill blackish. Legs and feet blue-black. Eyes deep brown.

GEOGRAPHICAL VARIATION None. Monotypic.

MEASUREMENTS Wing 122-140; tail of male 80-100, of female 77-93; bill of male 32.5-39.5, of female 26-28; tarsus of male 26-28, of female 23-24.5. Weight: 87-100.

VOICE The two most common calls are series of variable *wa wa wa* or *wu wu wu* calls when two birds meet, and a loud *ch-arrgh*, also in series of 3-8 notes. The latter calls are apparently used to maintain contact and may also promote recognition of sex or individual. The drumming consists of rolls which are slower than those of Red-bellied Woodpecker (51) and which may contain an initial beat or beats out of rhythm. Weak, short rolls are given at or in the cavity in mutual tapping.

HABITS Inconspicuous, although not shy, this woodpecker is most easily detected by its acoustic signals or when flying. Forages mainly on tree trunks and larger branches, but visits treetops to obtain fruits. Gleaning, probing and light pecking are the main foraging modes. Clings upside-down when obtaining fruit. Does not tarry long at one spot in its foraging routine, only clusters of fruits and fruit-bearing trees being revisited regularly. The flight is flapping, and its style resembles that of Lewis's (34) and White (33) Woodpeckers. Displaying Guadeloupe Woodpeckers behave rather like their congeners. Bill-raising/pointing, lateral swinging and more vertical bowing movements, with bill raised, have been observed. At close encounters wing-spreading may be shown. Many displays, including instrumental signals, are concentrated around the nest. Courtship behaviour includes mate-feeding.

FOOD Mainly insects, particularly beetle larvae (cerambycids and others), fruits and occasionally seeds.

BREEDING Practically all aspects of reproduction are as yet unknown. Breeds probably between April and August.

REFERENCE Short 1974a.

---

36 PUERTO RICAN WOODPECKER
Melanerpes portoricensis   Plate 9

IDENTIFICATION Length c. 22cm. Small, with longish, slightly chisel-tipped bill curved on culmen and fairly broad across nostrils. Unmistakable: the only woodpecker in Puerto Rico apart from very different Yellow-bellied Sapsucker (55), which is only a winter visitor. Has black upperparts with white forehead and rump; below, red from chin to belly, with sides of body buffish-brown.

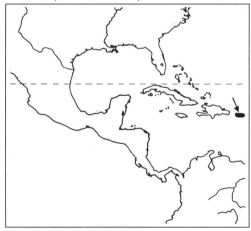

DISTRIBUTION Endemic to the West Indies, where found on Puerto Rico and Vieques in the east.

HABITAT Any wooded areas, from mangrove swamps and coconut plantations on the coast to montane forests. Appears, however, to be most common in the hills and lower mountains, including areas where coffee is grown.

DESCRIPTION
Adult male Forehead, lores and narrow circle of feathers around eye white, tinged buffish on forehead. Crown to hindneck, upper ear-coverts and narrow line beneath eye

black, glossed blue. Lower ear-coverts, moustachial region, side of neck, chin and throat bright red. Mantle, scapulars, upper back and upperwing-coverts glossy blue-black; lower back, rump and uppertail-coverts white. Flight feathers brownish-black, slightly glossed blue on edges, with a little white in carpal region and with variable amount of white at bases of inner webs of tertials; secondaries also sometimes narrowly tipped white. Uppertail glossy blue-black, outer feathers occasionally tipped white. Blue-black of rear neck extends somewhat onto breast side (occasionally with black-based feathers across entire breast), but breast otherwise bright red, this colour continuing down through central belly; entire flanks and thighs buffish-brown, paler on lower flanks; undertail-coverts pale brownish. Underwing brown, coverts black and white. Undertail as uppertail.

Adult female Smaller and shorter-billed than male. Generally has less extensive red, with chin and throat and often moustachial region largely brown; forehead more extensively pale (buffish); red area of belly usually narrower and may be paler (more orange/yellow).

Juvenile Much as adults, but less glossy, and with red of underparts less extensive and more orange-tinged. Males usually show a few red feather tips in crown.

Bare parts Bill blackish. Legs and feet greyish. Eyes dark brown.

GEOGRAPHICAL VARIATION None. Monotypic.

MEASUREMENTS Wing of male 118-129, of female 108-119; tail of male 71-81, of female 66-74; bill of male 27-29, of female 21-24; tarsus of male 21-24, of female 19-20.5. Weight: 45-72. Male about 12% heavier.

VOICE A number of harsh sounds, such as a rolling *gurrr-gurrr*. A wide variety of calls, the most common being *wek, wek, wek-wek-wek-wek-wek*, etc., increasing in volume and speed. Other vocalisations include *kuk* notes (like those of a domestic hen) and *mew* notes. Drums infrequently and weakly.

HABITS Found singly or in pairs, after the breeding season in small family groups of two to five birds, while later loose groups of up to ten individuals may be seen. Forages mainly on trunks and branches. Sexual differences exist in foraging strata and methods used: males tend to forage in the lower and middle parts of trees and they do more pecking and probing; females are more frequently found in the middle tiers and in the canopy and prefer to glean. These sexual differences are most pronounced in the harsh conditions of the dry season (54% gleaning and 31% pecking/hammering for females, versus 27% and 45% for males). Displays not described in detail. Individuals or groups gather at prominent (dead) trees for signalling. Territorial spacing seems to take place when the breeding season commences.

FOOD Wood-boring beetle larvae, ants and earwigs constitute the principal animal food, which may also include grasshoppers, bugs and the occasional frog or lizard. Vegetable matter constitutes about a third of the diet and comprises various seeds and fruits from palms, trees (figs) and shrubs, and possibly bark.

BREEDING Nest construction starts in January, nests being excavated in dead stumps usually high in trees. Four eggs are laid in April-May. Both parents feed the young and continue their care for two weeks after fledging, although family parties stay together for longer periods.

REFERENCES Raffaele 1989; Wallace 1974.

---

37 RED-HEADED WOODPECKER
Melanerpes erythrocephalus   **Plate 10**

IDENTIFICATION Length c. 24cm. Rather small, with long, chisel-tipped bill slightly curved on culmen and broad across nostrils and at base. Adult unmistakable: red head, neck and throat, white rump, large white wing patches and white underparts.

Prominently black and white in flight. Juvenile brown and white, but still shows large white areas above. A noisy, bustling woodpecker, often forages on ground or in sorties from perch; prefers clearings and open areas with dead trees.

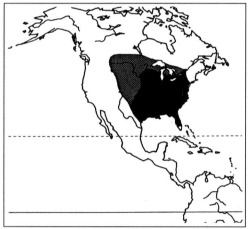

DISTRIBUTION Occurs from Canadian Lake Winnipeg (Manitoba) and southern Ontario south to the Gulf of Mexico and Florida. Western limits of the range are approximately along the line C Texas, New Mexico and C Colorado north to northern Montana; reaches the Atlantic coast in the east, from New Brunswick to Florida.

MOVEMENTS Northern populations migrate south more or less regularly; northwestern populations are particularly migratory. Winters south of Kansas, Iowa, Ohio and New Jersey. Returns from winter quarters in March (late February). Autumn dispersal and migration take place from August to November, and may be conspicuous when flocks of several hundred appear on passage.

HABITAT Frequents mainly old mature lowland forests with a sufficient amount of dead trees and with relatively open undergrowth. Basic requisites are old trees for nest sites, open areas for flycatching and access to the ground. Habitats frequented by this species include various types of wooded savannas, open woodland, riparian forests, pine

forests, villages, suburbs, orchards and agricultural land. Some regional differences exist in details of habitat preferences: in the east old mature woodlots with some undergrowth as found in suburbs and agricultural areas are important, while farther south clearings with some tall stumps are typical. The preference for tall mature forest is especially pronounced in the post-breeding season. Usually found in habitats that are less dense and possess less undergrowth than those frequented by Red-bellied Woodpecker (51). Where Lewis's (34) and Red-headed Woodpeckers occur together, the former tends to be more common in agricultural areas and on edges while the latter is found more commonly in riverine woodland and also in clearings.

DESCRIPTION
Adult Sexes alike in plumage, but female very slightly smaller. Entire head, neck, throat and upper breast bright red, rarely with admixed orange or yellow feathers; feathers of upper breast black subterminally, forming black border against pale underparts. Mantle and upper back glossy blue-black; lower back, rump and uppertail-coverts white, often with indistinct black shaft streaks. Upperwing-coverts glossy blue-black; primaries and outer secondaries brown; inner secondaries and tertials white, with indistinct black shaft streaks and occasionally with hint of barring. Uppertail blackish-brown with hint of blue gloss, narrowly tipped white on outer feathers; outermost rectrix edged white. Breast to belly white, usually with dull yellowish to reddish wash of variable intensity and extent; undertail-coverts white or creamy, often with narrow indistinct shaft streaks. Underwing as upperwing, but coverts black and white. Undertail as above, but duller.

Juvenile Similar in pattern to adults, but distinctly different in plumage coloration and with much individual variation (possible role of this conspicuous difference is in need of study). Top and sides of head grey-brown with dark brown feather tips, chin and throat greyish-white with heavy brown streaking; usually some indication of dull red on nape and/or around eye (can be lacking). Mantle, scapulars and back barred black-brown and greyish-white; rump and uppertail-coverts white. Upper breast barred black-brown and grey-brown, contrasting with white of remaining underparts, but has fairly heavy brown streaking on sides and flanks; breast, belly and undertail-coverts variably streaked, most individuals being pure white but some having entire underparts streaked. Upperwing-coverts dark brown, broadly tipped paler grey-brown; primaries and outer secondaries brown, narrowly margined whitish, inner secondaries and tertials white with black bars. Tail blue-black and suffused brownish, with off-white tip (soon abraded), and with outer rectrices tipped and edged white. Bill duller than on adult. Juvenile acquires adult plumage in gradual moult through autumn-winter: some (presumably from early broods) are fully adult by late September/October; by December, most show much red on head, largely unstreaked underparts and blue-black back; by January/February, can be aged by barring in secondaries (which may still be evident in May), some also showing faint flank streaking and possibly also barring on mantle and streaking on head.

Bare parts Bill bluish-grey, becoming paler towards base. Legs and feet olive-grey. Eyes brown.

GEOGRAPHICAL VARIATION Northwestern populations of the western Great Plains south and west to C Colorado have been separated as 'caurinus'; they are slightly longer-winged (surely a result of their more migratory habits) and perhaps with slightly deeper yellow wash below (though this varies greatly among all populations). Their racial separation seems unwarranted.

MEASUREMENTS Wing 127-150; tail 66-85; bill 21-30; tarsus 19-24.5. Weight: 56-97.

VOICE Many variable calls. Aggressive *quirr* calls are heard the year round and consist of fast series of 5-7 notes; they are most frequently uttered prior to intraspecific encounters or copulations. In the breeding season, and probably serving as announcement and as means of contact between the pair, very rapid series of notes are uttered, rendered *churr* or *kweer*, or, if the initial note is higher-pitched, *kwi-urr*; this call may be given by two birds simultaneously. Less loud and variable variants of these calls are exchanged in close encounters, and during copulation become chattering *er-er* or *er-r-r-r*. Nestlings 'beg' with *chee-chee*. Drumming rolls are delivered in the breeding season and are weak and short, the rhythm being about 20-25 strokes per second. Drumming occurs in similar context to churs. Mutual tapping, with one bird inside the hole and the other at the entrance, is typical for this species, as well as for some other melanerpine woodpeckers.

HABITS Most easily detected when flying over open parts of its habitat or when perched on prominent lookout. When foraging on trees, visits medium-sized branches of live deciduous as well as dead trees, preferring higher levels (12-18m) and most frequently utilising limbs of between 5 and 30cm in diameter; about a third to two-thirds of substrates visited while foraging are dead. Regularly descends to the ground. In the breeding season, the main foraging techniques are hawking flying insects and gleaning, with some occasional pecks during arboreal foraging. Pecking becomes more important during winter, when it is more often employed than is the case with Red-bellied Woodpecker. The young of hole-nesting birds are obtained by widening the hole entrance. Larger animal prey is pounced on and worked with blows of the bill. Hops on the ground and on horizontal branches, climbs in the usual woodpecker way and may cling to smaller twigs in a more tit-like fashion. Larger insects are placed in crevices or cavities as interim storages. Acorns, beechmast, corn and other nuts are stored in cracks and bark crevices during years with good mast crops, and are defended against all intruders. Harvesting occupies most of the active time in early autumn. Stores are any kind of natural or anthropogenic crevices, and holes and are not excavated by the woodpecker itself; if a piece of nut does not fit into the intended store, the nut is broken into pieces rather than the crevice being prepared to fit the food. Some stores are sealed with wood chips. The most commonly seen display is bobbing or bowing, which occurs both in intraspecific and interspecific encounters. In close encounters tail and/or wings are spread, and opponents are approached on the wing in a flight display. During copulation, the male shows a rapid, repeated sideward motion lasting a few seconds. Reversed mounting has been recorded. Many features of this species' social behaviour still await study. One particularly interesting aspect would be the structure of the breeding unit, which may possibly consist now and then of a pair augmented by an additional female or helper. Winter territories are established from September onwards. Winter-territory sizes vary between 0.04 and 2.0ha. Because of its size and aggressiveness, this species dominates other members of the bark-foraging guild, including the congeneric Red-bellied Woodpecker, in most of their habitats, causing them to shift habitat or foraging stratum. At the nest and at the storage site, starlings, nuthatches, titmice, jays, crows and other woodpeckers, even Pileated Woodpeckers (164) but least so Northern Flickers (146), are attacked. Interspecific and intraspecific aggression peaks immediately before incubation and around the time broods fledge. Hawking Red-headed Woodpeckers are themselves subject to attacks from larger tyrannid flycatchers.

FOOD About two-thirds of the diet is made up of animal matter in spring, seeds becoming the predominant food in winter. One of the most omnivorous woodpeckers with a really wide range of prey, including earthworms, lizards, mice, nestlings of hole-nesting and open-nesting birds, eggs, grasshoppers, crickets, beetles and their larvae, caterpillars, moths, butterflies and wasps. Generally, flying insects are more important than wood-boring larvae, which are virtually absent from the diet. Besides acorns and various types of nuts and corn, which are stored in the winter, a great variety of fruits is taken; these include dogwood and cherries, grapes and apples, and the like. Also eats bark.

BREEDING The breeding season spans April to August (September). Various species of trees are used for excavating the nest, among them cypress, oaks and palmettos. Typically, barkless trunks, stumps or branches hold the nest hole, which usually is initiated at an already existing crack. Nest heights vary from rather low, about 2m, to 25m. Red-headed Woodpeckers are flexible in their nest-site selection and also use natural holes, nest in buildings and other artificial structures (e.g. pumps), and allegedly even occupy jay nests. The task of excavation rests mainly on the male and takes about two weeks. Usually, the basic reproductive unit consists of a pair, but there are observations which indicate that sometimes more complex breeding units are established. Eggs are laid from April to July in the south, May-June being the main breeding season there, as also, apparently, in the northern parts of its range. Clutch size varies from 3 to 10 eggs, most commonly 4-5. Both parents incubate, the male staying in the nest at night, for 12-13 days. Both sexes also are involved in the care of the nestlings, brood and feed them and remove faeces (not in the last days before fledging). The work load is not evenly distributed between the partners (females seem to increase their effort in the second half of the nestling period), but general sex-related trends need to be established through extensive observations, and the role of the possibly greater contribution by the female in freeing the male to produce the next nest hole should also be elucidated. After about a month the young woodpeckers emerge from the nest. Commonly (in about 20% of cases), the pair starts on a second brood, usually in a newly made cavity, sometimes while still feeding fledglings of the first (but the young of the first brood are kept away from the second nest).

REFERENCES Bent 1939; Brackbill 1969a; Conner 1976, 1980; Gamboa & Brown 1976; Jackson 1976; Kilham 1958, 1959a, 1959b, 1959c; Moskovits 1978; Reller 1972; Roth 1978; Southern 1960; Williams 1975; Williams & Batzli 1979a, 1979b; Willson 1970.

38 ACORN WOODPECKER
Melanerpes formicivorus   Plate 10

IDENTIFICATION Length c. 23cm. Rather small, with moderately long, slightly chisel-tipped bill curved on culmen and broad across nostrils. Unmistakable: glossy black, with red on crown, white on face and underparts, black breast band and white primary patches; adult has very pale eyes. White rump and wing patches conspicuous in flight.

A well-studied, common and sociable woodpecker, usually found in small groups; noisy, with distinctive raucous call.

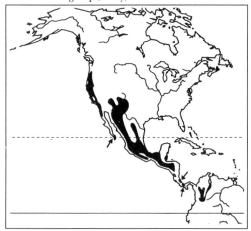

DISTRIBUTION Resident along the American west coast from southern Oregon through C America to Colombia. Ranges as far inland as New Mexico (isolated populations occur in Texas), and interior Mexico (Sonora, Coahuila, locally even farther east).

MOVEMENTS Some localities are used for breeding only and the woodpeckers leave them in autumn. Birds of southern Arizona and adjacent Mexican mountains winter possibly in northern Mexico (Sierra Madre?).

HABITAT A woodpecker of oak and pine-oak woodland. Numbers vary locally according to abundance and fruiting of oaks. From Arizona south to Belize, this woodpecker lives in pine and pine-oak forests of the highlands, sometimes in adjacent semi-open woodland and second growth. Its main habitats in C America and Colombia are forests, particularly highland oak stands, forest borders, open or light woodland, clearings and pastures with scattered dead trees. Occurs in California from sea level to 1800m, above 750m in Arizona, and in Mexico generally found at 500-3000m, locally lower on Caribbean slopes. Ranges from the tree line down to 1200m, straying to 900m, in tropical C America, and is found on both slopes of the Andes

between 1400 and 3500m farther south.

DESCRIPTION
M. f. formicivorus **Adult male** Crown to nape red; white of forehead extends in line through lores to cheeks and onto throat, where becomes pale yellowish; chin black. Area around eye and entire ear-coverts, rear and side of neck, mantle and upper back glossy black. Lower back, rump and uppertail-coverts white. Upperwing black or brownish-black, primaries with white at bases, coverts glossed purplish/greenish. Uppertail black or brownish-black, occasionally with white tips and subterminal spots to outer feathers; may show white shaft streaks at tail base. Black of neck extends across upper breast, upper border of which is broken by white streaks and spots (usually also with a few red feather tips in centre); lower breast white with variable black streaking, streaks extending onto flanks; rest of underparts white, undertail-coverts with black streaks or tear-shaped spots. Underwing as upperwing but duller, with white streaks on coverts. Undertail much as uppertail.

Adult female Bill about 10% shorter than male's. Red on head restricted to hindcrown, central crown being black.

Juvenile Similar to adults, but browner and less glossy above, with orangey central crown (orange may be less extensive on female); tinged buff below, with larger but less contrasting streaks/spots on upper breast, some barring across flank streaks and with heavily streaked undertail-coverts. Tail often has more white barring on outer feathers and more prominent white shaft streaks on central feathers.

Bare parts Bill black. Legs and feet grey to greenish-grey. Eyes white to yellow-white or pinkish-white; initially brown in juveniles, becoming greyish before turning white. Orbital skin grey, sometimes brown or blackish.

GEOGRAPHICAL VARIATION Quantitative analyses on large amount of material revealed both clinal and discrete variation in many characters. A number of races have been described, differing only moderately in plumage and to lesser extent in size. The following are considered the most valid. The first three (northern) races share sexual dimorphism in bill length, males being about 10% longer-billed.

> *M. f. formicivorus* (mainland Mexico from north of Chiapas northwest to Arizona, New Mexico and W Texas) Described above. The most variable race.
> *M. f. bairdii* (N Baja California north to Oregon) Slightly larger than other races, with particularly long and stout bill. Breast band well demarcated, with little streaking; moderately yellow throat; poorly streaked below, lower breast and belly appearing as large white area.
> *M. f. angustifrons* (extreme S Baja California) The smallest race, with relatively long bill. Throat yellower than in all races except *flavigula* and *striatipectus*; white of forehead much reduced. More heavily streaked below than nominate, and with more white in breast band (which therefore narrower). Females have red extending farther forwards on crown.
> *M. f. lineatus* (Chiapas to Guatemala and northern Nicaragua) Like *striatipectus*, but throat pale yellow and white primary patch larger and unbarred; breast band fully streaked.
> *M. f. striatipectus* (Nicaragua to W Panama) Throat very yellow; white primary patch narrower and often with some black barring.
> *M. f. albeolus* (E Chiapas, probably also Tabasco and Campeche, in Mexico, and NE Guatemala and Belize) Very like nominate *formicivorus* and *lineatus*, but throat the palest of all races; underparts with reduced streaking.

M. f. flavigula (Colombia) Male has red confined to hindcrown (as females of other races) and female lacks red altogether. Throat very yellow; underparts the most heavily streaked of all races; rump and uppertail-coverts have feathers tipped and edged black (barred). Juveniles of both sexes have completely red crown and nape.

MEASUREMENTS Wing 130-151; tail 65-86; bill 22-33; tarsus 19-24.5. Weight: 67-89.

VOICE This rather noisy woodpecker utters nasal whinny-ing, laughing or rattling calls. The most common call is rendered *whaaka-whaaka* or *wa-ka*, usually repeated several times, and is given by stationary birds when a group member lands, flies by or takes off. This call is delivered at high rates during territorial disputes; at full intensity it is terminated by a rasping sound, *wa-ka, wa-ka, wa-ka, trtrtr,* and may be accompanied by wing-spreading. Repeated *karrit-cut* or *rack-up, rack-up* or varied to a more rolling *r-r-r-rack-up* are delivered in synchrony with bowing displays; also heard in the presence of predators. General alarm is expressed with vibrating *karrit* calls. More intimate chat-ters, *hick a ick a ick,* are exchanged when members of the group come into close contact, for instance at the nest. In adult/young encounters *urrk* notes (not loud) are heard. Less vibrating than other calls are *garick* notes, which seem to be related to reproduction. Fledglings respond with *squee-trtr* when fed by an adult. Chatters when attacked, and about 60% of individuals trapped (or coming into physical contact with conspecifics) utter distress calls. Only terri-tory-owners (or members of an established group) drum, and this signal is restricted to territorial encounters.

HABITS Sociable and very active. Most often seen, singly or as a group comprising up to 15 birds, sitting conspicu-ously on an exposed perch. Seldom far from oaks; stores acorns whole or piecemeal in crevices of bark or wood, or amid epiphytes, or in specially made holes, the latter covering large areas of a tree (oaks, pines and others) and densely spaced, at about 28 mm nearest-neighbour dis-tances. Granaries may contain up to 40,000-50,000 holes, which take years for the woodpeckers to excavate. Stores are constantly looked after and tended. The acorns are col-lected in the trees or on the ground and are prepared in anvils for ingestion. Storage behaviour varies geographi-cally, however, and not all Acorn Woodpecker groups possess granaries. Sap holes, 3-19 mm deep and 5-15 mm wide, are drilled into live oaks and are arranged in a similar way to storage holes; sap-sucking is especially important in June and July (California). In addition, some probing (including into epiphytes) and gleaning for insects diversi-fies the diet on rare occasions. Occasionally descends to the ground to feed on ants. Acorn Woodpeckers are expert flycatchers, sallying from snags or fence posts, especially towards dusk, and catching just one insect on each flight; in spring (April, May), this foraging mode, which often involves the whole group, is most important, and the food thus obtained is also important for the nestlings. Animal prey is also stored in appropriate places. Territorial defence is centred around the food store and anvils, as well as sap trees and favourite hawking perches. Displays are similar to those of other melanerpine woodpeckers, but relatively poorly studied. They include bowing with simultaneous calls (bowing may also be silent) and a hunched posture with bill and head lowered; in these displays the head feathers may be raised, too. At encounters between perched and flying/landing birds wings are spread and often raised over the back, this behaviour being accompanied by *wa-ka* calls. Acorn Woodpeckers live in groups the size and composition of which depend on, among other things, the

acorn crop. The social system is characterised by the occurrence of a co-operative polygynandry and the pres-ence of non-breeding helpers recruited from the group's offspring, and has been extensively studied in recent years. Within groups, dominance hierarchies are established which probably regulate access to mates and which are not sex-related, at least among immature birds. Temporary breeding pairs are formed by birds that disperse individu-ally in autumn. The group members roost either in adja-cent holes or several birds in one hole, engaging in brief mutual mountings prior to roosting. Stores and holes are defended against all sorts of intruders, and interspecific interactions are an important constituent of this woodpeck-er's everyday life. Because conspecific intruders are pre-dominantly females, breeding females are involved in territorial defence significantly more. Home ranges vary between 5 and 52ha. Common recipients of interspecific Acorn Woodpecker attacks are starlings and tityras, which compete for nest sites, and Lewis's Woodpeckers (34), jays and squirrels, which pose a constant threat to the granaries. Defence is carried out by the whole group, and this may one of the reasons why the complex social system of this species arose. Groups usually comprise 1-4 reproducing related males and one breeding female; in about 20% of groups a second breeding female, usually a sister of the first, is present. Up to ten helpers, the group's offspring of previ-ous years, are attached to the group of breeders. Broodmates remain at the breeding territory for at least one year. Whether an individual Acorn Woodpecker stays with its family as a helper is influenced by the variation in quality of the territories available. Birds of high-quality territories tend to stay rather than to disperse, although data so far suggest that their lifetime fitness is lower. Females disperse earlier than males and try harder to enter another breeding group. Many broodmates stay together for their entire lives and share mates. Whether an Acorn Woodpecker breeds within its group is largely determined by its relatedness to other group members; if individuals of opposite sexes are closely related, e.g. brother/sister or parent/offspring, breeding is very unlikely.

FOOD The staple diet is dried acorns, but green acorns are taken as well; S American populations are less dependent on acorns and store rarely. Acorns make up about half of the nutriment of northern populations and are the basic energy source in winter. Other seeds, such as pine seeds, are also taken. Sap-sucking is also important, and Acorn Woodpeckers drink sugar water from feeders and eat fruit (berries, cherries, apples, figs) occasionally. Ants and other insects (beetles, moths, flies) are taken as well. This species eats other birds' eggs and nestlings now and then, and may grab the occasional lizard. The nestling food consists mainly of insects (hymenopterans, beetles, hemipterans, homopterans, caterpillars, dipterans); older broods are also fed with acorns and fruits.

BREEDING Breeds from April to August in C America, and in May and June (September) in Colombia. Californian and Arizonan birds breed from March (June in Baja California) to September. Second and replacement clutches occur regularly. Autumn breeding is rare and such nests are initiated in August and September. The nest hole is excavated 6-21m up in a dead, usually well-decayed tree. If a new nest is made, all group members participate in the task, which may take up to three months. One clutch of 4-6 eggs (average 5.06) is laid per season, clutch size correlating positively with latitude. Although females be-have very aggressively and destroy rival eggs, they are not able to prevent laying of eggs in their nest by subordinate females. Competition for breeding opportunities seems to be the crucial factor which determines breeding with other females. Such nests contain on average 2.5 more eggs. About two-thirds of the eggs hatch, of which again two-thirds eventually result in fledglings. Jointly nesting females raise about 35% fewer offspring per year than females which nest singly. Over the full lifetime, both female strategies result in about the same reproductive success, largely because females sharing the nest with another one survive marginally better. Joint nesting of females is also known to become more likely as population size increases. The eggs are incubated for 11-12 days, the chicks remaining in the nest for about a month after hatching. All group members care for the brood, hence up to ten or more birds may incubate and feed at the same nest. Female helpers make greater efforts in brood care than males, and females generally do not incubate at night and take no part in nest sanitation. Second and third broods are appended at about two-months intervals.

REFERENCES Benítez-Díaz 1993; Bennun & Read 1988; Blake 1965; Bock & Bock 1974; Hilty & Brown 1984; Howell & Webb in press; Kattan 1988; Koenig 1986; Koenig *et al.* 1983, 1984, 1991; MacRoberts 1970; MacRoberts & MacRoberts 1976; Mumme *et al.* 1988; Ridgely & Gwynne 1989; Ritter 1938; Russel 1964; Skutch 1969; Stacey & Bock 1978; Stanback 1994; Stiles & Skutch 1989; Trail 1980.

39 BLACK-CHEEKED WOODPECKER
Melanerpes pucherani   Plate 11

Other name: Pucheran's Woodpecker
Forms a superspecies with *chrysauchen*.

IDENTIFICATION Length c. 17-19cm. Small, with longish, almost pointed bill curved on culmen and broad across nostrils. Black upperparts and wings are narrowly but prominently barred white, with rump all white, while pale lower underparts are heavily barred, with belly red in centre; breast is olive-buff. Both sexes have a pale forehead and cheeks, black ear-coverts and rear neck sides, and a small pale streak behind eye; male has crown and nape entirely red, while female has pale forecrown, black central crown and large red nape patch.

Similar species Most likely to be confused with Golden-naped Woodpecker (40), although the ranges of the two appear not to overlap. Golden-naped differs in having a white panel from mantle to rump, with black wings almost unbarred, and has entire hindneck bright yellow.

DISTRIBUTION From southern Mexico (Veracruz, Chiapas) through C America to western Colombia and western Ecuador.

HABITAT Lives within humid and wet evergreen forest, and may also be found at forest borders, in the semi-open, on scattered tall trees in clearings, and in old secondary growth and abandoned banana plantations. Numbers decline with extensive deforestation. Replaces Red-crowned Woodpecker (49) in more wooded areas. Lowlands and foothills up to 700-900m (occasionally 1200m).

DESCRIPTION
Adult male Forehead golden-yellow; crown and nape red, with variable amount of black at sides of forecrown and often some white feathers at front edge. Small white line behind rear upper corner of eye. Narrow area around eye and band through upper ear-coverts and down rear neck side to hindneck black. Lores, cheeks, lower ear-coverts, chin and upper throat white, tinged buff to grey-buff on

rear ear-coverts and throat. Mantle and upper back black, barred white; scapulars black, unbarred or partly barred; lower back, rump and uppertail-coverts white, tinged pale buff, occasionally faintly barred/streaked blackish. Upperwing-coverts black, greaters and some medians spotted white; flight feathers black or brownish-black, narrowly tipped white when fresh, and with white bars on all but outer webs of outer primaries (bars broadest on tertials). Uppertail black, variably barred white on central feathers, and sometimes with indication of bars on outer feathers. Lower throat and breast olive-buff, tinged grey, feathers initially tipped yellowish; rest of underparts buffish-white, becoming red on centre of belly, all with strong arrowhead barring. Underwing barred dark and white. Undertail yellowish-brown.

Adult female Somewhat smaller than male. Has forecrown white to buffy-white, bordered by black which extends backwards and then across hindcrown, with red confined to nape.

Juvenile Duller than adults, and browner above with more diffuse barring, underparts with rather more widespread but duller barring, and with red of belly paler and less extensive. Both sexes have some orangey-red on nape and red on crown, female with far less red (and often barred) on crown. Males can be distinguished even as nestlings by their red feathers in the crown.

Bare parts Bill black, usually paler at base of lower mandible. Legs and feet grey, tinged green, or olive. Eyes brown. Orbital skin brown to greyish.

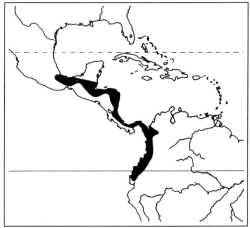

GEOGRAPHICAL VARIATION Monotypic. Prominence of white barring on upperparts and wings varies somewhat, perhaps tending to be stronger among northern individuals than in southern ones, but much overlap occurs and racial separation of northern population as '*perileucus*' is not sustainable.

MEASUREMENTS Wing 100-122; tail 48-63; bill 20.5-28.8; tarsus 17.5-21.8. Weight: 42-68.

VOICE Calls similar to but higher-pitched than those of Red-crowned Woodpecker and less nasal than Golden-fronted's (53). Most often heard is a series of about four short, rattling trills on the same pitch, *churrr, churrr, churrr* or *cherrr*. In addition, a longer, smoother rattle, a loud, full-toned *krrrr*, and a higher-pitched, piercing *chirriree* or *keereereek* recalling a Boat-billed Flycatcher *Megarhynchus pitangua* have been described. Both sexes drum.

HABITS Lives alone or in pairs, and occasionally larger family parties may be met with; also joins also mixed-species flocks. At fruiting trees 12 or more individuals may gather. Forages mostly in the upper and middle levels inside forests. Most frequently probes crevices and cracks in bark, bases of epiphytes, and pecks and hammers dead wood. Gleans insects from trunks, branches and lianas, often searches epiphytes for animal prey and seeds, and takes fruits regularly. Moves actively and peers, reaches and also clings with great agility on the underside of branches and twigs. Details of its displays have not been described, but probably similar to other *Melanerpes* species. Reversed mounting has been recorded. Strong interspecific interactions concern competition for nest sites with tityras.

FOOD Spiders, termites, beetles, grubs, ants, caterpillars, and aerial insects. Eats large quantities of plant material, including fruits, berries, seeds of large bromeliads (may even be fed to nestlings), arils and catkins of *Cecropia*. Also drinks nectar from large flowers of balsa and kapok trees.

BREEDING The breeding season in C America and Colombia extends from March to July. Nest hole 4-30m up in a dead trunk (including palms) or branch, and it is the hole in which the male sleeps, at least sometimes also joined by the female. Clutch consists of 2-4 eggs. Both sexes incubate, the young hatching after 14 days. Observations in captivity have shown that after the young have fledged, which takes about three weeks, they may return to the nest to roost. Captive birds may start a second brood and still tolerate the young of the previous one, even in a relatively small aviary.

REFERENCES Askins 1983; Blake 1965; Hilty & Brown 1984; Land 1963; Otvos 1967; Peterson & Chalif 1973; Ridgely & Gwynne 1989; Russel 1964; Slud 1964; Stiles & Skutch 1989; Wareman 1988; Wetmore 1968.

---

40 GOLDEN-NAPED WOODPECKER
Melanerpes chrysauchen   Plate 11

Other name: Beautiful Woodpecker (race *pulcher*)
Forms a superspecies with *pucherani*.

IDENTIFICATION Length c. 17-18cm. Small, with long-ish, almost pointed bill curved on culmen and fairly broad across nostrils. Has black upperparts and wings, with white central panel from mantle to rump (white area barred black in Colombian race *pulcher*). Underparts and head pattern are superficially similar to those of Black-cheeked Woodpecker (39), but both sexes of Golden-naped have bright golden-yellow on hindneck (extending up to nape on C American population).

Similar species Differs from Black-cheeked Woodpecker, which it appears not to meet, in having less barring on wings, more white in central upperparts, and different head pattern (with golden hindneck).

DISTRIBUTION The small disjunct range covers south-western Costa Rica and western Panama, and, some distance away, the Magdalena valley in northern Colombia.

HABITAT A resident of humid areas with dense tall rain forest, but increasingly extends into semi-open areas and scattered trees as forests shrink. Replaces Black-cheeked Woodpecker in drier areas, in Colombia. Its habitats also include edges of clearings, forest edge and plantations enclosed by forest. From lowlands to 1200m in C America, locally to 1500m, and from 400 to 1500m in Colombia.

DESCRIPTION
M. c. chrysauchen **Adult male** Forehead golden-yellow,

occasionally tinged orange; crown red, often with some olive-yellow feather bases visible; hindcrown, nape and hindneck golden-yellow. Short black-streaked white supercilium just behind eye. Small black streak on rear lores, black continuing narrowly around eye, across upper ear-coverts and down rear neck side. Front and lower part of lores, moustachial region, lower ear-coverts, chin and upper throat white, strongly tinged grey-buff at rear and on throat. Mantle and scapulars blue-glossed black, with narrow white panel down centre of mantle; back, rump and uppertail-coverts white, often tinged pale buffish. Upperwing-coverts black, glossed blue; flight feathers brownish-black (blacker towards bases), tipped narrowly white when fresh, inner webs with short white bars. Uppertail black, outer feathers often with one or two white bars/ spots. Lower throat and breast to upper belly olive-buff, washed grey; central belly orange-red; flanks, belly sides, thighs and undertail-coverts pale buffish-white, heavily marked with broad black arrowhead barring. Underwing brownish, blackish on coverts, barred white, with white marginal coverts. Undertail brownish-black.

Adult female Slightly smaller and shorter-billed than male. Head pattern differs: forehead and forecrown golden-yellow, central crown black (occasionally with a few red feather tips), and hindcrown, nape and hindneck golden-yellow.

Juvenile Duller than adults, with black areas browner; yellow of forehead paler and less extensive; below, barring duller and less contrasting, and belly patch smaller and more orange. Both sexes have red-tipped feathers on crown, less extensive on female.

Bare parts Bill black, paler at base. Legs and feet grey, sometimes tinged green or brown. Eyes brown.

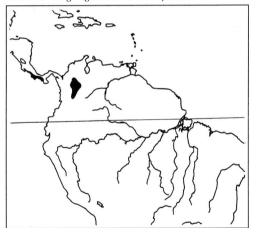

GEOGRAPHICAL VARIATION Two geographically discrete races.

> *M. c. chrysauchen* (SW Costa Rica to W Panama) Described above.
> *M. c. pulcher* (Colombia) Differs most obviously in pattern of upperparts, which have the white panel at least partly and sometimes fully barred black; also, forehead patch is paler, more buffish or creamy-white, and extends onto forecrown, while barring below extends across upper belly. Male has red of crown continuing to upper nape, with lower nape and hindneck golden; female has black across central crown, red hindcrown, and golden nape and hindneck.

MEASUREMENTS Wing 103-118; tail 50-61; bill 21.5-28.3; tarsus 18-21.2. Weight: 45-68.

VOICE A resonant churr, similar to that of Black-cheeked; a short, loud, rattling or laughing trill, three to five times in rapid succession on same pitch; also, several short rattles. Nestlings utter a squeaking buzz. Both sexes drum occasionally.

HABITS Lives in pairs or family parties of three to six individuals throughout year. Prefers canopy and middle levels of humid forest, constantly pecking and hammering into decaying trunks and branches. Frequently captures insects on the wing, and especially on wet evenings ascends above treetops to flycatch with great skill. Displays with deep bows which are accompanied by chur-calls. In close contact between two individuals wing-spreading occurs. Young remain with parents until the onset of the following breeding season. A whole family not only moves as a loose group during the day, but also roosts together in the same hole.

FOOD Wood-boring beetles and their larvae, winged termites and also other insects. Takes much fruit: *Cecropia*, figs, arillate seeds, bananas, oranges, palm fruits; also accepts these fruits on feeders.

BREEDING The breeding season spans March to June. Nest hole is built by male and female 5-30m up, usually in a massive dead trunk. As with other woodpeckers, several holes may be initiated in one season before one becomes the final nest, which can be completed in two weeks. A clutch of 3 or 4 eggs is laid. Male and female incubate in long sessions; both sexes sleep together in nest during breeding. The chicks stay 33-34 days in the nest, and two or three young fledge. Both parents feed them, but the male seems to be more involved in parental tasks. Fledglings are taken care of for up to three months and share the roost with their parents until the next breeding season. Rarely, two broods are raised in a season; in such cases, a young from the first brood may also incubate and feed the second brood, and roost in the same nest.

REFERENCES Hilty & Brown 1984; Ridgely & Gwynne 1989; Sassi 1939; Skutch 1948a, 1969; Stiles & Skutch 1989.

---

41 YELLOW-TUFTED WOODPECKER
Melanerpes cruentatus   Plate 11

Other name: Red-fronted Woodpecker (black-headed morph)
Forms a superspecies with *flavifrons*.

IDENTIFICATION Length c. 19cm. Small, with long, almost pointed bill curved on culmen and rather broad across nostrils. A dark-looking woodpecker, relatively easy to identify. Occurs in two morphs: one with all-black head and neck (male with red on crown), the other having bold white supercilium from just in front of eye and becoming yellow on lower nape (male with more red on crown and with yellow hindneck); intermediates also occur. Both sexes of both morphs have bluish-black upperparts (with white rump), wings and breast, red belly, and black-barred pale flanks. Ring of bare whitish skin around eye, accentuated by black face, is particularly striking.

DISTRIBUTION East of the Andes in S America, ranging from E Colombia to the Guianas and extending south to E Ecuador and eastern Peru, N and E Bolivia and in Brazil to Mato Grosso and NE Pará.

HABITAT Rain forest, secondary growth, forest edge, and (burnt-over) clearings with isolated trees. Tall dead trees

seem to be an important prerequisite of the habitat. Occurs from sea level up to 1200m.

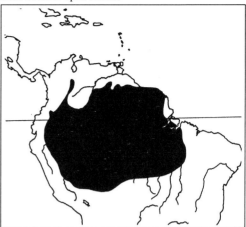

DESCRIPTION
Adult male: Black-headed morph (*'rubrifrons'*) Centre of crown red, often rather rounded in shape. Rest of head and neck, chin to breast, mantle, scapulars, upper back and upperwing-coverts blue-glossed black; lower back, rump and uppertail-coverts white, often with some hint of black barring, and with black shaft streaks on uppertail-coverts. Flight feathers blackish (slightly glossy), with short white bars on inner webs (on primaries, restricted to bases). Uppertail bluish-black, central pair of feathers usually with white spots on inner webs (outer feathers occasionally tipped white). Belly centre red, this extending as a wedge onto lower breast (but exact colour and extent of patch show considerable individual variation); lower breast sides, flanks, thighs, sides of belly and undertail-coverts white or pale yellowish-white, all with bold black arrowhead barring. Underwing barred black and white, browner at margins. Undertail brownish-black.

Yellow-tufted morph (*'cruentatus'*) Differs in having white (often yellow-tinged) supercilia from slightly in front of eye, over ear-coverts and meeting on lower nape, which is golden-yellow, sometimes orangey, this colour continuing down hindneck; red of crown on male is usually more extensive and less rounded. (Intermediates between the two morphs have a restricted or broken pale supercilium and less or little yellow on nape/hindneck.)

Adult female Slightly shorter-billed than male. Lacks red on crown. Female of yellow-tufted morph also has less golden-yellow on head.

Juvenile Duller than adults, with black areas much browner; underparts greyer, with barring more obscure and belly patch more orange-coloured. Both sexes have red in crown centre, and in yellow-tufted morph the white and yellow head markings are reduced.

Bare parts Bill black. Legs and feet grey to pinky-grey. Eyes pale yellow. Orbital skin very broad, whitish to pale yellow.

GEOGRAPHICAL VARIATION The black-headed morph appears to occur mostly from E Venezuela eastwards and across central N Brazil, where it is more numerous than yellow-tufted morph. The two morphs were formerly considered separate species, but they interbreed freely. There are no grounds for any subspecific divisions within this polymorphic woodpecker.

MEASUREMENTS Wing 106-121; tail 50-59; bill 21-26. Weight: 48-64.

VOICE Noisier than most of its congeners. Various loud and hoarse calls similar to Acorn Woodpecker's (38): single *chowp* notes and double-syllabled *r-r-r-aack-up*, *trrr-eh* or *churr-dówp*. Another call is described as a nine-syllable *ih-ih-ih-ih...* or *treh-treh-treh...*, slowing down towards the end. More rasping renditions of similar calls are heard during display. The bowing ceremony when two birds meet is accompanied by frequent *kat-sup*, *kat-sup* calls.

HABITS A very social woodpecker, usually found in pairs or groups of 3-5 birds, occasionally up to 12. Not difficult to detect when calling from treetops or when sitting conspicuously on high perches. Forages in the upper parts of tall, dead trees. Gleaning from the surface of trunks and branches and twigs and leaves of the canopy is the main foraging mode; flycatching is common in evening hours. Display, which occurs at various social encounters, involves conspicuous wing-spreading, whereby the wings are spread either laterally or over the back. At close distance, bowing movements and many variants thereof may be seen, which may include bill-pointing, turning the head away from the opponent; body-swinging and hunched postures may also occur in such situations. This species, too, is a communal breeder, with adult helpers. Up to five birds may share a roost. One individual may attend to three nests. Birds care for the brood individually or in groups. Further details of the obviously highly developed and complex social system are not known.

FOOD Insects (ants and others) and fruits (berries) are the main constituents of the diet. Other arthropods such as spiders and chilopods are also taken.

BREEDING Broadly, the breeding season spans December to September. Breeds between June and August in E Peru, Colombia and east to the Guianas, and in September along the Rio Negro. Localities where nesting occurs between March and June include again Colombia, Bolivia, and the Amazonian basin to Ecuador. Populations in SE Peru and the Mato Grosso breed from December to February. The nest is excavated in a dead tree or tall dead stump; several nests may be found in one neighbourhood. Care of the young seems to be shared by the entire social unit, thus an adult may feed at several nests.

REFERENCES Hilty & Brown 1984; Meyer de Schauensee & Phelps 1978; Parker *et al.* 1982; Short 1970a; Sick 1993; Snyder 1966.

---

42 YELLOW-FRONTED WOODPECKER
Melanerpes flavifrons   Plate 11

Forms a superspecies with *cruentatus*.

IDENTIFICATION Length c. 17cm. Small, with long, chisel-tipped bill barely curved on culmen and fairly broad across nostrils. Has blue-black upperparts and wings, but with white rump and broad white mantle streaks; breast is grey, bordered below by red which extends down belly, with pale flanks barred dark. A very broad black band through lores and ear-coverts contrasts with bright yellow forehead and throat, and also emphasises the broad ring of pale bare skin around dark eye. Male has red crown, nape and hindneck, these areas being glossy black on female. A relatively little-known woodpecker, but readily identifiable if seen well.

DISTRIBUTION Ranges over large parts of Brazil, Bahia, Goias, Minas Gerais to Rio de Janeiro and Rio Grande do

Sul, to eastern Paraguay and Argentina (Misiones).

HABITAT Humid forests and secondary vegetation, such as cane fields, palm groves and orchards; from sea level to 1800m.

DESCRIPTION
Adult male Forehead and forecrown golden-yellow, with white feather bases; central crown, nape and hindneck red. Entire lores, area around eye and upper ear-coverts glossy blue-black, this colour continuing down rear neck side to mantle. Chin and throat, moustachial region and lower ear-coverts pale yellow to deep golden-yellow, this sometimes reaching to upper breast. Mantle black, glossed blue, central feathers with white on one web and black on the other, creating pattern of broad white streaks; back, rump and uppertail-coverts white, usually with a few black spots (rarely, indication of bars), and with black shaft streaks on uppertail-coverts. Upperwing-coverts glossy blue-black; flight feathers black to brownish-black, glossed blue on edges, with white bars on inner webs of secondaries and tertials (bars forming larger patches on tertials). Uppertail black, central pair of feathers often with one or two white bars on inner webs, outer feathers tipped white when fresh. Lower neck sides and breast pale grey to yellowish olive-grey; belly centre orangey to crimson-red, this colour extending onto lower breast/breast sides (intensity and extent of red highly variable); flanks, thighs, belly sides and undertail-coverts whitish, often tinged olive or buffy-yellow, all with black arrowhead barring. Underwing brownish, barred white. Undertail brown, often olive-brown on outer feathers.

Adult female Somewhat smaller and shorter-billed than male. Lacks red on head, having central crown to hindneck blue-black.

Juvenile As adults, but black areas browner and less glossy; belly patch smaller and more orange in colour. Young males have red in crown and hindcrown, females generally in mid crown only.

Bare parts Bill black. Legs and feet olive, tinged green or brown. Eyes blackish to blue-black; brown in juveniles. Orbital skin whitish to orange-yellow.

GEOGRAPHICAL VARIATION Populations in northwest of range generally show much paler underparts than coastal populations, having yellowish throat, whitish-grey breast and orange belly patch, but considerable variation exists throughout entire range and subspecific division seems unsafe.

MEASUREMENTS Wing 110-127. Weight: 49-64.

205

VOICE A noisy species, with strident *kikiki, tsilidit* notes, or flight calls sounding like *benedito*. When two meet on a perch, series of *chlit* notes are uttered. Other calls are apparently aggressive *tweewetwee tweewetwee...* and *eeeuk eeeuk*. Drums, preferably on tall trees.

HABITS As other congeners, this species stores seeds. It also lives in groups, in which several birds may share a single roost and breed together; such groups may form loose colonies.

FOOD Fond of fruits, berries and seeds.

BREEDING Breeds from January to April (May) in the northern parts of its range, in southern Brazil and in Argentina, and in November in Espírito Santo. Communal breeding seems to be common. Up to three males and up to two females have been observed to attend a single brood. Fledglings return to the nest to roost.

REFERENCES Bolton 1984; Olrog 1984; Short 1970a; Sick 1993.

---

43   WHITE-FRONTED WOODPECKER
Melanerpes cactorum   Plate 12

IDENTIFICATION Length c. 16cm. Very small, with relatively short, almost straight, slightly chisel-tipped bill broad across nostrils. Largely black and white/whitish above and more or less plain pale buffish below, with black of central crown, ear-coverts and neck stripe contrasting with pale forehead, hindneck, sides of face and throat; rump, wings and wing-coverts and tail are strikingly barred. Sexes are virtually alike, but males have a very small patch of red in crown (often very difficult to discern in the field).

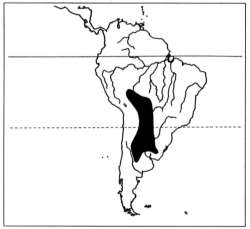

DISTRIBUTION Occurs from SE Peru and from Bolivia (Chuquisaca, Santa Cruz) to western Paraguay and Argentina (from the northwest to southern provinces, east to western Corrientes and Entre Ríos). Rather common.

MOVEMENTS Probably some seasonal movements take place.

HABITAT Within its range, a common bird of dry forests. Frequents forest edge, savannas, gallery forests, bush country (chaco) and montane scrub; also found in palm groves with trees. Also associates with cacti (*Cereus*). From lowlands to 1700m and locally (Bolivia) to 2500m .

DESCRIPTION
Adult male Forehead and forecrown, lores and moustachial region and lower ear-coverts white; narrow area around eye and back through upper ear-coverts and central crown to hindcrown blue-black, continuing as black stripe down rear neck side to mantle, crown with small, partly concealed patch of red near front. Nape white, faintly tinged buff or yellow, becoming pure white on hindneck. Chin and throat variably white, partly yellow, or entirely yellow or golden-yellow. Mantle and scapulars glossy blue-black, with heavy, broad, white or buffish-white streaks down centre of mantle (feathers having one web white, the other black); back, rump and uppertail-coverts white, barred or spotted black. Upperwing-coverts black, glossed blue, greaters spotted and tipped white, medians with white distal half spotted black; flight feathers blackish, browner on primaries, and barred white on both webs of secondaries and tertials and at bases of primaries. Uppertail black, tipped white (when fresh), and barred white across all feathers. Underparts buff, paler and greyer on belly, with slight arrowhead bars on lower flanks and undertail-coverts. Underwing brown, barred white, with coverts whiter and more or less unbarred. Undertail brownish-black, barred white.
Adult female On average, smaller and shorter-billed than male, and lacks red spot on crown.
Juvenile Much as adults, but browner and less glossy above and more barred below. Both sexes have some orange-red in crown centre.
Bare parts Bill black or grey-black. Legs and feet slaty-coloured. Eyes brown to red-brown.

GEOGRAPHICAL VARIATION Monotypic. Varies in throat colour, those in Bolivia and W Argentina having yellow throat, while those to the east of this have partly yellow throat in the north but are white-throated in south; this feature is not constant, however, and elsewhere in range individuals may be found with variable throat coloration.

MEASUREMENTS Wing 99-115; tail 68-75; bill 24-29; tarsus 20-22. Weight: 29-53.

VOICE A loud *weep-weep, wee-beep*, resembling call of Yellow-bellied Sapsucker (55); faster renditions of this call are heard from displaying birds. Drums in short and weak rolls near the hole early in breeding season.

HABITS Usually encountered in groups of 3-5 birds. Forages on palms, trunks and branches by gleaning, and probing. Bowing displays have been observed during encounters, which also involve much calling.

FOOD The diet includes insects and fruits. Ants seem to be important, and beetles have also been found.

BREEDING Breeds from September to December. The nest is excavated in trees, palms and cacti.

REFERENCES Olrog 1984; Short 1970a, 1975; Sick 1961, 1993.

---

44 HISPANIOLAN WOODPECKER
Melanerpes striatus   Plate 12

IDENTIFICATION Length c. 20-24cm. Small, with long, straight and broad bill (shorter on female). Restricted to Hispaniola, where the only true woodpecker and hence unmistakable; Yellow-bellied Sapsucker (55) may occur in winter, but is easily separated, while resident Antillean Piculet (32) is smaller and differs considerably in all respects. Hispaniolan Woodpecker is distinctive in appearance, with barred black and yellowish upperparts, plain dark buff underparts, and red crown to upper hindneck, the smaller female having black crown. Common throughout Hispaniola, where unusual in its gregarious behaviour and colonial nesting habits.

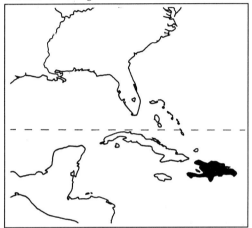

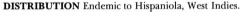

DISTRIBUTION Endemic to Hispaniola, West Indies.

HABITAT Occurs from lowland mangrove swamps and semi-arid country to the forested mountains. Also frequents pine woodland and occurs in human habitations so long as there are trees; particularly common in cultivated areas with trees and palms.

DESCRIPTION
Adult male Forecrown to upper hindneck bright red; rest of head, including forehead and superciliary area, pale buffish-white, greyer on ear-coverts, with chin and throat more olive-buff. Lower hindneck broadly striped black and yellowish-white (whiter laterally). Mantle, scapulars, back, upperwing-coverts and tertials black, broadly barred greenish-yellow to golden; rump yellow or greenish-yellow, feathers of lower rump tipped red, and faintly barred blackish (bars sometimes lacking); uppertail-coverts red, with black bases. Primaries and secondaries brownish-black, broadly barred yellowish, bars whiter on primaries. Uppertail brownish-black, outer feathers edged whitish. Underparts dark reddish-buff, washed grey, and with olive tinge to upper breast and belly; may occasionally have a few red-tipped feathers on belly and/or darker streaks on lower flanks (latter rarely with obscure narrow bars). Underwing barred brown and white, with plain olive coverts. Undertail brownish, outer feathers washed yellow. (In worn plumage, yellow barring on upperparts becomes paler and whiter and black bases of crown feathers may show, while face and underparts are greyer and can be stained rusty, sometimes distinctly so.)
Adult female Clearly smaller, less bulky, and shorter-billed than male. Has black crown, usually speckled white at sides.
Juvenile Much as adults, but with red of nape and tail-

coverts more orangey and less extensive. Both sexes have white-spotted black crown with a few red tips.
Bare parts Bill dark grey, blacker at tip. Legs and feet greenish-grey. Eyes white to pale yellowish.

GEOGRAPHICAL VARIATION Monotypic, with much individual variation.

MEASUREMENTS Wing of male 113-130, of female 108-127 (on average 5% shorter than male); tail of male 73-91, of female 72-95; bill of male 32-39, of female 25-28; tarsus of male 22-26, of female 20-23.5. Weight: males significantly heavier by almost a third, 83-92 versus 65-75.

VOICE Highly variable. Long series of up to 23 notes are used in long-distance communication. A common call consists of several connected *waa* notes and is uttered during encounters. Encounters are also the context of the (aggressive) *wup*, the more defensive *Ta* and *ta-a* calls. Three to five distinct notes are strung together in another call, *Bdddt*. Instrumental signals are delivered near the hole.

HABITS Occurs in pairs or in groups. Forages at all levels, mainly 7-20m above ground (but not on the ground), on trees, bushes, vines, poles and cacti. The main feeding techniques are gleaning, probing and pecking (which is less forceful than in Golden-fronted Woodpecker (53), as a comparison). Probing is directed at bromeliads and other large epiphytes, fruits (to obtain seeds and/or insects), crevices and holes. Females glean more (about one and a half times as much) than males and probe much less frequently (0.6% as against 34%; this difference may be reversed if other types of probing are included); males use hammering or pecking twice as much as females. Probably excavates sap wells. Often hangs upside-down, on twigs and pine cones, reaches for fruits, and also takes insects by hawking. Often forages in groups; particularly large aggregations form on fruiting trees. The most common displays are bowing and lateral swinging movements, which are associated with calls. Birds approaching their partner in flight stretch the wings upwards and glide the last few metres before landing. Mate-feeding seems to be part of the courtship. Several pairs form loose colonies of five and up to 20 or even more nests. Helpers seem to occur, but these appear not to be bound to one particular pair. Nest sites and prominent perches are defended against intruders or subdominants, and nest-site quality also seems to reflect social status. The highest holes are apparently occupied by dominant birds.

FOOD Various insects, but vegetable matter, including tree sap, seems especially important. Fruits and seeds, including corn, are readily taken. This species' predilection for fruits and seeds gives rise to problems, as it attacks oranges and cacao pods.

BREEDING Breeds all year round, but predominantly between February and July. As already mentioned, nests are clustered, usually in 1-3 (dead) trees, live or dead palms, cacti, stubs and telephone poles. Both sexes, but mainly the male, excavate the nest. The clutch contains 4-6 eggs. The nestlings are fed by regurgitation.

REFERENCES Bond 1985; Selander 1966; Short 1974a; Wallace 1974.

45 JAMAICAN WOODPECKER
Melanerpes radiolatus   Plate 12

IDENTIFICATION Length c. 24-26cm. Medium-sized, with long, more or less pointed bill curved on culmen and fairly broad across nostrils. Found only in Jamaica, where it is the only woodpecker apart from very different Yellow-bellied Sapsucker (55), which occurs only in winter. Has black upperparts very narrowly barred white, dark olive underparts with indistinct yellow to reddish belly patch and slight barring on lower flanks, and a white face with prominent red eye and with red crown to hindneck (crown dark grey on females). Very common.

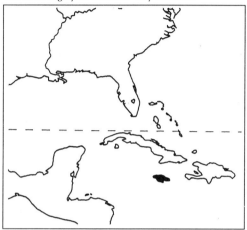

DISTRIBUTION Endemic to Jamaica, West Indies.

HABITAT Found in a variety of habitats, including mangrove woodland, wooded pastures, lowland copses, citrus groves and coconut plantations, dry and wet limestone forest, mist forest, and lower montane rain forest. Highest densities (0.91 individuals/ha) are reached in secondary mesophytic forest

DESCRIPTION
Adult male Forecrown to hindneck entirely red. Rest of head, including forehead, superciliary area, chin and throat (to uppermost breast) white, tinged greyish or olive on rear ear-coverts. Upperparts, upperwing-coverts and tertials black, narrowly barred white (often with olive/green tinge), bars broadest on rump and uppertail-coverts. Primaries and secondaries black, browner on primaries, all but outer primaries with well-spaced narrow white bars on both webs (broader on inner webs). Uppertail black, central feather pair finely barred white on inner (rarely, also outer) webs and outer pair with small white spots/bars on outer (sometimes also inner) webs. Underparts from breast olive-grey to olive-buff, feathers initially tinged greenish at tips, with diffuse yellow to reddish area in belly centre; lower flanks, vent and undertail-coverts black, barred white to olive-white. Underwing brownish-black, barred white. Undertail as uppertail, but more brownish-black and with outer feathers tinged olive.
Adult female Has crown grey to dark grey, sometimes buff-tinged or partly black.
Juvenile Duller than adults, with greyer underparts and yellower belly patch, and with flank bars more diffuse. Both sexes have red in crown, less extensive on female (which soon acquires grey coloration of adult).
Bare parts Bill black. Legs and feet slaty-black. Eyes red; brown in juveniles. Orbital skin grey to brown.

GEOGRAPHICAL VARIATION None. Monotypic.

MEASUREMENTS Wing 122-141; tail 78-94; bill 31-38.5; tarsus 23-26.5. Weight: 92-131 (males about 12% heavier than females).

VOICE Most frequent call a loud *kaaa*, which may be repeated two or three times in succession. Single *kao* calls are given during mild alarm, which, however, can be raised to a scold. A very loud *kaaaah* seems to be used for advertising the territory. *Wee-cha weecha* calls are heard during intraspecific encounters. During the breeding season, *krirr, krirr* and more intimate *whirr-whirr* calls are typical. Instrumental sounds include drumming, by both sexes, and mutual tapping near the nest hole.

HABITS Forages on trees, bromeliads and other epiphytes being important sites. Foraging height correlates with tree height; most foraging takes place in inner and outer branches of mid-crown, but some visits are also paid to the lower and upper crown and to vines. Food-seeking on trunks is rare. Snatching (when eating fruit) and probing predominate as feeding modes, followed by pecking (about 15%), gleaning and some occasional aerial feeding. No clear sexual difference in foraging behaviour seems to exist. Displays described for this woodpecker include crest-raising when disturbed or excited. Bill-waving occurs usually in connection with *weecha*-calls: tail is spread, the crest raised, and the head swings from side to side through a 180° angle. Jamaican Woodpeckers occupy overlapping home ranges, territorial defence being restricted to a radius of 40m around the nest. No interspecific aggression seems to occur, and even potential nest-hole competitors are not attacked.

FOOD Nestling diet consists of small invertebrates (snails, lepidopterans, othopterans, ants, coleopterans), vertebrates (*Anolis*) and fruits (*Cecropia, Ficus, Daphnopsis*). *Cecropia* and *Ficus* fruits form an important part of the vegetable content, which comprises almost half of all food eaten. Insects (*Orthoptera, Lepidoptera, Coleoptera*) form the major part of the animal prey: most are species which live on wood surfaces, in crevices, debris and epiphytes; wood-boring forms (e.g. Buprestidae) are rarely taken. Most prey items are in the 1-10mm size class.

BREEDING The breeding season spans December to August, but may sometimes be longer. Nests in trunks and branches of dead trees and dead branches of live trees, and in utility poles, most nests being 5-10m up. Nest-hole diameter averages 65mm (47-77mm). Male carries out approximately two-thirds of all the excavating. Clutch size 3-5 eggs, laid at daily intervals. Laying period ranges from January to beginning of July. Young hatch 13 day after the first egg is laid. Both sexes incubate, but only the male stays in the nest at night; during the day, both sexes take about equal share of breeding duties. The same applies to brooding, which ceases completely about three days before the young fledge. Young are fed at an average rate of 10.3 visits/hour (2-22), with peak activity in the middle of the nestling period (days 10-20), the male being slightly more active. Young are fed inside the nest up to the 17th day; the food is carried in the bill. Feacal sacs are removed by both sexes. Young fledge after one month, and remain with their parents for at least one further month. One pair may raise a second or even third brood in a season.

REFERENCES Bond 1985; Cruz 1977; Downer & Sutton 1990; Wallace 1974.

46 GOLDEN-CHEEKED WOODPECKER
Melanerpes chrysogenys   Plate 12

Other name: Gold-cheeked Woodpecker

IDENTIFICATION Length 19-22cm. Small, with long-ish, barely chisel-tipped bill curved on culmen and rather broad across nostrils. Barred black and white above, including on tail, and brownish below, with inconspicuous yellow belly patch and indistinct barring on lower flanks. Head shows golden cheeks and ear-coverts, black over and broadly around eye, and bright yellow hindneck; male has red crown and yellow to orange nape, female having grey-brown crown. In flight, shows broad white barring on wings and a white patch at primary bases. A little-known species.

Similar species Grey-breasted Woodpecker (47), which partly overlaps in range, is similar in appearance, but lacks yellow in the plumage; it also has a brownish head (male with small red crown patch), with less black around eye and usually with a few red feathers just below eye, and has less barring in tail.

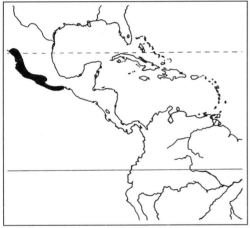

DISTRIBUTION Restricted to the Pacific slope and plain of Mexico from S Sinaloa, N and S Guerrero and to Oaxaca.

HABITAT Mesic to xeric forests and forest edge, forest patches, open areas with scattered trees and plantations. From sea level to about 1500m.

DESCRIPTION
M. c. chrysogenys **Adult male** Forehead whitish, with golden-yellow at base; crown red, becoming more golden-orange on nape, and bright yellow-gold on hindneck. Area from upper rear lores back along crown side and broadly encircling eye black. Lower lores, across cheeks, and ear-coverts deep golden-yellow, with broad area below this paler, more buffish/yellow-buff in colour. Chin and throat golden-buff. Upperparts black, narrowly barred white, becoming more black-barred white on rump and uppertail-coverts. Upperwing-coverts black, with large white spots and tips; secondaries and tertials black, barred white; primaries black, narrowly edged and tipped white (when fresh), and barred white on basal area, white bars forming a patch about halfway along feathers. Uppertail black, central feather pair broadly barred white, adjacent two pairs unbarred (third pair sometimes with a few bars), fourth pair with half-bars, and outer (large) pair fully barred white. Underparts grey-brown to brownish-buff,

strongly washed olive-yellow (feather tips yellowish), with orange patch of variable extent in belly centre, becoming paler and greyer in lower regions, with dark bars on thighs, flanks and undertail-coverts. Underwing brown, barred white, with white patch on primaries. Undertail as uppertail, but paler.

Adult female Slightly shorter-billed than male. Has grey-buff crown, often darker at sides, with orange-red nape patch; cheeks and ear-coverts tend to be paler and less golden than on male.

Juvenile Upperparts browner/greyer, with barring less contrasting; paler and greyer below, strongly suffused yellow, with obscure barring in lower regions. Both sexes have red in crown; young female has less red and often much black in crown, but red is soon lost.

Bare parts Bill black. Legs and feet green-grey. Eyes reddish to orange-brown. Orbital skin blackish.

GEOGRAPHICAL VARIATION Varies clinally, but with two apparent races.
> *M. c. chrysogenys* (northwest part of range, from Sinaloa to Nayarit) Described above.
> *M. c. flavinuchus* (south of nominate, from Jalisco to Oaxaca) Slightly larger and duller, with greyer underparts, less yellow on face and less bright nape patch. Northeastern populations (often separated as '*morelensis*') tend to be paler, with even less yellow and orange in plumage, but overlap greatly with other *flavinuchus* and are therefore included within latter.

MEASUREMENTS Wing 110-126; tail 62-78; bill 23.5-30.5; tarsus 19-23. Weight: 55-88.

VOICE Many churring calls and short series of notes, among them a nasal *ki-di-dik*, more explosive than call of Gila Woodpecker (50). A loud, nasal *cheek-oo, cheek-oo, cheek-oo, keh-i-heh-ek*, softer *keh-i-heh* or *kuh-uh-uh*. Drumming apparently not described.

HABITS Forages on trees by gleaning, probing and pecking; further details apparently not known.

FOOD Adults and larvae of beetles, and ants form part of this species' insect food. Feeds also on fruits and seeds.

BREEDING Breeds from May to July; nest holes are in trees or cacti. Eggs and clutch apparently undescribed.

REFERENCES Alden 1969; Howell & Webb in press.

47 GREY-BREASTED WOODPECKER
Melanerpes hypopolius   Plate 12

IDENTIFICATION Length c. 19-21cm. Small, with fairly long, slightly chisel-tipped bill curved on culmen and fairly broad across nostrils. Barred black and white above and on wings, with plain grey-brown underparts. The head is dull brownish-buff, white on forehead and throat, with a small area of black around eye and a few red feathers beneath it; males also have a red patch in centre/front of crown. A very poorly known Mexican species, somewhat resembling Golden-cheeked Woodpecker (46), but found mainly in cactus deserts.

Similar species Differs from Golden-cheeked, whose range partly overlaps, in lacking yellow/gold on head and neck and on belly and in having less red in crown of male and less white barring in tail; also, habitat preferences differ.

DISTRIBUTION Endemic to the interior of SW Mexico from N Guerrero and Morelos to C Oaxaca.

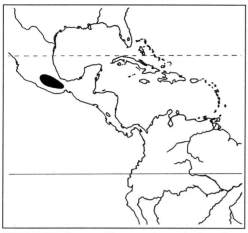

HABITAT Xeric areas with scattered trees, shrubs, or large organpipe cacti, and riverside groves. Avoids the latter in the presence of Golden-cheeked Woodpeckers. Hills between 900 and 1800m.

DESCRIPTION

Adult male Forehead white to buffish-white; central crown with patch of red, somewhat rounded in shape; narrow area of black around eye, with a few red feathers beneath eye (sometimes also in moustachial region, but occasionally red absent altogether). Rest of head and neck to uppermost mantle pale buff-brown to grey-brown, often slightly darker on rear ear-coverts and usually paler or whitish in malar region. Upperparts and upperwing-coverts black barred white to buffish-white; rump and uppertail-coverts white, with black markings in form of spots, streaks or arrowhead bars; flight feathers black, broadly barred white, primaries also tipped and narrowly edged white and with white bars sometimes forming a patch near base. Uppertail black, initially tipped white, central feather pair with large white spots on inner webs, outer pair barred white on outer webs. Underparts grey-brown, becoming paler and with variable black arrowhead barring in lower regions. Underwing brown, barred white, with white patch at base of primaries. Undertail as uppertail, but browner.

Adult female As male, but lacks red in crown.

Juvenile Duller than adults, browner and greyer, with less contrasting barring. Both sexes have red in crown.

Bare parts Bill blackish, paler on lower mandible. Legs and feet grey. Eyes reddish to brown.

GEOGRAPHICAL VARIATION None. Monotypic.

MEASUREMENTS Wing 116-131; tail 74-87; bill 23-26; tarsus 18-22. Weight: 46-54.

VOICE The variable calls are generally lower-pitched and harsher than those of Golden-fronted Woodpecker (53). They include nasal *yek-a yek-a* calls and series of dry *chi-i-i-ir churrs*.

HABITS Conspicuous and often in small foraging groups of up to ten birds. Roosts may be clustered and up to 26 birds gather at them; roost holes occupied by single individuals or up to four birds.

FOOD Probably similar to that of others in genus; fruits (*Ziziphus*) have been recorded.

BREEDING The breeding season extends from late April to July. Nest holes are built in trees and habitually in cacti.

REFERENCES Hendricks *et al.* 1990; Howell & Webb in press; Peterson & Chalif 1973; Selander & Giller 1963.

48 YUCATAN WOODPECKER
Melanerpes pygmaeus   Plate 13

Other name: Red-vented Woodpecker
Forms a superspecies wirh *rubricapillus*.

IDENTIFICATION Length c. 16-18cm. Very small, with long, almost pointed bill curved on culmen and broad across nostrils. Barred black and white above and on wings, with white rump, and buffish-brown to grey-brown below, with red belly patch and slight barring on lower flanks. The head is brownish-buff, with whiter forehead and supercilium, and usually with golden-yellow around the front of the face (including chin); males have red from crown to hindneck, while females have red only on nape and hindneck.

Similar species Differs hardly at all from Red-crowned Woodpecker (49), and often treated as conspecific with it, although the two are separated geographically by some 750km or more. Yucatan Woodpecker is slightly longer-tailed and generally shows a more extensive and more golden coloration in face, but some overlap occurs and occasional individuals may have the yellow much reduced; mainland birds seem generally to have less barring on tail, but this feature is variable in both taxa. The population on Guanaja Island off N Honduras is somewhat intermediate between those breeding to the northwest (in Yucatan) and the Red-crowned to the southeast (N Venezuela). The two species appear to differ little, if at all, in behaviour. The golden area on the face also helps distinguish Yucatan Woodpecker from the local race of Golden-fronted (53), which is bigger and has red at bill base.

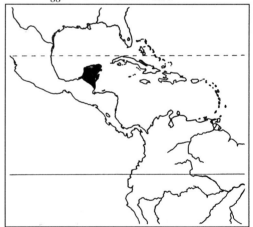

DISTRIBUTION Restricted to Yucatan peninsula (Mexico, Belize, NE Guatemala) and Cozumel and Guanaja islands.

HABITAT Deciduous forest, edge, clearings, second growth, and coastal scrub. Note that the similar Golden-fronted Woodpecker prefers higher forests.

DESCRIPTION

M. p. rubricomus **Adult male** Lower forehead, lores, front part of moustachial region and chin yellowish-gold to golden-orange; upper forehead, forecrown and narrow short supercilium whitish or buffy-white; central crown to nape and hindneck bright red. Rest of head and throat buffy-brown, tinged grey. Mantle, scapulars and upper back black, narrowly barred buffish-white; lower back, rump and uppertail-coverts white, rarely with a few black streaks/bars. Upperwing and its coverts black, barred narrowly white; primaries browner, tipped white (when fresh), and with bars restricted to bases. Uppertail black, barred/spotted white on outer webs of outer feathers. Underparts buffish grey-brown, paler in lower regions, with red patch in centre of belly (variable in extent); flanks and thighs to undertail-coverts variably barred black. Underwing brown, barred white. Undertail as uppertail, but browner.

Adult female Slightly shorter-billed than male. Has red on head restricted to nape and hindneck, and often less bright in colour.

Juvenile Duller than adults, with less contrasting barring above and with belly patch paler; head pattern more diffuse. Males have red on crown to hindneck; females have crown blackish, often barred, and occasionally with traces of red.

Bare parts Bill blackish. Legs and feet pale grey. Eyes red to brown.

GEOGRAPHICAL VARIATION Three races.

M. p. rubricomus (Yucatan peninsula, Belize and NE Guatemala) Described above.

M. p. pygmaeus (Cozumel Island, off Yucatan) As *rubricomus*, but a little smaller and darker.

M. p. tysoni (Guanaja Island, off N Honduras) Larger-billed than above two races. Has forehead less golden/orange, with restricted golden-yellow on front of face, and red area on head of male usually broken by buff-brown at rear; tail usually shows more white.

MEASUREMENTS Wing 95-102; tail 57-63; bill of male 20-23, of female 18-21; tarsus 17-20. Weight: 35-43.

VOICE Similar to that of Golden-fronted, but generally softer and less nasal. A soft, rolling *churr, pyurr-r-r,* and *chuh-uh-uh-uh-uh-uh* or *keh heh heh-heh heh-heh heh-heh.*

HABITS Forages habitually in lower levels than other congeners of the area. In other aspects of its behaviour probably very similar to Red-crowned Woodpecker.

FOOD Not recorded.

BREEDING Breeds April-May.

REFERENCES Howell & Webb in press; Peterson & Chalif 1973.

49 RED-CROWNED WOODPECKER
Melanerpes rubricapillus Plate 13

Other names: Wagler's Woodpecker (Panama); Little Red-headed Woodpecker
Forms a superspecies with *pygmaeus.*

IDENTIFICATION Length c. 16-18cm. Very small, with longish, slightly chisel-tipped bill curved on culmen and fairly broad across nostrils. Barred black and white above, with white rump, and grey to grey-brown below, often washed olive, with reddish belly and barred flanks. Face is rather pale grey-brown. Male has red crown, becoming paler red on nape and hindneck, some individuals/populations having grey-brown area at nape isolating the crown; females lack red on crown, and hindneck is often paler than male's. A common species, often noisy and conspicuous as it moves through the treetops.

Similar species See Yucatan Woodpecker (48). Overlaps in range with Hoffmann's Woodpecker (54) in Costa Rica, where the two often hybridise; Hoffmann's has similar crown pattern, but contrasting golden nape and hindneck, and golden-yellow belly patch.

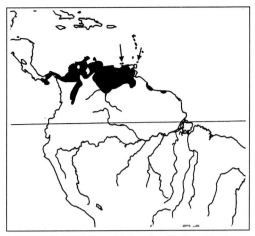

DISTRIBUTION From C America (Belize, Honduras, including Cozumel and Guanaja islands) through Costa Rica and Panama (and adjacent islands) to northern Colombia and Venezuela, east to Surinam. Common on Tobago and on Patos, absent from Trinidad, Monos, Huevos and Chacachacare.

HABITAT A resident of humid to dry semi-open country, avoiding heavy forest. Can be found in such habitats as lighter woodland, deciduous forest, arid and semi-arid scrub, dry woodland, shrubby clearings, mangroves, cultivated areas (coconut plantations), residential areas and gardens. Also frequents edges and more open parts of forest, gallery woodland with tall trees, semi-open areas and secondary growth. Locally common in tall cacti. Often increases following forest clearance. Ranges to higher altitudes in wooded habitats, often much lower in more open ones. Occurs from sea level to about 1600-1700m in Costa Rica and Colombia, to 1900m in Venezuela north of the Orinoco, and to 500m south of it.

DESCRIPTION

M. r. rubricapillus **Adult male** Nasal tufts and lower forehead pale yellow; upper forehead whitish; crown bright red, becoming somewhat more orangey-red on nape and hindneck. Rest of head greyish-buff, paler or whitish on lores and side of forecrown and on chin and throat (a very few individuals show faint hint of yellow on chin, lores and fore part of moustachial region). Mantle, scapulars and upper back black, barred white; lower back, rump and uppertail-coverts white. Upperwing and its coverts black, barred white; primaries browner, tipped white (when fresh), and with bars confined to bases and joining to form a white patch. Uppertail black, outer pair barred white on outer webs, remaining feathers with little or no white. Underparts buffish-grey to grey-buff, washed olive or yellowish (mainly when fresh), becoming paler in lower regions, with thighs and lower flanks to undertail-coverts barred black; centre of belly diffusely reddish to orange-red. Underwing brown, barred white, with white patch at base of primaries. Undertail brownish-black, washed yellow on outer feathers, with markings as above.

Adult female Slightly shorter-billed than male. Has crown concolorous with sides of head, or paler, with nape and hindneck reddish to orange-red.

Juvenile Duller and browner than adults, with less contrasting barring, and often slightly streaked below, with paler and usually mottled belly patch. Head pattern as respective adult, but red of male duller and nape/hindneck of both sexes paler or yellowish; females may have dark crown, often somewhat barred, and occasionally with a few reddish feather tips (soon lost).

Bare parts Bill blackish. Legs and feet grey. Eyes red to brown. Orbital skin grey-brown.

GEOGRAPHICAL VARIATION Four races are recognised here, though several others have been described.

  M. r. rubricapillus (range of species, apart from small areas occupied by following three races) Described above. Varies in depth of coloration (especially on underparts); populations of Tobago, NE Venezuela and Margarita Island (named as '*terricolor*') are somewhat larger, have white bars on outer webs of central tail feathers and seem to be constantly darker below, but similar individuals can be found in other parts of range. See also *M. r. paraguanae*, below.

  M. r. subfusculus (Coiba Island, Panama) Barely smaller than mainland nominate. Distinctly darker below, deep grey-brown on breast and sides.

  M. r. seductus (San Miguel Island, Panama) Shorter-winged than mainland nominate. Breast a shade darker; female has more red on nape.

  M. r. paraguanae (Paraguana peninsula, N Venezuela) Longer-tailed than nominate. Has broader white bars above; belly patch more golden-yellow (less orange/red). Tail usually with much white in centre and outer feathers all black. Lower forehead pale yellow; hindcrown/nape buff-brown, isolating red crown from yellower lower nape and hindneck (female has nape and hindneck pale orangey-brown). Note, however, that similar-plumaged individuals, with red of crown separated from nape, occur not uncommonly further east in northern S America.

MEASUREMENTS Wing of male 100-114, of female 96-110; tail of male 43-60, of female 43-58; bill of male 21.6-28.7, of female 20-25.3; tarsus of male 17.8-21.7, of female 17.4-20.1. Weight: 40-65.

VOICE Typical calls are a *churr, churr, krr-r-r-r*, often prolonged and with wavering pitch, ending abruptly with a sharp note. These and various other calls, such as a *wicka, wicka* during displays, resemble those of Hoffmann's Woodpecker and its N American congener the Red-bellied Woodpecker (51), and the chatters also resemble those of Boat-billed Flycatcher *Megarhynchus pitangua*. Both sexes drum during the breeding season, the rhythm of the rolls being slower than in Red-bellied Woodpecker. Mutual tapping at the hole also occurs.

HABITS This rather confiding and noisy woodpecker stays paired throughout year, but roosts solitarily. The pair maintains contact with *churr*-calls. Forages at various heights, middle and lower levels being preferred. Foraging techniques include hammering into bark, probing, gleaning from trunks, branches and foliage, and reaching for fruits; pierces the skin of larger fruit to obtain its contents. Readily takes fruit from feeders. Larger food items are secured in crevices and then processed with pecking. Displays include bowing and lateral swinging of the body with the bill held straight, for instance when cautiously approaching a feeding site or roost, but certainly also during social encounters. Upon landing at close distance to another woodpecker, in another type of display wings are held stiffly upwards. Territorial, at least during the breeding season, the pair members roosting in separate holes; rarely, two birds may share a roost. Possibly because roosts are often small or situated in a horizontal branch or stub, Red-crowned Woodpeckers frequently enter roosts tail first. Loses out to Golden-naped Woodpeckers (40) in interspecific encounters and also suffers severe nest- and roost-site competition

from tityras.

FOOD Ants, beetles, grubs, crickets, other small insects and spiders; wood-boring larvae play a minor role. Generally less dependent on arthropods than, for instance, Hoffmann's Woodpecker. Eats many fruits and berries, including papayas, cashews and bananas at feeders, and visits balsa flowers for nectar. Because of its fruit-eating habits often considered a nuisance in plantations and gardens.

BREEDING Breeding season spans February to June (July) in Costa Rica and Panama, May-June in Colombia, breeds May-November in Venezuela and March-July on Tobago. Nest hole 3-23m up, usually in slender dead tree or branch; sometimes in a large cactus or fence post. Both sexes take part in excavating, though the former roost of the male may become the nest hole, too. Clutch comprises 3-4 eggs, from which usually two young hatch after ten days of incubation. The young stay in the nest for 31-33 days. Both sexes partake in parental care. The male stays in the nest overnight. Food for the nestlings is carried in the bill. Nest sanitation is not neglected until immediately before the fledging of the young. The fledglings are cared for by the parents for a further month or so. Some pairs are double-brooded.

REFERENCES Belcher & Smooker 1936; Blake 1965; ffrench 1990; Haverschmidt 1968; Hilty & Brown 1984; Kilham 1972a; Meyer de Schauensee & Phelps 1978; Otvos 1967; Ridgely & Gwynne 1989; Skutch 1948a, 1969; Slud 1969; Snyder 1966; Stiles & Skutch 1989.

50   GILA WOODPECKER
Melanerpes uropygialis   Plate 14

IDENTIFICATION Length 21.5-24cm. Small, with long, barely chisel-tipped bill curved on culmen and fairly broad across nostrils. Barred black and white above and on wings, with less black on rump, and greyish to light brown on head and underparts, with yellow belly patch and barred flanks; tail is barred in centre and at sides. Male has a small patch of red in centre of crown. In flight, reveals dark primaries with white patch at base. A common woodpecker of arid habitats, not likely to be misidentified if seen well. Interbreeds to a limited extent with Golden-fronted Woodpecker (53) in NW Mexico.

DISTRIBUTION From SW USA (S California, S Arizona; S Nevada, New Mexico) south to Baja California, along the Pacific slope and adjacent highlands of W Mexico, down to Chalisco and Aguascalientes.

HABITAT Lives in arid to mesic areas with scattered trees or large cacti and also in somewhat more mesic habitats such as riparian woodlands (especially cottonwood), subtropical forests, and plantations. Where this species meets Golden-fronted Woodpecker it is restricted to drier habitats. Habitats span altitudes from sea level to about 900m, to 1600m at the southern tip of its range.

DESCRIPTION
M. u. uropygialis **Adult male** Small red patch in centre of forecrown. Rest of head pale greyish-brown (sometimes somewhat paler or darker), usually more whitish on forehead and upper lores (nasal tufts buffish, rarely pale yellow) and occasionally on chin; hindneck sometimes with yellowish tinge. Upperparts black, barred white (or bars grey-buff on uppermost mantle), becoming mainly white with narrow black bars on rump; uppertail-coverts white,

with narrow black arrowhead bars. Upperwing-coverts, tertials and secondaries black, narrowly barred white; primaries and their coverts brownish-black, primaries tipped white (when fresh) and with white bars at bases merging to form white patch on outer primaries. Uppertail black (tipped white when fresh), central feather pair barred white on inner webs and often with white streak bordering shaft on outer webs, outer large feathers barred white, and next innermost (fourth) pair barred white at tip of inner webs and on edge of outer webs. Grey-brown of head continues over underparts, becoming paler and with arrowhead bars in lower regions, and with yellow to golden-yellow patch in centre of belly. Underwing as upperwing, but paler, with black-barred white coverts. Undertail blackish-brown, patterned as above.

Adult female Smaller and shorter-billed than male, and lacks red on crown.

Juvenile Duller than adults, with white upperpart barring more buff-tinged, flank bars more diffuse, belly patch paler, and with throat/moustachial area often faintly streaked/barred; crown usually dark-barred. Males show some reddish in crown.

Bare parts Bill blackish. Legs and feet usually blue-grey. Eyes deep red.

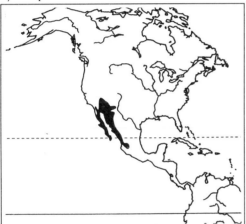

GEOGRAPHICAL VARIATION Varies mainly in darkness of head/underparts and width of black bars above, but individual variation quite widespread. Of four races recognised here, one may be untenable.

    M. u. uropygialis (SW USA to N Sonora) Described above. Varies somewhat, but generally relatively pale. Those in Colorado valley average a shade paler and shorter-winged than Arizona birds.
    M. u. brewsteri (S Baja California) Very like nominate, but clearly smaller.
    M. u. cardonensis (N Baja California) Darker, with heavier black barring above and brown head and underparts.
    M. u. fuscescens (S Sonora) Dark; very like *cardonensis*, and possibly not separable from it.

MEASUREMENTS Wing 117-140; tail 72-88; bill 28-35, of female 23.5-29; tarsus 20.5-25. Weight: 51-81 (males 20% heavier than females).

VOICE A vocal species with a wide range of variable calls (which even allow identification of some individuals by an experienced observer). Rolling *jurr uh-rr jurr uh-rr..* (more exactly *chürr*) calls, exhibiting a clear vibrato (i.e. regular frequency modulation) similar to Red-bellied Woodpecker

(51), serve as contact calls between members of a pair and as territorial advertisement and are most frequently uttered by males. The length (0.18-0.38sec) and the minimum pitch of this note show great variation among individuals. More rasping versions of this call, *rruhk-rruhk..*, are heard when birds are more agitated. When alarmed, also gives series of sharp *pip pip..* notes, uttered about twice as often by females as by males. Both sexes drum occasionally, the female even less frequently, in long regular rolls, especially in the pre-nesting period, when drumming usually precedes agonistic behaviour.

HABITS A conspicuous and noisy member of the desert bird community. Forages at all levels of its habitat, from treetops, cacti and bushes to the ground. Very versatile in its foraging techniques, this woodpecker obtains its food by gleaning and reaching, probing and pecking. Readily accepts feeders with suet, meat and fruit, and has been observed to feed young with pieces of bark or seeds soaked in syrup provided at a feeder. In alarm and in conflict situations, birds bob and swing their heads and bodies. These behaviours and bill-pointing are the displays most frequently seen in social interactions and are also associated with vocalisations. Generally a rather aggressive species which also attacks other species (predominantly flickers and starlings, but also thrashers and the like). Most aggression is part of nest-site defence in a radius of 40-50m around the hole. Family groups stay in a territory after nesting until the young disperse or are driven away prior to the next breeding attempt. Following dispersal of young and subdominant birds, local abundance may drop by 50%. The holes produced by this woodpecker provide quarters for many other bird species, mammals and reptiles, which also compete with it for nest sites.

FOOD This species is essentially omnivorous. The diet includes various kinds of insects, ants, beetles, grasshoppers, insect larvae obtained from surfaces, galls and so on; even earthworms and lizards are taken, as also are eggs and chicks of other birds. Fruits and seeds play an important role as a source of nutrition: fruits of cacti, berries, corn, fruits from gardens and plantations, and honey/sugarwater from feeders are included in the wide range of non-animal food.

BREEDING The breeding season commences in April and stretches to June; second clutches may be laid in July. The nest hole is excavated by both sexes in a cactus, a tree or palm stump at up to 10m (mean for cactus nests 7.2m); holes in living cacti can be used only after they have dried out. The clutch comprises 3-4 (6) eggs, later ones containing fewer eggs. So far as is known, both parents feed the young by carrying the food in the bill.

REFERENCES Antevs 1948; Bent 1937; Brenowitz 1977, 1978; Inouye *et al.* 1981; Rice *et al.* 1980; Selander & Giller 1963.

51 RED-BELLIED WOODPECKER
Melanerpes carolinus   Plate 14

Forms a superspecies with *superciliaris*.

IDENTIFICATION Length c. 24cm. Small, with long, slightly chisel-tipped bill curved on culmen and fairly broad across nostrils. Superficially similar in basic pattern to Gila Woodpecker (50), with boldly barred upperparts and wings, white rump and pale underparts; central tail feathers are largely white, with some black barring, and outer rectrices are barred black and white.

Reddish patch on belly may be rather difficult to see. Male has entire top and rear of head conspicuously bright red, female usually lacking red on crown (which is grey). In flight, shows white patch at base of primaries, as well as white rump.

Similar species In southwest, range overlaps with that of Golden-fronted Woodpecker (53), but local race of the latter is easily distinguished from Red-bellied by its very pale grey head and underparts, with yellow lower forehead and golden nape and hindneck, the male also having a small patch of red in centre of crown. Golden-fronted also has all-black central tail feathers.

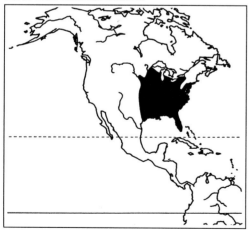

DISTRIBUTION Widely distributed in eastern N America from South Dakota, southern Minnesota through Michigan to southern Ontario, south to C Texas and Florida. Sometimes extends further north.

MOVEMENTS At least during severe winters, northern populations try to escape unfavourable conditions. Generally, Red-bellied Woodpeckers concentrate in opportune areas in winter and may by found more commonly in places where they were rare or absent in summer.

HABITAT Mesic habitats, dead trees, densely wooded lowlands, swampy woods, open deciduous or mixed coniferous woodlands with very large trees, and pecan groves; also found in heavy woods of oak and elm along rivers and creek bottoms, as well as at shade trees and dead trees in residential areas. Foraging and nesting habitats tend to be denser and can contain more understorey than those used by Red-headed Woodpecker (37). From sea level to 600m, locally to 900m.

DESCRIPTION

Adult male Lower forehead pinkish to reddish-orange; upper forehead, crown and entire rear of head to lower neck sides and uppermost mantle bright red, occasionally interrupted by grey feathering across central upper forehead (rarely, nape/hindneck may be more orange or, exceptionally, even yellowish). Sides of head and neck, including chin and throat, grey to whitish-grey, paler in superciliary and moustachial areas, and generally with tinge of orange or pinkish (varying in strength) to feathering from lores to cheeks and chin. Upperparts black, barred white, becoming white with variable black streaks and bars on rump; uppertail-coverts white, sometimes with a few indistinct black streaks or U-shaped markings. Upperwing-coverts, secondaries and tertials black, with white bars/spots; primaries and primary coverts black, with large area of white at base of primaries forming central patch. Uppertail black, central feather pair with white on inner webs (generally with a few black spots/bars) and outer pair barred black and white on outer webs. (In fresh plumage, all flight and tail feathers are tipped white.) Underparts pale grey, somewhat darker on breast, and normally tinged olive, buffish or pink, with pale red/pink (sometimes orange) patch on central belly diffusely bordered by yellowish wash; lower flanks to undertail-coverts with black V-shaped markings. Underwing grey, with white primary patch, coverts barred grey and white. Undertail as uppertail, but paler and greyer.

Adult female Somewhat smaller than male, and head lacks red on upper forehead and crown, which are grey (though occasionally shows small central patch of red); red/pink tones in loral and moustachial areas normally less extensive than on male, belly patch often smaller and/or paler, and reddish suffusion in general is less marked.

Juvenile Upperpart barring less contrasting than on adults, with white bars dirtier; underparts darker, with variable blackish streaking on (mainly) breast and usually more widespread but more diffuse barring in lower regions, with belly patch paler and often indistinct (especially on young females). Juvenile males have less extensive and paler red on crown and nape than adult, crown being mostly grey with black barring (occasionally, crown entirely black/blackish); females have even smaller amount of reddish on nape/hindneck, but have a small area of red in crown.

Bare parts Bill black. Legs and feet grey to green-grey. Eyes deep red to red-brown; brown in juveniles.

GEOGRAPHICAL VARIATION A monotypic species, showing relatively little variation. Northeastern populations tend to be longer-billed, while an east-to-west cline of increasing width of white barring on upperparts may be evident in long series of skins. S Florida population, slightly smaller and tending to show more white on upperparts, paler red on lower forehead and less white in tail, may perhaps be considered sufficiently distinct to be separated racially (as '*perplexus*').

MEASUREMENTS Wing of male 123-139, of female 122-133; tail of male 70-85, of female 68-84; bill of male 27.7-33, of female 25.5-30; tarsus 19.4-23. Weight: 56-91 (male 8-9% heavier than female).

VOICE Red-bellied Woodpeckers announce their presence and maintain pair contact with *churr* calls, which are essentially vibratos, given as single notes or in series of up to four, and also in association with other vocalisations and drumming. Long series of harsh, low-pitched notes, *cha-aa-ah*, are typically associated with territorial struggles. Alarmed or otherwise agitated individuals utter highly variable *chip* or *chup* calls, delivered as single notes or as sometimes long (8 secs) series. Close aggressive encounters are characterised by *chee-wuk* or *wuck-ah* calls, which also may comprise long series. At more intimate contacts quiet *grr* notes are exchanged. Drums in weak rolls at a steady rhythm, though a single introductory strike may be separated from the others by an appreciably longer interval. At a potential or actual nest site mutual (drum-)tapping occurs.

HABITS Prefers to feed in upper storeys of live and dead deciduous trees, particularly oaks, favouring medium-sized branches between 10 and 30cm in diameter; dead substrates constitute a third to more than half of those visited. The relative use of dead substrates, however, depends very much on local availability. Surface probing is most frequent, with some occasional pecking and hammering; gleaning is the main foraging technique during the breeding season, pecking or hammering constituting about 15%. Flycatches when the occasion arises, but far less commonly than the Red-headed Woodpecker. Sexual differences in foraging most pronounced in winter, when males more often search trunks for arthropod food. Seed-eating is rather important, especially in combination with this woodpecker's storing behaviour. Collecting and storing of acorns, nuts and various other seeds begins in autumn and continues to early winter, single food items being stored usually in crevices; insects and fruit are also occasionally cached. Visual displays comprise practically the full range of postures and movements typical of woodpeckers. Males, in particular, raise the head feathers in encounters, in which tail- and wing-spreading can also occur. Aggressive conflicts are expressed with bobbing and (slow) swinging movements and with various forms of bill-pointing. Immediately before alighting close to another woodpecker, wings may be held stiff and upwards, resulting in a conspicuous glide. Females often initiate copulations by mounting the male (reversed mounting); this behaviour may continue even after eggs have been laid, and it does not necessarily stimulate the male to copulate. When forced to compete with the superior Red-headed Woodpecker, this species moves to other sites rather than shifting to other strata; territories of the two species may, however, overlap broadly without any interspecific aggression. With Golden-fronted Woodpecker, by contrast, mutually exclusive territories are maintained. Besides other woodpeckers, starlings are important competitors for nest sites.

FOOD Omnivorous, with plant material constituting 40% (spring) to 80% (winter) of the diet. The insect food contains some wood-boring larvae, but the main bulk comprises ants, flies, grasshoppers, beetle larvae and caterpillars. Spiders are also taken, and bigger items are tree frogs, lizards, and bird eggs and nestlings. A great variety of fruits (e.g. apples, peaches, oranges) and berries (e.g. mulberries, juniper, blackberries, palmetto berries) is taken; Seeds and nuts become the major food in winter. The stores may contain acorns, pecan or hickory, hazelnuts, pine seeds, and others. Corn is important locally. Tree sap is also licked from tree wounds or sapsucker wells.

BREEDING Red-bellied Woodpeckers nest from late March to August. Usually, the male produces a new cavity as nest site, but sometimes his roost serves the purpose (roosts are often smaller than nest holes). The nest is situated in a dead

or, in one out of four cases, a live tree at 2-18m. Does not show the Red-headed Woodpecker's preference for trunks and branches without bark and apparently does not require a pre-existing crack for excavation. The female joins in the preparation of the cavity towards completion. Copulations peak when eggs are laid. The clutch contains 4-6 (3-8) eggs. Both parents incubate, the male at night, and the chicks hatch after 12 days. Both deliver food to the nestlings, carrying it in the bill, and both brood (female possibly more) the chicks when they are still small. Faeces are removed throughout almost the entire nestling period; reports that only females carry out this chore require corroboration. The male stays with the nestlings overnight almost until they fledge, which takes place about 22-27 days after hatching. The young remain in the natal territory. A second, and rarely a third, brood may be raised in late summer/early autumn.

REFERENCES Brackbill 1969b; Conner 1980; Gamboa & Brown 1976; Jackson 1976; Hauser 1959, Neill & Harper 1990; Selander & Giller 1959; Stickel 1965; Williams & Batzli 1979a, 1979b; Willson 1970.

52 WEST INDIAN WOODPECKER
Melanerpes superciliaris   Plate 14

Other names: Great Red-bellied Woodpecker; Cayman Woodpecker (race *caymanensis*)
Forms a superspecies with *carolinus*.

IDENTIFICATION Length c. 27-32cm. Small to medium-sized, with long, slightly chisel-tipped bill curved on culmen and fairly broad across nostrils. Entirely barred above, including on inner wings and tail, and greyish to yellow-buff on face and underparts, with small area of red on belly and some dark flank barring; black markings on white uppertail-coverts usually shaped like horseshoes. Males of most races have red at base of upper mandible, a pale forehead, and red crown to hindneck, with an area of black above and behind eye, while females have pale colour of forehead extending over forecrown and black above eye continuing over rear crown. Those on Grand Cayman Island, however, have the black over and behind the eye replaced by white, and females have rear crown greyish-buff/brown.

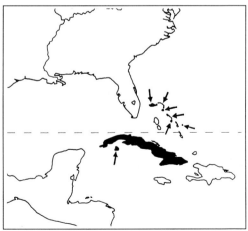

DISTRIBUTION Restricted to the West Indies, with main populations in Cuba, including Grand Cayman and Isle of

215

Pines, and several islands in the Bahamas, namely Grand Bahama, Abaco and San Salvador (Watling's Island). Has become scarce on Grand Bahama and San Salvador (race *nyeanus*), but very common in Cuba.

HABITAT Various types of wooded areas, including palms, forest and forest edge, palm plantations. On Grand Cayman, uncommon near human habitations and in grape-almond woodland and pure logwood forests, and fairly common in mangroves (winter and summer, suspected breeder), forest of logwood, thatch palm and red birch (winter, uncommon in summer) and limestone forest (common in winter). Occurs from lowlands to mountains.

DESCRIPTION

M. s. superciliaris **Adult male** Nasal tufts light red; forehead and sides of forecrown white to buffish-white; crown, nape and hindneck red. Area just in front of eye black, this colour continuing over eye and back along central crown side. Side of head and neck side, chin and throat pale grey to whitish with buffy or yellowish-brown tinge (mainly towards rear). Upperparts buffish-white (whiter when worn), barred black, bars fewer and narrower on rump; uppertail-coverts white, with narrow black horseshoe-shaped markings. Upperwing-coverts largely white, with narrow black bars; secondaries and tertials black, broadly barred white; primaries and their coverts black, tipped white (when fresh), and with white at primary bases forming fairly large patch. Uppertail black, central feather pair with very broad white bars on inner webs (white bars broader than black bars) and with white at base of outer webs, and outer pair barred white on outer webs. Underparts below throat greyish, strongly tinged buffy-brown on breast, becoming paler olive-yellow on lower breast, pale yellow-buff on sides and whitish on flanks and undertail-coverts, with belly centre diffusely red to orangey-red; flanks and undertail-coverts with black arrowhead barring. Underwing greyish, with coverts barred black and white. Undertail much as uppertail, but somewhat paler and with grey tone to outer tail.

Adult female Slightly shorter-billed and less bulky than male. Pale colour of forehead continues onto crown, becoming blackish on rear crown and meeting with black area behind eye.

Juvenile Similar to adults, but less contrastingly patterned and often with tinge of red to plumage of upperparts and with larger but more diffuse red area on underparts. Both sexes have red crown, the red interspersed with black feathering on female.

Bare parts Bill black. Legs and feet olive-grey. Eyes red-brown.

GEOGRAPHICAL VARIATION Five races, differing mainly in size but also in plumage coloration and pattern.

M. s. superciliaris (Cuba, Cantiles Keys and associated keys) Described above. The largest race on average, with noticeably long bill and wings.

M. s. murceus (Isle of Pines, Cayo Largo and Cayo Real) Plumage much as that of nominate, but averages smaller in bill, wing and, particularly, tail measurements.

M. s. nyeanus (Grand Bahama and San Salvador) Much smaller than nominate, particularly on Grand Bahama. Plumage rather variable, some lacking black behind eye and others showing a small amount (but always less than in nominate); underparts slightly greenish-tinged, and uppertail-covert markings more bar-like. Population on Grand Bahama, which averages slightly shorter-billed and a shade darker below and tends to show a little more black behind eye, is sometimes separated as

'*bahamensis*', but this seems unjustified in view of its otherwise identical appearance to San Salvador birds, which, in any case, show some variation.

M. s. blakei (Abaco Island in Bahamas) Averages somewhat bigger than *nyeanus*. Pale bars on upperparts, wings and tail narrower than in above three races, and often tinged greenish-buff on mantle, while face and underparts generally greyer and darker (appears darker overall). Red of nasal tufts paler and less extensive, but shows more black around and behind eye (as nominate).

M. s. caymanensis (Grand Cayman) Size as that of *blakei* or smaller, with shorter wing. Dark barring above and on wings much narrower and white on back often strongly buffish (appears predominantly pale above); tail more evenly barred, with white bars extending onto outer webs of central rectrices, and uppertail-covert markings more irregular. Lacks black around and behind eye, these areas being white, and red of nasal tufts is much paler and restricted; female has hindcrown greyish-brown (not black).

MEASUREMENTS Wing 115-159, 137-159 (*superciliaris*), 115-132 (*caymanensis*); tail 85-111 (*superciliaris*), 80-94 (*caymanensis*); bill of male 37.6-42.5 (*superciliaris*), 31-37 (*caymanensis*), of female 32.5-39.5 (*superciliaris*), 29-33.5 (*caymanensis*); tarsus 23-27 (*superciliaris*), 21-24 (*caymanensis*). Weight: 83-126 (*superciliaris*), 63-81 (*caymanensis*); males heavier by about 20%.

VOICE Similar to that of Red-bellied Woodpecker (51). Has a *churr*-call which is slightly higher-pitched than that of Red-bellied, *chup* series, and also *waa* notes as in Hispaniolan Woodpecker (44); also *key-on* and continuous *ke-ke-ke-ke* series. Drums in loud and steady rolls.

HABITS Spends much of its time gleaning arthropods, especially in bromeliads, and taking small fruits. Also descends to the ground to forage.

FOOD On Grand Cayman: 56% insects and spiders, especially Acrididae, and beetles; the rest of the diet is made up of fruit, including *Carica*, *Ficus* and papayas. Occasionally takes small vertebrates (*Hyla*), probably in bromeliads; also *Sphaerodactylus*.

BREEDING Nests are found from January to August. Nest excavated in a dead tree or palm at 2-6m; clutch of 4 eggs. A single female may incubate at two nests; most brood-feeding is done by male. Two broods may be raised in one season.

REFERENCES Bond 1985; Bradley 1985; Johnston 1975; Willimont *et al.* 1991.

53 GOLDEN-FRONTED WOODPECKER
Melanerpes aurifrons   Plate 15

Forms a superspecies with *hoffmannii*.

IDENTIFICATION Length c. 22-26cm. Small, with medium to long, slightly chisel-tipped bill barely curved on culmen and fairly broad across nostrils. A highly variable woodpecker with many races, including a number of island forms. All are densely barred black and white above and on inner wing (pale bars usually very narrow), with white rump, while face and underparts vary from very pale whitish-grey in the north to darker in most of the eastern parts of the range; a patch of yellow to orange or red in the centre of belly is often difficult to see in the field, and the barring on lower flanks may similarly not be obvious (can be imperceptible in northern populations). Black tail generally shows only little barring (on outer tail), but some southern and eastern populations have white also on central tail. Head pattern varies. The most widespread, northern, race is very pale on face and underparts, male having yellow-orange nasal tufts, small red patch in centre of crown and orangey hindneck, female lacking the red and having a paler, yellower hindneck. Further south, on Atlantic slope and eastwards, males have red nasal tufts and red crown and nape, becoming orange on lower hindneck (nasal tufts yellow and nape/hindneck more orange from C Guatemala to Honduras), while in SE Mexico they have yellower nasal tufts, red crown merging with orangey nape and yellower hindneck; females of all these have pale crown, lacking red. In flight, the white rump and white primary patch are often striking.

The various races tend to intergrade where they come into contact, so intermediates are common. The species also interbreeds with a number of other woodpeckers. For further details of above-mentioned mainland populations, and also island races, see Geographical Variation.

Similar species Nominate race is easily distinguished from partly overlapping Red-bellied Woodpecker (51) by its distinctive head pattern and unbarred central tail; further south, in Yucatan, Yucatan Woodpecker (48) is smaller and smaller-billed than local race *dubius* of Golden-fronted, and has yellow around bill base; in extreme south-east, Hoffmann's Woodpecker (54) is smaller, more broadly barred above, paler below, and has yellow (less orange-red) nape and hindneck. For hybridisation with these and also with Gila Woodpecker (50), see Geographical Variation. Golden-cheeked (46) and Grey-breasted (47) Woodpeckers, which meet Golden-fronted in Mexico, should not cause any confusion in good views.

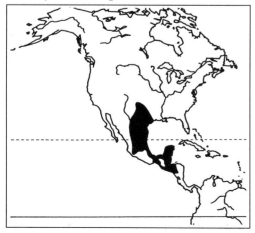

DISTRIBUTION Found in southern USA and C America, ranging from NW Texas and SW Oklahoma southwards through E and C Mexico to Jalisco, and then east to Veracruz and south and east to the Yucatan peninsula (including Cozumel Island and Turneffe Islands), W Honduras (including islands of Utila, Roatán and Barbareta) and NW Nicaragua. A fairly common or common species in most of its range.

HABITAT Although this species may enter mesic and humid habitats in some parts of its range and may be found at the edge of rain forest, typically it is a resident of arid or semi-arid districts with sparse to tall second-growth woodland. Often fairly abundant in towns as well as in rural areas, and also enters coconut groves. In Texas, frequents xeric vegetation, with mesquite often a dominant element, riparian cottonwoods, mixed oak, large mesquite, and juniper country, being found also in pecan groves and in open situations on floodplains; occurs in small numbers in areas of live oaks, elms and other mesic types in residential districts, especially where these are adjacent to stands of mesquite, deciduous oak and/or juniper. From sea level to 2500m.

DESCRIPTION
M. a. aurifrons **Adult male** Nasal tufts yellow (rarely, orange-gold); centre of crown with small red patch (very occasionally larger, extending to nape); nape golden-orange (occasionally yellow), becoming more orange-yellow on lower hindneck and (often) uppermost mantle. Rest of head, including chin and throat, pale grey, darkest on hindcrown and palest on fore region from forehead to chin (rarely, with faint yellowish wash). Upperparts, including upperwing-coverts, barred black and white, white bars as broad as black ones or almost so; rump and uppertail-coverts white, rarely with dark shaft streaks. Flight feathers black, secondaries and tertials barred white, outer primaries tipped white (when fresh) and with white at bases forming patch. Uppertail black, tipped white (when fresh), outermost feathers barred white on outer webs and sometimes also at tip of inner webs. Pale grey of head continues over entire underparts, with narrow diffuse area of yellow (occasionally more golden-yellow) on central lower belly; thighs, lower flanks and undertail-coverts barred blackish (flank bars often indistinct). Underwing greyish, with white primary patch and barred coverts and inner wing. Undertail as uppertail but paler, and often tinged buffish at sides.

Adult female Somewhat smaller than male. Has pale grey crown, lacking red (may rarely show some red feathers), and often (especially younger females) has nape and hindneck paler than on male.

Juvenile Duller overall than adults, with less contrasting and less well-defined markings, broader dark bars above, dusky barring on forehead/forecrown, streaked breast and paler belly patch. Young males have a reddish crown patch (smaller than adult's); females either lack red or have a few scattered red feather tips in crown (rarely a larger area of red, approaching that of male), and generally have paler nape and hindneck.

Bare parts Bill black to grey-black. Legs and feet grey, usually with greenish tinge. Eyes deep red or red-brown; brown in juveniles. Orbital skin grey to grey-brown.

GEOGRAPHICAL VARIATION A highly variable species, with a number of mainland races and island forms. Main differences involve head colours and pattern, width of pale upperpart bars, colour of face and underparts, and tail pattern. The races are themselves variable to a greater or lesser degree, and the mainland forms also intergrade in contact zones, producing populations of intermediate appearance. Furthermore, the species hybridises with a number of other congeneric woodpeckers.

M. a. aurifrons (northern part of range, south in E Mexico to southern Tamaulipas) Described above. Very pale, with the broadest white upperpart barring of all races. Tends to become paler towards west of range. Intergrades with *grateloupensis* hybridises to limited extent with Gila Woodpecker in NW Mexico, and has interbred with Red-bellied Woodpecker in Texas.

M. a. grateloupensis (E Mexico, from around central San Luis Potosí and southernmost Tamaulipas to S Veracruz) Pale upperpart bars tend to be rather narrow, and nasal tufts sometimes red. Possibly no more than an intergradient population, being closer to nominate in north and to following race in south, but also intergrading with *polygrammus* in Isthmus of Tehuantepec.

M. a. dubius (Tabasco and NE Chiapas in Mexico, through Yucatan peninsula to Belize) Long-billed. Pale upperpart bars much narrower than on nominate, and face and especially underparts generally darker, more buffy-grey; belly patch red, sometimes with diffuse golden border; outer-tail bars very narrow (sometimes absent), and white primary patch smaller. Both sexes have red nasal tufts (often paler on female); male has red crown to hindneck, with golden-orange band across lower hindneck/uppermost mantle, while emale has nape and hindneck more orangey. Intergrades with above race in west of range and with *polygrammus* and *santacruzi* in south and east.

M. a. polygrammus (SW Oaxaca and interior Chiapas, Mexico) Pale upperpart bars slightly broader than in *dubius*, and face and underparts somewhat paler, with golden-yellow belly patch; central tail feathers normally barred white on inner webs, and uppertail-coverts usually have dark submarginal lines. Nasal tufts yellow or occasionally orange-tinged; male usually has orange-red crown grading into yellower nape and hindneck (though sometimes broken at hindcrown/upper nape), while female, which is shorter-billed than male, has grey-buff crown and nape and orange-yellow hindneck. Intergrades with *grateloupensis* and with *santacruzi*.

M. a. santacruzi (S Chiapas, Mexico, to SW Honduras and W Nicaragua) Relatively short-billed and short-tailed. Plumage rather variable. Generally similar to *dubius*, but somewhat darker below and with belly patch more golden-orange or orange-yellow; pale upperpart bars sometimes tinged brownish, and central rectrices usually with some white markings on inner webs. Head pattern similar to that of *dubius*, but nasal tufts yellow or yellow-orange, and red coloration usually paler, and female generally has pale of crown continuing onto upper nape. Intergrades with *dubius* and with *polygrammus*; interbreeds with Hoffmann's Woodpecker in small area of overlap.

M. a. pauper (coastal N Honduras) As *santacruzi* but much shorter-winged, and pale upperpart bars normally very narrow.

The following four races are confined to islands off the Caribbean coast:

M. a. leei (Cozumel Island) Long-billed and long-tailed. Comparatively dark (the darkest race on average), with very narrow pale (brown-tinted) barring above, and brownish below with dark red belly patch; uppertail-coverts dark-barred, and white outer-tail bars very narrow or even absent. Head pattern much as *dubius*, but red of male's crown reaches farther

forwards, sometimes meeting red of nasal tufts.

M. a. turneffensis (Turneffe Islands) As *leei*, but pale bars above slightly broader and underparts rather paler, with belly patch more orangey; nasal tufts paler, and crown more orange.

M. a. insulanus (Utila Island, off N Honduras) Resembles mainland *pauper*, but bigger and with longer tail.

M. a. canescens (Roatán and Barbareta Islands, east of Utila) Very long-billed. Face and underparts very pale, as nominate, but belly patch and head pattern/coloration more as *dubius*, pale bars above narrow, but broader than in *dubius*.

MEASUREMENTS Wing of male 128-140, of female 125-134; tail of male 76-85, of female 69-80; bill of male 24-29, of female 22-28; tarsus of male 20-26, of female 21-24. Weight: male 73-99, female 63-90.

VOICE Possesses the same range of calls as Red-bellied Woodpecker, though in general these differ in being louder and harsher. The *churr*-call, a tremulous rolling *pwurr-rr-rr*, is slightly shorter and higher-pitched than Red-bellied's. Also a flicker-like *kek-kek-kek-kek*, and other nasal and rolled calls. Drums occasionally.

HABITS Generally shyer than Red-bellied Woodpecker. Most foraging takes place on medium to large branches and on trunks. Gleaning and searching (50%), pecking and hammering (28%), and probing in crevices and holes (13%) constitute the most important feeding techniques; some flycatching, ground feeding and picking of fruits also occur. Slight sexual differences exist, with males pecking less frequently than females and visiting small twigs rarely. As observations of storing corn obtained from a feeding station suggest, this woodpecker occasionally stores food in crevices and cracks in early winter. Displays not well described for this species, but available records suggest close similarity to congeners. Roosts singly. Interspecific territories with Red-bellied Woodpeckers are maintained. Other bird species are attacked at fruit trees or near seed stores.

FOOD Rather omnivorous like its congeners. Various kinds of insects and their larvae, including those of wood-boring beetles, ants, and grasshoppers. Fruits, berries, nuts (e.g. pecan) and various seeds, particularly acorns and corn, also mesquite, are readily taken.

BREEDING Breeding season stretches from late March to June in Texas, commences in January in Chiapas, and spans February to August in Guatemala. Nest excavated by both sexes in large stubs and often at top end of a telephone pole (formerly persecuted because of this), at almost any height up to 7m from ground; the work may be completed in less than two weeks. May also, however, use old holes for nesting. Clutch contains mostly 4 (7) eggs (average 4.65), clutch size increasing somewhat with latitude. Eggs are incubated by both parents during the day, by the male during the night, for 12-14 days. Both parents also feed the young with insects and fruit carried in the bill. The male also stays with the nestlings for almost the full nestling period, which lasts for about a month. A second, and even a third brood may be produced; these are initiated about three weeks after the young of the previous one have left the nest.

REFERENCES Askins 1983; Bent 1939; Blake 1965; Howell & Webb in press; Koenig 1986; Leck 1969; Martin & Kroll 1975; Peterson & Chalif 1973; Russel 1964; Selander 1966; Selander & Giller 1959, 1963; Skutch 1948a; Sutton & Pettingill 1942; Wallace 1974.

54 HOFFMANN'S WOODPECKER
Melanerpes hoffmannii   Plate 15

Forms a superspecies with *aurifrons*.

IDENTIFICATION Length c. 19-21cm. Small, with fairly long, barely chisel-tipped bill slightly curved on culmen and rather broad across nostrils. Fully barred black and white above, including on inner wing and most of tail, with white rump, and pale greyish-buff on face and underparts, with yellow or golden belly patch and dark-barred flanks and ventral region; belly patch is diffuse and often indistinct (underparts frequently sullied brownish). Nasal tufts pale golden-yellow, often indistinct (especially on female); male has red crown and golden-yellow nape and hindneck, sometimes with intervening grey area on hindcrown, female having grey hindcrown/nape and yellow hindneck. In flight, shows prominent white rump but only small white primary patch.

Similar species Overlaps in range with Golden-fronted Woodpecker (53) in S Honduras and with Red-crowned (49) in C Costa Rica; interbreeds with both and may even be conspecific with Golden-fronted. Local race of latter has narrower white barring above and on wings, usually less white in tail, and much redder or more orange-red nape/hindneck; Red-crowned also has much redder nape and hindneck, and belly patch is reddish. See also Geographical Variation.

DISTRIBUTION C America, from Pacific slope of Honduras and Nicaragua to Costa Rica, where also reaches Caribbean slope in the north. Common throughout most of range.

HABITAT A resident of xeric to mesic open and semi-open country. Deciduous forest, light woodland, secondary growth, shade trees in coffee plantations and gardens, scattered trees in pastures, and hedgerows are the habitats typically frequented; often found near human habitation. Avoids dense wet forest, but may invade when forest has been cut. Found from sea level up to 200m in Honduras and mostly at 600-2150m in Costa Rica, where also lower in the north.

DESCRIPTION
Adult male Nasal tufts pale golden-yellow; crown patch red; nape and hindneck golden-yellow to orange-yellow, sometimes with a few scattered red feather tips, becoming paler on uppermost mantle; rest of head, including chin and throat, pale greyish-buff to brownish-grey (this colour frequently continuing at least partly over hindcrown), becoming paler, whiter, at front of face and often with pale yellow feather tips in loral/chin area. Upperparts black, narrowly barred white; rump and uppertail-coverts white, occasionally with the odd black spot or bar. Upperwing-coverts black, barred white (usually fewer white bars than on back), greater coverts with broad white bars; secondaries and tertials similarly barred, white bars broadest on tertials; primaries black, tipped white (when fresh), outer feathers broadly barred white at base of inner webs (may form small patch). Uppertail black, central feather pair having inner webs white with black half-bars and outer webs with some white at base, and outermost pair narrowly barred white on outer webs. Greyish colour of head continues over underparts, becoming slightly olive-tinged on breast and whiter on flanks (often yellowish) and undertail-coverts, with diffuse area of golden-orange or orangey-gold on central belly; thighs, belly sides, flanks and undertail-coverts with blackish arrowhead bars. Underwing dark brownish, barred white. Undertail as uppertail, but paler, with browner sides.

Adult female Slightly smaller and shorter-billed than male. Nasal tufts often paler than on male, and lacks red on head, having crown and nape concolorous with head sides.

Juvenile Duller and darker than adults, with upperpart barring less sharp; underparts more olive-toned, with paler belly patch, and streaked/mottled dark on belly and flanks (sometimes also on breast). Head pattern similar to that of respective adult, females perhaps occasionally with hint of red on crown.

Bare parts Bill black. Legs and feet grey. Eyes red, sometimes red-brown; brown in juveniles. Orbital skin brownish.

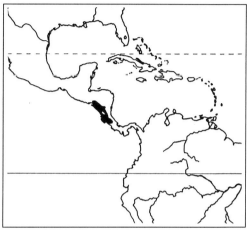

GEOGRAPHICAL VARIATION No races are recognised, but in the two zones of hybridisation, with Golden-fronted Woodpecker in S Honduras and with Red-crowned in C Costa Rica, many individuals show intermediate characters. For example, in Costa Rica, the majority of those found between Tárcoles and Parrita/Quepos show an orange hindneck and belly patch.

MEASUREMENTS Wing 109-128; tail 50-62; bill 22-28; tarsus 19-21. Weight: 62-84 (males 15% heavier than females).

VOICE Most common calls are loud to quiet churrs, resembling those of Golden-fronted Woodpecker. A hard metallic rattle, in repeated short bursts; a prolonged, nasal rattle or splutter, wavering in pitch. In excitement, a querulous, grating *woick-a-woick-a-woick-a...* or *wit wit wit...*, often with visual displays. Also drums.

HABITS Usually seen in pairs and hard to overlook. Largely an arboreal woodpecker, but often comes down below eye level on fence posts and stumps. Pecks and hammers wood, flakes off pieces of bark, and probes. Can cling head downward to obtain berries, reaching for them with stretched neck. When startled, hides behind a branch or trunk in the usual woodpecker style. Known displays consist of bobbing of the entire body accompanied with calling and wing-spreading. Paired throughout year, but usually sleeps singly in holes; rarely, two individuals roost together overnight. Before the breeding season often involved in conspicuous pair-pair encounters. Quick to mob pygmy owls *Glaucidium*.

FOOD Insects, particularly ants, beetles, lepidopterans, and their larvae. Eats many fruits, including figs, *Cecropia* catkins, and arils. Drinks nectar of balsa, African tulip tree, and other large flowers.

BREEDING The breeding season extends from February

to July. Nest hole 1.5-9m up in a dead trunk or branch, sometimes only 1m up in fence post. Clutch of 2-3 eggs is laid. Details of its breeding poorly known, but probably not too different from Golden-fronted Woodpecker and Red-crowned Woodpecker. Apparently regularly double-brooded.

REFERENCES Howell & Webb in press; Otvos 1967; Sassi 1939; Slud 1980; Stiles & Skutch 1989.

---

55   YELLOW-BELLIED SAPSUCKER
Sphyrapicus varius   Plate 16

Other name: Common Sapsucker
Forms a superspecies with *nuchalis* and *ruber*.

IDENTIFICATION Length c. 19-21cm. Small to very small, with relatively short, straight, chisel-tipped bill broad across nostrils. Within its range, a common and highly distinctive migratory woodpecker, unlike any other apart from the very similar Red-naped Sapsucker (56); despite its bold plumage pattern, often surprisingly inconspicuous. Dark above, with white mottling/barring and white rump, and pale below with black breast (barred paler when fresh) and dark streaking; white-barred wings with large white covert patch. Has characteristic head pattern, with black and white stripes on head and neck, black-bordered red crown (may be black or partly so on female), and red (male) or white (female) throat enclosed by black moustache which joins with black upper-breast band. Juveniles, which do not acquire full adult plumage until spring of second calendar-year, are much browner in overall appearance, with pale bars above and with dark scallop markings below, but lack black breast patch; young males gain some red on throat at an early stage, but the adult head pattern is acquired only gradually during the first winter.

Similar species Red-naped Sapsucker is very similar to Yellow-bellied and sometimes considered conspecific with it; the two meet each other in SW Alberta, where they occasionally interbreed. Red-naped differs most obviously in its distinctive red nape patch (both sexes), though on a very few individuals this may be much reduced or even virtually lacking, and in its smaller amount of white in the wings and upperparts (white on back forms two lines down sides); in addition, male has more red on throat, usually concealing the black moustache, and female has lower half or so (rarely, almost entire throat) red. Juvenile Red-naped also resembles juvenile Yellow-bellied, but tends to be darker above, with white spots (rather than bars) on mantle and back, and with more extensive flank barring; the moult into adult plumage takes place much earlier than that of young Yellow-bellied, and by early autumn the head and throat patterns are much as those of the adults (by start of second calendar-year, young Red-naped are virtually identical to adults in the field). Red-breasted Sapsucker (57) is easily distinguished by its all-red head (with white moustache in southern race) and breast, juveniles (identical to adults by late summer) having the red replaced by brown-black and with reddish wash to throat/breast; interbreeds only rarely with Yellow-bellied. The other sapsucker species, Williamson's (58), is also easily distinguishable: males are largely black and white, with a yellow belly, showing no red apart from a small red throat patch; females are barred dark brown and white, with yellowish belly, and lack the characteristic white wing-covert panel of all other sapsuckers.

DISTRIBUTION A woodpecker of the forests of northern N America east of the Rocky Mountains; across Canada from northeastern British Columbia to S Labrador and Newfoundland. The southern boundary of the range runs through northern USA, from S Alberta and North Dakota to New York and Connecticut, and from there along the Appalachians to E Tennessee and NW Georgia. Common.

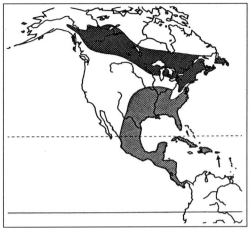

MOVEMENTS Sapsuckers are highly migratory and winter far south of their breeding ranges. Ranges in winter from Texas to Mexico (E Chihuahua, S Sinaloa to Tamaulipas and to Yucatán and Chiapas) and further through C America to Costa Rica and rarely to W Panama. The entire West Indies are also included in the winter range. Females winter farther south, and males return to the breeding grounds earlier than females. Autumn migration starts late August and may continue into early November. Arrival at breeding grounds from late April to May. Vagrants have also reached Europe (Britain, Ireland and Iceland).

HABITAT Lives in northern deciduous and mixed coniferous forests in summer; desires the presence of aspen *Populus*, an important nesting tree, other important tree species being birch *Betula* and hickory *Carya*. Winters in forests, usually not in pure conifer stands, and forest edge and various semi-open habitats, at which season found in montane forests (chiefly 900-3000m, but also to 3500m and to sea level) and visits larger trees in pastures, clearings, semi-open sites, and even suburban areas; occasionally, and during passage, in lowlands and coastal palm groves. In Puerto Rico, inhabits sparsely wooded areas, though it may well occur in mountain forests. On Grand Cayman, common in grape-almond woodland in winter.

DESCRIPTION
Adult male Forehead and crown bright red (very rarely, yellow) with complete black border, black becoming broader on rear crown side and across hindcrown. Stripe from above eye white, broadening at rear and over nape (nape rarely with trace of red), and continuing down side of hindneck to side of mantle; hindneck narrowly black. Black line across lower forehead extends slightly below eye and as broad band through ear-coverts and down neck side, bordered below by white stripe from nasal tufts/lores which expands on side of neck and continues to breast side. Black submoustachial stripe extends to meet broad black band across upper breast, enclosing red chin and throat. Mantle and innermost scapulars to upper rump white (tinged yellow-buff when fresh), heavily patterned with irregular black barring (appearing mottled black and white); outer scapulars black; lower rump and uppertail-coverts white, with black outer webs. Upperwing-coverts black,

with large amount of white across most of median and central greater coverts (forming elongated white panel on closed wing); flight feathers black, tipped white, with white spots on both webs forming bar-like pattern, but innermost tertials largely white with black barring. Uppertail black, central feather pair with white inner webs (with a few black bars/spots) and sometimes with some white at tips of outer webs, and outer two or three pairs often with a few white marks near tips, outermost also with narrow white edge to outer web. Underparts below black of breast pale yellow, becoming white or pale buffish-white on flanks and ventral region; breast sides to flanks and undertail-coverts with narrow blackish arrowhead markings and (usually) shaft streaks. Underwing barred greyish and white, with largely dusky-whitish coverts. Undertail much as uppertail. (Note that, when fresh, white parts of plumage show a yellow or buffish tinge, sometimes strongly, especially on upperparts, head and over underparts, and black breast patch and underpart markings are partly obscured by broad yellowish feather fringes; yellow tones, however, soon disappear through wear, and by winter most birds appear much more black and white.)

Adult female Differs from male in having entirely white chin and throat. Red of forehead and crown usually slightly paler than on male and often less extensive, sometimes with black admixed with the red or with red restricted to a few patches on forehead; occasionally lacks red altogether, having top of head all black (or with a few buffy streaks/spots). May also have slightly smaller wing-covert panel, with some black feather bases showing.

Juvenile Differs considerably from adults. Initially, both sexes are mainly dark olive-brown, with upperparts (including rump) barred and mottled blackish and pale, breast with scaly pattern and central belly pale yellowish-white, and with wings and tail similar to adult's but tail more extensively barred; chin whitish or pale buff, and head shows pale streaks/spots on crown and sides with narrow whitish-buff supercilium behind eye and whitish moustache. Although males may gain some red feathers in throat at an early stage, moult to full adult plumage is protracted and is not completed until spring of second calendar-year (on the wintering grounds); characteristic head pattern develops slowly through the first winter, generally not being recognisable until about March/April, and the black breast patch appears last of all (being barred brownish well into the spring).

Bare parts Bill slaty-grey to blackish. Legs and feet blue-grey to greenish-grey. Eyes deep brown.

GEOGRAPHICAL VARIATION Monotypic. Southern Appalachian population is perhaps a shade darker and very slightly smaller than northern populations, but considerable overlap exists and subspecific recognition (as 'appalachiensis') is not justified.

MEASUREMENTS Wing 115-131; tail 59-78; bill 21-25.5; tarsus 18.5-22. Weight: 40-62 (large-sample mean Pennsylvania, 50.3).

VOICE Vocalisations of this species have a rather nasal, cat-like quality and are sometimes compared with the hissing sound of bellows. At start of breeding season single or grouped squealing notes, naaah, owee-owee, wee-wee-wee-wee or kwee-urk, can be heard; this seems to be a general-purpose long-distance signal, which is often interspersed with drumming. When alarmed, gives a soft view, becoming louder, hoarser and vibrant with increasing excitement (this call is lower-pitched in the other members of the superspecies). In more aggressive contexts, weetick-weetick calls are uttered. During encounters, juk-juk-juk calls are associated with the

visual displays. Soft, intimate notes, mjuk, are given when pair members meet at the nest or in comparable situations. Similar notes may be heard from flying sapsuckers. The nestlings maintain an incessant chatter, yip-yip-yip-…. This species' drumming is very distinctive, consisting of a roll with clearly separated taps at the end, and sometimes also at the beginning, tap-tap-trrrrrrrrr-ta-ta-tat--tat--tat. Both sexes drum. Ritual tapping at the lower rim of the nest hole is a rather common acoustic signal.

HABITS Rather solitary outside the breeding season, though small groups form during migration. Rather inconspicuous on its wintering grounds. Live branches in the lower canopy are the preferred foraging stratum in spring. Drills shallow holes in many tree species for sap and bast; these holes may be arranged in vertical columns, as horizontal bands or, on twigs, in spiralling bands. In spring, uses old sap wells or other sources of sap on bruised parts of a tree; during late summer and autumn (sometimes earlier when insect food is scarce because of adverse weather), sap and cambium are the staple food, and fresh wells are made. A variety of birds, insects and mammals scrounges at the sap wells. Sap is sought at all levels of the habitat, on tree trunks as well as in the crown. When hunting carpenter ants, sapsuckers descend to the ground. In spring, when arthropods dominate the diet, this species forages like a typical woodpecker, excavating in dead or dying wood, flaking off bark to expose ants and their brood. Flycatching also plays an important role; sallies occasionally from an exposed perch, returning to the same or another perch. Hangs on the outermost tips of twigs when reaching for buds. Reports of food-storing have involved sapsuckers placing fruits, nuts or acorns in crevices; whether this behaviour is true storing or just use of crevices as anvils requires corroboration. This species displays with stiff body and bill pointing vertically upwards, even on a horizontal perch, while it jerks left and right rhythmically with tail spread; crown and throat feathers are erected, and wings are slightly spread at the carpal or are flicked. In close contact with an opponent or partner, the bill is pointed in the latter's direction and up-and-down bobbing movements may be shown. During ritual tapping, the crest and throat feathers are also raised, and at higher intensities of the display the wings are extended laterally and dropped at the carpal.

FOOD Beetles, their larvae, ants and their brood, moths, and dragonflies. Except during the nesting season, when insects comprise almost half the diet, sap constitutes an important part of the nutrition: sap trees used include numerous deciduous and coniferous species, very common being poplar, willows, birch, maple, hickory and alders, as well as pines, spruces and firs. In spring, buds of trees are eaten. Berries are occasionally taken, and, in times of food shortage, even fed to the nestlings. Fruits are mostly taken in October-February.

BREEDING The majority of nests are built into live trees at heights between 3 and 14m. Trees with rotten heartwood are favoured and may be used in consecutive years, although a fresh nest is ordinarily excavated in such a tree. Usually, the male selects the nest site, and also carries out most of the construction, completing this within 15-28 days. Both sexes continue to excavate somewhat when the chicks have hatched. Clutch size increases from south to north and averages 4.93 eggs. Both sexes share incubation, which lasts 12-13 days, and provide equal food for the nestlings. The male carries out most of the nest sanitation; because of the often liquid food, faecal sacs rupture easily (or are lacking). The young leave the nest 25-29 days after hatching, becoming fully independent after two weeks.

REFERENCES Conner & Kroll 1979; Howell 1952, 1953; Howell & Webb in press; Johnston 1975; Kilham 1962a, 1971, 1977; Koenig 1986; Lawrence 1967; Raffaele 1989; Ridgely & Gwynne 1989; Tate 1973; Williams 1975, 1980.

---

56 RED-NAPED SAPSUCKER
Sphyrapicus nuchalis   Plate 16

Forms a superspecies with *varius* and *ruber*.

IDENTIFICATION Length c. 19-21cm. Small to very small, with comparatively short, straight, chisel-tipped bill broad across nostrils. Very similar to Yellow-bellied Sapsucker (55), with which sometimes treated as conspecific. Main differences shown by Red-naped in the field are: its red patch on nape (both sexes), though in rare cases this may be lacking; its more extensive red on throat, obscuring most of black moustache (male; female also has at least some red on lower throat, and has crown as fully red as male); and the reduced amount of white above, with tendency to give impression of two broad pale lines down sides of mantle and back. Juveniles are also very like juvenile Yellow-bellied, but darker and less barred (more spotted) above and more heavily barred below; the post-juvenile moult progresses far more rapidly, however, so some red is usually visible on crown and throat by late summer.

Similar species See Yellow-bellied Sapsucker, and also Description (below). Red-naped hybridises rather frequently with the easily separable Red-breasted Sapsucker (57) where the ranges of the two overlap, producing individuals showing variable (often minimal) degrees of intermediacy in plumage, but apparently no stable hybrid population. Williamson's Sapsucker (58) is also very different from Red-naped, but interbreeding between the two has occurred on rare occasions.

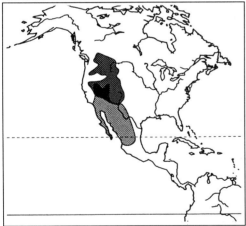

DISTRIBUTION The breeding range covers the Rocky Mountains of western USA and SW Canada, from SE British Columbia and SW Alberta, through Nevada, Utah to C Arizona, New Mexico and Texas.

MOVEMENTS Less migratory than Yellow-bellied Sapsucker; winters September-April from Arizona south to NW Mexico (Baja California, and from Sonora and Nuevo León to Jalisco), and may, at least occasionally, reach Guatemala and Honduras. Females tend to migrate farther than males. Red-naped Sapsuckers return to their breeding grounds in March-May and leave them in September.

HABITAT Found in forests containing aspen (*Populus tremuloides*) or in pure aspen stands; also coniferous forests (e.g. with Douglas fir, larch; spuce and fir), particularly if aspen is present. Does not breed in oak or oak-pine forests. Montane habitats to 2900m. Winter habitats in Arizona are oak-juniper, pine-oak and pure oak woodland in mountains to 1700m; found in its Mexican winter quarters from sea level to 2500m.

DESCRIPTION
Adult male As Yellow-bellied Sapsucker, apart from following differences. Head: nape red (very rarely, red much reduced or almost invisible); red of chin and throat more extensive, covering most of malar and moustachial region and reaching further downwards onto upper breast (so black breast patch therefore less deep); black ear-coverts often with some red feather tips. Upperparts: fewer pale markings, appearing pale-spotted rather than mottled or barred and with white bands down sides of mantle and back. Upperwing: shows reduction in white markings, sometimes with far fewer bars on flight feathers, and white covert patch is somewhat smaller.

Adult female Differs from male mainly in having less red on throat: chin and upper throat usually white and lower throat red, with complete black moustache meeting black of breast. Amount of red varies, however, and some females may approach or, rarely, even match males in this respect.

Juvenile Very like juvenile Yellow-bellied but darker, lacking or having only few pale markings on blacker crown and with pale spots (instead of bars) on blackish upperparts; flanks generally more heavily and more extensively barred, leaving smaller pale area on belly. Red on crown and throat is evident to varying extent, and females soon show signs of white on upper throat. By late summer/early autumn both sexes resemble respective adult, apart from having black of breast barred buff-brown, acquiring full black breast band by January of second calendar-year.

Bare parts Bill black to dark slaty. Legs and feet greyish. Eyes deep brown.

GEOGRAPHICAL VARIATION Monotypic, showing relatively minimal variation.

MEASUREMENTS Wing 118-133; tail 67-69 ; bill 20-26 (locally, females have significantly shorter bills); tarsus 19-22. Weight: 36-61 (large-sample mean 52.4).

VOICE Calls similar to those of Yellow-bellied Sapsucker, particularly a mewing *meeah* (lower-pitched than Yellow-bellied's); shorter, more vibrant versions of this call are given in flight. The squealing series are uttered mainly by males in the early breeding season. Single notes in these series are shorter and delivered at a faster rate than in Williamson's Sapsucker. Low calls are given during changeovers at the nest. Both sexes drum: rolls consist of an initial burst, followed by irregular, slower burst of 2-3 strokes, and are delivered at a rate of 8-9 per minute.

HABITS Uses sap holes throughout the year, exploiting various conifers and deciduous trees and bushes on the breeding grounds. In winter quarters, prefers oak for feeding. Displays much as Yellow-bellied Sapsucker, for instance with swinging and bowing movements. As prelude to copulation, the male approaches the female with wings lowered and head feathers raised. In areas of sympatry, interspecific territories with congeners are established. Other woodpeckers, e.g. Hairy Woodpecker (116), are attacked in the vicinity of the nest.

FOOD Relies very much on conifer sap during spring. Ants (*Camponotus*) seem to be important as nestling food. Otherwise, food requirements presumably rather similar to those of Yellow-bellied Sapsucker.

BREEDING The nest is excavated in aspen, paper birch, larch and other trees at 1-25 m; trees with some dead parts are preferred. Several holes may be initiated in one season, the final hole often being one started the previous season, but even old holes may be used for nesting. The clutch comprises 4-6 (3-7) eggs, laid in May-June, from which a mean of about three chicks fledges. Incubation (by both sexes) takes about 13 days, the nestlings fledging after 25-28 days. The male roosts in the nest and takes a greater share in nest sanitation. Nest success 1-6 young per nest. The young quickly become independent, and both they and adults soon leave the nest area. The pair may reunite in the following season.

REFERENCES Bock & Larson 1986; Crockett & Hadow 1975; Howell 1952, 1953; Howell & Webb in press; Johnson & Johnson 1985; Johnson & Zink 1983; Martin & Li 1992; Miller pers. comm.; Tobalske 1992.

---

57   RED-BREASTED SAPSUCKER
Sphyrapicus ruber   Plate 16

Forms a superspecies with *varius* and *nuchalis*.

IDENTIFICATION Length 20-22cm. Small to very small, with rather short, straight, chisel-tipped bill broad across nostrils. A very distinctive woodpecker, adults of both sexes easily identified by their red head, neck and breast (red brightest in spring), black upperparts with pale mottling, and the white wing-covert panel typical of the genus; a small amount of white is present just above the bill and a small black spot in front of the eye, while the generally paler southern race *daggetti* has a white moustache of varying length. On juveniles, the red is replaced by dark brown or blackish with a red wash, but adult coloration is soon acquired.

Similar species Adults are unmistakable. Juveniles are very like those of Red-naped Sapsucker (56), but have a blacker, red-washed head and more obvious white across the top of the bill (and sometimes a short white moustache); throat much darker than on juvenile Red-naped.

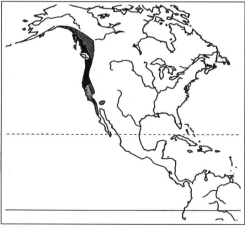

DISTRIBUTION Western N America. Nominate form breeds along the Pacific coast from SE Alaska to S Oregon, along the western slope of the Cascade Range, occasionally east of it, and in C British Columbia; the range of *daggetti*

extends from the Cascade Mountains south, its main breeding region being the Sierra Nevada in California and Nevada, west across N California to the coast. Reasonably common throughout most of its range.

MOVEMENTS Less migratory than its congeners; nominate *ruber* virtually sedentary. Winters south to northern Baja California, stragglers sometimes venturing further south to about 29°N. Remains in its winter quarters from October to March and returns to the breeding grounds at the beginning of April.

HABITAT Coastal populations inhabit humid forests dominated by conifers. Elsewhere, Red-breasted Sapsuckers are found in mixed deciduous and coniferous forests and forest edge, particularly aspen-ponderosa (*Populus tremuloides-Pinus ponderosa*) associations. Ranges up to 2900m during the breeding season and occurs at 500-3000m in its winter quarters.

DESCRIPTION

S. r. daggetti **Adult male** Sexes alike. Nasal tufts and front of lores white, this extending as fairly broad moustachial stripe of variable length; small black area in front of and below eye. Entire remainder of head and neck to central breast and lower breast sides red, sometimes tinged pale purple. Upperparts black, with lines of buffish-white bar-like spotting on mantle, back and upper rump; lower rump and uppertail-coverts white, with black on outer webs of feathers. Upperwing-coverts black, with white across distal half of median and central greater coverts; flight feathers black, tipped white and narrowly barred white. Uppertail black, central feather pair with narrow white bars on inner webs, and outermost with narrow white edge to outer web. Underparts below red of breast pale yellow to yellowish-white, becoming white in lower ventral region, with irregular, rather coarse arrowhead markings most prominent on flanks. Underwing barred grey and white, with more uniformly dusky coverts. Undertail much as uppertail. (In fresh plumage, in autumn, the red coloration appears duller and darker, becoming brighter through winter and spring as browner feather tips wear away; when very worn, in summer, the red may be very bright but some black feather bases often show through on crown and breast.)

Juvenile Pattern similar to that of adults, but coloration differs considerably. Head and upper breast, including throat, dark brownish with (often strong) tinge of red, and with whitish nasal tufts and short moustache; underparts extensively barred, with paler unbarred central belly; upperparts and wings similar to adult, but with indication of barring on rump. Acquires adult plumage very rapidly, the ages being indistinguishable in the field by late summer/autumn.

Bare parts Bill black. Legs and feet grey to greenish-grey. Eyes deep brown.

GEOGRAPHICAL VARIATION Two races, intergrading completely in southernmost Oregon, and both interbreeding to an extent with Red-naped Sapsucker (but species limits are genetically stable).
 S. r. daggetti (California and Nevada) Described above.
 S. r. ruber (Alaska south to W Oregon) Slightly bigger and darker than *daggetti*. Red coloration somewhat deeper in tone and reaches further down on breast, where more sharply demarcated, and belly tends to be yellower; pale upperpart markings fewer and more like spots than bars. Head has white nasal/loral area, but lacks moustachial extension of *daggetti*. Juvenile plumage darker than that of *daggetti*.

MEASUREMENTS Wing 118-128; tail 71-79; bill 22-26; tarsus 19-22. Weight: 40-55.

VOICE Similar to that of Yellow-bellied Sapsucker (55): a mewing, rather drawn-out *meeah* and quiet *puc* or *pwuc* notes and the other call types described for the former species. Both sexes drum: rolls consist of an initial burst, followed by irregular, slower burst of 2-3 strokes.

HABITS Similar to those of Yellow-bellied and Red-naped Sapsuckers. Because of the former merger of this species with *S. varius*, specific differences have not been unravelled. Generally, differences are probably only quantitative in nature; for instance, the description of the copulatory behaviour, male with drooping wings and erect head feathers, agrees with what is known for the other species within the superspecies.

FOOD Lives on sap, as its close relatives. Insects, especially ants, are an important nestling food.

BREEDING Differences from other sapsucker species not well documented. Conifers seem to be preferred nesting trees.

REFERENCES Howell 1952, 1953; Howell & Webb in press; Johnson & Johnson 1985; Johnson & Zink 1983.

---

58 WILLIAMSON'S SAPSUCKER
Sphyrapicus thyroideus   Plate 16

IDENTIFICATION Length c. 21-23cm. Small, with shortish, straight, chisel-tipped bill broad across nostrils. A mountain-forest woodpecker with striking sexual plumage dimorphism (sexes were long thought to represent two different species). Male has glossy black head, breast and upperparts, with white supercilium, moustache, rump and wing panel and with small red throat patch (latter often hard to discern in the field), and yellow belly with flanks heavily striped and barred black and white. Very different female has a brownish head with obscure paler and darker moustachial stripes, heavily barred upperparts and wings and a white rump (but no white wing panel), and a blackish breast (often obscured by barring when fresh) with yellow belly and heavily barred flanks. Juveniles resemble respective adult, males having white throat and more white on nape/hindneck and females lacking black breast patch.

Similar species Males are unmistakable. Females are somewhat similar to juvenile Yellow-bellied Sapsucker (55), but lack the white wing-covert panel and are more extensively barred.

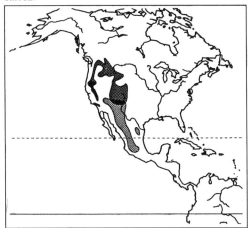

DISTRIBUTION Western N America, from interior S British Columbia, W Montana and Wyoming south to S California, C Arizona and W New Mexico, in the west breeding also in NW Mexico in the San Pedro Martír mountains of N Baja California. A fairly common species.

MOVEMENTS Mostly resident, but some movement does occur and flocks of about a dozen birds can be observed. Range shifts from C Washington in summer south to C California. Females seem to be more nomadic than males and tend to migrate farther south. Arrives at breeding grounds from mid April onwards in NC Colorado.

HABITAT Mixed forests at higher elevations where spruce, firs and pines predominate, occurring also in mixed stands of aspen and fir. Typical trees in these habitats are ponderosa pine *Pinus ponderosa* and Douglas fir *Pseudotsuga*, also larch *Larix*, and other pines. The bottom of drainages is preferred over slopes and ridges. In its Mexican range found at 2000-3000m. Winters in humid to mesic habitats. Found then in pine-oak and oak-juniper woodland at higher elevations of up to 1830m in Arizona and at 1000-3500m in Mexico, but vagrants (females) may also turn up in low desert habitats.

DESCRIPTION
S. t. thyroideus **Adult male** Nasal tufts, lores and long moustachial stripe white; narrow white supercilium from above eye, curving downwards on nape side; chin and upper throat red. Rest of head and neck, breast and most of upperparts glossy black, blue gloss strongest on head, scapulars and mantle; rump and uppertail-coverts white, with black on outer webs of feathers. Upperwing-coverts black, with large amount of white across median and central greater coverts; flight feathers black, primaries with small white spots on outer webs and tertials narrowly tipped white, and with small white spots on inner webs of primaries and secondaries. Uppertail black, either unmarked or with a few white bars/streaks on central feathers. Lower breast to lower belly unmarked bright yellow, with breast sides, thighs, flanks and undertail-coverts having broad black streaks or arrowhead marks on a white ground colour. Underwing barred dark grey and white, with coverts more uniform. Undertail much as uppertail or browner.

Adult female Differs substantially from male in plumage pattern and coloration. Head rather variable, and may show very faint indication of male pattern, but basically brownish or buffish, usually streaked darker (sometimes with appearance of broad blackish bands on crown sides meeting across nape/hindneck), with paler buff moustachial area and dark-streaked or fully blackish submoustachial region; throat centre generally yellowish-brown, sometimes buff with blackish chin (may rarely show very small area of red). Upperparts buff, broadly barred black-brown, with rump and uppertail-coverts white (as male). Upperwing and its coverts dark brown, barred buff to white, and lacking male's white covert patch. Uppertail brownish-black, barred buffish-white on central and outer feathers. Underparts barred black and buffish, breast tending to appear as a more solid black patch (especially when worn), and with unmarked pale yellow central panel from lower breast to lower belly; a few females may have brighter yellow belly, more solid black on breast area and a rather streaked pattern at sides, and can somewhat resemble males in this respect.

Juvenile Juvenile male resembles adult, but is duller and unglossed, with white (not red) throat and paler yellow belly, and with more barring on wings and tail; upperparts often show a few small white spots, and some white is generally present on hindneck and nape sides, usually meeting white of rear supercilium (and often forming a pale patch). Juvenile female resembles adult, but is duller and browner overall, with heavier and more widespread barring (head and throat often streaked/barred); below, unmarked area of belly is more restricted and a much paler yellow or whitish, while breast is fully barred and does not give impression of a black patch. Both sexes are much as adults by late summer/early autumn.

Bare parts Bill black. Legs and feet grey. Eyes deep brown to dark chestnut.

GEOGRAPHICAL VARIATION Two races, differing only in bill size.

    S. t. thyroideus (western part of range, from British Columbia south through Cascade mountains to N Baja California) Described above.

    S. t. nataliae (eastern part of range, from British Columbia south through Rockies to Arizona and New Mexico) As nominate, but with longer, broader and deeper bill

MEASUREMENTS Wing 128-143; tail 76-90; bill 23-28.5; tarsus 20-23.5. Weight: 44-64.

VOICE Explosive noisy, pulsating, single calls are distinctive; also a low-pitched guttural *k-k'-r-r-r*. The squealing call series are slower and possess shorter elements than in Red-naped Sapsucker (56). Calls given in close encounters between pair members are low, have a nasal quality, and recall similar calls given by Yellow-bellied Sapsuckers. Nestlings utter a whinnying chorus of cries when fed and chatter in the nest constantly. Drumming is most distinctive: a roll commences with a burst, which is followed by several rhythmically delivered (but distinctly slower than in other sapsuckers) groups of 2-4 strokes. About five rolls per minute are given in a drumming sequence.

HABITS Like the other species of its genus, it drinks sap from various tree species, among them lodgepole pine, alpine hemlock, red fir, white fir, Jeffrey pine and quaking aspens. Some sexual differences seem to exist, females foraging more on oaks and trunks while males prefer pines and glean more on limbs and on the ground. Forages for insects mostly by gleaning; other foraging techniques are bark-scaling, hawking, probing and pecking. In winter, when sap does not flow, the birds forage for insects and their larvae hidden in bark crevices. Displays comprise largely the general melanerpine repertoire. Head feathers are raised in mild excitement. Throat and breast feathers are erected and wings are raised when an individual alights near another. Swinging motions, combining lateral and bobbing elements, are carried out with head and breast feathers erect, the bill pointed upwards, and they are associated with chattering calls. Fluttering aerial displays are also known, particularly if a bird approaches its mate on the wing, but also upon departure from its partner. In sympatry with other sapsucker species, interspecific territories are maintained.

FOOD Nestling food consists of large wood ants. Takes sap, and insects and their larvae. Fruits (junipers) are occasionally taken in winter.

BREEDING Nest holes are drilled into snags, but also in live trees with rotten cores, most commonly in quaking aspen *Populus tremuloides*, also in larch (tamarack), at 0.8-26m. Nests of individual pairs are 175-375m apart. The pair copulates in the vicinity of the nest, but apparently never in the nest tree. Clutch contains 3-7 (most commonly 5 or 6) eggs, which are white and ovate; laid in the last quarter of May to almost the end of June, with a peak in first week of June. Both sexes incubate, the male seeming to take the slightly greater share, sitting on the eggs overnight and

attending to them slightly more during the day. Incubation lasts about 13 days, and the young remain in the hole for about a month. They are fed by both parents, which also share brooding and nest sanitation; again, males tend to be marginally more attentive. Occasionally, unmated males may feed larger nestlings, although such helpers are not tolerated by the parents. Feeding rates drop two or three days prior to fledging.

REFERENCES Bent 1939; Bock & Larson 1986; Conway & Martin 1993; Crockett & Hadow 1975; Crockett & Hansley 1977; Howell & Webb in press; Martin & Li 1992.

---

59   CUBAN GREEN WOODPECKER
Xiphidiopicus percussus   Plate 16

IDENTIFICATION Length c. 21-25cm. Small, with short, straight, slightly chisel-tipped bill fairly broad across nostrils. An unmistakable species, with small crest, short wings and long tail. Green above and dark-streaked yellow below, with barred flanks; wings barred black and white. Head is mostly white, with black band behind eye and black chin and red throat; male has narrow red band through crown to hindneck, female having most of crown black.

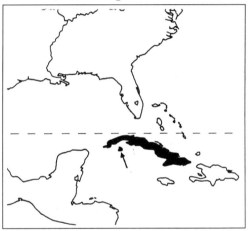

DISTRIBUTION Endemic to Cuba and its adjacent islands (Isle of Pines, Cantiles Key and others). Stragglers may reach other islands of the West Indies (e.g. Hispaniola). Reasonably common.

HABITAT Forests and woodland at any elevation, also in tall mangroves and fairly open woodland with palms. A shy bird, but found near human habitations in rural areas.

DESCRIPTION

X. p. percussus **Adult male** Narrow band of red from crown to nape and short crest and down hindneck, usually with some black feather bases visible (especially on forecrown); rather narrow blackish stripe from just in front of eye continues behind eye, around rear of ear-coverts and down rear neck side; rest of face, including forehead, white. Chin and throat centre black, this expanding on lower throat sides and on uppermost breast centre, with feathers of lower throat and breast broadly tipped red and forming red patch. Upperparts, including upperwing-coverts and tertials, green, variably tinged yellow or grey, becoming yellower on rump, latter usually showing some pale and dark bars and dark shaft streaks (bars occasionally prominent); uppertail-coverts paler, barred dark. Primaries and secondaries dark brown, broadly barred white, bars tinged green on outer webs of secondaries. Uppertail dark brown, washed buffy-grey or pearl-grey in centre, with rather broad pale brown bars on outer three or so feathers (occasionally extending onto all feathers). Breast (below red patch) and breast sides to belly yellow, strongly streaked/striped blackish except on lower breast and belly (which are sometimes tinged orange); flanks, thighs and lower underparts paler, whitish (often with pale green wash), heavily barred black. Underwing fully barred brown and whitish, coverts with greenish tinge. Undertail brown, outer three or so feathers barred paler.

Adult female Smaller and shorter-billed than male. Most of crown narrowly black, with very fine white streaks (streaks often invisible in the field); unmarked yellow area below smaller, with barring more extensive.

Juvenile Duller and more barred than adults. Upperparts narrowly barred darker, more heavily on rump, with fully barred tail; underparts more barred and streaked, with belly patch smaller but brighter (often orange or orange-red); throat and uppermost breast much less red, more brownish-black; may show hint of red on mantle. Both sexes have adult-like head pattern, but with more black in forecrown, female soon acquiring white-streaked black crown feathers.

Bare parts Bill bluish-black. Legs and feet greenish to greyish-olive. Eyes brown.

GEOGRAPHICAL VARIATION Shows much variation, both in size and in colour, but in most characters considerable overlap exists between different populations. Only two races seem to be tenable.

    X. p. percussus (range of species, apart from Isle of Pines and Cantiles Keys) Described above. Highland populations, sometimes separated as '*monticola*', tend to be larger and perhaps brighter, especially in eastern Cuba.

    X. p. insulaepinorum (Isle of Pines and Cantiles Keys) Averages smaller than nominate (but much overlap) and paler, especially below (belly paler yellow), with smaller red throat/breast patch; tail barred also on central feathers. Cantiles population, with slightly smaller bill, is sometimes separated as '*gloriae*', but differences seem insignificant.

MEASUREMENTS Wing 102-139; tail 72-98 ; bill of male 17.1-28, of female 16.4-23.5; tarsus 20.5-25.5. Weight: 48-97. Generally highly variable in size, with larger birds occurring in the highlands and males being significantly heavier.

VOICE A mewing or squealing and rather nasal *ta-há*, or *gwuk* in loose series. The *wicka*-type calls *chwet-chwet*, may be combined with low *gwurrg* notes, which are also given on their own.

HABITS Usually occurs singly or in pairs, but may sometimes be seen in parties of 3-5 individuals. Forages among vines and creepers and on trunks and in the canopy with gleaning and pecking. Attacks other woodpeckers, e.g. West Indian Woodpecker (52), in the vicinity of the nest.

FOOD Available reports stress the relatively large size of the insects taken.

BREEDING The nesting season spans February to August, possibly with a peak in May-June. Nests mostly in palms, but also in other trees, and apparently sometimes in nests of arboreal termites, at 4-5m or occasionally higher. Clutch generally of 3-4 eggs. Both parents feed the young about equally.

REFERENCES Barbour 1923; Bond 1985.

60 FINE-SPOTTED WOODPECKER
Campethera punctuligera   **Plate 17**

Forms a superspecies with *nubica*, *bennettii* and *scriptoricauda*.

IDENTIFICATION Length c. 22cm. Small, with medium-long bill with slightly decurved culmen and broad base but narrower across nostrils. Bright yellow and green above, and pale yellowish-white below, with delicate 'pinhead' spotting (mostly on breast). Rather pale-faced, but male shows prominent red moustache; red on top of head, restricted to hindcrown and nape on female.

Similar species Unlikely to be confused with other woodpeckers within its range. Overlaps with Little Green (67) and race *permista* of Green-backed (68), both of which are smaller, darker-faced, heavily barred below, and lack male's red moustache, and with Golden-tailed (64), which is heavily streaked/blotched below. Range of Nubian Woodpecker (61) may approach that of Fine-spotted, when latter told by whiter face, 'cleaner-looking' appearance and much more delicate breast spotting. Several *Dendropicos* species occur within same range, but all are smaller, less barred and/or less green above, lack male's red moustache and have bolder underpart markings.

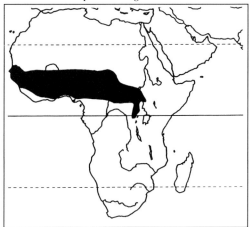

DISTRIBUTION Western Africa from SW Mauretania (c. 60km north of Rosso) and Senegambia, east through S Mali and C Chad to SW Sudan, extending south to C Ivory Coast (Lamto) and Ghana (Mole), S Nigeria (Abeokuta), Mount Zoro and Mbakaou in C Cameroon and across to NE Zaïre (upper Uele valley region). Common locally within this range.

HABITAT Inhabits wooded savannas and acacia grasslands with sometimes widely scattered trees and patches of bare ground.

DESCRIPTION
C. p. punctuligera **Adult male** Forehead to nape red, crown feathers with small grey bases. Lores, narrow supercilium and ear-coverts white, supercilium faintly streaked behind eye; blackish rear eye-stripe. Moustachial stripe red, spotted black. Chin white, occasionally with fine black spots. Neck sides and throat buffy-white, spotted black. Upperparts green or yellow-green, feathers tipped yellow, and with yellowish-white of shafts extending onto feathers to form variable number of bars; rump narrowly barred. Upperwing-coverts as back, but less barred; flight feathers brown, barred yellowish-white or white. Uppertail barred brown and yellow, with prominent yellow shafts. Underparts below throat yellowish-white, becoming whiter on belly and

lower flanks, and with delicate black spots on breast sometimes extending more sparsely to flanks (where may form bars). Underwing pale yellowish-white, barred dark. Undertail as uppertail, but paler.

Adult female As male, but forehead and forecrown black with white streaking, and moustachial area spotted/streaked black and white.

Juvenile As adult female, but darker, more olive, above and with darker barring, and more buffish below. Both sexes have unstreaked black forehead and forecrown, blacker and more obvious eye-stripe, and more prominent black moustachial stripe.

Bare parts Bill slate-grey, tipped black. Legs and feet greenish-grey; more brownish or bluish-tinged (less green) on juveniles. Eyes reddish (varying from pinkish-red to violet); brownish-grey in juveniles.

GEOGRAPHICAL VARIATION Two races.

C. p. punctuligera (entire range of species except Sudan and NE Zaïre) Described above. Varies clinally from west to east and intergrades with the following race where their ranges meet.

C. p. balia (S Sudan to NE Zaïre) Slightly smaller than nominate, with upperparts greener, less yellow, and with larger spots on whiter (less yellow) underparts. Female has black forehead and forecrown distinctly spotted (not streaked) white.

MEASUREMENTS Wing 102-125; tail 60-69; tarsus 19.9-22.3. Weight: 56-74.

VOICE An often repeated *kweeyer* or *peer*, to European observers reminiscent of the calls of Eurasian Wryneck (1) or Common Kestrel *Falco tinnunculus*. Pairs keep contact with more complex, *wik-wik-whew-wee-yeu, wee-yweu*. During encounters, soft *nyaa, nyaa, nyaa* or *tik-tik-tik-tik* calls are given. Voice very similar to that of Nubian Woodpecker.

HABITS Commonly found in pairs or family parties of up to four birds; sometimes joins mixed-species flocks. Forages in trees and bushes, and often searches the base of trees (seems to prefer the bases) and descends to the ground.

FOOD Ants and their larvae, as well as termites, form the bulk of the food, including that of nestlings.

BREEDING The breeding season is from November through early April to June in Zaïre and April-August in Nigeria to Senegambia (sometimes February in Nigeria). Nest excavated in tree. Clutch consists of 2-3 eggs. Families stay together for a long time.

REFERENCES Bannerman 1933; Bates 1930; Chapin 1939; Short 1988.

---

61 NUBIAN WOODPECKER
Campethera nubica   Plate 17

Forms a superspecies with *punctuligera*, *bennettii* and *scriptoricauda*.

IDENTIFICATION Length c. 23cm. Small, with medium-length, fairly straight bill with broad base and broad across nostrils. Combination of distinctly brownish-toned upperparts with prominent, irregular pale barring, clearly barred tail and conspicuous large spots on underparts should prevent confusion with most other *Campethera* species. Male has red forehead to nape, red moustache and white supercilium; on female, forehead, forecrown and moustache are black, spotted with white. Rather vocal, with loud ringing calls.

Similar species Overlaps with Reichenow's Woodpecker (63) in Tanzania (Kilimanjaro); Reichenow's is very similar but has more regular barring above, less contrasting tail bars and paler face (but with dark stripe behind eye). Golden-tailed (64) and Mombasa (65) Woodpeckers are both greener/yellower, less brown, above with less prominent markings, have less contrasting tail bars, and are streaked (not spotted) below. In northwest of range, may almost come into contact with Fine-spotted Woodpecker (60); both have loud screaming calls, but Fine-spotted has paler face, is much greener/yellower above, and has much smaller spots on breast.

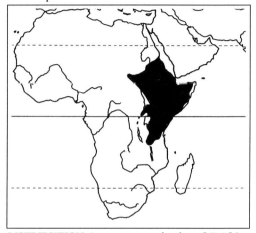

DISTRIBUTION A common woodpecker of E Africa, whose range extends from WC to NE Sudan and east to NW Somalia, south to W Uganda and adjacent NE Zaïre (Beni, Rutshuru Plain), and from S Somalia through Kenya to C and SW Tanzania (Morogoro; Rukwa valley).

HABITAT A common bird of drier bushland, bushy grassland, riverine woods and open woodland, being virtually allopatric with Bennett's Woodpecker (62). Found in *Euphorbia-Acacia* woodland, open acacia savannas, also in areas with extensive growth of elephant grass. The altitudinal range may extend to 1800m in Ethiopia, and from sea level to 2300m elsewhere in E Africa, but does not exceed 1530m in the Ruwenzoris.

DESCRIPTION

C. n. nubica **Adult male** Forehead to nape red. Lores and supercilium white. Ear-coverts white, slightly streaked at rear; streaky black eye-stripe from just in front of eye to rear of ear-coverts. Moustachial stripe red, spotted with black. Neck sides and hindneck white, heavily spotted with black. Chin buffish-white, occasionally slightly spotted black (e.g. Ethiopian breeders); throat whitish, spotted black. Upperparts including wing-coverts heavily barred olive-brown, white and yellow, white bars on mantle and back tending more towards spots (hence barring somewhat irregular compared with that on rump). Flight feathers dark brown, barred yellow or whitish. Uppertail contrastingly barred brown and yellow. Underparts below throat pale buff-white or yellowish-white; large black spots on breast and upper flanks, becoming more barred on lower flanks and with small spots on undertail-coverts (belly usually unmarked). Underwing barred yellow and brown (sometimes unbarred yellowish). Undertail as uppertail, but brown bars duller and less contrasting.

Adult female As male, but forehead, forecrown and moustachial stripe black with white spots.

Juvenile Generally darker than adults, and with heavier

underpart markings; breast markings often more as streaks, often extending to throat and chin. Both sexes have forehead and crown black (spotted or unspotted), and white-spotted moustachial stripe.

Bare parts Bill grey to dark horn (sometimes blackish), tipped black. Legs and feet grey, tinged olive. Eyes red to pinkish; greyish or grey-brown in juveniles. Orbital skin grey.

GEOGRAPHICAL VARIATION Two races, not well marked, and situation complicated by apparent habitat-conditioned variation in nominate form.

    C. n. nubica (range of species, except S Somalia) Described above. Throughout its range this race varies according to habitat: those in higher-lying areas are darker above and have heavier spotting below, while those in arid lowlands are very close to (or virtually identical to) race *pallida* in colour and are less heavily spotted below. Also, chin pattern varies somewhat, being slightly spotted on some, particularly those in Ethiopia.

    C. n. pallida (S Somalia) Averages slightly smaller than nominate, and paler above, with less strongly spotted underparts.

MEASUREMENTS Wing 95-118; tail 57-72; tarsus 18.7-22.9. Weight: 46-71.

VOICE A shrill, metallic, accelerating *weee-weee-weee...kweek*, dying away at the end. Pairs keep close contact with this call by responding immediately to the partner's call. Various low *kwick* and *kweek* notes are given at close encounters.

HABITS Mainly seen singly, the pair members keeping vocal contact, however. Forages on trunks and limbs of trees; occasionally ventures down to the ground. Pays most attention to cracked bark, stubs and the like, wherever its main prey may dwell. Feeding techniques include gleaning and pecking. Roosts individually. Territories large. Nests parasitised by honeyguides (*Indicator minor, I. variegatus*).

FOOD Almost entirely ants; also termites, other insects and spiders.

BREEDING In E Africa, during or shortly after main rainy season or in the little rains. November-March in Ethiopia; January-February in Somalia, June-July in Uganda, and February in Zaïre. A new hole is produced every season and excavated mainly by male in a rotten stump, fence post, or in the trunk of a tree or palm, where construction is easier owing to natural cavities already present. Normal clutch size is 2-3(5) eggs. Both sexes incubate, the male roosting in the nest. Both parents feed the young and guide them sex for sex in the post-fledging period.

REFERENCES Beals 1970; Chapin 1939; Short 1988.

---

62 BENNETT'S WOODPECKER
Campethera bennettii   Plate 17

Forms a superspecies with *punctuligera*, *nubica* and *scriptoricauda*.

IDENTIFICATION Length c. 24cm. Small, with medium-length pointed bill narrow between nostrils and moderately curved on culmen. A brownish-yellow species of southern Africa, with heavily spotted underparts. Male has red forehead to nape and red moustache, with unmarked white ear-coverts. Female differs from all similar woodpeckers in region in having brown throat and ear-coverts. Generally arboreal, but feeds markedly more often on ground than

other *Campethera* species.

Similar species Overlaps widely with Golden-tailed Woodpecker (64), from which male best distinguished by much browner upperparts, unmarked white ear-coverts and spotted (not streaked) breast; male Golden-tailed usually shows more black in forehead, and habitat preferences differ. In north, range approaches those of Nubian (61) and Fine-spotted (60): former is browner and more irregularly barred above, and has more patterned ear-coverts; latter is much greener/yellower above, with a fairly obvious eye-stripe, and has much finer spotting below. At northeastern limits of range meets very similar Reichenow's Woodpecker (63), for distinctions from which see latter.

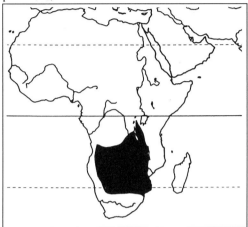

DISTRIBUTION A patchily distributed woodpecker of open woodlands in southern half of Africa. Ranges from WC Angola and NE Namibia through SE Zaïre and E Rwanda (may reach Uganda in the Merama Hills) to W and S Tanzania, W Malawi and S Mozambique, and south to S Botswana, Transvaal and NE Natal. Throughout this range it varies in abundance, being common in some places, rare in others, and totally absent from large areas (note that map shows range, not exact distribution).

MOVEMENTS Those in the most arid areas have been recorded making short-distance movements to more moderate climates after the breeding season, but this hardly represents true migration (and similar movements are no doubt performed by other woodpeckers when circumstances dictate).

HABITAT Inhabits well-developed and mature woodland and bush country. Found in miombo (*Brachystegia*) and in gusu (*Baikiaea*) woodland; in dry *Acacia* woodland, occurs mainly in the taller patches. In parts of Zimbabwe, it appears to replace Golden-tailed Woodpecker in *Brachystegia* woodland on sandy soils and in less diverse closed woodland, although the two coexist in many other areas and particularly in valley woodlands. Occurs up to 1600m in E Africa.

DESCRIPTION
C. b. bennettii **Adult male** Forehead, crown and hindneck red, forehead with small grey feather bases. Short black stripe in front of eye (not reaching bill). Rest of side of head (including thin supercilium) and chin and throat unmarked white, separated by broad red moustachial stripe with scattered black feather bases (note that a few individuals may show traces of brown on ear-coverts and throat, though much less extensive than on females, or have yellowish-buff throat). Entire upperparts and upperwing-coverts barred brown, yellow and white (those inhabiting

arid zones may have very pale and unbarred rump and uppertail-coverts), coverts usually more spotted and pale-fringed. Flight feathers brown, edged greenish, with yellowish-white bars on inner webs. Uppertail variably barred brown and dull yellow. Underparts below throat pale yellowish, often tinged golden-buff on breast, with bold, dark, round to elongated spots on breast, usually becoming bars on flanks; undertail-coverts white, often spotted or barred. Underwing much as upperwing or paler. Undertail yellowish, often tipped black.

Adult female Differs from male in head pattern. Forehead and crown black, spotted white; ear-coverts brown to blackish-brown, tipped white at top and rear, and with dark colour extending forwards beneath eye to base of upper mandible; moustachial stripe white, often flecked black; chin and throat brown to brownish-black (as ear-coverts).

Juvenile Upperparts somewhat darker and more spotted (less barred) than on adults, and underparts with coarser spotting. Forehead and crown black, finely spotted white (spots sparse or absent on males). Young males have blackish moustachial stripe; young females show at least an indication of adult's brown head markings.

Bare parts Bill slaty-grey, paler towards base. Legs and feet bluish-green to grey-green. Eyes red; dark brown in juveniles.

GEOGRAPHICAL VARIATION Two races are recognised, both of which show some variation.

C. b. bennettii (most of species' range, except S Angola, SW Zambia and northern parts of Namibia and Botswana) Described above. A general cline occurs in colour of female's throat and ear-coverts, these being palest brown in the east. Some males throughout range show suggestion of female's head/throat pattern.

C. b. capricorni (southwest of range, in S Angola and SW Zambia and adjacent N Namibia and N Botswana) Slightly larger than nominate, and with paler (whiter) rump and uppertail-coverts; underparts generally deeper yellow and with fewer, sparser spots (sometimes lacking). Females of this race have much blacker ear-coverts and throat on average (but pale lores), although paler-coloured individuals overlap with darkest-throated nominate females. As with nominate race, some males can show some brownish on throat and ear-coverts.

MEASUREMENTS Wing 108-130; tail 60-75; bill 24-30; tarsus 18-23. Weight: 61-84.

VOICE Most frequent calls are *chuur* notes, and a long call-series varying from *wi-wi-wi-wi..* or *kee-kee-kee-...* to *ddrahh, ddrahh, ddray-ay, ddray-ay, dray-ay*. During encounters, a chattering, high-pitched *wirrit-wirrit...* or *whirrwhirrwhirr whir-it-whir-it-whir-it-wrrrrrrrrrr...* and *wicka*-type calls. Seems to drum rarely, and then only softly.

HABITS A rather social woodpecker, regularly found in pairs or family parties of about three to five birds. Frequently follows glossy starlings *Lamprotornis* when foraging. Arboreal feeding takes place mostly on the trunks and larger branches of trees, where gleaning and probing in cracks seem to prevail. This species is, however, highly terrestrial, and commonly frequents lawns and other grassy sites, ground feeding constituting 70-85% of its foraging. Usually bare ground or patches with short grass are visited. When disturbed it retreats to a nearby tree, but readily returns to the ground, where it hops clumsily in search of food. Bill-pointing, wing-flicking, wing-waving/spreading and tail-spreading displays together with calls are characteristic in interactions between two or more individuals.

FOOD Mainly ants, and termites and their eggs; occasionally other insects and larvae.

BREEDING Has been found breeding from August to February; nesting season culminates in October and November in Zimbabwe and Transvaal. Holes are excavated in dead trees or dead sections of live trees at 2-10m. Reuses holes from previous years, and often uses holes made by other species of woodpecker or natural cavities. Usually lays 3 eggs, but clutches of 2 and 5 have been recorded as well. Both parents incubate for 15-18 days, and provide for the young, which stay with parents until the initiation of the next brood.

REFERENCES Britton 1980; Clancey 1964; Harwin 1972; Irwin 1978, 1981; Maclean 1985; Newman 1989; Roberts *et al.* 1981; Short 1971a, 1971c, 1971e, 1988; Short *et al.* 1990; Tarboton 1990.

63 REICHENOW'S WOODPECKER
Campethera scriptoricauda **Plate 17**

Other names: Speckle-throated Woodpecker, Tanzanian Woodpecker

Forms a superspecies with *punctuligera, nubica* and *bennettii*.

IDENTIFICATION Length c. 22cm. Small, with medium-length, slightly curved bill narrow between nostrils. Often considered a race ('megasubspecies') of Bennett's Woodpecker (62) (Short *et al.* 1990) or even a race of Nubian Woodpecker (61). Closest to Bennett's, and in most plumage features largely inseparable from nominate race of that species. Differs, however, from latter in being slightly smaller and shorter-winged, and has different head pattern: both sexes have stripe behind eye formed by dark brown feathering, rear ear-coverts slightly to moderately streaked blackish, and also chin and throat clearly spotted with black; females thus lack brown ear-coverts and throat of female Bennett's. Underparts are much as on Bennett's, but spots perhaps larger and more rounded (more as Nubian); upperparts as Bennett's (i.e. less greenish and more regularly barred than on Nubian). Bill similar to Bennett's, but with extensive pale yellow or yellow-green on proximal half of lower mandible. Female is further distinguished from female Nubian Woodpecker by white moustachial area (blackish on Nubian).

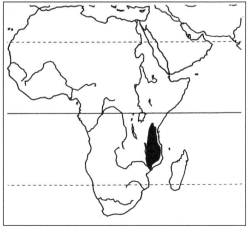

DISTRIBUTION Restricted to a small area of E Africa. Occurs from inland eastern and S Tanzania through N

Mozambique south to 17/18°S, and in the west from Lake Malawi south to around 17°S in Nsanje area.

HABITAT Frequents open woodland, savanna and thorn scrub. At its southern limits, found in open *Brachystegia* woodland with tall-grass ground cover.

DESCRIPTION Essentially as Bennett's Woodpecker (62), apart from differences given above.

GEOGRAPHICAL VARIATION None reported.

MEASUREMENTS Wing 103-117; tail 63-64; bill 25-27.

VOICE Similar to the vocalisations of Bennett's Woodpecker, which see.

HABITS A quiet bird; even its pecking is very subdued. Often backing up when searching for food.

FOOD Mainly ants and their larvae.

BREEDING The breeding season spans October-November (Malawi). The nest is excavated in a dead tree or palm trunk. Lays 3 eggs.

REFERENCES Maclean 1985; Roberts *et al.* 1981; Short 1988; Short *et al.* 1990; Vincent 1935.

64 GOLDEN-TAILED WOODPECKER
Campethera abingoni   Plate18

Forms a superspecies with *mombassica* and *notata*.

IDENTIFICATION Length . 20-23cm. Small, with moderately long, broad-based bill with slightly curved culmen. Variably greenish-toned above, ranging from yellow-green to grey-green or even olive-brown, with distinct pale yellowish and greenish-yellow bars. Underparts whitish with heavy broad blackish streaks, latter sometimes merging in breast area to form blotchy pattern. Ear-coverts vary from plain white to dark-streaked, and normally shows fairly distinct white supercilium and pale line below eye. Male has red tips to blackish forehead and crown feathers, red nape and largely red moustache. Female and juvenile have forehead, crown and moustache patterned black and white. A rather unobtrusive species, preferring denser vegetation and often remaining hidden for long periods.

Similar species Combination of barred greenish upperparts and streaked underparts generally separates it from most other woodpeckers within its range. A number of other sympatric or partly sympatric species are greenish-backed, but most of these lack distinctive barring above. Bennett's (62), Reichenow's (63) and Nubian (61) Woodpeckers are all somewhat browner and more heavily barred above and are spotted (not streaked) below, and female Bennett's has diagnostic brown ear-coverts and throat. Fine-spotted Woodpecker (60) has a paler face and is delicately speckled below, while smaller Green-backed (68) is spotted (or almost barred) above but has spotted underparts. Mombasa Woodpecker (65) is very like Golden-tailed, and until recently was considered conspecific with it, but has brighter, more golden-green upperparts with small yellow spots (not bars) and the crown feathers have olive-green rather than blackish bases.

DISTRIBUTION Recorded in Senegambia and N Guinea, but, apart from one report from Ghana, apparently absent between there and N Central African Republic, and then again absent before reappearing in S Sudan and adjacent NE Zaïre and NW Uganda; from there, range continues south through westernmost Uganda, Rwanda, SW Kenya

(east to Mara river), Tanzania (except extreme northeast), S and SE Zaïre southwards to Natal (Durban area) and northern parts of S Africa, west through NE Namibia and Angola and north to westernmost Zaïre and the lower Congo river. Within this range it is locally common.

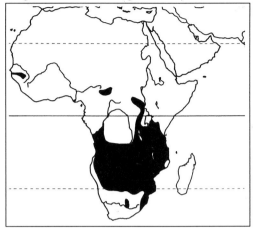

HABITAT Inhabits all kinds of woodland and forest edge with the possible exception of *Brachystegia*, where it is replaced by Bennett's Woodpecker. Exhibits some preference for vicinity of rivers in more open regions, but always in areas of dense trees and thickets. Occurs in coastal forest, evergreen forest and thickets, riparian fringing forests, and in savanna with dense *Acacia* bush. Among the habitats recorded for this species are rich miombo woodland and montane forest, where it keeps mostly to the edge. Occasionally visits parks and large gardens and exotic trees. Ranges from sea level up to about 1400m in Natal, and to 1800m in Zimbabwe and 2000m in E Africa, to 2200m in Malawi.

DESCRIPTION

C. a. abingoni **Adult male** Forehead to nape red, feathers of forehead and crown with greyish-black bases. Neck sides white, streaked blackish. Narrow, indistinct white supercilium with dark upper border. Lores white; thin black-streaked white line below eye. Ear-coverts white or whitish, with broad dark eye-stripe behind eye. Short moustachial stripe red with dark feather bases. Chin and throat black, heavily spotted with white. Upperparts including upperwing-coverts olive-brown, narrowly barred pale yellow-white and greenish-yellow, pale bars becoming broader on rump and uppertail-coverts; wing-coverts spotted and tipped yellowish. Flight feathers brown, barred whitish, bars broader on inner webs. Uppertail brown, barred yellowish-white (bars sometimes obscured by overall yellow suffusion). Underparts below throat white, tinged yellow on breast and flanks, with heavy blackish streaking on breast becoming spots/bars on flanks and spots/streaks on belly. Underwing as upperwing, but paler. Undertail yellowish-brown, obscurely pale-barred.

Adult female Differs from male in having forehead and crown black with fine white spots, and moustachial stripe streaked black and white with no red.

Juvenile Both sexes as adult female, but appear less yellow above and with spots and streaks rather than bars, and more heavily streaked below, with flanks and belly more barred. Moustache mostly black, spotted white.

Bare parts Bill slaty-black, often tinged green at base of lower mandible. Legs and feet dark greenish, usually tinged olive or grey. Eyes reddish but rather variable, from hazel to black; brown or brownish-grey in juveniles (some brown-eyed individuals are possibly subadults).

GEOGRAPHICAL VARIATION Six races are recognised, differing mainly in tone of upperparts and degree of markings below.

  C. a. abingoni (lower Congo and western Zaïre, Angola and NE Namibia east to Ruwenzori area of E Zaïre and western Tanzania, NW Zambia, Zimbabwe and N Transvaal) Described above.
  C. a. chrysura (Senegambia, Guinea, Central African Republic, S Sudan, NE Zaïre and W Uganda) Smaller than nominate and greener above, with streaked ear-coverts; blacker on throat and breast.
  C. a. kavirondensis (eastern Rwanda, NW and NC Tanzania and SW Kenya) Pale barring above broader, and underparts paler (more narrowly streaked); ear-coverts streaked.
  C. a. suahelica (Tanzania from Kilimanjaro south, through Zambia, Malawi, Mozambique and E Zimbabwe to E Transvaal and N Swaziland) As *kavirondensis*, but upperparts yellower-toned.
  C. a. constricta (Natal, Zululand, S Swaziland and S Mozambique) Very like *suahelica*, but less yellow (more green) above.
  C. a. anderssoni (SW Angola, Namibia except northeast, SW Botswana, and northern Cape Province to SW Transvaal) As nominate *abingoni*, but upperparts greyer, rump pale, and underpart markings heavier (throat and breast can be almost wholly black).

MEASUREMENTS Wing 103-124, 103-112 (*chrysura*), 112-124 (*abingoni*); tail 59-72; bill 24-30; tarsus 17-21. Weight: 51-58 (*chrysura*), 61-83 (*abingoni*, *suahelica*).

VOICE Call loud and distinctive: a single plaintive *dreee-aw* or *weeea*, often by male. Long-distance call a series of 2-12 *yaooaak-yaaaaaak* notes. More aggressive notes sound like ...*weet-wit-wit*... and *kyek*. Intimate notes *pew-pew-pew*. Drums in long (1.5sec), slow rolls.

HABITS Usually a quiet species which generally lives singly or in pairs. Visits even rather isolated trees, where it explores larger branches and twigs, often moving along their underside. Most easily detected when hammering forcefully (this foraging mode seemingly commoner than in congeners) on dead tree trunks or branches affected by wood-boring larvae; probing and gleaning are, however, the dominant feeding techniques. Hunts particularly for arboreal ants. Flies quite far between foraging sites, and lives in rather large territories (10-15ha). Often associates with Cardinal Woodpecker (76), which hammers more and can exploit very small twigs. Nest parasitised by honeyguides *Indicator*.

FOOD Insects and their larvae, but mainly ants; also millipedes.

BREEDING Breeding extends from August to December. Nest holes are drilled into trees at moderate heights, 1-5m. Clutch comprises 2-3(5) eggs and is incubated by both sexes, by the male at night. Both parents brood, and feed the young by regurgitation. Nestling period 22-25 days.

REFERENCES Britton 1980; Chapin 1939; Clancey 1964; Cyrus & Robson 1980; Dowsett-Lemaire 1989; Irwin 1978, 1981; Maclean 1985; Roberts *et al.* 1981; Short 1971f, 1988; Short *et al.* 1990; Tarboton 1990; Wood 1989.

65 MOMBASA WOODPECKER
Campethera mombassica   Plate 18

Forms a superspecies with *abingoni* and *notata*.

IDENTIFICATION Length c. 22cm. Small, with medium-length broad-based bill with slightly decurved culmen. Until recently, regarded as a rather distinctive race of Golden-tailed Woodpecker (64). Differs from latter, however, in somewhat smaller size, bright golden-green upperparts with small yellowish-white spots (not bars), paler throat, and in forehead and crown feathers of both sexes having olive-green (not blackish) bases; voice also differs, and appears not to drum (or does so only very rarely). Confined to central part of E African coast and NE Tanzania. Apparent hybrids have been recorded between this species and race *suahelica* of Golden-tailed, but the two have also been found together in NE Tanzania with no indication of interbreeding.

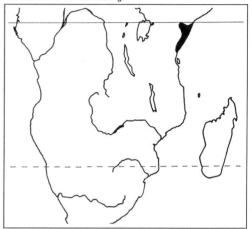

DISTRIBUTION Fairly common in southernmost Somalia, and coastal Kenya from Lamu south to NE Tanzania (Dar es Salaam); inland, recorded in the Arabuko-Sokoke Forest, the W Usambara Mountains, and Mount Kilimanjaro (eastern part).

HABITAT Coastal forest and woodland.

DESCRIPTION
Adult male Forehead and crown olive-green with red feather tips; nape red. Lores buffish; sides of head and neck whitish with black streaking (including on ear-coverts); short white supercilium. Short red moustachial stripe streaked black. Chin and throat whitish, sometimes with a few dark streaks/spots. Upperparts including upperwing-coverts golden-green, with fine yellowish-white spots and shaft streaks. Flight feathers brown, with some spots forming bars (similar to Golden-tailed). Uppertail golden-green to olive-brown, unbarred except faintly on outer feathers. Underparts below throat as nominate Golden-tailed, white or buffy-white with yellowish tinge to breast and flanks, with fairly broad blackish streaks becoming narrower on flanks and belly. Underwing as upperwing, with paler coverts. Undertail brownish, suffused yellow.

Adult female Differs from male in having forehead and crown dark olive-green with small yellowish-buff spots, and moustachial stripe olive-grey with black and white streaks/spots.

Juvenile Both sexes resemble adult female, but are duller and more spotted above and more heavily streaked below, sometimes with some barring on lower underparts.

Bare parts Bill slate-grey, with distinct green tone to lower mandible, especially proximal half. Legs and feet greenish to olive or olive-grey. Eyes dark reddish; more brownish or greyish in juveniles.

GEOGRAPHICAL VARIATION None reported within its small range, but intermediates (apparent hybrids) between this species and race *suahelica* of Golden-tailed have been recorded from EC Tanzania and from just south of Kilimanjaro.

MEASUREMENTS Wing 100-108. Weight: 50-71.

VOICE Distinctly different from that of Golden-tailed Woodpecker. Accelerating call-series ends with a short *yuk*. Call notes less buzzing at beginning. Intimate calls include a grating *drrrdddt*. Apparently does not drum.

HABITS Similar to those of Golden-tailed Woodpecker, which see.

BREEDING Breeding season December-February.

REFERENCES Clancey 1988; Short 1988; Short *et al.* 1990.

---

66 KNYSNA WOODPECKER
Campethera notata   Plate 18

Forms a superspecies with *abingoni* and *mombassica*.

IDENTIFICATION Length 20-22cm. Small, with rather long, narrow bill with slightly curved culmen. A relatively dark-looking woodpecker, especially in worn plumage, confined to S Africa. Green above, finely spotted; pale yellow-buff breast, with prominent large dark brown spots which extend to sides of neck and to flanks. Male has red forehead to nape and spotted red moustache.

Similar species Very closely related to and possibly conspecific with Golden-tailed Woodpecker (64); range of nominate race of latter almost meets that of Knysna, but apparently does not overlap. Best separated from nominate Golden-tailed by much darker overall appearance, greener and less barred (more spotted) upperparts and strongly spotted (not barred) underparts and neck sides. Olive Woodpecker (86) overlaps almost completely in range, but is much more uniform, less green and more golden-olive above, has grey face, red rump and centre of belly, and lacks spots.

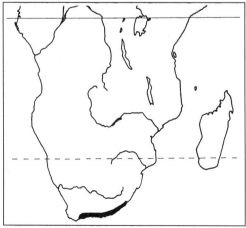

DISTRIBUTION Endemic to S Africa, occurring from Swellendaam region of southern Cape Province east to

southernmost Natal between 30° and 31°S. Locally common.

HABITAT A species confined to coastal areas. Frequents light forest, evergreen forest, dense bush, and riparian woodland and bush. Also found in comparatively open country where there are large trees, and in *Euphorbia* scrub; occasionally enters gardens.

DESCRIPTION

Adult male Forehead, crown and nape red, feathers of forehead with extensive dark olive-brown bases. Narrow short white supercilium heavily obscured by dark spotting; lores buffish-white. Sides of head buffish-white, heavily streaked/spotted dark. Neck sides whitish, with prominent black spots. Moustachial stripe red, but feather bases heavily spotted white and black (moustache sometimes obscure). Chin and throat whitish, heavily streaked and spotted black, especially on throat. Hindneck olive, spotted pale; rest of upperparts green or yellowish-green, finely spotted pale yellow (rarely, spots form broken bars), very occasionally with slight trace of red on mantle, and rump and uppertail-coverts finely and indistinctly barred whitish. Scapulars and upperwing-coverts as mantle, with small pale spots often elongated and streak-like; flight feathers dark brown, edged green and barred white, bars broader on inner webs. Uppertail yellowish-olive, narrowly barred yellowish. Breast buffish-tinged white, becoming whiter on lower underparts, with large, bold, dark brown spots on breast and flanks becoming narrower streaks on belly and undertail-coverts. Underwing much as upperwing, but paler. Undertail washed yellow, with barring much obscured.

Adult female As male, but forehead and crown olive-brown, finely spotted pale yellowish to white; also lacks red in moustache, which is spotted black and white (appears as a dusky stripe).

Juvenile Both sexes resemble adult female, but are greener, less yellow, above, with fewer spots, and have larger spots and barring below.

Bare parts Bill dark slate-grey, tipped black. Legs and feet green-grey. Eyes reddish.

GEOGRAPHICAL VARIATION Much individual variation, some individuals being darker and/or more heavily spotted overall, but such differences range throughout population and no subspecies are recognisable.

MEASUREMENTS Wing 101-114; tail 66-77; bill 19-24; tarsus 19-23. Weight: 62.

VOICE The usual call, an almost whistled *wliee* or *peeeah*, is weaker and more shrill than the similar call of Golden-tailed Woodpecker. Series of triple notes, *weee-we-wi*, and *kra kra kree-kree-kree-kree kra kra*, in sound somewhere between croaking and whistling. Nestling calls have been likened to a puffing engine.

HABITS An unobtrusive woodpecker which lives singly or in pairs, and may also be met with in small family parties. Occasionally accompanies mixed-species flocks. Forages in (often dead) trees on branches at medium heights and on trunks. Frequently pecks and probes among lichens. Movements quick, and perches crosswise occasionally.

FOOD Mainly ants and their brood, and wood-boring beetles and their larvae.

Breeding Breeding takes place August-November. Nest is constructed in a dead trunk or branch of a tree by both sexes. Lays 2-4 eggs. Incubation period probably 12 days. The chicks are fed by regurgitation, by both parents, which also both tend to nest sanitation. Nestling period 3-4 weeks.

REFERENCES Clancey 1964; Maclean 1985; Roberts *et al.* 1981; Short 1988; Sinclair *et al.* 1993; Tarboton 1990.

67 LITTLE GREEN WOODPECKER
Campethera maculosa   Plate 19

Other name: Golden-backed Woodpecker
Forms a superspecies with *cailliautii*.

IDENTIFICATION Length c. 16cm. Small and rather small-headed, with short and relatively broad-based bill fairly broad across nostrils. A little-known species with a restricted range in W Africa. Green-backed, black-tailed, with completely barred underparts; no moustache. Underwing unmarked yellow. Male has indistinct reddish on crown and a somewhat more obviously red nape; female lacks red and has a spotted head.

Similar species Within its range, likely to be confused only with extremely similar western race *permista* of Green-backed Woodpecker (68). Differs from latter in having bronze or yellowish tinge to upperparts, less well-defined red on head (male), black tail (more yellowish on *permista*), and in underwing-coverts being unmarked or nearly so (this feature of limited use in the field); note also that female Green-backed has red nape (buff-spotted olive on female Little Green). Has hybridised with Green-backed in Ghana.

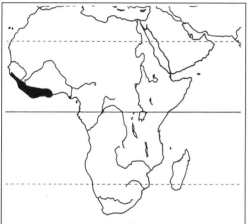

DISTRIBUTION A West African endemic, occurring from western Guinea-Bissau eastwards along coastal zone to C Ghana (in Aburi region); extends inland to just south of Mount Nimba. Not uncommon locally, but little known and possibly overlooked.

HABITAT Inhabits primary and secondary forest edge, clearings with secondary growth and dead trees, and forest-shrub mosaic. From lowlands to mountain ridges above 1000m.

DESCRIPTION
Adult male Forehead and crown olive-blackish with small red feather tips; nape red but rather ill-defined. Rest of head, neck, chin and throat buff, densely spotted with brown. Entire upperparts and upperwing-coverts yellowish-green to bronze-green, rump slightly barred (occasionally a few whitish spots on mantle, and some may show slight traces of red on upperparts). Flight feathers brown with pale buffish bars, latter broadest on inner webs. Uppertail blackish, with indistinct yellow shafts; outer

feathers green. Underparts from throat buffish, becoming greenish-white below breast, all heavily barred deep olive. Underwing-coverts pale yellowish-white and unmarked, or with just a few indistinct broken bars. Undertail blackish with yellow tinge.

Adult female Lacks red on head: forehead and crown olive-black, becoming deep olive on nape, all spotted with buff; greater tendency towards some spotting on upperparts.

Juvenile Much as adults, but upperparts less bronzy, more green, and usually with some paler streaks on mantle/back; underparts generally paler and less buff/green, with more irregular barring.

Bare parts Bill dark olive-green to blackish, with bluish or olive tint on lower mandible. Legs and feet olive-grey or greenish. Eyes brown or pinkish-brown; dark brown in juveniles.

GEOGRAPHICAL VARIATION None known within small range.

MEASUREMENTS Wing 96-107; tail 53-65; bill 21; tarsus 16.6-17.7. Weight: 54.

VOICE Common call a regular series of 3-4 ascending notes, *teeay teeay...*, faster than in Green-backed Woodpecker. Also an aggressive (?) *teerweet-teerweet-....*

HABITS Virtually unknown; tame and inconspicuous, moving without haste.

FOOD Ants, primarily *Crematogaster* species.

BREEDING Nesting recorded in August in Senegambia; possibly also March-April.

REFERENCES Bannerman 1933; Colston *et al.* 1986; Short 1988.

68 GREEN-BACKED WOODPECKER
Campethera cailliautii   Plate 19

Other name: Little Spotted Woodpecker
Forms a superspecies with *maculosa*.

IDENTIFICATION Length c. 16cm. Small and small-headed, with short and broad-based bill. A variable species, green above (unmarked, spotted or barred) and pale below (spotted, semi-barred or, on western race, heavily barred); yellowish undertail and barred yellowish underwing. Males have red forehead to nape; females have red only on nape. An inconspicuous bird, easily overlooked, but its loud calls may attract attention to it.

Similar species Races in eastern parts of range have upperparts barred or spotted and are spotted below: separated from similar-sized Cardinal Woodpecker (76) by greener, less black-and-white, appearance, lack of dark moustache, and spotted rather than streaked underparts; from larger Golden-tailed Woodpecker (64) by similar criteria; and from Bennett's (62) and Nubian (61) by smaller size, less brownish and less barred upperparts, facial spotting, and again lack of any moustache. In extreme west of range, race *permista* overlaps with (and has hybridised with) highly similar Little Green Woodpecker (67), from which best told by less bronzy tone to upperparts, paler tail, better-defined red on head of male, and red on nape of female (female Little Green lacks all red); similarly small Buff-spotted Woodpecker (70) has dark underparts with pale spots and male has red confined to nape (female lacks all red), and is often found in denser growth; where overlaps with Cardinal, Gaboon (78) and Speckle-breasted

(74) Woodpeckers, Green-backed (*permista*) differs from all these in having entire underparts heavily barred rather than streaked or spotted.

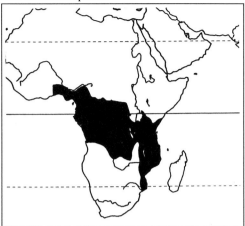

DISTRIBUTION An isolated population is found in SW Ethiopia. Main range extends from E Ghana, eastwards through S Nigeria across to southernmost Sudan, down to SW Uganda and across to southwest Lake Victoria, then S Kenya (north to Kabarnet) and north to Juba river in S Somalia; southern limits are in N Angola across to N and NW Zambia, and in the east south to the Limpopo river in Mozambique. This species varies from being common or locally common, as in parts of Cameroon and C Malawi, to uncommon, as in W Kenya and Mozambique.

HABITAT Occurs over a wide range of habitats, from forest to thornbush country; near water in dry country. Occupies, for instance, rich *Brachystegia* (miombo) and mahobohobo (*Uapaca*) woodland in the southern parts of its range; elsewhere, it frequents the edges of lowland or other evergreen forest, woodland, wooded grassland and, locally, palm groves. In E Africa found at up to 2100m (Bwamba region), in Zimbabwe to 1000m, and locally to 1200m.

DESCRIPTION
C. c. loveridgei **Adult male** Forehead and crown feathers black, tipped red; nape red. Entire sides of head to chin and upper throat buffish-white, whiter on supercilium, with all but lores densely spotted with black. Neck sides and hindneck buffish, heavily spotted black. Upperparts including upperwing-coverts yellowish-green (yellower on rump and uppertail-coverts), all with whitish bar-like spotting, becoming more green-barred on rump. Flight feathers brown, edged yellow-green on outer webs, and barred white, barring heaviest on inner webs. Uppertail yellowish-green. Underparts from throat greenish-white, tinged buff on breast and becoming yellower on belly, with dark brown spots on throat and breast becoming smaller and sparser on belly and more bar-like on flanks. Underwing-coverts pale yellowish, spotted blackish. Undertail yellowish, tipped darker, sometimes vaguely barred at base.

Adult female Differs from male in having forehead and crown black, spotted with buff.

Juvenile Greener, less yellow, above than adults, with less obviously barred flanks. Both sexes have forehead and crown as adult female, but with spots finer and whiter; red on nape often much reduced or even lacking.

Bare parts Bill grey or blackish with dark tip, and with greenish or horn-green base to lower mandible. Legs and feet variably grey, green or olive-grey, sometimes tinged yellow. Eyes reddish to brownish; less red, more brown (or even greyish), in juveniles.

GEOGRAPHICAL VARIATION Four races, generally fairly distinct, and western race highly distinct.
    C. c. loveridgei (C Tanzania around Kilosa, south to Limpopo river in Mozambique and west to Mount Zelinda in easternmost Zimbabwe) Described above.
    C. c. cailliautii (coastal zone from S Somalia through E Kenya to NE Tanzania, including Zanzibar) Slightly smaller than *loveridgei* and with more spotted, less barred, upperparts and browner tail; underpart spots more evenly dispersed.
    C. c. nyansae (SW Kenya and NW Tanzania south to N Zambia, and west through E and SE Zaïre to NE Angola; also SW Ethiopia) Slightly longer-winged than *loveridgei*. Upperparts greener, less yellow, and with markings in form of narrow streaks; underparts more heavily spotted, spots tending to form bars. Also bill broader across nostrils, more as *permista*. Intergrades with latter race in Angola and S and E Zaïre.
    C. c. permista (E Ghana across to extreme SW Sudan, SW Uganda, through C Zaïre to NW Angola) Differs conspicuously from other races in unmarked green upperparts and completely dark-barred underparts; in S Nigeria, some may have paler underparts with narrower barring. Bill also broader across nostrils.

MEASUREMENTS Wing 88-108; tail 58-66; bill 14-15; tarsus 15-17.4. Weight: 34-57.

VOICE A thin, plaintive *hee* or *hlieee*, repeated about 4-12 times at regular intervals. In encounters, gives grating *grrrr* or *dddn* calls, including on the wing, and *tew-a*, *wik-a* and variations thereof, sometimes accelerating into series. At intimate contacts, *aaaa* or *aa-aa*. Drumming rolls short and soft.

HABITS This retiring woodpecker lives singly or in pairs. Stays high in the canopy of the forest. Visits live and dead sections of trees, including ant and termite nests. Gleaning seems to be the major foraging mode; also pecks. Has also been seen attacking seed-pods in search of insects.

FOOD Feeds largely on arboreal formicid ants and on termites.

BREEDING Nesting activities are confined to the period September-November in east of range. Probably breeds March-September in Zaïre; egg-laying associated with rainy seasons. Nests in trees and palms. Clutch contains 2-3(4) eggs. Both sexes incubate and feed (probably by regurgitation) the nestlings.

REFERENCES Bannerman 1933; Britton 1980; Chapin 1939; Irwin 1981; Maclean 1985; Roberts *et al.* 1981; Short 1988; Tarboton 1990.

69 TULLBERG'S WOODPECKER
Campethera tullbergi   Plate 20

Other name: Fine-banded Woodpecker (eastern races)

IDENTIFICATION Length c. 18-20cm. Small, with medium-long bill slightly curved on culmen and fairly narrow across nostrils. A rather distinctive green-backed woodpecker of mainly highland areas, confined to three well-separated regions of W and E Africa. Males have red forehead to nape, females have red nape, and both sexes lack moustache. Western race has finely spotted face and breast, spotted yellow underparts, and red on carpal area (unique among woodpeckers). Eastern populations have face and underparts narrowly vermiculated and barred. A little-known woodpecker, generally foraging at high levels and difficult to observe. Reasonably easy to identify once seen well.

Similar species Nominate western race unlikely to be confused. Eastern races also distinctive, and occur at higher elevations than other woodpeckers in range; race *permista* of Green-backed (68) may possibly be found in similar habitat, but is smaller, shorter-billed, has coarser barring below and has spotted (not vermiculated) face.

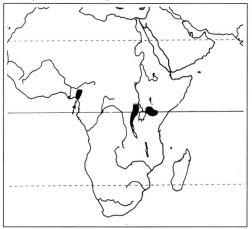

DISTRIBUTION An African endemic with three discrete populations: on the Obudu Plateau of SE Nigeria, in adjacent W Cameroon and on Bioko Island; in easternmost Zaïre, SW Uganda, W Rwanda and Burundi, and Mount Mahari in westernmost Tanzania; and from central E Uganda to the central highlands of Kenya.

HABITAT Seems to prefer ravines and edges, but also visits dead trees away from main forest cover. Confined to moist mountain forests between 900 and 3000m.

DESCRIPTION

C. t. taeniolaema **Adult male** Forehead and crown feathers black-based and red-tipped; nape red. Chin and sides of head greyish-white, finely vermiculated black, sometimes with dark post-ocular patch or spots. Neck sides and hindneck yellow-green, barred black. Upperparts yellow-tinged green, rump occasionally barred or streaked paler. Upperwing-coverts green, edged yellow; flight feathers brown, outer webs edged yellow-green, and with inner webs barred yellowish-white. Uppertail dark brown, tipped yellow, with feathers green-edged. Underparts pale greenish-yellow, paler on belly, all with narrow black barring. Underwing-coverts yellowish. Undertail yellowish, sometimes faintly barred brownish.

Adult female Differs from male in having forehead and crown feathers black with white spotting, and almost invariably has reddish feathers on upper lores.

Juvenile Has greyish tone to green upperparts, which are also variably pale-spotted; barring below heavier. Both sexes have forehead and crown olive-black and finely spotted, but males soon acquire red feather tips.

Bare parts Bill slaty to black, with bluish-grey or green-grey lower mandible. Legs and feet dull olive-green or yellow-green. Eyes red; brown in juveniles.

GEOGRAPHICAL VARIATION Three races, the nominate highly distinctive (other races were formerly regarded as constituting a separate species).

C. t. taeniolaema (E Zaïre and W Uganda south to W

Tanzania, also E Uganda to Kenya west of Rift Valley) Described above.

C. t. hausburgi (Kenya east of Rift Valley) Differs from *taeniolaema* in yellower upperparts and underparts and in narrower barring below. Some may have barring more broken, approaching pattern of *tullbergi*.

C. t. tullbergi (Nigeria, Cameroon, Bioko) Highly distinctive in plumage, and averages slightly larger and longer-billed than above two races (which were formerly combined as a separate species). Greener, less yellow, above, and with vermiculation of head to breast replaced by fine spots and remaining underpart barring by larger spots/broken bars; outer lesser upperwing-coverts heavily spotted and tipped red.

MEASUREMENTS Wing 100-116; tail 63-72; tarsus 18-20. Weight: 43-66.

VOICE A call-series, *kweek-kweek-….*

HABITS Joins mixed-species flocks. Forages in the canopy, where it probes into epiphytes (moss, lichens). Seems also to be attracted by trees killed by fire. Nests parasitised by honeyguides (*Indicator variegatus*).

FOOD Mainly ants; also caterpillars.

BREEDING Egg-laying season probably October-November. Nest excavated in tree.

REFERENCES Britton 1980; Jackson 1938; Short 1988; Short *et al.* 1990; Taylor & Taylor 1988.

70   BUFF-SPOTTED WOODPECKER
Campethera nivosa   Plate 20

IDENTIFICATION Length c. 14-16cm. Very small, with short bill slightly curved on culmen and narrow across nostrils. Unmarked green above, with underparts dark olive or yellowish-olive with pale spots and/or bars. Crown distinctively dark olive (males with red, but on nape only); lacks moustache. Rather quiet and unobtrusive; frequently perches across branches.

Similar species Sympatric Brown-eared Woodpecker (71) is somewhat similar but noticeably bigger, and is easily separated by its brown ear-coverts bordered by long pale supercilium. Little Green Woodpecker (67) and western race *permista* of Green-backed Woodpecker (68) are almost as small, but both have paler and prominently barred underparts and different head pattern.

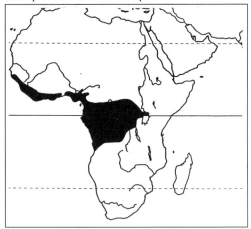

235

DISTRIBUTION Known range extends from Senegambia through coastal W Africa to SE Nigeria, south to NW Angola, and east through southern Cameroon to the Bangangai Forest of southwesternmost Sudan, NE Zaïre and across C Uganda to the Nandi Forest in W Kenya and to NW Zambia in the south. Despite being common, this species is easy to overlook and possibly occurs more widely than indicated on the map.

HABITAT A common but inconspicuous African woodpecker which has similar habitat requirements to those of the larger and longer-billed Brown-eared Woodpecker. In primary and dense secondary lowland and montane forest at up to about 950 (1800)m; also in *Gmelina* woodlands, forest patches interspersed with shrub and grassland, and in gardens.

DESCRIPTION
C. n. nivosa **Adult male** Forehead and crown dark green-olive or somewhat darker; nape red. Lores, chin and sides of head whitish (sometimes buff-tinged), all heavily streaked olive; may show slight trace of pale supercilium behind eye. Entire upperparts, including wing-coverts, bronze-green, very occasionally with some pale spots. Flight feathers brown, edged green, barred yellow-green on inner webs and pale-spotted on outer webs. Uppertail blackish-brown. Underparts dark olive-green, with buffy-white spots from throat to lower breast tending more towards bars on flanks and lower underparts. Underwing yellowish. Undertail blackish-brown, with yellowish outer feathers.

Adult female Has entire top of head blackish-olive, lacking red on nape.

Juvenile Less bronze-tinged above, and browner below with spots tending towards bars. On both sexes, forehead to nape greyish-olive (lacks red).

Bare parts Bill slaty-black, lower mandible bluish- to greenish-grey. Legs and feet olive to greenish. Eyes reddish-brown to red; brown in juveniles. Orbital skin dull olive.

GEOGRAPHICAL VARIATION Three races are known, one an island form, with a possible fourth, larger, one.
    C. n. nivosa (Senegambia east to Cameroon and W Zaïre and south to Angola and NW Zambia) Described above. This form has recently been reported in the northern part of Ivory Coast as well as in NW Zambia. Intergrades in northeast of its range with *herberti* (intermediates were formerly named '*efulensis*').
    C. n. poensis (Bioko Island) Differs from nominate *nivosa* in whiter belly, somewhat yellower tail, and breast markings tending more towards bars.
    C. n. herberti (Central African Republic and Sudan to Kenya and south to C and E Zaïre) Slightly smaller than nominate. More green, less bronzy, above; underparts yellower, with breast spots more bar-like and belly paler-looking (broadly pale-barred); uppertail greener. Wing and tail feathers have more yellow on shafts.
    C. n. maxima (N Ivory Coast) Known only from two specimens from isolated gallery forest. Differs from nominate only in size, measurements being about 10% greater. Validity doubtful, and may represent simply a larger form of nominate (latter has recently been found in northern part of Ivory Coast).

MEASUREMENTS Wing 76-95; tail 40-48; bill 19-22; tarsus 15.8-16.8. Weight: 30-49.

VOICE Calls *preeeew* and a trilled *dee-dee-dee-*...; during encounters, *te-te-te-*....

HABITS Met with mainly in pairs, and regularly joins mixed-species flocks. Although not shy, its unobtrusive habits and rather silent nature render this species inconspicuous. Joins mixed-species flocks. Forages in the lower storeys (but also up to canopy) of the forest on trunks and vines, by gleaning and pecking. May spend longer periods exploiting arboreal termite and ant nests. Moves rapidly and often perches crosswise. Displays with wing-spreading and head/body-swinging. Most likely brood parasite of this woodpecker is the Spotted Honeyguide *Indicator maculatus*.

FOOD The main food is (black) ants (*Crematogaster*) and termites.

BREEDING Breeding season spans November to June. Birds with enlarged gonads have been found in March and April in Liberia, eggs in April in Nigeria; probably breeds in November-January and respectively in March-June in Cameroon, January-May in Zaïre, and December-March in Uganda and Kenya. Carves its nest in trees into the nests of arboreal ants and termites, occasionally into wood. Clutch size 2 eggs.

REFERENCES Britton 1980; Chapin 1939; Colston *et al.* 1986; Short 1988; Walker 1939.

---

71 BROWN-EARED WOODPECKER
Campethera caroli   **Plate 20**

IDENTIFICATION Length c. 18cm. Small, with longish bill fairly narrow across nostrils. A rather dark-plumaged woodpecker, distinguished at all times by large brown area on ear-coverts bordered by long pale supercilium. Dull greenish above with blackish tail; has prominent large spots on dark underparts, which may be stained green from algae. Lacks moustache, but male shows some red on nape. A shy species, difficult to observe and easily overlooked.

Similar species Buff-spotted Woodpecker (70) occurs in same range, but is smaller and has different head pattern. Golden-crowned Woodpecker (82) is also dark-looking, but is bigger, with striking black and white head pattern (male also with yellow crest), and is a noisier and more conspicuous bird.

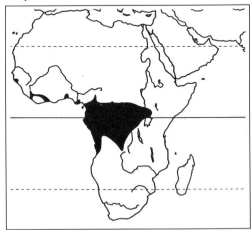

DISTRIBUTION An uncommon woodpecker with two apparently discrete populations: occurs patchily in W Africa, in Guinea-Bissau and from Sierra Leone (and possibly Guinea) to Ivory Coast; further east, recorded in Benin and S Nigeria and occurs more continuously from Cameroon across southernmost Central African Republic to SW Sudan, Uganda (except northeast) and W Kenya

(Kakamega, at up to 1800m), and south to NW Angola, central S Zaïre and NW Zambia, W Burundi and Rwanda and NW Tanzania (Bukoba). May also extend outside this range, but inconspicuous and easily overlooked.

HABITAT A resident of lowland primary forests, dense secondary growth, forest-shrub-grassland mosaic and plantations; also found less commonly in riverine gallery forest. Stays below 1800m.

DESCRIPTION
C. c. caroli **Adult male** Feathers of forehead to nape olive to blackish-olive, tipped red on hindcrown and with broad red tips on nape. Ear-coverts brown. Supercilium from eye and curving around rear of ear-coverts buffish, streaked (often quite extensively) olive, and sometimes rather obscured through green algal staining. Neck sides and hindneck olive-green with paler spots. Lores, chin and throat olive, spotted buffish-white (this colour often stained green). Upperparts including upperwing-coverts green, mantle usually tinged bronze and occasionally with some indistinct yellow spots, rump and uppertail-coverts often with whitish spots. Flight feathers brown, edged green and barred paler, bars on inner webs broad and often joining to form pale patch. Uppertail blackish, edged green, outer feathers spotted/barred greenish. Underparts below throat olive to dull green, heavily spotted with buffish-white, spots tending more towards bars on lower underparts. Underwing yellowish-white. Undertail yellowish-black.

Adult female Lacks all red on crown and nape; otherwise as male.

Juvenile Greener above, lacking bronze tinge, with pinkish tinge to brown ear-coverts; chin pale-streaked, breast spots larger and whiter, and belly/flanks more barred.

Bare parts Bill grey-black, with olive or greenish tinge at base of lower mandible. Legs and feet greyish to olive-yellow. Eyes reddish to brown; brown in juveniles. Bare orbital skin greyish to olive.

GEOGRAPHICAL VARIATION Two fairly well-differentiated races.
    C. c. caroli (main range of species, excluding W Africa) Described above.
    C. c. arizelus (Guinea-Bissau, Sierra Leone to Ivory Coast) Upperparts less bronzy-yellow, more deep olive, than nominate; underparts less heavily spotted (three spots on each feather, compared with five on nominate).

MEASUREMENTS Wing 94-108; tail 52-64; bill 28-30; tarsus 17.4-18.9. Weight: 50-68.

VOICE Common call a slurred *kwaa-kwaa-kwaa.*

HABITS Shy and inconspicuous; may join mixed-species flocks. Searches dead branches in the canopy, and low in forest, on trunks, vines and saplings. Probing, gleaning and pecking are the major foraging modes.

FOOD Mainly (small black) ants; insects and larvae.

BREEDING Not well known; breeds in August-February. Nest in trees; clutch size 2-3 eggs.

REFERENCES Chapin 1939; Colston *et al.* 1986; Short 1988.

72 GROUND WOODPECKER
Geocolaptes olivaceus Plate 17

Other name: African Ground Woodpecker

IDENTIFICATION Length 22-30cm. Small, but the largest of Africa's woodpeckers; bill long and pointed with curved culmen, and very narrow between nostrils. In both plumage and habits unmistakable. Pinkish-red underparts with barred flanks contrast with brownish to greenish upperparts with red rump and barred tail, and with plain greyish head with dark moustache. Entirely terrestrial (even nests and roosts in ground holes), feeding in small groups.

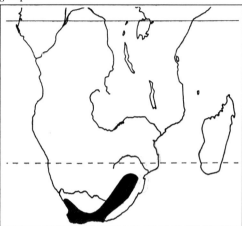

DISTRIBUTION A South African endemic. Confined to area from NW Cape Province (almost to Namibia) east to Orange Free State and north to northern Transvaal, W Swaziland and W Natal; entirely absent from eastern coastal strip (forest) from Port Elizabeth northwards. Common.

HABITAT A resident of open rocky terrain in uplands, such as grassy boulder-strewn slopes and hillsides, open grassy country with rocky ridges, mountain slopes, barren or eroded areas, and has been recorded around reedy marshes. Reaches to about 2100m, in the hills and uplands of Natal from 1200m upwards; rarely recorded as low as about 600m, but also descends to sea level in southwest of range, choosing similar type of rocky habitat (e.g. roadsides).

DESCRIPTION
G. o. olivaceus **Adult male** Forehead and crown brownish-grey, becoming browner on nape (where may show slight trace of red). Sides of head and neck grey. Moustachial stripe dark greyish, feathers finely tipped red (red visible only at close range). Chin and throat white. Mantle, scapulars and back greyish-brown to dull green-brown (in fresh plumage feathers pale-tipped, forming small pale spots and hint of barring); rump red; uppertail-coverts brown, barred white. Upperwing-coverts greyish-brown, indistinctly spotted/barred pale; flight feathers dark brown, tertials tinged greenish/greyish, all barred whitish. Uppertail brown, with prominent but narrow white bars. Breast feathers white, broadly tipped pinkish-red with some pale streaking, becoming deeper crimson with pale bases on belly and undertail-coverts; flanks barred grey-brown and whitish, barring often extending to undertail-coverts. Underwing brown and yellowish-white. Undertail light brown, barred yellowish-white.

Adult female Very like male, but lacks red tips to moustachial feathers.

Juvenile Pattern as adults, but duller overall, though usually with some red on nape. Underparts paler, more light pinkish.

Bare parts Bill black, greyer at base. Legs and feet grey. Eyes pink, becoming white or whitish towards pupil; all white in juveniles.

GEOGRAPHICAL VARIATION Two races.
G. o. olivaceus (C and W Cape Province) Described above.
G. o. prometheus (rest of species' range) Much paler, especially below (note that upland populations tend to be darker overall).

MEASUREMENTS Wing 118-140; tail 64-101; bill 29-41; tarsus 21-27. Weight: 105-134.

VOICE When startled or alarmed, blurts out loud, harsh screams, *peer, peer, peer* to *pee-aa-r-g-h*. A loud series of up to five *chick-scream* or *ree-chick, ree-chick* notes, recalling the noise produced when sharpening a saw with a file, seems to serve as contact and territorial call. Also a falcon-like *krrrreee* when joining the group. Displaying birds utter *chew-kee* calls. Long-distance calls are delivered from a prominent perch, such as a rock pile.

HABITS Usually seen in pairs or small parties of about six birds, such groups occupying areas of between 21 and 70ha. Relatively easy to detect when perching upright on large boulders or flying rather heavily from one rocky outcrop to the next. On boulders, hides and peeks as other woodpeckers do on tree trunks. Occasionally may sit in sturdy bushes or forage on dead trees. Preferred resting sites during the day are boulders, even along roadsides, where they remain indifferent to traffic. Ground Woodpeckers direct their attention to any fault, crevice or hole in the substrate, and explore the interfaces between stones and the soil, applying single inquisitive pecks; debris is swept away with the bill. Penetrates the soil with heavy pecks when it hits upon an ant colony. The final feeding posture is a characteristic stance, with head down and beak deeply planted into the ground, the continuous activity of the tongue with which the prey is collected indicated only by jerky movements of the tail. Surface gleaning is not an important feeding technique of this woodpecker, its efforts being concentrated on subsurface ant nests. Wood-dwelling ants (*Crematogaster*) are also pursued: these are not obtained by pecking or hammering, but instead by probing into dead wood. Moves on the ground primarily by hopping, but on more level terrain also by walking. During arboreal foraging, does not cling to the underside of branches. Even during the cooler season, this woodpecker requires only about a third of the total daylight hours to procure sufficient food: the main activity is in the morning hours, with a further peak in late afternoon. During these periods, the woodpeckers fill the glandular proventriculus with large quantities of ants, which are subsequently digested slowly. Groups seem to know the exact locations of ant nests within their home range, and spend at most three days in a particular place. In display, birds simultaneously sway body and head and call; during interactions, wing-flicks may also be seen. In aggression, points with the bill at the opponent. Before copulation, male may display in an upright stance with spread wings.

FOOD The Ground Woodpecker is highly specialised on ants, ant broods and alates. Eight ant genera make up 95% of the food: among them are *Camponotus, Anoplolepis, Acantholepis, Tetramorium, Crematogaster* and *Pheidole*. A total of about 60 ant species has been recorded in the diet; termites are regularly included, but form only a small proportion (1.25%) of total food intake. Beetles, other insects and mites are probably taken accidentally.

BREEDING Nests from August to September in Cape Province and Transvaal, and from August to December (mainly October-November) in Natal. During breeding season, pairs or trios construct burrows for nesting, copulations occurring in this phase of the cycle. Nest is dug mainly by male into a bank, often in road cuttings, in the vertical wall of a donga, and among rocks: the tunnel is usually about 1m (50-120cm) long, 7.5cm in diameter, and is enlarged at the end to form a nest chamber (15cm diameter). The same nest site may be used over several breeding seasons. Tunnels dug into the ground also serve as roosts. Clutch is of 2-5 eggs, usually 3. Both parents, and possibly one helper, incubate. Young are fed by parents and helper, and stay with the family until the next breeding season.

REFERENCES Clancey 1964; Cyrus & Robson 1980; Earlé 1986; Maclean 1985; Oatley *et al*. 1989; Roberts *et al*. 1981; Short 1971a, 1971e, 1971f, 1988; Sinclair *et al*. 1993.

73 LITTLE GREY WOODPECKER
Dendropicos elachus   Plate 21

IDENTIFICATION Length 12-14cm. Very small, with relatively long and proportionally broad bill. A rare and little-known species of NC African steppes. Combination of small size, very pale coloration with poorly marked head (weak moustache), and red rump (noticeable in flight) easily distinguishes both sexes from other woodpeckers in its range. Upperparts barred grey-brown and white; underparts white, with brown spots on breast. Male has red hindcrown and nape.

Similar species Overlaps in range with nominate race of Brown-backed Woodpecker (87), but latter appears much darker, with plain dull brown upperparts with brown-streaked white rump, and has contrastingly brown and white face pattern.

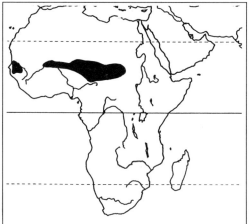

DISTRIBUTION Occurs in sahel and subdesert bordering southern edge of the Sahara, from about 17˚N in SW Mauretania to Senegambia, and from C Mali through SC Niger (where ascends to 1600m), NE Nigeria (to Aliya) and northernmost Cameroon (south to around 10-11˚N), and

238

C Chad to western C Sudan; possibly present between Senegambia and C Mali, but this requires confirmation. Sparsely distributed and in many parts of range rare.

HABITAT Lives in lightly wooded steppe, dry stream beds and wadis.

DESCRIPTION

Adult male Forehead to mid crown pale brown; hindcrown and nape dull red. White supercilium from behind eye to rear of ear-coverts. Lores, ear-coverts and neck sides pale brown, with whitish stripe from lower lores running below ear-coverts. Narrow dingy brown moustachial stripe. (Note that head markings fade rapidly, leaving plain-faced appearance.) Chin and throat white, indistinctly streaked brown in fresh plumage. Mantle, scapulars and back greyish-brown, barred white; rump and uppertail-coverts red. Upperwing-coverts brown, barred off-white and tipped white; flight feathers brown, barred whitish. Uppertail brown, barred off-white. Underparts whitish, spotted (or sometimes vaguely barred) brown on breast, spots becoming smaller and very faint on flanks and belly. Underwing whitish, spotted brown. Undertail as uppertail. (In fresh plumage, all brown pigments are darker, producing more contrasting pattern, but fading occurs very quickly and most individuals look very washed out and pale.)

Adult female As male, but with entire crown and nape brown.

Juvenile Much as adults, but duller.

Bare parts Bill grey, becoming paler towards base (where almost whitish on lower mandible). Legs and feet greenish-grey. Eyes brown.

GEOGRAPHICAL VARIATION None. Monotypic.

MEASUREMENTS Wing 71-80; tail 34-41; tarsus 13.1-14.1. Weight: 17-21.

VOICE Common call a grating, often repeated, rattle, *skree-eek-eee-eee-eeee-ee-eee-eeek*. Also a softer *tee-tee-tee-*.... In interactions, low whirring *wi-i-i-*... to *ch-ch-ch-ch*; also louder rattling series of *wi* or *wik* notes.

HABITS Almost unknown; forages in trees (*Balanites*, acacias) by pecking and hammering.

BREEDING Breeds January-February in Senegambia and Mali, March-May in Niger, about October in Chad. Nest in dead branch of acacia.

REFERENCE Short 1988.

---

74 SPECKLE-BREASTED WOODPECKER
Dendropicos poecilolaemus   Plate 21

Other name: Uganda Spotted Woodpecker

IDENTIFICATION Length c. 15cm. Very small, with fairly long bill broad across nostrils. Yellow-green above with weak barring, and with red rump (in fresh plumage); yellowish below, with scattered spots on breast and/or variably barred (barring usually very faint). Small and indistinct dark moustache, but facial markings poorly defined. Male has red hindcrown and nape; female has top of head and nape all dark. Not a well-known species.

Similar species Separated from most other woodpeckers in its range by small size, ill-defined face pattern, and spotted/barred rather than streaked breast. Similar-sized Gaboon Woodpecker (78) has entire underparts heavily

spotted/streaked, and sympatric races of Cardinal Woodpecker (76) are streaked below, while Green-backed (68) is entirely spotted below and spotted above or (in west) entirely barred below.

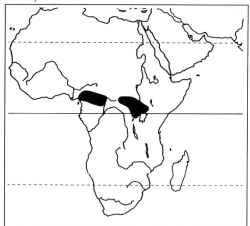

DISTRIBUTION Ranges from southernmost Nigeria (Serti) through C Cameroon, north of main forest region, to SW Central African Republic, N Congo and NW Zaïre and adjacent parts of Central African Republic and S Sudan, through W and C Uganda to Nandi and Kabarnet in westernmost Kenya; presence in intervening parts of Central African Republic and northern Zaïre probable, but requires confirmation. Locally common.

HABITAT Prefers forest edge and clearings, particularly where bordering cultivations with trees. Also inhabits upland savanna with forest, and riverine forest, at up to 2100m in west of range; in the east found at 700-2100m.

DESCRIPTION

Adult male Forehead to mid crown brown; hindcrown and nape red. Ear-coverts and neck sides white, streaked brown (perhaps more heavily immediately behind eye), with hardly defined brown-streaked white supercilium from eye backwards. Lores brownish and white, extending into whitish moustachial stripe streaked with brown (better defined and sometimes more solid along lower edge). Chin and throat white, sometimes lightly spotted grey. Upperparts yellow-green, with faint hint of dark barring on rump and uppertail-coverts (occasionally also on mantle); rump and uppertail-coverts initially have red tips, but these soon wear off. Upperwing-coverts brown, spotted and tipped dull yellow; flight feathers brown, edged yellowish-green and barred yellowish-white. Uppertail brown, sometimes with faint dull greenish bars. Underparts below throat pale greeny-yellow, usually suffused grey, and with scattered dark spots on breast and hint of barring on flanks (but markings vary: some may have narrowly barred breast, with broader pale grey flank bars and faint belly streaking). Underwing barred brown and yellowish-white. Undertail yellowish-brown.

Adult female Lacks red on head, brown of forehead darkening to black on nape. Upperparts show blackish barring (more distinct than on males).

Juvenile Greyer above than adults, lacking yellow tone, and with mantle indistinctly barred black; may have small red tips to uppertail-coverts. Underparts greyish-white, lacking green or yellow tones, and with less obvious markings. Both sexes have red on crown (more restricted on females), and black nape and rear crown sides.

Bare parts Bill dark grey or brownish-grey (sometimes paler, blue-grey), paler on culmen and at base. Legs and feet greenish to olive or olive-grey. Eyes red, sometimes brown; brown in juveniles.

GEOGRAPHICAL VARIATION None. Monotypic.

MEASUREMENTS Wing 79-91; tail 43-49; tarsus 14.9-16.1. Weight: 25-30.

VOICE A dry *che che che che....* is the only known vocalisation.

HABITS Visits (dead) trees, often isolated ones, and even visits elephant grass. Obtains its food by pecking and hammering.

FOOD The diet comprises beetle larvae, caterpillars and ants.

BREEDING Breeding season presumably May-September in Zaïre, March-September and November-January in Uganda. Nest excavated in trees.

REFERENCES Britton 1980; Chapin 1939; Short 1988.

---

75 ABYSSINIAN WOODPECKER
Dendropicos abyssinicus   Plate 21

Other names: Golden-backed Woodpecker, Gold-mantled Woodpecker
Sometimes regarded as forming a superspecies with *fuscescens.*

IDENTIFICATION Length c. 16cm. Very small, with longish, fairly broad bill. Unmistakable within its range. Golden-yellow above, with bright red rump and barred wings and tail; underparts pale, heavily streaked dark. Striped head pattern, male also with red hindcrown and nape. A little-known species.

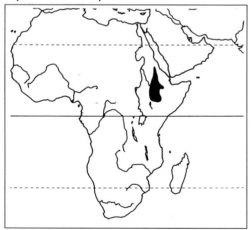

DISTRIBUTION An uncommon Ethiopian endemic, found in the highlands from upper Anseber river in Eritrea east to Harar region and south to Alata. Range likely to be somewhat diminished through recent habitat destruction, since more and more native woodland is being turned into eucalypt plantations.

HABITAT Inhabits mostly juniper woods and *Hagenia* forest, but also areas of Euphorbia, mostly between 1600 and 3000m, occasionally higher; has also been found in wooded savanna, including at slightly lower elevations.

Largely separated by altitude from Cardinal Woodpecker (76).

DESCRIPTION
Adult male Forehead to mid crown pale brown; hindcrown and nape red. Ear-coverts (extending to neck side) and broad moustachial stripe brown. Rest of face, including long supercilium from eye to hindneck, white. Chin and throat white, streaked brown. Lower hindneck and upper mantle greenish-brown; feathers of lower mantle, scapulars and back with broad yellowish-golden tips (occasionally some reddish-green tips) concealing brown bases (can appear quite mottled when worn); rump and uppertail-coverts red. Inner upperwing-coverts as scapulars, outers brown and broadly tipped white; flight feathers dark brown, edged yellowish and barred white, bars broadest but duller on tertials. Uppertail brown, narrowly barred white. Underparts below throat white, tinged yellow, and streaked blackish-brown, streaks broadest on breast and flanks. Underwing-coverts off-white, barred/streaked brown. Undertail yellowish-brown, obscurely barred paler.

Adult female Lacks red on head, having hindcrown brown and merging into darker nape.

Juvenile Upperparts less golden, more greenish, than on adults, and rump paler red; underparts whiter, heavily streaked, and with indication of barring on belly. Both sexes have red crown (slightly reduced on female) and black nape.

Bare parts Bill dark grey. Legs and feet lead-grey. Eyes brown to reddish.

GEOGRAPHICAL VARIATION None.

MEASUREMENTS Wing 87-96; tail 43-51; tarsus 14.1-15.5. Weight: 23-26.

VOICE Not recorded.

HABITS Little known. A quiet bird, which forages on trees by probing into mosses.

FOOD Not known.

BREEDING Nesting season probably spans December-May.

REFERENCES Benson 1946; Short 1988; Urban & Brown 1971.

---

76 CARDINAL WOODPECKER
Dendropicos fuscescens   Plate 21

Sometimes regarded as forming a superspecies with *abyssinicus.*

IDENTIFICATION Length 14-16cm. Very small, with longish, broad bill. Africa's most widespread woodpecker, occurring in most of the continent south of the Sahara, and generally the commonest. A variable species with a number of races, using a variety of habitats. In very general terms, upperparts vary from green and unbarred in the northwest of the range to barred blackish and white in the southernmost parts; those in the northeast are somewhat browner and pale-coloured, while most of those in the intervening (central) part of the range are more yellowish-green above with variable barring. Underparts vary from white to yellow, with heavy to rather light streaking, and usually with at least a trace of barring on flanks. All races have (often prominently) barred wings and tail. Rump and uppertail-coverts are normally somewhat yellower than the rest of the upperparts, and uppertail-coverts are usually indistinctly tipped red (red generally absent on green-backed races). Variably distinct white supercilium, and sides of head usually whitish with rather obscure streaks. Males have brown forehead and crown, with red hindcrown and nape, while females have black crown and nape; juveniles have red central crown and blackish nape. All individuals show a moustache, varying in prominence. This species tends to move rather quickly through its habitat when foraging, uttering frequent contact calls, and often joins mixed-species feeding flocks (as do some other similar species).

Similar species If good views are obtained, there should be no major identification problems. Cardinal overlaps with a number of similar small woodpeckers, however, and perhaps the most likely confusion species are the following. In the northwest and north-central part of Cardinal's range, Melancholy (77) and Gaboon (78) Woodpeckers both have a stronger facial pattern (especially the former), are more heavily marked (spots or thick streaks) below, and lack wing and tail barring, Speckle-breasted (74) has unbarred tail and very fine spots below (largely confined to breast), and Little Green (67) is barred below, has a plain black tail and lacks moustache. Almost meets Little Grey Woodpecker (73) in northwest, but that species is very pale and has red rump and brownish (but often faded) ear patch. Where range overlaps with that of Elliot's Woodpecker (83), latter is bigger and has plain buffish face lacking moustache, black forehead and largely unmarked brown wings and tail. In Ethiopia, Abyssinian Woodpecker (75) has golden mantle, long dark ear-covert patch and red rump, and is usually found at higher elevations. Overlaps widely with Green-backed (68), but latter is heavily spotted or barred (not streaked) below, has much less prominent wing and tail barring, lacks moustache, and (except in north of its range, though there it has distinctive barred underparts) is spotted above and has black tail; in the south, Green-backed looks much less black-and-white than Cardinal Woodpecker.

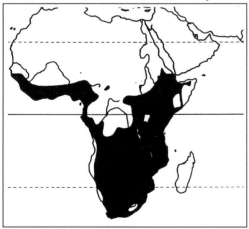

DISTRIBUTION Widespread in most of Africa south of the Sahara. Extends from Senegambia through W Africa to S Sudan, N Ethiopia, Djibouti and NW Somalia, and southwards, including Zanzibar, to the Cape; absent from S Nigeria (and probably also S Togo and S Benin), most of Central African Republic (except west and extreme southeast and Bamingui-Bangoran National Park in north), N and SE Cameroon and E Gabon through NW and C Zaïre, NE and C Somalia, most of Angolan coast and NW and SW Namibia, and the Lesotho highlands. See also Geographical variation. A generally common resident (e.g. the commonest woodpecker in E and S Africa).

HABITAT A wide-ranging bird of open and dense woodland, wooded grassland and bushland, only mountain forests being avoided. Inhabits riparian fringing forests, edges of lowland forest, and montane forest in highlands (where they are drier). Such formations are represented for instance by *Euphorbia-Acacia* woodland in Ethiopia and by *Brachystegia*, especially if not disturbed by human activities, in Zambia. Does not shun areas influenced by man, such as plantations, orchards, parks and gardens. The race *lepidus* is more of a forest bird than the other races, and *hemprichii* and its allies inhabit arid scrub. At about 1800m in Ethiopia; up to 2600m in E Africa, up to 2100m in Malawi, to 1800m in Zimbabwe, and in Zaïre ascends to 3500m.

DESCRIPTION
D. f. fuscescens **Adult male** Forehead to mid crown medium-brown; mid crown to hindneck red. Supercilium behind eye white, extending broadly (but less obvious) around rear of ear-coverts. Lores buffish or white. Ear-coverts and area below eye off-white or greyish-white, very finely and often inconspicuously streaked dark. Long, broad moustachial stripe brownish-black, extending to and expanding on lower neck sides. Chin and throat white, sometimes finely spotted/streaked brown. Upperparts closely barred dark brown/blackish and white to pale olive-white, becoming yellower overall on rump and uppertail-coverts, latter tipped light reddish. Upperwing-coverts blackish-brown, strongly spotted (barred) white or yellowish-white; flight feathers black-brown, barred whitish. Uppertail brown, barred yellow-white, with pale shafts. Underparts below throat white (often tinged yellow-buff when fresh), streaked brownish-black, streaks heaviest/broadest on breast, becoming more barred on lower flanks, belly and undertail-coverts. Underwing greyish-black with white coverts. Undertail dully barred. (In worn plumage becomes duller overall, with less of an olive or yellow tinge to pale areas, and can appear very black-and-white.)

Adult female Differs from male in having darker brown forehead merging into black on rear crown and nape.

Juvenile Duller and greyer than adults, and less contrastingly patterned. Both sexes have red patch in centre of crown (somewhat smaller on female), and black nape and hindneck.

Bare parts Bill blackish, sometimes with blue or brown tones, or horn-brown, normally with paler lower mandible. Legs and feet greenish-grey to green-brown. Eyes red to reddish-brown; brown or grey-brown in juveniles.

GEOGRAPHICAL VARIATION Varies widely geographically, especially in upperpart coloration and degree of barring, as well as in size to some extent. A large number of races have been described, but many of these are too poorly differentiated to warrant recognition or represent intergrades between better-defined races. Here, we follow Short (1982, and in Fry *et al.* 1988) in recognising nine races, these being broadly divided into three groups (though these groups also intergrade and even interbreed in places).

(a) Southern *fuscescens* group (largest, with most prominent barring above):

D. f. fuscescens (northern C Namibia through most of S Africa to S Transvaal and W Natal) The most obviously 'black-and-white' race. Described above.

D. f. intermedius (Transvaal and Natal north to Zambezi river in Mozambique) Barring above more olive-black and yellowish-white than in nominate, and underpart streaking narrower.

D. f. centralis (NW Angola east to W Tanzania, south to Zambia and N Namibia) Upperparts more brown, less black, than in nominate, with barring more yellow; underparts more yellow than in above two races, with

241

less barring, and streaks somewhat finer than in nominate.

D. f. hartlaubi (E Africa, from Kenya-Tanzania border south along coast to Zambezi in Mozambique, and west inland to C Tanzania, Malawi and just into E Zambia) Smaller, especially coastal populations, than above races. Upperpart barring olive-brown and pale yellowish-olive, and underparts yellow with olive-brown streaks.

(b) Western and central *lafresnayi* group (smaller, and green above without bars or only weakly barred; intergrades with *fuscescens* group and interbreeds with *hemprichii* group):

D. f. lafresnayi (Senegambia east to Nigeria) Green above with, at best, obscure bars; yellowish below, with fine dark streaks.

D. f. sharpii (Cameroon and Central African Republic to S Sudan, south to W Zaïre and northernmost Angola) As *lafresnayi*, but streaks below broader.

D. f. lepidus (E Zaïre, and highlands of Uganda, Ethiopia, W and C Kenya, NW Tanzania and Rwanda) Larger than last two races, and generally unbarred above (but somewhat more barred, especially on females, in Kenyan highland population); pale below, with streaks very narrow.

(c) Northeastern *hemprichii* group (smallest, brownest/palest, and conspicuously barred above, approaching nominate *fuscescens*):

D. f. massaicus (S Ethiopia at middle elevations, and inland and western Kenya and C Tanzania at lower altitudes than *lepidus*) Entirely barred above, and tinged yellow both above and below, but still looks more black-and-white than *lepidus* (with which interbreeds where the two meet). Those at higher elevations are larger and darker.

D. f. hemprichii (Ethiopia below *massaicus*, Somalia, and N and E Kenya) Slightly smaller than *massaicus*, and paler, with narrower dark barring above; lacks yellow tinges. Intergrades with *massaicus*, and also with *hartlaubi*, in region of SE Kenya/NE Tanzania.

MEASUREMENTS Wing 74-86 (*sharpii*), 84-94 (*lepidus*), 84-97 (*intermedius*), 87-100 (*fuscescens*), 82-100 (*centralis*); tail 40-54 (*fuscescens*); bill 11.2-15.2 (*fuscescens*); tarsus 15-17.8 (*fuscescens*). Weight: 20-31 (*lepidus*), 29-37 (*fuscescens*).

VOICE A shrill chittering *kweek-eek-eek-ik-ik* is given by both sexes. Utters a *creek, creek, creek* and *kweek-a, kweek-a* in aggression. Nestlings call with *kee-kee-kee…*. Screams in emergency. Drumming is rapid and not very loud.

HABITS Encountered in pairs or family parties, which keep contact by calling, and often joins bird parties. Seeks its food mainly at lower levels in large and small trees, vines, bushes, reeds and euphorbias; also forages on dry stalks of cultivated maize and seed-pods, such as those of *Swartzia madagascariensis*. Although often at base of trees or even on the ground, it also searches the outer canopy, where it favours small branches and twigs. Pecks in short bursts, less frequently and mor weakly than its congeners, and probes commonly. Moves quickly, and when searching twigs it frequently works over them upside-down, examining them from all sides. During encounters, calls and may perform wing-flicks, tail-spreading, conspicuous crown-raising and bobbing (with some lateral swinging component); also, the bill is pointed at the opponent, which is frequently of the same sex. Sometimes joined by Golden-tailed Woodpeckers (64), which peck less, and do not follow Cardinal Woodpeckers to the very small twigs. Subordinate to Bearded Woodpeckers (80) when the two meet. Interacts also with hole competitors, such as barbets and sparrows.

The nest may be parasitised by honeyguides *Indicator*.

FOOD Insects and their larvae, particularly beetles; also caterpillars. In addition, termites, grasshoppers and fruits have been recorded.

BREEDING In southern Africa, breeds all year round except in February and March, with most pairs nesting from August to October; breeds throughout year in E Africa, with great local variation and, overall, with no clear association with rainy/dry seasons; in W Africa, about February-July. Holes are bored into dead trunks or branches of trees, both sexes taking part in the task, which lasts about two weeks. Lays 2 or 3 eggs (rarely, 1 or 5). Incubation lasts 10-13 days, begins with first egg, and is shared by both sexes. The male may feed the female at the nest. Nestling period 27 days; both sexes feed the young, and divide the fledged brood between them (sex for sex), caring for them another 8-10 weeks.

REFERENCES Atwell 1952; Bannerman 1933; Beals 1970; Belcher 1930; Britton 1980; Chapin 1939; Cyrus & Robson 1980; Irwin 1981; Maclean 1985; Newman 1989; Roberts *et al.* 1981; Short 1971f, 1988.

77 MELANCHOLY WOODPECKER
Dendropicos lugubris   Plate 22

Forms a superspecies with *gabonensis*.

IDENTIFICATION Length c. 17-18cm. Small, with shortish bill fairly broad across nostrils. A rather insignificant woodpecker of W African lowlands, often considered a race of Gaboon Woodpecker (78) as the two intergrade (see Geographical Variation). Bronzy-green above, with black tail, and broadly and heavily streaked brown below (appears darkish). Head pattern distinctive, with long pale supercilium, broad area of brown on ear-coverts extending well to rear and bordered below by broad white stripe, and quite prominent brown moustache. Male has red on nape.

Similar species Gaboon Woodpecker lacks bronze tinge above, has less black tail, is pale yellowish below with narrower streaks or spots, and has very different head pattern. Brown-eared Woodpecker (71) is somewhat bigger, has dark underparts with pale spots, and pale markings on head are streaked olive (and often stained green).

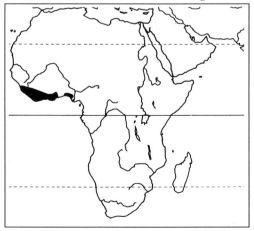

DISTRIBUTION Breeds from Sierra Leone to SE Ghana and in SW Nigeria. Rather uncommon throughout.

HABITAT Inhabits open forest, forest edge, clearings, secondary growth and *Gmelina* woodlands, from lowlands to about 1200m.

DESCRIPTION
Adult male Forehead and crown olive-brown; nape red. Supercilium from rear of eye to sides of nape and lower hindneck white. Ear-coverts brown, curving diffusely into white of neck sides at rear, bordered below by broad white stripe extending to lower lores. Moustachial stripe brown and broad. Chin and throat white, often with some dark spots/streaks. Lower hindneck and entire upperparts, including wing-coverts, bronzy-green, occasionally with paler feather tips forming very indistinct bars. Flight feathers brown, edged greenish-bronze, and barred or spotted white on inner webs (bars thus not visible in field). Uppertail black. Underparts below throat pale greenish-yellow and heavily and broadly streaked brown (feathers with broad dark centres), streaks continuing to lower underparts. Underwing pale yellowish-white, spotted brown. Undertail grey-black.

Adult female As male, but with nape blackish (not red).

Juvenile Duller than adults, lacking bronze tone above. Both sexes have black nape and small red patch on hindcrown.

Bare parts Bill greyish to blackish, with paler base and lower mandible. Legs and feet greenish, with brown, olive or yellow tinge. Eyes red to reddish-brown; brown in juveniles.

GEOGRAPHICAL VARIATION No races, but in east of range, in SW Nigeria, intergrades with race *reichenowi* of Gaboon Woodpecker (which see), although interbreeding not proven. Latter race is intermediate between Melancholy and nominate Gaboon, which is taken by many authors as good grounds for treating the two species as conspecific.

MEASUREMENTS Wing 76-83.

VOICE Common call as that of Gaboon Woodpecker, which see. A fast rattle *bdddddddddddddd-d-it* or *br-r-r-r-r-ip*. Also *rrek-rrek-rrek-rrak-rrak* and low *pit* to *pa-bit* during encounters.

HABITS Occurs mainly in pairs. Does not often hammer or peck forcefully.

FOOD Insects, ants and beetle larvae.

BREEDING Possibly breeds December-March.

REFERENCES Bannerman 1933; Colston *et al.* 1986; Rand 1951; Rand *et al.* 1959; Short 1988; Walker 1939.

---

78 GABOON WOODPECKER
Dendropicos gabonensis   Plate 22

Forms a superspecies with *lugubris*.

IDENTIFICATION Length c. 16-17cm. Small, with rather short bill fairly broad across nostrils. Green and unbarred above, with plain darker tail, and heavily spotted/streaked below on yellowish ground colour. Top of head brown to blackish, male with red on hindcrown and nape. Moustache narrow and indistinct or lacking.

Similar species Combination of unmarked green upperparts and heavily streaked underparts distinguishes this from other small woodpeckers in its range. Most likely confusion is with Cardinal (76) and Speckle-breasted (74): former, however, has prominently barred wings and tail and much lighter streaking below, while latter has very fine

pale spots or speckles below (largely confined to breast) and shows barred wings. Larger and longer-tailed Elliot's Woodpecker (83) has black forehead (also crown and nape on female) and plain buffish face, and occupies different habitat (dense forest). Note that western race *reichenowi* of Gaboon Woodpecker intergrades with Melancholy Woodpecker (77); see latter species, and also Geographical Variation below.

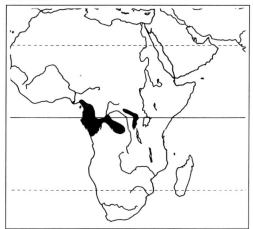

DISTRIBUTION Found from S Nigeria to S Cameroon (north to Buedun), Congo and N Zaïre (Semliki valley) to Bwamba in SW Uganda, south to Cabinda, lower Congo river and, in C and E Zaïre, to the Western Kasai and the west slope of the Ruwenzoris; presence in parts of Congo and Zaïre is uncertain. Uncommon to locally common.

HABITAT Frequents forest edge, tall secondary growth and edges of cultivation, generally below 1400m; seems to avoid open savanna-type habitats and riverine forests, as well as denser woodlands.

DESCRIPTION
D. g. gabonensis **Adult male** Forehead and forecrown olive-brown (rarely with pale streaking); hindcrown and nape red. Neck sides buffy green-brown, streaked darker. Ear-coverts whitish, heavily streaked brown (especially at rear), bordered above by indistinct dark-streaked white supercilium and below by dark-streaked whitish stripe. Lores buffish. Indistinct brown moustachial stripe invaded by white streaks. Chin and throat white, spotted/streaked brown. Lower hindneck and entire upperparts, including wing-coverts, green (mantle and rump may rarely show faint barring). Flight feathers brown, edged green, with barring on inner webs (not visible in field). Uppertail olive, edged greenish-brown and tipped dark, occasionally with hint of pale green barring. Underparts below throat pale yellowish, with fairly narrow and short spot-like streaks on breast, becoming spots on lower underparts and bars on lower flanks. Underwing yellowish-white, spotted brown. Undertail yellow-green.

Adult female Lacks red on head, having crown and nape blackish-brown.

Juvenile Duller than adults, and greener above. Both sexes have red patch on central crown, with black nape.

Bare parts Bill dark grey to blackish, with paler base and lower mandible. Legs and feet brown-green to yellow-green. Eyes red to reddish-brown; brown in juveniles.

GEOGRAPHICAL VARIATION Two well-differentiated races.

   D. g. gabonensis (S Cameroon excluding southwest

corner, to S Congo, Zaïre, westernmost Uganda and Cabinda) Described above.

D. g. reichenowi (S Nigeria to southwest corner of Cameroon) Differs from nominate in having more strongly indicated brown moustachial stripe, darker tail, broader underpart streaks, and male has slightly less red on hindcrown. Consequently, is intermediate in plumage between nominate *gabonensis* and Melancholy Woodpecker, and intergrades with the latter in SW Nigeria.

MEASUREMENTS Wing 76-86 (*gabonensis*), 72-79 (*reichenowi*); tail 37-41; bill 11.7-13.3; tarsus 13.7-15.1. Weight: 24-30.

VOICE Common call a single buzzing *zh-dzeeeep*, or rapidly repeated *dzhaah, dzhaah, dzheep* (and variations). Series of these calls contain fewer notes and give a noisier impression than voice of Cardinal Woodpecker.

HABITS Forages by probing and gleaning. Also pecks and prises off pieces of bark or wood.

FOOD Insects and their larvae, particularly wood-boring ones, and ants.

BREEDING Probably breeds September-October in west of range, June in Uganda.

REFERENCES Britton 1980; Rand *et al.* 1959; Short 1988.

79 STIERLING'S WOODPECKER
Dendropicos stierlingi   Plate 23

IDENTIFICATION Length c. 17-18cm. Small, with long and fairly broad bill. A generally rare and little-known species with a very small range in SE Africa. Combination of plain brown upperparts (blackish upper mantle) and tail, bold head pattern with broad dark ear-covert patch and moustache, barred and streaked underparts forming scaly pattern, and small size easily separates this from all other woodpeckers in its range. Male has red hindcrown and nape. Restricted to *Brachystegia* woodland, where flies in characteristic twisting fashion among the trees.

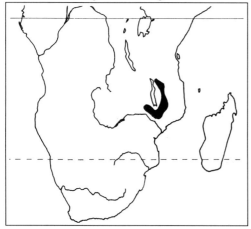

DISTRIBUTION Found only in S Tanzania (Songea, Lindi), N Mozambique and adjacent SW Malawi (and possibly E Zambia?). A scarce to rare woodpecker, only infrequently observed. Exact status requires further investigation.

HABITAT Inhabits *Brachystegia* (miombo) woodland at up

to 1500m.

DESCRIPTION
Adult male Forehead and forecrown brown with narrow pale feather edges (scaly); hindcrown and nape red. Earcoverts dark brown, enclosed by white supercilium from behind eye and extending down neck sides to join white stripe running forward to lores. Prominent dark brown moustachial stripe expands on neck side and extends down to breast side. Chin and upper throat white, lower throat chequered white and dark brown. Hindneck and uppermost mantle black; rest of upperparts, including most of wing-coverts, olive-brown, tipped slightly paler when fresh, with indistinct pale barring on uppertail-coverts (latter occasionally tipped reddish when fresh). Flight feathers and some outer wing-coverts brown, edged olive, and barred white on inner webs. Uppertail plain brown, tipped yellow. Entire underparts below throat white, barred dark brown and with brown shaft streaks (appears scaly). Underwing white, spotted brown. Undertail yellowish-brown.

Adult female Lacks red on head, having indistinctly pale-streaked brown crown, becoming blacker on nape.

Juvenile Duller than adults, less uniform above, and with underpart markings more irregular. Both sexes have red in centre of crown (or more extensive).

Bare parts Bill slate-grey, paler at base of lower mandible. Legs and feet olive-green to greyish-green. Eyes red to reddish-brown; brown in juveniles.

GEOGRAPHICAL VARIATION None.

MEASUREMENTS Wing 95-106; tail 44-52. Weight: 25-31.

VOICE Common (territorial, long-distance) call a somewhat wavering *pi-di-di, da-di-di, da-da-da-da, da-da*. Also soft single or repeated *pik* notes, sometimes strung together in short bursts. Aggressive calls sound like *bdddt*. Irregular *weep* series have also been recorded. Drums about five rolls per minute; rolls rapid and loud.

HABITS Associates loosely with mixed-species flocks. Forages in medium to upper levels of the forest, where it searches large to medium-sized branches, less frequently twigs. Main foraging mode is powerful pecking, whereby bark may be deeply excavated; also probes in bark. May spend considerable time at one foraging site.

FOOD Insect larvae, occasionally centipedes.

BREEDING Breeds March-October. Nests in trees.

REFERENCES Britton 1980; Short 1988; Short & Horne 1981.

80 BEARDED WOODPECKER
Dendropicos namaquus   Plate 23

IDENTIFICATION Length 24-27cm. Small for a woodpecker, but, together with the Ground Woodpecker (72), the largest in Africa. Bill very long and broad. Rather dark-plumaged, especially in south of range, with entire upperparts and underparts narrowly barred. Highly distinctive head pattern, with black crown and very broad black eye-stripe and moustache contrasting with white supercilium and cheeks; male has red hindcrown. Maintains large territory, and drums frequently and loudly.

Similar species Relatively large size and dark, barred plumage, with distinctive head pattern, make confusion with other species improbable. Golden-crowned Wood-pecker (82) is only a little smaller and is superficially similar in plumage, but lacks obvious barring above, is spotted (not barred) on breast, and male has yellow crown; is also much more of a forest bird, and the two are unlikely to meet. (Note, incidentally, that the rattle call of Bearded Wood-pecker could be confused with the song of Grey-headed Kingfisher *Halcyon leucocephalus*, which overlaps in range.)

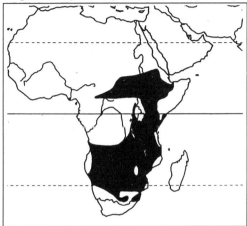

DISTRIBUTION A resident of central and southern Africa. Occurs from western Central African Republic east to Eritrea and SW Somalia, south through NE Uganda and Kenya (apart from east, but with extension along coast to S Somalia), then from SW Uganda, E Rwanda and Burundi and Tanzania south (with a few gaps) to Lesotho border (and possibly to Grahamstown area in eastern Cape Province); in west, from about 9°N in Angola and southern Kivu in SE Zaïre, extends south to 23-24°S in Namibia (absent from much of coastal area) and southeast to Orange Free State in S Africa. Rather common in many parts of range, but often local.

HABITAT Any woodland with large trees, although principally in the drier savannas such as mopane and on the edges of riparian fringing forest and taller *Acacia* on alluvium. Regularly in *Brachystegia* (miombo) woodland, *Euphorbia-Acacia* woodland, and bushland, least common in richer types of woodland, and avoids moist mountain slopes. Wide-ranging from sea level to 3000m (to 1800m in Ethiopia), but curiously local and seldom numerous.

DESCRIPTION
D. n. namaquus **Adult male** Forehead and forecrown black with small white spots; hindcrown red, sometimes with admixed yellowish at fore edge; nape and hindneck black. Lores whitish, with short black stripe in front of eye. Broad white supercilium from eye, curving around rear of ear-coverts and meeting broad white stripe extending from bill base. Ear-coverts black. Submoustachial stripe black, broadening on throat side. Chin and throat white, sometimes with a few dark streaks or bars. Uppermost mantle black; rest of upperparts yellow-brown, paler on rump, and narrowly barred white; uppertail-coverts grey-brown, tipped yellow (or reddish). Upperwing-coverts brown, pale-fringed, and spotted/barred white; flight feathers brown, heavily barred whitish on both webs. Uppertail brownish, barred whitish, and with prominent yellow shafts. Underparts below throat grey with olive tinge, becoming browner in lower regions, all barred white. Underwing barred blackish and grey-white. Undertail dull yellowish-brown, barred paler.

Adult female Similar to male, but with slightly shorter bill, and lacks red on head.

Juvenile Upperparts tinged green and more diffusely barred than on adults. Both sexes have red patch on crown which may extend to nape, but red is admixed with black and usually heavily spotted white.

Bare parts Bill grey-black, paler at base of lower mandible. Legs and feet grey, often with olive or green tinge. Eyes reddish-brown or red; usually more greyish to red-brown in juveniles.

GEOGRAPHICAL VARIATION Three well-defined races, tending to intergrade where ranges meet.
    D. n. namaquus (most of species' range, but excluding S Africa, S Mozambique, and the northeast from Ethiopia to N Kenya) Described above.
    D. n. coalescens (S Africa and S Mozambique) Somewhat darker overall: upperparts distinctly olive-brown and with barring broken, and underparts darker grey (especially on breast, where bars again broken). Intergrades with nominate in C Mozambique, Transvaal and Orange Free State.
    D. n. schoensis (Ethiopia, Somalia and N Kenya) Relatively shorter-winged than nominate. Dark brown (less yellow) above, with narrower pale barring; darker below, especially on breast, with markings more as spots or arrowhead bars (breast usually sparsely spotted). Rear of ear-coverts sometimes joined to moustache by broad black bar on neck side. Intergrades with nominate where ranges meet.

MEASUREMENTS Wing 124-140; tail 60-79; bill 27-36; tarsus 17-22.2. Weight: 61-89.

VOICE Common call is an accelerating series of 5-15 notes, *wik-wik-wik-...* (this rattle call is rather similar to calls of Grey-headed Kingfisher *Halcyon leucocephala*). Chattering *wickwickwickwick-wick-wick* series seem to belong to the *wicka-quee* continuum. Also *chip chip chip*. A loud nasal scream has also been recorded. Nestlings produce a piping cackle. Drums loudly, each roll followed by four regular taps: *trrrrrrr-tap-tap-tap-tap*, rolls longer than those of Fire-bellied Woodpecker (81).

HABITS Seen mostly singly and in pairs, which keep contact with their common call. Forages on dead trees (prefers larger ones), often high on trunk, on larger and smaller branches; otherwise visits all levels, from ground to canopy. Sexual differences apparently exist, females preferring smaller trees and smaller branches. Excavates with vigorous pecking and hammering, probes, and also gleans to some extent. Spends a long time at one site, and may cover large distances when moving to another. Flicks its wings when calling and the partner is close by; displays also with head-swinging and bill-directing. Foraging ranges are large, which contributes to its apparent rarity. Has many nest competitors, among them rollers, starlings, owlets, kingfishers and, most commonly, squirrels.

FOOD Insects and their larvae, particularly wood-boring beetles and their larvae, caterpillars, ants and spiders. May even hunt geckos or small lizards and feed them to the young.

BREEDING Breeds January in Somalia, (April)May-June in Ethiopia, April-October in Kenya, June-November in Tanzania, and June-December in Zimbabwe, Zambia and Malawi; in S Africa, breeding takes place from May to November (in Natal, breeds rarely in November, but more commonly during the cooler months from May onwards). Nesting hole is drilled in dead wood 2-20m up in a tree. The same nest may be used several times. The entrance is relatively large and vertically oval in shape (7.5 x 5.5cm). Clutch contains 2-4, mostly 3, eggs. Both parents incubate for 13 days and provide equally for the chicks, which remain around 27 days in the nest.

REFERENCES Beals 1970; Belcher 1930; Britton 1980; Clancey 1964; Cyrus & Robson 1980; Irwin 1981; Maclean 1985; Newman 1989; Roberts *et al.* 1981; Short 1971f, 1988; Short & Horne 1981; Tarboton 1970, 1990.

---

81 FIRE-BELLIED WOODPECKER
Dendropicos pyrrhogaster Plate 23

Forms a superspecies with *xantholophus.*

IDENTIFICATION Length c. 24cm. Small, but the largest forest woodpecker in its African range. Bill long and broad. Combination of broad black and white stripes on head, red rump, and broad red stripe down underparts is diagnostic. Upperparts excluding rump bronze-green, with longish unbarred blackish tail; breast sides and flanks barred. Male has red crown and nape. Tends to feed in upper levels of forest, and drums frequently and loudly.

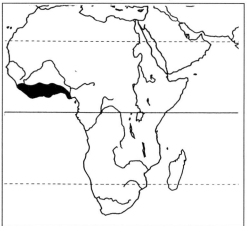

DISTRIBUTION A common W African endemic, found from Sierra Leone and southern Guinea east to the Niger delta in S Nigeria; has also been reported a couple of times from S Cameroon, including once at 2300m, but these records (especially the high-altitude one) seem unlikely and require better documentation.

HABITAT Primary and secondary forest in lowlands. Prefers vicinity of large trees and, although very much a forest species, will sometimes visit tall, often dead (particularly fire-killed) trees along rivers or growing in isolated patches, clearings, forest edges and forest-grassland mosaic.

DESCRIPTION

Adult male Forehead brownish-black; crown to nape red (very occasionally buffish-yellow in crown centre), with black feather bases (black more obvious in worn plumage). Lores white, with dark spot before eye. Ear-coverts black and curving down at rear, bordered above by broad white supercilium which continues downwards to meet broad white stripe from neck side to bill. Submoustachial/malar stripe black, paler-streaked near bill, and continuing onto breast side, where breaks up. Chin and throat white. Nape sides and hindneck black. Mantle, scapulars and back bronze-green, often with some indistinct bars and red tips

when fresh; rump and uppertail-coverts red, with black feather bases. Upperwing-coverts brownish bronze-green, narrowly fringed paler, with a few pale spots on median coverts; flight feathers brown, narrowly edged paler, inner webs with broad white bars and outers with narrower yellow-white bars. Uppertail olive-black, unbarred. Centre of breast to undertail-coverts broadly red; upper breast sides with broad black streaks, becoming off-white with heavy arrowhead barring on flanks. Underwing whitish. Undertail dull yellowish-green.

Adult female Slightly shorter-billed and relatively longer-tailed than male. Lacks red on head, having black forehead to nape.

Juvenile Duller, less bronzy above, and with all black areas of plumage browner; red areas duller and less extensive. Both sexes have red on crown (less extensive than on adult male), young female having much brown admixed with the red.

Bare parts Bill dark grey, with paler lower mandible. Legs and feet green to grey-green. Eyes brown to red; brown in juveniles.

GEOGRAPHICAL VARIATION None known.

MEASUREMENTS Wing 106-122; tail 60-74; bill 30-33; tarsus 20.2-22.3. Weight: 63-74.

VOICE A sharp *wip*, which also introduces the long-distance call, *wip-wi-di-di-di-dit*. Drums in clearly accelerating rolls, which also weaken towards the end; rolls shorter than those of Golden-crowned Woodpecker (82).

HABITS Often in pairs. Forages in the upper levels, but may descend to fallen logs. Excavates with pecking and hammering.

FOOD Insects, larvae of beetles and white ants.

BREEDING Nestlings have been recorded in March in Liberia; breeds October-May in Nigeria.

REFERENCES Bannerman 1933; Colston *et al.* 1986; Rand 1951; Short 1988; Walker 1939.

---

82 GOLDEN-CROWNED WOODPECKER
Dendropicos xantholophus Plate 23

Other name: Yellow-crested Woodpecker
Forms a superspecies with *pyrrhogaster.*

IDENTIFICATION Length c. 25cm. Small, but among the largest of Africa's woodpeckers. Bill long and broad. A relatively big, dark, strong-billed species of C African forests. Striking black and white head pattern is its most obvious feature. Upperparts dark brown, with minimal yellow on rump and with black tail; dark olive below, spotted pale on breast and pale-barred on flanks and lower underparts. The only African woodpecker in which both sexes lack all red in plumage: male has yellow on hindcrown (but note that yellow very occasionally replaces, at least in part, the red of red-crowned species). Noisy, tapping and drumming loudly and frequently in upper levels of trees.

Similar species Unmistakable in good views. If seen briefly or in poor light could perhaps be confused wth Fire-bellied Woodpecker (81), but latter always shows much red in plumage and does not overlap in range. Bearded Woodpecker (80) also has black and white head stripes, but is fully barred above (including tail) and below (appears very dark), and avoids dense forest; the two may just possibly meet at forest edge, but ranges barely overlap.

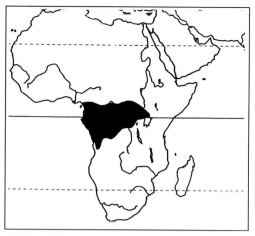

DISTRIBUTION A common forest woodpecker distributed from SW Cameroon eastwards through southwesternmost Central African Republic to S Sudan, W and C Uganda and just into Kenya (Kakamega and Nandi Forests), and south to Cabinda and NW Angola (to about 90°S) and across C Zaïre; unconfirmed sight records from Nigeria are thought to be unreliable.

HABITAT Inhabits mainly areas with large trees in lowland forest, forest edge, but also occurs in nearby thick secondary growth and occasionally densely wooded areas and cultivated plantations (e.g. coffee, cocoa), and may visit isolated large trees outside forest. Altitudinal range extends from 700 to 2150m in the east.

DESCRIPTION
Adult male Forehead brown, merging into blackish crown, latter with a few white speckles; hindcrown feathers black with yellow tips; nape and hindneck black. Lores white, with black spot in front of eye. Ear-coverts black, curving downwards at rear, bordered above by broad white supercilium which continues around rear ear-coverts to meet broad white area from neck side to bill. Submoustachial stripe black, broadening on throat side. Chin and throat white, lower throat tinged olive and crossed by row of black spots. Uppermost mantle black; rest of upperparts olive-brown (sometimes with a few indistinct paler bars on mantle), rump and uppertail-coverts with narrow yellow tips. Upperwing-coverts olive, with variable number of pale tips and subterminal spots; flight feathers brownish-black, narrowly edged and tipped green, and barred white on both webs. Uppertail black, unbarred. Underparts below throat blackish, becoming greenish-olive from lower breast, breast with white spots and flanks to belly and undertail-coverts barred whitish. Underwing dull off-white. Undertail dull blackish.

Adult female Slightly shorter-billed than male, and without yellow on crown.

Juvenile Duller and greener above, and greyer and more barred below. Both sexes have hindcrown feathers tipped yellow, less extensively on females.

Bare parts Bill dark grey to black, with paler cutting edges and paler lower mandible. Legs and feet green to olive or brownish. Eyes red to brown; less red in juveniles.

GEOGRAPHICAL VARIATION None. Monotypic.

MEASUREMENTS Wing 104-123; tail 65-78; bill 27-35; tarsus 20.4-21.7. Weight: 50-73.

VOICE Single notes to fast bursts, *dit, dit-it*, to purring

ddditrrrrr and grating *grrrrr*. Also very fast *dddit, graa* and *a-wik a-wik...* during encounters. Both sexes drum in accelerating rolls, which also weaken towards end (longer than rolls of Fire-bellied Woodpecker).

HABITS Visits the middle and upper storeys, where it pecks strongly and hammers or removes bark. Also takes prey on the wing. Moves down trees by fluttering.

FOOD Diet consists largely of wood-boring beetles and their larvae; also other insects (ants), and spiders.

BREEDING Breeds probably in October-March in Cameroon, and January-April and September in other parts of W Africa; September-March in Uganda and adjacent Kenya. Both sexes excavate nest in a dead tree or dead section of a tree at up to 17m.

REFERENCES Britton 1980; Short 1988.

83 ELLIOT'S WOODPECKER
Dendropicos elliotii   Plate 22

IDENTIFICATION Length c. 20-22cm. Small, but relatively large within its African range. Bill rather long and broad. Plain greenish upperparts, long unbarred tail, unmarked buffish face and black forehead, and yellow underparts with variably heavy to virtually invisible streaks combine to give distinctive, if modest, appearance. Male has red hindcrown and nape; female has forehead to nape solid black. If seen well in its dense forest habitat, unlikely to be mistaken for any other woodpecker within its range.

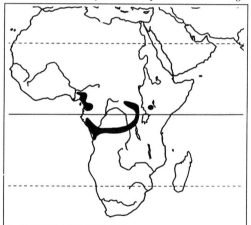

DISTRIBUTION A forest woodpecker, with range extending from SE Nigeria and W Cameroon, including Bioko Island, south to NW Angola and east through SC Zaïre to SW Uganda (Kibale Forest) and NE Zaïre, with an isolated population on Mount Elgon in E Uganda (see also Geographical Variation). In much of this range, however, distribution is patchy and incompletely known; range less contiguous than shown on map. Rather uncommon.

HABITAT Occupies dense primary forest, in northwest of range at up to 2320m in moist, gloomy, mossy montane forest, elsewhere being found down to lowlands; occasionally ventures out into secondary forest with tall trees.

DESCRIPTION
D. e. elliotii **Adult male** Forehead and forecrown black; hindcrown and nape red. Lores reddish-buff; rest of sides of head, including crown sides, buff, tinged greenish

247

(sometimes strongly) on rear ear-coverts and neck sides. Chin and throat white, narrowly streaked olive. Hindneck and entire upperparts, including wing-coverts, plain green with bronze or brownish tinge. Flight feathers brown, broadly edged bronzy-green on outer webs and white on inner webs. Uppertail brown, feathers edged green, outers occasionally barred buff at base. Underparts below throat pale yellowish to yellow-brown, broadly streaked brown or olive, streaks often becoming bars on flanks and belly. Underwing yellowish-white. Undertail yellow-brown.

Adult female Lacks red on head, forehead to nape being entirely black.

Juvenile More streaked on underparts than adults, and duller overall. Both sexes have red on crown, restricted to rear crown on females.

Bare parts Bill greyish to black, often tipped yellowish, and with paler lower mandible. Legs and feet grey or green with olive or brown tinge. Eyes red-brown to red; browner in juveniles.

GEOGRAPHICAL VARIATION Three races, differing mainly in amount and intensity of streaking on underparts.
    D. e. elliotii (lowland SW Cameroon, south discontinuously to Cabinda and across parts of SC Zaïre to NE Zaïre and SW Uganda; also Mount Elgon in E Uganda) Described above.
    D. e. gabela (NW Angola south to Gabela area) As nominate, but has narrower streaks on underparts.
    D. e. johnstoni (highlands of SE Nigeria, SW Cameroon and Bioko Island) Underpart streaking very fine and much sparser than on nominate, or may even be lacking (leaving plain yellow underparts). Mount Kupé population is sometimes separated as '*kupeensis*', but appears intermediate between nominate race and *johnstoni* (which interbreed in region of Mount Kupé and base of Mount Cameroon).

MEASUREMENTS Wing 83-95 (*johnstoni*), 89-97 (*elliotii*); tail 63-69; tarsus 16.9-17.5. Weight: 32-40.

VOICE Apparently similar to that of Grey Woodpecker (84). A call-series and shrill *bwe-bwe* notes have been reported. Apparently drums in weak rolls.

HABITS Met with singly or in pairs, and joins mixed-species flocks (occasionally including other woodpecker species as well). Forages at all levels of the forest, including in the understorey. Pecks powerfully and probes into epiphytes (mosses) on branches and on very large leaves. Moves rapidly, without staying at a single site for long.

FOOD Larvae of beetles, and other insects.

BREEDING Probably breeds in September-October in west of range.

REFERENCES Chapin 1939; Short 1988.

84 GREY WOODPECKER
Dendropicos goertae   **Plate 24**

Other names: Eastern Grey Woodpecker, African Grey Woodpecker
Forms a superspecies with *spodocephalus* and *griseocephalus*.

IDENTIFICATION Length c. 20cm. Small, with longish, straight, broad bill. Obscurely pale-striped grey head (male with red hindcrown and nape), unbarred green or brownish-green upperparts with red rump, barred brown tail, grey underparts with orange to yellow belly patch and some barring on flanks, and barred wings make this a fairly distinctive species among African woodpeckers. Sahel race *koenigi* is paler, with more barring below and on lower back, and frequently lacks belly patch. Gives long, loud territorial rattle call, but otherwise rather unobtrusive.

Similar species Forms a superspecies with Grey-headed (85) and Olive (86) Woodpeckers, and has often been treated as conspecific with them (especially with Grey-headed). Olive Woodpecker is best distinguished by its darker grey head, contrasting with generally unbarred and distinctly greenish or olive underparts with red belly patch (patch lacking in eastern Tanzanian race), and its darker, unbarred tail; the two scarcely overlap in range, but apparently interbreed in N Angola and in Rwanda/Burundi. Grey-headed is very like Grey in all respects (race *abessinicus* of Grey is intermediate between the two), but has larger area of red (not orange/yellow) on central lower underparts, generally much yellower upperparts (except nominate), only outer rectrices barred, less barring on wings, and an even more uniform face with no (or only very slight) indication of pale markings. Grey-headed has the same long territorial rattle as Grey, but this call is lacking in Olive Woodpecker's repertoire. Great care and good views are required when identifying these three species, the problems being exacerbated by the existence of hybrids. For further details on the complexities of this superspecies, see references.

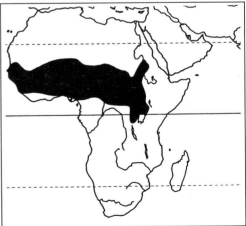

DISTRIBUTION Ranges from SW Mauretania and Senegambia in a broad band south of the Sahara to S Sudan and W and N Ethiopia (but absent from most of Liberia, southern half of Ivory Coast, coastal Ghana and Niger delta area), extending south to northern Cameroon, N and NE Zaïre, Uganda, E Rwanda, NE Burundi, NW Tanzania and W Kenya; also two apparently isolated populations, one extending from S Gabon through the lower Congo region to NW Angola (south to 10-11 °S, possibly to around 14 °S), and the other in the Kasai and Shaba regions of SC Zaïre. A fairly common species.

MOVEMENTS Some movement occurs in non-breeding season, with one record between 20° and 21°N in Mauretania (at Atar, well north of breeding range), as well as isolated occurrences in S Nigeria and on Ghana coast.

HABITAT Common and wide-ranging in woodlands, wooded grasslands and pastures, riverine woodland, thickets with larger trees, gardens, forest edges and cultivation with trees; also frequents mangroves in west of range. From sea level to 3000m; at 700-3000m in E Africa.

DESCRIPTION
D. g. goertae **Adult male** Forehead and forecrown grey; hindcrown and nape red, sometimes with grey feather bases showing through on hindcrown. Rest of head grey (may be darker on ear-coverts), often tinged buffish/olive on hindneck and neck sides, and with obscure white supercilium behind eye and faint white moustachial stripe extending to lores and base of forehead. Chin and throat pale grey. Mantle, scapulars and back variably bronzy-green to olive-green or brownish-green; rump and uppertail-coverts red. Upperwing-coverts as back, but edged and tipped paler and with hint of pale bars; flight feathers brown, barred pale on both webs (strongest on inner webs). Uppertail brown, with pale bars not quite meeting in centre. Underparts pale grey, normally tinged slightly pale yellow, with variable (usually rather weak) white and yellowish-white barring on flanks and lower ventral region, and with small yellow or orange-yellow patch (rarely, with some admixed red) in belly centre. Underwing barred black and white. Undertail brown, obscurely barred pale and suffused yellow.
Adult female Slightly shorter-billed than male, with head all grey (lacks red).
Juvenile Duller above than adults, lacking bronze tinge, with red of rump paler, and usually with more obvious pale facial markings; tends to show more barring below, with smaller, paler belly patch. Both sexes have red in crown centre, more extensive on males.
Bare parts Bill slaty-grey to black, paler on lower mandible. Legs and feet greenish-grey, suffused chalky, with whitish joints. Eyes red to brown; grey-brown in juveniles.

GEOGRAPHICAL VARIATION Four races, one fairly distinctive.
   D. g. goertae (most of species' range from W Africa to Sudan and south to NE Zaïre, Tanzania and Kenya, but excluding sahel zone occupied by following race) A variable race, described above.
   D. g. koenigi (Sahel zone across central parts of E Mali, Niger and Chad to W Sudan) Noticeably paler than nominate, with pale barring above (mainly on lower back and wing-coverts) and somewhat stronger pale markings on face; belly patch small and yellow, but more often lacking altogether. Intergrades with nominate in south, and with *abessinicus* in east of range (Nubian desert, where can show small red belly patch).
   D. g. abessinicus (E and N Sudan and N and W Ethiopia) Has modest-sized red belly patch; shows hint of flank barring and of pale supercilium and moustachial stripe. Appears intermediate between Grey and Grey-headed Woodpeckers (strengthening case for conspecificity).
   D. g. meridionalis (SC Zaïre and, presumably this race, S Gabon to NW Angola) As nominate, but browner above and lacking yellowish tinge below.

MEASUREMENTS Wing 102-117. Weight: 40.5-52.5.

VOICE Long-distance call a series of 20-30 notes, *wik wik*.... During interactions, irregular series of *week* or *weeka* notes. Also *pew* and *pit-it*. Drums rarely.

HABITS Seen in pairs or family groups. Forages on live and dead trees, on larger branches and trunks; also descends to ground. Mainly pecks, excavating for prey. Some prey is taken on the wing. Moves rapidly.

FOOD Ants, termites, beetle larvae, and other insects.

BREEDING Breeds December-June in west of range, December-February and July-September in Zaïre, and February-July and September-November in E Africa. Nest excavated by both sexes in a dead tree or dead section of a tree, at 0.3-20m. Clutch comprises 2-4 eggs.
REFERENCES Britton 1980; Prigogine & Louette 1983; Rand *et al.* 1959; Short 1988; Short *et al.* 1990.

85 GREY-HEADED WOODPECKER
Dendropicos spodocephalus Plate 24

Forms a superspecies with *goertae* and *griseocephalus*.

IDENTIFICATION Length 20cm. Small, with fairly long, straight, broad bill. Yellow-green upperparts with red rump and barred outer tail contrast with unmarked pale grey head and underparts, latter with usually large patch of red in ventral region. Male has red on hindcrown and nape.

Similar species Very like Grey Woodpecker (84), with which considered conspecific on good evidence presented by Short & Horne (1986). Differs in having generally brighter upperparts, even more uniform grey head and underparts, and larger, red (not orange or yellow) belly patch; also has tail barred only on outer feathers and shows less barring on wings than Grey. The two species are identical in voice and behaviour. Note also that race *abessinicus* of Grey is intermediate between the two species. Olive Woodpecker (86) is also superficially similar, and its range (race *kilimensis*) may overlap slightly with that of Grey-headed in NE Tanzania, but differs mainly in being darker overall, with darker grey head, olive underparts (these lacking red on belly in area of possible overlap), and dark unbarred tail.

DISTRIBUTION A fairly common species in E Africa, ranging from eastern Sudan and N Ethiopia southwards through the highlands to C and SE Kenya and N Tanzania east of Lake Victoria (Kilimanjaro, Lake Manyara).

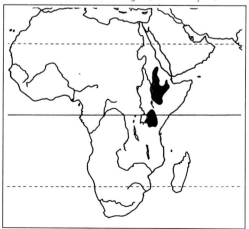

HABITAT Moist forest, forest edge and riverine forest; highlands.

DESCRIPTION
***D. s. rhodeogaster* Adult male** Hindcrown and nape red, sometimes with some grey feather bases visible (especially when worn); entire rest of head, including forehead and forecrown, hindneck, chin and throat, grey (sometimes slightly darker on ear-coverts) and unmarked. Mantle, scapulars, back and upperwing-coverts yellowish-green, most feathers edged and/or tipped brighter yellow (very bright-looking when fresh); rump and uppertail-coverts red. Flight feathers dark brown, outer webs edged yellowish-green (broadly on tertials), primaries and secondaries barred whitish on inner webs. Uppertail dark brown, outer feathers barred white on outer webs. Grey of head extends over underparts, which have red patch from central belly to undertail-coverts; flanks may have faint indication of pale bars. Underwing barred blackish and white. Undertail brown, barred yellowish on outer feathers.

Adult female Slightly shorter-billed than male and with no red on head.

Juvenile Duller than adults, lacking yellow tones above and with red of rump paler, but with obscure whitish supercilium; stronger indication of barring below, with smaller red belly patch. Both sexes have red in crown centre, more extensive on males.

Bare parts Bill slaty-grey to black, with paler lower mandible. Legs and feet chalky greenish-grey with white joints. Eyes red to brown; greyish-brown in juveniles.

GEOGRAPHICAL VARIATION Two races.
   D. s. rhodeogaster (highlands of C and SE Kenya and NC Tanzania) Described above.
   D. s. spodocephalus (C and S Ethiopian highlands) As *rhodeogaster*, but lacks bright yellow feather tips to upperparts.

MEASUREMENTS Wing 103-118; tail 55-62; bill 16-18; tarsus 19-20.4. Weight: 43-52.

VOICE Very much as those of Grey Woodpecker.

HABITS Very much as those of Grey Woodpecker.

FOOD Diet includes Geophilidae, lepidopteran pupae and larvae.

BREEDING Breeding season spans August to April in Ethiopia, and peaks April-May and July-October (may breed in all seasons) in Kenya and N Tanzania.

REFERENCES Prigogine & Louette 1983; Short 1988; Short & Horne 1986.

86 OLIVE WOODPECKER
Dendropicos griseocephalus Plate 24

Forms a superspecies with *goertae* and *spodocephalus*.

IDENTIFICATION Length 20cm. Small, with longish, straight, broad bill. Unmarked dark grey head (male with red on nape), plain olive upperparts with red rump, dark unbarred tail, and olive underparts with or without red belly patch distinguish this from all other African woodpeckers. An upland species in most of its range, usually found in denser forest. Often forages in small groups, and frequently joins mixed-species feeding flocks.

Similar species Unmistakable throughout most of range, provided good views obtained. May overlap very slightly with Grey Woodpecker (84) in Angola, SW Uganda and Rwanda/Burundi, and with Grey-headed (85) in Tanzania (Mount Kilimanjaro). Best told from both by somewhat longer and completely unbarred tail, deeper grey head, and olive/greenish underparts with golden-tinged breast; also lacks long territorial rattle call given by both those species. Note, however, that occasional hybrids occur which can confuse the issue.

DISTRIBUTION In northern part of range, resident from Angolan highlands east through SE and E Zaïre to W Tanzania (Kibondo), Burundi and Rwanda, and to Ruwenzoris and Impenetrable Forest of SW Uganda, and from Mount Kilimanjaro across SC Tanzania to NW Malawi, extending south to SE Angola, Caprivi Strip of NE Namibia and adjacent northwest corner of Zimbabwe, and SC Zambia; southern part of range, in S Africa, extends from N and E Transvaal and Lebombo mountains on Mozambique border south through Natal and along coast to the Cape. A variably common to uncommon woodpecker; common in S Africa.

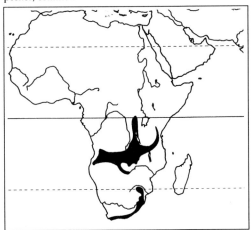

HABITAT Frequents forests, evergreen thickets and dense woodlands of highlands and those fringing watercourses, usually in more open parts, as in *Hagenia* forest. Seems to prefer forest patches over closed forests. Rather common inland in evergreen forest and less common in thick coastal bush; in S Africa, the only woodpecker species likely to be observed in latter type of habitat. Found at altitudes of between 450 and 3700m (on Kilimanjaro, usually found higher up and in denser forest than Grey-headed Woodpecker); low-level records may involve stragglers.

DESCRIPTION
***D. g. griseocephalus* Adult male** Hindcrown and nape feathers grey at base, often with some fine black subterminal

bars, and broadly tipped red (when worn, black or grey often shows through, producing mottled/barred effect); rest of head, including forehead, hindneck, chin and throat, rather dark grey. Mantle, scapulars and back dull olive-green, tinged bronze (brighter in east of subspecies' range); rump and uppertail-coverts red, latter sometimes showing dark bases. Upperwing-coverts dull green (as back), edged paler bronzy-green; flight feathers dark brown, sometimes with some pale spots on inner webs, and with olive-green (sometimes reddish-tinged) edges, latter broadest on tertials. Uppertail blackish-brown or black, feathers edged olive. Underparts below throat bronzy-olive, breast with distinct golden tinge, becoming much greyer on belly and undertail-coverts and occasionally with very small patch of red on belly; a few individuals have rather obscure whitish bars on flanks. Underwing pale brownish. Undertail brownish, with yellow tinge to outer feathers.

Adult female Shorter-billed than male, with head entirely grey (lacks red).

Juvenile Duller than adults, greener (less bronzy) above and greyer below, with paler red on rump; usually shows more distinct barring below (can extend to belly), and red belly patch, when present, is paler and very insignificant. Both sexes have red in crown centre, more extensive on males, the red usually obviously barred with black.

Bare parts Bill grey to blackish, paler and tinged blue or greenish on lower mandible. Legs and feet grey to greyish-olive or olive-grey. Eyes brown.

GEOGRAPHICAL VARIATION Three races, one fairly well differentiated.

D. g. griseocephalus (eastern S Africa and Lebombo mountains) Described above. Those in north and east of range tend to be brighter, more yellow, than southern populations.

D. g. ruwenzori (most of species' range, but excluding S Africa and highlands of NE Tanzania south to Uzungwas) Brighter than nominate, with yellower or more golden tinges above and golden or yellow-olive breast; primaries and secondaries more clearly barred (occasionally on both webs); has red patch on belly, sometimes fairly extensive (paler and much reduced, or lacking, on juveniles).

D. g. kilimensis (Tanzanian highlands: Mount Kilimanjaro, Mount Meru, and mountains of north Pare, Usambara, Uluguru and Uzungwa) Averages slightly smaller than above two races, and has less yellow in upperparts; underparts greyer, and always lacks red on belly. Some may have red eyes.

MEASUREMENTS Wing 97-105 (*kilimensis*), 104-116 (*ruwenzori*); tail 60-72; bill 12.3-17.8; tarsus 18-21.2. Weight: 33-51.

VOICE A long, slightly nasal, whistled trill, *whee-whee-whee*, of 3-4 notes. Conversational notes among birds in a group are rendered *pep* to *pep-pep-pep*. In alarm, a soft *tick* is given which may be followed by a contracted trill, *chi-r-r-r--re*. Also, *tweet* when taking off and *wat-chew* on the wing; a repeated *wer chick* uttered with head movements; and, when two individuals are at close distance, quiet *kiwi-kiwi-kiwi* may be heard. Nestlings utter soft, high-pitched twitters, *kee-kee-kee-kee*.... Drums in soft, rapid rolls.

HABITS This quiet woodpecker is found singly or in pairs, sometimes in parties of up to six, and is often difficult to detect in its misty habitats. It is strictly arboreal and forages on upper trunks and on branches, preferring small trees and small branches in larger trees. Foraging

heights span the range 1-24m, the modal foraging height is 12m, and preferred heights are between 10 and 15m. Pecks, often with lateral blows, excavating for large larvae, probes frequently among mosses, and gleans the bark. Moves quickly through a tree, often sidling or backing up. In display, the head is swung from side to side and the woodpecker calls. Territories small in forest patches (2.2 pairs/10 ha) and large in forests (0.2-0.3 pairs/10 ha). Nests parasitised by honeyguides (e.g. *Indicator variegatus*). Social organisation obscure; (male) helpers occur.

FOOD Insects (beetles, Scarabaeidae) and their larvae, particularly ants.

BREEDING Nests possibly in April-June in Tanzania, and breeds July-September in Malawi, September in Natal and Zululand, and October-November in the Cape; June in Angola. Nest holes are excavated at 1.5-18m in dead trunks or dead branches (sometimes on underside of horizontal branches), male doing most of the work. Most clutches contain 2-3 eggs. Both sexes incubate for 15-17 days, and both (and possibly 1-2 helpers) feed the young and take care of nest sanitation. The female may feed the brood more frequently, but often with smaller loads, and collects nestling food close to the nest, whereas the male makes longer foraging trips. Female and male roost together in the nest during egg and nestling stages. After young fledge, the whole family may roost together in the former nest for three months and more; this seems to occur regularly if only one fledgling is produced (which appears most commonly to be the case).

REFERENCES Britton 1980; Chapin 1929; Clancey 1964; Cyrus & Robson 1980; Dowsett-Lemaire 1983, 1989; Irwin 1981; Koen 1988; Maclean 1985; Roberts *et al.* 1981; Short 1971f, 1988; Tarboton 1990.

87 BROWN-BACKED WOODPECKER
Picoides obsoletus   Plate 25

IDENTIFICATION Length c. 13-16cm. Very small, with longish, straight, chisel-tipped bill broad across nostrils. Brown and white plumage, with prominent white supercilium and moustache enclosing dark ear-coverts, together with unmarked back and strongly barred wings and tail, characteristic; most races also have spotted upperwing-coverts. Male has red hindcrown and nape. Underparts are whitish, with amount/intensity of dark streaking varying racially. Ngorongoro race *crateri* is much darker, almost black, above and has heavy streaking below (forming patch on breast).

Similar species Generally distinctive within African range, but heavily worn individuals can be very pale, approaching sympatric (unworn) Little Grey Woodpecker (73), but lack latter's red on uppertail-coverts and have unbarred back.

DISTRIBUTION Inhabits sub-Saharan bush savanna from the Gambia south to C Sierra Leone and N Liberia and eastwards to W Ethiopia, north to Eritrea, and then south to northern Zaïre, C and E Uganda, east through C Kenya to Thika (SE Kenya), with extension into N Tanzania (Loliondo), and with isolated population just south of there in region of Nou Forest and Ngorongoro; also wanders east to Mombasa and Shimba Hills in SE Kenya. Rather local and uncommon, though has increased recently in suburbs of Nairobi; may disappear from suitable areas for several years, before returning.

HABITAT Uncommon and local in drier areas, favouring scrubby terrain, wooded grassland, edges of cultivation,

Combretum woodland and *Hagenia* forests, but also occurs in suburban gardens and even in open savanna with scattered trees. Found in highlands up to 2300m, locally to 3000m (Mount Kenya), but also down to sea level.

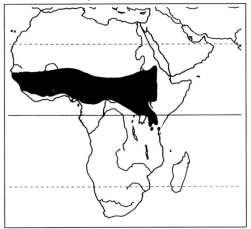

DESCRIPTION

***P. o. obsoletus* Adult male** Forehead pale brown, becoming darker on crown; hindcrown and nape red. Supercilium from behind eye white, extending as stripe around rear of ear-coverts and down neck side to breast; rear lores and ear-coverts brown. Moustachial stripe white, broadening at rear and continuing to breast side, bordered below by dark brown submoustachial stripe which also expands on upper breast side. Chin and throat white, sometimes with small dark spots. Hindneck, mantle, scapulars and back unmarked dull brown; rump and uppertail-coverts white, streaked brown. Upperwing-coverts as back, but feathers tipped white (amount of spotting variable); flight feathers dark brown, barred white. Uppertail brown, barred white. Underparts below throat whitish, often sullied buffy-brown on breast, and lightly streaked brown (streaks occasionally almost absent). Underwing barred brown and white. Undertail yellowish-brown, barred paler. (When worn, plumage becomes much paler and less contrasting.)

Adult female Hindcrown and nape brown, not red; averages shorter-billed than male.

Juvenile Somewhat darker above than adults, and with greyish tinge to plumage; underparts usually show some barring. Both sexes have red on hindcrown, more extensive on male.

Bare parts Bill blackish, with paler, greyer, lower mandible. Legs and feet grey, often tinged green. Eyes red-brown; brown in juveniles.

GEOGRAPHICAL VARIATION Four races, differing in size, in darkness of upperparts, and in amount of streaking below; one race lacks wing-covert spots.

   P. o. obsoletus (from W Africa east to W Sudan and Uganda, east to Teso) Described above.

   P. o. heuglini (E Sudan and N Ethiopia) Larger than nominate. Lacks or has much-reduced spotting on wing-coverts, but more heavily streaked below.

   P. o. ingens (C and S Ethiopia, NE Uganda and Kenya south to Loliondo in N Tanzania) Includes '*nigricans*'. As *heuglini*, but darker above, especially on crown, and has spotted wing-coverts.

   P. o. crateri (N Tanzania, in Nou Forest, Crater Highlands and Ngorongoro) Larger and darker than other races, with upperparts almost black; underpart streaks very broad and dark, meeting to form patch on breast.

MEASUREMENTS Wing 75-86 (*obsoletus*), 83-91 (*crateri*); tail 30-40 (*obsoletus*), 39-44 (*crateri*); bill of male 9.5-12.5, of female 9.2-12.2; tarsus 13.7-14.9. Weight: 18-25.

VOICE Single clicking calls, a weak high-pitched trill, and *kweek-week...* (in flight). Drums.

HABITS Usually seen singly or in pairs; occasionally joins mixed-species flocks. Forages with gleaning and pecking on trunks and branches of trees, and on saplings.

FOOD Lepidopterous and coleopterous larvae and various adult insects.

BREEDING Breeds December-June in west of range, January-April and August in east. Both sexes excavate hole in (often isolated) tree or stub at 2-7m. Clutch size 2 eggs. Both parents incubate and feed the young.

REFERENCES Bannerman 1933; Chapin 1939; Serle 1957; Short 1988; Short *et al.* 1990.

88 SULAWESI WOODPECKER
Picoides temminckii   Plate 25

Other names: Celebes Pygmy Woodpecker, Temminck's (Pygmy) Woodpecker
Forms a superspecies with *maculatus*.

IDENTIFICATION Length c. 13-14cm. Very small, with longish, almost pointed bill slightly curved on culmen and broad across nostrils. A short-tailed species confined to Sulawesi and easily identified, being the only woodpecker of its size on the island. Barred dark and pale above and on wings, and buffish with darker streaking below. Both sexes have a dark crown and ear-coverts, latter bordered by white supercilium above and broad area of white below, and male has a small patch of red on nape (often confined to sides). A little-known species.

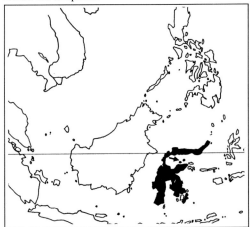

DISTRIBUTION Endemic on Sulawesi, including Buton (Butung) and the Togian archipelago. Not uncommon.

HABITAT Inhabits wooded areas, forests and riparian woodland, orange and coffee plantations in the cultivated lowlands, large trees along roadsides, and gardens. Also in the deforested hills and in primary montane forest edge up to 2300m.

DESCRIPTION

Adult male Lower forehead buffy-brown; rear lores, upper forehead and crown dark brown, with grey feather bases (in worn plumage, latter showing as streaks); nape band narrowly red, broader on nape sides (red often lacking on central nape); upper hindneck brown. Narrow white supercilium from front edge of eye to nape side. Ear-coverts dark brown (streaked grey when worn). Front of lores, moustachial area and cheeks broadly white, this colour extending to neck side and behind lower ear-coverts, and usually also onto central hindneck. Malar stripe brown, thinly barred white. Chin and throat dull grey-brown, sometimes with off-white markings. Lower hindneck, mantle, scapulars and back olive-brown, sometimes tinged green, all barred very pale brownish-tinged white; rump whitish, barred dark brown, occasionally pale yellowish-white and/or unbarred; uppertail-coverts barred brown and white. Upperwing-coverts and tertials dark brown with faint hint of olive, coverts tipped white and tertials barred white; primaries and secondaries darker brown, barred white on both webs. Uppertail brown, with buffish or buff-white bars of variable width. Underparts from breast pale buffish-olive to yellowish-grey, broadly streaked brown or olive-brown, somewhat paler and more narrowly streaked in lower regions. Underwing barred brown and whitish. Undertail as uppertail, but paler and usually with slight yellowish wash.

Adult female Slightly longer in wing and tail than male, but lacks latter's red on nape.

Juvenile Differs from adults only minimally, having barring above and streaking below less contrasting (with more of a brown tone).

Bare parts Bill black, with paler, greyer base to lower mandible. Legs and feet olive-green. Eyes red to light brown.

GEOGRAPHICAL VARIATION None as regards plumage. Southern and upland populations tend to be somewhat larger than northern and lowland ones, though this seems insufficient ground for racial separation.

MEASUREMENTS Wing 71-86; tail 30-40; bill 14-19; tarsus 13.5-14.5.

VOICE Most common call a sharp *tirr-tirr*, also a rapid, thin *geegeegeegeegeegeegee*. Drums in loud rolls in the breeding season.

HABITS Almost nothing is known, but presumably not very different from those of its closest relative, the Philippine Woodpecker (89). Spends most of its time high up in the treetops, calling irregularly.

BREEDING Drumming and copulations have been recorded in August and young have been found in November; probably also breeds early in the year. Nest is constructed in a dead tree (preferentially in rain-tree, *Pithecolobium*, but also in mango and the like) or a dead branch.

REFERENCES Meyer & Wigglesworth 1898; Stresemann 1940; Voous 1947; White & Bruce 1986.

89 PHILIPPINE WOODPECKER
Picoides maculatus   Plate 25

Other names: Philippine Pygmy Woodpecker; Ramsay's Woodpecker (race *ramsayi*)
Forms a superspecies with *temminckii*.

IDENTIFICATION Length c. 13-14cm. Very small, with fairly long, slightly chisel-tipped bill barely curved on culmen and broad across nostrils. A rather variable species, but the only woodpecker of its size in the Philippines and, as such, not confusable. Generally, has pale-barred dark upperparts and wings, pale underparts with dark spots and streaks, and black and white bands on head, including a usually prominent dark moustache; male has a small, sometimes invisible, patch of red on nape sides. Those in the Sulu Islands, however, are browner-looking and unbarred, instead having much white streaking above and a largely white rump, and are more or less unstreaked below, but with an orangey-yellow band across the breast; males also have more red on head, extending to hindcrown. Active and agile, but relatively poorly known.

DISTRIBUTION Confined to the Philippines, where it is common, and the most abundant woodpecker, on all the main islands, including the Sulu archipelago, but not extending to Palawan.

HABITAT Light to dense primary and secondary forest to cloud forest, mature mahogany plantations, forest edge, woods along rivers, and grassy clearings with scattered trees. Typically, dead, often rather small, trees are numerous in localities visited by this species. Altitudinal range (85)590-1350m, locally to 2500m.

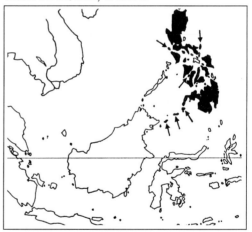

DESCRIPTION
P. m. maculatus **Adult male** Forehead to hindcrown dark brown, blacker at sides, and with small red patch at side of hindcrown (sometimes extending right across rear nape). White supercilium from rear of eye to nape side. Ear-coverts and backwards to hindneck blackish-brown. Upper lores buffish-brown; lower lores and broad band through cheeks and moustachial area to lower neck side white. Submoustachial stripe dark brown, variably spotted/streaked white. Chin white, becoming greyish on throat and uppermost breast, with brown spotting on lower throat and throat sides. Hindneck and upperparts dark brown, barred white on lower mantle, scapulars and back, with rump whiter and with a few dark spots/bars; uppertail-coverts white, broadly streaked dark. Upperwing brown, darker on primaries and secondaries, coverts narrowly tipped white and flight feath-

ers narrowly barred white. Uppertail dark brown, barred white. Underparts below throat pale buffish-white, washed yellow-buff on breast, with dark brown spots on breast becoming streaks on belly and flanks; undertail-coverts whitish, broadly streaked dark. Underwing brown, barred white. Undertail yellowish-brown, barred as above.

Adult female Slightly larger than male in bill, wing and tail lengths; lacks red on hindcrown sides.

Juvenile Much as adults, but upperparts browner and with heavier pale barring, and underpart markings less sharp.

Bare parts Bill dark grey, paler at base. Legs and feet brownish to olive-brown. Eyes brown to brownish-red.

GEOGRAPHICAL VARIATION Four races appear to be separable.

  P. m. maculatus (Panay, Sibuyan, Cebu, Guimaros and Negros) Described above. Birds from Negros are sometimes separated as '*menagei*'.
  P. m. validirostris (Luzon, Mindoro, Lubang, Marinduque and Catanduanes Islands) Shorter-tailed than nominate and darker above, with rump more barred (often completely so); white supercilium usually more extensive, continuing around rear of ear-coverts. Male has reduced red line on side of hindcrown.
  P. m. fulvifasciatus (Bohol, Leyte, Samar, Basilan and Mindanao) Still darker than *validirostris*, almost black above, with unmarked rump and more white behind ear-coverts (often a large white patch meeting white of supercilium); has buffish nasal tufts, buff tinge to pale upperpart barring, and stronger buff wash below. Birds from Leyte are sometimes separated as '*leytensis*'.
  P. m. ramsayi (Sulu Islands and Siassi) Highly distinctive. Browner and unbarred above, but with broad, irregular white streaking on mantle and back (rump mostly white); pale markings on wings reduced to small bars on inner webs of flight feathers (both webs of tertials). Underparts show much reduced streaking and few/no spots, but instead a brownish band across breast bordered below by yellow or golden colour. Supercilium normally extends back to hindneck, and male's red extends over entire nape and along rear crown sides. Birds from Siassi are sometimes separated as '*siasiensis*'.

MEASUREMENTS Wing 81-90; tail 36-43; bill 17.5-20.2; tarsus 14. Weight: 22-30.

VOICE Calls *pit* and more commonly *pitit* when foraging near conspecifics; single *chrrit* notes seem to be used as long-distance signals. Call-series resembling those of Lesser Spotted Woodpecker (93) in timbre are given in spring (February, March). Also drums.

HABITS A small and very agile woodpecker, seen singly, in pairs or in small family parties of up to five birds. Often joins mixed-species flocks with tits, nuthatches and other small birds. Forages mostly in upper levels (above 9m) of the forest on twigs and smaller branches. Dead trees or trees with dead branches are clearly favoured. Ventures out into (recently burned) clearings where dead trees are present. Pecks and hammers, and gleans from bark and foliage.

FOOD Ants form the bulk of its insect food, which also comprises grubs and other larvae.

BREEDING Nestlings have been found in February; this and other records and our own observations indicate breeding in February-August.

REFERENCES Goodman & Gonzales 1990; Rabor 1977.

90 BROWN-CAPPED WOODPECKER
Picoides moluccensis   Plate 26

Other names: Sunda Woodpecker, Malaysian (Pygmy) Woodpecker (nominate group); Indian Pygmy Woodpecker (*nanus* group)

IDENTIFICATION Length c. 13cm. Very small to tiny, with shortish, rather straight, slightly chisel-tipped bill broad across nostrils. A diminutive, comparatively dingy-looking species. Western populations, often treated as a separate species, have white-barred black or blackish-brown upperparts, wings and tail and pale to very pale underparts with relatively little or no streaking; forehead to nape is brown to blackish, and a dark band through ear-coverts continues down side of neck; no moustache; has red ring around eye. Male has a small red line on side of hindcrown, generally invisible in the field. Eastern races are more streaked below and have a prominent broad moustache, but lack red eye-ring. All juveniles are streaked below.

Similar species Overlaps partly in range with Grey-capped Woodpecker (91). In the west, distinguished from latter by its smaller size, smaller bill and paler, less contrastingly patterned appearance, with paler and less streaked underparts, and its white-marked central tail; in the east, also by its broad dark moustache.

DISTRIBUTION Two discrete populations. In the west, occurs from Haryana, Rajasthan and Gujarat in NW India, east through the lower parts of Nepal to Bangladesh and south throughout peninsular India to Sri Lanka; earlier reports of its presence in N Pakistan appear to be erroneous. In the east, found in coastal W Malaysia, Singapore, Sumatra, including the Riau archipelago, Bangka and Belitung, Java, Bali, Borneo (mainly coastal, and including Maratua, off Kalimantan), and the Lesser Sundas from Lombok east to Alor. Common to fairly common in most its range, but rather local in parts (e.g. Sri Lanka); status in Bangladesh unclear, but appears to be at best uncommon.

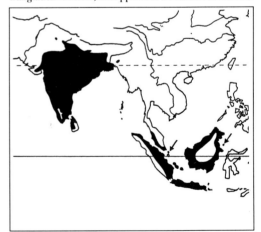

HABITAT Generally found in secondary forest and open-wooded park-like country. Frequents neglected estates with plenty of dead trees, plantations, gardens, and particularly coastal scrub, casuarina stands and mangrove. Increases in numbers in some areas where forests are opened up. A woodpecker of low elevations and coastal districts, also inhabiting hillsides at up to 1200m in Sri Lanka and up to 2300m in the Lesser Sundas.

DESCRIPTION
P. m. nanus **Adult male** Forehead to nape and hindneck

brown, sometimes tinged yellowish, with small red line at rear crown sides (usually concealed by overlying feathers). Broad dark brown band through ear-coverts, continuing irregularly down neck side, bordered above and to rear by broad white band. Lores, cheeks, moustachial area, chin and throat white or pale buffy-white. Upperparts blackish-brown, barred white; rump and uppertail-coverts white, spotted/barred blackish. Upperwing and its coverts blackish, coverts with elongated white spots or broad streaks at tips and flight feathers with white spots forming bars (spots smaller or lacking on outer webs of outer primaries). Uppertail blackish-brown, central feathers with white bar-like spots and outers barred white. Underparts white or off-white, with narrow brown streaks. Underwing and undertail barred brown and white.

Adult female Slightly larger than male. Lacks red on hindcrown.

Juvenile Very like adults, but browner and less contrastingly patterned. Males have orangey red patch on nape (more extensive than on adult).

Bare parts Bill grey, with pale inner half of lower mandible. Legs and feet greyish to green-grey. Eyes white to light brown. Orbital skin red.

GEOGRAPHICAL VARIATION Two discrete groups of races, often treated as two separate species.

(a) Western *nanus* group (lacks moustache, less streaked below; has red eye-ring):

    P. m. nanus (N India to Bangladesh and most of peninsular India, excluding southwest) Described above. Becomes darker clinally southwards ('*hardwickii*').

    P. m. cinereigula (SW India, in Kerala and W Tamil Nadu) Darker than *nanus*, especially on crown, and with underpart streaking very fine (can appear unstreaked). Juveniles more heavily streaked.

    P. m. gymnopthalmus (Sri Lanka) Small. Darker, more sooty-black, above, with blackish crown, and with less white in wings (but broader bars on secondaries); underparts washed with yellowish-brown and virtually unstreaked (except on juveniles).

(b) Eastern nominate group (shows strong moustachial stripe and heavier underpart streaking; darker eyes, lacking red orbital ring):

    P. m. moluccensis (Malaysia, Singapore and Greater Sundas) Blackish-brown crown; prominent dark moustache, continuing to breast side; underparts heavily streaked.

    P. m. grandis (Lesser Sundas: Lombok, Sumbawa, Flores, Lomblen and Alor) Bigger and longer-tailed than *moluccensis*; underparts often washed dirty yellow-buff and more finely streaked; moustache usually less solid (white-streaked), rump and uppertail-coverts generally less barred, but pale wingbars broader. Some clinal variation, tending to become larger and less heavily streaked from west to east.

MEASUREMENTS Wing 74-83 (*nanus*), 71-79 (*moluccensis*), 84-89 (*grandis*); tail 35-42 (*nanus*), 40-43 (*moluccensis*), 43-48 (*grandis*); bill (from skull) 14-17 (*nanus* group), 18-20 (*grandis*); tarsus 13-15 (*nanus* group). Weight: 13-18.

VOICE A common call is rendered *clickr-r-r*; also a weak *ti-ti-ti-ti-ti-ti-ti* or *kee-kee-kee-kee-kee-kee*. Drums at a rate of about seven rolls per minute; sound and tempo similar to drumming of Lesser Spotted Woodpecker (93), but longer and faster than Downy Woodpecker's (113).

HABITS Usually solitary, but also in pairs, family parties, and joins mixed-species flocks with tits and nuthatches.

Behaves in manner typical of a small woodpecker. Moves slowly over dead trees or dead parts of trees when foraging for ants and other insects. Prefers the smaller branches and twigs high up in the trees, and also forages on the thin stems of shrubs close to the ground. Hammers feverishly and loudly, but mostly only a few pecks are delivered. Gleaning from surfaces seems to be the most common feeding method; probing and prying under superficial layers of bark may also be observed. Flight rather like that of a small passerine.

FOOD Feeds on various insects, particularly ants and other hymenopterans, beetles and their larvae, caterpillars. Takes fruits and berries and flower nectar.

BREEDING Nests in (January)March-April(July) in India; in Sri Lanka in the same period, and under favourable conditions also October-December; March-July in Burma and Malaysia; and in the Greater and Lesser Sundas April-July, some in October. Hole is excavated in a dead branch, often on its underside, at 2-12m. Clutch comprises 2-3(4) eggs. Both sexes share hole construction and brood care.

REFERENCES Bernstein 1861; Henry 1971; MacKinnon 1990; Medway & Wells 1976; Phillips 1978; Rensch 1931; Short 1973a; Smythies 1981.

---

91 GREY-CAPPED WOODPECKER
Picoides canicapillus   **Plate 26**

Other name: Grey-headed Pygmy Woodpecker

IDENTIFICATION Length c. 14-16cm. Very small, with fairly long, almost straight, very slightly chisel-tipped bill broad across nostrils. Basically black and white in appearance, especially in northeast of range, with pale underparts streaked dark; has grey crown, dark band through ear-coverts and down neck side, and rather obscure dark moustache. Tail is black, with pale bars confined to outer feathers, but some SE Asian populations (Assam to Laos) have bars/spots also on central feathers. Males have a small red patch on nape side, generally invisible in the field, but those from E Nepal to N and W Assam have a larger (though still relatively small) area of red across the nape. Similar species See Brown-capped Woodpecker (90). In northeast, overlaps in range with Pygmy (92) and Lesser Spotted (93) Woodpeckers; Grey-capped differs from both in being slightly bigger and in having more black above, with white back and rump and mainly white wing-coverts, while Lesser Spotted also has a different head pattern.

DISTRIBUTION Ranges from lower Himalayas in N Pakistan and Himachal Pradesh, India, east through lower parts of Nepal and Bhutan to Arunachal Pradesh and south from Nagaland to Bangladesh, then east through Burma, S, C, E and NE China to Ussuriland and Korea and to Taiwan, extending south to Hainan and throughout SE Asia to Sumatra (including Riau archipelago and Nias) and Borneo. Locally common to fairly common in much of range, but uncommon in Hainan and rare and local in extreme northeast and northwest; apparently more common than Brown-capped Woodpecker in Bangladesh.

MOVEMENTS Minor altitudinal movements to lowlands take place in winter in the northern parts of its range.

HABITAT Corresponding with its wide distribution, is found in a great variety of forests and woodlands. In northern parts of range inhabits oak, deciduous and mixed forests. In Nepal, and Sikkim to SE Asia, occurs in closed as well as in more open forests, including sal forest, deciduous and open evergreen woodland, secondary growth, scrub and gardens; very dense (evergreen) forests are avoided. In mainland SE Asia also in shore vegetation, including casuarina and mangroves. In the Greater Sundas it frequents lowland forest, montane forest and pine forest and is found in jungle clearings. In Nepal, it is common in lowlands to 400m and infrequent at higher elevations up to 1350m. Ascends to 1830m in SE Asia, in Borneo it inhabits mainly the lowlands up to 1680m, and in Sumatra is found at 1000-2800m.

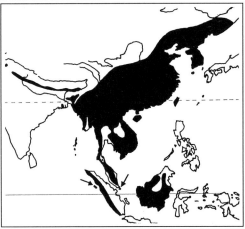

DESCRIPTION

P. c. semicoronatus **Adult male** Nasal tufts and lower forehead pale buff-brown; upper forehead and crown ash-grey, darker and blacker at sides, including on rear lores; rear crown sides red, meeting in narrow band across nape. Band through ear-coverts and down neck side to mantle dark brown, bordered by fairly broad white supercilium from above eye which continues as broad patch down rear neck side. Fore lores, cheeks and lower ear-coverts buffy-white, with thin, rather obscure submoustachial stripe. Chin and throat whitish, usually with some indistinct grey streaking. Hindneck narrowly black; upperparts black, barred white; uppertail-coverts black, occasionally with some white barring. Upperwing-coverts black, with variable amount of white at tips; flight feathers black, tipped white, and with white spots (forming broad bars on inner wing). Uppertail black, outer two or three feathers barred buffish-white. Underparts below throat whitish, strongly tinged yellow-brown or buff, sometimes even orangey, and streaked brown (streaks most pronounced on breast). Underwing brown, barred/spotted white. Undertail brown, often more buff at sides, and barred paler.

Adult female Averages slightly larger than male. Red of male's crown sides and nape replaced by black.

Juvenile Darker above than adults, with blackish crown, and darker below (never red), with heavier streaking and often a hint of barring. Males have orange-red on nape and rear crown sides, often more extensive than the red on adult.

Bare parts Bill grey to blackish, paler at base and on lower mandible. Legs and feet greyish to olive-grey. Eyes grey-brown to reddish-brown, sometimes paler grey or whitish. Orbital skin slate-grey.

GEOGRAPHICAL VARIATION

A very variable species, both in size and in plumage. Only the first race has red across the nape (males), all others having red reduced to a small spot or streak (often concealed) on nape side.

P. c. semicoronatus (easternmost Nepal east to W and N Assam) Described above. Intergrades with following race in E Nepal and with *canicapillus* in east of range.

P. c. mitchelli (N Pakistan, NW India and most of Nepal) Very like *semicoronatus*, but with red on male's nape restricted to a narrow lateral streak; brown of ear-coverts may extend to crown side.

P. c. canicapillus (E Assam, Bangladesh, C and S Burma, most of Thailand and Laos) Shorter-tailed than above races, and with brown tinge to plumage; tail barred or spotted on central feathers.

P. c. delacouri (Cambodia and S Vietnam) As *canicapillus*, but larger and with broader dark streaking below.

P. c. auritus (S Thailand and W Malaysia) As *canicapillus*, but slightly shorter-tailed and with blacker (less brown-toned) plumage; central tail barred on some, unmarked on others.

P. c. volzi (Sumatra) Lower underparts orangey or orange-gold on adults; central tail unmarked.

P. c. aurantiiventris (Borneo) Much as *volzi*, but longer-billed, shorter-tailed and slightly smaller (the smallest of all races). Submoustachial/malar stripe often more pronounced; central tail usually unmarked.

P. c. doerriesi (E Siberia, E Manchuria and Korea) The largest race. Distinctive. Mantle and upper back black, lower back and rump white, and uppertail-coverts black; wing-coverts with much white, forming patch, and wingbars broad; tail mostly black, with little or no white on outer feathers; pale below, with rather narrow streaking.

P. c. scintilliceps (N and E China, from Liaoning south to Sichuan and Zhejiang) Similar to *doerriesi*, but slightly smaller. Upper back barred white, and shows less white in wings (coverts with large spots towards tips); darker and more heavily streaked below.

P. c. kaleensis (SE China, from W and S Sichuan to Fujian, Taiwan, N Burma and northernmost Vietnam) As *scintilliceps* but more streaked below.

P. c. swinhoei (Hainan) Slightly smaller than *kaleensis*. Paler, whiter, below, with narrower streaking; more white in wings.

MEASUREMENTS Wing 81-87 (*auritus*), 83-91 (*canicapillus*), 84-94 (*mitchelli*), 90-105 (*scintilliceps*), 92-102 (*kaleensis*), 100-108 (*doerriesi*); tail 40-47 (*mitchelli*), 55-69 (*scintilliceps*), 61-64 (*kaleensis*); bill 17 (*mitchelli*), 15-20.5 (*scintilliceps*), 19-21.5 (*doerriesi*); tarsus 14.6-17 (*scintilliceps*). Weight: 20-27 (*mitchelli*), 21-32 (*scintilliceps*).

VOICE Call is a short, soft *cheep* or *pic* or *tzit*; as double-call *chip-chip*, the second note shorter and lower-pitched. When given in flight, call is uttered in unison with flight dips. The rattle, described as *tit-tit-erh-r-r-r-r-h*, *pic-chirru-chirru-chihihihi...* or *click-r-r-r*, is usually introduced by a call note, and contains six to about 20 variable call-note-like elements; similar rattles are given in interspecific encounters. Irregular series of squeaking notes, *kweek-kweek-kweek*, are associated with rattles and are uttered during encounters, e.g. between fledglings and adults. Low chirps are exchanged between members of a pair in close contacts. Nestlings call only when an adult is present. Drumming is muted, but may carry a long distance.

HABITS Solitary, but also in pairs and small family groups. Forages in crowns of tall trees and at edge on saplings and in bushes, where seeks out dead twigs or stubs, but most foraging is on (outer) twigs and branches, with little or no effort devoted to larger branches and tree trunks, from which it is also driven away by larger Fulvous-breasted Woodpecker (95). Does not peck and hammer at one spot for very long; does much gleaning, and occasionally removes a piece of bark or a lichen and probes into crevices and at the base of leaves. Frequently perches crosswise and hangs on twigs and leaf clusters, often upside-down. Altogether, this diminutive woodpecker gives a very active and agile impression as it moves through the canopy or hurries up a trunk, not pausing at any one site, often flying from branch to branch, and even fluttering to catch less accessible items. Excited and displaying birds raise their crest, in what is not a very conspicuous display. Bill-directing and slow body-swinging and tail-spreading during encounters are more obvious behaviours, the latter of which may also be performed in flight. Interspecific encounters involve Fulvous-breasted Woodpecker, which in most cases is superior.

FOOD The diet includes caterpillars, homopterans, small beetles, insect pupae, grubs, diptera, ants, and fruits. Seeds (grass) and other plant matter (e.g. carmine cherries) of some importance in winter.

BREEDING Breeds March-May in India and Borneo, one month earlier in Burma, and somewhat later in the northern parts of its range. Nest excavated by both sexes high up in a tree at 2.5-15m, in a branch, particularly on its underside. Clutch consists of 3-5 eggs in south of range and of 6-8 in north. It is incubated for 12-13 days by both sexes; both also feed the young and remove faeces except during the last two days before fledging (records of adult attendance during the night are doubtful and need study). The nestling period is about 21 days, and fledged young presumably stay with their parents for some time.

REFERENCES Ali 1962; Ali & Ripley 1970; Cheng 1964; Diesselhorst 1968; Fleming *et al.* 1984; Gore & Pyong-Oh 1971; Gyldenstolpe 1916; Inskipp & Inskipp 1991; King & Dickinson 1975; Knystautas & Sibnev 1987; Lekagul & Round 1991; MacKinnon 1990; MacKinnon & Phillipps 1993; Medway & Wells 1976; Poliwanowa *et al.* 1974; Roberts 1991; Robinson 1927; Short 1973a; Smythies 1953, 1981; Stanford & Mayr 1941; Winkler & Short 1978.

---

92 PYGMY WOODPECKER
Picoides kizuki　　　　　Plate 27

Other name: Japanese Pygmy Woodpecker

IDENTIFICATION Length c. 13-15cm. Very small, with short, straight, slightly chisel-tipped bill fairly broad across nostrils. A brownish, grey/black and white species with barred back and wings. Has characteristic head pattern, with grey crown and brown ear-coverts, with white above eye and on neck sides, white moustache and brown/grey malar. Dark colour of ear-coverts and malar extends onto breast sides, and breast is often suffused brownish, forming breast band and isolating unmarked white throat (spotted on juveniles), with rest of underparts pale and variably streaked. Male has small red patch on nape sides, this normally concealed by overlying feathers. Usually occurs in pairs throughout year, and joins mixed feeding flocks when not breeding.

Similar species Overlaps partly in range with Grey-capped Woodpecker (91) in E Siberia, where latter is slightly but noticeably bigger and has much more black above (with white back and rump) and large area of white above ear-coverts. In same region may meet similar-sized Lesser Spotted Woodpecker (93), which appears much more black-and-white and has very different head pattern.

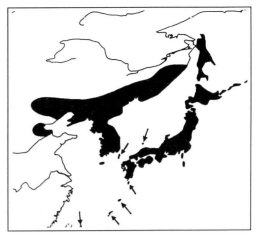

DISTRIBUTION Korea, NE China and the Ussuri and Amur regions of SE Siberia, and from Sakhalin and the southern Kuriles south through Japan (including most of its islands) to Iriomote in the Ryukyu Islands. Fairly common, and in Japan the commonest woodpecker (found even in the centre of Tokyo), but rarer in south of range.

MOVEMENTS Some altitudinal movements to the lowlands take place in winter, at least in the continental parts of its range.

HABITAT The habitats of this common woodpecker range from lowland woods to subalpine mixed-coniferous forest, and from subtropical evergreen to northern boreal forests with firs and birches. It occupies broadleaf deciduous and mixed forests in the riverine lowlands of Ussuri region. Besides deciduous woodland, it may occupy light pine (*Pinus densiflora*) stands in Japan and dense, montane coniferous forest in Korea. In Japan it has extended its range to parks and gardens, even in major cities. Ranges from sea level to 1300m on the mainland and to just above 2100m in Japan.

DESCRIPTION
P. k. ijimae **Adult male** Forehead and crown grey-brown, becoming browner at rear and on hindneck. Thin white supercilium from above rear of eye, very narrow (sometimes interrupted) at nape, continuing as broad white band down rear neck side to side of breast; small red patch at side of nape. Ear-coverts to front edge of neck side brown (greyer near eye), this colour continuing to breast side. Lores whitish, joining with white moustachial stripe, latter bordered below by grey-brown malar stripe. Chin and throat white. Upper mantle dark brown; lower mantle, scapulars, back and rump darker brown, all barred white; uppertail-coverts blackish-brown. Upperwing-coverts and flight feathers brownish-black, barred white (coverts with large subterminal white spots). Uppertail blackish on central feathers, adjacent two pairs with white at tip, outer two pairs white with dark brown bars. Underparts white, with pale brown suffusion on breast and upper belly, and streaked brown on breast, upper flanks and belly, streaks coalescing on breast. Underwing barred brown and white. Undertail as uppertail, but paler.

Adult female Slightly larger than male in wing, bill and tail. Lacks red spot on nape sides.

Juvenile Underparts greyer than on adults, with streaked/spotted throat. Male has small patch of red in crown centre.

Bare parts Bill grey-black, paler at base. Legs and feet grey.

257

Eyes brown to red-brown.

GEOGRAPHICAL VARIATION Varies clinally, becoming smaller and more saturated dark from north to south. Four races are recognised here; a number of island races have been described, but these differ insignificantly from populations on main islands.

P. k. ijimae (S Ussuriland, probably NE Korea and adjacent eastern Manchuria, also Sakhalin, southern Kuriles and Hokkaido) Described above. Largest and palest race.

P. k. seebohmi (Korea except northeast, also Quelpart Islands and Honshu) Smaller and darker than *ijimae*, with less white on upperparts and wing-coverts; heavier streaks below.

P. k. amamii (Amami and Tokunoshima in N Ryukyus) Blacker above, and with rich buff-brown on flanks; undertail-coverts barred.

P. k. kizuki (NE China; Tsushima, Kyushu, Shikoku, Izu Islands, and all but smallest islands south to Iriomote) Smaller and darker than *seebohmi*, with much brown on neck side and and with heavy streaking on flanks; undertail-coverts slightly barred. Most populations on the smaller islands are a trifle larger, equal to *seebohmi*.

MEASUREMENTS Wing 79-95; tail 43-54; bill 15.5-18; tarsus 13-15. Weight: 18-26.

VOICE Calls are a single, unmistakable *khit* or *khit-khit-khit* and, even more common, buzzing *kzz, kzz* notes. Drumming, which commences in late winter and continues to the breeding season, is weak and does not carry far; it consists of very short bursts delivered in rapid succession.

HABITS Met with singly, in pairs or in family parties, frequently in mixed-species tit and nuthatch flocks. An active little woodpecker, it hammers and excavates the bark of thin trunks and twigs and also visits stronger herbaceous plants. During the breeding season, gleaning in the canopy is the predominant foraging method.

FOOD Mainly arthropods, namely insects and their pupae, caterpillars, weevils, aphids, small ants (*Lasius, Formica*), and spiders. Exceptionally, small lizards. Some berries (*Rhus*) are taken.

BREEDING Breeding season in Japan commences in March in the south and in late May/early June in the north; in the Amur-Ussuri region, it starts in late April and extends to end of May. Nests are dug into soft, rotten stumps at heights of 2-7(10)m. Clutch consists of 5-7(9) eggs, which are incubated for 12-14 days. The chicks fledge after three weeks. One instance of helping by a third adult has been recorded.

REFERENCES Brazil 1991; Chiba 1969; Dement'ev & Gladkov 1966; Gore & Pyong-Oh 1971; Ishida & Ueta 1992; Knystautas & Sibnev 1987; Matsuoka 1979; Voous 1947; Yamagami 1992.

93 LESSER SPOTTED WOODPECKER
Picoides minor   Plate 27

IDENTIFICATION Length 14-16cm. Very small and compact, with short, chisel-tipped bill broad across nostrils. Essentially a 'black-and-white' woodpecker, with strikingly barred back and wings distinctive in the field. Underparts variably whitish to brown-buff, usually with at least some streaking. Strong black moustache contrasts with pale buffish/dusky ear-coverts and white patch on neck sides. Male has red on crown, often mottled pale, this area being white or dusky white on female. In west of range, small size, barred upperparts and lack of red or pink on vent easily identify it. Often unobtrusive, however, and easily overlooked; often feeds in tops of trees. Drums fairly frequently, but rather weakly.

Similar species None in west; in eastern parts of range, may overlap slightly with equally small Pygmy Woodpecker (92), but latter has extensive brown on ear-coverts and upper breast and both sexes have grey-brown crown. Also in east, Grey-capped Woodpecker (91) is somewhat bigger, has white patches in wing, and both sexes have very dark grey crown and broad dark eye-stripe.

DISTRIBUTION Immense range extends from W Europe, including Britain, in the west, all across Russia to Kamchatka and E Siberia in the east. Reaches N Africa in south; southern limits otherwise Eurasia from Spain, through Anatolia, the Caucasus, Iran, Mongolia and Manchuria, to N Korea and Japan (Hokkaido).

MOVEMENTS Northern populations partly migratory; N European birds may get into C Europe and to the Black Sea. Migration often of an irruptive nature, parallel with the movements of Great Spotted Woodpeckers (104). Autumn migration mainly late August to November.

HABITAT In the northern Palearctic this small woodpecker is restricted to temperate and boreal deciduous woodland of the lowlands, responding negatively to forest fragmentation and admixture of conifers, at least for breeding. Open forests with softwood deciduous trees are preferred. Occurs also at forest edge, in parks, orchards, and in gardens. A good number of snags, as found in old stands or in riparian woodland, are also required. In N Africa, restricted to cork-oak forest. In Polish primeval forest, found mainly in ash-alder and oak-hornbeam stands, where mean density about 0.25 territories/10ha, maximum 0.8/10ha (ash-alder), densities elsewhere usually being below 0.1/10ha. Inhabits lowlands and foothills at up to 850m, locally to 1260m, in Europe. Found at higher elevations in the Caucasus (up to 1400-2000m), the Altai (1700m) and in Mongolia (1400m); to 1300m in N Africa.

DESCRIPTION

P. m. minor **Adult male** Forehead and lores white, tinged buff; crown crimson-red, usually with some pale feather bases showing through, bordered by narrow black lines which broaden on nape sides; nape and hindneck black. Sides of head (including patch behind upper rear of eye) and neck sides white, with buff tinge to ear-coverts. Moustachial stripe from lower bill base black, expanding on neck side and extending slightly upwards around rear of ear-coverts and irregularly down neck side to upper breast side. Chin and throat white. Upper mantle and scapulars black; lower mantle and lower scapulars to upper rump white, barred black; lower rump and uppertail-coverts black. Upperwing-coverts black, median and greater coverts with broad white spots/bars near tips; flight feathers, including tertials, black, broadly barred white. Uppertail

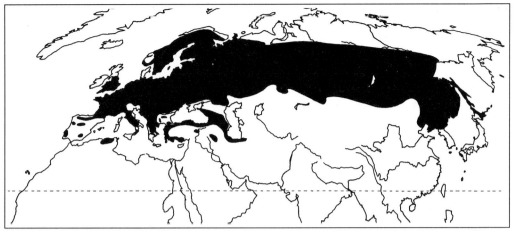

black, outer feathers mainly white with two or three dark bars near tip. Underparts from breast white, with slight buff tinge, breast sides and flanks with narrow black streaks and undertail-coverts usually spotted black. Underwing barred grey and white. Undertail as uppertail. (In worn plumage, buff tinges to pale areas are lost, producing much whiter appearance.)

Adult female As male, but lacks red on head: has forecrown white or buffish-white, bordered at sides by black which extends across hindcrown (white area thus smaller than male's red).

Juvenile Duller than adults, with black areas tinged brown, and pale forehead patch obscured by darker feather tips; underparts more heavily streaked, but streaks duller and less well defined. Male has pinkish-red forecrown mottled grey/brown, less extensive than adult's red; female has pale forecrown obscured by dark feather tips and usually with a few reddish tips.

Bare parts Bill dark grey to blackish, with paler base to lower mandible. Legs and feet greenish-grey. Eyes red-brown or brownish.

GEOGRAPHICAL VARIATION Many races have been named over this species' huge range, but often on very weak grounds. Intergrading populations occur in many parts, while differences are often part of a clinal variation. We recognise 11 races here: three 'northern' and eight 'southern' ones. For fuller treatment of subspecies, see Vaurie (1965) and Roselaar (in Cramp & Simmons 1985).

(a) 'Northern' races:

P. m. minor (Scandinavia and N Continental Europe, east of Baltic, to Urals) Described above. A large and long-tailed race. N Scandinavian (Lapland) populations tend to be whiter and less streaked (sometimes separated as 'transitivus' = 'lonnbergi'). Intergrades with *hortorum* in south and with *kamtschatkensis* in east.

P. m. kamtschatkensis (Urals east to Kamchatka and Anadyr river) The largest race, long-winged, and with proportionately longer bill than nominate. Very pale, with dense, fluffy plumage: pale areas of plumage more or less white, with white bars on upperparts very broad (back almost all white), and virtually unstreaked below; white outer tail feathers with only one small bar. Populations in easternmost Siberia (often separated as 'immaculatus') are particularly white, especially on back and underparts, and completely unmarked below.

P. m. amurensis (lower Amur river, Ussuriland, NE Manchuria, NE Korea, Sakhalin and Hokkaido) Very like nominate, but more heavily barred with black

above and slightly greyer below, where usually somewhat more streaked. Intergrades with previous race in west of range.

(b) 'Southern' races:

P. m. hortorum (from France east to Poland and south to Hungary and Switzerland) Has slightly less white on back than nominate; underparts distinctly darker, buff or light brown, sometimes with pink tinge on throat/upper breast, flanks more heavily streaked, and outer rectrices more barred. Intergrades with nominate in north and east of range and with *buturlini* in south.

P. m. buturlini (Iberia, southern France, Italy, Greece and Romania) Smaller and shorter-tailed than nominate. Even darker and more heavily streaked below than *hortorum*, with which intergrades in southern France.

P. m. ledouci (NW Africa) A doubtful race. Very like *buturlini*, but usually has all-black bill, pale areas of head and throat/breast perhaps even darker (buff-brown), and may be more heavily streaked below; may show some black at rear of ear-coverts. Often, however, indistinguishable from *buturlini* (especially Iberian populations of latter).

P. m. comminutus (Britain) Slightly smaller than *buturlini* but similarly dark below, though with much fainter streaks; pale bars above slightly narrower than in *hortorum*.

P. m. danfordi (Greece and Turkey) Size as *comminutus*. Very like *buturlini*, but a touch browner below; has (usually complete) black band from hindcrown around rear ear-coverts to rear moustache. Intergrades with *buturlini* in north of range.

P. m. colchicus (Caucasus and Transcaucasia, except Lenkoran region) Slightly bigger than *danfordi* and with more white above; has some black at rear of ear-coverts (sometimes as broken band, less complete than in *danfordi*). Those in Transcaucasia resemble eastern populations of *buturlini* (though latter lack black behind ear-coverts).

P. m. quadrifasciatus (Lenkoran area of SE Transcaucasia) Small and short-billed. Similar to *buturlini*, but pale areas slightly darker buff-brown; spots/bars on wings narrower (appears blacker), and median coverts wholly black; some may show hint of black band joining moustache with nape. Flanks heavily streaked dark, sometimes with some barring, and outer rectrices heavily barred black.

P. m. morgani (NW Iran and Zagros mountains) A highly distinctive race. Bill very long and narrow.

Upper breast (sometimes also chin and throat) deep buffish-brown, contrasting with rest of underparts, which are white, with breast and flanks very sharply and heavily streaked black. Broad black band joins rear moustache with nape. Intergrades with *colchicus* in NW Iran (where population sometimes separated as '*hyrcanus*').

MEASUREMENTS Wing 83-86 (*ledouci*), 85-94 (*hortorum*), 90-100 (*minor*); tail 49-51 (*ledouci*), 48-57 (*hortorum*), 56-65 (*minor*); bill 14-18 (*hortorum*), 15.5-19 (*minor*); tarsus 13.8-15.2 (*ledouci*), 14-17 (*hortorum*), 14-16.5 (*minor*). Weight: 16-25 (*hortorum*), 18-22 (*comminutus*), 19-26 (*minor*).

VOICE Single call note *gig*, rarely heard. A series of notes, *gee-geegeegee...*, is most common. Utters *whuit* or *shwicka* notes in aggressive encounters, and low notes, soft *keer-keer* and *sht-sht*, during changeovers at nest and during copulation. Displays at nest include demonstrative tapping. Both sexes drum; The high-pitched, long rolls, delivered at a rate of 14-19 per minute, are distinctive and often interspersed with call-series at the height of the courtship period. Acoustically most active in the breeding season, from March to May.

HABITS Mostly met with singly; may join (generally singly) tit flocks in winter. Because of its small size and its quiet nature when foraging in the canopy or dense vegetation, this species is easily overlooked. Prefers to seek its food from (vertical) twigs (1-3cm in diameter) in the canopy, rarely on the trunk or base of large trees; descends to lower levels mainly to visit bushes and stalks of various plants, particularly reed and occasionally corn. Foraging techniques include gleaning, hammering, series of pecks to dislodge large pieces of bark, and probing. As with other species, is very opportunistic when needing to provide food for chicks, although gleaning prevails. Even persistent probing at the base of large trunks can be observed when weather conditions prohibit proficient use of other foraging techniques. May also flycatch and visit the sap holes made by other woodpecker species (Great Spotted, Middle Spotted), but does not seem to ring trees itself. Moves restlessly through the canopy, stopping only for extended hammering. Most conspicuous displays are wing- and tail-spreading and a characteristic flutter-aerial display, a gliding flight with wings held well above back, particularly upon landing. Stabbing bill movements, gaping, crest-raising, wing-flicking and wing-spreading are commonly employed behaviours in agonistic situations. Interactions occur with Great Spotted Woodpeckers, flycatchers and starlings at holes.

FOOD Small insects comprise the main bulk of the diet. Caterpillars, aphids, ants, beetles (e.g. chrysomelids) and other surface-dwelling arthropods are taken mainly in summer; in winter, wood-boring larvae (e.g. cerambycids) and those living under the bark (e.g. Ipidae) become important. Eats hardly any vegetable matter, but occasionally takes fruit and berries, and consumes seeds at feeders.

BREEDING Significant courtship activities begin in February; the breeding season extends to May. Both sexes (male's share often greater) work on the nest for (from six days to) 2-4 weeks. Roost and nest holes are excavated in the soft wood of a dead or decaying trunk, stump or the underside of a branch; rarely, will accept a nestbox for roosting or breeding. Nest height 0.4-20m, mostly 2-8m; in primeval forest of Poland, mean nest height 11.1m. Copulations (10-15 secs duration) take place close to the nest and are often interspersed with hole construction. Clutches of 5-6 (4-9) eggs are produced end of April to mid May (June). Incubation by both sexes (male's part often

greater), for 10-12 days; the male usually roosts in the nest. Chicks stay 19-21(23) days in the nest, and are cared for by parents for a further week or two.

REFERENCES Bezzel 1985; Blume 1968; Brazil 1991; Cramp 1985; Dement'ev & Gladkov 1966; Glutz & Bauer 1980; László 1988; Miech 1986; Olsson *et al.* 1992; Pynnönen 1939; Short 1988; Spitznagel 1993; Vaurie 1965; Wesolowski & Tomialojc 1986; Wiktander *et al.* 1991; Winkler 1972a; Winkler & Short 1978.

94 BROWN-FRONTED WOODPECKER
Picoides auriceps   Plate 28

IDENTIFICATION Length 19-20cm. Small, with medium-long, slightly chisel-tipped bill with barely curved culmen and broad across nostrils. Barred black and white above and heavily streaked below, with pinky-red down centre of belly and on undertail-coverts. The face is white with a darker patch on ear-coverts and a black moustache, latter with extension onto breast side. Both sexes have brown forehead, male with yellow crown becoming red on nape, female with duller yellow crown and nape. Drums frequently at start of breeding season.

Similar species Fulvous-breasted Woodpecker (95) is similar in size but longer-billed, less streaked below, and has red or black crown. Slightly smaller Yellow-crowned Woodpecker (97) is confusable, but has upperparts more spotted or 'marbled' (less barred), more closely barred wings and brighter crown (feathers often raised), and lacks dark moustache (but has dark on throat and sides of neck). Larger Himalayan Woodpecker (108), found at higher elevations, and Sind Woodpecker (107) are easily distinguished by their unbarred back, large white wing patches, red or black crown, and unstreaked underparts.

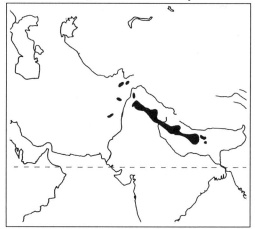

DISTRIBUTION A locally common woodpecker, occurring from Nuristan in Afghanistan, eastwards through parts of Pakistan and N India to E Nepal.

MOVEMENTS Descends to lower altitudes in winter.

HABITAT Resides in coniferous and pine-oak forest and montane dry deciduous forests; can also be found in park-like woodland and secondary growth. In Pakistan, confined to the subtropical 'Chir' pine belt (*Pinus roxburghii, P. longifolia*) and also frequents *P. gerardiana* forests and cedar stands. Breeds to at least 2100m in Afghanistan, at

900-1800m in Pakistan, with stragglers recorded at up to 3000m, and reaches 3100m in Nepal.

DESCRIPTION

Adult male Forehead and forecrown dull brown to yellow-brown, becoming yellower from mid crown and with orangey-red nape patch. Supercilium and sides of head and neck white, with grey-brown feather tips forming darker patch on lores and ear-coverts. Narrow submoustachial stripe buffish browny-grey, becoming black and broader at rear and continuing down onto upper breast side. Chin and throat white, tinged brown or grey (only when fresh?). Central hindneck and entire upperparts black, barred white on mantle and back. Upperwing-coverts black, greaters and some medians tipped white; flight feathers brownish-black, barred/spotted white. Uppertail black, outer feathers barred white. Underparts from breast white, tinged yellow on lower breast and flanks and becoming pink or orangey on central belly and undertail-coverts; broadly streaked black on breast, streaks becoming paler and narrower on lower underparts and sometimes lacking on belly. Underwing barred dark grey and white. Undertail as uppertail.

Adult female As male, but shorter-billed and longer-tailed, and with different head pattern: crown duller yellow, sometimes greener, this colour continuing to hindcrown/nape (thus lacks red, though occasionally shows hint of orange).

Juvenile Duller than adults, with darker (browner) ear-coverts, and greyer below (lacks yellow tinge) with paler pink ventral area. Crown pattern much as adult female's, but sometimes streaked, males with trace of red in hindcrown and females with orange/yellow in hindcrown.

Bare parts Bill slate-grey to horn-blue, darkest on culmen and tip, with paler base to lower mandible. Legs and feet grey-green to slate-grey. Eyes red-brown to red (duller in females).

GEOGRAPHICAL VARIATION Monotypic. Size decreases clinally from west to east. Some females in C Nepal have brighter, more golden-yellow nape than those further west, but this feature is not constant.

MEASUREMENTS Wing 105-130; tail 68-73; bill 21-24; tarsus 18-20. Weight: 37-50.

VOICE The call note is rendered as *chick* or *peek*, and is more squeaky than Himalayan Woodpecker's, resembling call of Rufous-bellied (99). The rattle is described as kingfisher-like, *chitter-chitter-chitter-r-r-rh* or *cheek-cheek-cheek-rrrr*. The *wicka*-call is a *tu-whit*. Drums frequently in the breeding season.

HABITS Forages singly or in pairs, and often joins mixed flocks of tits and minivets. Foraging is mostly confined to trees and bushes. Alleged sap-sucking requires corroboration. Nestboxes are accepted for roosting.

FOOD Insects and their larvae; caterpillars, grubs. Commonly takes vegetable matter, fruits, berries and pine seeds.

BREEDING Breeding season spans April to July. Nest holes are excavated in the (dead) trunks or in (the underside of) large branches of pines, elms and presumably other tall trees, at 2-12 m. Clutch comprises 3-5, mostly 4, eggs. The chicks are fed by both parents.

REFERENCES Christison & Ticehurst 1943; Diesselhorst 1968; Fleming *et al.* 1984; Inskipp & Inskipp 1991; Löhrl & Thielcke 1969; Proud 1958; Roberts 1991; Whistler 1930; Whistler & Kinnear 1946.

95 FULVOUS-BREASTED WOODPECKER
Picoides macei **Plate 28**

Other names: Streak-bellied Woodpecker, Spotted-breasted Pied Woodpecker
Forms a superspecies with *atratus*.

IDENTIFICATION Length 18-19cm. Small, with long, straight, chisel-tipped bill broad across nostrils. Looks pale-faced with contrasting black moustache and red or black crown; upperparts strongly barred black and white (white bars at least as wide as black ones). Red or pink on lower belly and undertail-coverts. In western populations, which generally lack barring on uppertail-coverts and central tail, underparts are fairly strong buff with rather distinct streaking on breast sides; eastern populations have upper-most mantle unbarred but wholly barred uppertail-coverts and tail, and much paler underparts with smaller dark spots/streaks across breast. Usually rather tame. Drums weakly, and has soft chattering call when foraging.

Similar species In west of range may occur in same areas as Brown-fronted Woodpecker (94), though latter is usually found at higher altitudes and is best distinguished by much shorter bill, heavier streaking on under parts, and yellow and red (male) or dull yellow (female) crown. In east, overlaps somewhat with Stripe-breasted Woodpecker (96), which, however, has very bold stripes over almost entire underparts, broader black bars above, unbarred central tail and (male) more red on head, and also tends to occur at higher elevations.

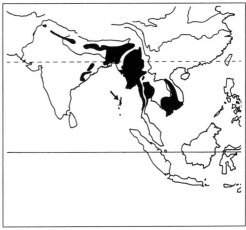

DISTRIBUTION Inhabits S Asian lowlands and foothills, from N Pakistan east to Arunachal Pradesh and then south to Orissa and NE Andhra Pradesh, continuing eastwards to Burma, NW and C Thailand, the southern half of Laos, Cambodia, and southern Vietnam (south Annam, Cochinchina), and also the Andaman Islands, Java and Bali; also recorded in Sumatra, but status there uncertain. Common to locally common, but uncommon in e.g. Thailand and rare in Pakistan.

HABITAT Prefers open forest, forest edge, secondary forest, open country with scattered trees, plantations, and gardens. Also occurs in bamboo stands, sparse woodland, single trees and larger bushes along dry river beds. In the Himalayas, it is found in tall stands of deciduous forest, especially mixed *Bombax-Ficus* woods; in Pakistan, also occurs in tropical dry deciduous scrub. Habitats cover a wide altitudinal range from lowlands to hills and mountains: in SE Asia below 1200m (usually below 600m in Thailand to Vietnam), but up to 2000m in the Greater Sundas and in the Himalayas, where it occasionally reaches 2440m and even higher elevations (2750m).

DESCRIPTION

P. m. westermani **Adult male** Lower forehead buffish; upper forehead, crown and upper nape crimson-red, with some black feather bases showing through. Lores, sides of head and neck sides white, tinged pale buffish (especially on ear-coverts). Moustachial stripe black, expanding at rear and continuing slightly onto upper breast side. Chin and throat unmarked buffish. Lower nape, hindneck and upperparts black, with very broad white bars from mantle to upper rump; lower rump and uppertail-coverts black. Upperwing-coverts black, tipped broadly white; flight feathers black, barred white. Uppertail black, outer one or two feather pairs barred white. Underparts from breast buffish-brown, occasionally tinged reddish, sometimes becoming browner on belly and flanks, and with central lower belly to undertail-coverts red; sides of breast streaked blackish, lower flanks and belly sometimes barred (faintly or more obviously). Underwing barred dark grey and whitish. Undertail as uppertail. (In worn plumage, becomes whiter, less buff, with streaking more distinct.)

Adult female As male, but entire top of head black.

Juvenile Duller above and below than adults, and with only small area of pink (not red) on undertail-coverts. Both sexes show some red in crown centre, greatly reduced on females.

Bare parts Bill blackish-grey, paler (sometimes bluish) at base. Legs and feet grey-green to dark greenish-slate. Eyes red-brown. Orbital skin slate-coloured.

GEOGRAPHICAL VARIATION Five races are recognised, in two main groups.

(a) Western *macei* group (less barred above and on tail, darker below, and proportionately longer-tailed):

    P. m. westermanni (Pakistan to western Nepal) Described above.

    P. m. macei (C Nepal and E India east to N Burma) Shorter-winged, shorter-tailed and shorter-billed than *westermanni*, and slightly paler on throat, which contrasts more with breast. A few may show some spots/bars on central tail feathers.

(b) Eastern *analis* group (uppertail-coverts and tail completely barred, paler below with more markings on breast, and proportionately shorter-tailed):

    P. m. analis (Java and Bali) Fully barred from mantle to tail; entire nape black; ear-coverts with distinct buff-brown tinge. Below, has white throat and only pale yellow-buff tinge to breast, latter with small blackish spots/streaks forming indistinct 'necklace', and much reduced streaks/bars on belly and flanks; lower ventral region pink (red in all other races).

    P. m. longipennis (S Burma east to Vietnam) Underparts have even paler yellowish tinge than in *analis*, but undertail-coverts a deeper red-pink; markings below more prominent, with broader spots/streaks forming 'necklace' (extending to lower breast) and thin bars on flanks. Some have virtually unspotted central tail feathers (approaching *macei* group).

    P. m. andamanensis (Andaman Islands) A distinctive pale-billed race with proportionately longer tail than others in this group. Throat white with a few spots on lower part, upper breast with large rounded or heart-shaped spots, lower breast with faint streaks, and upper belly and flanks prominently barred; neck sides slightly streaked black. Males have entire nape as well as crown

strongly red, and female has distinct brown tone to crown.

MEASUREMENTS Wing 100-120 (*macei*), 93-102 (*analis*); tail 54-71 (*macei*), 55-60 (*andamanensis*); bill 21-30 (*macei*), 17-20 (*andamanensis*); tarsus 17-18 (*macei*). Weight: 38-53 (*macei*).

VOICE Call note is an explosive *tchick*, sharper than that of sympatric Grey-capped Woodpecker (91), but less sharp and less loud than Stripe-breasted Woodpecker's, and is uttered as single note or in indistinct series. Infrequently, these calls are given as double *pik-pik* or *chik-it-chik-it*. The rattle commences with a call note and contains about a dozen similar, slightly lower-pitched *pit*-like notes, terminating with a call note separated by a short pause; slower than the rattle of Grey-capped. During prolonged encounters squeaking calls can be heard, and a soft chattering *chik-a-chik-a-chit* represents this species' *wicka*-call. Drums weakly in short rolls of 1-2 secs duration.

HABITS May be observed singly or in pairs, or in family parties of five or six individuals, and in mixed-species flocks. An arboreal species favouring tall trees, which may be isolated in open areas near forest. Forages on trunks and larger branches and also way up under the crown and in the foliage of the crown on small branches and large twigs; rarely at lower levels (maybe more so on islands, e.g. Andamans), or on the ground in search of ants. Feeding techniques include gleaning, probing and strong pecks and hammering, and bark is prised off. Less agile than sympatric and smaller Grey-capped Woodpecker, lingering occasionally at one site; in latter situation, has been recorded being supplanted by Grey-capped (pers. obs.). Displays with crest-raising, swinging movements, bill-directing, tail-spreading, wing-flicks, and wing-spreading. In intense display the tail may be spread, the body held straight with the bill in line and pointing upwards, and the head swung moderately from side to side. A fluttering aerial display has also been described. May interact with Grey-capped Woodpecker, which it normally supplants.

FOOD Feeds on ants, a variety of other insects, (large) larvae, and small scorpions. Berries and fruits are also taken.

BREEDING Breeds from April to June in Pakistan, India, Nepal and Burma, and from January to March in Thailand and in the Andamans; in Java mostly between April and October, rarely January. The nest, in a branch (often on underside) of a free-standing tree, in a fence post or palm stub in open ground at the edge of the forest, is excavated by both sexes at 1-5m. Clutch contains 2-5, normally 3, eggs. Both parents incubate and feed the young.

REFERENCES Abdulali 1964; Ali & Ripley 1970; Diesselhorst 1968; Fleming *et al.* 1984; Herbert 1926; Inskipp & Inskipp 1991; King & Dickinson 1975; Lekagul & Round 1991; MacKinnon 1990; MacKinnon & Phillipps 1993; Osmaston 1906; Proud 1936; Roberts 1991; Short 1973a; Smythies 1953; Stresemann & Heinrich 1940; Tikader 1984; Winkler & Short 1978.

96 STRIPE-BREASTED WOODPECKER
Picoides atratus   Plate 28

Forms a superspecies with *macei*.

IDENTIFICATION Length 21-22cm. Smallish, with long, straight, chisel-tipped bill broad across nostrils. A broad-bodied species with boldly barred upperparts and conspicuously striped underparts (in worn plumage stripes even more striking, resemble tyre marks). Has whitish face with contrasting black moustache and bright red (male) or black (female) crown and nape. Only outer tail is barred white. Red on undertail-coverts. Frequently utters loud, positive *chik* call typical of genus, stronger than that of Fulvous-breasted Woodpecker (95).

Similar species Likely to be confused only with Fulvous-breasted in east of latter's range. Eastern Fulvous-breasted, however, is much less heavily marked below, and has even broader white bars above (looks more white than black), fully barred tail, less intense red on undertail-coverts, less red on head (male) and a weaker-looking bill, and generally occurs at lower elevations.

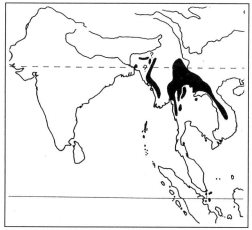

DISTRIBUTION From NE India in Khasi and Cachar hills, Manipur and possibly Nagaland (also reported from C and SE Bangladesh) to S and E Burma and SW Yunnan, south to NW Thailand and Laos. Fairly common locally to uncommon.

HABITAT A woodpecker of open oak and pine woodland in hill evergreen forest; prefers pine forest, but also occupies edges of open broadleaf forest. Also occurs in cultivated areas and in clearings with scattered trees. Found at altitudes between 800 and 2800m, but mostly above 2000m.

DESCRIPTION
Adult male Lower forehead dark; upper forehead to nape bright red (rarely with some admixed yellow), usually with some black streaks (especially at sides of crown). Sides of head, to just above eye, and neck sides white, usually with a few narrow black streaks. Moustachial stripe black, expanding on neck side and with extension to upper breast side. Chin and throat white, lower (and sometimes upper) throat sparsely streaked black. Central hindneck and entire upperparts black, broadly barred white from lower mantle to upper rump. Upperwing-coverts black, with large white subterminal spots (much smaller on lesser coverts); flight feathers black, barred white (broadly on tertials). Uppertail

black, with white bars on outer two (sometimes three) feather pairs. Underparts from breast pale greyish-yellow, yellower on upper belly, with long, broad, black streaks over entire area down to lower belly (occasionally lacking on central belly), and slightly barred on flanks; undertail-coverts tipped bright red, this colour extending to lowermost belly. Underwing dark grey, barred whitish. Undertail much as uppertail, but paler. (In worn plumage, sides of head appear very white and underparts are paler, off-white, with striped effect even more obvious.)

Adult female Slightly shorter-billed but longer-tailed than male. Lacks red on head, crown and nape being entirely black.

Juvenile Duller than adults, greyer below and with lower underparts more orangey; more broadly but more obscurely streaked below. Males have dark red on crown; females have a few red-tipped feathers in mid crown only.

Bare parts Bill horn-brown to dark grey, sometimes tinged greenish, with paler (sometimes yellowish) base to lower mandible. Legs and feet grey, often tinged blue or greenish. Eyes brown to brownish-red.

GEOGRAPHICAL VARIATION None known. Monotypic.

MEASUREMENTS Wing 110-120; tail 65-72; bill 24-26; tarsus 18-19. Weight: 42-52.

VOICE Calls with an explosive *tchick*, very like that of Great Spotted Woodpecker (104) and typical of the genus; this call is heard frequently when parents accompany young. Also a whinnying rattle call, and a squeaking call of unknown context. Probably drums.

HABITS Little known. Pecking and hammering seem to be rather important feeding modes. Adults and young seem to keep close together, giving frequent contact calls.

FOOD Insects, particularly beetle larvae and ants.

BREEDING Breeding recorded in N Thailand in February, fledged birds in March; breeds March-May in India and April-May in Burma. Nests in stump, usually below 4m, but also rather high up (to 20m) in a tree. Clutch comprises 4-5 eggs and is incubated by both sexes.

REFERENCES Ali & Ripley 1970; King & Dickinson 1975; Lekagul & Round 1991; Smythies 1953; Stresemann & Heinrich 1940.

97 YELLOW-CROWNED WOODPECKER
Picoides mahrattensis   Plate 28

Other names: Yellow-fronted Woodpecker, Mahratta Pied Woodpecker

IDENTIFICATION Length c. 17-18cm. Small, with long, fairly straight, slightly chisel-tipped bill broad across nostrils. Strongly black and white above, with mainly white rump, and barred wings and tail. Has obscure pale moustache, but shows much dark brown on face and underparts, with orangey-red on belly (not extending to undertail-coverts). Forehead and crown are golden-yellow, on males becoming red at rear and on nape (which has slight crest), while females have a much browner hindcrown and nape. Fairly tame, but tends to keep to middle and upper levels of trees; often rather silent and easy to overlook.

Similar species Very like Brown-fronted Woodpecker (94), but latter is somewhat bigger, has more barred (less scaly or 'marbled') upperparts, dark moustache, pinkish undertail-coverts, and only outer tail barred; where the two overlap, Brown-fronted generally occurs at higher elevations.

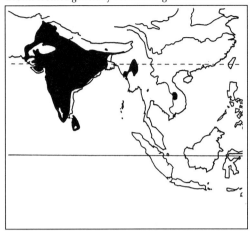

DISTRIBUTION A mainly lowland, arid-country species, occurring from the plains of the Indus in Pakistan (north to about 35°N), through most of India to Sri Lanka and east to Assam, and in W, C and S Burma, WC Thailand and S Laos. Common in Indian subcontinent but only locally so elsewhere, and rare in east of range.

HABITAT Occupies dry to very dry open woodland and desert scrub, its habitats including deciduous woodland, scrub, riverine forest, wild-olive woodland, plantations and trees along roadsides or watercourses; also found in cultivations and gardens. Prefers these habitats to dense forest, and, locally, shows a predilection for the big *Euphorbia antiquorum* which are abundant in dry districts of Sri Lanka. Confined to elevations below 1000m in most of its range, only occasionally being observed higher up, to 1700m, in Nepal.

DESCRIPTION
P. m. mahrattensis **Adult male** Forehead and forecrown golden-yellow, becoming red on hindcrown and nape. Sides of head white, but tinged/streaked brownish below eye and on ear-coverts; rear malar stripe rich brown and continuing upwards from lower neck side to rear of upper ear-coverts and downwards onto upper breast side. Chin and throat white, sometimes tinged brown. Hindneck dark brown. Upperparts blackish-brown or black, feathers broadly edged white near tips, with rump largely white; uppertail-coverts white with black central 'wedge'. Upperwing brownish-black to black, with coverts tipped white and flight feathers barred white. Uppertail dark brown-black, fully barred white. Underparts from breast whitish, streaked dark brown or blackish, streaks often lacking or indistinct in breast centre but broad on breast sides and upper flanks; centre of belly orangey-red. Underwing brown, barred white. Undertail as uppertail.

Adult female Slightly longer-tailed than male. Crown yellowish, lacking red (or with just a few red tips), and nape brownish.

Juvenile Duller than adults, more brownish above, and with underpart streaks more diffuse and belly pinker (less red). Males have some orange-red on crown and often on nape, and females a few orange-red feathers in central crown.

Bare parts Bill slate-grey to horn, with paler base to lower mandible; usually paler on juveniles. Legs and feet blue-grey. Eyes brown to red-brown; brown in juveniles.

GEOGRAPHICAL VARIATION Two races.
P. m. mahrattensis (range of species, except Pakistan and N India) Described above. Varies in size clinally, being slightly larger in north and northeast. Intensity of colour varies greatly among individuals, but no clear geographical pattern exists to justify further subdivisions.
P. m. pallescens (Pakistan, N and NW India) Paler than nominate, with larger white markings on upperparts (rump can be completely white), paler head markings, and underpart streaking a lighter brown.

MEASUREMENTS Wing 94-110; tail 54-64; bill (from skull) 21-28; tarsus 15-21. Weight: 28-46.

VOICE Gives a feeble *peek* or a sharp *click, click*, and *click-r-r-r'*, *kik-kik-kik-r-r-r-h*. Drums.

HABITS Forages singly or in pairs, which stay in loose contact vocally, and also joins mixed-species flocks. Stays mostly in the crown of trees and on trunks, and comes down to the ground rarely. Rather typical *Picoides* in its foraging, agile, and regularly clinging upside-down. Excavating bark and dead wood for insect larvae seems to be a common method of procuring food, even in the breeding season. Has been observed to pierce holes in pods of *Cassia*, presumably to get at insects hidden within. There is an obscure indication that a pair may share a common roost (previous nest). Interspecific interactions with parakeets have been reported; seems to be locally separated from sympatric Sind Woodpecker (107).

FOOD Bark-dwelling insects, fruits and nectar comprise its diet. In particular, caterpillars (Geometridae), grubs (Elateridae, Curculionidae, Buprestidae), and dragonflies have been reported.

BREEDING On the continent the breeding season extends from February to April-May, most clutches being produced in March; nests March-July in Sri Lanka. Nest is a typical woodpecker hole, in a dead section of a live tree, often on the underside of a sloping branch, at 4-9m. The 3 eggs are incubated for 13 days by both sexes (male's share may be greater); both also feed the young, which may stay with parents until they are driven off at the onset of the next breeding cycle.

REFERENCES Ali & Ripley 1970; Eates 1937; Ganguli 1975; Henry 1971; Inskipp & Inskipp 1991; King & Dickinson 1975; Lekagul & Round 1991; Mason & Lefroy 1912; Phillips 1978; Roberts 1991; Smythies 1953; Whistler 1930; Whistler & Kinnear 1946.

---

98 ARABIAN WOODPECKER
Picoides dorae   Plate 28

IDENTIFICATION Length 18cm. Small, with fairly long, almost straight, chisel-tipped bill broad across nostrils. A brownish to olive-grey woodpecker, barred only on wings and outer tail, and with paler underparts. Has red on nape (male) and belly, and faintly barred flanks. Unmistakable: the only woodpecker in Arabia apart from totally different Eurasian Wryneck (1), which occurs only on passage.

DISTRIBUTION Endemic to the southwest Arabian peninsula, in a narrow band from just north of Mecca south through C Yemen to western 'South Yemen' (formerly Aden Protectorate). Locally common in wooded areas.

MOVEMENTS There are seemingly some seasonal altitudinal movements. These woodpeckers may be found down to the lowlands (Tihama) in winter, and at least part of the population moves upslope for about 350m in summer.

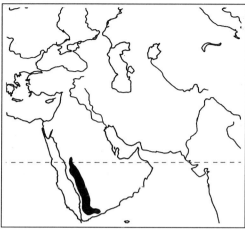

HABITAT Inhabits riparian woodland dominated by *Cordia abyssinica*, in well-mixed and dense stands of predominantly *Juniperus*, *Olea* and *Nuxia* on mountain slopes, in pure stands of *Acacia origena*, and also in very scattered acacias (predominantly *A. iraquensis*) in rather flat desert areas. Palm and fig groves with adjacent acacias are the habitat at the base of the escarpments. Breeds mainly in valleys, on slopes and in highlands at 1200-2400m; at least outside the breeding season, from sea level to 3000m.

DESCRIPTION

Adult male Hindcrown and nape crimson-red. Rest of head brownish to grey-brown or dark brown, with paler streaks on ear-coverts and sometimes in superciliary area; malar region (and sometimes to rear of ear-coverts) often paler. Chin and throat whitish to pale brownish. Hindneck and upperparts, including scapulars and lesser coverts, brown to olive-brown or grey-brown (often tinged golden), darker on rump and uppertail-coverts. Upperwing (except lesser coverts) blackish, coverts tipped white and flight feathers barred white. Uppertail blackish, outer rectrices barred white and second-outer with a few white bars. Underparts pale olive-brown to greyish-brown, with red or orange-red patch on central belly, faintly barred brown and white on flanks and lower belly; undertail-coverts browner, spotted/barred white. Underwing white, flight feathers barred brown. Undertail as uppertail, but paler. (Plumage coloration varies according to degree of wear and fading: paler in first half of year, and can appear rather dark in winter.)

Adult female Slightly smaller and shorter-billed than male, lacks red on hindcrown and nape, and tends also to be somewhat duller, with less prominent red on belly.

Juvenile Much as adults, but greyer below, with some streaking apparent, and belly more pink than red. Males have patch of orangey-red on crown.

Bare parts Bill slate-grey to horn, usually paler at base of lower mandible. Legs and feet grey. Eyes greyish-brown or whitish.

GEOGRAPHICAL VARIATION None. Monotypic.

MEASUREMENTS Wing 108-115; tail 60-66; bill 20-25; tarsus 19-20.

VOICE The long-distance call consists of a highly variable introductory note followed by a series of 7-12 notes, dropping slightly in pitch at the end, and terminates with 3-4 still lower-pitched and shorter notes, *pweek pit-pit-pit-pit-pit-pit-pit-ptptpt*. These calls are associated with long-distance movements and given mostly upon alighting, rarely at take-off and never during flight. Single call notes or alarm notes seem to be rare or lacking. A call uttered on the wing resembles the rattle call of Great Spotted Woodpecker (104) in sound quality, but more continuous, *chrrrt…chrrrt*, sometimes squeakier. Very quiet and low-pitched notes are heard from pair members in close contact. Nestling calls are quite similar to those of other pied woodpeckers and change with the age of the nestlings. Drums feebly and apparently only occasionally.

HABITS Mostly met with singly or in pairs, which maintain loose vocal contact; a partner responds to a call by calling itself within about 5 seconds, or by approaching. Not very shy, but because of large home ranges and foraging habits more likely to be heard than seen. Forages most often in *Acacia*, followed by *Olea*, *Nuxia*, *Ziziphus* and fig trees (*Ficus salicifolia*), in well-mixed mountain and riverine woodland. Decaying junipers, which are abundant locally, and which show signs of heavy infestation with beetle larvae, may be visited occasionally. These woodpeckers forage commonly in the crown of trees on medium to thin branches and twigs, frequently along their underside; also descends to ground. The predominant foraging mode, at least in early spring, is hammering; the holes thus produced are small in diameter and go straight into the bark or wood. Flaking off bark is used only moderately. Probing in crevices is also frequently observed; pierces figs to obtain insects living in these fruits. Gleaning becomes the dominant foraging mode in the nesting season. Drills sap wells into the bark of a living acacia: wells are generally stained at their edges and on the area below by the oozing sap, such marks being either single, irregularly scattered, or forming the characteristic horizontal rows known from other sap-sucking woodpeckers; marks are concentrated on a single tree or a few trees within one site (apparently all territories contain at least one such tree). When foraging, stays in one patch for a long time and then moves to another tree, in most cases not to a neighbouring one but instead to a tree at least 40m away. Movements within trees are slow and deliberate. Changes sites often by dropping down from the crown, followed by a low forward flight and an upsweep into the crown of another tree; this flight style appears to be especially suited for the dense and thorny crowns of acacias. Longer distances are covered in a virtually noiseless flight with shallow undulations. During encounters with a female, male may raise his crown feathers. Other bird species compete for the holes made by Arabian Woodpeckers: in drier wadis House Sparrows *Passer domesticus* are the main occupants of their holes; in other areas Violet (Amethyst) Starlings *Cinnyricinclus leucogaster* seem to be a potential threat and are correspondingly attacked by the woodpeckers.

FOOD Larvae of wood-boring insects, fig wasps, and aphids and other winged insects have been recorded as adult and nestling food. Observations suggest that ants living in the base of acacias may play an important role. Tree sap probably forms an important constituent of the diet in winter; whether the pulp of figs is taken requires confirmation.

BREEDING Breeds from (February) March to May; possible breeding in November (Yemen) needs to be corroborated. The actual onset of nesting varies locally and is apparently closely related to the appearance of leaves on acacias, which probably triggers insect production. The male, and very likely the female as well, excavate the nest low in a tree trunk or limb in live or dead wood, mostly at

0.5-6m. Holes (for roosting only?) are also found in palm stumps and at up to 9 (25)m. Hole entrances are often irregularly shaped. Clutch, of 3 eggs, is incubated by both sexes, only the male staying in nest overnight. The young hatch after 11 days and are fed and brooded by both parents, which also remove faeces. Young fledge after about 22 days in the nest, and remain in the nesting area for at least two more months.

REFERENCES Everett 1987; Hollom *et al.* 1988; King 1978; Martins 1988; Meinertzhagen 1954; Phillips 1982; Stagg 1985; Winkler *et al.* in press.

---

99 RUFOUS-BELLIED WOODPECKER
Picoides hyperythrus
Plate 29

IDENTIFICATION Length 20-25cm. Smallish, with long, almost straight, chisel-tipped bill broad across nostrils. Combination of white-barred black upperparts, wings and outer tail, white face patch, and unmarked chestnut to rufous or rusty-buff neck and underparts with red undertail-coverts is diagnostic. Male has extensive red from forehead to nape, the red covering the entire hindneck on some western populations, which are also a deeper chestnut below. Female has forehead to nape black, heavily spotted with white. Rather silent, but has distinctive dry rattle call; drums frequently during courtship and nesting periods.

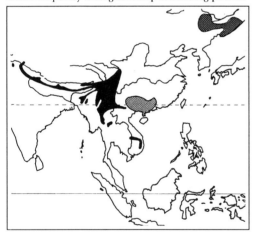

DISTRIBUTION Inhabits foothills and mountains, from NE Pakistan and Kashmir eastwards across N India and Nepal, Sikkim and to Arunachal Pradesh (extending south to northern Bangladesh, Mizoram and Manipur), northern Burma, NW Thailand and northernmost Vietnam northwards through W and SE Tibet and western China (Yunnan, N Sichuan); isolated populations are present in Manchuria (NE Heilongjiang) to S Ussuriland, and in E Thailand through S Laos to S Vietnam. Rather uncommon to scarce in most of range, but may be more common locally in western parts and perhaps elsewhere.

MOVEMENTS Northeastern populations (Manchuria, Ussuriland) are migratory, passing through C China in May and again in August-September, and wintering in S and SE China. In Korea, this is a rare vagrant only. Possibly some altitudinal movements in Nepal, with descent to 2000m outside the breeding season.

HABITAT Occurs in broadleaf forest and in mixed and coniferous forest. In Pakistan, prefers deciduous forest with Himalayan Poplar *Populus ciliata* and False Dogwood *Cornus macrophylla*. Farther east, it is found in evergreen montane and cloud forests, in oak, chestnut, silver fir and pine forests, in mixed forest and in rhododendron. Occurs in oak and alder stands in northern Burma, and frequents open woodlands of oak, pine and dry dipterocarp trees elsewhere in SE Asia. This is essentially a woodpecker of high elevations: in Pakistan, between 1520 and 1980m; in Nepal and Sikkim, breeds much higher up, between 2100 and 4100m (records below 3000m in Nepal fall outside the breeding season); in NW Burma, most common between 2000 and 2800m; and in other parts of SE Asia it ranges between 500 and 1200m.

DESCRIPTION
P. h. hyperythrus Adult male Forehead to nape extensively bright red (sometimes tinged orange on nape), often with a few black feather bases showing on crown, and bordered by thin black line from forehead to mid crown (in western populations, red of nape often continues around rear of ear-coverts). Lores, area below eye to fore ear-coverts and thin line over and just behind eye white, with a few greyish marks in loral area. Malar region whitish with dusky streaks. Rear ear-coverts and neck sides, chin and throat rufous-chestnut. Lower hindneck and entire upperparts black, barred white from mantle to upper rump (bars broadest, almost meeting, on upper back). Upperwing, including coverts, deep black, with white spots forming bars (spots sometimes reduced on coverts). Uppertail black, outer two feather pairs barred white. Rufous-chestnut of neck/throat continues over entire underparts, apart from pinky-red lower belly and undertail-coverts, with narrow area of black and white bars on lower belly sides and flanks. Underwing dark grey, barred white. Undertail as uppertail. (In worn plumage, colour of underparts becomes paler, noticeably so when heavily worn; in fresh plumage, appears much deeper-coloured below.)

Adult female Much as male, but with different head pattern: forehead to hindneck black, with regular white spots (occasionally with a few red feather tips admixed).

Juvenile Noticeably different from adults. Initially, throat is heavily streaked brown and white, underparts barred brownish, black and white, with paler (pinkish) undertail-coverts, and sides of head streaked/barred; wings brownish-black and upperparts more spotted than barred. Crown is black with white spots, males also with many orange-red feather tips and females with fewer orange tips. Adult plumage is acquired gradually, and obvious traces of juvenile plumage may still be evident on some in January.

Bare parts Bill black or blackish, with lower mandible pale yellow or greenish-yellow (greener at base). Legs and feet olive to greenish-grey or slaty. Eyes red-brown to pale reddish or deep brown; darker brown in immatures.

GEOGRAPHICAL VARIATION Considerable individual variation exists, particularly in tone of underparts, but four races are recognisable, two being noticeably and constantly paler below (but note that plumage of all races becomes much paler when worn).
> *P. h. hyperythrus* (Nepal east to Sichuan and NW Thailand) Described above. In west of range, a few males show tendency towards expansion of red on nape and neck sides. Slight increase in size clinally northeastwards.
> *P. h. marshalli* (Pakistan and N India) Similar to nominate but larger. Male has considerable amount of red on head, this covering entire nape and hindneck

and rear neck sides.

P. h. subrufinus (Manchuria and Ussuriland; winters S China) Larger than other races (though some *marshalli* possibly as large). Plumage as nominate, but paler, more rufous-buff, below.

P. h. annamensis (E Thailand to S Vietnam) Longer-billed than nominate. Otherwise much as *subrufinus*, but somewhat smaller.

MEASUREMENTS Wing 109-122 (small races), 119-136 (larger races); tail 69-87, 74-90; bill 23-28, 24-29; tarsus 19-22. Weight: 42-53, 53-74.

VOICE The rattle is a *chit-chit-chit-r-r-r-r-h*, usually given three times in succession; reminiscent of that of Greater Flameback (199), but weaker. Very fast *ptíkitititit...* in alarm. Pair members give a *chwecka-chwecka* call in close contacts. Both sexes drum in the breeding season, female's rolls being lower and shorter; a roll consists of 5-15 beats, fading towards the end, *dáddddddd*.

HABITS Usually met with singly or in pairs, which maintain loose contact; outside the breeding season, may associate with flocks of small insectivorous birds. Forages on tree trunks, in the canopy, by hammering, probing and gleaning; sometimes catches prey on the wing. Observations and anatomical evidence indicate, however, that probing, typically with turning of the head sharply to the side, is the major technique for obtaining food, rather than excavating for wood-boring larvae. Pecks at loose bark or probes under loose edges of bark, into crevices and at ant workings. Hammering at one spot seems to be absent or rare. In spring, sap-sucking seems to be of some importance: creates sap wells by drilling densely spaced rows of 8-10 small holes girdling the trunks of deciduous oaks (*Quercus kerrii*) and other trees (e.g. *Abies, Tristania rufescens*, Myrtaceae), or drills single, large deep holes through thick bark of *Quercus kerrii*; actual construction of sap holes has apparently not yet been observed and seems to take place during brief period in spring. Many ringed trees, covered with sap wells, are found in a territory. When drinking sap (observations at solitary wells), visits wells about every 20 minutes, a visit lasting only about one minute. Solitary outside breeding season, at onset of which, however, pairs or trios and aggressive encounters can be observed.

FOOD The essential components of its diet are insects and vegetable matter. Ants and beetles (Carabidae), other small insects, a katydid, caterpillars and butterflies have been reported. During migration in China, insects, predominantly ants, form the main sustenance. Feeds on sap in spring.

BREEDING Nesting season spans April to May in Nepal and India; nest construction may start in March in Thailand. Nest is a typical woodpecker hole high in a tree (about 5m has been reported). Clutch size 4 or 5 eggs. Both sexes care for the brood.

REFERENCES Abdulali 1968; Ali 1962; Ali & Ripley 1970; Cheng 1964; Dieselhorst 1968; Gore & Pyong-Oh 1971; Inskipp & Inskipp 1991; Lekagul & Round 1991; Martens & Eck in press; Osmaston 1916; Proud 1958; Roberts 1991; Stanford & Mayr 1941; Stresemann & Heinrich 1940; Whistler 1930; Zusi & Marshall 1970.

100 CRIMSON-BREASTED WOODPECKER
Picoides cathpharius   Plate 29

Other name: Lesser Pied Woodpecker

IDENTIFICATION Length c. 17-19cm. Small, with relatively short, chisel-tipped bill with slightly curved culmen and broad across nostrils. A highland species of mountain slopes. Occurs in two racial groups, both with black upperparts, white patch in wings, moderately barred wings and tail, and black moustache to neck side and continuing down to breast side, but differing in underpart patterning and in head markings of male. Southwestern populations (east to Burma and SE Tibet) are well streaked below, and breast shows variable amount of red (sometimes very little or none) which is bordered by only a little black, while undertail-coverts are orangey-red or have small orange-red tips; males have red from nape extending well down hindneck and also forwards to rear of ear-coverts. In east, populations are darker, again with variable amount of red on breast, but bordered by much more black (on some forming black patch at side of and below the red), with a pinkish tinge to red of undertail-coverts, and is heavily streaked below (though in C Hubei they are very pale below, with less black on breast sides and with fewer streaks on flanks); males have red on head restricted to a patch on nape. Females of all populations have red of nape/neck replaced by black. Juveniles are darker below and lack all red on breast. A rather little-known species, much of whose behaviour (including acoustic signals) is unknown.

Similar species Only real confusion risk is with Darjeeling Woodpecker (101), the range of which overlaps quite widely. Darjeeling is larger and clearly longer-billed, has bright yellow on neck sides, lacks any indication of red on breast, and black streaks on breast never merge to form black patch; male also has smaller area of red on nape. Darjeeling often occurs at higher elevations than Crimson-breasted, and drums loudly in breeding season.

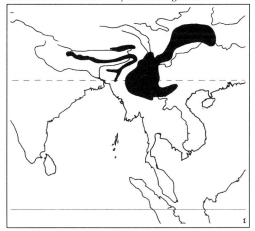

DISTRIBUTION Occurs in mountain and hill forests, ranging from NC Nepal and NE India east to Arunachal Pradesh, northwards in mountain zones to SE Tibet and W and C China (SW Gansu, S Shaanxi, C Hubei, Sichuan, N Yunnan), and in the south to Meghalaya and Mizoram, C Burma, northernmost Thailand, N Laos and NW Vietnam (NW Tonkin). Generally uncommon throughout range.

HABITAT Frequents evergreen and deciduous forests with oaks, rhododendron and *Castanopsis* at 700-3000m or higher, but generally on lower and middle mountain slopes between 1200 and 2800m, below Darjeeling Woodpecker (though the two may overlap). Occurs above 1400m in Thailand, and in Nepal is most common above 1500m.

DESCRIPTION

P. c. cathpharius **Adult male** Forehead buffish-white (with indistinct dark central line to crown). Crown black, often down to eye level. Nape, hindneck and rear neck sides red, slightly tinged orange. Lores, area below eye, supercilium behind eye and entire ear-coverts white, ear-coverts with faint buff tinge and sometimes a few very faint dark streaks. Moustachial stripe black, joining with black patch on neck side which extends down to meet breast streaking. Chin whitish. Upperparts black. Outer upperwing-coverts black, inners mainly white; flight feathers black, with small white spots forming narrow bars. Uppertail black, outer three feather pairs barred whitish (amount of barring decreasing inwardly). Underparts below chin pale buffish (often more yellowish on belly and flanks), with small ill-defined patch of orangey-red in breast centre (red may be virtually or totally lacking), broadly streaked black on breast sides, streaks becoming thinner from lower breast and mid flanks; lowermost belly and undertail-coverts streaked black and broadly tipped orange-red. Underwing dark grey, barred white. Undertail much as uppertail.

Adult female Similar to male, but red on head replaced by black (may show hint of red bordering rear ear-coverts).

Juvenile Much as adults, but underparts darker and duller, lacking red on breast, and red of undertail-coverts much paler or virtually absent. Male lacks red on neck, but has orangey-red from mid crown to nape; female has less extensive area of orange-red.

Bare parts Bill grey to blue-grey on upper mandible, with lower mandible very pale grey to whitish. Legs and feet dull grey to grey-green. Eyes brown to red-brown. Orbital skin slate-grey or paler.

GEOGRAPHICAL VARIATION Six races, some reasonably distinct, forming two fairly well-defined groups.

(a) Southwestern *cathpharius* group (smaller, paler, with less black on breast, males with much red on rear head):
  P. c. cathpharius (Nepal east to N Assam) Described above.
  P. c. pyrrhothorax (S Assam and adjacent N Burma west of Chindwin river) Somewhat longer-billed than nominate. Face and underparts paler (less buffy), with obvious, well-defined orangey-red patch on breast and much more red on undertail-coverts.
  P. c. ludlowi (SE Tibet) Much as *pyrrhothorax*, but darker on face and underparts.

(b) Northeastern *pernyii* group (larger, darker, with more black on breast, males with red on head restricted to nape or occasionally with faint red bordering rear ear-coverts):
  P. c. pernyii (NW Yunnan to N Sichuan and SW Gansu) Darker and greyer below than *cathpharius* group, with red on breast bordered at sides and below by fairly solid black areas, and undertail-coverts much redder.
  P. c. tenebrosus (C and S Yunnan to N Burma and N Thailand, east to N Vietnam) As *pernyii* but slightly smaller, with shorter tail and smaller bill. Heavily streaked below, but with slightly less black in breast area.
  P. c. innixus (S Shaanxi, NE Sichuan, C Hubei) Resembles *pernyii*, but much paler (whitish) below, with less black on breast and with streaks on flanks very narrow or absent. May have ivory-coloured lower mandible.

MEASUREMENTS Wing 94-110; tail 57-66; bill 16-19.5; tarsus 15-17. Weight: 25-35.

VOICE A loud monotonous *chip* or *tchick*, somewhat higher-pitched than call of sympatric Darjeeling Woodpecker and less sharp, represents the call note of this species. A very short, fast and descending rattle has also been reported, as well as a shrill *kee-kee-kee*.

HABITS Details of this species' behaviour are little known. Seems to forage with frequent pecking and hammering.

FOOD Insects and their larvae; nectar.

BREEDING Nesting takes place in April-June. Clutch of 2-4 eggs.

REFERENCES Ali 1962; Ali & Ripley 1970; Inskipp & Inskipp 1991; King & Dickinson 1975; Lekagul & Round 1991; Short 1973a; Stanford & Mayr 1941; Winkler & Short 1978.

101 DARJEELING WOODPECKER
Picoides darjellensis Plate 29

Other name: Brown-throated Woodpecker

IDENTIFICATION Length c. 25cm. Smallish, with rather long, straight, chisel-tipped bill broad across nostrils. A largely mountain-dwelling species of the Himalayan region and eastwards. Black above, with white patch on barred wings, barred outer tail, and black moustache; underparts heavily streaked, with dark throat and red undertail-coverts. In reasonable views, a golden or orangey-yellow patch behind ear-coverts is conspicuous and diagnostic. Male has small red nape patch.

Similar species Crimson-breasted Woodpecker (100) is superficially very similar, but smaller and shorter-billed, usually with at least some red on breast (sometimes bordered by black), male has more red on head, and both sexes lack golden colour on neck sides. Where the two overlap, Darjeeling usually occurs at higher elevations.

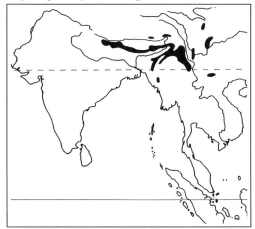

DISTRIBUTION Ranges from northern C Nepal east to Arunachal Pradesh and continuing south to the Cachar hills and Mizoram, also north to SE Tibet and S Sichuan and south through W Yunnan to northern Burma; also in N Vietnam (NW Tonkin).

MOVEMENTS Seems to remain at high elevations even in winter.

HABITAT Within its range this species breeds in almost every kind of woodland, favouring dank evergreen and coniferous forest, often with moss-covered trees, and also rhododendron woods. It is found in evergreen broadleaf cloud forests, closed forests to open woodland, with dominant tree species including deciduous trees and conifers, oaks as well as firs or rhododendron. A high-altitude woodpecker, not found below 1200m in SE Asia, and in Nepal occurring mainly between 1800 and 3500m, reaching almost 4000m in Sikkim.

DESCRIPTION

Adult male Lower forehead whitish; upper forehead and crown to about eye level black; nape narrowly red. Lores, area below eye and ear-coverts white, tinged buff (sometimes strongly) below eye and on rear ear-coverts. Sides of neck behind ear-coverts golden-yellow to deep orange-buff. Moustachial stripe black, extending to lower rear ear-coverts and then down onto upper breast side. Chin and throat to upper breast brownish-buff to buff-brown, diffusely bordered paler. Hindneck and upperparts black. Upperwing black or brownish-black, inner coverts largely white, with flight feathers narrowly barred white. Uppertail black, barred white to pale buff on (up to three) outer feathers. Underparts brownish-buff, becoming paler on lower breast and more yellow on flanks and belly, with heavy black streaking from breast sides and lower breast becoming somewhat narrower (and often forming bars) on flanks and belly; undertail-coverts pinkish-red. Underwing dark brown, barred white. Undertail as uppertail.

Adult female Slightly smaller than male, and with red of nape replaced by black.

Juvenile As adults, but lacks golden patch on neck; underparts duller, with streaked throat, more obviously barred belly and flanks, and duller, paler red on undertail-coverts. Males have dull red crown; females have black crown with small red central patch or red-tipped feathers, but occasionally red may be lacking altogether.

Bare parts Bill dark grey to blackish on upper mandible, with pale grey lower mandible, latter with greener (or even ivory-coloured) base. Legs and feet grey-green. Eyes red to reddish-brown; dark brown in juveniles. Orbital skin slaty-grey.

GEOGRAPHICAL VARIATION Northeastern populations average slightly smaller, particularly in bill length, and have been separated as '*desmursi*'. Differences, however, are probably due to clinal variation, and grounds for subspecific treatment are insufficient.

MEASUREMENTS Wing 119-134; tail 76-86; bill (from skull) 30-36.5; tarsus 21.5-25. Weight: 61-87.

VOICE Single *tsik* calls, resembling those of Great Spotted Woodpecker (104), are heard most commonly; may be delivered in fast series in alarm. The rattle is trill-like and is the common mode of communication between distant members of a pair; occurs in a long and in a short version, *di-di-di-d-dddddt*. Loud or soft *tchew-tchew-tchew-tchew* calls mark close encounters between individuals. Drums frequently in the breeding season; both sexes may drum, rolls resembling those of Great Spotted Woodpecker but slightly longer.

HABITS Usually forages singly or in pairs, which keep loose contact; may also join mixed-species flocks. Exploits all levels of the habitat: fallen logs, tree trunks and the canopy are visited, mossy and dead surfaces are carefully inspected, debris is removed, and forceful pecking is rather common, as well as gleaning and probing. Moderate crest-raising is the only visual display so far described.

FOOD What has hitherto been reported on its diet corresponds to what is known of its foraging behaviour. Larvae of wood-boring insects, insect larvae, beetle larvae, pupae, and insects have been found.

BREEDING The breeding season starts in late March and April, extending to June, with first nestlings found in May. The nest, excavated low (to 5m) in a dead tree, contains a clutch of 2-4 eggs. The young are fed by both parents.

REFERENCES Ali 1962; Ali & Ripley 1970; Diesselhorst 1968; Inskipp & Inskipp 1991; King & Dickinson 1975; Martens & Eck in press; Short 1973a; Smythies 1953; Stanford & Mayr 1941; Winkler & Short 1978.

---

102 MIDDLE SPOTTED WOODPECKER
Picoides medius Plate 30

IDENTIFICATION Length c. 20-22cm. Small, with medium-length, rather pointed bill with slightly curved culmen and broad across nostrils. Black above, with wings heavily barred white and with white patch on inner coverts; pale buffy-yellow below, quite heavily streaked dark, and with large diffuse area of pink from lower belly to undertail-coverts. Head pattern distinctive: both sexes have red crown and nape (on female, nape yellower or browner), and black mark on neck extending slightly up around rear ear-coverts (rarely, almost to nape) and down onto breast side, but lack or have only indistinct dark moustache (producing 'gentle-looking' expression), though front part of head often appears distinctly sullied. Can look very round-headed. Spends much time in upper level of trees, where very restless, fluttering from one spot to another. Has characteristic, nasal, territorial call, heard frequently in first half of year.

Similar species The other pied woodpeckers within its almost solely W Palearctic range are easily distinguished when seen well. Adult males of Lesser Spotted (93) and White-backed (103) have red crown, but former is smaller and lacks pink on vent, latter is clearly bigger and longer-billed, and both have complete dark moustache but lack obvious white patch on inner wing-coverts. Juveniles of Great Spotted (104) and Syrian (105) Woodpeckers have red on crown (bordered with black), but both are bigger, have obvious moustache and are generally unstreaked or only faintly streaked on flanks. Note that Middle Spotted appears dirtier below, especially when seen in flight, than these larger species, and has a much more 'open-faced' look about it.

Great Spotted (above) and Middle Spotted (below) in gliding phase of flight (wings closed).

269

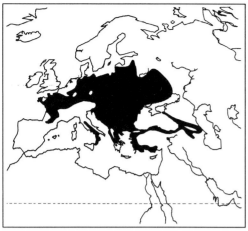

forming 4-6 broken bars across entire wing. Uppertail black, outer two rectrices with white tips and outer webs, these with 2-3 dark bars. Underparts white, strongly tinged yellow-buff on breast and flanks, becoming pinkish on upper belly and lower flanks, with vent and undertail-coverts darker pink; breast sides and flanks with long black streaks, usually well defined. Underwing barred black and white, coverts and axillaries mottled grey and white. Undertail as uppertail (white of outer feathers more obvious). (In worn plumage, black of upperparts distinctly brown-tinged, and underparts dirty-looking with more extensive streaking; grey feather bases more obvious on head, including crown, and on lower underparts, producing mottled effect.)

Adult female As male, but red of crown often paler and becoming browner to golden at rear; pale areas of head often somewhat more buff. Some are virtually identical to male.

Juvenile Duller than adults, especially on head (where crown feathers shorter and less narrow), and with pale areas of body having brownish feather tips; black areas browner. Some brown marks in white of scapulars and wing-coverts. Underparts less buff, more grey, with pink area paler and reduced in extent, and streaking more diffuse and usually with indication of thin bars on flanks. Male has red crown, mottled grey, becoming blackish with admixed red feather tips on nape; female has smaller area of duller red, with hindcrown mostly black.

Bare parts Bill lead-grey or darker, with paler (sometimes pink- or yellow-tinged) base to lower mandible. Legs and feet lead-grey, sometimes tinged greenish. Eyes red-brown or red; often grey-brown in juveniles.

GEOGRAPHICAL VARIATION Four rather poorly differentiated races.

P. m. medius (Europe, including NW Turkey) Described above. North Spanish population is somewhat more saturated black above, deeper yellow-buff below and with brighter pink-red in ventral area, while those in SE Europe are similar, with heavier and darker flank streaking; sometimes separated as '*lilianae*' and '*splendidior*' respectively, but differences seem to result from clinal variation.

P. m. caucasicus (N Turkey, Caucasus and Transcaucasia; probably this race in NW Iran) Brighter below than nominate, more golden-yellow on breast and belly and pink of ventral region less extensive but redder; breast sides and flanks more heavily streaked, and outer rectrices more strongly and symmetrically barred. Those in N Turkey are closer to nominate.

P. m. anatoliae (W and S Asia Minor) Smaller than *caucasicus* but otherwise very similar, and possibly better placed within it. May show rather heavier streaking below (perhaps with hint of barring on flanks) and slightly paler pink vent.

P. m. sanctijohannis (Zagros mountains of Iran; probably this race in northern Iraq) Similar to *caucasicus* but much whiter on head and underparts, with pale yellow restricted to band across lower belly, and with deeper pink-red on vent and undertail-coverts; flanks show more contrasting narrow black streaks. Those in N Iraq appear intermediate between this race and S Turkish breeders.

MEASUREMENTS Wing 120-135; tail 77-87; bill 22-26.2; tarsus 20-23. Weight: 50-80(85).

VOICE The characteristic vocalisation all year round is the rattle call *Kig-gag-gag-gag-gag....*, which is most common in its short form containing three or four elements. It could be confused, if at all, only with series of call notes or *gwig*

DISTRIBUTION Range covers large parts of Europe to W Asia. Breeds from NW Spain, through France to S Sweden (where recently became extinct), in C Europe, Italy, the Balkans, W Turkey and Anatolia and through the Caucasus to W Iran. Eastern parts of the range include Lithuania, Latvia (first bred in 1985, now widespread), Belarus (Belorussia), W Russia, Moldova (Moldavia), and Ukraine. Locally common, but rather scarce to rare in some parts.

MOVEMENTS Although generally sedentary, some short-distance dispersal is apparent. A couple of records in coastal S Sweden after species' extinction in that country may have involved wanderers from Latvia, where this woodpecker is expanding its range. Single records in the Netherlands in May 1992 and February 1994 are only the third and fourth there since 1980.

HABITAT Restricted to mature deciduous forests. Prefers oak-hornbeam (1.0 territories/10ha) and ash-alder (swampy, no oaks; 0.7 territories/10 ha) in primeval Polish forests. Floodplain forests and hillsides covered with mature beech or oak were probably its original habitat in the north and in C Europe, where beech may dominate locally. Nowadays, this woodpecker depends on the presence of oaks in large parts of its C European range, their rough bark combined with a fair amount of dead branches providing the substrate for surface-dwelling arthropods. In parts of Germany, Switzerland and Austria, old open orchards bordering deciduous woodland are of some (although dwindling) importance. Occupies beech, mixed oak-beech and oak forest in the south, and beech forests in NE Anatolia and in the Caucasus; also in olive groves in Turkey. This is a bird of the lowlands in C Europe, where it occurs below 600m, locally reaching 700m or more (900m). In S Europe, Italy, occurs at 300-1700m, and to 1300m in Anatolia; reaches 2300m in SW Iran.

DESCRIPTION

P. m. medius **Adult male** Forehead buffish-white; crown and nape feathers long and narrow, crimson-red. Sides of head and neck white, streaked/mottled greyish on ear-coverts; faint moustachial stripe buff or pale greyish, but expanding into large and prominent black patch on neck side which curves up in narrow stripe around rear ear-coverts (normally about halfway up, but occasionally almost to nape) and downwards as broader band onto upper breast side. Chin and throat white. Hindneck, mantle and inner scapulars to uppertail-coverts dull black (unglossed). Outer scapulars and inner greater and inner median upperwing-coverts mainly white, with some black at base; flight feathers, including tertials, black, all with large white spots calls of Great Spotted Woodpecker. Double-calls, *kik-gook*, are also heard frequently. In spring, long-drawn, nasal and loud *gwaaag · gwaaag · gwaaag...* series are a sure and unmistakable indication of this woodpecker's presence; this call may be associated with a flutter-aerial display. The soft single call notes are uttered only occasionally; only when scolding are they given in series, which may resemble the corresponding vocalisation of Great Spotted. Low *gad* calls are heard during changeovers at the nest or in the course of mating. Nestlings chirp very much as other pied woodpeckers, and similarly the fledglings' calls become squeaky when an adult approaches. Instrumental signals include a loud tapping, mostly near or at the nest hole, and drumming, which is rather rare (rolls over 2 secs long, relatively slow and with even rhythm). Acoustically most active in March and April.

HABITS Despite its brilliant coloration, this species is an only moderately conspicuous woodpecker and not so easily detected as Great Spotted. Forages mostly singly; may join mixed-species flocks with tits and other woodpecker species. Over the seasons, different parts of a tree are preferred for foraging: in winter, larger branches of the lower crown and trunks are searched, trunks becoming most important in late winter/early spring, whereas in late spring use of the crown increases. Thin twigs are visited only rarely, but it often searches the underside of larger branches. About a third of foraging takes place on dead wood. Rarely descends to the ground. Probing (50-90% of foraging time) and gleaning are the most characteristic foraging techniques employed. Pecks frequently, but usually this does not turn into persistent hammering; flycatches to some extent. Use of anvils not very frequent and not well developed. Ringing of trees and sap-sucking is common in early spring. Movements appear fast, mainly because this species stops only briefly to take prey; frequently covers short distances within the crown by flying, and moves long distances among trees. Crest-raising is a rather conspicuous display in this species, which also exhibits wing- and tail-spreading in agonistic encounters. Flutter-aerial display is often shown during hole demonstration by the male, which also includes tapping and drumming. Female has been recorded mounting the male after copulation. Breeding densities vary greatly, from 0.1 territories/10ha to 2.4/10ha in optimal habitats. Inferior to Great Spotted Woodpecker in direct competition for nest sites, otherwise relatively few conflicts with this species. Interacts also with squirrels and starlings.

FOOD Bark-dwelling arthropods, various beetles, caterpillars (even hairy ones), dipterans, aphids; wood-boring larvae rare. Plant material is taken mainly in winter, but sometimes fruits (cherries) are eaten and even fed to the nestlings. In winter, nuts (acorns, hazel nuts, walnuts, beech, rarely seeds of conifers) are of some importance.

BREEDING Tends to breed earlier than Great Spotted Woodpecker, from mid April to beginning of May (later records most likely refer to replacement clutches). Nest excavated by both sexes in the trunk or in larger branches of deciduous trees, mainly in dead or decaying wood, within 8-20 days; frequently, however, uses old holes. Nest height 1-20m, mostly 5-10m (higher than Great Spotted); mean in primeval forests of Poland 14.9m. Clutches of 5-6 (range 4-8) eggs are laid from mid April to May. Incubation, by both sexes, takes 12 (11-14) days; both also contribute to nest sanitation and feed the young. Male sleeps in the nest overnight. A male helper, observed at one nest, even contributed more food than the apparent primary male. The young fledge after 20-26 days, and are cared for by the parents for a further 8-11 days. Losses in winter correlated

with number of cold days (Sweden).

REFERENCES Ahlén *et al.* 1978; Bezzel 1985; Blume 1968; Christie 1990; Christie & Winkler 1994; Cramp 1985; Dement'ev & Gladkov 1966; Feindt 1956; Feindt & Pettersson 1985; Gebauer *et al.* 1984, 1992; Glutz von Blotzhein & Bauer 1980; Günther 1993; Hochebner 1993; Jenni 1983; Miech 1986; Pasinelli 1993; Pettersson 1983; Reblin 1959; Ruge 1970, 1973; Serez 1983; Spitznagel 1993; Wesolowski & Tomialojc 1986; Winkler 1973; Winkler & Short 1978.

103 WHITE-BACKED WOODPECKER
Picoides leucotos   Plate 30

Other name: Owston's Woodpecker (race *owstoni*)

IDENTIFICATION Length c. 23-28cm. Small to medium-sized, with long, chisel-tipped bill slightly curved along culmen and broad across nostrils. The largest of the pied woodpeckers, and highly variable. Most races are essentially black and white, with broadly white-barred wings, wing-coverts and outer tail, a white-looking face with prominent black moustache and black patch on sides of neck and breast, and streaked underparts with pink to reddish ventral region. Males have entire crown red. The back and rump are plain white in northern populations, but variably barred in others and virtually all black in the endangered Amami Island race *owstoni*. The latter is highly distinctive and possibly a full species (but closely approached in darkness by some SE Chinese birds): upperparts are entirely black, white in wings and tail is much reduced, and underparts are very dark, with breast more or less black. The white back of those races possessing it is rarely obvious on perched birds in the field, and a better feature is the white barring across the wings and coverts (especially median coverts) and corresponding lack of a white inner-wing patch. Rather fearless, but secretive and difficult to locate (occupies very large territories); has become rare in most of western parts of range owing to destruction of habitat.

Similar species A number of rather similar woodpeckers occur within its range, all of them smaller than White-backed. Only Middle Spotted (102) has a red crown, but is considerably smaller and shorter-billed, has white inner-wing patch and lacks an obvious black moustache. Red-crowned juveniles of Great Spotted (104) and Syrian (105) also have obvious white wing patches, are less streaked (or unstreaked) below, and the latter has less white in outer tail and at least a hint of a pinkish breast band; black-crowned females are distinguished by similar criteria and by their unmarked underparts with darker red vent. (Beware confusing white wing patch with broad white median bar of White-backed.)

DISTRIBUTION Ranges across the Palearctic in a continuous band from Fennoscandia (where generally declining except in W Norway) and Poland through the southern taiga to Kamchatka and Japan. In west of range, isolated populations are found in the Pyrenean mountains, Corsica (?), the Alps, the Carpathian mountains, the Appenines, the Balkans and Peloponnes, N Anatolia and the Taurus, and W Caucasus. Isolated populations in the east occur in NW Fujian and W Sichuan on the continent; island populations are found on Taiwan, Shikoku and Quelpart Islands, Dagelet Island, and Amami Island. Seems to be at best uncommon in most of its range and in many parts rare or extremely rare (e.g. Sweden; declined to 11 nesting pairs in

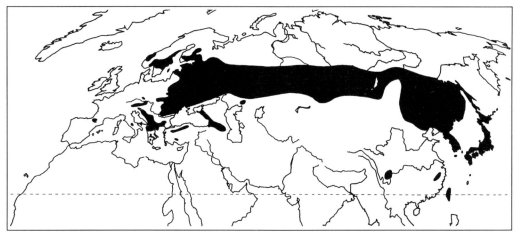

Finland in 1994), but in southern C Siberia said to be the commonest woodpecker species in the upper Ket' river region; possibly overlooked in places owing to its unobtrusive habits and low density. Endangered wherever forest management, including introduction of conifers, is intense.

MOVEMENTS Resident, with some local movements. Some individuals seem to be carried along with migrating Great Spotted Woodpeckers; such movements are occasionally of an irruptive nature, when relatively large numbers from Russia move west/south in autumn (e.g. major influxes in Finland and Sweden in 1993, involving up to 140 individuals).

HABITAT Lives in mature but relatively open deciduous and mixed forests with high proportion of dead trees and fallen timber, which are often found only on steep slopes or near water. In primeval E European forests, prefers swampy ash-alder and oak-hornbeam stands; occasionally in coniferous stands. In Scandinavia, depends on natural forests containing many dead branches and decaying deciduous trees. Spruce may cover considerable portions of the forests; the more important deciduous trees are birch, sallow (*Salix capra*), aspen, alder and oak. Forest-wetland ecotones which have not been thinned or cut for a long time, islands of old deciduous stands, and even clearings near old forests are favoured. Alpine and Pyrenean populations live in light, sunny mixed forests (beech-fir, maple-spruce and the like) little affected by management (more than 40 years old, stands older than 80 years being favoured). Oak forests are the main habitat in NE Anatolia. Japanese populations depend to a great extent on natural beech forests. Requires large continuous areas of suitable habitat. A bird of the lowlands in eastern Europe; between 500 and 1500 m in the Alps; on the Peloponnes, Greece, closely associated with mature montane forests between 860 and 1740 m dominated by the fir species *Abies cephalonica;* and at 1600-2000m in N Anatolia and down to 300m in the south. In Japan, found from sea level to montane deciduous or mixed forest, preferring sections with many fallen and dead trees; Owston's or Amami Woodpecker (race *owstoni*) is confined to old mature evergreen broadleaf forest in the hills of Amami-oshima, where population is estimated at fewer than 630 pairs.

DESCRIPTION

P. l. leucotos **Adult male** Forehead and lores white, tinged grey or buff; forecrown to upper nape bright red, often with some black of feather bases visible. Sides of face and rear neck sides white, often with pale buffish area behind eye, and divided by fairly large black patch on side of neck that extends up behind ear-coverts (not reaching nape), down onto breast side and forwards as moustachial stripe to bill base. Chin and throat white to pale creamy. Lower nape, band down central hindneck, mantle and most of scapulars black (slightly glossed); back and rump white, this extending partly onto lower scapulars (some dark feather bases usually visible); upperwing-coverts black. Upperwing black, greater and especially median coverts (and some lessers) with large white spots at tips forming broad bars; flight feathers with broad white spots, these extending also to both webs of tertials, forming prominent bars. Uppertail black on central two feather pairs, third pair tipped white, outers largely white with 3-4 narrow black bars. Underparts whitish (tinged creamy when fresh), with extension of black neck patch breaking up into streaks that continue to flanks and belly sides; belly to undertail-coverts and often lower flanks reddish-pink. Underwing barred grey and white, with pale coverts. Undertail as uppertail.

Adult female Slightly smaller than male, and with entire top of head black, not red.

Juvenile Duller and browner than adults, and with pale areas tinged grey or buff; markings below more diffuse and red of ventral area paler and less extensive. Both sexes have red or orange-red on crown, usually admixed with black, but red reduced on females.

Bare parts Bill dark slate-grey. Legs and feet dark grey. Eyes red-brown or red.

GEOGRAPHICAL VARIATION Ten races. Varies quite widely in plumage coloration and markings, and also in size.

P. l. leucotos (Europe, except south and southeast, and eastwards in Asia to Kamchatka, Sakhalin, Korea and N China) Described above. Several other races have been described within this area, but they probably represent merely variation within the range of nominate. Populations from the southern Urals east to at least C Siberia ('*uralensis*') average slightly larger and are generally whiter-looking, with more white in wings and less streaking below, while those in northern China ('*sinicus*') are perhaps more sharply streaked below.

P. l. lilfordi (S and SE Europe, Asia Minor, Caucasus and Transcaucasia) Only just larger than nominate, but darker: pale of head is buff-tinged, and black on neck sides and ehind ear-coverts more extensive; rump mostly black and back barred black; less white in wings; ground colour of underparts more buff, with heavier black streaking (flanks faintly barred). Intermediates between this and nominate occur in northern parts of range of *lilfordi*.

P. l. subcirris (Hokkaido, Japan) As nominate but slightly bigger, with buff tinge to face and more black on neck and breast; ventral region paler, pinker.

P. l. stejnegeri (northern Honshu, Japan) A trifle smaller than *subcirris*, and darker; rump partly barred, more black on neck sides with heavier streaking below, and ventra region darker, redder; less white in wing-coverts.

P. l. namiyei (southern Honshu, Kyushu, Shikoku and Quelpart Islands) As *stejnegeri*, but darker still: more buff on head (especially ear-coverts and throat), back fully barred, breast side more black with heavier streaking below it, ventral region darker red; even less white in wing-coverts and flight feathers.

P. l. takahashii (Dagelet Island in Sea of Japan) Close to *stejnegeri*, but wing and bill shorter and face and underparts paler.

P. l. owstoni (Amami-oshima in northern Ryukyus) Largest and darkest of all races. Upperparts all black (occasionally a few white spots); underparts very dark, with breast mainly black with broad streaks below it; face and throat pale buff, and much less white in wings and tail.

P. l. tangi (Sichuan, China) A little-known race. Apparently close to the following race, but larger and with somewhat less black below.

P. l. fohkiensis (Fujian, SE China) Nearly as dark as *owstoni* but clearly smaller, with paler throat, less black on breast and some white on back; shows large area of black on side of neck.

P. l. insularis (Taiwan) The smallest race. Similar in plumage to *namiyei*, but with more white on back.

MEASUREMENTS Wing of male 141-159, of female 139-154; tail 83-91 (*leucotos*), 85-94 (*lilfordi*); bill (male's significantly longer) 34-40 (*leucotos*), 32-37 (*lilfordi*); tarsus 22-26 (*leucotos*), 25-27 (*lilfordi*). Weight: 99-112 (*leucotos*, Europe, Russia), 92-158 (*leucotos*, China), 115 (*lilfordi*).

VOICE Most common call a surprisingly soft and low *gig*. A series of *kyig gyig...* notes is given in alarm. The long-distance call is *gig gig kwerrrr*, and *gaee* calls are interspersed with drumming. Also *weecha-wecha.., chud-chud·..., k-k-k*- notes in aggressive encounters. Low *djad* calls are exchanged when partners meet. Drums in long, moderately fast and slightly accelerating rolls (note that Great Spotted Woodpecker rolls are short, fast bursts, Three-toed (118) delivers slower and slightly shorter rolls, while those of Grey-faced Woodpecker (194) are most similar but do not accelerate); female's rolls often somewhat shorter than male's.

HABITS Although not shy, this is a very elusive species, mostly met with singly. Most foraging takes place on dead trees, least so in late spring and summer. Various techniques used to obtain its main food (wood-dwelling insects) include stripping off bark, hammering holes through bark, and hammering on already exposed wood. In the latter case, either deep conical holes are made or very distinctive shallow and horizontal marks on the wood are produced. On very soft, decaying wood, appears more to dig than to excavate. Morphological differences between the sexes (males larger, with larger bills) are associated with differences in foraging: males hammer more strongly and are more persistent (for instance, about 6.3min, versus 4.6min in females; winter data), visit live and taller trees more often, and forage on larger branches. Foraging techniques change with the seasons, gleaning being most common in the post-breeding season, when it comprises about a quarter of all techniques used; occasionally hunts aerial prey. Hammering deeply into the wood drops from about 20%

in winter to about 12% in the post-breeding season. Both sexes prefer the trunk as a foraging site (53% of observations made by Aulén & Lundberg 1991), particularly in winter when they are after big cerambycid larvae that may be present low in the trunks of small trees. Uses all sorts of crevices as anvils to process unwieldy food items. When gleaning, moves swiftly through the canopy, also visiting thin twigs. Displays with bill-pointing, relatively slow lateral head/body-swinging and flutter-aerial display. Home range large, approximately 100-250ha. Interspecific encounters mainly with Great Spotted Woodpecker, which seems to be dominant.

FOOD Specialises on large wood-boring insect larvae, which even make up more than half of the nestling diet. Larvae of coleopterans predominate (*Aromia, Necydalis, Rhagium, Sapersda, Strangalia*); other insects, including adult beetles and ants and their larvae (e.g. *Cossus*), are also important. Takes some plant material, wild cherries and prunes, berries (*Rhus*); acorns and hazel nuts in summer. Visits feeders.

BREEDING Significant courtship activities begin in February; the breeding season extends to June. Breeds about two weeks earlier than other woodpeckers in same habitat, which may relate to the emergence of coleopterous larvae. Both sexes work on the nest for two to four weeks, excavating in the soft wood of a dead or decaying trunk, stump or branch, or in a utility pole. In primeval forest of Poland, mean nest height 17.8m; range 1.8-16m in Scandinavia, (1)3-20m in the Alps, 0.8m in Anatolia, 6.5-20m in Japan; generally higher than Great Spotted Woodpecker. Clutch of 3-5 eggs produced mid April to early May. Incubation by both sexes for (12)14-16 days, male staying in the nest during the night. Chicks remain 27-28 days in the nest and are tended by both parents, with the female's share often less.

REFERENCES Ahlén *et al.* 1978; Andersson & Hamilton 1972; Aulén & Lundberg 1991; Bezzel 1985; Brazil 1991; Chiba 1969; Christie & Winkler 1994; Franz 1937; Glutz von Blotzhein & Bauer 1980; Hågvar *et al.* 1990; Håland & Toft 1983; Hölzinger 1990; Ishida 1989, 1990a; Matsuoka 1979; Nuorteva *et al.* 1981; Rogacheva 1992; Scherzinger 1982; Serez 1983; Stenberg 1990; Wesolowski & Tomialojc 1986.

---

104 GREAT SPOTTED WOODPECKER
Picoides major   Plate 31

Forms a superspecies with *syriacus, leucopterus, assimilis* and *himalayensis*.

IDENTIFICATION Length c. 20-24cm. Small, with rather short to medium-length, moderately chisel-tipped bill almost straight on culmen and broad across nostrils. A prominently pied woodpecker, the commonest and most familiar one within much of its range. Black post-auricular bar extends to nape, isolating white patches on cheeks and on side of neck; male has red nape patch. Bold black and white pattern, with large white inner-wing patch and wingbars; underparts mainly white to buffish, with variable extension of black onto breast and with deep red ventral area. N African populations show some black or black and red across breast, while Far Eastern birds are distinctly darker below. Juvenile somewhat duller, but with red crown; has pinker vent and often a degree of streaking below.

Similar species Confusion most likely with Syrian Woodpecker (105) and White-winged Woodpecker (106). Syrian

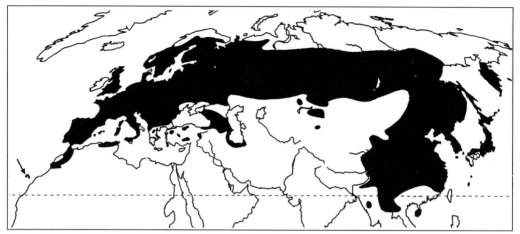

has more white on sides of head, pink rather than red ventral area, largely black outer tail feathers, and (on male) larger red nape patch; White-winged is slightly smaller, with less heavy bill, and has much more white in wings and more extensive red below. Red-crowned juvenile Great Spotted is distinguished from Middle Spotted Woodpecker (102) by larger size, much heavier bill, complete black moustache reaching bill, cleaner underparts/face, and less active behaviour; from White-backed Woodpecker (103) by white wing patches, dark back and lack of obvious streaking below.

DISTRIBUTION The immense range covers almost the entire Palearctic, from Britain in the west (but absent in Ireland) to Japan in the east, reaching Palearctic N Africa and the Canary Islands (Tenerife, Gran Canaria) in the southwest. From there, extends through S Europe to Turkey (N Anatolia, Taurus), the Caucasus, N Iran and SW Turkmenia; to Tien Shan; and, in the east, south through E and C China to Hainan, N Indochina, N Burma and NE India (Nagaland, Assam, Manipur). See also Geographical Variation, below. Common throughout its range in suitable habitat, and in many places very common.

MOVEMENTS Northern populations are subject to irruptive migrations, triggered by poor crops of pine or spruce seeds; these movements start in late summer (late July), reach islands (e.g. Ireland, Faroes), and individuals may stray more than 3000km. Juvenile dispersal often over 100km, and up to about 600km. Some movements also take place in the Far East, with stragglers found even on remote islands. Populations in mountainous areas descend somewhat to the valleys in winter.

HABITAT Within its vast range this species may be found in virtually any kind of woodland and forest, from pure broadleaf forest to unmixed stands of conifers; also rather common in copses, parks and gardens. In primeval forests of Poland, highest densities are reached in ash-alder (0.9 territories/10ha) and in oak-hornbeam (0.7 territories/10ha) stands, but rather uniformly distributed over all types of forest. Extremely high densities of up to 5 territories/10 ha are attained in parks or denser park-like forests with many old trees (7.2-7.6 territories/10ha; Berlin, Vienna). In N Africa, found in olive and poplar plantations and up to cedar, pine, pine-oak and cork-oak woods. In northern Burma, found in alder and rhododendron; in Japan, common in deciduous, mixed or coniferous woods. This species is also distributed over a wide range of altitudes: occurs from sea level to the timber line in Europe, where breeding has been recorded at over 2000m; in N

Africa reaches 1000m (Tunisia) and 2200m (Morocco), and in C Asian mountains 2500m; in SE Asia (race *cabanisi*) occupies forests above 1800m, and is found at up to 2300m in northern Burma and in Japan.

DESCRIPTION
P. m. major **Adult male** Forehead white to buffish; crown blue-glossed black; nape bright crimson-red. Lores, narrow supercilium and sides of head white to creamy, bordered below by black stripe from nape to base of lower mandible, black broadening in centre and extending to breast side. Chin and throat white or whitish. Hindneck black, with large white patch on each side. Mantle to uppertail-coverts bluish-black, rump often showing greyish feather bases; inner scapulars bluish-black, outer scapulars white. Upperwing black or brownish-black, with up to six white spots on flight feathers forming prominent bars; wing-coverts glossy black, innermost greater and median coverts white and joining with outer scapulars to form large white patch; some white in primary coverts. Uppertail black, with off-white bars at tips of rectrices increasing in size from second-innermost outwards, two largest outermost pairs largely white with two or three black bars. Underparts generally white, pale greyish-white or buff-white, with black extending onto breast sides from above and with bright scarlet vent and undertail-coverts. Underwing greyish-black, barred white, with coverts largely off-white to buffy-white. Undertail much as uppertail. (In worn plumage, black areas become duller and brown-tinged; underparts dirtier, greyish or creamy, and often stained.)

Adult female Much as male, but crown to upper mantle uniform, lacking red on nape.

Juvenile Lacks adult male's red nape, instead having red crown narrowly edged black (red usually less extensive on juvenile female). Black of upperparts less glossy, more brown-tinged, and bases of white scapulars often with some black barring (visible when plumage worn); black moustache less sharply defined, post-auricular bar narrower and sometimes not extending to nape. Underparts dirtier, often showing variable dusky streaks on sides and flanks, latter sometimes barred; ventral area pink rather than red, occasionally even buff/whitish; rarely, may show some pinkish colour on breast.

Bare parts Bill blackish-grey, lead-grey or slate-grey, paler at base of lower mandible. Legs and feet slate-grey, tinged olive or brown. Eyes deep red or reddish-brown; browner in juveniles.

GEOGRAPHICAL VARIATION Marked variation, both in size and in plumage as well as in length and shape of bill, throughout the species' extensive range. Generally, northern populations are bigger, with a shorter and heavier bill, and whiter below. Variations are mostly clinal, however, making racial boundaries difficult to define, and the situation is further complicated by much individual variation and the existence of many intermediates. Hybridisation has been recorded (rarely) between this species and White-winged, White-backed and Syrian Woodpeckers. Historical aspects of racial differentiation have been discussed by Voous (1947) and Winkler (1979b). The following 14 races are recognised here (following Short 1982).

P. m. major (Scandinavia and Siberia south to N Poland and northern Ukraine and east to Urals) Described above.

P. m. pinetorum (Britain and France east to Don and Volga rivers and south to Italy, Balkans, Turkey and southern Ukraine) Slightly smaller than nominate, but with much longer and narrower bill, and more buff or greyish below. Intergrades with nominate *major*. British and southern European individuals average smaller than intervening population. Romanian population ('*candidus*') slightly whiter than those in western Europe. Birds from Crimea, Caucasus and Transcaucasia may be intergrades between *pinetorum* and *poelzami*, but largely indistinguishable from former.

P. m. brevirostris (W Siberia south to C Tien Shan and Mongolia, and east to lower Amur, Manchuria and Sea of Okhotsk) Not well defined. Very like nominate race, very white (perhaps even whiter) below, very slightly bigger and with deeper red vent. Plumage noticeably dense and fluffy.

P. m. kamtschaticus (Kamchatka peninsula and northern Okhotsk coast) Similar to nominate *major* and *brevirostris*, but even whiter below and with very large white wing patch; outer tail feathers white, with at most just a few black spots.

P. m. hispanus (Iberia) Poorly defined. Darker than *pinetorum*; similar to *harterti* but smaller, more cream/less grey below (some are buff-brown or greyish-white), and with paler cheeks; rarely, may show hint of red on breast.

P. m. harterti (Sardinia and Corsica) Larger than S European *pinetorum* (closer in size to those from C Europe), and obviously darker greyish-brown below, with very dark red vent; less white on flight feathers. Corsican population ('*parroti*') averages slightly larger, but much overlap precludes subspecific recognition.

P. m. canariensis (Tenerife) As *harterti*, but with ventral region orangey-red and more black on outer tail, and with pale areas of wing less buffy; flanks pale, contrast with dark (deep brown to grey-brown) belly.

P. m. thanneri (Gran Canaria) As *canariensis*, but generally paler brown, less grey-buff, below, with white of flanks extending to breast.

P. m. mauritanus (Morocco) Resembles *hispanus* but slightly smaller, generally paler below and often with red on central breast. High Atlas population ('*lynesi*') tends to be slightly bigger and slightly darker below, but variation apparently clinal, with much overlap.

P. m. numidus (northern Algeria and Tunisia) As *mauritanus*, but larger, and with complete black breast band partly obscured by (variably prominent) red feather tips; generally buff below (some are paler), with vent a deeper red and this colour extending further up on belly.

P. m. poelzami (southern Caspian region and Transcaspia) Smaller than *pinetorum*, but with bill averaging longer than latter's (and longer than in nominate *major* or *brevirostris*); bill of male up to 11%

longer than female's. Markedly brown below.

P. m. japonicus (E and C Manchuria, Ussuriland, Korea, Sakhalin, Kuriles, Hokkaido, Honshu and Tsushima) Blacker above than *brevirostris*, with narrower bill, and with less white on scapulars and tail but more white on flight feathers; darker below. Becomes darker from north to south; intergrades with *cabanisi*, but generally much paler than latter.

P. m. cabanisi (southern Manchuria south through eastern China to eastern Burma, northern Laos, N Vietnam, SE China and Hainan) Very dark buff-brown below and very black above, with pale areas of head buffy-brown; increases in darkness southwards. Often some red on breast. Hainan population ('*hainanus*') slightly shorter-winged/-tailed.

P. m. stresemanni (SE Tibet, Sichuan, Qinghai, Gansu and Shaanxi to Yunnan, NE Burma and NE India) Even darker than *cabanisi*, and similarly becoming darker southwards. May have some red on breast.

MEASUREMENTS Wing 119-134 (*mauretanus*), 120-130 (*poelzami*), 123-136 (*cabanisi*), 132-141 (*pinetorum*), 135-150 (*major*); tail 79-89 (*numidus*), 84-93 (*cabanisi*), 82-95 (*pinetorum*); bill 31-36 (*poelzami*, *numidus*), 26-31 (*major*, *cabanisi*); tarsus 19-23 (*cabanisi*), 22-26 (*pinetorum*). Weight: 66-98 (*cabanisi*), 72-93 (*pinetorum*), 70-98 (*major*).

VOICE The most common call is a single, sharp *kix*, which may be delivered in rapid series when alarmed at the nest. A wooden *krrarraarr* of varying length and introduced by a *kix* represents a stronger form of announcement. A not very loud *rrrrr* (recalling Mistle Thrush *Turdus viscivorus*) may be given in agonistic situations, when other, softer calls can also be heard. Pair members exchange intimate *djad* at changeovers at the nest and before coition. In the courtship season, especially during flutter-aerial display, series of *gwig* notes are delivered which may be mistaken for calls of Middle Spotted Woodpecker. In distress, a piercing shriek is uttered in panting series. Nestlings utter a rasping chatter almost constantly, even in the absence of the parents. At the nest hole, rhythmic taps may be delivered. Both sexes drum before the breeding season, starting in winter, until about the time the young fledge, males drumming much more frequently; rolls are rather short, slightly accelerating, and, when drumming at fullest intensity, are given at a rate of about six per minute. Acoustically most active during and before the breeding season.

HABITS Rather conspicuous. Mostly seen singly, but pair members keep in contact before and during the breeding season, and in areas of high density short interactions in the canopy are commonly witnessed. Although it makes use of all strata, this is mainly a bird of the tree crowns in winter and may resort more frequently to the lower trunk in summer; in the canopy, branches and small twigs are visited. Pecking and hammering are most common in winter (65-95% of all foraging techniques), but do not altogether lose their importance when nestlings are being fed, especially if surface arthropods are not readily available (e.g. because of weather or habitat quality). Generally rather opportunistic, and seasonal and local differences are marked. Hammers quite persistently into hard and soft wood, up to 10cm deep in the latter. Prises, tears and pecks off pieces of bark. Gleaning and probing are more important at times of high food availability (and are also more prevalent among subspecies of milder climates, e.g. N African *numidus*). Sexual differences are minimal. Drilling of sap holes and sap-sucking is a very common habit of this woodpecker. Another very important feature of its behaviour is the use of anvils to work on unwieldy arthropod prey, fruits and, most important of all, nuts and pine, spruce or larch cones; certain anvils may be used for years (always by the same individual?). Harvests cones by holding the cone with one foot and pecking at the stalk until it breaks: then, transports cone in the bill and fixes it in the anvil, cones from previous activities being removed; seeds are then extracted, with the cone being rotated at regular intervals. One main (with up to 5500 processed cones) and several ancillary anvils are maintained. Climbs quickly, mostly straight up, but often backwards and downwards; in the crown, prefers to climb rather than to use its wings. May cling to twigs and leaf clusters in tit-like fashion; occasionally even hovers briefly, and sallies for aerial prey. Sexual differences in foraging very slight in C European and northern populations; they are more pronounced in *P. m. numidus* of N Africa, in which females are found mainly in the crown, preferring thinner branches. Displays in agonistic situations include forward pointing of the bill and moderate lateral swinging movements of the body. Wing-spreading with bill open, head feathers more or less erected, is more common. During courtship, a flutter-aerial display is exhibited by birds (mostly males) flying away from the partner: the wingbeats are shallow, the tail fully spread and turned upwards, and *gwig* call-series may be delivered as well; upon landing, the bird may demonstrate a prospective breeding hole, or drums. Roosts singly in old holes, or in cavities constructed for the purpose in late summer and autumn (mainly first-year birds?). Interspecific interactions are numerous and concern mainly hole competitors, primarily starlings, and sympatric woodpeckers.

FOOD Has a very varied diet, with clear seasonal changes in more seasonal habitats. Plant material rich in fat, mostly in form of coniferous seeds and various nuts (e.g. hazel, walnut, beech, hornbeam) and acorns (particularly in Caucasus), becomes prominent in winter. Seeds usually contribute about 30% but often up to 80% of the energy intake in winter (the equivalent of up to 1700 pine or 1440 spruce seeds); other vegetable matter includes buds and, of major importance locally and seasonally, tree sap, and possibly nectar. The animal food consists mainly of larvae of wood-boring beetles, lepidopterous larvae and pupae, plant lice, beetles, hymenopterans, hemipterans, spiders and many other arthropods, and even crustaceans; ants may form a substantial part of the diet, with smaller species (e.g. *Lasius*) being favoured over larger ones (e.g. *Formica*). Notorious for taking eggs and young of other hole-nesting birds and of open-nest breeders, and seems to be a key predator on nests of Penduline Tits *Remix pendulinus*.

BREEDING Courtship activities may commence in December; egg-laying period mid April to June. Shows great flexibility in choice of nest site. Male plays the most active part in selection of the nest, in which it also roosts throughout the breeding cycle, at least until two days before the young leave the nest. In most cases, a new nest is constructed annually in dead or living (much more so than its sympatric congeners) trees or large bushes, at usually 3-8m (range 0.3-26m; mean in primeval forest of Poland 12.0m, lower than Middle Spotted or White-backed). Entrance circular or slightly oval. Both sexes excavate the hole, the male taking the major share in most cases. Rarely, breeds in wooden nestboxes. Clutch of 4-8 (generally (5-7) eggs (geographical variation in clutch size not well documented). Both sexes incubate for 10-12 days. The young fledge after 20-23 days, are divided up between the parents and remain near nest for two or three weeks, although the parents cease to feed them after ten days.

REFERENCES Bardin 1986; Bezzel 1985; Blume 1961, 1968; Brazil 1991; Conrads & Mensendiek 1980; Cramp 1985; deBruyn *et al.* 1972; Dement'ev & Gladkov 1966;

Gebauer 1984; Glutz von Blotzheim & Bauer 1980; Hågvar *et al.* 1990; Heim de Balsac & Mayaud 1962; Hogstad 1971a, 1971b; Jenni 1983; László 1988; Miech 1986; Pflumm 1979; Pynnönen 1939; Ruge 1973; Spitznagel 1993; Stanford & Mayr 1941; Voous 1947; Wesolowski & Tomialojc 1986; Winkler 1973, 1979b; Winkler & Short 1978; Witt 1988.

---

105 SYRIAN WOODPECKER
Picoides syriacus   Plate 32

Forms a superspecies with *major, leucopterus, assimilis* and *himalayensis*.

IDENTIFICATION Length c. 23cm. Small, with rather long, almost straight, chisel-tipped bill broad across nostrils. A typical pied woodpecker, having black upperparts, white-barred wings with large white patch on inner coverts, and unmarked pale underparts (some show a few flank streaks/bars) with pinkish-red undertail-coverts. Prominent black moustache extends down onto breast side but does not reach rear of head, so looks very white about face. Male has red nape patch. Juveniles have black-bordered red crown.

Similar species Most likely to be confused with very similar Great Spotted Woodpecker (104) where ranges overlap. Syrian is best distinguished by its having greater area of white on rear of head (from behind, this makes Syrian look longer- and thinner-necked), less white in outer tail, duller, less glossy upperparts and pinker, less red vent; pale of forehead usually extends further up, and male has more red on nape. Juveniles of the two are very similar, but young Syrian generally shows more white on head and less in tail, more streaking below, and usually a stronger indication of pink on breast. Syrian also has a different (softer), call, distinguishable once known. In southeast of range overlaps with slightly smaller Sind Woodpecker (107), which is separated by its smaller moustache only just extending onto breast (but connecting with base of hindneck) and by its greater amount of white in outer tail; male Sind also has entire crown red.

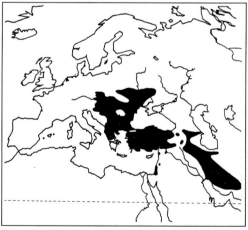

DISTRIBUTION Ranges from SE C Europe (Austria, Czech Republic, Slovakia, Hungary) east to S Poland, W and S Ukraine and southernmost Belorussia, and southeast through the Balkans to Turkey, Syria, Israel, Palestine (to N Sinai), N Iraq, Transcaucasia and from N and W to SE Iran. In the last century, has extended its range: formerly a woodpecker of the eastern Mediterranean, it spread via the Balkans to C Europe. Agricultural development and other human activities probably fostered this range expansion, which seems to be continuing to some extent (e.g. in region north of Black Sea). Common in most parts of range.

MOVEMENTS Despite its open habitat and its proven ability to cover long distances during dispersal, no seasonal movements have been documented.

HABITAT A woodpecker of open country. Inhabits oak woodland and light montane forests in the southeast; in Turkey, also breeds in coniferous forest at lower levels. Often found in plantations of all kinds, including olive, pecan and avocado in the south, and vineyards in C Europe, where found also in native trees, groups of trees, mainly near habitations, forest edge, parks and gardens. Visits reedbeds in winter. Habitat overlap with Great Spotted greatest in winter, when the latter often occurs closer to human settlements. Reaches at least 2000m in N and W Turkey and 2700m in 3 Iran.

DESCRIPTION
Adult male Lower forehead buffy, remainder white to creamy; crown black (rarely, with a few scattered red feathers), central hindcrown and nape red. White of forehead continues to lores, below eyes, as a line above eye and back to rear neck side. Moustachial stripe black, expanding a little upwards on neck side and continuing down onto upper breast side. Chin and throat off-white to pale buff. Central hindneck, mantle and inner scapulars, back and uppertail-coverts dull black. Outer scapulars and innermost greater coverts (plus some medians) white, remaining upperwing-coverts black (but outer primary coverts mostly white); flight feathers black, with large white spots forming three wingbars (usually four or five bars on Great Spotted). Uppertail black, outer feathers with a few white spots or white tip and next inner rectrix sometimes with one white spot/bar. Underparts from breast white to pale creamy, becoming pinkish-red on lower belly to undertail-coverts; lower flanks often faintly streaked or barred dusky grey. Underwing broadly barred grey and white, with off-white or buffy-white coverts. Undertail much as uppertail.

Adult female As male, but lacks red on nape.

Juvenile Slightly duller than adults, but often with some pinkish feathers across upper breast (may rarely form complete band); flank streaks/bars usually present and more extensive, sometimes reaching breast sides. Both sexes have black-bordered red crown (nape black).

Bare parts Bill dark grey to slaty-blue, paler at base of lower mandible. Legs and feet slate-grey, tinged blue, brown or olive. Eyes red-brown, in adult sometimes deep red.

GEOGRAPHICAL VARIATION Slight. Those in N Iran and Transcaucasia are smaller and frequently show more white in outer tail, while latter population and also those from Asia Minor tend to be darker, more brown-buff, below. Overlap exists, however, and racial separation seems unwarranted. Hybridises with Great Spotted Woodpecker, and apparently also with Sind Woodpecker.

MEASUREMENTS Wing 124-139 (Iran), 131-137 (C Europe); tail 79-85; bill 27-33; tarsus 22.5-25. Weight: 55-63 (Iran), 70-82 (C Europe).

VOICE The most common call is a single *kewg* (a better rendering would be *püg*, or *puc* pronounced as in French 'duc'), which may be delivered in rapid series when alarmed at the nest. A loud *kweg-kweg kriririrrrr* is more commonly heard than the equivalent call of Great Spotted Woodpecker. In agonistic situations, loud *gweeka-gweeka..* may be

given. Pair members exchange intimate *djad* calls in changeovers at the nest and before coition. During courtship, loud series of distinct *kweek* notes are characteristic. Both sexes drum, but it is mainly the male that delivers the accelerating rolls, which are longer (up to twice as long), and often higher-pitched, than those of Great Spotted; as a rule, less persistent than in latter species, with rolls given at a rate of five or six per minute. Nestlings utter a rasping chatter, mostly in the presence of a parent. In distress, a piercing shriek is uttered in panting series. Acoustically most active during and before the breeding season.

HABITS Usually a conspicuous bird, most easily detected by its voice or when covering large distances in its open habitat on the wing. The usually low breeding densities (0.05 territories/10 ha), however, make it often difficult to find. Lives singly or in pairs, which keep loose contact before and during breeding season. Forages at all levels, from ground to canopy, but almost half of all foraging takes place in the lower strata. Marked seasonal changes, from more crown foraging in winter to opportunistic habitat use during nesting season. Pecks and hammers less often than Great Spotted Woodpecker. Especially in summer, gleaning and probing (probes more than Great Spotted, but less than Middle Spotted, 102) account for 40-50% of all foraging activities, which include up to 20% flycatching. Anvils are used frequently to process large insects (beetles), fruits and nuts. Has also been observed taking sap on ringed trees. Hops on the ground, and moves swiftly during arboreal feeding. Has to cover relatively large distances between feeding sites, and between them and the nest. Displays similar to those of Great Spotted: raises neck feathers, spreads and flicks wings, opens bill and exhibits lateral swinging movements with bill-pointing in aggressive encounters. Home ranges large, densities about 0.05-0.1/10 ha. Interspecific territories are maintained with Great Spotted (each reacts to the other species' drumming), from which Syrian is behaviourally isolated through different calls, but no interactions with Middle Spotted Woodpecker. Main hole competitor is the Common Starling *Sturnus vulgaris*, whose range has locally expanded possibly with the arrival of this woodpecker and the consequent new breeding opportunities.

FOOD Animal food and a relatively large amount of plant material. Beetles and their larvae, ants, lepidopterous larvae (even hairy ones) and pupae; spiders. Almonds (causes some damage to plantations), walnuts, pecans, hazel nuts, apricot stones, acorns, pine seeds, sunflower seeds, pistachios and the like comprise the seeds which are eaten in summer (in some cases, as with apricots and prunes, ripe fruits are taken to get at the seeds), as well as in winter. Also takes the flesh of cherries, mulberries, raspberries, citrus fruits (*Melia azedarach*) and others, which may also be fed to the nestlings.

BREEDING Breeding season extends from mid March (Israel) or mid April (C Europe) to May, rarely to June. A wide variety of tree species is used for nesting; also uses utility poles and similar structures. Nest holes are excavated, mainly by the male, in the trunk or a large limb 1.5-6m above ground; nests may be reused. Most frequent clutch size usually 4 (Israel) or 5 (Hungary) eggs, but 3 and 7 eggs have been recorded as well. Both sexes take part in incubation, the male sitting overnight; the chicks hatch after 9-11 days. The parents also share nest sanitation (ceases at end of nestling period) and feeding, with a slight tendency for the female to do less. The young fledge after about 20-26 days, and stay with the parents for a further two weeks.

REFERENCES Bezzel 1985; Cramp 1985; Dement'ev &

Gladkov 1966; Desfayes & Praz 1978; Glutz von Blotzheim & Bauer 1980; Moran 1977; Paz 1987; Ruge 1969, 1970a; Serez 1983; Vaurie 1959a; Voous 1947; Winkler 1968, 1971, 1972b, 1973; Winkler & Short 1978.

106 WHITE-WINGED WOODPECKER
Picoides leucopterus   Plate 31

Other name: White-winged Spotted Woodpecker
Forms a superspecies with *major, syriacus, assimilis* and *himalayensis.*

IDENTIFICATION Length c. 22-23cm. Rather small, with medium-long, straight and slightly chisel-tipped bill fairly broad across nostrils. A pied woodpecker of SC Asia, best told by its extensive long white patch on the inner wing and scapulars and broad white wingbars (wings can appear mostly white), and the red of the ventral area extending to the central breast; male has red nape band. Head pattern is much as that of Great Spotted Woodpecker (104). Juvenile is also similar to that of Great Spotted, but usually distinctly buff below (with pinkish vent).

Similar species Distinguished from sympatric race *brevirostris* of Great Spotted Woodpecker by much more extensive white in wings, larger white patch on rear neck side (difficult to judge), and slightly smaller size, with somewhat shorter and narrower bill (and adult often even purer white below).

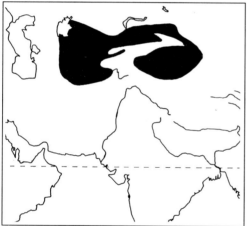

DISTRIBUTION Resident from Aral Sea, SW Turkmenistan (Turkmenia) (possibly also extreme NE Iran) and NE Afghanistan eastwards through S Kazakhstan, Uzbekistan and lower parts of Kyrgyzstan (Kirgizia) to southern tip of Lake Balkhash, and continuing to Xinjiang, W China (north to around Karamay, east to about Lop Nur and south to the edge of the Kunlun Shan). Common.

MOVEMENTS Somewhat nomadic outside breeding season, but essentially non-migratory.

HABITAT In the plains, inhabits riparian woodland with poplars and other softwood, willows, saxaul (*Haloxylon ammodendron*) scrub in deserts, and frequently orchards and gardens. Also found in broadleaf montane forests, often containing hazel and fruit trees or mixed with fir or juniper, and in juniper stands. Generally at lower elevations than Great Spotted Woodpecker (which in same region prefers coniferous areas), but reaches 1050m in several places and over 1800m on northern slopes of

Kunlun Shan.

DESCRIPTION
Adult male Forehead white; crown black; nape red. Narrow supercilium, cheeks and ear-coverts white (often stained). Black moustachial stripe from base of lower mandible, curving up behind ear-coverts to join upper nape, broadening on neck side and extending down onto breast and backwards to join mantle sides, isolating large white patch on side of rear neck. Chin and throat white. Hindneck and mantle to uppertail-coverts black. Upperwing black, with large area of white on scapulars and inner wing-coverts, broad white bars on primaries and secondaries, and outer webs of tertials edged white; marginal coverts white. Uppertail black, with broad white bars towards tips of outer two or three pairs of rectrices. Underparts white (sometimes with faint grey or buff tinge/staining), with black extending from neck to breast sides, and red-pink from central lower breast to vent and undertail-coverts; a few individuals have trace of pink on breast. Underwing mostly white, with greyish-black bars and tips to flight feathers. Undertail as uppertail, but greyer.

Adult female Bill averages about 10% shorter than male's. Lacks red nape band.

Juvenile Duller, more brown-black above and clearly buffish below, with ventral area pink rather than red and sometimes black streaks on breast sides. Primaries tipped white; often more white in wings and tail, though occasionally white scapulars finely barred black. Juvenile male lacks red on nape, but has crown red admixed with some black and white feathers; female has crown black or, more often, with variable amount of red in forecrown.

Bare parts Bill greyish-black, paler at base of lower mandible. Legs and feet dull blackish or dark grey. Eyes deep red, red-brown or brown.

GEOGRAPHICAL VARIATION Minor variation insufficient to warrant racial division. Birds of the hills and mountains of Turkestan tend to be less white. Hybridises very occasionally with Great Spotted Woodpecker (race *brevirostris*), with which possibly conspecific; Great Spotted Woodpeckers from Tien Shan named as '*tianshanicus*' are presumed to be offspring of such mixed pairs.

MEASUREMENTS Wing 122-133; bill 27-32.5. Weight: 67.

VOICE Not well described; common call seems to be similar to that of Great Spotted Woodpecker. Drums.

HABITS Probably rather similar to those of other members of the superspecies. Since it is smaller and has a weaker and more slender bill than the form of the Great Spotted Woodpecker with which it comes into contact, more gleaning and probing may be expected.

FOOD Not recorded.

BREEDING Egg-laying extends from late March to April. Nests in softwood trees (poplar, willow) at heights between 1 and 5m; also recorded nesting in the slope of a sandhill. Clutch 4-6(7) eggs.

REFERENCES Dement'ev & Gladkov 1966; Vaurie 1959a.

107 SIND WOODPECKER
Picoides assimilis   Plate 32

Other name: Sind Pied Woodpecker
Forms a superspecies with *major, syriacus, leucopterus* and
himalayensis.

IDENTIFICATION Length c. 20-22cm. Small, with longish, almost straight, slightly chisel-tipped bill broad across
nostrils. Black above with white inner-wing patch and
white-barred flight feathers, and white below with red
undertail-coverts. Looks very pale in area of head, with
forehead, face and neck sides unmarked white apart from
isolated black moustache. Male has crimson crown and
nape, these being black on female. A restless and very active
bird, often encountered singly.

Similar species In Iran meets Syrian Woodpecker (105),
from which told by slightly smaller size, smaller (thinner)
bill, and moustache extending downwards only just onto
breast, but rear moustache joined to upperparts by black
band; also, male Syrian has red on head restricted to nape,
though juveniles (both sexes) have red crown bordered
with black. The two species may occasionally interbreed. In
west of range overlaps partly with Himalayan Woodpecker
(108), which is bigger, less pure white below, has black line
joining rear moustache with crown but moustache not
normally connecting with hindneck base, has dark mark
behind eye, and has more white on outer tail. Himalayan
is also usually found at higher elevations.

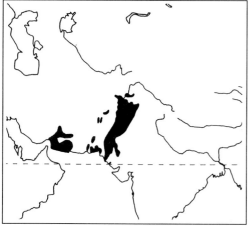

DISTRIBUTION Generally prefers dry areas at lower
levels, occurring in SE Iran and in Baluchistan, Sind and
Punjab regions of Pakistan. Locally distributed, and common in some parts (e.g. Punjab).

HABITAT Frequents riverine forests, thorn scrub, and
desert wadis with scattered acacias and other trees, as well
as roadside trees and irrigated plantations (especially of
mulberry); in Iran, also frequents palm stands and enters
gardens. Scattered and stunted thorn trees (*Prosopis spicigera,
Acacia modesta, A. senegal*) and euphorbias are sufficient for
this woodpecker in arid habitats; wild olives (*Olea cuspidata*),
pistachio *Pistacia integerrima*, and ash *Fraxinus excelsior*
occur in the hilly parts of its range. Apparently absent from
pine-juniper woodland, where Brown-fronted Woodpecker
(94) may be met with. Found mainly in lowlands, but in
Pakistan ascends to 1600m in the Salt Range and perhaps
to 2200m in Baluchistan.

DESCRIPTION
Adult male Forehead, lores, superciliary area, cheeks, ear-
coverts and neck sides white, normally stained buffish on
forehead/lores and sometimes with dusky area in centre of
ear-coverts. Crown and nape red, usually with at least some
black and/or grey of feather bases visible. Black moustachial
stripe extends to rear lower edge of ear-coverts, from where
black band continues to upper mantle and narrow stripe to
uppermost breast side. Chin and throat white, often stained
pale buff. Hindneck and upperparts blue-glossed black.
Upperwing-coverts black, with large area of white on
mostly inner coverts and extending just onto outer scapulars;
flight feathers brownish-black, broadly barred white.
Uppertail black, outer two rectrix pairs with broad white
bars (rarely, bars much reduced or almost absent). Underparts white (occasionally with very faint grey or buffy
tinge), with minimal black flank streaking, and with pink
in centre of lower breast and belly and on lower flanks,
becoming red on undertail coverts. Underwing white,
barred greyish-black on flight feathers. Undertail dark
brown with white barring.

Adult female Slightly shorter-billed than male, and with
entire crown and nape deep black.

Juvenile Duller than adults, with black areas browner,
white areas buff-tinged and undertail-coverts pink rather
than red. Both sexes have red in crown centre, more
restricted on females.

Bare parts Bill slate-grey, paler on lower mandible. Legs
and feet grey to blue-grey. Eyes red-brown to brown.

GEOGRAPHICAL VARIATION Monotypic. Hybridises
rarely with Syrian Woodpecker.

MEASUREMENTS Wing 111-123; tail 65-73; bill of male
28-32, of female 24-27; tarsus 20. Weight: 42-64.

VOICE A single call note, a weak rattle, *chir-rir-rirrh-rirrh,*
and a *wicka, toi-whit toi-whit toi-whit.* Young are noisy when
older, and are fed at the hole entrance. Both sexes drum.

HABITS An active woodpecker, usually met with singly,
which forages by hammering and probing. Uses branches
and twigs of *Acacia, Pistacia* and other trees, as well as
euphorbias and fence posts. Often near the ground and on
fallen trees.

FOOD Ants, especially *Camponotus,* and larvae of wood-
boring beetles form the diet.

BREEDING Breeding season extends from March (egg-
laying) to April. Holes are sometimes rather low, about 1-
4m from the ground, in trunks and dead branches, often
of tamarisk (*Tamarix*). Both sexes take part in nest excavation. Usual clutch size 3 or 4 eggs. Incubation lasts 15-16
days and is undertaken by both parents.

REFERENCES Ali & Ripley 1970; Christison & Ticehurst
1943; Roberts 1991; Vaurie 1959a; Whistler 1930.

108 HIMALAYAN WOODPECKER
Picoides himalayensis   Plate 32

Other name: Himalayan Pied Woodpecker
Forms a superspecies with *major, syriacus, leucopterus* and *assimilis*.

IDENTIFICATION Length 23-25cm. Small, with long, almost straight, chisel-tipped bill broad across nostrils. A typical pied woodpecker of the Himalayas, with black upperparts, large white inner patch on white-barred wings, and largely white outer tail; underparts are pale buffish or greyish, generally unmarked, with red lower belly and undertail-coverts. Both sexes have pale forehead and whitish face, with black patch behind eye, and with black moustache extending at rear slightly down onto breast and upwards (often as broken band) around rear of ear-coverts. Males have red crown and nape.

Similar species The only similar pied woodpecker within its range is Sind Woodpecker (107), which is found at lower levels. Sind is slightly smaller, with whiter underparts, and has whiter face lacking black between eyes and hindneck.

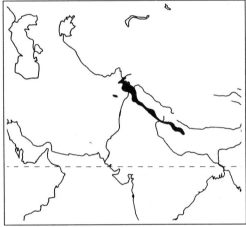

DISTRIBUTION A western Himalayan species found in the Safed Koh of extreme NE Afghanistan and adjacent Pakistan, in NE Pakistan and east through Kashmir and the N Indian foothills to western Nepal just beyond 83°E. The commonest woodpecker in most of its range.

MOVEMENTS Some local movement to lower hills (1370m or sometimes lower) may occur in winter.

HABITAT Habitats include rather dense coniferous, oak and rhododendron mountain forests, this woodpecker being found in spruce, pine, cedar or other extensive forests, and locally in smaller patches of mixed pine and juniper. It lives in a zone between 1970 and 3200m, regionally up to the tree line.

DESCRIPTION
P. h. himalayensis **Adult male** Forehead pale buffy-white; crown to upper nape crimson-red, usually with at least some black/grey feather bases showing, especially at forecrown and crown sides. Lores, superciliary area, area below eye, and ear-coverts white, tinged buff, with black patch behind eye. Complete moustachial stripe black, this colour expanding on neck sides and continuing down slightly onto upper breast side and up behind ear-coverts (where often broken) to meet rear crown. Rear neck sides white or whitish. Chin and throat buff. Hindneck and entire upperparts black. Upperwing black, inner coverts with much white, and

flight feathers barred white. Uppertail black, but outer two feathers largely white with black at base and a few black bars at tip, and next inner ones with white bars at tip (amount of white in outer tail varies, however, some having more black barring). Underparts pale buff or greyish-brown (breast often sullied yellowish-brown), becoming yellower on belly and red on lower belly and undertail-coverts; generally unmarked, but may show hint of streaks or bars on lower flanks. Underwing greyish-black, barred white. Undertail as uppertail, but duller.

Adult female Somewhat smaller and shorter-billed than male. Lacks red on head.

Juvenile Duller than adults, with black areas browner, and has red of ventral area pink and not reaching to belly; some streaking on upper flanks and barring on lower flanks (faint bars sometimes present on breast). Both sexes have white spotting on forecrown and orange-red in crown centre, red more restricted on female.

Bare parts Bill blackish to dark grey, often paler on lower mandible. Legs and feet grey to dull green or green-brown. Eyes red-brown.

GEOGRAPHICAL VARIATION Two races.
  P. h. himalayensis (W Nepal and adjacent parts of N India) Described above.
  P. h. albescens (NE Afghanistan east to Himachal Pradesh) Paler than nominate, with forehead white and underparts pale greyish-white (lacking buff or brown tinges of nominate); white bars in tail average narrower. Intergrades with nominate where ranges meet.

MEASUREMENTS Wing 123-136; tail 74-85; bill 27-33; tarsus 20.5-24. Weight: 57-85.

VOICE A single call note, *kit*, strongly resembling Great Spotted Woodpecker's (104), with a slight tendency towards Syrian's (105). A *tri-tri-tri-tri* call has been described and may represent a long-distance signal. The *wicka*-call of this species is a rapid, high-pitched *chissik-chissik*. Drums in rapid short rolls.

HABITS An arboreal woodpecker, rarely descending to the ground. Forages singly, typically so in winter, or in pairs, and is occasionally seen within mixed-species flocks of tits and warblers. Anvils are used for processing pine cones. It is quite possible that this species also drinks sap from specially excavated sap wells. The pair engages in aerial pursuits near the nest tree, during which *wicka*-calls are uttered.

FOOD The diet consists of insects and their larvae and plant matter. Takes wood-boring beetle larvae, weevils, spiders and caterpillars; acorns (*Quercus dilatata*) and pine seeds (*Pinus wallichiana, P. longifolia*) are important in winter.

BREEDING Eggs are laid in the second half of April and first half of May. Nest in dead (but often also living) wood in main trunk or large limb at 1.5-12m; male does most of the excavating. Locally, deciduous trees, especially cherries (*Prunus cornuta*) are preferred. Copulation may last 30secs. Clutch of 3-5 eggs. Both sexes incubate, the young hatching after about two weeks. Both also feed the young, which take about three weeks to fledge.

REFERENCES Ali & Ripley 1970; Inskipp & Inskipp 1991; Löhrl & Thielcke 1969; Macdonald & Henderson 1977; Osmaston 1916; Roberts 1991.

109 STRIPED WOODPECKER
Picoides lignarius   Plate 33

Forms a superspecies with *mixtus*.

IDENTIFICATION Length c. 15-16cm. Very small, with longish, virtually straight, chisel-tipped bill broad across nostrils. Strongly black and white in appearance, with heavy barring above and on wings and entire tail; underparts white or whitish with prominent streaking. Dark crown, ear-coverts and small moustache. Male has small amount of red on nape and usually has pale streaks/spots on crown; female lacks red and generally also has unstreaked crown.

Similar species Checkered Woodpecker (110) is extremely similar to Striped and may well be conspecific with it. The two are often inseparable in the field, even with good views. Striped is slightly larger, has a slightly longer bill, is rather more heavily marked below and more clearly barred above (dark bars broader than on Checkered), and is a shade darker overall (Checkered being a little browner, less deep black); in addition, nape of male Striped tends to show a little more red, which is somewhat darker in tone. In direct comparison, these minor differences should together be sufficient, but ranges appear not to meet (although more field research is required to confirm this).

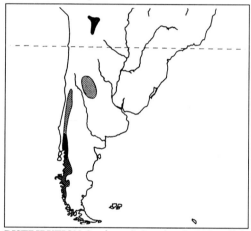

DISTRIBUTION Southern S America, in WC Bolivia (Santa Cruz; Cochabamba, Tunari range) and SW Bolivia (Potosí, Tarija), and in the Andes in S Chile (Bío-Bío to Magallanes) and SW Argentina (Neuquén to Santa Cruz).

MOVEMENTS Southern populations migrate to WC Argentina (La Rioja, Cordoba).

HABITAT Rather versatile, this species inhabits humid to xeric forests, *Nothofagus* forest, open types of forest or the edge of dense forest, open stunted forest, but also in the interior of tall wet forest. In north of range, occurs in dry areas with scattered trees (*Acacia*) and cacti. Also in pastures with shade trees, plantations and orchards. At 1600-4000m in Bolivia, Chilean and Argentinian populations reaching 1800m.

DESCRIPTION
Adult male Forehead and crown black, latter with variable amount of streaking/spotting (often rather indistinct); sides of nape dark red (sometimes orange-tinged), red generally meeting across lower nape. Ear-coverts dark brownish-black, faintly spotted white. Lores and supercilium white, latter continuing down around rear ear-coverts to join broad white line from bill. Moustachial stripe blackish, mixed with white feathering, and heavily streaked white

near bill. Chin and throat whitish, finely streaked/spotted black. Hindneck and upperparts dark brownish-black, narrowly scalloped white to pale brownish-white. Upperwing brownish-black, flight feathers barred white and coverts with large white spots (form broken bars). Uppertail dark brownish-black, all feathers narrowly but distinctly barred white or buff-white. Underparts from breast white, often tinged yellow or buff, and heavily and rather coarsely streaked blackish, streaks finer on belly, and becoming barred black on lower flanks (arrowhead marks) and undertail-coverts. Underwing and undertail as above, but paler.

Adult female Shorter-billed than male and lacks red on nape; usually lacks white crown spots/streaks, but may show some on forecrown.

Juvenile Duller and browner than adults, and with heavier underpart streaking and barring; upperparts more irregularly barred. Both sexes have red on crown, male having entire crown red, but on young females this is much less extensive.

Bare parts Bill black, paler at base and on lower mandible. Legs and feet grey or grey-brown. Eyes deep brown.

GEOGRAPHICAL VARIATION None recognisable. Monotypic.

MEASUREMENTS Wing 89-97; tail 56-59; bill 20-21.2. Weight: 35-39.

VOICE Common call a loud *peek*; also a trilling long-distance call, lower, less harsh than that of Checkered Woodpecker.

HABITS A shy and quiet bird which lives solitarily. Occasionally joins mixed-species flocks, e.g. with the ovenbird *Aphrastura spinicauda* (Thorn-tailed Rayadito). Resembles Lesser Spotted Woodpecker (93) in foraging behaviour; mainly gleans and probes, but also pecks and hammers to excavate.

BREEDING Bolivian populations breed probably in June-September, Chilean and Argentinian birds from October (north) to January (south). Nest is built into tree or cactus, and contains a clutch of 3-5 eggs.

REFERENCES Fjeldså & Krabbe 1990; Johnson 1967; Olrog 1984; Short 1970a; Vuilleumier 1967.

---

110 CHECKERED WOODPECKER
Picoides mixtus   Plate 33

Other name: Checked Woodpecker
Forms a superspecies with *lignarius*.

IDENTIFICATION Length c. 14cm. Very small, with long, straight, slightly chisel-tipped bill broad across nostrils. A barred and streaked woodpecker very closely related to and possibly conspecific with Striped (109), which it greatly resembles in basic plumage pattern. Male has red to orange-red on nape often restricted to sides only (not meeting across nape).

Similar species Often indistinguishable in the field from Striped Woodpecker, which is barely larger and only slightly darker; northern race *cancellatus* of Checkered, however, is much browner overall and has much more white in plumage, with reduced markings below. For differences see Striped Woodpecker, and also Description and Geographical Variation below. Note that the ranges of the two species appear not to overlap.

DISTRIBUTION Southern S America: Uruguay, Argentina (south to N Chubut), Paraguay, SE Bolivia and central

S Brazil (S Mato Grosso, Goiás, Minas Gerais, São Paulo, Rio Grande do Sul).

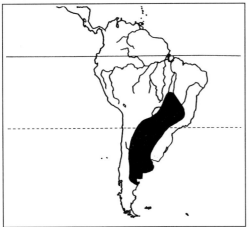

MOVEMENTS Individuals of southern populations may migrate a short distance in autumn. Leaves the Mato Grosso in May, returning in January.

HABITAT This species is found in various types of dry, open woodland. It occurs in savannas, and in arid bush country with spiny *Prosopis* species. Up to 610m in Bolivia.

DESCRIPTION
P. m. mixtus **Adult male** Forehead and crown blackish-brown, streaked white or buffish-white (some crown feathers occasionally tipped red); nape red or orange-red, but this colour often restricted to nape sides. Ear-coverts dark brown. Lower lores and supercilium white, latter continuing around rear ear-coverts to join broad white band from bill. Narrow, weak moustachial stripe of dark brown streaks and spots. Chin and throat white, faintly streaked brown. Hindneck and upperparts blackish-brown, barred/scalloped whitish or brownish-white, bars appearing more irregular or more spot-like on mantle. Upperwing and its coverts deep brown, barred white throughout (bars more as spots on coverts). Uppertail brownish-black, all feathers narrowly but distinctly barred white. Underparts from breast white, tinged pale yellow or buff, and with dark brown streaks especially on breast and flanks (lower belly/flanks sometimes with hint of barring); undertail-coverts whitish, with fine brown spot-like streaks. Underwing and undertail as above, but paler.

Adult female Slightly smaller than male. Lacks red on nape and pale streaks on crown, but occasionally shows slight streaking on forehead/forecrown.

Juvenile Duller and darker than adults, with barring on upperparts usually broken; underparts dull white, more heavily streaked and barred. Both sexes have red on crown (not nape), this colour being reduced (and often as scattered red tips) on young female.

Bare parts Bill black, with paler base and lower mandible. Legs and feet pale greyish. Eyes deep brown to reddish.

GEOGRAPHICAL VARIATION Four races are recognised, the first three below forming a homogeneous group and the fourth being well differentiated.
    P. m. mixtus (Parana river and Buenos Aires Province, Argentina) Described above.
    P. m. berlepschi (Argentina, from Cordoba south through San Luis, La Pampa and southern Buenos Aires to Neuquén and Río Negro) Very like nominate, but longer-billed; somewhat darker above, crown

streaks sometimes limited to forecrown, more extensive dark colour on ear-coverts, and ground colour of underparts cleaner white.
    P. m. malleator (Chaco region of northern Argentina, Paraguay and SE Bolivia) Averages slightly smaller than above two races, but plumage very close to nominate; underparts more heavily streaked than latter, and usually with some barring.
    P. m. cancellatus (Brazil) Shorter-tailed than above races and much browner, less black, overall, with crown distinctly browner (especially on female); white bars on upperparts broader than dark ones; underparts much whiter, with far fewer and smaller, finer streaks. Intergrades with *malleator* in NE Paraguay.

MEASUREMENTS Wing 78-91; tail 62; bill 18-22. Weight: 29.8-37.

VOICE Single *peek*, similar to call of Downy Woodpecker (113), also a trilling long-distance call, *ti-ti-ti-ti-ti...*; and *we-we-we....* Drums.

HABITS Occurs singly or in pairs. Works over twigs and small branches of bushes and trees. The most common feeding techniques employed are gleaning and probing; also pecks weakly.

FOOD Insects, seeds.

BREEDING Breeds September-November. Nest is excavated by both sexes in a tree or palm at 3-6m. Clutch of 4 eggs.

REFERENCES Gore & Gepp 1978; Marelli 1919; Olrog 1984; Peña 1994; Short 1970a; Sick 1993.

---

111 NUTTALL'S WOODPECKER
Picoides nuttallii   Plate 33

Forms a superspecies with *scalaris*.

IDENTIFICATION Length c. 19cm. Small, with fairly long, straight, chisel-tipped bill broad across nostrils. A very black-and-white woodpecker, barred above and on wings and with limited spots and barring below; has much black on face. Male has prominent red patch on hindcrown and nape. Confined to California and Baja California.

Similar species The only really similar species within its range is the very slightly smaller and much more widespread Ladder-backed Woodpecker (112). Nuttall's is best separated by the greater extent of black on its head and neck sides (extending to mantle sides), the broad area of unbarred black on the upper mantle, the broader bars above, the more barred appearance of the flank region, and by its more contrastingly black and white appearance; males also have less red on the crown. In addition, Ladder-backed is much more a bird of arid country, which Nuttall's generally shuns, and also has a different call. Note that Nuttall's may hybridise with Ladder-backed and also, rarely, with Downy Woodpecker (113), producing offspring of intermediate appearance.

DISTRIBUTION Restricted to coastal California (USA) and N Baja California (Mexico). Casually recorded in other parts of California, adjacent Arizona, S Oregon, Idaho, and British Columbia and Alberta (Canada). Fairly common to common.

HABITAT Arid to mesic woodlands, riparian woodland, open oak woodland (main habitat in California), shrub. From sea level to 1250 (2000)m.

DESCRIPTION
Adult male Forehead and forecrown black (contrasting

strongly with white nasal tufts), well streaked with white, especially on forecrown; hindcrown and nape red, normally with a few white spots. Ear-coverts black, bordered above by narrow white supercilium which curves down onto rear neck sides and below by white stripe running backwards from lores. Thin black moustachial stripe expands on neck sides into large patch, this joining with rear ear-coverts and also extending back to meet mantle sides. Hindneck and upperparts black, with lower mantle to upper rump broadly barred white. Upperwing-coverts black, spotted white; flight feathers black, narrowly barred white. Uppertail black, with outer feathers white (often with one or two black spots) and next two inners barred black and white at tips. Underparts white, lightly tinged creamy-buff, with spots on breast sides becoming bars on flanks, lower belly and undertail-coverts. Underwing and undertail as above, but paler. (In worn plumage, ground colour of underparts very white and crown streaking often lost.)

Adult female Clearly shorter-billed than male, and lacks red on head; forehead to nape usually unmarked black, but some variable white spotting may be present on fore and rear areas, and rarely crown may be entirely white-streaked.

Juvenile Duller and less contrastingly patterned than adults; upperparts have more white (but duller, greyer), and underparts are dull buff to greyish with more diffuse spots and more obvious bar marks. Both sexes have red on crown centre, on males speckled with white and on females less extensive and more broken.

Bare parts Bill blackish-grey to dull greyish-horn, paler at base and on lower mandible. Legs and feet greyish or grey-olive, sometimes dark horn. Eyes deep brown.

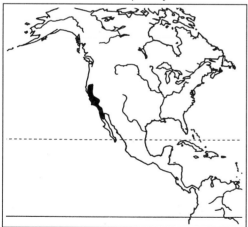

GEOGRAPHICAL VARIATION None. Monotypic.

HYBRIDS Hybridises with Ladder-backed (which see) and Downy Woodpeckers.

MEASUREMENTS Wing 96-107; tail 59-72; bill 18-24.2 (male's longer than female's by about 1.4 on average); tarsus 17.5-19. Weight: 28-47.

VOICE Single *pit* calls are less common than *pitit* notes, which are sometimes followed by a rapid (long or short) rattle, *itititit*..., as long-distance signal. Variable *kweek* series accompany encounters, in which also various *ta-wick* to *tew-tew-tew* calls and (more intimate) smacking notes are exchanged. Both sexes drum, the male more frequently, in relatively long rolls.

HABITS Most feeding takes place in oaks (*Quercus douglasii, Q. agrifolia*) and other trees with dense foliage

(e.g. blueblossom and relatives); also on mesquite and yuccas. Relative use of tree species changes somewhat with season. Gleaning and probing are the most common feeding techniques; pecks and hammers to excavate and flycatches occasionally. Sap wells of sapsuckers are also visited. Sexual differences more or less well expressed, but not consistent in direction among localities/studies (probably most marked outside breeding season). Often moves laterally and flutters to move within the crown of a tree, where it often perches crosswise and balances with the wings; plucks fruits while hanging upside-down. Displays as Ladder-backed, though crest-raising and head-bobbing seem to be more common. Interacts with other small woodpeckers in areas of contact, and with sapsuckers, Hairy Woodpeckers (116) and Acorn Woodpeckers (38), as well as with passerine hole competitors.

FOOD Mainly animal matter, with beetles predominating; also hemipterans, caterpillars and ants. Berries, seeds, acorns and nuts play a small role.

BREEDING Reproductive behaviour begins in February, with egg-laying season in April-May. Nest is excavated mainly by the male, more or less significantly assisted by the female (more so in latter stages), in a tree stub or fence post at 1-11m. A new nest is constructed each year. Copulations and egg-laying commence in the last days of hole excavation. Normal clutch size (3)4-5(6) eggs. Both sexes incubate for 14 days (the male at night and a majority of the day), and together feed the young and keep the nest clean. The young fledge after a 15-day nestling period, remaining with their parents for several weeks.

REFERENCES Block 1991; Jenkins 1979; Miller & Bock 1972; Short 1971b.

112 LADDER-BACKED WOODPECKER
Picoides scalaris Plate 33

Forms a superspecies with *nuttallii.*

IDENTIFICATION Length c. 18cm. Small, with long, rather straight, chisel-tipped bill broad across nostrils. A fairly typical pied woodpecker in appearance, prominently and heavily barred black and white above and on wings and outer tail, and with face striped black and white; pale underparts are spotted/streaked with blackish on breast and flanks and usually with at least a hint of bar-like markings in lower regions (but markings highly variable). Male has much red on crown/nape, this extending as spots onto forehead, but red area is reduced with wear.

Similar species Likely to be confused only with the closely related Nuttall's Woodpecker (111), with which it occasionally hybridises. Ladder-backed, however, has less black on sides of head and neck, has more numerous bars on upperparts (which extend to uppermost mantle) and on outer tail, and appears less clean, more buffy, below and with smaller dark spots/streaks; males normally show rather more red on head, this often extending to forehead. Nuttall's appears more hunched than Ladder-backed, and the calls of the two species also differ.

DISTRIBUTION SW USA and C America, from S California, Baja California (including Tres Marías and other islands), S Nevada, SW Utah, SE Colorado, W Oklahoma and Texas, southwards through Mexico to NE Nicaragua, and on some islands (Cancún and Holbox, off N Yucatan peninsula). Common to fairly common in northern half of range, becoming less common and much more local in southernmost part.

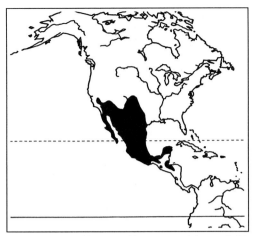

HABITAT Found in very arid country and deserts, habitats usually avoided by Nuttall's Woodpecker. Open to semi-open woodland and woods along (seasonally dry) rivers, with deciduous trees (e.g. sycamores) or cacti; also in pine-oak woodland. Southern populations (Belize) are found mainly in pinelands; Mexican Ladder-backed Woodpeckers are found commonly in oaks and become rarer towards the oak-pine woodland at higher altitudes, and locally are found also in clearings of humid forests; in mangroves in Honduras. From lowlands to 3000m in Baja California, at 1500-2100m in NE Mexico, and from sea level to 1800m in Guatemala.

DESCRIPTION

P. s. cactophilus **Adult male** Forehead and forecrown black, feathers narrowly tipped with red and white; central crown to nape red, fore part spotted with white. Broad supercilium from above eye white, continuing as wide band down rear neck side to breast side; broad black eye-stripe extends across upper ear-coverts, bordered below by white band from lower lores. Moustachial stripe black, bending upwards at rear to meet black eye-stripe and usually continuing downwards a little onto upper breast. Chin and throat white, tinged buffy or grey-brown on throat and usually unmarked. Hindneck and entire upperparts black, barred white from upper mantle to upper rump (some individual variation in width of bars). Upperwing black, coverts spotted with white and flight feathers white-barred. Uppertail black, outer two feathers normally barred white (outer rectrix sometimes all white) and next inner barred at tip. Underparts below throat pale buffish-white to pale greyish-brown, with breast sides (sometimes also centre) and upper flanks finely streaked or spotted, marks becoming rather more bar-like on lower flanks and undertail-coverts (markings below, however, vary greatly individually, both in size and in extent). Underwing barred dark grey and whitish. Undertail as uppertail, but paler. (In worn plumage, forehead and forecrown can be mostly or almost unmarked black, with some black feather bases visible at sides of rear crown and nape; also, ground colour of underparts becomes paler, whitish.)

Adult female Smaller and shorter-billed than male. Has forehead brownish-black and crown to nape black, sometimes with a few white spots on forehead and forecrown (rarely, spots more numerous and extensive).

Juvenile Dark areas duller than on adults, and barring above diffuse; underparts generally more buff, more heavily marked with dull brown streaks and with more barring. Both sexes have red in crown centre (not nape), usually less extensive on females, and normally have some white spots on forehead/forecrown.

Bare parts Bill blackish to dark brown-grey or grey, paler at base and on lower mandible. Legs and feet greyish-olive. Eyes brown to red-brown, sometimes dull reddish.

GEOGRAPHICAL VARIATION Although a great many races have been described, most are too poorly or too inadequately differentiated to warrant recognition. The following seem most worthy of subspecific status (but note also that a good deal of individual variation exists within all forms of this species).

P. s. cactophilus (N American part of species' range and south in Mexico to Guanajuata, Puebla, Nayarit and Michoacán) Described above. Tends to have broader white bars above than other races (except *lucasanus*), but this feature is highly variable.

P. s. eremicus (N Baja California) Larger, longer-tailed and longer-billed than *cactophilus*, and darker above (broader dark bars) and below, with stronger dark barring on lower underparts. Great variation in amount of white in outer tail.

P. s. lucasanus (S Baja California) Smaller and whiter than *eremicus*, with white bars above broader and underparts paler.

P. s. graysoni (Tres Marías Islands, off Nayarit) Resembles *lucasanus*, but slightly smaller and shorter-tailed, with underparts more buff (less grey-brown) and with thinner streaks on breast sides.

P. s. sinaloensis (S Sonora to Guerrero, SW Puebla and C Oaxaca) Smaller than *cactophilus* (which occurs nearby), and with moustache interrupted towards bill; underparts streaked rather than spotted.

P. s. scalaris (Veracruz and Chiapas) Smaller than *cactophilus* (which occurs nearby), with buffish forehead and with moustache broken by white near bill; underparts narrowly streaked on breast.

P. s. parvus (Yucatan) Smaller and darker than nominate *scalaris*, with black forehead, more black in moustache, and broader black bars above; underparts are spotted rather than streaked, but belly is more obviously barred.

P. s. leucoptilurus (Belize and Guatemala to NE Nicaragua) The smallest race, just smaller than *parvus*, and with more white on upperparts; darker, more buff, below and poorly marked, with little spotting on breast and relatively indistinct barring on lower belly.

Hybrids Hybridises with Nuttall's Woodpecker. Male hybrids can be detected by intermediate crown coloration, and hybrids are intermediate also in other characters (e.g. outer tail), each of which is well within the existing range of character overlap of these two species. Hybrids can therefore be evaluated only by using several characters together.

MEASUREMENTS Great variation among subspecies; the following data refer to *cactophilus*. Wing 96-107; tail 52-68; bill 17.5-27 (male's longer than female's by about 2.9 on average); tarsus 16-19.6. Weight: (21)25-41(48).

VOICE Usual call note is *peek*, often repeated in alarm. Long-distance signal is a series of similar, but slightly longer notes, accelerating and dropping in pitch at the end, *cheekeekeekee...keekikk*; this series is slower and longer than that of Nuttall's. There is also a short version of this call. Often given in association with drumming or aerial display are series of variable *kweek* notes. Variable smacking calls denote the various forms of close contact. Drums uncommonly, in shorter and faster rolls than Nuttall's.

HABITS Usually seen singly or in pairs, but also found in groups of up to four after the breeding season. Forages on trunks and branches of broadleaf and coniferous trees, mesquite, bushes, on yuccas and cacti, and occasionally on the ground. Females differ from males in utilising more branches and twigs. The two sexes also differ greatly in use of plant species (these preferences vary with location and season). These sexual differences are apparently maintained through aggression by the male, which also is more of a generalist. Among the various foraging techniques, gleaning, probing, sweeping away debris, reaching, and removing bark prevail; excavating is uncommon and more often performed by males. Movements are rapid, and also covers greater distances between foraging sites than does related Nuttall's Woodpecker; turns, twists, sidles, and flutters even more than the latter, and hops are longer. Displays with bill-directing, head-swinging and bobbing, and freezes with bill raised over body axis. These displays are associated with crest-raising and tail-spreading, and wings may be flicked or conspicuously spread. Flutter-aerial displays are seen mainly during the mating period. Males clearly dominate the smaller females, and intraspecific encounters are usually sex for sex. Copulations may be associated with such encounters, when the individual's own partner is nearby. Interacts interspecifically with Nuttall's in area of contact; interspecific territories are maintained.

FOOD The diet is mainly animal matter; it comprises larvae and adults of (wood-boring) beetles, caterpillars, ants and hemipterans. Also takes (cactus) fruit.

BREEDING Eggs are laid from March to beginning of June (in latter part of this range in S Mexico). Nests are excavated in dead parts of trees, stubs, fence posts, yuccas, agaves and large cacti, at (0.9)2-4.5(10)m. The male is joined in its efforts by the female to some extent. Clutch comprises (2)3-4(7, egg-dumping?) eggs. Both sexes feed the young. Fledglings stay with the parents for an undetermined period.

REFERENCES Austin 1976; Bent 1939; Blake 1965; Howell & Webb in press; Miller 1955; Russel 1964; Short 1971b; Winkler & Short 1978.

---

113 DOWNY WOODPECKER
Picoides pubescens　　　　　Plate 35

IDENTIFICATION Length c. 15-17cm. Very small, with short, almost straight, slightly chisel-tipped bill broad across nostrils. A common woodpecker with contrasting (especially when worn) black and white plumage. Upperparts and wings are black, with a broad white band down back and with much or just a little white in wings; underparts very pale whitish to pale buffish or browny-grey, and unmarked. Most have the outer tail white with obvious black barring. The head pattern is strongly black and white, and males have a small red nape patch.

Similar species The basic plumage pattern, including the pale back, is very like that of Hairy Woodpecker (116), with which it overlaps in many areas. Downy is best separated by its clearly smaller size and, especially, its much smaller and shorter bill, as well as its black-barred outer tail and its lack of moustachial extension to breast sides. Female Downy is also somewhat similar to female Three-toed Woodpecker (118), but the latter is easily distinguished by its much larger size, barred flanks and much longer bill. Note also that both Hairy and Three-toed show a strong preference for mature coniferous forest and have a different call. Downy has hybridised with Nuttall's Woodpecker (111), producing offspring with black and white bars on back and streaked/barred underparts.

DISTRIBUTION Widespread over wooded N America, from SE Alaska across Canada (S Mackenzie, Alberta, Saskatchewan, S Quebec) to Newfoundland in the north, and from S California, C Arizona and N New Mexico, through Oklahoma and SC Texas, to the northeast Gulf of Mexico coast and Florida. Common.

MOVEMENTS Northern and montane populations are locally partially migratory. Movements may be observed particularly along the Atlantic coast and may take individuals as far as 1200km away from their breeding grounds. Stragglers outside breeding range reach NW Mexico.

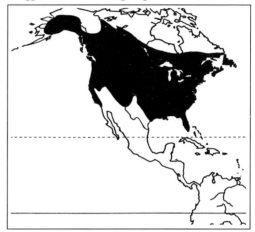

HABITAT Generally favours deciduous forests and woodlands and is common in cultivated areas. Among these habitats are mixed forests with hemlock, second growth, and suburban areas. In the (south)western and southern parts of the range, partial to riverine woodland; selects moist aspen and willow stands in the coniferous zone. Habitats range from sea level to 1860-2750m in (south)western mountains.

DESCRIPTION
P. p. pubescens **Adult male** Nasal tufts whitish; forehead to hindcrown black; nape red. Supercilium from above eye white, broadening at rear to meet nape; ear-coverts black, upper edge extending to lower nape; lores and band beneath eye white, becoming broad white patch on rear neck sides, and bordered below by black moustachial stripe (often broken near bill) which continues back mantle sides. Chin and throat white or greyish-white. Hindneck and upperparts black, except for white central panel from mid mantle to lower back. Upperwing black, coverts with large white subterminal spots, and flight feathers with spots on outer webs and bars on inner webs. Uppertail feathers black, all but central pair with white at tip, white increasing in extent towards outers (which mostly white), and with variable but often prominent black bars in outer white areas. Underparts unmarked white to greyish-white, undertail-coverts sometimes with faint streaks/spots. Underwing grey and white. Undertail as above, but paler.

Adult female Lacks red on nape, which is instead black or white-streaked black (supercilia may occasionally virtually meet on nape).

Juvenile Black areas duller, browner, and white of back streaked darker; underparts are dirtier, greyish or buffish, and finely streaked on breast sides (sometimes also centre) and flanks and variably barred on lower flanks. Males have red feather tips on crown, especially at rear (but not on nape), with variable white spotting on forecrown; female has crown brownish-black, either unmarked or lightly or

285

heavily streaked/spotted pale buffish or white.

Bare parts Bill dark grey or blackish, with paler base and lower mandible. Legs and feet olive-grey or grey. Eyes deep brown or red-brown; paler, greyish or olive, in juveniles.

GEOGRAPHICAL VARIATION Variation involves mainly size, amount of white in wings, and tone of underparts. Size increases clinally from south to north. Western races have less white on wing-coverts and (apart from Rocky Mountains population) darker underparts. Variation in wing length has been particularly well studied; it shows a clear inverse relationship with air temperature and humidity (combining to produce the annual total heat of air).

P. p. pubescens (eastern North Carolina south to Florida and southern Alabama and west to eastern Texas) Described above. Intergrades widely with the following race from east of Rockies across to Maryland.

P. p. medianus (Nebraska east to northern Virginia and northwards, east of Rockies, to C Alaska, Canada and Newfoundland) Larger and paler than nominate, with which it intergrades widely in central USA.

P. p. leucurus (Rocky Mountains, from SE Alaska south to NE California, Arizona and New Mexico) The largest and whitest race, pure white below with undertail-coverts unstreaked, and little black in outer tail; wing-coverts have few or no white spots.

P. p. glacialis (coast of SE Alaskan) Very like *leucurus*, but underparts a shade darker, more pale buffy-white; outer tail shows more bars.

P. p. gairdneri (western British Columbia south along coast to NW California) Darker below than other races, being brownish-grey; wing-coverts largely unspotted, but outer tail strongly barred.

P. p. turati (inland Washington and Oregon, and California except northwest and northeast) As *gairdneri*, but smaller and with slightly paler, pale buffish-grey, underparts.

MEASUREMENTS Wing shortest (86) in S Florida, longest (over 94) in northeast (e.g. New England); the following data refer to *medianus*. Wing 92-99; tail 50-61; bill 14.4-18.1; tarsus 15.9-17.1. Weight: 20.7-32.2 (large-sample mean 27.0).

VOICE The call note is a not very loud *pik*, which may be delivered at high rates in alarm. The long-distance signal is a characteristic series of notes, dropping in pitch at the end, *peet-peet-peet-…pit-pit-pitpit*. In the breeding season, series of *check* to *kweek* notes, often with aerial display, are delivered. Variable, short notes, like soft, grating *chirrr* and a *twit*, are given in close contacts. Chirping of nestlings varies with age; squeaky notes are uttered by fledged young. Squeals loudly in distress. Both sexes drum in short rolls (normal rate 9-16 per minute), particularly when unpaired; slow rolls are given at the nest.

HABITS Mostly solitary during the winter, pairs roaming through the territory with onset of courtship behaviour; the two often join mixed-species flocks. Foraging is rather flexible, and substrate use shifts with seasons, supply, and under the influence of intraspecific and interspecific competition. Usually favours live wood over dead (portions of) trees, but may occasionally shift completely to dead (including fire-killed) trees. Generally, limbs of small diameter (<25cm) are preferred, and foraging may take place at all heights in a tree, with some emphasis on the lower canopy, but also descends to fallen logs. In winter, larger trees and those with more furrowed bark are favoured. Males utilise smaller branches than females (laboratory results suggest the opposite) and concentrate their foraging more on the upper levels; females forage from middle levels down to the tree base (niche breadth greater than in males). The male maintains this segregation through supplanting attacks on the female. Pecking is the most common technique, followed by hammering and probing, with subcambial excavation generally being more common in winter; in summer, some flycatching occurs in addition. Males and females differ in the seasonal course of these changes. Bark and wood are not deeply excavated. Commonly removes bark, and on dead trees in particular this may amount to more than half of foraging activity. In aggressive encounters, Downy Woodpeckers demonstrate postures with bill-pointing along body axis, and perform rapid bill-pointing (sometimes with bill slightly open) with wing-flicking; at highest intensity, wings are held fully extended, the tail is also spread, the legs are extended, and the bird sways laterally (bill-waving dance). Most conflicts are between two males or two females. During courtship, the nape feathers are erected. Flutter-aerial displays are shown mainly by the male and frequently targeted at the female or prospective hole. Downies roost singly (the male in the nest), and new roosts may be produced in autumn (particularly by young birds). In winter, lives solitarily and may defend locally concentrated resources (e.g. insect-infested trees). Interspecific interactions are often related to hole competition and involve sapsuckers and flying squirrels. Other, larger woodpeckers, such as Red-headed (37) and Hairy, are usually dominant when encountered. Interactions are numerous at feeders.

FOOD Mainly insects, with wood-boring larvae being an important component. Bark beetles (*Scolytus*), spiders, ants and moths are fed to the nestlings. Berries, as from red-berried elder (*Sambucus pubens*), are taken when available; plant material becomes more important in winter. Readily accepts suet from feeders.

BREEDING Breeding-related behaviour may start in late winter. Egg-laying season is April-May in Florida, May-July in British Columbia, and in between in the intervening parts of the species' range. Nests are inevitably in dead trees or at least in a dead part (e.g. with fungal heart rot) of a tree at (1.5)3.5-9(18)m, and frequently located just beneath the broken-off top of a stub; other sites are fence posts and utility poles. The female seems to select the nest site more often than is the case with other woodpeckers; both sexes announce their choice with drumming. Male does most of the excavating (as copulations become frequent, females may work more) and completes the hole within 13-20 days. Copulations (4-10, up to 16 seconds long) take place mainly from the end of excavation to the fifth day of incubation, mainly during egg-laying, close to the nest. Males may copulate with intruding females, but defend the nest against them. Clutch of (3)4-5(6) eggs (mean 4.81), with a tendency for clutch size to increase with latitude (to 7 eggs in British Columbia). Male and female share breeding duties (incubation, brooding, feeding, nest sanitation), the female often reducing her effort towards the end of the nestling period. The young hatch after 12 days and are cared for by both adults; the nestling period lasts 20-23 days. After emerging from the hole, the young are accompanied by their parents for up to three weeks. More than one brood may be raised within a season.

REFERENCES Askins 1983; Conner 1980; Conner *et al.* 1975; Gamboa & Brown 1976; Jackson 1970b; James 1970; Kilham 1961, 1962b, 1970, 1974b, 1974c; Koplin 1969; Lawrence 1967; Martin & Li 1992; Matthysen *et al.* 1991; Travis 1977; Williams 1975; Williams & Batzli 1979a, 1979b; Willson 1970; Winkler & Leisler 1985; Winkler & Short 1978.

114 RED-COCKADED WOODPECKER
Picoides borealis   Plate 34

IDENTIFICATION Length c. 22cm. Small, with fairly long, chisel-tipped bill slightly curved on culmen and broad across nostrils. A rare and endangered pied species of pine woods of the SE USA. Within its range, this relatively long-tailed woodpecker is distinguished from all others by the black and white barring of its upperparts and wings and its black and white head pattern (male has a very small area of red at each side of the nape, but this is rarely visible in the field, being often concealed by the overlying crown feathers). Outer tail white with several black bars. Underparts white, with prominent black spots on breast sides and flanks. Highly distinctive nest site, with sap flowing from holes drilled around the entrance hole and much bark removed from trunk, gives away the species' presence in an area.

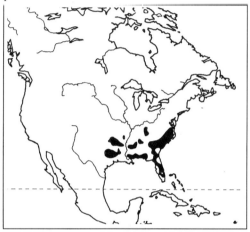

DISTRIBUTION Patchily distributed in the USA, from Atlantic coast in southeast (S Virginia, North and South Carolina, Georgia, N and C Florida), west to Oklahoma and Texas and north to Kentucky. Distribution closely associated with the occurrence of certain pine species (see below). Because of its strict habitat requirements, it is endangered throughout its range. The largest population lives in N Florida. Populations in Maryland recently became extinct, Tennessee population is about to go the same way, few remain in Kentucky, and populations continue to decline elsewhere.

HABITAT Adapted to open mature pine and pine-oak forests, which form a unique ecosystem in SE United States. Open pine stands with a park-like structure are the required nesting habitat. Also uses adjacent stands of cypress (*Taxodium*), cornfields and orchards for foraging. Dense hardwood midstorey is detrimental to this endangered species, and keeping hardwood low and small, at least around nest sites, is one of the most important (although somewhat controversial) management practices. There seem, however, to be regional differences in the negative effects of hardwood admixture; up to 52% non-pine species have been registered in Kentucky habitats. Naturally, these habitats assumed their typical structure through frequent fires, to which the pines are well adapted. A clan of three or four birds needs about 58-91ha of proper habitat for its survival (genetically healthy populations possibly require more than 25,000ha). This woodpecker is dependent on a few species of pine belonging to the longleaf pine savanna of the SE USA; these are primarily longleaf pine *Pinus palustris*, slash pine *P. elliottii*, shortleaf pine *P. echinata*, but also loblolly pine *P. taeda*, pitch pine *P. rigida* and pond pine *P. serotina*. These pines are suitable for the particular nest-site requirements described in detail below. Habitat fragmentation, clearcutting and midstorey encroachment of hardwood are important reasons for the decline of this species, which also suffers locally from the devastating effects of hurricanes. Irregular shelterwood-cutting seems to be less detrimental, and even beneficial. Restricted to the Atlantic coastal plain and hills below 500m.

DESCRIPTION
Adult male Forehead to hindneck, short stripe behind eye, plus lores and broad moustachial stripe deep black, moustache broadening on neck side and extending slightly onto upper breast side. Small red spot at side of nape. Rest of head, including short supercilium, white, with ear-coverts sometimes tinged grey or buffy. Chin and throat white. Upperparts black, barred/vermiculated white from central mantle to upper rump. Upperwing black, coverts with white subterminal spots and flight feathers barred white. Uppertail black, with white at tips increasing in extent from second/third pair outwards and reaching base on outer tail, and with dark bars or half-bars on outer two feathers. Underparts white, often sullied buffish or pale grey; black moustachial extension breaks up into large black spots/streaks on breast sides, these becoming smaller/ narrower on flanks and sometimes thin bars on lower flanks and undertail-coverts. Underwing grey, barred white. Undertail as uppertail, but duller.

Adult female A trifle larger than male; lacks red spot at nape sides.

Juvenile Duller and browner above than adults, with dusky cheek patch, and duller and more diffusely marked below. Males have a dull reddish crown centre, but on females this is absent (there are conflicting statements in this in the literature: Short (1982) maintains that some females are indistinguishable from males, whereas Ligon (1970) and Gowaty & Lennartz (1985) believe that the sexes are clearly different in the way described above).

BARE PARTS Bill blackish-grey. Legs and feet olive-grey. Eyes dark brown.

GEOGRAPHICAL VARIATION None. Monotypic.

MEASUREMENTS Wing 95-126; tail 70-82; bill 19-23.1 (large-sample mean: male 22.6, female 21.8); tarsus 17.7-21.1. Weight: 40-55.

VOICE The most common call of self-announcement and alarm is a distinctive *shrrit*, which structurally resembles the chur calls of many melanerpine woodpeckers (i.e. it shows a clear vibrato or regular frequency modulation), but is higher-pitched and shorter and thus sounds rather different to the human ear. Call notes are given singly or in groups or series, depending on context. The rattle, much rarer and obviously a long-distance signal, commences with a call-note-like preamble, which is followed by up to 30 notes (shorter and lower-pitched versions of the call note). Shorter and more variable forms of the rattle are given by fledged young. Birds in groups are rather vocal, and frequently utter a wide range of twittering calls and chortles which are low and short to clear *wic-a wic-a* notes. Low and soft notes characterise intimate contacts, especially at the nest or roost. Whether there really is a genuine and distinct warning call for aerial predators, described as *shurz-u*, merits closer study, since such calls have not been described for other woodpeckers. Two types of nestling call are recognised, which change considerably in the course of the chicks' development; nearly fledged young already utter the adult form of the call note. The shrieks given when caught show the same vibrato as the call notes. Drumming is infrequent and often not loud; both sexes produce this signal in the course of disturbances at the nest, and in territorial context either when entering a new territory or as response to a drumming intruder.

HABITS Roams through its often large territory singly, in pairs or in groups, and accompanies mixed-species foraging flocks in winter. Pines are the main tree species utilised by this woodpecker (larger ones preferred over smaller ones), but other trees (e.g. cypresses) and orchards are utilised as well. Cornfields are entered when infested with earworms (*Heliothis*). Live and dead trees are visited to about the same extent, although local differences seem to exist in this respect, with live and only recently dead pines being preferred in some places. Most foraging takes place on tree trunks. Although Red-cockaded Woodpeckers do not sport conspicuous sexual badges, there are clear sexual differences in foraging, most pronounced in January-March, which are associated with only slight mensural differences. Males use mainly the upper trunk and branches, while females tend to feed on the lower trunk; the sexes overlap greatly in their use of the mid trunk. Consequently, sexes differ in foraging height by about 3-7m. Food is frequently obtained by removing bark, which is achieved by grasping pieces with the bill, by prying it off, and often by grabbing bark with both feet and tearing it off by making a short flying leap or by scratching with both feet. Exposed prey is then gleaned. Scaled trees give away this species' presence. Also probes crevices and needle and cone clusters, and males in particular peck to some extent, excavating decayed wood. Occasionally sallies in the air to catch flying insects. Males, which feed more often on limbs, frequently move along the underside of branches.

The basic social unit of this species is termed a clan and consists of three or four adults. Clan members roost in close proximity to each other, normally each individual in its own hole. In the morning the group assembles with much calling and then takes off for the daily routine; except in adverse weather conditions, the birds of a clan usually forage 500-1200m away from the roosting site, covering an area of about 70ha daily outside the breeding season. Territory varies greatly, however, from 50 to 150ha or more, poorer habitats demanding larger territories. The territory is maintained all year round, and all activities of a clan take place within its boundaries. Single intruders are attacked by both members of the established pair. Territorial conflicts with neighbouring clans may last half an hour or so and are accompanied by much calling, drumming and visual displays. The latter comprise crest-raising (a general and frequent sign of excitement) in which the red cockade of the male is apparent, tail-spreading, wing-flicking combined with jabs at the opponent, and conspicuous open-wing displays during which the wings are extended over the back. A flutter-aerial display is shown in the early breeding season. The roost is the centre of life for each individual, each excavating its own. Roosts are entered around sunset, earlier on overcast days or in adverse weather conditions, and left around sunrise. Hole construction may take weeks or even months. Availability of suitable trees for setting up roosts (and nests) determines group size and successful breeding. Suitable trees contain up to five holes. Aggregations of cavity trees used by groups of Red-cockaded Woodpeckers are termed clusters (also colonies). The cavities are renowned for their peculiar features, created by the woodpeckers as apparent means of defence: an array of sap wells is made around the hole entrance from which sticky and mildly poisonous resin oozes constantly (since creating new wounds is part of the routine prior to entering

the roost). Hole sites are thus recognised by a broad, whitish coat of resin flow around and particularly below the hole entrance. Only a small zone around the entrance is kept free, as the bark there has been removed by the bird. Loose bark is also scaled off other parts of the cavity trunk and even off adjacent trees. Because of these peculiar habits, only living pines are selected as sites for hole construction; for this, however, the heartwood of the trunk has to be soft through the action of a fungal disease (*Phellinus pini*) which afflicts mainly mature trees. The resin flow is supposed to ward off ants, hole competitors and predators; if it is a defence at all, it is only relative, since ants and flying squirrels have been found in holes with the resin still flowing, although it does seem to be an effective protection against snakes (*Elaphe*). Another suggested function of the resin cover is that the woodpeckers may find their holes more easily in their typically uniform habitat. Because holes require so much time to construct, they are a key feature in understanding this woodpecker's biology. Holes and clusters are easily lost, but new colonies are hard to establish, when no holes at all exist in an area. Red-cockaded Woodpeckers provide holes for many other species in their unique ecosystem, and hence suffer from nest competitors, which occupy up to a quarter of the available holes. Red-bellied Woodpeckers (51) pose a great threat and require constant vigilance and vigorous defence of the hole. Interference at the nest by other woodpecker species which share their habitat seems to be insignificant, although nests are occasionally lost to Red-headed Woodpeckers (37) and interactions with Hairy Woodpeckers (116) do occur. Other hole competitors are flying squirrels and to a lesser extent other birds (e.g. bluebirds). In some areas, especially those where hardwood understorey is extensive, Pileated Woodpeckers (164) damage up to 40% of Red-cockaded Woodpecker cavities. Interference at foraging sites mainly involves the congeneric Hairy and Downy (113) Woodpeckers.

FOOD The diet consists mainly of insects, their larvae and other arthropods. Wood roaches, ants (may predominate at times), termites, beetles, moths, damselflies, spiders and millipedes have been recorded as nestling food. Fruits (e.g. cherries) and berries of various species (e.g. *Vaccinium, Myrica*) are taken to some extent and are even fed to the nestlings. Pine seeds are taken mainly in winter. Other plant food comprises nuts (pecans).

BREEDING The basic reproductive unit is the pair, but about a third of all pairs share their territory with helpers. The unit is completely sedentary (at least on the male's part) once a nest and proper roosts have been established. Females often break away from the breeding unit; this is associated either with mate death or incest avoidance, or with moving to another group even after successful breeding (possibly, females are often forced out by other group members or intruders). As already explained, this woodpecker is dependent on live mature pines for excavating nests and roosts. Holes are mainly at (0.7)9-15(31)m, low in younger pines and high in old ones, and in most cases with no branch (which would make them more vulnerable to climbing predators) below them. Artificial cavities are also accepted. The male's roost becomes the nest by default. Male and female, as well as helpers, take part in nest construction; often, no special nest-building activity precedes breeding activities. The egg-laying season commences around 20 April and ends about 5 June. The pair itself is essentially monogamous in behaviour. Males external to the group, not male helpers, are responsible for exceptional extra-pair fertilisations. Clutch contains (1)3-4(5) eggs. Both members of the pair share incubation, which begins with the second egg, about equally, the male staying in the nest overnight. Helpers, which also develop small brood patches, may also incubate. The chicks hatch after 10-11(13) days, the sex ratio being biased in favour of males in some areas (59% in a South Carolina study, but 49.6% in North Carolina). They are brooded almost continuously for the first four days. Both parents feed the nestlings; as with other species, some variation exists as to the share each sex takes. Helpers contribute as much to nest sanitation, brooding and brood-feeding as the parents. The nestlings fledge after (22)26-29 days. Parents and helpers continue to feed the young for up to five or six months. Occasionally, second broods are undertaken. The positive effects of helpers on chick survival are small and due mainly to reduced predation owing to better resistance to disturbance. Young males follow one of two options: either they disperse to other areas (up to 22 km) to search for a breeding opportunity (31% of males employ this strategy in a particularly well-studied North Carolina population), or they delay reproduction, wait for a breeding vacancy and meanwhile stay within the natal territory to become helpers to their parents in the next breeding cycle. The two groups are roughly equivalent in terms of relative fitness. Most helpers are males, the oldest of which inherits the territory if the breeding male disappears, while others may become breeders in an adjacent territory. Dispersers often remain unmated territory-holders, establish themselves as helpers in a non-natal group, or become floaters. Females stay with their natal group in only 1% of cases, and disperse farther than males (up to 32 km).

REFERENCES Collar *et al.* 1992, 1994; Conner & Locke 1982; Conner *et al.* 1991; Gowaty & Lennartz 1985; Haig *et al.* 1993, 1994; Hooper & Lennartz 1981; Jackson 1974, 1977, 1994; James 1991; Kalisz & Boettcher 1991; Kelly *et al.* 1993; Labranche & Walters 1994; Lennartz & Harlow 1979; Lennartz *et al.* 1987; Ligon 1968b, 1970; McFarlane 1992; Morse 1972; Nesbitt *et al.* 1978; Porter *et al.* 1985; Reed *et al.* 1988; Richardson & Smith 1992; Rudolph *et al.* 1990; Walters 1990, 1991; Walters *et al.* 1988, 1992a, 1992b; Winkler & Short 1972.

---

115 STRICKLAND'S WOODPECKER
Picoides stricklandi   Plate 34

Other names: Brown-backed Woodpecker, Arizona Woodpecker

IDENTIFICATION Length c. 18-20cm. Small, with longish, straight, chisel-tipped bill broad across nostrils. Rather distinctive, with brown or dark brown upperparts, brown crown and ear-coverts, barred outer tail, and heavily spotted and barred underparts. Male has red nape patch. In northern and western populations (formerly considered a separate species, 'Arizona Woodpecker'), the entire upperparts are either solidly brown or show some indication (occasionally strong) of paler barring on back. Nominate southeastern birds are darker, more blackish-brown (paler when worn), are prominently barred dark brown and white from central mantle to rump, and have narrow pale bars on flight feathers. Unlikely to be confused with other woodpeckers.

DISTRIBUTION Southwest N America and Mexico, from SE Arizona south through adjacent Sonora to Chihuahua, Sinaloa and from Durango to Nayarit, Jalisco and Michoacán. Isolated populations are found in Morelos, Distrito Federal, and Veracruz and Puebla. Fairly common to common throughout range.

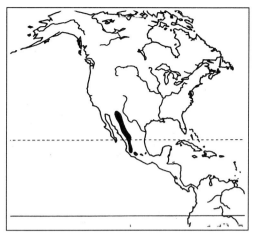

HABITAT Race *arizonae* occurs in mixed pine-oak woodland in north of range (Arizona) and W Mexico at 1200-2400m, usually below Hairy Woodpecker (116) in the same area (some overlap in the non-breeding season); habitats are almost entirely pine woods in southeast. Race *stricklandi* inhabits the higher mountains of the central volcanic belt in C and E Mexico, in woods dominated by pines, mixed with firs, oaks, cypresses and alders (above sympatric Hairy Woodpecker, but these relationships require clarification), at 2500-4000m (Veracruz and Puebla).

DESCRIPTION
P. s. arizonae Adult male Forehead and crown medium to darkish brown; nape red. Upper rear lores and ear-coverts dark brown, bordered by white band from above eye, broadening behind and below ear-coverts and continuing forwards to join white lores. Moustachial stripe brown, streaked with white, and continuing back to lower hindneck. Chin and throat whitish, latter variably spotted or streaked brown. Hindneck dark brown; upperparts dark brown (but a shade paler than hindneck), unmarked or with some indication, occasionally strong, of white vermiculations. Upperwing brown, flight feathers with white bars on inner webs and with small spots on outer webs of primaries (bars and spots sometimes much reduced). Uppertail dark brown, darker than back, outer two or three feather pairs barred white. Underparts below throat whitish, variably but usually heavily marked with dark brown spots on breast, which become arrowhead bars on flanks and lower underparts. Underwing pale brown, barred whitish. Undertail as above, but paler. (In worn plumage, brown areas become paler and underpart markings appear darker and even heavier.)

Adult female Shorter-billed than male, and with brown (not red) nape.

Juvenile Duller than adults and clearly darker below, with heavier and more extensive markings (including streaking) and much barring; has less white in tail and on sides of neck. Both sexes show orangey-red on crown, which is less extensive on female and usually restricted to hindcrown (with scattered red feather tips along crown sides).

Bare parts Bill blackish, with paler (horn-brown/grey) base and lower mandible. Legs and feet greenish-grey. Eyes dark brown.

GEOGRAPHICAL VARIATION Two main types occur, one in the southeast with much darker coloration and distinctly barred back, and the other paler and browner with plain or less obviously barred back. The latter type is also divided into two rather poorly defined races.

    P. s. arizonae (SE Arizona to northern Sinaloa and

neighbouring parts of Durango) Described above. Has been considered to form, with the following race, a separate species. Male and female more dimorphic in bill size than other subspecies.

P. s. fraterculus (southern Sinaloa and adjacent Durango south to Michoacán) Averages smaller than *arizonae* in all measurements (but a cline is evident), but very similar in plumage, although possibly a shade darker brown. Many individuals of this race (and also of *arizonae*) show at least a hint of barring above, some approaching nominate race (see below).

P. s. stricklandi (southeast part of range, from México region east to Puebla-Veracruz border) Much darker, more blackish-brown, than above races, and always has mantle to rump barred dark and white; also smaller-billed and with less obvious barring in outer tail. Males tend to have more red on nape, extending onto hindcrown, but this apparently variable. Underparts show tendency towards less heavy markings in eastern populations, but this character seems to vary clinally (intermediates occur).

MEASUREMENTS Wing 103-121; tail 56-71; bill 18-28; tarsus 17-21. Weight: 34-51.

VOICE The common call is a single *peep*, a distinctive rattle is used as long-distance signal, *peep chree-chree-chree....* Series of variable *kweek* notes intergrade with *twuit* notes. More twittering notes accompany head-swinging displays; intimate calls sound like *tyet* or *thsd*. Nestlings' calls similar to those of Hairy Woodpecker. Both sexes, but mainly the male, drum loud rolls (longer than Hairy's) in long series at a rate of 3-4 per minute. Signal tapping occurs at the prospective nest.

HABITS Mostly met with singly; pairs, however, use the same territory and keep vocal contact over long distances. Sometimes joins flocks of small passerines. Forages mainly on pines (less selective during the breeding season, especially in north of range, where other tree species, such as oaks, and agaves are available; may concentrate on particular dead trees for several days). Forages on trunks, branches and twigs, the female more on twigs, especially in the breeding season. Trunk foraging clearly predominates during early spring, at which time pecking and hammering (to excavate or to remove bark, which is also removed with feet) are most common, followed by probing, gleaning and flycatching. Surface feeding more common in summer. Displays include head-swinging, wing-spreading and a flutter-aerial display (directed at mate/hole) during courtship activities. Meets Hairy Woodpecker (and Acorn Woodpecker, 38), apparently without much overt interference.

FOOD Insects, mainly beetle larvae, and some fruits and seeds (acorns).

BREEDING Nesting activities take place mainly in April-May. The nest is excavated by both sexes, mainly by the male, in a dead tree or into the dead section of a live one at 2.5-15m, or lower into an agave stem. Both sexes incubate the clutch of 3-4 eggs; both also tend the young, which stay in the family group until summer.

REFERENCES Davis 1965; Howell & Webb in press; Ligon 1968a, 1968b; Winkler 1979; Winkler & Short 1978.

116 HAIRY WOODPECKER
Picoides villosus   **Plate 35**

IDENTIFICATION Length c. 16.5-26cm. Small to very small, with long chisel-tipped bill slightly curved on culmen and broad across nostrils. Mainly a black and white species, though colour of pale areas varies from pure white to greyish and even brown; size also varies considerably. Basic plumage pattern resembles that of Downy Woodpecker (113), including almost wholly pale back, and like Downy has variable amount of white in wings (southwestern and southern populations of Hairy show little or no white in wing-coverts); outer tail is generally plain white.

Similar species Overlaps in range with superficially similar Downy Woodpecker, from which it is best told by its larger size, distinctly longer, more powerful bill, unbarred white outer tail feathers, black extending from neck side to upper breast, as well as by its less confiding habits and its different habitat preferences and voice. Female is confusable with that of Three-toed Woodpecker (118), but is distinguished by the broad white band extending from bill across lower face to rear neck and the broader white supercilium (Three-toed looks much blacker on the head), and also by the lack of heavy barring on body sides (juvenile Hairy shows some hint of or even strong barring on flanks, but not extending to breast sides).

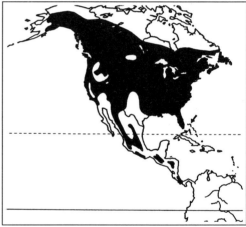

DISTRIBUTION Widely distributed in the forests of N and C America. From the tree line in the north across Alaska and Canada, south to the highland forests of Panama, this species avoids only deserts and grassland and tropical lowland forests. It occurs in all states of the USA and is distributed through the Mexican highlands to Nicaragua, Costa Rica and W Panama. Also reaches the Bahamas. Fairly common in most of range, but uncommon to rare in SE USA.

MOVEMENTS Northernmost populations show some seasonal movements, and highland populations move downslope in winter.

HABITAT Occupies a wide range of forest types and woodlands, with some predilection for pines. Occurs in the NW USA in Douglas Fir/Western Hemlock forests, preferring the former species for foraging. In the west, also in open juniper woodland; in the plains, in riparian forests; in the east, in virtually all types of forest. In West Indies, mainly pine woods. In Mexico and Guatemala restricted to the highlands and rather common in pine-oak and oak (and other broadleaf) forests, cypress stands, and second growth.

In Costa Rica and Panama, occurs in wet, epiphyte-laden highland forests, up to the stunted forests at the timber line, and in neighbouring clearings and semi-open areas, with main abundance centred in oak forests of higher elevations; in latter, often found with Acorn Woodpecker (38). May concentrate locally in areas where forest fires have occurred. Altitudinal range changes towards the tropics, from sea level to high mountains. In the northern parts of the continent, this species is found from sea level to 2900m in the western mountains (to the timber line in the east). Farther south, the lowlands are avoided: in Arizona usually above 2000m, in Mexico at 1200-3500m, in Guatemala at 900-2900m, in Costa Rica and Panama at (1200)1500-3400m, in valleys and sheltered places generally not below 1800m.

DESCRIPTION

P. v. villosus **Adult male** Nasal tufts white; forehead and crown black; nape narrowly red, sometimes tinged orange. Supercilium from above eye white, continuing back to nape; small area in front of eye and broad band covering ear-coverts black, meeting nape at rear; lores and wide band below eye and ear-coverts and broadly down rear neck side white. Moustachial stripe black, usually partly obscured by white near bill, expanding on neck side and continuing back onto mantle and down to upper breast side. Chin and throat white. Hindneck, sides of mantle and back, and rump and uppertail-coverts black, with contrasting broad white panel on central upperparts from mid mantle to lower back. Upperwing black, coverts with large white subterminal spots (forming bars) and flight feathers barred white. Uppertail black centrally, with white tips to remaining feathers increasing in extent outwards; outermost feathers all white. Underparts from breast white with very slight grey tinge, unmarked (rarely, may show a few streaks from moustachial extension and/or faintly on flanks). Underwing barred black and white, with white coverts. Undertail as uppertail or paler.

Adult female Shorter-billed and smaller (less bulky) than male; lacks red on nape, which is black or mixed black and white.

Juvenile Duller than adults, with black areas browner and underparts somewhat darker; also shows at least some streaking/barring below and some bars on outer tail feathers. Both sexes have orange or red on crown, often quite extensive on male but normally very restricted on female. White eye-ring of juvenile is a reliable indication of age for several weeks.

Bare parts Bill dark grey to blackish, paler at base and on lower mandible. Legs and feet grey or bluish-grey, sometimes darker or green-tinged. Eyes deep brown or red-brown; greyer in juveniles.

GEOGRAPHICAL VARIATION Most variation is clinal, associated with temperature and moisture, large and pale birds being in the dry-cold areas. A large number of races have been described, but many of these differ only minimally from or fall within the range of variation of other, better-marked races. The situation in many areas is complex, however, and a number of intergrading forms occur. More research is required to clarify racial divisions. A total of 14 races is recognised here, differing mainly in size, colour of pale areas and amount of white in wings. (It should be borne in mind that, in all races, juveniles are darker below than their parents.)

P. v. villosus (northeast part of species' range, from eastern North Dakota to Nova Scotia south and west to eastern Colorado, C Texas, the Ozark Plateau of Missouri and northern Virginia) Described above. One of the larger and whiter races. Intergrades with

audubonii across EC USA.

P. v. terraenovae (Newfoundland) Slightly greyer (and buff-tinged) below than nominate, with fine flank streaks; has less white in wings, narrower white face stripes, narrower and somewhat black-streaked white back panel, and often some bars on outer tail. Juveniles are very dark-looking, and have buff underparts with obvious streaks on breast sides and barred flanks (closely resembling Three-toed Woodpecker).

P. v. audubonii (southeast part of range, from E Texas, W Kentucky, southern Illinois and SE Virginia southwards) Smaller and darker than nominate (with which intergrades in northern parts); has greyish-buff underparts.

P. v. septentrionalis (from northern tree line in Alaska, east across southern Canada to Lake Superior, south to Montana and North Dakota, and in the west to SC British Columbia and south inland to Colorado and northern New Mexico) The largest and whitest race, and large-billed. White of supercilium and of neck sides may just meet at rear.

P. v. picoideus (Queen Charlotte Islands, off British Columbia) Pale area of back is barred dark (recalls Three-toed Woodpecker), and underparts are dark buffy-brown with obvious streaking on flanks; outer tail barred, sometimes strongly.

P. v. sitkensis (coast of SE Alaska and northern British Columbia) Near *septentrionalis* in size. Resembles *harrisi*, but has more white in wings and underparts are more buff, less grey-brown, in tone.

P. v. harrisi (coastal region from southern British Columbia to NW California) Smaller than *sitkensis*, but with longer bill, and with white in wing very much reduced; pale parts of plumage are dark grey-brown.

The following five southern and western forms all have pale wing-covert spots greatly reduced or absent:

P. v. hyloscopus (W California south to N Baja California) A trifle smaller than *harrisi*, and paler, more buff (less grey-brown) below, with whitish suffusion.

P. v. orius (Cascade Mountains in British Columbia south through C Oregon to SE California, C Arizona, New Mexico and westernmost Texas) Intermediate in measurements between *septentrionalis* and *hyloscopus*, but bill as long as former's. Buff below, but somewhat paler than *hyloscopus*.

P. v. icastus (SE Arizona and SW New Mexico south through western Mexico to Jalisco) Somewhat shorter in wing and tail than *orius*, and much shorter-billed; also darker, buffer, below (closely approaching *hyloscopus*). Intergrades with following race.

P. v. jardinii (C Mexico from San Luís Potosí, Tamaulipas and Veracruz to Jalisco, Guerrero and Oaxaca) Smaller than *icastus* and much darker (deep buff-brown) below, with a few streaks on breast sides; pale head markings narrow.

P. v. sanctorum (C America, from Chiapas in S Mexico through Guatemala to western Panama) Smaller than *jardinii* and the smallest of all races. Darker below (brown), sometimes with pale flanks (especially in Nicaragua), and with streaks on breast sides, but variable. Supercilium very narrow at rear and tinged buff.

The following two races, isolated in the Bahamas, are almost as small as *sanctorum*:

P. v. piger (Abaco, Mores and Grand Bahama) Has brownish throat, paler breast and dusky flanks, latter streaked/barred blackish; pale back is slightly dark-streaked, and usually has a couple of dark bars in outer tail.

P. v. maynardi (Andros and New Providence Islands) Differs from *piger* in unstreaked back, paler and unmarked underparts (but with buff tinge to breast) and plain white outer tail. Resembles mainland form (*audubonii*), but smaller and shorter-billed, and slightly buff (less grey) on breast.

MEASUREMENTS Wing 115-124 (*villosus*), 97-111 (*sanctorum*), 108-118 (*audubonii*), 127-138 (*septentrionalis*); tail 65-83 (*villosus*), 49-65 (*sanctorum*), 57-70 (*audubonii*), 71-92 (*septentrionalis*); bill 24.9-33 (*villosus*), 21-27 (*sanctorum*), 24.9-30.5 (*audubonii*), 29-39 (*septentrionalis*); tarsus 20.1-23.1 (*villosus*), 17-20.5 (*sanctorum*), 19-23 (*audubonii*), 22-26.3 (*septentrionalis*). Weight: 42 (*sanctorum*), 59-80 (*villosus*).

VOICE Common call a rather high-pitched *k(ee)k*; calls of Panama birds are higher-pitched and more subdued than those of N American races. This note also introduces the rattle (whinny, sputter), *keek kit-kit-kit-kit…kt*. Series of variable notes, *kweek kweek…*, are often associated with flutter-aerial display and occur in the breeding season, whereas head-swinging is accompanied by *wick-a-wick-a* calls, which intergrade with intimate *teuk* notes. Nestlings utter the well-known 'begging' chirp; fledglings react to the approach and food delivery of an adult with squeaks. Both sexes drum in short rolls (normal rate 4-9 per minute), which are as long as but faster than Downy Woodpecker's; rolls tend to slow down at the end. Taps at the nest.

HABITS Mostly met with singly, the pair members keeping only loose contact. Sometimes in mixed flocks. Live trees seem generally to be visited more often (but less than with Downy in same habitat), except during the winter, although often forages on dead branches. Mean foraging height does not differ clearly from that of its smaller edition, the Downy Woodpecker, and shifts seasonally (higher in winter). Snags without branches are more frequently visited in winter. Large trees are preferred in either season. Parts of the trees below the crown and which do not have limbs are the favoured foraging substrate. Patches of exposed wood, for instance those excavated by Pileated Woodpeckers (164), attract this species. Visits Joshua trees in California, and in C America also utilises bamboo (*Chusquea*), old stalks of giant thistle and stems of soft shrubs such as *Senecio*. Also descends to the ground, most frequently in early spring. Pecking and hammering are characteristic foraging activities, by which bark is removed or funnel-shaped holes are drilled into the bark. Also probes and prises or tears off bark. Although the various studies are not easy to compare, seasonal changes in foraging are clear cut, and involve mainly an increase in probing from winter to spring and a parallel addition to the repertoire of gleaning and searching; pecking and hammering, very important in winter, are consequently reduced in spring, although pecking and excavating by vigorous hammering comprise major foraging activities at all seasons. Whenever food is scarce, Hairy Woodpeckers resort to foraging for wood-boring grubs. Males use more subsurface feeding than females. Individuals use separate holes for roosting. During aggressive/social encounters, alternates phases of 'freezing', in which bill points obliquely upwards, with spasmodic displays. The latter include lateral swinging movements of the head, countercurrent flips of the spread tail and wing-flicks. The wings are fully spread in a more defensive attitude. During courtship, the male erects the red parts of the nape feathering and spreads the tail fully; in the breeding period, flutter-aerial display (fluttering or floating flights) is exhibited while approaching the mate or (prospective) nest. Roosts singly in old holes or holes produced for the purpose. Holes are lost to many avian competitors, from toucanets to starlings, but also to other animals, e.g.

squirrels. Interacts also with other woodpeckers, from sapsuckers to flickers, and with its sympatric congeners (subordinate apparently only to larger Black-backed Woodpecker, 119).

FOOD Beetles and their grubs, crickets, flies, spiders and vegetable matter comprise the diet of this versatile species. More than 80% consists of animal food: larvae of wood-boring beetles, especially cerambycids and buprestids, but also curculionids, scolytids, siricids and others, constitute about half of this, the remainder being made up of caterpillars, even hairy ones, and other arthropods (spiders, millipedes). The diet also includes fruits and seeds, mostly coniferous, particularly in winter. Sap is taken at sapsucker wells. Southern subspecies seem to be more fond of fruit and berries than the northern races, and may even feed young with figs. Wild raspberries and blackberries and certain hardy fruits, such as cornel berries, acorns, and the stones of the islay, or evergreen cherry (*Prunus ilicifolia*), are eaten in summer; in winter, takes Virginia creeper berries and apples. Readily accepts suet from feeders.

BREEDING Breeding season varies relatively little; pair-formation starts 2-3 months before nesting. In Costa Rica nests are found February-April, in California end of March to June (peak April-May), and in British Columbia and Ontario April-June. 50% to over 90% of nests are excavated into live trees (but in a dead part or in wood afflicted with fungal heart rot), at heights between (0.9) 3 and 20(38)m. Nests have also been found low in utility and fence poles. The male is mostly responsible for nest-site selection and excavation, the latter taking 17-24 days. Signal tapping and copulations peak before or during the egg-laying phase. Clutch size is 2-5 eggs, increasing northwards; about 3 eggs in Costa Rica, while in the main part of the range the mean is 3.93 eggs. Male and female incubate and feed the nestlings with about the same effort for 14 days. The male alone incubates and broods during the night. Both also remove the faeces for about 17 days. Males feed the brood less frequently, but with larger prey. The young leave the nest after 28-30 days. The fledged brood is divided between the parents, which accompany the young for two weeks and more.

REFERENCES Askins 1983; Bent 1939; Blackford 1955; Blake 1965; Bond 1985; Conner 1980; Gamboa & Brown 1976; Howell & Webb in press; Jackson 1970a; Kilham 1965, 1966, 1968; Koenig 1986; Land 1970; Lawrence 1967; Lundquist & Manuwal 1990; Martin & Li 1992; Morrison & Whit 1987; Otvos 1967; Ridgely & Gwynne 1989; Sassi 1939; Skutch 1955; Stiles & Skutch 1989; Villard & Beninger 1993.

117 WHITE-HEADED WOODPECKER
Picoides albolarvatus　　　　Plate 34

IDENTIFICATION Length c. 24cm. Small, with longish, slightly curved, chisel-tipped and broad-based bill. A very distinctive, long-tailed coniferous-forest species of the western N American mountains. Plumage mostly black, but with contrasting white crown, face and throat and white wing patch; white areas conspicuous in flight. Males have red on nape. Unmistakable.

DISTRIBUTION Mountains of western N America, from southern interior British Columbia through Washington, N Idaho and Oregon to S California. Local and rare in north of range, but fairly common elsewhere.

MOVEMENTS Some downslope movement in winter.

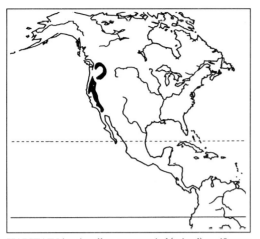

HABITAT Lives in tall open-canopied (mixed) coniferous forests, particularly with ponderosa pine (*Pinus ponderosa*), Coulter pine (*P. coulteri*), Jeffrey Pine (*P. jeffreyi*), and fir (*Abies*). Both managed and unmanaged forests are inhabited; mature, more or less open stands at 1000-2750m are preferred.

DESCRIPTION

P. a. albolarvatus **Adult male** Forehead, crown, lores, ear-coverts, chin and throat white, usually tinged faintly greyish on crown and buffy on forehead/lores; very thin dark line behind eye (often obscured); nape red. Rear neck sides, hindneck, entire upperparts, and underparts from breast black, slightly glossed bluish on upperparts and breast; one or two white feather edges sometimes apparent on underparts. Wings black, coverts blue-glossed; most of primaries have white bases, on some extending almost to tip on outer web and with two or three small white spots near tip of outer web on central primaries. Tail black. (In worn plumage, black areas are duller and some black feather bases are usually evident in crown and around ear-coverts.)

Adult female Slightly smaller than male, and with black (not red) nape.

Juvenile Much browner than adults, and sometimes with obscure paler barring on belly; white wing patch somewhat larger, but interrupted by dark barring across some or most feathers. Males have orangey-red patch from crown centre to nape; females have less red, usually restricted to hindcrown region, and rarely may lack red altogether.

Bare parts Bill dark grey. Legs and feet grey-olive or greyer. Eyes deep brownish-red or dull red.

GEOGRAPHICAL VARIATION Two races, differing only in size.

P. a. albolarvatus (most of species' range) Described above.

P. a. gravirostris (mountains around Los Angeles and San Diego) Plumage as nominate (from which geographically isolated), but significantly longer-tailed and longer-billed. In addition, male's bill is much longer than female's in *gravirostris* than in nominate.

MEASUREMENTS Wing 118-131; tail 74-90; bill of male 27-32, of female 24-29; tarsus 20-23.5. Weight: (50)52-68(79).

VOICE Common call *peek-it*, with intergrades with the rattle, *kit-kit-kit-kit...*, through short rattles. Variable series of *kweek* notes characterise encounters and accompany flutter-aerial displays. Twittering *twit-it* notes are associated with swinging displays. Intimate *tyet* notes are given at close encounters between pair members. Both sexes drum in long rolls, somewhat slower than those of Hairy Woodpecker (116). The prospective nest site is marked with slow, rhythmic tapping.

HABITS Forages mainly on the lower trunks of large trees for animal food; also descends to the ground. Regularly takes pine seeds from cones in the canopy. Favoured foraging stratum shifts moderately with season, foraging in the crown becoming more frequent in early summer. Sexual differences in foraging most pronounced in south of range: females feed more on trunks, males more on cones, particularly the huge ones of the Coulter pine. These differences are apparently maintained by male aggression. Foraging modes include removal of bark, probing and pecking. Displays include bill-pointing (bill in line with body axis) and mainly lateral swinging movements (bill straight). During courtship or pair-pair disputes, males flying away from the partner and the scene of the melee give flutter-aerial display with shallow wingbeats and uttering *gwig* call-series. Upon landing, the bird demonstrates the hole which is the current centre of activity of the pair.

FOOD Pine seeds, insects (wood-boring beetles) and spiders.

BREEDING Nests are found in May-July in snags (frequently with broken top), sloping logs, stumps, or in live trees but with soft centre caused by heart rot, relatively low at 2.5-9(29)m. Nest site frequently in open part of the habitat or on edge, and even in fence posts. Clutch comprises (3)4-5(7) eggs and is incubated by both sexes for at least 14 days. Both also care for the nestlings, which leave the nest after about 26 days.

REFERENCES Koch *et al.* 1970; Ligon 1973; Marshall in press; Milne & Hejl 1989; Morrison & With 1987; Winkler & Short 1978.

118 THREE-TOED WOODPECKER
Picoides tridactylus Plate 36

Other name: Northern Three-toed Woodpecker

IDENTIFICATION Length c. 20-24cm. Small, with longish, straight, chisel-tipped bill very broad across nostrils. Has only three toes. The only woodpecker occurring in both the New and the Old Worlds. Lacks red in all plumages. In the Palearctic this is a characteristic bird of the taiga, but is also found in mountains farther south: black and white overall, with large white panel down back (white largely obscured in southern races) and heavily to very heavily barred flanks (but unmarked or virtually so in northernmost populations east of Urals), and head appearing mostly dark with relatively narrow white bands; SW Chinese population is especially dark-bodied, mainly blackish below with narrow pale barring. N American populations are blacker on head, with white bands much narrower, and have narrower white back panel (barred in westernmost populations and greatly obscured in northern and eastern birds). All races have white bars on flight feathers, but wing-coverts unmarked (or with a few white spots in palest races), and have white bars on outer tail (outer rectrices all white in palest races). Males have yellow on crown; females have black crown, almost always streaked/spotted pale grey or white. Generally a tame woodpecker, not afraid of man, but very unobtrusive and difficult to locate; in many areas frequently forages low down near base of trunks, but slow in its movements and often remains in one place for lengthy periods. Drums loudly and relatively slowly.

Similar species In Palearctic, unlikely to be confused with

293

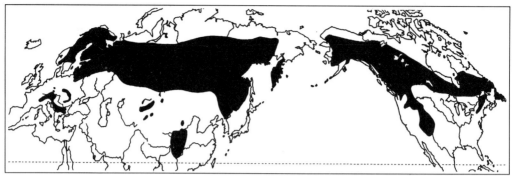

any other species when seen well. In Nearctic, the closely related Black-backed Woodpecker (119) is similar in general appearance, but is larger, has solidly black upperparts, and has largely black head (lacks white supercilium and white rear neck sides) but with more pronounced white band running backwards from lores. Female Hairy Woodpecker (116) is possibly confusable with Three-toed, but has much more white on head and more white in wings, and lacks heavy barring on sides of body.

DISTRIBUTION The huge range covers boreal forests in the north and at higher mountainous elevations in Eurasia and N America, and coincides largely with the distribution of spruce (*Picea*). Widespread from Scandinavia through the Eurasian taiga to Kamchatka, this species also reaches Japan (Hokkaido), and disjunct populations inhabit the mountains of C and SE Europe, the Tien Shan, and W China. In N America, scattered over the boreal zone from Alaska to Newfoundland; reaches farther south in the Rocky Mountains, through Oregon (absent from the Sierra Nevada) to high ranges in Arizona and New Mexico, and in the east occurs south to New England and upstate New York. Uncommon generally, and often local.

MOVEMENTS N Eurasian and eastern N American populations may perform irruptive migrations, whereas mountain populations (Alps, Tien Shan, Altai) are sedentary. In Scandinavia, most juveniles move out of the nesting area and appear far from their breeding areas. Siberian populations (*crissoleucus*) regularly migrate greater distances. Concentrates locally in areas of insect infestations.

HABITAT This woodpecker is a denizen of mature boreal and montane conifer forests. Although the range corresponds considerably with the distribution of spruce, it also inhabits other (mixed) conifer forests. Three-toed Woodpeckers are closely associated with spruce in Europe. In E European natural forests, territories are found in the wettest parts of ash-alder, coniferous, and oak-hornbeam stands; in Siberia, occurs primarily in larch taiga. In N America, there is again a clear general preference for spruce, but in NW USA, for instance, forests containing fir (*Abies*) or lodgepole pine (*Pinus contorta*) are inhabited as well. Does not occur in stands of Douglas fir (*Pseudotsuga menziesii*) or ponderosa pine (*Pinus ponderosa*). For further details, see Black-backed Woodpecker. Forest with a good proportion of insect-infested dead trees and fallen timber and which are often dense and shady are favoured. Outside the breeding season, also in more open areas or brush. May concentrate locally in burned sites or windfall areas, and may also take advantage of forests damaged by insect plagues or pollution. Found in the Alps from 650m and to over 1900m; at 3300-4000m in SE Tibet; in W USA above 1300m to 2750m, and at 360-1250m in the east.

DESCRIPTION

P. t. tridactylus **Adult male** Forehead and fore lores black,

mottled whitish; central forecrown brassy-yellow or pale lemon-yellow, usually with some black and white of feather bases showing through; crown sides and hindcrown and band down to central hindneck deep glossy black, crown usually with some white streaks. Supercilium from rear top of eye white, broadening backwards and extending down rear neck side to meet white of mantle. Area in front of and just below eye, and ear-coverts and neck sides deep glossy black, bordered below by white band from lores back to front edge of black on neck. Moustachial stripe deep black, obscured by white tips near bill, extending back to broad area of black on neck side and continuing irregularly down onto upper breast side. Chin and throat white, tinged creamy. Central mantle, innermost scapulars, back and rump white, with a few dull black spots/bars at margins; mantle sides, remaining scapulars and uppertail-coverts dull brownish-black. Upperwing dull brownish-black, flight feathers with variably sized white spots (largest on inner webs, including those of tertials) forming prominent barred pattern; coverts usually unmarked, but outers occasionally with white dots. Uppertail black, outer three pairs with increasing amount of white, barred black, at tip. Underparts white, faintly tinged creamy-buff (when fresh), with black from neck sides breaking up into streaks on sides of breast and belly, becoming variably barred on flanks and undertail-coverts. Underwing barred grey and white. Undertail as uppertail. (In worn plumage, becomes blacker, less glossy, around head, underpart markings are blacker, and yellow of crown fades and may even be lost altogether when heavily worn.)

Adult female Somewhat smaller and shorter-billed than male, and lacks yellow on crown; has forehead and crown black, with variable amount of white spots and streaks (sometimes forming contrasting white patch).

Juvenile Duller, browner, than adults and with white of back less extensive and sometimes barred; underparts duller, buffer, with heavier but more diffuse markings. Forecrown dull yellow, smaller in extent than on adult male, and probably reduced on young females; some (presumably females) lack yellow altogether.

Bare parts Bill slaty-grey, darker at tip, with paler (sometimes horn-coloured) base to lower mandible. Legs and feet slate-grey. Eyes deep red or brown-red; paler in juveniles.

GEOGRAPHICAL VARIATION Marked variation, mainly in size and in pattern of upperparts and underparts.

(a) Palearctic races:

> *P. t. tridactylus* (N Europe east across southern taiga to the Altai, N Mongolia, Manchuria, Ussuriland and Sakhalin) Described above. Easternmost populations average slightly larger and longer-billed than European ones. Wide individual variation also, especially in extent of white on head and upperparts (and also on underparts).

P. t. crissoleucus (northern taiga from Urals to Sea of Okhotsk) Only just bigger than nominate. Plumage more fluffy, and with more white on head, back and flight feathers; has less black in outer tail, and very few or no markings below.

P. t. albidior (Kamchatka) Averages smaller than above two races. Plumage as *crissoleucus* but even whiter, with pure white outer tail and underparts; much white in wings, including spots on coverts.

P. t. alpinus (mountains of C, S and SE Europe, Tien Shan, NE Korea and Hokkaido) Darker overall than above races, with white of back narrower and barred/spotted black; underparts pale-barred dark at sides, leaving narrow central band of white, and outer tail more broadly barred black. Juveniles mostly dark above and below, with pale restricted to throat, spots on mantle and mottling on underparts. Populations of the Tien Shan have been separated as '*tianschanicus*', which may be justified on grounds of isolation, although characters hardly differ from those of European *alpinus*.

P. t. funebris (SW China to Tibet) Considerably darker overall: black above, with narrow area of white or a few pale bars, and thin white bars in outer tail and on flight feathers; throat pale buffish, contrasting with finely pale-barred black of remaining underparts.

(b) Nearctic races (generally smaller and darker):

P. t. dorsalis (Rocky Mountains, from Montana south to Arizona and New Mexico) Darker on head than Palearctic races, with white bands narrower, and white of back less broad; compared with *alpinus*, is usually less barred above, less strongly marked below, and lacks bars in outer tail.

P. t. fasciatus (Alaska and Yukon south to Oregon) Averages smaller than *dorsalis*, with narrower white head markings and with more heavily barred back; body sides strongly barred.

P. t. bacatus (Alberta east to Labrador and Newfoundland and south to Minnesota and New York) The smallest of all races, slightly smaller than *fasciatus*. Differs from latter in having white face markings even narrower (supercilium broken or even absent) and back mostly black with a few small bars or spots; female has crown all black or with just a few white speckles.

MEASUREMENTS Wing 126-129 ('*tianschanicus*'), 114-132 (*tridactylus*), 109-119 (*bacatus*); tail 82.5 ('*tianschanicus*'), 70-93 (*tridactylus*), 65-77 (*bacatus*); bill 31-34 ('*tianschanicus*'), 25-34 (male *tridactylus*, mean 30.7), 24-29 (female *tridactylus*, mean 26.9), 25-29 (*bacatus*); tarsus 18-22 (male *tridactylus*, mean 21), 17-21 (female *tridactylus*, mean 19.1), 20.1-22.3 (*bacatus*). Weight: male 65-74 (*tridactylus*), female 54-66 (*tridactylus*); 46-76 (species range).

VOICE Single call notes, *kip* (higher-pitched in American birds), given in series when alarmed. Rattles are relatively short, *kri-kri-kri*.... In encounters, series of *twuit* notes are uttered in association with head-swinging displays. Low *dwach..dwach..* notes are heard in intimate contacts between pair members. Nestlings chirp unrelentingly. Fledglings utter frequent short rattles and squeaky call notes. The distress call is loud and raucous. Both sexes drum, rolls being between those of Great Spotted (104) and White-backed (103) Woodpeckers in length and slightly accelerating at the very end; not unlike roll of Black Woodpecker (169), but only about half as long. Compared with Black-backed Woodpecker, rolls are slower and shorter.

HABITS This species is not very conspicuous in its demeanour, but not particularly shy either. Except in the breeding season, mainly single birds are met with. Leads a largely arboreal life and rarely descends to the ground. Prefers trunks of dead trees and stubs, tending to forage higher up than sympatric Black-backed Woodpecker, but in the Old World most foraging takes place at 1-3m, lower than Great Spotted Woodpecker and occasionally on the ground. Males forage lower than females, mainly on trunks, and prefer large trees, while females forage higher up and have a greater niche breadth, using also relatively thin trees and branches and more frequently live trees (in summer). Both sexes forage lower in winter. When pairs forage together, females restrict their feeding to higher levels. Pecking, hammering and especially stripping off bark are the predominant techniques used; works over one particular tree persistently before choosing another site. Gleaning and probing (e.g. into lichens) are much less common. This species takes sap from wells drilled into a wide range of tree species (mainly conifers, locally *Tilia*), which become covered with sap holes from the base of the trunk up into the crown; this habit seems to be particularly common in the subalpine zone (American birds take sap from sapsucker wells). Relatively frequently moves down backwards; dead trees may be revisited over several days until they are entirely stripped of bark. Displays with bill-pointing, an apparently submissive bill-lowering. The crest is fully erect in head-swinging displays, which are accompanied by *wicka*-calls, and in which the bill is raised more and more above the body axis with increasing intensity. Threatens with spread tail and spread wings, and shows a flutter-aerial display. Breeding densities range from 0.001 pairs/10ha (or lower) to 0.15 pairs/10ha. Home ranges of male and female do not overlap greatly. Interacts with sympatric congeners, particularly with similar Black-backed Woodpecker, which is dominant in general. Other interactions relate to hole competitors (squirrels, pygmy owls, tree swallows).

FOOD Larvae and pupae of beetles living beneath the bark form the bulk of the diet, and are also important as nestling food. Other insect larvae (hymenopterans) and imagoes and spiders are taken, too. This species is an important predator of insects which are subject to 'plagues'; examples are *Polygraphus* and *Ips* (both in Eurasia) and spruce bark beetle (*Dendroctonus obesus*, USA). Apart from sap, vegetable matter plays no role, although berries (e.g. *Sorbus*) and spruce seeds are occasionally taken.

BREEDING Courtship activities start in the second half of March, but take place mainly from mid April to mid May, when egg-laying commences. Both sexes participate in nest construction. The hole is excavated in dead trees or (rarely) in sections of live trees with heart rot, spruce and other conifers being preferred; mean nest height 2.0m (Norway), or 4m (Alps), to 10.2m (Poland); range 1m (or lower) to 21m. A new nest is usually made each year. Clutch size varies from 3 to 4 eggs in the Alps, and from 3 to 6 (rarely 7), mean 4.1, in Scandinavia; 3-4(5) in N America. Both sexes incubate the eggs, about 60% of which hatch after 11-14 days. As with most other woodpecker species, the male sits with the eggs/chicks overnight, at least for the first two weeks of the nestling period. The nestlings are fed by both parents for 22-26 days, the female sometimes reducing her effort (completely) towards the end of that period. Fledglings are accompanied by their parents for up to a month.

REFERENCES Bezzel 1985; Blackford 1955; Bock & Bock 1974; Cramp 1985; Dement'ev & Gladkov 1966; Hågvar et al. 1990; Hogstad 1970, 1971a, 1976, 1977, 1991; Koplin 1969; Marshall in press; Ruge 1968, 1971, 1971a, 1973; Scherzinger 1972; Short 1974c; Wesolowski & Tomialojc 1986; West & Speirs 1959; Winkler & Short 1978.

119 BLACK-BACKED WOODPECKER
Picoides arcticus   **Plate 36**

Other names: Arctic Woodpecker, Arctic Three-toed Woodpecker, Black-backed Three-toed Woodpecker

IDENTIFICATION Length c. 23-25cm. Small, with longish, straight, flattish, chisel-tipped bill broad across nostrils. Has only three toes. A coniferous-forest inhabitant of N America, entirely glossy black above and white below, with regular and prominent barring from breast sides to flanks. Flight feathers are narrowly barred white and outer tail plain white. Head mostly dark, apart from contrasting broad white band from lores to lower neck side, male with bright yellow patch on crown; female lacks yellow crown and is one of the plainest of all N American woodpeckers.

Similar species Three-toed Woodpecker (118) is slightly smaller, less uniformly patterned, has white supercilium and white behind ear-coverts, and usually has at least some white on back. Black-backed is closest to very dark and almost fully black-backed individuals of eastern race *bacatus* of Three-toed, but latter shows some contrast between deep glossy black of head and duller brownish-black of upperparts and also has some white on rear neck sides (but a narrower white band from lores than Black-backed).

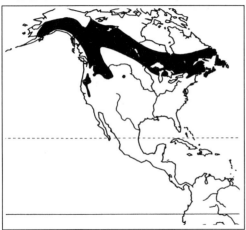

DISTRIBUTION Broadly sympatric with Three-toed Woodpecker, but does not occur so far north, the northern limits of its range corresponding closely with the presence of closed pine (*Pinus*) forests. Occurs across N America from Alaska through Canada to S Labrador and Newfoundland, its southern limits including Montana, Wyoming, South Dakota through N Michigan and S Ontario to New York. In the Rocky Mountains, ranges north to NW Wyoming and South Dakota and south into the Sierra Nevada (Nevada, C California). In the east, found south to N New England and upstate New York. Uncommon in general, but seems to outnumber Three-toed Woodpecker in eastern parts of range.

MOVEMENTS Normally non-migratory, this species is, however, subject to irregular dismigration possibly caused by regional population increase due to very favourable conditions (such as outbreaks of spruce budworm or following fires).

HABITAT Northern and montane dense coniferous forests. Burned and windfall areas and those afflicted by outbreaks of forest pests (e.g. spruce budworm, *Pissodes* and other bark beetles) are particularly favoured. Compared with its close ally the Three-toed Woodpecker, this species

is not particularly tied to spruce and frequents a wider set of habitats. It is found regularly in pine (*Pinus*, mainly *P. banksiana* and *P. contorta*) forests and in other types of conifers (e.g. larch *Larix*, firs *Abies*), typically those which are also found at lower elevations. In particular, it enters forests of Douglas fir (*Pseudotsuga menziesii*) and ponderosa pine (*Pinus ponderosa*) in areas of overlap with its sibling species. Ranges from sea level to 1300m in the east and is restricted to the mountains in its western range: to 1200-2400m in S Oregon, above 1350m in Montana, and to 1200-3100m in California.

DESCRIPTION
Adult male Forecrown yellow to golden-yellow; lores and band running back below ear-coverts to neck side white, sometimes also a very fine pale line behind eye. Rest of head, including moustache (latter usually mixed with white near bill), and entire upperparts deep blue-glossed black (rarely, a few pale tips to rump feathers). Upperwing black, coverts glossed blue (occasionally with a few small white spots), primaries and usually also secondaries with small white spots forming narrow bars. Uppertail black, with white at tip of third rectrix increasing in extent outwards to almost all-white outer tail. Chin, throat and rest of underparts white, washed greyish in lower regions, and with black of upper mantle/moustache extending down to breast side and breaking up into bars, which become very regular on flanks and belly sides. Underwing barred dark grey and white. Undertail as above, but paler.

Adult female Slightly smaller than male, and with entire crown black.

Juvenile Duller, browner, than adults, with more white in wings and with less regular, less black and more diffuse markings below. Young males have some yellow or orange-yellow on crown, less extensive than on adult; young females usually have a few small spots of yellow, but may lack these.

Bare parts Bill slaty-grey, paler on lower mandible (where may be horn-coloured at base). Legs and feet dark grey or slaty. Eyes red-brown to brown; paler in juveniles.

GEOGRAPHICAL VARIATION None. Monotypic.

MEASUREMENTS Wing 119-134; tail 73-85; bill 28.5-35; tarsus 21-24.9. Weight: 61-88.

VOICE Call note a distinctive short and high-pitched double click. The rattle is a peculiar, long, grating snarl, varying in pitch in the course of delivery and changing from a fast series of clicks ('scream') into a fast rasping snarl. Variations of this call seem to cover all the functions of the louder calls of congeners. In encounters between members of the pair, soft *yek* notes are given. Nestlings chirp incessantly. Drumming rolls are faster than those of Three-toed Woodpecker and slower than Hairy Woodpecker's (116), and tend to accelerate at the end. Responds more readily to drumming (playback) than its sibling species.

HABITS Forages mostly on tree trunks, to some extent on large limbs, and on fallen timber; where available, fire-killed trees (e.g. *Pinus strobus*) are strongly preferred. Generally, about half to two-thirds of trees visited are dead, and pines seem to be selected as feeding stations even when not the dominant tree species. Predominant feeding techniques, especially in winter, are pecking, including blows which remove pieces of bark and other forms of scaling, and hammering, whereby the woodpecker excavates deeply into the wood of dead trees; these foraging modes remain important throughout the year, although gleaning and probing increase during the breeding period. Flycatching is rare. Displays with bill-directing, raises the bill in same way as Three-toed Woodpecker, and exposes the (raised) crown feathers in a bill-lowering posture, which may be combined with a hunch. Swinging head movements are not very prominent, but conspicuous tail- and especially wing-spreading is common. The flutter-aerial display is directed at the partner/nest. This species appears to avoid interspecific encounters with Hairy Woodpeckers, yet encounters with this and other congeners are not rare; other species involved are flickers, sapsuckers, squirrels and tree swallows.

FOOD Largely wood-boring beetle larvae; particularly, the large grubs of *Monochamus scutellatus* (white-spotted sawyer), an insect confined to burned forests, and bark-dwelling beetles (*Pissodes*). Also takes other insects and spiders, and some fruits and seeds are eaten occasionally.

BREEDING Nest is excavated in dead or live (with heart rot) trees at 0.6-5(25)m. May also use cavities from previous years or holes of other similar-sized woodpeckers as nest. Commonly, the bark around the entrance is removed and the exposed wood renders nests rather conspicuous (compare with similar behaviour of Red-cockaded Woodpecker, 114). Clutch consists of (2)3-4(6) eggs; both sexes incubate, the male at night and apparently more than the female during the day as well. Both parents provide for the young, but the male seems to bring more and larger food items.
REFERENCES Blackford 1955; Bock & Bock 1974; Marshall in press; Mayfield 1958; Short 1974c; van Tyne 1926; Villard & Beninger 1993; West & Speirs 1959.

120 SCARLET-BACKED WOODPECKER
Veniliornis callonotus   Plate 37

IDENTIFICATION Length c. 13cm. Very small, with fairly long, broad bill with straight or slightly curved culmen. A very distinctive species, red above and on wings and white below (lightly barred in southern populations); flight feathers and tail are dark, and dark ear-coverts stand out against pale face. Female has contrasting black forehead to nape. A rather poorly known species, but unmistakable.

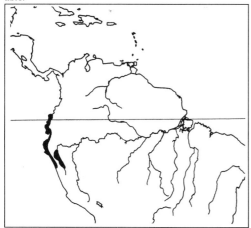

DISTRIBUTION West-central S America, from W Ecuador to N and NW Peru. Apparently uncommon.

HABITAT Occurs in arid tropical lowlands, where it frequents desert scrub with scattered trees and cacti, dry

deciduous forests, and dense growth along watercourses.

DESCRIPTION
V. c. callonotus **Adult male** Feathers of forehead to nape black-based and extensively red-tipped. Ear-coverts greyish-brown; rest of face, including very thin line below eye, white, side of rear neck often dirtier or even brown, and sometimes with a slight indication of a thin dark moustachial line. Hindneck and upperparts, together with upperwing-coverts, brownish-scarlet (browner when worn), usually with some brown feather bases showing through. Flight feathers dark brown or blackish-brown, becoming redder on secondaries and tertials. Uppertail blackish-brown, blacker on central rectrices, and with outer feathers whitish-yellow and barred black. Underparts entirely white with very light (variable) pale buff wash, sometimes almost imperceptibly vermiculated darker. Underwing and undertail as above or paler.

Adult female Has forehead to nape wholly black, often with some white feathers at rear.

Juvenile Has red of upperparts heavily mottled with olive or greyish, and underparts buffish-white; head pattern generally less obvious, more diffuse. Males have small red feather tips on forecrown.

Bare parts Bill yellowish, usually darker at base and sometimes dark-tipped. Legs and feet greenish-grey. Eyes deep brown (occasionally deep red, or tinged bluish).

GEOGRAPHICAL VARIATION Two intergrading races.
  V. c. callonotus (northern part of range) Described above. Intergrades with following race, and the two interbreed in southern Ecuador.
  V. c. major (southern part of range) As nominate, but has noticeably darker ear-coverts, and underparts are narrowly vermiculated/barred blackish. Intermediates, with partly and/or more obscurely barred underparts, occur in overlap zone.

MEASUREMENTS Wing 71-81. Weight: 23-33.

VOICE Unknown.

HABITS Unknown.

FOOD Unknown.

BREEDING Breeding most likely between January and July; no details known.

REFERENCES Parker *et al.* 1982.

121 YELLOW-VENTED WOODPECKER
Veniliornis dignus   Plate 37

IDENTIFICATION Length c. 15-17cm. Small, with shortish to long, straight bill broad across nostrils. A little-known species of forested hill slopes. Like most of its genus, a rather dark-looking woodpecker with greenish tone to upperparts and heavily barred underparts. Both sexes have blackish ear-coverts bordered above and below by whitish stripes, and also deep red hindneck, rear neck sides and upper mantle, and yellowish ground colour to belly. Male has red of hindneck extending to forecrown.

Similar species Bar-bellied Woodpecker (122) is very similar, but has far less distinct pale face stripes, red does not reach onto neck sides (female lacks red altogether), and is less yellow but more barred below; it also occurs at higher altitudes.

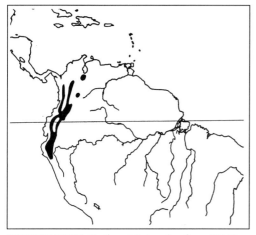

DISTRIBUTION Northwest S America, from SW Venezuela along the Andes in the submontane zone through NC Colombia to E Peru. Probably uncommon.

HABITAT Humid and wet forest, especially cloud forest, and forest edge. Found rarely outside primary forest, for instance in overgrown abandoned coffee plantations. Occurs at altitudes between (700) 1200 and 2700m.

DESCRIPTION

V. d. dignus **Adult male** Forehead greenish-buff; crown, nape and rear neck sides to upper mantle deep crimson, with some black feather bases showing through (especially on crown). Ear-coverts olive-tinged black, bordered above by white/whitish stripe behind eye and below by white stripe from lores. Chin blackish, vermiculated or spotted whitish. Lower mantle to uppertail-coverts dark yellowish-green with bronze tinge, with red of upper mantle evident on lower mantle as red tips/edges; rump and uppertail-coverts barred paler and dark olive. Upperwing brownish-olive, browner on flight feathers, which have small pale bars on inner webs; median and sometimes also lesser coverts with pale yellow (often red-edged) central area forming triangles, spots or streaks. Uppertail blackish, suffused yellow, outer two feather pairs barred pale. Underparts below chin greenish-white, becoming yellow on belly and flanks, and throat, breast and upper flanks with heavy olive-blackish arrowhead marks forming bars. Underwing barred brown and yellow-white. Undertail as uppertail.

Adult female Has forecrown to nape blackish, tinged olive, but retains red on neck.

Juvenile Duller and less yellow, more green, above. Both sexes have some red tips to crown feathers.

Bare parts Bill blackish, with paler base. Legs and feet dark olive-grey. Eyes brown to red-brown.

GEOGRAPHICAL VARIATION Three rather poorly differentiated races, differing in bill length and in degree of barring below.

> *V. d. dignus* (Venezuela and Colombia) Described above. Includes Venezuelan 'abdominalis'. Bill medium-long.
> *V. d. baezae* (Ecuador) Shorter-billed than nominate, and with underpart barring darker and tending to be more extensive on flanks.
> *V. d. valdizani* (Peru) As nominate, but with longer bill and with rump barring more obscure.

MEASUREMENTS Wing 92-102. Weight: 35-40 (*dignus*), to 46 (*valdizani*).

VOICE This small woodpecker does not call often. The rattle is weak, nasal and high-pitched.

HABITS Usually seen alone or in pairs; occasionally joins mixed foraging parties. Forages in the middle level of trees up to the canopy. Seems to hammer a lot, although with weak blows, spending long periods at one spot; this activity may take place high up on a tree trunk, on limbs and smaller branches.

FOOD Unknown.

BREEDING From the scant information, a breeding season from March to August is inferred.

REFERENCES Hilty & Brown 1984; Meyer de Schauensee & Phelps 1978; Miller 1963; Parker *et al.* 1982.

122 BAR-BELLIED WOODPECKER
Veniliornis nigriceps Plate 37

IDENTIFICATION Length c. 19cm. Small, with longish, straight bill broad across nostrils. A very poorly known inhabitant of humid montane forest. Very like Yellow-vented Woodpecker (121), but pale head stripes much narrower and less obvious. Bronzy yellow-green or olive above, and heavily and broadly barred over entire underparts; has indistinct pale supercilium and very indistinct pale line below ear-coverts. Male has red from forehead to hindneck, these areas being olive-tinged black on female.

Similar species Yellow-vented Woodpecker has much stronger head pattern, more red on neck (both sexes), less barred underparts and pale spots on wing-coverts, and is found at lower elevations. Very similar Dot-fronted Woodpecker (125), which approaches range of Bar-bellied in the south, is slightly smaller, has pale spots on wing-coverts and scapulars and lightly spotted/barred mantle, and has white-spotted forehead (male) or crown (female).

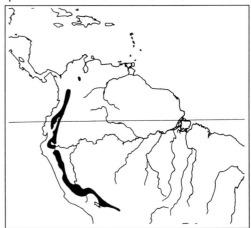

DISTRIBUTION Central Andes of western S America, from Colombia to Ecuador and along the eastern slopes from Peru to Bolivia (Cochabamba, Santa Cruz). Appears to be not uncommon.

HABITAT Humid and wet forest, forest edge, stunted forest at the tree line and on mountain ridges, and occasionally above the tree line in patches of *Polylepis* woodland. Prefers stands with dense (bamboo) undergrowth. Ranges from (2000) 2600 to 3600m (4000m in Ecuador).

DESCRIPTION

***V. n. equifasciatus* Adult male** Forehead olive, with extensive red feather tips; crown to central hindneck red, with some black feather bases visible on crown. Ear-coverts dark olive-brown, finely streaked pale, bordered above by very narrow and short pale supercilium from above eye and below by equally narrow or even thinner pale line. Sides of neck dark olive, with feathers whitish-edged/barred and variably golden-tipped. Chin and throat blackish-olive, chin streaked/mottled and throat barred pale. Upperparts dark olive with bronze tinge, often with a few scattered dull red feather tips on mantle, and rump and uppertail-coverts with obscure paler spots or bars. Upperwing olive-brown, all feathers edged and tipped bronze-olive, coverts sometimes with very narrow pale central streaks. Uppertail blackish, outer two feather pairs barred pale. Underparts from throat buffish-white, tinged olive, all broadly barred dark olive (pale and dark bars about equal in width). Underwing barred brown and whitish. Undertail much as uppertail.

Adult female As male, but has forehead to nape blackish to olive-black, often with a few red feather edges.

Juvenile Duller and greener than adults, with more barring in tail. Both sexes have red on crown (not nape), that on female being more restricted and with darker, blacker feather bases than on adult.

Bare parts Bill dark grey to bluish-grey, paler on lower mandible. Legs and feet grey to olive-grey. Eyes deep red to brown.

GEOGRAPHICAL VARIATION Three races, the southern two more heavily barred.

    V. n. equifasciatus (Colombia to Ecuador) Described above.

    V. n. pectoralis (S Ecuador and Peru) Darker below, with dark bars much broader than pale ones.

    V. n. nigriceps (Bolivia) Very heavily barred below, as *pectoralis*; females have darker (black) crown.

MEASUREMENTS Wing 95-106. Weight: 39-46 (*pectoralis*).

VOICE A high-pitched descending sputter, *kzrrrrr*.

HABITS This quiet woodpecker is found alone and regularly in mixed-species flocks. Pecks on bark, removes it, and probes among mosses on (horizontal) branches from lower levels up to the canopy.

FOOD Unknown.

BREEDING Breeds February-March in Ecuador and April-May in Bolivia. August birds from Peru (race *pectoralis*) reported with large testes (AMNH specimens).

REFERENCES Fjeldså 1991; Fjeldså & Krabbe 1990; Hilty & Brown 1984; Parker *et al.* 1982.

123 SMOKY-BROWN WOODPECKER
Veniliornis fumigatus   Plate 37

Other name: Brown Woodpecker

IDENTIFICATION Length c. 16cm. Very small, with rather long, straight bill broad across nostrils. A fairly uniformly patterned brown or brownish woodpecker, with darker wings and tail; belly is usually paler than rest of underparts, and ear-coverts generally paler than rest of face (with northern populations also very whitish around eye). Male has top of head red, this area being blackish-brown with olive feather edges on female. Inconspicuous but probably not uncommon, and unmistakable: the only plain brownish woodpecker within its range.

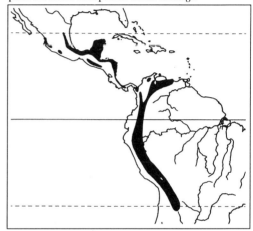

DISTRIBUTION C America and western S America, from S Mexico, through Panama, N Venezuela, Colombia and Peru along the eastern slopes of the Andes to Bolivia (Tarija) and NW Argentina (Jujuy). Fairly common to common in C America, perhaps somewhat less common further south.

HABITAT Humid and wet forests, cloud forests and dry cloud forests in mountain terrain, and occasionally above the tree line in patches of *Polylepis* woodland. In lowlands, prefers forest edge and clearings, and occurs along wooded streams, in shady and tall second growth, in thickets, lighter woodland and woodland borders, and coffee plantations. In Mexico from almost sea level to 1500m; in C America in lowlands to middle elevations (750m), locally up to 1850m, and apparently absent from some wetter lowlands. In Venezuela occurs from 800 to 2700m; in Colombia and Peru mostly between 1200 and 2800m, occasionally lower (600m) or higher (3500m to above 4000m in Peru, Cordillera Blanca); and in Argentina it is found between 1700 and 2500m.

DESCRIPTION

***V. f. oleagineus* Adult male** Forehead to nape red, with dark grey feather bases showing on forehead and crown. Rest of head and neck olive-brown, paler on ear-coverts and whitish on lores and around eye. Chin brown, obscurely barred blackish. Upperparts brown to olive-brown, mantle tinged red or with some golden to orange feather edges when fresh; rump and uppertail-coverts duller brown. Upperwing dark brown, coverts tinged greenish and often with some red edges; flight feathers barred pale on inner webs. Uppertail blackish-brown, becoming paler brown on outer feathers. Underparts from throat olive-brown, paler on lower regions, latter occasionally with faint, obscure

299

darker bars. Underwing barred whitish and brown. Undertail much as uppertail.

Adult female Lacks red on head, forehead to nape being olive-tinged dark brown to black-brown, occasionally with a few white speckles; feathers dusky at base.

Juvenile Similar to adults but duller, lacking fresh-plumaged adults' red tinges above; young males are darker-coloured, more sooty-brown, showing white bars on inner webs of secondaries in flight. Both sexes have dull red on crown, sometimes reaching nape on male, on female normally restricted to forecrown.

Bare parts Bill blackish, paler on lower mandible. Legs and feet dark greyish. Eyes deep brown to red-brown.

GEOGRAPHICAL VARIATION Five races, some intergrading, varying mostly in tone of plumage and in wing length.

> ***V. f. oleagineus*** (E Mexico) Described above. Longer-winged than all races except *obscuratus*.
> ***V. f. sanguinolentus*** (C and S Mexico to W Panama) Smaller, shorter-winged and a richer brown than *oleagineus*, ear-coverts paler than rest of head, but lacks obvious whitish colour around eye.
> ***V. f. reichenbachi*** (E Panama and N Venezuela, and south through Colombia to E Ecuador) As *sanguinolentus*, but slightly longer-winged and duller brown.
> ***V. f. fumigatus*** (upper Amazonia) Similar to *oleagineus*, but smaller and without white around eyes.
> ***V. f. obscuratus*** (NW Peru to NW Argentina) Similar to *reichenbachi*, but longer-winged and with darker, more grey-brown, not golden, plumage tone.

MEASUREMENTS Wing 80-98 (*sanguinolentus*), 92-101 (*reichenbachi*), 94-105 (*oleagineus, obscuratus*); tail 40-55 (*sanguinolentus*), 46-58 (*oleagineus, reichenbachi*); bill 18.5-24.2 (*sanguinolentus*), 19.6-23.9 (*reichenbachi*), 21-24.5 (*oleagineus*); tarsus 16.8-19 (*oleagineus*), 15-18.8 (*sanguinolentus*), 18.1-20.9 (*reichenbachi*). Weight: 31-40 (*sanguinolentus*), 36-42 (*oleagineus*), 35-50 (*reichenbachi*).

VOICE Single call a metallic *wick, peek* or *pwik*, softer and more slurred than note of Hairy Woodpecker (116). Rattle described as being higher-pitched and piping or as a hard, rolling, gravelly *keer-keer-keer-keer, zur-zur-zur-zur*, or *krrr-krrr-krrr*, at higher intensities. *tchip, tchip zr-r-r-r uh kuh-kuh-kuh-kuh-kuh-kuh*. In interactions, a squeaky, sucking *wick-a wick-a* or *tsewink tsewink*. Drums in prolonged, very rapid tattoos.

HABITS Inconspicuous and not often seen. Although paired throughout the year, often met with singly. Found in family groups following breeding, and often with mixed-species flocks. Forages high in broken canopy or lower at edges and in undergrowth, often in vine tangles or on slender branches and among foliage, mostly at middle and low levels; also visits isolated trees in the open. Pecks and hammers industriously on thin stems to large branches and vines. Probing infrequent, and gleaning seems to be almost absent. Moves along branches with many sideward lunges. Spreads wings when attacked, as other woodpeckers. Roosts singly.

FOOD Small wood-boring beetles and their larvae comprise the major part of the diet, which is occasionally supplemented with fruits.

BREEDING Breeding season February-June in C America, February-March in N Venezuela, and October-April in Colombia. Nest hole 1.5-8m up in a dead limb, tree trunk or fence post. Both members of the pair work on the hole. Clutch contains four eggs.

REFERENCES Askins 1983; Blake 1965; Fjeldså 1991; Hilty & Brown 1984; Howell & Webb in press; Meyer de Schauensee & Phelps 1978; Miller 1963; Olrog 1984; Parker *et al*. 1982; Peterson & Chalif 1973; Ridgely & Gwynne 1989; Russel 1964; Skutch 1969; Slud 1964; Stiles & Skutch 1989; Wetmore 1968; Zimmer 1942.

124 LITTLE WOODPECKER
Veniliornis passerinus   Plate 37

Forms a superspecies with *frontalis*.

IDENTIFICATION Length c. 14-15cm. Very small, with fairly long, straight bill broad across nostrils. A variable species, basically dark above, dull yellow-green to bronzy-olive, sometimes somewhat barred, and barred olive and whitish below; wings (narrowly barred) and tail (outer feathers narrowly barred) are darker, and wing-coverts have small pale spots. Very thin, indistinct pale supercilium and moustachial line, often difficult to see in the field, and one or both are absent in some races. Males have usually grey-brown forehead and variable amount of red on crown, red extending to nape on some; females have entire head top dark grey-brown to brown.

Similar species Dot-fronted Woodpecker (125) has red extending to forecrown (male), speckled forehead, more obviously barred tail, and longer supercilium than partly sympatric race *olivinus* of Little.

DISTRIBUTION S America, from Colombia, Venezuela and the Guianas in the north, through N Brazil and along eastern slopes of the Andes to Rio Grande do Sul (Brazil), Paraguay, Argentina (Santa Fe, Corrientes), and Bolivia (Santa Cruz). Appears to be not uncommon.

HABITAT The Little Woodpecker is rather versatile in the habitats it occupies, generally preferring edge and second growth over forest. It is found at edges of humid forest, including cloud forest, in gallery forest with bamboo along swampy lagoons and rivers, deciduous woodland, mangroves, second growth, as well as transitional forests, densely wooded savannas, light second growth, shrubs (caatinga) and sparsely wooded savannas. To 850m in N Venezuela, to 400m farther south, and to 900 and 1200m in Peru and Colombia, respectively.

DESCRIPTION
V. p. olivinus **Adult male** Forehead and forecrown brownish-grey, usually finely pale-spotted; hindcrown and nape

red (a few dark bases visible). Short, thin, pale supercilium behind eye (but often absent) and thin whitish moustachial line (often partly lacking); otherwise, face plain olive-brown to olive-buff, ear-coverts very lightly streaked. Neck sides greyish-olive with paler feather tips. Chin olive, spotted or barred pale. Upperparts bronzy olive-green, sometimes with a few red feather tips, and with variable obscure paler barring (most evident on rump, but still indistinct). Upperwing-coverts as back, median coverts usually with small subterminal streak-like spots; flight feathers brown, edged green (broadly on secondaries and tertials), with narrow whitish bars on inner webs of primaries and secondaries. Uppertail dark brown, outer feathers usually with some thin pale bars. Underparts from throat dark olive, entirely barred with buffish-white (bars arrowhead-shaped on flanks and belly). Underwing barred olive-brown and pale. Undertail much as uppertail.

Adult female Lacks red on head, having forehead to nape greyish olive-brown, usually with indistinct pale spots.

Juvenile Similar to adults but duller, less bronzy, and barring on breast less regular. Both sexes have dull red on crown (not nape), less extensive on females.

Bare parts Bill blackish, paler on lower mandible. Legs and feet dark grey. Eyes deep brown; paler or greyish in juveniles.

GEOGRAPHICAL VARIATION Nine races, differing mainly in nature of barring below, in tone of upperparts and amount of spotting on wing-coverts, in extent of red on head of male, in presence of facial stripes, and in size.

V. p. olivinus (S Bolivia, S Brazil, Paraguay and N Argentina) Described above. The largest race. Intergrades with following race in EC Brazil.

V. p. taenionotus (E Brazil) Smaller than *olivinus* and yellower-toned above (often with scattered red feather tips and stronger hint of barring), and with larger spots on wing-coverts, including on greater coverts; pale bars on underparts noticeably broader than in *olivinus*. Red of male's head extends to forehead.

V. p. tapajoensis (C Brazil) Rather bright yellow-tinged above, with some red spots. Red of male's head extends to forecrown.

V. p. insignis (WC Brazil) Small. Lacks pale facial stripes; no spots on wing-coverts; pale bars below broad. Red extends to central crown on male.

V. p. diversus (N Brazil) Lacks or has only faint indication of facial stripes; wing-coverts sometimes with very narrow pale shaft streaks; wide pale bars on underside; dark bars tend to form arrowhead markings on breast. Red on crown of male extends further forwards (to central crown) than in *olivinus*.

V. p. passerinus (NE Brazil and the Guianas) Smallest race (as *insignis*). Lacks pale facial stripes; rather pale-billed. Red of male's head extends to forecrown.

V. p. modestus (NE Venezuela) Moustachial line fairly prominent, but lacks pale supercilium; wing-coverts with obvious pale spots; grey-brown below, with breast barring irregular; pale bars relatively narrow. Red on male extends to forecrown.

V. p. fidelis (W Venezuela to E Colombia) Breast barring broken or scallop-shaped; pale supercilium and moustache much more marked, and wing-covert spots larger. Red of male's head reaches to forecrown.

V. p. agilis (E Ecuador to N Bolivia and W Brazil) Supercilium and moustachial stripes well developed. Male has red extending to forecrown.

MEASUREMENTS Wing 71-97; tail 40-63; bill 16-22; tarsus 15. Weight: 24-37.

VOICE High-pitched *ki, ki, ki, ki* or *wi-wi-wi-wi-wi-wi-wi*, also associated with drumming, seem to represent this species'

long-distance calls. Gives *wicka* or *wik-wik-wik...* in encounters.

HABITS Found singly, in pairs or in small groups; sometimes joins mixed-species flocks. Forages from low in the undergrowth, preferentially on bamboo, to upper heights in trees. Foraging techniques include vigorous pecking and hammering on bark, branches and limbs, around bamboo nodes, and on saplings; small holes are drilled through the latter activity. Displays include wing-spreading and swinging of the head, with tail-spreading.

FOOD Ants, termites, beetles and their larvae and various other insects.

BREEDING Breeds September-December in French Guiana and October-March in Argentina; copulation observed in February in Colombia. Nest built in a stub, palm or bamboo at 5-13m. Observations of nest excavation and brood care have so far related to males only.

REFERENCES Dubs 1983, 1992; Hilty & Brown 1984; Meyer de Schauensee & Phelps 1978; Olrog 1984; Parker *et al.* 1982; Reiser 1929; Short 1970a; Sick 1993; Tostain *et al.* 1992; Zimmer 1942.

125 DOT-FRONTED WOODPECKER
Veniliornis frontalis   Plate 37

Forms a superspecies with *passerinus*.

IDENTIFICATION Length c. 16cm. Very small, with fairly long, straight bill broad across nostrils. A little-known species of the Andes, very similar in plumage to Little Woodpecker (124). Yellow-green upperparts are marked with paler bars or rows of pale spots and have golden feather tips when fresh, but in worn plumage much of this pattern disappears; wing-coverts have more prominent pale triangular spots and streaks. Wings and tail darker and barred pale. Underparts are largely olive-grey, narrowly barred whitish. The head shows a thin white supercilium behind eye and a thin white moustache; forehead heavily spotted with white, male having a red crown and nape and female a white-spotted crown and nape.

Similar species Just overlaps in range with Little Woodpecker of race *olivinus*, which has somewhat plainer upperparts, lacks or has only indistinct pale speckling on forehead, and has more uniform ear-coverts and neck sides. In addition, note more obvious barring on tail of Dot-fronted and more extensive red on male's head (reaches to forecrown; limited to hindcrown and nape on male *olivinus*).

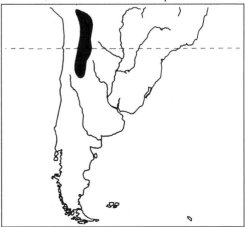

DISTRIBUTION Southern S America, from Bolivia (Cochabamba, W Santa Cruz) to Argentina (Tucumán). Uncommon.

MOVEMENTS Some downslope movements occur outside the breeding season.

HABITAT Transitional and humid forests of Andean slopes at up to 2000m.

DESCRIPTION
Adult male Forehead olive to grey-brown, heavily spotted with white; forecrown to nape red, with extensive dark grey feather bases showing. Ear-coverts and neck sides light olive-brown, streaked buffish, with neck sides barred pale, and bordered above by long but thin white supercilium from above eye and below by thin white line from lores (pale stripes often partly obscured by darker spotting). Chin and malar region whitish, broadly streaked/spotted olive-grey. Hindneck and upperparts yellowish-olive, latter barred and streaked pale and with golden feather tips (pattern much less obvious in worn plumage). Upperwing-coverts yellowish-olive, medians with pale wedge-shaped spots (extending to outer scapulars) and greaters with narrow pale central streaks; flight feathers brown, broadly edged yellow-green, with primaries and secondaries narrowly pale-barred on inner webs. Uppertail dark brown, barred whitish (barring less distinct on central feathers), all suffused yellow. Underparts from throat to undertail-coverts olive-grey, all narrowly barred whitish. Underwing barred dusky and pale. Undertail as uppertail, but paler.

Adult female Lacks red on head, having crown to nape olive-brown with white spots (nape more streaked).

Juvenile Duller and greyer than adults. Both sexes have red on crown (not nape), less extensive on female.

Bare parts Bill slate-grey to blackish, paler on lower mandible. Legs and feet dark grey. Eyes dark brown.

GEOGRAPHICAL VARIATION None. Monotypic.

MEASUREMENTS Wing 89-97. Weight: 30-40.

VOICE Not known.

HABITS Forages on limbs and small trunks, often near ground.

FOOD Not known.

BREEDING Presumably breeds November to February.

REFERENCES Olrog 1984; Wetmore 1926.

---

126 WHITE-SPOTTED WOODPECKER
Veniliornis spilogaster   Plate 37

IDENTIFICATION Length 16-19.5cm. Very small, with rather short to longish, straight bill broad across nostrils. A rather dark olive-coloured woodpecker, but with very prominent pale barring both above and below and on wings and tail; has dark crown and ear-coverts with pronounced white supercilium and moustache, latter dark-bordered below. In reasonable views, combination of all these features renders identification relatively straightforward.

DISTRIBUTION Central-southern S America, from S Brazil (Rio de Janeiro, Minas Gerais, São Paulo) to adjacent Paraguay, Argentina (Misiones, E Corrientes) and Uruguay. Common, and locally very common.

HABITAT Various types of forest and woodland, from humid lowland forests, riverine forests and isolated forest patches to open and very open woodland and open parkland country with low and spiny trees.

DESCRIPTION
Adult male Forehead buffy to olive; crown blackish-brown, very narrowly streaked dark red when fresh. Ear-coverts brownish, spotted white, bordered above by narrow white supercilium and below by thin moustachial stripe, latter edged with a dark brown or mixed brown-and-white submoustachial stripe. Chin and sides of neck white or whitish, striped dark olive-brown. Upperparts olive-green, with pale yellowish-white feather edges forming bars, bars sometimes becoming spots on rump. Upperwing-coverts dark olive, tipped whitish (forming bars); flight feathers dark brown, barred whitish. Uppertail dark brown, narrowly barred off-white. Underparts from throat dark olive, heavily streaked yellowish-white on throat, becoming barred or spotted on breast and heavily barred in lower regions (flank feathers clearly edged and tipped, producing scaly pattern). Underwing barred brown and white. Undertail much as uppertail. (In worn plumage, crown and ear-coverts become plainer and less patterned, barring above and on wings conspicuously whiter and less yellow, and underparts more narrowly barred and hence darker.)

Adult female As male but noticeably shorter-billed, and has crown olive-brown and finely spotted white.

Juvenile Much as adults, but barring above less obvious and less regular, more spotted.

Bare parts Bill blackish-grey, paler at base and often with yellowish base to lower mandible. Legs and feet olive or olive-grey. Eyes deep chestnut-brown.

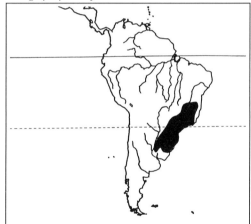

GEOGRAPHICAL VARIATION None. Monotypic.

MEASUREMENTS Wing 90-105. Weight: 35-45.

VOICE Single call notes (mild alarm), *pic*, and a great variety of other distinctive calls: a sharp *cheékit* and *ti-rra-rra*, *prio-rr-rr-rr-rr*, *reh-reh-reh-reh*, or *cheékit ch che che che che che*. Nestlings utter a variable, high-pitched, almost whistled chittering. Also described is a gentle signal tapping, in groups of 2-4, with pauses and single taps.

HABITS Not much is known about this locally very common woodpecker. Has been observed foraging on tree trunks, saplings and fence posts. Forages by pecking, and hammers vigorously to excavate bark. Also plucks berries.

FOOD Insect (beetle) larvae; berries are also taken.

BREEDING Breeding seems to span August to October (early November). Holes are carved low down (one at 2.2m) into a stub, the chamber occupying most of the heartwood.

REFERENCES Belton 1984; Gore & Gepp 1978; Olrog 1984; Short 1970a; Sick 1993.

127 BLOOD-COLOURED WOODPECKER
Veniliornis sanguineus   Plate 38

IDENTIFICATION Length c. 13cm. Very small, with relatively long, straight bill broad across nostrils. A lowland species restricted to the Guianas, where it is fairly common and unmistakable. Dark crimson-red above, with darker brown wings and tail, and closely barred pale on dark over entire underparts. Red extends over the crown on male, while female has a white-spotted brown crown. Plumage becomes much browner when worn.

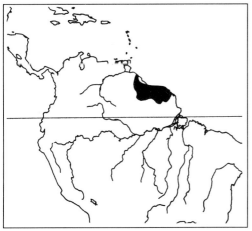

DISTRIBUTION Northeast S America in the Guianas, mainly in the (coastal) lowlands. Reasonably common.

HABITAT Mangrove and swampy forests, also coffee plantations; a bird of the lowlands.

DESCRIPTION
Adult male Forehead brown, spotted white; crown to nape crimson-red, with much brown of feather bases and centres usually fairly visible. Superciliary area, ear-coverts and neck sides brown, ear-coverts finely streaked whitish. Chin, throat and moustachial region barred dark and pale brown. Entire upperparts from hindneck to uppertail-coverts dark crimson-red with extensive greenish-brown feather bases. Upperwing-coverts dark brown, broadly edged/tipped crimson, medians with a few very small white spots; flight feathers dark brown, primaries edged greenish-brown and secondaries and tertials broadly edged/tipped crimson. Uppertail dark brown. Underparts from breast dark brownish, barred off-white, pale bars becoming broader on belly. Underwing entirely barred brown and whitish. Undertail much as uppertail. (In worn plumage, red areas become duller and much browner, especially on head, and underparts even more boldly barred.)
Adult female As male, but has crown brown with fine white feather tips.
Juvenile As adults, but duller and browner, with looser feathering; usually shows larger pale spots on wing-coverts.
Bare parts Bill dark grey, paler at tip. Legs and feet blackish. Eyes dark red-brown.

GEOGRAPHICAL VARIATION None. Monotypic.

MEASUREMENTS Wing 72-79. Weight: 23-30.

VOICE The common call is represented by single *keek* notes. Also gives a fast series of about 16 notes, *wih-wih-wih*.... Both sexes drum. Nestlings produce a rattling noise.

HABITS Usually seen singly or in pairs. Forages in various kinds of trees and shrubs. The pair members roost together, and may share the roost with another individual, presumably a young of the previous brood, until the next brood is initiated.

FOOD Ants, beetles (Cerambycidae), caterpillars.

BREEDING Breeding records from February-March and May-November in Surinam. Hole excavation may take two months and is carried out by both sexes. The hole is situated in a stump or larger branch. The pair may copulate before entering the common roost. Nest not very high (e.g. 1.4m). Both parents incubate the clutch of 1-2 (3) eggs. The nestlings are apparently fed with single food items by both sexes, with the male accounting for a slightly larger share.

REFERENCES Haverschmidt 1953, 1968; Tostain *et al.* 1992; Snyder 1966.

128 RED-RUMPED WOODPECKER
Veniliornis kirkii   Plate 38

Other name: Kirk's Woodpecker
Forms a superspecies with *chocoensis, cassini, affinis* and *maculifrons.*

IDENTIFICATION Length c. 15-16cm. Very small, with longish, straight bill broad across nostrils. Yellowish-green to olive-brown upperparts have contrasting red rump, and underparts are entirely barred; wing-coverts usually show some pale spots, and flight feathers and outer tail are pale-barred. Male has red on crown and nape, these areas on female being blackish with pale feather tips on nape. Forages mostly in the canopy, where constant loud tapping and pecking give away its presence.

Similar species Golden-collared (130), Red-stained (131) and Yellow-eared (132) Woodpeckers are all superficially similar to Red-rumped, but all lack the red rump and do not overlap in range. Choco Woodpecker (129) does overlap with Red-rumped in W Colombia, but again lacks red on the rump and has a more variegated ear-covert pattern.

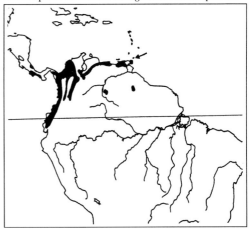

DISTRIBUTION Neotropics, patchily from Costa Rica and panama (including Coiba Island) to lowland Colombia and W Ecuador, also from W Venezuela, east to NE Venezuela (easternmost Sucre, Monages) and Trinidad and Tobago. Isolated populations on Cerro Paraque (NW Amazones, Venezuela) and Mount Roraima and Cerro Vei-tepui (SE Gran Sabana, Venezuela). Fairly common to uncommon.

HABITAT In lowland wet forest, adjacent second growth and overgrown clearings, open woodland, and edge of mangroves. Found in gallery forest, xerophytic areas, dry deciduous forests, tall open woodland, savannas, plantations (coconut), and cemeteries. Ascends to 900m in Panama, to 1000m in N Venezuela (found at the higher altitudes only in Táchira and Barinas), and to 1500-1750m in the tepuis south of the Orinoco.

DESCRIPTION

V. k. kirkii **Adult male** Forehead, lores and superciliary area buffish; crown dusky brown or dark grey with red feather tips, tips becoming yellower on nape. Lower nape to upper neck sides golden-coloured. Ear-coverts olive-brown with whitish shaft streaks. Chin, throat and moustachial area barred dark olive and whitish. Hindneck and upperparts to lower back golden olive-brown with paler yellow shaft streaks (latter often obscure), sometimes with some red feather edges/tips; rump and uppertail-coverts bright crimson-red. Upperwing-coverts as back, with pale buff wedge-shaped spots (mostly on medians); flight feathers dark brown, broadly edged greenish-olive (edges broadest on secondaries and tertials), with pale bars on inner webs of primaries and secondaries. Uppertail dark brown, paler and barred pale buff on outer feathers (bars continue obscurely across central tail). Underparts entirely barred olive-brown and whitish, pale bars becoming broader in belly region. Underwing barred dark brown and whitish. Undertail as above, but paler.

Adult female As male, but lacks red on head, having crown dark brown (some green tinge), more orangey and spotted on nape.

Juvenile Resembles adults, but both sexes have red feather tips on crown, less extensively on female.

Bare parts Bill blackish, paler on lower mandible. Legs and feet dark greyish, tinged green, olive or blue. Eyes dark brown to red-brown (occasionally with paler orbital ring).

GEOGRAPHICAL VARIATION Five races.

V. k. kirkii (Trinidad and Tobago and NE Venezuela) Described above. A large race.

V. k. monticola (Mount Roraima in SE Venezuela) Large, as nominate or larger, and with heavy, very dark (blackish) barring below.

V. k. continentalis (N and W Venezuela) Smaller, with pale bars below broader.

V. k. cecilii (E Panama to W Colombia and W Ecuador) Smaller than above races, with paler, less patterned chin/upper throat (sometimes pure white); wing-coverts less spotted.

V. k. neglectus (SW Costa Rica and W Panama) Much as *cecilii*; usually lacks spots on wing-coverts.

MEASUREMENTS Wing 78-97, 80-87 (*neglectus*), 91-92 (*kirkii*); tail 45-58; bill 16.5-23; tarsus 15.2-16.2. Weight: 30-42.

VOICE A nasal *keer*, tapering in intensity, and softer than note of Rufous-winged Woodpecker (133), recalling kiskadee *Pitangus* or even Golden-olive Woodpecker (141). Similar mewing notes are strung together in shrill and ventriloquial series of 2-4(16), *wih-wih-wih-wih-wih...* or *quee-quee-quee*, becoming louder and expressive at the end, when weak, sawing and throaty *yuk* or *yk* may be added; also a repeated *kee-yik kee-yik....* Drumming is rapid, noisy and often prolonged.

HABITS Usually seen singly or in pairs, or in small groups; joins mixed-species flocks. Inconspicuous, unless detected by sound of its frequent pecking and hammering. Mainly in mid levels and canopy of forest, coming lower in adjacent second growth and overgrown clearings only. Visits trees both within forest and at borders, but rarely ventures outside forest. Foraging takes place on trunks to smaller branches, often among thick foliage. Hammers steadily but not very loudly to expose larvae and adults of small wood-boring beetles.

FOOD Larvae and adults of small to medium-sized wood-boring beetles and other insects.

BREEDING Birds in breeding condition found in January and September in Colombia and Ecuador; December-February (possibly March) in Panama and in Trinidad and Tobago, February-March in N Venezuela. Nest hole 3-8m up in a living tree or palm, even slender ones, often at edge of forest. Clutch contains 2-3 eggs.

REFERENCES ffrench 1973; Hilty & Brown 1984; Marin & Carrion 1991; Meyer de Schauensee & Phelps 1978; Parker *et al.* 1982; Ridgely & Gwynne 1989; Slud 1964; Snyder 1966; Stiles & Skutch 1989; Wetmore 1968.

129 CHOCO WOODPECKER
Veniliornis chocoensis   Plate 38

Forms a superspecies with *kirkii, cassini, affinis* and *maculifrons*.

IDENTIFICATION Length c. 16cm. Very small, with rather short, straight (or slightly curved) bill broad across nostrils. Has a small range, restricted to Pacific coast of Colombia. Formerly considered a race of either Golden-collared (130) or Red-stained (131) Woodpeckers, and is very similar to both, but is separated from them by the Andes chain. Golden-green upperparts with faint red suffusion and barred rump, heavy barring below, and yellowish nape and neck sides with red (male) or dark brown (female) on crown all recall its close relatives (Choco is especially similar to race *orenocensis* of Red-stained, with which most likely conspecific).

Similar species Apart from the above-mentioned allopatric species, Choco also resembles Red-rumped Woodpecker (128). Race *cecilii* of latter occurs sympatrically with Choco, but is readily distinguished by its red rump.

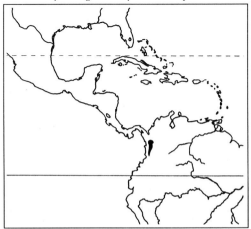

DISTRIBUTION NW Colombia. Rare.

HABITAT Forests.

DESCRIPTION

Adult male Forehead buffish and crown blackish, with broad red feather tips; nape and upper neck sides dull golden. Lores, superciliary area, ear-coverts and area below eye brownish-buff, obscurely streaked darker at rear, often with some pale tips (can appear spotted or variegated). Chin and upper throat pale buffish, spotted/barred darker (can be almost fully dark). Upperparts bronzy golden-green, often suffused red on mantle/scapulars, with obscure pale yellow shaft streaks; rump and uppertail-coverts barred olive and yellowish. Upperwing-coverts as back, but with little or no red suffusion, and with small, obscure pale yellow spots (mostly on medians); flight feathers dark brown (inners sometimes red-tinged), edged olive-yellow, and barred buffish. Uppertail dark brown, barred yellowish (bars most pronounced on outer tail). Underparts from throat to undertail-coverts barred olive and whitish-buff. Underwing barred pale and dark. Undertail much as uppertail.

Adult female As male, but crown dark olive-brown, becoming yellow-streaked on nape.

Juvenile As adults, but looser-plumaged and with face sides streaked. Both sexes have red-tipped crown feathers, red confined mostly to central area on females.

Bare parts Bill dark, with paler lower mandible. Legs and feet dark olive, tinged grey or green. Eyes red-brown to brown.

GEOGRAPHICAL VARIATION None. Monotypic.

MEASUREMENTS Wing 94-101. Weight 24-38.

VOICE Not known.

HABITS Not particularly known; presumably as for Red-stained Woodpecker.

FOOD Not known.

BREEDING Presumably as Red-stained Woodpecker.

REFERENCES Short 1974b.

---

130 GOLDEN-COLLARED WOODPECKER
Veniliornis cassini   Plate 38

Forms a superspecies with *kirkii*, *chocoensis*, *affinis* and *maculifrons*.

IDENTIFICATION Length c. 14cm. Very small, with rather long, straight bill fairly broad across nostrils. A very poorly known canopy-dwelling woodpecker of northern S American lowlands. Rather plain yellowish-green above, with bright golden nape and neck sides and with pale-spotted wing-coverts, and prominently barred black and whitish below; ear-coverts are pale-coloured. Tail is obscurely barred, but usually with obvious white notches on outer feathers. Male has red on crown and female has dark crown spotted pale at rear, in both cases contrasting with golden nape area.
Similar species In south of range overlaps slightly in range with Red-stained Woodpecker (131), from which it differs in having more regular and more contrasting barring below, brighter and more extensive golden-yellow on nape/neck, paler ear-coverts and usually white notches on outer tail: all features that are very difficult to confirm in the field.

DISTRIBUTION Northern S America, in S and SE Ven-

ezuela (Bolívar, Amazonas), the Guianas, and Brazil N of the Amazon, from Rio Negro to Amapá. Not uncommon.

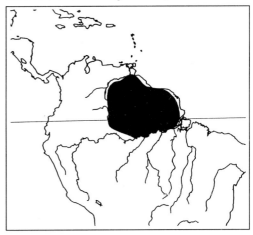

HABITAT Rain forests, clearings, open terrain with trees, and shrubbery, to 1500m.

DESCRIPTION

Adult male Lower forehead and lores buffish; upper forehead and crown greyish-black with narrow red feather tips, tips becoming larger on upper nape. Lower nape golden-yellow, this colour extending onto neck sides and rear superciliary area. Ear-coverts and supercilium behind eye buffish-white, finely streaked darker. Chin whitish, lightly barred/spotted dark. Upperparts yellowish-green, slightly bronzed, rump sometimes with vague yellowish barring. Upperwing-coverts as back, medians (and some greaters) with rounded pale buff subterminal and sometimes also basal spots; flight feathers dark brown, edged greenish (broadly on inner secondaries and tertials), with white bars on inner webs of primaries and secondaries. Uppertail dark brown, obscurely barred paler, outer two feather pairs more clearly marked with whitish notches. Throat and moustachial area to undertail-coverts white to pale buffish-white, all barred black/brownish-black, dark bars becoming narrower in lower regions. Underwing barred dark brown and white. Undertail as uppertail, but barring more obvious.

Adult female Differs from male in having crown green-tinged brown with profuse pale whitish-yellow spots at rear, merging with golden-yellow of nape.

Juvenile Greener, less yellow, above than adults, with duller, less golden, nape and darker face; wing-coverts more streaked. Both sexes have some red on crown.

Bare parts Bill dark grey, paler at tip and on cutting edges. Legs and feet olive to dark grey or blackish, sometimes tinged blue. Eyes probably deep brown or darker, or red-brown.

GEOGRAPHICAL VARIATION None. Monotypic.

MEASUREMENTS Wing 91-101; tail 53. Weight: 24-38.

VOICE Not known.

HABITS Solitary, often in treetops.

FOOD Beetles (Cerambycidae).

BREEDING Details apparently unknown.

REFERENCES Haverschmidt 1968; Meyer de Schauensee & Phelps 1978; Snyder 1966.

---

131 RED-STAINED WOODPECKER
Veniliornis affinis   Plate 38

Forms a superspecies with *kirkii*, *chocoensis*, *cassini* and *maculifrons*.

IDENTIFICATION Length c. 17cm. Very small, with fairly long, straight bill broad across nostrils. Much more widely distributed than but very similar to previous three species. Green or bronzy-green above, with or without red suffusion, and with golden nape/hindneck contrasting with red (male) or blackish (female) crown; underparts are strongly barred. Southeastern populations have fairly pronounced pale spots on wing-coverts, but, as with the other species, variations in posture and amount of wear often render this and other features of limited use in the field. Difficulties in obtaining good views in the species' forest habitat add to the problems, and consequently this woodpecker, although probably not uncommon, is not well known.

Similar species Overlaps quite widely in range with very slightly smaller Little Woodpecker (124), but latter lacks yellow on nape, usually has extensive greyish forehead/forecrown, and some races show at least an indication of thin white supercilium and/or moustachial line. Only just overlaps with extremely similar Golden-collared (130) and possibly with Yellow-eared (132) Woodpeckers: differs from former in having less bright and less extensive golden colour on nape, less contrasting barring below (pale bars more buff-tinged), and darker face; and from Yellow-eared in being darker and generally plainer above, and in lacking pale spots on forehead and thin white moustache and line behind eye (though latter features of little use in the field).

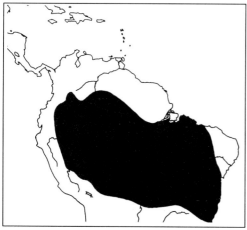

DISTRIBUTION S America, from C Venezuela and Colombia to Amazonian Brazil and south to the provinces of Pernambuco, Espírito Santo and Mato Grosso, in the west extending through E Ecuador and Peru to N Bolivia. Seems to be not uncommon.

HABITAT Tall rainforest; less common at forest edge, or in second growth and scrub. Found at altitudes between 100 and 500m in Venezuela, and lives at up to 500m on the eastern slope of the Colombian Andes and to 1000m on the Pacific slope.

DESCRIPTION
V. a. orenocensis **Adult male** Lower forehead and lores cinnamon-buff; upper forehead and crown with black-based feathers broadly tipped red, becoming golden-yellow on nape/hindneck (yellow reaching a little onto feather edges of upper neck sides). Sides of face dark buffish, streaked olive on ear-coverts. Chin buffish-white, spotted/barred darker. Upperparts greenish, sometimes suffused red, with very faint pale yellow shaft streaks; rump and uppertail-coverts variably barred. Upperwing-coverts as back, with barely visible yellowish subterminal spots, rarely with very faint reddish tips (red normally absent); flight feathers dark brown, broadly edged green (broadest on tertials), and barred buffish-white on primaries and secondaries. Uppertail dark brown, barred yellowish (bars strongest on outer tail). Throat and moustachial region to undertail-coverts cinnamon-buff, becoming whiter on lower underparts, all barred dark olive-brown, dark bars somewhat more widely spaced on belly/flanks. Underwing barred dark brown and whitish. Undertail much as uppertail or paler.

Adult female As male, but crown dark olive-brown, sometimes faintly pale-streaked at front, and with distinct golden-yellow streaks on hindcrown merging with golden nape.

Juvenile As adults, but with face darker, more streaked. Both sexes have red on crown, on females generally restricted to central area.

Bare parts Bill blackish; lower mandible paler, silvery to slaty-black, with black tip. Legs and feet olive-grey or greenish-grey. Eyes brown to red-brown.

GEOGRAPHICAL VARIATION Four races, largely intergrading.
   V. a. orenocensis (E Colombia to S Venezuela and N Brazil) Described above. Intergrades with following race in SE Colombia ('*caquetanus*').
   V. a. hilaris (E Ecuador through E Peru to N Bolivia and W Brazil) Larger than *orenocensis*. Plumage similar, but more bronzy or yellow above and has prominent broad red tips to wing-coverts. Intergrades with *orenocensis* in SE Colombia and with following race in C Brazil.
   V. a. ruficeps (C and E Brazil) Size as *hilaris*, but wing-covert spots much larger and obvious, though red covert tips slightly less marked; pale shaft streaks on upperparts often more obvious.
   V. a. affinis (E Brazil) Similar to *ruficeps* but smaller, and with red on wing-coverts much reduced or absent.

MEASUREMENTS Wing 85-102; tail 51-56; bill 19-21. Weight: 32-44.

VOICE A series of high-pitched notes, *ghi-ghi-ghi*.

HABITS Lives singly, being met with in pairs only occasionally. Foraging strata include canopy down to middle levels; will venture down to lower levels, especially at forest edge. Also accompanies army-ant processions to obtain flushed arthropods.

FOOD Arthropods; also fond of fruit.

BREEDING Presumably January to September.

REFERENCES Hilty & Brown 1984; Meyer de Schauensee & Phelps 1978; Parker *et al.* 1982; Sick 1993; Willard *et al.* 1991.

132 YELLOW-EARED WOODPECKER
Veniliornis maculifrons   Plate 38

Forms a superspecies with *kirkii, chocoensis, cassini* and *affinis.*

IDENTIFICATION Length c. 15cm. Very small, with long, straight bill quite broad across nostrils. A very little-known woodpecker with a restricted distribution in eastern Brazil. Has the same basic pattern as many others of its genus, greenish above and barred below; like the previous four species it also has a yellow nape, but in addition has a thin white moustache and a very narrow, short white supercilium behind eye (very difficult to see in the field). Both sexes have white spots on forehead/forecrown, but these are hard to discern (and soon lost with wear).

Similar species Of those similar-looking species, only Little (124), White-spotted (126) and possibly nominate Red-stained (131) appear to overlap in range. Little lacks yellow on nape and is darker, less green, above, often with scattered red feather tips. Red-stained is extremely similar to Yellow-eared, but tends to have darker upperparts, deeper yellow (more golden) nape, and lacks white forehead/crown spots and short supercilium, though latter characters not always visible. White-spotted Woodpecker is more readily distinguished by its dark olive plumage, heavily barred pale above and below, and its dark head (little or no red visible) with stronger white supercilium and moustache.

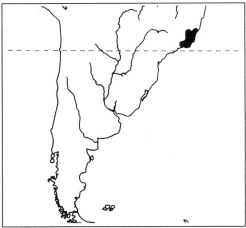

DISTRIBUTION Eastern S America, in the Brazilian provinces of Rio de Janeiro, Minas Gerais and Espírito Santo. Common, at least in southern part of range.

HABITAT Secondary forest and parks in lowlands and hills.

DESCRIPTION
Adult male Forehead, loral and crown feathers brown, tipped white on forehead, streaked white and tipped red on forecrown (red lost when worn) and becoming largely red on hindcrown. Nape pale golden-yellow, extending to neck sides. Thin, short white supercilium from rear upper edge of eye; ear-coverts olive-brown, streaked whitish. Chin and moustachial region whitish, spotted/barred olive, usually with very thin white moustachial line. Upperparts yellowish-green, sometimes slightly bronzed, and faintly spotted or barred, becoming more distinctly barred on rump. Upperwing-coverts and tertials as back, median coverts with very faint streaks or spots; flight feathers darkish brown, barred white. Uppertail dark brown, barred paler. Throat to undertail-coverts off-white, all narrowly barred olive (dark bars broader on breast and flanks). Underwing barred brown and white. Undertail as uppertail, but bar-

ring more obvious.

Adult female As male, but crown olive, spotted white, with golden tips to hindcrown merging with yellow nape.

Juvenile Duller and more barred above than adults, with duller yellow nape; underpart barring more irregular and coarser. Crown possibly shows some limited red (on forecrown), but details insufficiently known.

Bare parts Bill blackish. Legs and feet probably olive or grey and eyes presumably deep brown/reddish, but information on bare parts is lacking.

GEOGRAPHICAL VARIATION None known.

MEASUREMENTS Wing 90-96; tail 56-60; bill 22-23.5.

VOICE A long series of vibrating and sonorous *ew* notes, first rising, then descending. Also a quite different call in the breeding season. Drums.

HABITS No information available.

FOOD Not known.

BREEDING Presumably breeds in September and October.

REFERENCES Sick 1993.

133 RUFOUS-WINGED WOODPECKER
Piculus simplex   Plate 39

Forms a superspecies with *callopterus, litae* and *leucolaemus.*

IDENTIFICATION Length c. 18cm. Small, with fairly short bill slightly curved on culmen and relatively narrow across nostrils. This and the following three species, all of which are rather little known, are very similar to each other in appearance and were formerly considered conspecific, but they differ in the important parameters of head pattern and voice. All have yellowish bronzy-green upperparts, a greenish breast with barred lower underparts, and darker wings and tail, the wings with a cinnamon-rufous patch on the flight feathers. Males of all four have much red on a slightly crested head, a broad red moustache, and a whitish or dull greenish chin and throat; females have most of the red replaced by green. Fortunately, the ranges of the four do not overlap. Male Rufous-winged is characterised by the red of its forehead and moustache meeting on the lores, and both sexes by their uniform green ear-coverts lacking a paler stripe on the lower edge (though an indication of a stripe is present on juveniles) and also by their pale eyes.

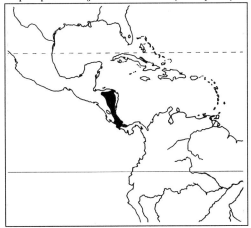

DISTRIBUTION C America, from Honduras (?) through Nicaragua to Costa Rica and W Panama (W Chiriquí, W

307

Bocas del Toro, Atlantic slope of Veraguas). Uncommon to fairly common.

HABITAT Frequents canopy and edge of humid forest, sometimes large trees in adjacent semi-open areas. Lowlands and foothills, on Caribbean slope locally to 750m, on Pacific slope to 900m.

DESCRIPTION
Adult male Forehead to hindneck red, this colour also extending across lores and into broad moustachial band. Ear-coverts brownish-green, sometimes with some red feather tips towards eye. Chin pale brownish-green. Upperparts bronzy-green, generally unmarked. Upperwing-coverts and tertials similar; flight feathers mostly cinnamon-rufous, with dark olive-brown outer webs and bars on inner webs. Uppertail blackish, often with an element of cinnamon-rufous in outer feathers. Throat and upper breast olive-green, feathers of upper breast with pale buffish-yellow subterminal spots or wedges and darker tips; lower breast to undertail-coverts pale yellow-buff, barred dark olive. Underwing-coverts cinnamon-rufous. Undertail much as uppertail or paler.

Adult female Differs from male in having head plain brownish olive-green, apart from red nape/hindneck.

Juvenile Duller, greyer and greener, than adults, with throat to breast somewhat mottled or spotted buffish-green and barring below uneven; often shows a very short, narrow yellowish-white stripe above moustachial region. Young males have red only on rear crown to hindneck.

Bare parts Bill blackish, with paler grey lower mandible. Legs and feet olive to greyish. Eyes pale bluish or yellowish to white.

GEOGRAPHICAL VARIATION None confirmed, but northernmost populations may differ slightly. Treated as monotypic.

MEASUREMENTS Wing 104-119; tail 55-67; bill 18-24; tarsus 17-19.4. Weight: 51-55.

VOICE A loud, sharp, nasal *deeeah*, more drawn out and higher-pitched than note of Golden-olive Woodpecker (141) and clearer, less nasal, than that of Slate-coloured Grosbeak *Pitylus grossus*. Also a loud, emphatic series of jay-like, downslurred, slightly nasal notes: *heew heew heew heew....* Drums in prolonged tattoos. (Vocalisations are said to differ substantially from those of Stripe-cheeked Woodpecker, 134.)

HABITS A forest-based species, seen singly or, less often, in pairs; occasionally accompanies mixed-species flocks. Prefers forest interior over edge and forages high in trees, but also at or below middle levels, pecking into mossy and rotting branches, lianas, and dead wood trapped in vine tangles; taps incessantly and irregularly.

FOOD Ants, beetles and their larvae.

BREEDING February to May. Nest hole is excavated 2.5-5m up in a recently dead tree or rotten stub. Eggs 2-4.

REFERENCES Ridgely & Gwynne 1989; Slud 1964; Stiles & Skutch 1989.

134 STRIPE-CHEEKED WOODPECKER
Piculus callopterus Plate 39

Forms a superspecies with *simplex*, *litae* and *leucolaemus*.

IDENTIFICATION Length c. 17cm. Small, with fairly short bill slightly curved on culmen and rather narrow across nostrils. Very like Rufous-winged Woodpecker (133), particularly juveniles of latter, differing only in minor details of head pattern, wing barring and underpart barring. Vocalisations also apparently differ.

DISTRIBUTION Panama: Veraguas, Caribbean slope of the Canal Zone to Darién. Uncommon.

HABITAT Uncommon and local in humid forest and forest borders in foothills on Caribbean slope, ranging between 300 and 900m.

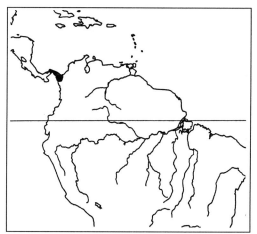

DESCRIPTION
Adult male Upper forehead to hindneck red. Lower forehead, lores and sides of head greenish-yellow, with short, narrow yellowish-white stripe at lower front edge of ear-coverts, bordered below by broad red moustachial band reaching well onto neck side. Chin pale greenish. Upperparts, upperwing-coverts and tertials bronzy-green. Primaries and secondaries much as on Rufous-winged, but barring less extensive (though still present). Uppertail as on Rufous-winged. Throat and upper breast greenish-olive, with pale yellowish spots on breast tending to form bar-like pattern (barring usually more marked than on Rufous-winged); rest of underparts pale yellow, barred greenish-olive. Underwing as upperwing, coverts showing some cinnamon-rufous. Undertail much as uppertail.

Adult female As male, but lacks red on top of head and in moustache.

Juvenile Duller than adults and more irregularly barred below, with mottled/barred upper breast. Males lack red moustache and crown.

Bare parts Bill blackish, paler on lower mandible. Legs and feet dark olive-grey or darker. Eyes red-brown to dark brown.

GEOGRAPHICAL VARIATION None. Monotypic.

MEASUREMENTS Wing 102-110; tail 54-60; bill 20-22.6; tarsus 17-20.

VOICE Allegedly different from that of Rufous-winged Woodpecker, but published data apparently lacking.

HABITS Rather quiet and inconspicuous; usually found singly or in pairs, and with mixed-species flocks. Forages on lower or middle parts of trees. Pecks steadily.

FOOD Small ants are the only food items on record.

BREEDING No relevant information available. Presumably much as for rest of superspecies.

REFERENCES Ridgely & Gwynne 1989; Wetmore 1968.

135 LITA WOODPECKER
Piculus litae   Plate 39

Forms a superspecies with *simplex, callopterus* and *leucolaemus*.

IDENTIFICATION Length c. 20cm. Small, with shortish bill slightly curved on culmen and fairly narrow across nostrils. Greenish above, with much red and yellow on head, and strongly barred on belly, this species is very similar to White-throated Woodpecker (136) and was until recently regarded as conspecific with it, but the two are separated by the Andes chain, Lita being found on the western side.

Similar species See also Yellow-throated Woodpecker (137), a possible new race of which appears to overlap with Lita Woodpecker in SW Colombia.

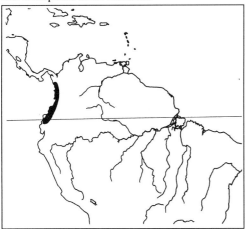

DISTRIBUTION Pacific slope of the northern Andes, from Serranía de Baudó in Colombia south to NW Ecuador. Uncommon.

HABITAT An uncommon woodpecker of humid and wet forests, inhabiting the western slopes of the Andes at 800-1800m.

DESCRIPTION
Adult male Forehead to nape red. Upper lores and ear-coverts green to golden-green, bordered below by golden-yellow stripe and with slightly shorter broad red moustachial band and thin yellow malar. Centre of chin and upper throat white to pale or darker greenish. Hindneck and upperparts, upperwing-coverts and tertials bronzy-green (feathers tipped yellower when fresh). Flight feathers dark brown, with pale cinnamon-rufous area on inner webs. Uppertail feathers blackish, edged greenish. Lower throat and upper breast yellowish-green, spotted pale yellow and tipped darker on breast; lower breast to undertail-coverts whitish, barred olive. Underwing as upperwing, with rufous on coverts. Undertail much as uppertail.
Adult female Much as male, with red nape but without red

crown and moustache.
Juvenile Duller and darker generally than adults, and without red moustache or red crown.
Bare parts Bill blackish to dark grey, paler on lower mandible. Legs and feet bluish-grey to blackish. Eyes dark brown to red-brown.

GEOGRAPHICAL VARIATION None. Monotypic

MEASUREMENTS Wing 105; tail 60; bill 20; tarsus 15.

VOICE Probably similar to that of other members of the superspecies.

HABITS Probably similar to those of other members of the superspecies.

FOOD Not known.

BREEDING Breeding season presumably extends from January to August.

REFERENCES Hilty & Brown 1984.

136 WHITE-THROATED WOODPECKER
Piculus leucolaemus   Plate 39

Forms a superspecies with *simplex, callopterus* and *litae*.

IDENTIFICATION Length c. 20cm. Small, with fairly short, pointed bill with slightly curved culmen and broad across nostrils. Very like Lita Woodpecker (135), but found on the eastern side of the Andes. Like Lita, has striking red, olive and golden head pattern.

Similar species In much of range overlaps with similar Yellow-throated Woodpecker (137), the latter being separated by its greater extent of yellow on head (all yellow, apart from red/green crown to nape and often red/greenish moustache), yellow chin and throat and more regularly patterned yellower upperparts.

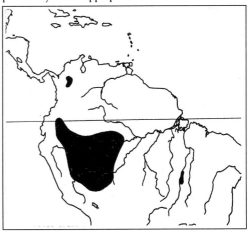

DISTRIBUTION S America, in C and W Amazonian Brazil, E Peru and N Bolivia also NW Colombia (Cundinamarca) and Ilha do Bananal (Goiás, Brazil). Appears to be rather uncommon.

HABITAT Tall, humid *terra firme* forests and lowland humid, seasonally inundated forests along rivers.

DESCRIPTION
Adult male Forehead to nape bright red. Lores and backwards through ear-coverts yellowish-green, bordered below

by golden-yellow band from bill base across lower ear-coverts and expanding on rear neck sides; broad red band covers moustachial and malar region. Chin and upper throat white. Hindneck and upperparts, upperwing-coverts and tertials bronzy-green (feathers tipped/edged yellow when fresh). Flight feathers dark brown, with pale cinnamon area on inner webs. Uppertail blackish, edged greenish. Lower throat and upper breast yellowish-green, feathers with paler centres and darker tips; lower breast to undertail-coverts white, barred olive. Underwing as upperwing, with cinnamon on coverts. Undertail much as uppertail.

Adult female Lacks red crown and moustache, red being restricted to small patch on nape.

Juvenile Greener than adults, and without male's red moustache and crown.

Bare parts Bill blackish to grey. Legs and feet dark olive to blackish. Eyes dark brown to red-brown.

GEOGRAPHICAL VARIATION Varies slightly in depth of coloration (as do most woodpeckers), but with no obvious geographical pattern. Monotypic.

MEASUREMENTS Wing 119-121; tail 59-60; bill 21-22. Weight: 69.

VOICE Probably similar to that of other members of the superspecies.

HABITS Probably similar to those of other members of the superspecies.

FOOD Not known.

BREEDING Apparently not recorded.

REFERENCES Parker *et al.* 1982; Sick 1993.

---

137 YELLOW-THROATED WOODPECKER
Piculus flavigula   Plate 39

IDENTIFICATION Length c. 20cm. Small, with shortish, pointed bill slightly curved on culmen and narrow across nostrils. The distinctive red and golden head pattern (on female, mostly golden), yellow-green upperparts, yellow or red throat and regular wavy barring or spotting on underparts are characteristic, making this a brighter-looking bird than White-throated Woodpecker (136). Like latter, shows some cinnamon on wings. A recently discovered form of *Piculus* from SW Colombia, tentatively treated within Yellow-throated, has a black throat (see Geographical Variation).

Similar species Overlaps in range with White-throated Woodpecker, from which best told by wholly yellow throat and ear-coverts, lack of or much smaller red moustache, and stronger patterning on underparts.

DISTRIBUTION Northern S America, from Colombia east of Andes (new subspecies/allospecies west of Andes; not shown on map), through Venezula south of the Orinoco to the Guianas and Amazonian Basin, Through N Mato Grosso to E Peru and to NW Bolivia in the west; also in N Brazil from Pernambuco to São Paulo. Rather common throughout most of range.

HABITAT Tall, humid *terra firme* forests and lowland humid, seasonally inundated forests along rivers; also forest edge. In the east, also in drier forest types (caatinga).

DESCRIPTION
P. f. flavigula **Adult male** Forehead to nape bright red with dark feather bases; lores yellowish-green. Rest of head,

including chin and throat, bright golden-yellow, apart from short red moustachial band. Upperparts, upperwing-coverts and tertials yellowish-green (brighter when fresh), brighter on mantle/back, and occasionally with a few paler spots on rump. Flight feathers brownish-black, inner webs with cinnamon patches. Uppertail black, edged greenish. Underparts below throat green, with triangular or more rounded whitish feather centres and dark tips on breast, pattern becoming more barred or scaly on belly and undertail-coverts. Underwing as upperwing, with paler coverts somewhat barred. Undertail much as uppertail, but paler.

Adult female Lacks short red moustache and red on crown, having these areas respectively greenish or golden and yellow-tipped green; red nape.

Juvenile Duller and greener, less yellow, above and on head than adults, and darker and less marked below (but still with yellow throat). Young males may have some red on crown; females have all-green crown, lacking adult's yellow tips.

Bare parts Bill black, paler on black-tipped lower mandible. Legs and feet dark green-grey. Eyes brown.

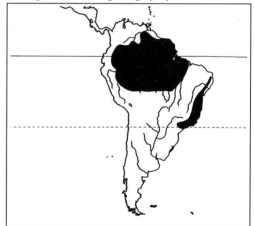

GEOGRAPHICAL VARIATION Three well-differentiated races, plus a possible fourth.

P. f. flavigula (Colombia and N Amazonia east to the Guianas) Described above. Intergrades with following race.

P. f. magnus (SE Colombia to NE Bolivia and NE Brazil) Male lacks red moustache, having this area golden-yellow, as female. Intergrades with nominate race in region of NE Brazil.

P. f. erythropis (E Brazil) Smaller than above two races and highly distinctive. Male has red extending variably over neck sides and from malar region over chin and throat, while female has golden-yellow forecrown, moustache and throat, the latter usually with some red markings. Both sexes have entire underparts more obviously barred (rather than spotted/scaly).

P. f. ssp. nov. A form of *Piculus* very recently discovered in SW Colombia (i.e. west of the Andes) is tentatively assigned to this species, although it may prove to be a full species (its voice apparently differs) or perhaps more closely related to another species within this genus. Both sexes differ most markedly in having a fully black throat. Male has red head top and broad red moustache, while female has forehead and crown yellow, with red confined to hindcrown and nape, but apparently (and surprisingly) also has a red moustache; underparts appear to be closest to those of *erythropis*.

Juveniles are greener generally above and below and on head, with no red, but with a very large yellowish-golden area from lores to rear neck side, and have a pale-barred dull olive throat.

MEASUREMENTS Wing 104-128, 104-118 (*erythropis*), 112-120 (*flavigula*); tail 68. Weight: 48-63 (*flavigula*).

VOICE The rattle-type call is 6-8 secs long, *kee kee kee...*, slowing down towards the end. Another call is described as *queea queea* or *shaa, gheh*.

HABITS Met with singly or in mixed-species flocks. Forages at middle levels in the subcanopy up to the treetops, on limbs, branches and trunks. Very little is known about other aspects, but more vigorous feeding techniques such as pecking and hammering seem to prevail.

FOOD Mainly ants (*Camponotus, Pheidole, Crematogaster*).

BREEDING In Colombia and Venezuela, presumed to breed in November; breeds May-July in the Guianas, and August-December in Brazil to Bolivia. Hole is built into a stub, at various heights apparently not very high up, rarely to 15m.

REFERENCES Haverschmidt 1968; Hilty & Brown 1984; Meyer de Schauensee & Phelps 1978; Parker *et al.* 1982; Sick 1993; Tostain *et al.* 1992; Willard *et al.* 1991.

---

138 GOLDEN-GREEN WOODPECKER
Piculus chrysochloros   Plate 40

Forms a superspecies with *aurulentus*.

IDENTIFICATION Length c. 18-21cm. Rather small, with longish, slightly curved bill broad across nostrils. A highly variable species, but basically olive-green or yellowish-green above, with evenly barred pale yellowish and dark underparts, and with distinctive striped head pattern. Males have red forehead to nape, a dark olive band from lores to nape bordered below by a narrower yellowish stripe, and with a red or red-and-green moustache. Females usually lack the red crown (some may have red on nape) and have a green moustache. The eyes are white.

Similar species Could be confused with closely related Yellow-browed Woodpecker (139) in southeast of range, but latter is separated by its long pale supercilium, less yellow tone to underparts (which have broader dark barring), and dark eyes (and female Yellow-browed always have red in nape and moustache).

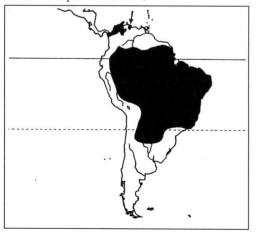

DISTRIBUTION Southeastern C America and S America, ranging from E Panama to Colombia, the Guianas, the Amazonian Basin, south to Rio de Janeiro on the east coast, and to N Argentina (Formosa to Santiago del Estero, Santa Fe) in the west interior. Possibly not uncommon.

HABITAT This species can be found in humid *terra firme* and *várzea* forest, and rain forest, but also occurs in deciduous forest, patches of wood in savannas and in xerophytic vegetation, where it also visits forest edge, tall trees in clearings and pastures, often near water or marshy ground. Is at home in lowlands at elevations of up to 450m in Venezuela north of the Orinoco, 100-650m south of it, and at up to 500m in Colombia.

DESCRIPTION

P. c. capistratus **Adult male** Forehead to nape red. Upper lores, area around eye, ear-coverts and line back to lower nape olive-green, bordered below by pale yellow stripe from lower lores to hindneck. Short red moustachial stripe, bordered below by olive-green, extending as olive-green band to side of neck. Chin, throat and neck sides greenish-white, barred olive (chin and throat sometimes only lightly barred). Hindneck and upperparts olive-green. Upperwing including coverts dark olive-brown (occasionally some barring on primary coverts). Uppertail dark olive-brown, tinged greenish. Underparts whitish to pale greenish-white, entirely barred olive-green. Underwing with large area of cinnamon (unbarred). Undertail much as uppertail.

Adult female Lacks red on head, having forehead to nape brownish-green and entire moustache greenish-olive.

Juvenile Much as respective adults, but duller and less regularly marked.

Bare parts Bill dark grey to blackish, paler at base. Legs and feet greyish-green. Eyes white or bluish-white; darker in juveniles.

GEOGRAPHICAL VARIATION Varies greatly in plumage tone and markings and also in size. Considerable individual variation also occurs, partly obscuring racial differentiation.

    P. c. capistratus (C Colombia to NW Brazil and Surinam) Described above. A large race, with barred throat.

    P. c. aurosus (Panama) Small, and very yellow in tone. Has much golden-yellow on face, unbarred golden-yellow throat and yellow ground colour below. Female has yellow on crown.

    P. c. xanthochlorus (NE Colombia and NW Venezuela) Small and very yellow, as *aurosus*, but generally duller in colour.

    P. c. guianensis (French Guiana) Large, and greener (less yellow) in tone, as *capistratus*, but usually with unbarred throat.

    P. c. laemostictus (W Brazil) Much as *guianensis*.

    P. c. hypochryseus (W Brazil to N Bolivia) Much as *guianensis*.

    P. c. chrysochloros (C and S Brazil to Bolivia and N Argentina) Small, as *aurosus*, and with yellow ground colour to underparts, but with much less yellow on head and throat.

    P. c. polyzonus (SE Brazil) As *chrysochloros* but large, perhaps with paler yellow coloration; may show barred, pale primary coverts. Male has extensive dark red in moustache.

    P. c. paraensis (NE Brazil) Intermediate in size. Much yellow or cinnamon-buff on head, throat and breast, and often over entire underparts. Male lacks red in moustache.

MEASUREMENTS Wing 115-152, 115-127 (*chrysochloros*),

120-125 (*aurosus*), 133-147 (*capistratus*), 150-153 (*polyzonus*); tail 60-68 (*aurosus*), 72-78 (*chrysochloros*), 80-87 (*polyonus*), 75-83 (*capistratus*); bill 21-25 (*chrysochloros*), 23.7-27.1 (*aurosus*) 31-32 (*polyzonus*), 25-30 (*capistratus*); tarsus 20-21 (*aurosus*). Weight: 55 (*chrysochloros*), 62-91 (*capistratus*).

VOICE Not described.

HABITS Met singly, in pairs, or in mixed-species flocks. Forages rather high in the subcanopy of the forest interior; rarely ventures to edge or into the open. Gleaning seems to be its common feeding technique. Also pecks and excavates to obtain subsurface prey, by intensive use of the tongue.

FOOD Ants (*Camponotus*).

BREEDING Records from Colombia suggest that breeding takes place from February to March; September in Argentina. Nest in trees and arboreal insect nests.

REFERENCES Haverschmidt 1968; Hilty & Brown 1984; Meyer de Schauensee & Phelps 1978; Olrog 1984; Parker *et al.* 1982; Ridgely & Gwynne 1989; Short 1970a, 1975; Sick 1993; Wetmore 1968.

139 YELLOW-BROWED WOODPECKER
Piculus aurulentus   Plate 40

Other name: White-browed Woodpecker
Forms a superspecies with *chrysochloros*.

IDENTIFICATION Length 21-22cm. Small, with medium-length bill slightly curved on culmen and fairly broad across nostrils. A little-known woodpecker closely related to Golden-green (138), which it much resembles in appearance. Green above and heavily barred below and on underwings, with boldly striped head pattern; has a long, narrow pale supercilium and a barred pale cinnamon patch on wing. Both sexes have red in the moustache, but this is not always obvious in the field.

Similar species In north of range may possibly come into contact with Golden-green Woodpecker, from which best separated by its pale supercilium and its much broader dark barring on underparts (which lack obvious yellow tone, so that it appears generally greener and blacker below). Yellow-browed is also somewhat bigger.

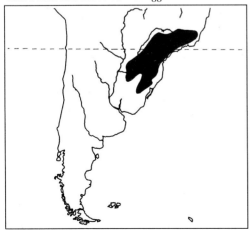

DISTRIBUTION East-central S America, from Brazil (Minas Gerais, Espírito Santo and Rio de Janeiro south to

Rio Grande do Sul) west to E Paraguay and NE Argentina (Misiones, NE Corrientes). Rather uncommon.

HABITAT Humid montane forests, forests and woodland, forest edge and dense second growth.

DESCRIPTION
Adult male Forehead to nape bright red, with very thin olive border. Narrow supercilium from front edge of eye pale yellowish-white, extending well back to nape side. Upper lores, area around eye, ear-coverts and rear neck sides dark olive-green, bordered below by broad pale yellow band from lores to side of neck. Moustachial stripe red (red often extending onto chin), becoming green at rear. Chin and throat pale golden. Hindneck, upperparts and tertials olive-green, sometimes with faint bronze tinge. Upperwing-coverts dark olive-green; flight feathers dark brown, edged greenish, with dark-barred cinnamon-rufous patch on inner webs. Uppertail blackish. Lower neck sides and underparts below throat whitish, densely and broadly barred dark olive. Underwing cinnamon-rufous, mostly barred black. Undertail much as uppertail.

Adult female Similar to male, but forehead and crown olive, occasionally with golden feather tips. Has red on nape and usually on front part of moustache.

Juvenile Much as respective adults, but duller and with coarser barring.

Bare parts Bill blackish-grey, paler at base of lower mandible. Legs and feet greenish-grey or darker. Eyes chestnut-brown. Orbital ring dark gray.

GEOGRAPHICAL VARIATION None. Monotypic.

MEASUREMENTS Wing 115-124. Weight: 52-68.

VOICE A single, sharp and loud note and a descending series of plaintive notes, *eeeww, eeeww, eeeww....* Drums in rapid, regular rolls.

HABITS This apparently shy species is found singly or in pairs. Forages in the middle tiers by gleaning and pecking.

FOOD Ants and their larvae and eggs.

BREEDING September in Argentina. Nest high (7m) up in a tree.

REFERENCES Belton 1984; Olrog 1984; Short 1970a; Sick 1993.

140 GREY-CROWNED WOODPECKER
Piculus auricularis   Plate 41

Forms a superspecies with *rubiginosus*.

IDENTIFICATION Length c. 16-17cm. Small, with medium-length, straight, narrow bill. A very poorly known species confined to western Mexico. Has greyish-green, barred upperparts and barred underparts, and in all plumages lacks red on top of head, but male has a red moustache. Golden-tinged wings usually show a small area of yellow in flight feathers.

Similar species Closely related to and possibly conspecific with Golden-olive Woodpecker (141). Both occur in Mexico, but do not appear to meet. Grey-crowned is, in any case, smaller and never has red on nape.

DISTRIBUTION Endemic to the Pacific slopes of W Mexico, from S Sonora to Oaxaca. Fairly common to common.

HABITAT Humid to mesic forests and forest edge form

the main habitats. Locally, this species also inhabits high-land pine-oak forest and tropical deciduous oak forest, at altitudes ranging from the lowlands to the foothills, from 900 to 2400m.

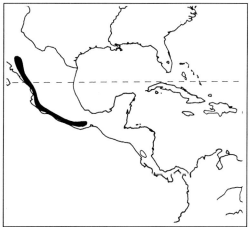

DESCRIPTION
Adult male Forehead to nape grey, often with green tinge. Lores, area around eye and ear-coverts buffish-grey (paler than crown), ear-coverts barred darker. Moustachial stripe red (often also has small patch of red on lores, sometimes protracted into thin line over eye). Chin streaked/barred olive and white. Neck sides and hindneck olive, barred paler. Upperparts green to greyish-green (greyer when worn), faintly barred. Upperwing and its coverts dark olive, tinged deep golden; flight feathers darker and with greenish-yellow area on inner webs. Uppertail brown, feathers edged greenish. Underparts below throat pale greenish-white, with broad olive bars throughout. Underwing pale yellowish. Undertail yellowish.

Adult female As male, but has moustache barred olive and whitish (not red).

Juvenile Insufficiently known. Probably much as adults but duller and greyer, with more obscure, more irregular barring.

Bare parts Bill blackish. Legs and feet green-grey. Eyes hazel-brown.

GEOGRAPHICAL VARIATION None. Monotypic.

MEASUREMENTS Wing 115-125; tail 67-72; bill 23-26; tarsus 17-24. Weight: 52-68.

VOICE Calls comprise a single, explosive *kee-ah* and a mewing *growk*; also a rapid and shrill rattle, similar to that of Golden-olive Woodpecker.

HABITS Probably similar to those of Golden-olive Woodpecker.

FOOD The diet also includes berries.

BREEDING Presumably similar to Golden-olive Woodpecker.

REFERENCES Baptista 1978; Blake 1965; Howell & Webb in press; Peterson & Chalif 1973.

141 GOLDEN-OLIVE WOODPECKER
Piculus rubiginosus   Plate 41

Other names: Green Woodpecker, Bronze-winged Woodpecker, Blue-headed Woodpecker
Forms a superspecies with *auricularis*.

IDENTIFICATION Length c. 18-21cm. Small, with generally medium-length, broad bill with curved culmen. Highly variable in general plumage tone (see Geographical Variation), but essentially bronzy-green above and on wings and heavily barred below; has pale ear-coverts. Males have a red moustache and nape, with a varying amount of red on the crown (often confined to sides, but some races have forehead to nape entirely red). Females lack the red moustache but have some red on nape/crown, though less extensive than on males.

Similar species Most resembles Grey-crowned Woodpecker (140) of Mexico, but latter is smaller and always lacks red on crown and nape. Absence of prominent yellow on head of Golden-olive Woodpecker helps distinguish it from other superficially similar woodpeckers in S America.

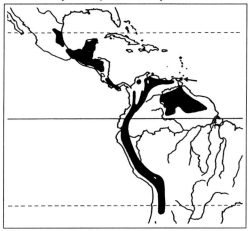

DISTRIBUTION Neotropics, from Mexico (Tamaulipas, Veracruz, Oaxaca and provinces south) through C America to S America, where it occurs from Venezuela south along the Andes from Colombia, through Peru, to Bolivia and Argentina (Tucumán) and east along the coastal ranges to Trinidad and Tobago; also recorded in the Guianan Highlands of Venezuela, N Brazil, and the Guianas. Common throughout most of range.

HABITAT The wide range of habitats this species occupies comprises not only rain and cloud forests, dry cloud forest, heavy epiphyte-laden forests, and their edges, but also adjacent clearings and semi-open parts with scattered trees, and second growth. Also inhabits dry deciduous oak forests, oak-pine woodland, riparian thickets, and mangroves; commonly associated also with trees bordering fields and coffee plantations with shade trees, as well as with clearings with scattered trees in mountainous terrain. In Mexico, the race (or possible allospecies) *aeruginosus* occurs in lowlands and foothills with cottonwoods, mesquite and cacti, from near sea level up to about 1800-2100m. In C America, inhabits foothills and highlands from sea level, but more common above 1000m, in Guatemala; and farther south from 750m (rarely about 400) to 2000m on the Caribbean slope, and occurs at altitudes from 1050 to 2150m on the Pacific slope. In Venezuela, this species is found at 750-2800m in the north and northwest, at sea level in the Orinoco delta, and from 350 to 2100m elsewhere. It occurs between 900 and 3100m in Colombia, and to at least 2300m in Peru and Bolivia. In Argentina, found in humid forests between 1000 and 2500m.

DESCRIPTION

P. r. yucatanensis **Adult male** Forehead and crown dark slaty-grey, bordered at sides and across nape by crimson-red. Lores, area around eye, superciliary area and ear-coverts pale greenish-buff. Broad red moustachial stripe, expanding slightly at rear. Neck sides barred yellow-buff and olive. Chin and upper throat pale buffy-white, streaked blackish. Upperparts, upperwing-coverts and tertials bronzy-olive (rump paler and with some olive barring), often with faint tinge of red to feather tips. Flight feathers dark brownish-olive, edged bronze-green, with yellowish on shafts extending slightly onto inner webs of primaries (forming paler area). Uppertail dark olive-brown. Underparts from throat pale buffish-yellow, becoming paler lower down, and entirely barred olive-green. Underwing largely yellow. Undertail dusky olive, with yellowish inner part.

Adult female Lacks red moustache, which is instead patterned as throat, but has some red on nape and sides of hindcrown.

Juvenile Much as respective adults, but much duller overall, with less regular patterning; often with area of black in loral region.

Bare parts Bill slaty to black. Legs and feet grey or olive-grey. Eyes deep dull red.

GEOGRAPHICAL VARIATION A very variable species with a large number of races, differing mainly in tone of plumage above and below, strength of barring, throat colour, and amount of red on crown of male. Note, however, that there is much individual variation in pattern and coloration even within races, and the following should be regarded as a general guide only.

(a) C America, two races:

P. r. yucatanensis (Oaxaca, Mexico, south to Panama) Described above. Size varies: those breeding in highlands of W Guatemala and Chiapas, Mexico ('*maximus*'), tend to be slightly larger (and a shade greener) than lowland populations, and lowland breeders show a decrease in size from north to south.

P. r. aeruginosus (E Mexico) Has distinctly green back, poorly barred rump, and bronze-edged green wings; underparts with more scallop-like markings, rather than bars. Red on crown sides of male reaches only to eye region and not to forehead; on female a narrower U-shaped band. Proportionately long-tailed.

(b) S America, 17 races:

The following eight northern races tend to show blackish breast barring, a white-spotted black throat, little/no rump barring, and reduced red in crown:

P. r. alleni (Santa Marta area of Colombia) Large. Bronze-gold above with some red tinges; blackish breast barring narrow; moderate red on male's crown.

P. r. tobagensis (Tobago) Breast bars less black, more green, but broader.

P. r. trinitatis (Trinidad) As *tobagensis* but much smaller, with less heavy bill.

P. r. deltanus (Delta Amacuro in Venezuela) Small. Greener back and larger white throat spots.

P. r. paraquensis (mountains of SC Venezuela) Large. Strong bronze tinge to back; very dark crown with much-reduced red (some females have no red in crown).

P. r. viridissimus (Auyen tepui of S Venezuela) Large. Very green on back; ground colour of breast whitish,

with very black barring; reduced red on male's crown.

P. r. guianae (E Venezuela and adjacent Guyana) Large. Back somewhat bronzy-green; throat black with fine white spots; moderate red in crown.

P. r. nigriceps (Acarai mountains of Guyana, Surinam) Much as *guianae*, but bronze tinge more or less lacking.

The next three races have greener breast bars, white-streaked black throat, more barred rump, and moderate red in crown:

P. r. buenavistae (E Colombia, E Ecuador) Very large. Back bronzy with reddish tinge.

P. r. meridensis (NW Venezuela) As *buenavistae* but somewhat smaller, with less bronzy back.

P. r. rubiginosus (NC and NE Venezuela) As *meridensis* but smaller, with greener back and blacker breast bars; less red in male's crown.

The next two races are black-throated, duller yellow on belly, and males have crown entirely red:

P. r. gularis (S Colombia, including Cauca valley) Rather large. Throat black, finely spotted white (rarely, no spots).

P. r. rubripileus (SW tip of Colombia, NW Peru, W Ecuador) As *gularis* but smaller, with breast bars blacker.

Three races in Peru and Bolivia have less barred/unbarred, brighter yellow belly and barred/scaly rump:

P. r. coloratus (NC Peru) Bright yellow belly with barred flanks; only slightly bronzy above; restricted red on male's crown.

P. r. chrysogaster (C Peru) Yellow belly generally unbarred; back very bronzy-red; much red on male's crown (fully red).

P. r. canipileus (N and SE Bolivia) Belly only weakly barred; crown moderately red.

The southernmost race is fairly distinctive:

P. r. tucumanus (S Bolivia to NW Argentina) Large, with thin bill. Green-backed and greyish, less bronze; breast barring blackish; olive tone to ear-coverts.

MEASUREMENTS Great size variation, particularly among insular forms. Wing 96-137, 98-116 (*trinitatis*), 115-119 (*rubiginosus*), 116-124 (*yucatanensis*), 126 -130 (*canipileus*) 127-137 (*aeruginosus*); tail 47-66 (*trinitatis*), 61-73 (*rubiginosus, yucatanensis*) 78-90 (*aeruginosus*); bill 17-23 (*trinitatis*), 20-24 (*rubiginosus*), 22-26 (*canipileus*), 23.7-29 (*yucatanensis*) 23-29 (*aeruginosus*); tarsus 17-26. Weight: 51-68 (*trinitatis*), 51-72 (*meridensis*), 69-82 (*aeruginosus*), 74-84 (*gularis*), 77-88 (*rubripileus*), 78-86 (*yucatanensis*).

VOICE Call note a loud, clear *deeeeh, keeeep*, or *kelee…klee*. The long-distance call is a prolonged clear trill, higher-pitched and more rapid than that of a *Melanerpes* (113), more like a Downy Woodpecker's (113), but remaining uniform to the end, *trrrrrrr te te te*. Also *churr, choo-úr* (first note longer than second). Observers have noted that the voice of this species recalls a jay, kiskadee *Pitangus* or flicker. In interactions, a liquid *woick-woick-woick….*, or *utzia-deek*, may be heard. In intimate encounters, low, whirring notes are uttered. Voice of *aeruginosus* apparently distinct; more intensive studies are clearly most desirable. Also drums.

HABITS Generally seen singly, or in pairs maintaining loose contact, or in mixed-species groups. These rather secretive woodpeckers can be found in the interior of forests, but are most frequently seen in more open places near tall forest. Has the flicker-like habit of sitting quietly on a horizontal perch in the top of a tree. Usually forages at middle levels to the upper canopy (where also utters its long-distance signal), on limbs, branches and vines, and on tree trunks. Although usually on large trees, will also descend to low stubs and fence posts along hedgerows and edges, but seems not to feed on the ground. Commonest feeding techniques are pecking, hammering (live soft bark, soft green wood), pecking with probing, surface probing, prying into crevices; gleaning plays a minor role. In particular, this woodpecker may be seen probing among vines, dense foliage or into clusters of epiphytes or on mossy branches; also tears apart bromeliads to get at food. Opens (infested) cocoa pods. Moves slowly when working up a tree. In encounters, involving three or more birds, various displays are exhibited, including wing- and tail-spreading and bobbing and bowing body movements, all these turbulent actions being accompanied by frequent vocalisations; bouts of such displays are interspersed with pauses in which the birds freeze. Roosts solitarily throughout the year.

FOOD Ants, termites, beetles and their wood-boring larvae, and rarely fruits and berries.

BREEDING The breeding season extends from January to May (June) in C America through Colombia to Trinidad; breeding recorded in October in Ecuador and Guyana. Holes are excavated 1.2-18m up in a dead or live stub or tree (palm). Clutch contains 2-4 eggs. Both sexes incubate, in long stints. The nestlings are fed at long intervals by regurgitation, the male apparently with greater effort. Nest sanitation ceases at the end of the nestling period.

REFERENCES Askins 1983; Blake 1965; ffrench 1973; Fjeldså & Krabbe 1990; Hilty & Brown 1984; Howell & Webb in press; Junge & Mees 1958; Land 1970; Meyer de Schauensee & Phelps 1978; Miller 1963; Olrog 1984; Parker *et al.* 1982; Peterson & Chalif 1973; Ridgely & Gwynne 1989; Russel 1964; Sick 1993; Skutch 1956, 1969; Slud 1964; Snyder 1966; Stiles & Skutch 1989; Sutton 1953; Sutton & Pettingill 1942; Tostain *et al.* 1992; Wetmore 1968.

---

142 CRIMSON-MANTLED WOODPECKER
Piculus rivolii
Plate 40

IDENTIFICATION Length c. 22-26cm. Small to medium-sized, with shortish to fairly long, broad-based bill with curved culmen. Red upperparts (more olive when worn) with contrasting yellow face, dark throat and breast, golden belly and black rump and tail, together with red area in wings, make this a rather distinctive species, unlikely to be confused in reasonable views. Males have a red moustache, lacking on females. Females also have a black crown, as do both sexes of the southernmost population, which in addition is less red and more bronzy-green above and on wings (and also differs in underpart markings). An unobtrusive woodpecker, easily overlooked as it forages among mosses and brightly coloured epiphytes in its montane-forest habitat.

DISTRIBUTION Andes of S America, from NW Venezuela (Trujillo, Táchira; Perijá mountains), Colombia (eastern slopes and central and western Andes), through Ecuador (west and east Andes) and Peru (eastern slopes) to Bolivia (Cochabamba). Fairly common.

HABITAT This species frequents tall humid and wet montane forests, favouring mossy and epiphyte-rich rain and cloud forests, but also exploits forest edge, clearings containing some trees, dry cloud forest, and dwarf forest at the timber line, where it ventures into adjacent páramos as well. As a result of these habitat preferences, it is found from 950 to 3700m in Venezuela, and from 1800 (regionally 700) to 3200m in Colombia and Peru.

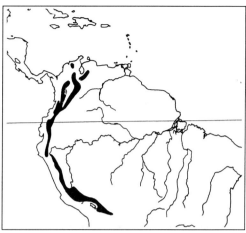

DESCRIPTION
***P. r. rivolii* Adult male** Forehead to hindcrown feathers black, broadly tipped red; nape, hindneck and lower neck sides bright red. Lores, area around and below eyes, and ear-coverts pale yellowish-white. Moustachial stripe black, broadly tipped red. Chin and upper throat black, speckled with white. Upperparts red, with olive feather bases variably visible, but lower back olive (often black-barred) and rump and uppertail-coverts black. Upperwing-coverts mainly red, with olive bases and inner webs; flight feathers dark brown, edged olive, and with outer edges of secondaries dark red (forming panel). Uppertail black. Feathers of lower throat and breast black, edged whitish and red, appearing decidedly scalloped; belly to undertail-coverts golden or golden-buff, usually with a few pale and black bar-like spots on upper belly and upper flanks (sometimes extending further down). Underwing with at least some yellow. Undertail blackish, with yellow at base. (In worn plumage, with brighter feather tips lost, crown becomes more black, upperparts more olive, and throat and breast more or less solidly black.)

Adult female As male, but lacks red on moustache and crown, which are instead solid black (still has red hindneck).

Juvenile Duller than adults throughout plumage, appearing mottled blackish, olive and dull red above, and with all-blackish breast and more brownish-buff belly. Males have a few narrow red tips to crown feathers.

Bare parts Bill blackish. Legs and feet grey or brown-grey. Eyes red-brown to brown.

GEOGRAPHICAL VARIATION Five races, one highly distinct.
> ***P. r. rivolii*** (W Venezuela to EC Colombia) Described above.
> ***P. r. meridae*** (W Venezuela) Very like nominate. Shorter-billed, but averages longer in wing.
> ***P. r. quindiuna*** (NC Colombia) Much as nominate. Females show some red in crown.
> ***P. r. brevirostris*** (SW Colombia to C Peru) More or less intermediate between above races and *atriceps*.
> ***P. r. atriceps*** (SE Peru and N Bolivia) Distinctive. Noticeably shorter-billed. Both sexes have black forehead and crown and olive-tinged ear-coverts, are darker, more bronzy-olive (less red), above, and have little or no red in flight feathers; ground colour of underparts is paler, breast feathers have only pale yellow edges (lack red tips), and bar-like spotting tends to reach further down on flanks.

MEASUREMENTS Wing 120-145, 128-139 (*meridae*), 136-143 (*rivolii*); tail 93-107 (*rivolii*), 88-103 (*meridae*); bill 34.5-37.5 (*rivolii*), 29-33 (*meridae*). Weight: 85-97 (*brevirostris*), 100-112 (*rivolii*).

VOICE Does not call very often. A loud, sonorous and flicker-like (*chrrr-r-r...*)*kre-ep* or *ka-weep*..., rising a little. Long-distance calls *kick-kick-kick-kick-kick-kick-kick* and *wik-wik-wik....* Both sexes drum: described as either slow (tapping?) or as fast, short bursts.

HABITS Found alone, in pairs or in family groups, and often joins mixed-species flocks. Quiet and, despite its coloration, inconspicuous. Forages in dense vegetation, on the thicker branches on surfaces overgrown with moss and epiphytes, at practically all levels; now and then descends to the ground to search for ants or to feed at *Puya* and *Espletia* flowers of the páramo. Gives particular attention to bases of epiphytes and leaves. Probes, gleans and pecks, but does not typically hammer. Moves slowly.

FOOD Ants and their brood, beetle larvae, and occasional spiders or millipedes. Some fruit is also consumed.

BREEDING Breeding is recorded in February and March in Colombia, June-November in Peru.

REFERENCES Hilty & Brown 1984; Meyer de Schauensee & Phelps 1978; Parker *et al.* 1982; Short 1970a.

---

143 BLACK-NECKED WOODPECKER
Colaptes atricollis   Plate 42

Other name: Black-necked Flicker

IDENTIFICATION Length c. 25cm. Smallish, with medium-long, pointed bill with curved culmen and narrow across nostrils. A little-known, long-tailed scrubland woodpecker found only in Peru. Black-barred green or brownish above, and very pale below with arrowhead markings forming black-barred pattern. Both sexes have black from chin to upper breast and red hindcrown, and male also has rather indistinct red moustache. Eastern race *peruvianus* is paler and more barred above, with wing-coverts appearing paler-edged, and also paler below. No other superficially similar woodpecker within its range has black from chin to breast.

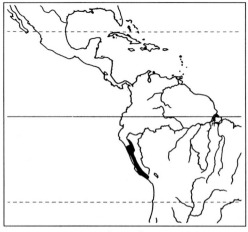

DISTRIBUTION Peruvian Andes, S America, on eastern slopes from the province of Piura (Marañón valley) to La Libertad, Ancash and NW Huánuco, and on western slopes

from La Libertad and Ancash (Cordillera Negra) south to W Arequipa. Locally common.

HABITAT Occurs in arid to semi-arid areas, where it inhabits dry cloud forest, montane scrub with large cacti, desert scrub, and wooded areas; also found in riparian vegetation, irrigated areas, orchards, tree plantations and gardens. Ventures locally into high altitude *Polylepis* woodland. Altitudinal range spans 500-2800(3400)m on west Andean slopes, locally (Cordillera Blanca, Ancash) to 4000m; at 1700-4300m around Marañón valley.

DESCRIPTION
C. a. atricollis **Adult male** Forehead to hindcrown dark grey, tipped red on forehead and crown sides (occasionally over entire crown); hindcrown and upper nape red. Lores and line above eye yellowish-white; ear-coverts similar but somewhat darker, tinged buffy-olive. Moustachial stripe red with black feather bases. Chin, throat and upper breast black, becoming more olive-grey and black-barred on neck sides. Hindneck and upperparts, including upperwing-coverts and tertials, bronze-green with narrow blackish bars, paler and with paler bars on rump and uppertail-coverts. Flight feathers dark brown, barred yellowish, with olive-yellow shafts often forming paler panel. Uppertail dark brown, barred pale on outer web of outermost and on central feathers. Underparts below breast pale yellow, with black of breast becoming bars on lower breast and black arrowhead marks on flanks and belly to undertail-coverts (belly more weakly marked). Underwing yellow, barred darker on primary coverts. Undertail brown, yellower at base, barred whitish-yellow.

Adult female Has red restricted to hindcrown and no red moustache.

Juvenile Duller and darker-faced than adults, but with top of head often wholly red and dark-barred; variably and more diffusely barred above and below. Moustache mixed red and black or (perhaps females only?) all black.

Bare parts Bill black, paler at base. Legs and feet green-grey. Eyes brown or chestnut-brown.

GEOGRAPHICAL VARIATION Two well-differentiated races.
  C. a. atricollis (western slope of Andes) Described above.
  C. a. peruvianus (Marañón valley) Smaller and shorter-billed than nominate, with browner upperparts; lacks olive on feather shafts; wing-coverts are broadly edged and tipped yellowish-white, and underparts are paler, with reduced markings.

MEASUREMENTS Wing 113-125; tail ; bill 21-26; tarsus 22-25. Weight: 73-90 (*atricollis*).

VOICE A short and repeated *peah* and *chypp* are commonly heard and specifically given in alarm. A loud, clear and long call-series corresponds to and resembles the similar, even longer calls of Northern Flicker (146), *wicwicwicwic....* The corresponding call of Andean Flicker (150) is also longer, and more ringing.

HABITS Usually seen singly or in pairs. Basically, this is an arboreal species, but it also forages near or on the ground, often among bushes. Gleaning and probing, including into the soil, with some occasional pecking, have been recorded as foraging modes.

FOOD Ants and their larvae and pupae.

BREEDING Probably breeds in June-July, and September (Marañón valley). Roosts and nest holes are excavated in trees and telephone poles (*atricollis*), and in large cacti (*peruvianus*).

REFERENCES Fjeldså 1991; Fjeldså & Krabbe 1990; Koepcke 1983; Parker *et al.* 1992; Short 1972a.

144 SPOT-BREASTED WOODPECKER
Colaptes punctigula   Plate 42

Other name: Spot-breasted Flicker
Forms a superspecies with *melanochloros*.

IDENTIFICATION Length c. 18-21cm. Small, with short, pointed bill curved on culmen and narrow across nostrils. A fairly common, highly variable species, generally bronzy-green or yellower above with black barring, and yellowish with dark breast spots below; the throat is patterned black and white, and the white face sides contrast with the dark crown and moustache. Both sexes have front half of crown black and rear half red, males also with a red moustache.

Similar species Not likely to be mistaken within its range. Green-barred Woodpecker (145) is bulkier and generally greener, but its range does not appear to overlap with that of Spot-breasted.

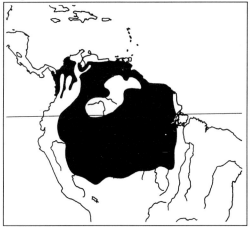

DISTRIBUTION Northern S America, from Panama (rare) and NW Colombia, through E Peru and N Bolivia in the west, east through Venezuela, the Guianas and Amazonian Brazil to Pará and N Mato Grosso in the southeast. Rather common, at least in eastern parts of range.

HABITAT Found in a wide array of wooded and open habitats, though generally not a forest species and most common in sparsely wooded regions. It occurs in rain, deciduous and gallery forests, second growth, open woodland, mangroves, swamp edges, llanos, forest edge, open terrain with large trees, scrub, clearings, moriche palm groves, coffee plantations and other cultivations with sufficient trees. Primarily a bird of the humid lowlands, it ranges to altitudes of up to 600m in Venezuela and to 1500m in Colombia.

DESCRIPTION
C. p. punctigula **Adult male** Forehead and forecrown black, becoming red on hindcrown and nape (exceptionally, red extends forwards along crown sides or even over entire crown). Lores, area above and below eye, and ear-coverts white. Moustachial stripe red, with black feather bases. Chin and throat black, spotted white. Hindneck and upperparts, including upperwing-coverts and tertials, bronzy-green, barred brownish-black, with rump paler and less barred. Flight feathers brown, indistinctly barred

paler, with yellow shafts often forming panel on closed wing. Uppertail brown, strongly barred green to yellow on outer feathers (and sometimes, less strongly, on central pair). Neck sides and underparts below throat dull yellow-olive, becoming paler downwards, and with fine black spots on breast and, more sparsely, on flanks; undertail-coverts yellowish, spotted black. Underwing pale yellowish. Undertail yellow-brown, barred brown.

Adult female As male, but lacks red in moustache and always has red restricted to rear crown and nape.

Juvenile As adults, but duller and greener above, and duller, less yellow, below with larger spots. Males show some red in moustache.

Bare parts Bill blackish. Legs and feet greenish-grey, tinged yellow. Eyes rufous-brown.

GEOGRAPHICAL VARIATION Six races.
    C. p. punctigula (Guianas) The smallest race. Described above.
    C. p. striatigularis (Panama and WC Colombia) Throat very white, with few black streaks, and spotting below fairly heavy; shows strong reddish tinge to breast and rump.
    C. p. ujhelyii (N Colombia) Very bright, with red/orange on breast and with barring above much reduced or lacking; throat as *striatigularis*. Crown of male may be almost entirely red.
    C. p. zuliae (NW Venezuela) Very small. Dull above; relatively little black on throat, and breast spots sparse.
    C. p. punctipectus (Venezuela except northwest) Green above, lacking bronzy tone, and dull below with fewer, small spots; throat generally black, with large white spots.
    C. p. guttatus (Amazonia) Rather variable. Generally very olive on breast and with relatively heavy spotting below; rump contrasts less with rest of upperparts; throat black, with large white spots.

MEASUREMENTS Wing (99)102-113(118); tail 62-74; bill 21.5-25.7; tarsus 20.4-23.9. Weight: 50-70 (*punctigula*), 75-79 (*guttatus* from upper Amazonia).

VOICE A whistled *whew* is given during courtship or in agonistic encounters. When alarmed, may utter *peek* notes in series. In encounters, series of *ta-wick* or *week-a* notes are associated with visual displays. In such situations, or in response to calls of other individuals, fast series of *wick* notes, which may commence with *ka-wick* elements, are typical. Low and soft *pee-ya* calls are characteristic of intimate meetings, e.g. during changeovers at the nest. A rather high-pitched, weak and nasal *wha-whe-whe-whe-whe-whe-whe-whe-wha* (8-10 notes), with the first and second notes slightly lower, sounds mechanical and rather resembles Northern Flicker's (146) but more so Campo Flicker's (151) long call-series, although it is somewhat shorter.

HABITS This flicker lives in pairs or family groups. Arboreal foraging takes place at medium heights and lower; also descends to the ground among scattered trees to forage in anthills. When foraging in trees, gleaning, probing and occasional light pecking prevail. On the ground, this woodpecker probes into the soil and sweeps away ground litter. In close encounters, displays with head-swinging and head-bobbing, and spread tail.

FOOD Ants and their brood.

BREEDING The breeding season seems to span October-May in Colombia, June-July (August) in the Guianas, and April-October in the Amazonian basin, and nesting takes place in February-September in Peru. Both sexes excavate nest in live or dead trees, and even in fence posts.

REFERENCES Darlington 1931; Haverschmidt 1968; Hilty & Brown 1984; Meyer de Schauensee & Phelps 1978; Parker *et al.* 1982; Ridgely & Gwynne 1989; Short 1972a; Sick 1993; Wetmore 1968.

145 GREEN-BARRED WOODPECKER
Colaptes melanochloros   Plate 42

Other names: Green-barred Flicker; Golden-breasted Woodpecker (*melanolaimus* group)
Forms a superspecies with *punctigula*.

IDENTIFICATION Length c. 27-30cm. Small to medium-sized, with fairly long, pointed bill curved on culmen and narrow across nostrils. A variable species, with barred green to buffish upperparts and spotted pale green to whitish underparts; has red hindcrown and nape, and male has red moustache. The forest and savanna populations (*melanochloros* group) are greener above with olive-toned ear-coverts, while those inhabiting pampas, chaco woodlands and scrub (*melanolaimus* group) are browner above with white ear-coverts and have golden/orange on the breast. The latter group is partly terrestrial and often associates with Campo Flickers (151).

Similar species Closely related to the smaller but otherwise similar Spot-breasted Woodpecker (144), but their ranges appear not to overlap.

DISTRIBUTION Central and eastern S America, from NE Brazil to Patagonia: from Marajó Island to Rio Grande do Sul (Brazil), Uruguay, Argentina (to S Buenos Aires, Río Negro) west to Mato Grosso (Brazil), Bolivia, and to the Argentinian Andes (La Pampa, Neuquén). Common.

MOVEMENTS Southernmost populations and highland populations from Cordoba (Argentina) at least partly migratory, moving north to Santiago del Estero (Argentina).

HABITAT Occurs in a variety of habitats, from forests to desert scrub in the Andes. Members of the race *melanolaimus* are generally found in woodland, savannas, open country and arid bushland; *nattereri* inhabits savannas and caatinga; subtropical humid forests and transitional forests, especially when mixed with bamboo, are the abode of nominate *melanochloros*. Green-barred Woodpeckers can be found in lowland areas and at elevations of up to 3000m (*melanolaimus*).

DESCRIPTION
C. m. melanochloros **Adult male** Forehead and forecrown

black; hindcrown and nape red. Lores, superciliary area, cheeks and ear-coverts whitish, ear-coverts strongly tinged olive. Moustachial stripe red with black feather bases. Chin and throat whitish-green, streaked black. Hindneck and upperparts, including upperwing-coverts and tertials, yellowish-green, barred dark brown, with rump paler and less barred; uppertail-coverts buff, tipped/barred black. Flight feathers greenish-brown, narrowly barred paler, and with olive shafts. Uppertail black, with at least outer feathers barred pale. Neck sides and underparts below throat pale green, usually somewhat darker and brighter on breast, and with prominent black spots, latter often tending towards bars on flanks but becoming smaller or obsolete on belly. Underwing yellowish-white, sometimes spotted on primary coverts. Undertail black, barred yellowish.

Adult female Proportionately longer-tailed than male. Lacks red in moustache, which is instead mostly black with white streaks.

Juvenile Duller than adults, and with broader barring above; markings below tend towards bars.

Bare parts Bill black. Legs and feet grey, usually with greenish or yellow tinge. Eyes brown to chestnut-brown.

GEOGRAPHICAL VARIATION Five races are recognised, forming two intergrading groups.

(a) Arboreal *melanochloros* group of forest and savanna, greener above and below, with darker ear-coverts, and no golden/orange on breast (two races):
>   *C. m. melanochloros* (SE and S Brazil, SE Paraguay, and Misiones, Argentina) Described above.
>   *C. m. nattereri* (N, NE, SC, WC Brazil; Santa Cruz, Bolivia) As nominate, but smaller, shorter-billed and more yellow; spots on breast/belly often very small or streak-like. Intergrades with nominate over a wide area.

(b) Partly terrestrial *melanolaimus* group of pampas, scrub and chaco woodland, generally browner and less green above and below, with white rump, white ear-coverts, yellow upperwing shafts, golden colour on breast, and black streaks tending to merge on lower throat sides (three races):
>   *C. m. melanolaimus* (upland valleys of Bolivia) Longer-billed. Fairly green in tone, and with golden tinge to breast; black throat markings tend to form patch on throat sides and rear moustache; rump with reduced spotting; tail less barred.
>   *C. m. nigroviridis* (N Argentina, S Bolivia and W Paraguay) As *melanolaimus*, but with tendency to more greenish coloration above, less golden on breast and with less black on throat sides; spots below are larger; tail strongly barred.
>   *C. m. leucofrenatus* (C Argentina, S Brazil; riverine and isolated woodland in pampas and arid inland scrub south to Patagonia) Large. Browner above (some even golden-brown), with white rump and whitish bars and edges; breast golden to orange, flanks strongly barred, and rest of underparts with large spots or arrowhead marks.

MEASUREMENTS Wing of male 111-143 (*nattereri*), 138-162 (*leucofrenatus*); tail of male 71-100 (*nattereri*), 88-108 (*leucofrenatus*), 101-118 (*melanochloros*); bill of male 19-26 (*nattereri*), 21-32 (*leucofrenatus*); tarsus of male 21-26 (*nattereri*), 26-33 (*leucofrenatus*). Weight: 104-150 (lighter forms), 154-178 (*leucofrenatus*).

VOICE Call similar to that of Campo Flicker, *kwiek-kwik-kwik*. Other vocalisations are an alarmed *peah* or screechy *wheéo* recalling Northern Flicker (146), and *krrew...*, *bewtra*, *pikwarrr* calls. Alarm is expressed in loose series of *peek* notes, probably also given singly. Notes sounding like *ta-wick* or *ker wick* and variations thereof are virtually indistinguishable from corresponding calls of Northern Flicker, though may be somewhat sharper on average, with the first note starting with a sound like two sticks being whacked together. Like Northern Flicker, this species also possesses a long call-series, which again is rather similar to the former species' calls. Both sexes drum, with slower rolls than those of Northern Flicker.

HABITS Mostly encountered individually, sometimes in pairs. Single birds join groups of the larger and more wary Campo Flicker (151) feeding on ants on the ground. Exhibits both arboreal and terrestrial habits; at any rate, requires the presence of trees in its habitat. Forages regularly in lower and middle sections of trees and palms, in low bushes, bamboo and on the ground. Probing and gleaning are the main techniques in trees. Breaks through the surface with a few pecks; if prey, such as ants, are detected, considerable time may be spent removing them with the tongue. Takes fruits and their sap. Hops through the crown of trees like a jay, and also hangs on the underside of branches when foraging. On the ground, leaps in long bounds or moves in short hops. Has been observed dustbathing. Calls for prolonged periods from tops of trees or palms. Displays with wing flicks, spread tail and swinging and bobbing head-and-body movements. In territorial clashes, opponents are attacked sex for sex.

FOOD Ants and their brood are the predominant and almost exclusive (spiders have also been recorded) constituent of the diet: the genera *Camponotus*, *Crematogaster*, *Paracryptocerus* and other, mainly arboreal-terrestrial species have been identified. Also takes cactus fruits and berries.

BREEDING The breeding season starts August-September in the south of the range and extends into January; breeds earlier in the north. Nest holes are made in dead trees or dead stumps, palms, cacti, and telephone poles, at heights between 2 and 6m. The clutch comprises 4 eggs. Both parents incubate, and feed the young by regurgitation.

REFERENCES Belton 1984; Gore & Gepp 1978; Olrog 1984; Short 1969, 1972a, 1975; Sick 1993.

---

146 NORTHERN FLICKER
Colaptes auratus   Plate 43

Other names: Common Flicker; Yellow-shafted Flicker (*auratus* group); Red-shafted Flicker (*cafer* group); Cuban Flicker (*chrysocaulosus* group); Guatemalan Flicker (*mexicanoides* group)
Forms a superspecies with *chrysoides*.

IDENTIFICATION Length c. 30-35cm. Medium-sized, with fairly long, pointed bill curved on culmen and narrow across nostrils. A highly distinctive, common and well-known woodpecker breeding throughout most of N America, where its plumage pattern and habits immediately separate it from all other species. Upperparts are dark-barred brown with plain white rump, and underparts boldly spotted on a pale background and with a prominent black crescent on breast. The head pattern and the feather-shaft and underwing colours vary geographically: in the north and east, the face is brown, the crown grey with a V-shaped red patch across the nape, the male has a black moustache, and the shafts and underwing are golden-yellow; in the west, the face is grey, the crown brown with

no red on nape, the male has a red moustache, and the shafts/underwing are salmon-pink; those in Cuba and Grand Cayman are similar to eastern mainland birds, but have golden shafts (and also differ in several other respects); and the highland populations in C America, generally brighter in appearance, have a grey face, rusty crown with no red on nape, males have a red moustache, and the shafts/underwing are orange. Females of this last group have a cinnamon moustache, but all others generally lack the moustache (though some western females may show signs of one). Hybrids are common, especially between the eastern *auratus* group and western *cafer* group, and show intermediate characters. In all cases, however, the species is instantly identifiable by the basic features outlined above, but see Gilded Flicker (147). This is a noisy and conspicuous woodpecker and highly terrestrial (except in Cuba and Grand Cayman), and in flight shows a striking white rump and strong yellow, pink or orange on underwings and base of undertail.

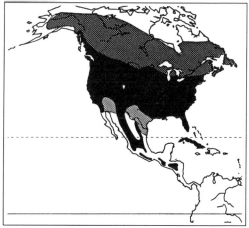

DISTRIBUTION Widespread over N America (occurs in all mainland states of the USA), from the tree limit in the north to the highlands of Nicaragua, wherever trees are present; not found in treeless plains. Has reached many islands, too, so this species is found on Grand Cayman, Cuba, and some of the Florida Keys. Common throughout range, and locally very common.

MOVEMENTS Those breeding north of a line joining the northern parts of California, Arizona, Oklahoma and Georgia are migratory. Autumn migration begins towards the end of August and lasts to late October (November), peaking in September. Flickers migrate during the day, in sometimes large flocks, low over the ground. Wintering birds concentrate in the USA from the southwestern states through Texas to Florida; those of the *auratus* group winter in October-March in N Mexico (Sonora east to Tamaulipas). Northern populations arrive back on their breeding grounds from early March to May. Vagrants have reached Europe (Ireland, Britain, Denmark), but perhaps only ship-assisted.

HABITAT Generally a bird of open areas and forest edge, this woodpecker frequents a broad range of habitats, provided access to open ground is available. Open forests, younger (2-6 years) clearcuts, burnt areas, farmland, pastures and residential areas form the chief habitats in the main part of the range. The natural habitats of northern birds comprise, for instance, aspen-lodgepine parkland, ponderosa pine forests, alpine meadow edge, riparian woodland, and forest edge. In the Great Plains, occurs in woodland along streams. In Mexico, flickers inhabit the oak and pine-oak zone; in Guatemala and Honduras, second growth in the cloud forest belt, in addition. A wide variety of habitats is used in winter also. In the temperate zone, visits denser habitats in winter than at other seasons. On Grand Cayman, for example, fairly common in grape-almond woodland in winter (uncommon suspected breeder there in summer), fairly common in mangroves (winter and summer, suspected breeder), in forest of logwood, thatch palm and red birch (winter, uncommon in summer) and in limestone forest (common in winter), and uncommon in pure logwood forests and human habitations. Northern birds breed from sea level to 2100m. In Mexico, nests at 750-3300(4000)m; in Guatemala and Honduras, occurs above (620) 900m and to 3200m.

DESCRIPTION

C. a. auratus **Adult male** Forehead to hindneck and rear neck sides grey, with a patch of deep red on lower nape extending to sides of nape (forming V shape). Moustachial stripe black. Lores, area around eye, ear-coverts, chin, throat and upper breast cinnamon, usually somewhat darker around eye and often more greyish on rear ear-coverts. Upperparts to back brown, barred blackish; rump unbarred white (occasionally with variable black marks), and uppertail-coverts white with black subterminal marks. Upperwing-coverts as back; flight feathers dark brown, narrowly barred pale brown, and with yellow shafts. Uppertail blackish-brown, initially tipped and edged buffy, with hint of pale bars on outer web of outermost feather, and with centre of shafts yellow. Underparts with broad black crescent across centre of breast; below this, white with pale buffish-yellow wash, and with rounded black spots becoming more crescentic on flanks and more bar-like or V-shaped on undertail-coverts. Underwing yellowish, darker at tip and on trailing edge, and with spots/bars on primary coverts. Undertail yellow, with black tip.

Adult female Slightly smaller than male and with breast crescent a little less deep. Lacks black moustache, this area being instead concolorous with throat.

Juvenile As adults, but head often with more greyish colour, crown sometimes barred, and usually with black loral patch. Above, dark bars much broader and uppertail-coverts with more black; below, breast crescent smaller, spots larger and less rounded, and underwing duller yellow. Young males tend to have strong dull red tinge on crown, and black moustache somewhat obscured; females usually show some red on crown and at least an indication of a black moustache.

Bare parts Bill black or slaty-black. Legs and feet grey, tinged green. Eyes deep brown.

GEOGRAPHICAL VARIATION Varies greatly over its huge range, but appears to fall into four racial groups.

(a) *auratus* group (northern and eastern N America) Southern nominate *auratus* is described above. Northern *luteus* is somewhat larger, but variation is clinal.

(b) *cafer* group (western N America and Mexico) Differs from above group in having brown crown and hindneck without red nape patch, grey face and throat to breast, red moustache on male (some females show cinnamon moustache), and salmon-pink shafts and undersurfaces of wings and tail. Northwestern coastal *cafer* is dark; inland and in California, *collaris* is paler; *mexicanus* of Mexican highlands south to Oaxaca is smaller and browner; greyer *nanus* of NE Mexico is still smaller; while rufous-crowned *rufipileus*, formerly of Guadeloupe, with short wings and tail and a rather long bill, is now extinct.

(c) *mexicanoides* group (highlands from Chiapas in S

Mexico to Nicaragua) A single-race group. Large and brightly patterned. Head pattern as *cafer* group, but with rusty or rufous-chestnut forehead to hindneck and with male's red moustache often mixed with black; upperparts and upperwings more heavily marked, with buff, grey-brown and blackish bars (dark bars broadest); breast patch deeper, less crescent-shaped, and spots below often larger or bar-like; shafts and undersurfaces of wings and tail orange-red. Females of this group have a pale cinnamon-brown moustache, often finely streaked darker. The wings are shallowly rounded.

(d) *chrysocaulosus* group (Cuba and Grand Cayman) A highly arboreal pair of races, with tail proportionately longer and wings more rounded than in *auratus* and *cafer* groups. As *auratus* group in head pattern, but upperparts more olive/greenish (even occasionally tinged reddish), rump more heavily barred/spotted, breast crescent deeper and spots below broader (less rounded); yellow of shafts and undersurfaces more golden in colour. Cuban *chrysocaulosus* is bigger and longer-tailed than *gundlachi* of Grand Cayman.

(Note that the '*chrysoides* group' of southern deserts is here treated as a separate species, Gilded Flicker.)

Hybrids The racial groups interbreed freely and without assortative mating wherever they meet, and an extensive and fairly stable hybridisation zone exists from British Columbia to Texas where the *auratus* and *cafer* groups overlap. Many hybrids show a mixed black-and-red moustache (males), incomplete red nape patch, pinkish or orange shafts or an odd-coloured feather or two on the underwing, intermediate head pattern and a number of other features indicating their mixed parentage. However, allozymatic homogeneity prevails among the populations of the Northern Flicker; thus, the hybrid zone represents no strong barrier to gene flow.

MEASUREMENTS Wing 122-133 (*gundlachi*), 132-149 (*chrysocaulosus*), 137-155 (*auratus*), 146-161 (*nanus*), 150-171 (*luteus*); tail 75-95 (*gundlachi*), 88-115 (*auratus*), 96-115 (*chrysocaulosus, luteus*); bill 22-26.2 (*gundlachi*), 25-30.4 (*chrysocaulosus*), 28-36 (*auratus*), 31-40 (*luteus*), 40-43 (*mexicanoides*); tarsus 25-28.5 (*chrysocaulosus*) 22-25 (*gundlachi*), 25-29 (*auratus*), 26.4-31.5 (*luteus*), 23-28 (*chrysocaulosus*). Weight: 121-167 (*collaris*), 106-164 (*auratus*), 88 (*gundlachi*), 105-126 (*nanus*).

VOICE A common, rather variable call is a descending *peah* or *klee-yer*. A characteristic vocalisation of this species is a long call-series of 3-70 or so notes, *whit-whit-whit...*, given throughout the breeding season to autumn, which may be imitated by whistling. During aggressive or courtship encounters, utters variations of *wicka* notes which may be rendered as *ew-i, cha-week-a, wee-cha, wik-up*, and so forth, varying in intensity. A flicker approaching its mate calls a soft *wee-tew*, or, on the wing or when mildly disturbed, *wa-wa-wa*. Nestlings at first give low hissing sounds, which eventually grow louder and variable. Although flickers do drum, this is a less important signal than in many other woodpeckers; rolls are not very loud and are slower than the similar rolls of Hairy Woodpecker (116), but do not change in rhythm.

HABITS Encountered in pairs, family groups, or in flocks during migration. Flickers feed commonly (12-75%) on the ground, on the forest floor, roadsides, lawns and the like. In arboreal foraging, dead trees or the broken ends of dead branches form important sites (about three-quarters of observed cases); trees and bushes are also visited for harvesting fruits and other plant matter. The insular *chrysocaulosus* of Cuba is more arboreal than its continental relatives. Sweeps away ground litter and digs into ant nests with the bill. Most of the prey is secured with the tongue. Berries are also collected on the ground. Gleans and probes, and catches prey on the wing. On the ground, flickers advance by hopping; in trees, may move in tit-like fashion among the twigs, frequently perching crosswise. The male's moustache serves as a sexual character in displays. Aggression directed mainly at individuals of the same sex. In agonistic and social contexts, displays are characterised by the bill being pointed steeply (but not quite vertically) upwards and the tail being spread. Depending on intensity of the display, the bill describes circles or figures-of-eight or, at high intensities, is involved in the bobbing movements of the bird, which keeps wings raised and spread; the tail is also spread and contorted, so that the underside is visible. Wing-flicking often precedes an assault, which often involves stabbing at the opponent, and finally a supplanting attack. Appears to remain paired for life. Reduced aggression during brood care may be one reason for locally high breeding densities (4.8 pairs/ 10ha). In many cases, flickers are forced to succumb to hole competitors (other woodpeckers, owls and starlings).

FOOD The staple food (about 75%) of this species is ants and their brood. Also takes termites, caterpillars, beetles and their larvae, wasps, crickets and grasshoppers, aphids, and spiders. Fruits and berries (e.g. dogwood, Virginia creeper, poison ivy, sumac, hackberry, cherries, black-gum) are important components of the diet, as well as seeds, and acorns and other kinds of nut kernals. Visits feeders.

BREEDING Nesting season spans February to July: February-March in the southern USA, June in the north; other temperate populations and those of C America breed April-May. Nests are excavated in dead trees (30-75%) or in dead parts of live trees, and most are located close to the distal end of a stub. Nest height varies from ground level, frequently below 3m, up to 27m; range in forests smaller, about 6-12m. Males rather commonly select old cavities for nesting. Because of the low inclination to excavate, many other, often peculiar, nest sites have been recorded: fence posts, utility poles, nestboxes, clothesline poles, marine breakwater pilings, silt or clay cliffs, haystacks, and suitable structures on buildings. If a new nest is constructed, which takes 5-19 days, the male is about twice as active as the female; the nest also forms the male's roost. Copulations are frequent. Clutch size varies between 3 and 12 eggs, 4-9 being most common; the average of a large sample (n = 411) was 6.5 ± 1.4 eggs. Larger clutches, e.g. 17 eggs, are probably laid by more than one female. One to ten chicks (mostly five to seven) hatch from a clutch, on average 1.1 fewer than eggs produced. So far, no effects on clutch size of hybridisation between Red-shafted and Yellow-shafted Flickers have been detected, although hybrid males tend to sire smaller broods. As with many other birds, early clutches and broods are larger than late ones. On top of these seasonal effects some geographical variation exists, larger clutches being laid in areas with higher summer productivity and more pronounced seasonality; these factors contribute to an increase of about one egg per 10° of latitude. Both sexes incubate, for 11-12 days, the male taking a greater share. The chicks are fed by regurgitation, the male seeming also to feed the nestlings at a higher rate than the female; feeding is reduced at the end of the nestling period. Faeces are removed at the beginning and during the main part of the nestling period, which ends after 25-28 days. The young stay with and call for the parents for a long time, and the family gathers at favourable feeding sites. A second brood may be reared in the same season. Later in summer, family groups cluster for migration.

REFERENCES Bent 1939; Bock 1971; Conner 1980; Conner & Adkisson 1977; Conner *et al.* 1975; Fletcher & Moore 1992; Gamboa & Brown 1976; Johnston 1975; Kilham 1973a; Koenig 1984, 1986; Lawrence 1967; Miller 1955; Moore & Koenig 1986; Noble 1936; Short 1965a, 1965b, 1967, 1972a.

147 GILDED FLICKER
Colaptes chrysoides   Plate 43

Forms a superspecies with *auratus*.

IDENTIFICATION Length c. 26-30cm. Medium-sized, with medium-long, pointed bill slightly curved on culmen and narrow across nostrils. Resembles Northern Flickers (146) of *cafer* group, but has forehead to hindneck more rusty, upperparts generally paler and more heavily barred, undertail with more black at tip, black breast patch deeper, and shafts and undersurfaces of wings and tail yellow. Lacks red on nape, and male has red moustache (some females may have pale cinnamon moustache). Closely associated with cactus and yucca plants. Although Gilded Flicker and the *cafer* group of Northern can and do hybridise when they meet, they appear to be segregated to a fair degree in the breeding season by habitat (Northern Flicker occupying higher elevation forests). Interbreeding is consequently very limited, and Gilded is now regarded by a number of authorities as a separate species, although others prefer to lump the two. The two associate freely outside the breeding period. Genetically, Gilded Flickers are not significantly divergent from red-shafted Northern Flickers of the SW USA (Fletcher & Moore 1992).

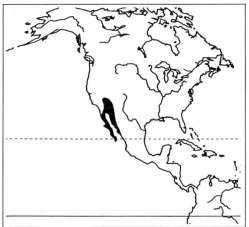

DISTRIBUTION Resident from extreme SE California and Baja California, SE Nevada, through C Arizona to NW Mexico (Sonora and N Sinaloa). Common.

HABITAT Arid scrub and riverine woodland (cottonwood, willows) with large cacti; from sea level to 250m in Baja California, to about 900m farther east.

DESCRIPTION Essentially as *cafer* group of Northern Flicker (which see), apart from differences given above.

GEOGRAPHICAL VARIATION Four races.
> *C. c. mearnsi* (northern part of range) The largest race. Rather pale.
> *C. c. tenebrosus* (NW Mexico) Smaller, and heavily barred.
> *C. c. brunnescens* (C Baja California) Browner above, with moderate barring.
> *C. c. chrysoides* (S Baja California) Small and pale.

MEASUREMENTS Wing 127-156; tail 85-109; bill 22.8-40.5. Weight: 92-129 (*mearnsi*).

VOICE As that of Northern Flicker (146).

HABITS Much as Northern Flicker. Found singly or in pairs, and forages frequently on the ground. Suffers greatly from nest competition from Common Starlings, ever since the latter conquered the habitats of the Southwest.

FOOD Ants and their brood and other insects. Takes fruits (e.g. cactus fruits) and berries (also from feeders), and may cause some damage to pecan and walnut plantations.

BREEDING Egg-laying season spans February to June. Nest most frequently sited in the upper 3m of a giant cactus, less commonly in cottonwood and willow trees and stubs at 1.5-8m. Usual clutch size 3-5 eggs.

REFERENCES Bent 1939; Fletcher & Moore 1992; Howell & Webb in press; Phillips *et al.* 1964.

148 FERNANDINA'S FLICKER
Colaptes fernandinae   Plate 44

Other name: Cuban Flicker

IDENTIFICATION Length c. 30cm. Medium-sized, with long, pointed, curved bill narrow across nostrils. A rare Cuban endemic. Pale yellowish, with dense blackish-brown barring above and more widely spaced brown bars below; top of head is buffish-cinnamon and ear-coverts yellower. Has long, fully barred tail. Male has a black moustache, that of female being heavily streaked white. Unlikely to be misidentified within its limited range; Cuban race of Northern Flicker (146) has very different plumage pattern and, unlike Fernandina's, is largely arboreal.

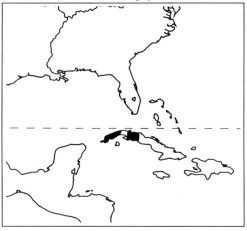

DISTRIBUTION Restricted to Cuba, where formerly common and widespread, but now survives very locally and only in the west. The population seems to have shrunk to around 300 pairs, most of these being in Zapata Swamp (Matanzas). Listed as endangered by Birdlife International.

HABITAT Chiefly palm groves in open, dry country, savannas, pastures, swamps, forest edge and dense woodland.

DESCRIPTION
Adult male Forehead to nape/hindneck buffy-cinnamon

(occasionally with a hint of red on nape), finely streaked black. Lores, narrow line over eye and below eye whitish-buff; ear-coverts buffish-yellow, becoming more cinnamon at rear. Moustachial stripe black, sometimes with admixed red. Chin and throat white, heavily streaked black, becoming black-spotted on lower throat and throat sides. Upperparts, upperwing-coverts and tertials pale yellow to buffish-yellow, paler on rump, and densely barred blackish-brown (bars narrower on rump and uppertail-coverts). Flight feathers dark brown, narrowly barred yellow-buff. Uppertail brownish-black, with narrow buffy-yellow bars across all feathers. Underparts below throat pale yellowish-buff (colour strongest on flanks), all with brown arrowhead marks or bars, markings being weaker on belly. Underwing yellow, with rather obscure barring. Undertail yellow.

Adult female Very like male, but moustache is heavily streaked white; never shows any hint of red on nape.

Juvenile Duller and browner than adults, with broader markings below and less barring above.

Bare parts Bill black. Legs and feet dark grey. Eyes deep brown (or red-brown?).

GEOGRAPHICAL VARIATION None. Monotypic.

MEASUREMENTS Wing 138-157; tail 102-130; bill 36.5-42.5; tarsus 27-31.8.

VOICE Like a Northern Flicker. Long call lower-pitched and slightly slower than latter's. Also has a trill.

HABITS A rather tame, usually quiet woodpecker. Often feeds on ground, apparently more so than local race of Northern Flicker, where it probes into the soil and under leaves.

FOOD Presumably, ants among other insects dominate the diet.

BREEDING Nesting season is March-June. Nest carved relatively low down into dead palms and dead trees. The same hole may be used in successive years. Nests may be locally clustered. Clutch consists of 4-5 eggs.

REFERENCES Bond 1985; Collar *et al.* 1992, 1994; Short 1965b.

149 CHILEAN FLICKER
Colaptes pitius   Plate 44

IDENTIFICATION Length c. 30cm. Medium-sized, with fairly long, pointed bill with curved culmen and narrow across nostrils. General plumage pattern, with barred upperparts and underparts, is not unlike that of the geographically remote Fernandina's Flicker (148), but Chilean has dark slaty crown, white rump, only central and outer tail feathers barred, and pale eyes. Within its range it is the only terrestrial woodpecker (though it also forages in trees) and, as such, unmistakable.

DISTRIBUTION Southwest S America, from C Chile (Atacama) through Llanquihue to S Chile (Chiloé, Magallanes), and adjacent SW Argentina (Neuquén to Santa Cruz). Common.

HABITAT Inhabits woodland and open wooded country, including open areas within *Nothofagus* forest, forest edge, riparian woodland, tree plantations and various types of scrubby vegetation. Ranges in altitude from 600m to over 1000m.

DESCRIPTION
Adult male Forehead to nape/hindneck dark slaty-grey,

blacker at sides, nape rarely with a hint of red. Lores, area around eye, and ear-coverts buffish. Moustachial region buffish, finely spotted black (or black and red). Chin and throat buffish-white, spotted black on lower throat. Upperparts, upperwing-coverts and tertials barred broadly with blackish-brown and narrowly with white to buffy-white, but rump unmarked white (some have a few black spots/bars). Flight feathers dark brown, primaries notched whitish with pale shafts, and secondaries narrowly barred whitish-buff. Uppertail brown-black, outer and central feather pairs narrowly barred white. Underparts below throat whitish, broadly barred blackish-brown, bars tending to merge on breast and to become smaller, or spots (or be lacking), on belly. Underwing yellowish, with darker tip, and with some bars on primary coverts. Undertail yellowish, obscurely barred. (When worn, may lose much of the white barring on mantle, back and wing-coverts, which thus become much browner.)

Adult female As male, but lacks black/red in moustache; never shows any red on nape.

Juvenile As adults, but more broadly barred above and more spotted below; crown blacker, with narrow buff feather tips (appears faintly barred).

Bare parts Bill black. Legs and feet grey or green-grey. Eyes yellowish; brown in juveniles.

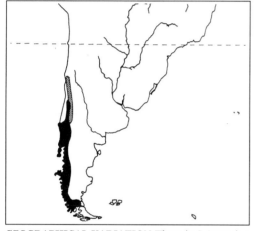

GEOGRAPHICAL VARIATION Those in S Argentina ('*cachinnans*') seem to have a proportionately shorter tail than Chilean birds but do not differ otherwise, and the species is treated as monotypic.

MEASUREMENTS Wing 145-160; tail 114-118; bill 38-40. Weight: 146-163.

VOICE A distinct repeated *piteéu*; a whistled, variable *kwee*, singly or in series. The latter resembles the whistling notes of Andean Flicker (150), but is less loud, more variable, and raucous. During encounters, birds utter *week-a, week-a* calls resembling those of Northern Flicker (146), but higher-pitched. Similar comparisons hold for the long call-series, *wic wic wic ...*, which in this species are also less clear in sound.

HABITS Easy to detect when roving about in noisy family groups. Forages mainly on the ground, but never far from trees. Rarely forages in trees, and then rather unenthusiastically, but resorts to their shelter when alarmed, and on such occasions some agitated pecking may be observed. Hops on the ground, where feeds by poking, sweeping away debris, and digging into the soil; also on fallen logs and stumps. Head-swinging/bobbing with tail-

spreading are the known displays. Seems to be highly territorial, and there are no indications of group formation or coloniality.

FOOD Almost exclusively ants and their brood. Occasionally takes other food items, such as scorpions and grubs.

BREEDING Breeding has been reported from October to December. Nests are excavated in dead trees and stubs, or banks. Clutch size 4-6 eggs.

REFERENCES Fjeldså & Krabbe 1990; Johnson 1967; Olrog 1984; Short 1972a.

---

150 ANDEAN FLICKER
Colaptes rupicola   Plate 44

IDENTIFICATION Length c. 32cm. Medium-sized to rather large, with extremely long, pointed bill with curved culmen and narrow across nostrils (but broad-based). A very distinctive pale-eyed terrestrial woodpecker with barred upperparts and buffish underparts, with spotted breast; dark grey or blackish forehead to hindneck and dark moustache contrast with pale face. Shows pale rump in flight. This noisy and conspicuous woodpecker, common in wet grassland with rocky slopes, where it feeds exclusively on the ground, is unmistakable within its range.

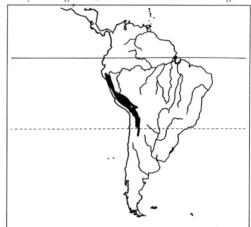

DISTRIBUTION High Andes of west-central S America, from N and C Peru (E Piura through W Amazonas to Pasco), through SE Peru and adjacent Bolivia (east to Santa Cruz) to N Chile (Tarapacá) and NW Argentina (south to Catamarca). Common.

MOVEMENTS There are probably some seasonal movements, cold or snow forcing these high-altitude birds to retreat to somewhat lower elevations.

HABITAT A woodpecker of open land and forest edge at high elevations. Within its range, it is common in the grassland of the Andean puna and less common in the humid grass-shrub of the *páramo*. Broken, rolling country is favoured over entirely flat land. Inhabits stony steppes and gorges, montane scrub, and *Polylepis* woodland. Throughout the puna zone between 2000 and 5000m. Reports of Andean Flickers at elevations as low as or below 2900m may refer to foraging parties of non-breeders, which probably return to higher elevations.

DESCRIPTION
C. r. rupicola **Adult male** Forehead to hindneck dark slaty-

grey, blacker at sides, sometimes with a trace of red on nape. Short, thin moustachial stripe black, tipped red. Rest of face, including line above eye, neck sides, and chin and throat unmarked pale buffish-white, slightly darker on ear-coverts. Upperparts, upperwing-coverts and tertials barred brown, light brown and buffish-white, becoming plain buffish-white (occasionally with a few bars) on rump, and white, narrowly barred dark, on uppertail-coverts. Flight feathers dark brown, narrowly barred pale buff. Uppertail black, thinly barred on outer and central feathers. Under-parts below throat whitish, washed orange-buff on breast (colour variable in strength), and with blackish spots or small V marks on breast and sometimes extending to neck sides and/or flanks; undertail-coverts occasionally with short bars. Underwing pale buffy-yellow, darker at tip and trailing edge, and with a few spots on primary coverts. Undertail much as uppertail, but often yellowish at sides.

Adult female Very like male, but lacks red in black mous-tache; never has any red on nape.

Juvenile Duller than adults, but usually with some red on nape (males) and with indistinct, narrow buff feather tips to rear crown; markings below more bar-like and often extending to flanks and belly.

Bare parts Bill black. Legs and feet yellowish-grey to greyish-pink. Eyes pale lemon-yellow; reddish-brown in juveniles.

GEOGRAPHICAL VARIATION Three fairly well-de-fined races.

C. r. rupicola (Bolivia, N Chile and NW Argentina) Described above. Interbreeds with *puna* in north of range.
C. r. puna (C and S Peru) Similar to nominate, but darker above and often also below, with larger breast markings, and both sexes have a dark red patch on lower nape/hindneck; tail usually less barred. Fe-male's moustache often indistinct. Legs dull greenish. Interbreeds with *cinereicapillus* in C Peru.
C. r. cinereicapillus (N Peru) Larger than above two races, and distinctive. Face and underparts deep cin-namon, with breast markings in form of thin horizon-tal bars, and throat partly grey; tail barring irregular. Lacks red on nape. Legs are paler, more orange-yellow.

MEASUREMENTS Wing 156-190; tail 92-128; bill 32-49; tarsus 26-33. Weight: (142)152-190(204), females about 5% lighter than males.

VOICE A loud whistled *tew-tew-tew*, very like the three- or four-note calls of Greater Yellowlegs *Tringa melanoleuca*. Single or grouped *peek* or *kek* notes, thought to serve as location calls and given in alarm, apparently exhibit some racial differences (being shorter and higher-pitched in *cinereicapillus*). Often interspersed with these during en-counters are single notes or series of notes sounding like *cloit* or *quoi-ik-ik* (race *puna*). Low *peea* notes may be heard when two birds meet; in display, louder *kwa-kwa-kwa*, *wee-a*, *wee-a* or *kway-áp* calls are given. A loud, clear and descending trill, *brrrridip*, often given from a rock when disturbed, is presumably used for long-distance communi-cation; this call, about 2.5 secs long, may contain about 70 elements, but tends to be shorter, higher-pitched and slower in *puna*.

HABITS Andean Flickers are wary birds, difficult to approach. Their foraging is decidedly terrestrial, occa-sional pecks on an arboreal perch being signs of excitement and alertness rather than true feeding. Behaviour while foraging closely resembles that of other flicker species. With their remarkably long bill they probe into the soil and brush away earth, pebbles and debris to get at food, digging

up the ground to obtain larvae hidden deep (e.g. 5cm) in the soil. Food is sought at the bases of tussocks. When alarmed, they retreat to a nearby lookout; structures used as vantage points include cliffs, rocks, stone walls, build-ings, road cuttings and river banks, with trees, where present, used as lookouts and signalling posts (trilling calls). Preferred feeding grounds are therefore grassy areas around rocky outcrops and other such structures as men-tioned above, from which the birds start ground-foraging and to which they return immediately after feeding or at the slightest sign of danger. A feeding area is scoured evenly and, unlike with other ground-feeding species, searches are not restricted to certain areas such as ant and termite hills. On the ground, characteristically walks rather than hops; in steep, rocky or densely grass-covered terrain, however, also hops. Feeding areas may be far from nesting grounds or roosts, and may be situated at lower altitudes. As other terrestrial woodpeckers, this species is rather social: 8-10 individuals may be seen foraging together (such parties may move considerable distances as a group) and nests may be close together, forming small colonies (even if farther apart, for instance in more rocky terrain, neighbours may be seen foraging together in loose groups). In display, birds raise (to a vertical position) and lower their heads, flick the wings and call. Head-swinging/bobbing and tail-spreading are also part of their repertoire.

FOOD Insects and large lepidopterous and coleopterous larvae. Beetles (Scarabidae, Melolonthinae, Rutelinae) and noctuid moths have been recorded as components of the diet.

BREEDING The breeding season probably spans Septem-ber to November (C Peru) and January to March, but nesting possibly occurs also at other times of the year. Cold and snowfall in the wet season are certainly of great influence. Nests, dug into earth banks, cliffs and other rocky terrain, consist of a horizontal or slightly upward-sloping entrance tunnel, about 1m long, and a nest cham-ber. Roost holes are often excavated in native buildings, especially abandoned ones; over the years, 30-60 such holes may have been dug into a hut. Ten or more pairs may share the same bank, thus forming a colony. Nests rarely exca-vated in trees (*Polylepis*). Both parents feed the 2-4 young and remove faeces.

REFERENCES Dorst 1956; Fjeldså 1991; Fjeldså & Krabbe 1990; Johnson 1967; Koepcke 1983; Olrog 1984; Parker *et al.* 1982, 1985; Short 1971a, 1971e, 1972a.

151 CAMPO FLICKER
Colaptes campestris   Plate 44

Other names: Campos Flicker; Field Flicker (race *campestroides*)

IDENTIFICATION Length c. 28-31cm. Medium-sized to large, with longish, pointed bill curved on culmen and narrow across nostrils (but broad-based). Another highly distinctive and long-tailed, ground-foraging woodpecker of open lowland country, heavily barred above and below and with deep golden-buff face, neck and breast; forehead to nape is black, and males have some red in moustache. The throat is black in northern populations and whitish in southern *campestroides*. In flight, shows pale underwing and white (variably barred) rump. Often forages in small groups, not uncommonly joined by Green-barred Wood-peckers (145). Its large size, terrestrial habits, shape and coloration make this species unlikely to be misidentified.

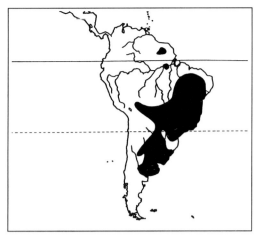

DISTRIBUTION Central S America, where patchily distributed in the savannas of Surinam and the lower Amazonas (Pará, Brazil), with range more continuous from E Brazil (Maranhão, Mato Grosso to Rio Grande do Sul), including some offshore islands, through Uruguay, Paraguay, south through Corrientes to C Argentina (Río Negro to Mendoza) and west to Bolivia. Range expands with deforestation in Brazil, particularly along the big highways, where vast areas are cleared and rendered wasteland. Common to very common.

HABITAT Race *campestroides* lives at forest edge and in clearings, and is a characteristic bird of open level country. Typically, it inhabits the open pampas, sub-arid scrub (caatinga) and areas above the tree line. Forest and woodland edge and tree plantations in these open areas seem to be especially attractive; also favoured are locations with termite nests, fence posts, trees and similar structures suitable for nesting. Deforestation allows this species to invade new areas, and it can thus be observed in clearings in subtropical moist forest. Overgrazed areas and wastelands along major highways are other secondary habitats in which this species can be found. Lowlands, reaching 600m in C Argentina. Generally common.

DESCRIPTION
C. c. campestris **Adult male** Forehead to nape black. Lores and area around eye buffish-white, becoming golden-buff on ear-coverts, neck and upper breast. Chin and throat black, chin often flecked white, bordered above by buffish and red tips to black moustachial stripe. Mantle, back, scapulars, upperwing-coverts and tertials barred dark brown and narrowly light brown and whitish, pale bars broader on scapulars and coverts; rump white, variably (occasionally quite heavily) spotted or barred dark; uppertail-coverts barred brown and white. Flight feathers dark brown, thinly barred buffish-white. Uppertail brown-black, with narrow buff bars on outer webs (but also on inner webs of central feathers). Underparts from lower breast white, tinged pale yellow, all with narrow arrowhead barring. Underwing yellowish with darker tip and trailing edge, with some spots on primary coverts. Undertail as uppertail but duller, with pale bars more obscure. (Owing to ground-feeding habits, underparts usually become very dirty, this soiling being common to many woodpecker species.)

Adult female As male, but lacks red tips in moustache, having this area whitish and black.

Juvenile Duller overall than adults, with dark bars broader and with golden-buff areas paler, more yellow and less extensive.

Bare parts Bill black. Legs and feet green-grey to pink-tinged. Eyes chestnut to red-brown.

GEOGRAPHICAL VARIATION Two races, differing mainly in throat colour.
  C. c. campestris (northern part of range) Described above.
  C. c. campestroides (S Paraguay, Uruguay and N Argentina) Differs from nominate mainly in having chin and throat white to buffy-white, not black, but does have moustache as nominate (but more conspicuous owing to pale throat); underparts often less marked, more narrowly barred, with belly virtually plain. Sometimes considered a separate species, but hybridisation between this race and the nominate occurs in Paraguay, and probably elsewhere.

MEASUREMENTS Wing (143)153-166(177); tail (94)104-116(122); bill (23.7)25-30(32.5); tarsus 27-34. Weight: 145-192, females may be about 15g lighter (*campestroides*); about 155 (*campestris*).

VOICE A loud double- or triple-note whistle is heard infrequently, the notes run together more than in the corresponding vocalisation of Andean Flicker (150). A wavering *wewww...*, *gwik*, *ewuh*, and *pya* or *kyow*. Series of *week* or *keep* notes may serve as a location call. Wavering *we-a*, *kwih* or *kya-wi* notes resemble low versions of the *wicka* calls of Northern Flicker (146). Fast series of *wick* notes (these slightly lower-pitched in nominate race) are typical of birds in close contacts. Long or short series of fairly clear notes, *oo oo oo oo ee oo oo ee oo ee oo oo oo ee oo oo*, delivered more slowly than in Andean Flicker, also occur. Nestling calls have been likened to sound of a kettle boiling.

HABITS Often lives in small groups; loose parties of up to eight individuals may be seen foraging together or concentrated at a particular anthill. Such groups may be joined by Green-barred Woodpeckers. A conspicuous bird which forages virtually exclusively on the ground, among stones, close to decaying fallen logs, and on roads; also visits termite mounds or anthills and other prominent structures, such as isolated trees, utility or fence poles, cacti and rocks, from where it surveys its environment. Although forest edge is used, for instance as a nest site, this woodpecker never ventures into the forest interior. Regularly perches on wires. Typically, opens the large mounds of terrestrial termites; sometimes breaks into nests of Rufous Hornero *Furnarius rufus* to get at the nestlings. Also known to hammer holes, up to 7cm in diameter, into buildings, but the scant reports on this behaviour leave it open to question whether such holes are intended as roosts or for securing food. In the tall grass of their habitat Campo Flickers primarily walk when searching for food, and hop to cover long distances; they also hop to ascend termite hills and similar structures, and along branches. Displays with fluttering or spreading the wings, whereby the bright yellow shafts are clearly visible. Head-swinging displays not very conspicuous; points motionless with the bill at an opponent, or stabs at it. Roosts also on buildings. Dustbathes. In suitable areas Campo Flickers form loose colonies, the members of which may share a common feeding ground.

FOOD Ants, termites and their brood predominate in the diet (more than 2000 ants have been found in one stomach); also adult beetles and crickets. Also takes nestlings of ovenbirds.

BREEDING Availability of nest sites is probably a crucial factor in this species' distribution patterns and social behaviour. In the breeding season, August-November in Argentina and January-April in Surinam, parties of three or four birds are more commonly seen than pairs or solitary individuals; the exact relationships within such groups are not well known. Nest is built in trees, also in various types of larger poles where available; trunks and dead stumps are preferred, but cavities are occasionally constructed in the nests of arboreal termites (*Constrictotermes cypergaster*). Nest heights of up to 12m have been recorded. In treeless country, nests are dug into the mounds of terrestrial termites (*Cornitermes cumulans*) and in banks. Although nests of different pairs may be not far apart, seems to avoid breeding in dense colonies. However, 5-6 nests per 100m may be found along lines of trees. Clutch contains 4-5 eggs, which are incubated by both partners. Family parties stay together for an extended period.

REFERENCES Aravena 1928; Belton 1984; Gore & Gepp 1978; Olrog 1984; Short 1969, 1971a, 1971e, 1972a, 1975; Sick 1993.

---

152 RUFOUS WOODPECKER
Celeus brachyurus   Plate 61

IDENTIFICATION Length c. 25cm. Fairly small, with short black bill slightly curved and rather narrow-based. Rufous to dark chestnut plumage heavily barred dark above, with variable dark barring on flanks and lower belly; throat usually shows streaks or scallop markings. Male has inconspicuous patch of red below eye. Much individual variation, however, some individuals appearing very dark, almost blackish, above, with rufous barring. Closely associated with nests of tree ants, and plumage often becomes contaminated with formic acid and other matter. Has characteristic drumming, which comes to a faltering halt like a stalling engine.

Similar species Within its range, likely to be confused only with Bay Woodpecker (205). Latter is bigger, with much larger, pale yellowish bill, and male has larger area of red on side of neck.

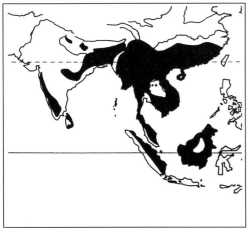

DISTRIBUTION Widespread in S Asia, from southern slopes of the Himalayas in Kumaon and W Nepal eastwards to Arunachal Pradesh and S China, including Hainan, south to Sri Lanka and south through Burma, Thailand and Indochina to Sumatra (including its offshore islands of Bangka, Belitung, Nias), W and C Java and Borneo. Locally common in India, Nepal, Borneo and Sumatra.

HABITAT Inhabits primary as well as secondary evergreen and deciduous forest. Prefers open forests, second-

ary forest, forest edge, and scrub, habitats including sal forest; at least locally, this species exhibits a predilection for bamboo jungle. May also visit reedbeds and mangroves. Occurs mostly well away from human habitations in some areas, but may be found in plantations, palm groves and gardens in others. Resident from plains up to 610m in Sri Lanka, to 1530m in Nepal, to 920m in SE Asia, and up to 1740m in Borneo.

DESCRIPTION
Adult male Highly variable (see Geographical Variation). Crown and short crest vary in colour from buffish to sooty or even blackish (can be contrastingly darker or paler than upperparts), unstreaked or with variable amount of dark streaking; lores, sides of head and neck generally unstreaked buffish to chestnut, with irregular and inconspicuous patch of dull red (formed by feather tips) below eye and on fore ear-coverts. Throat buffish to pale brown, with variably-sized dark streaks, feathers sometimes suffused with rufous (can appear dark when worn). Mantle to rump vary from rufous/chestnut, usually with black barring, to sooty-grey or blackish, narrowly barred rufous; uppertail-coverts barred rufous and black. Upperwing and its coverts barred rufous and black, but individuals with barring on upperparts often have barring on wing-coverts and secondaries obscure. Uppertail rufous or chestnut, narrowly or broadly barred black. Underparts below throat vary from rufous to dark/sooty-chestnut, with flanks and lower belly barred blackish (barring can be obscure or even lacking); undertail-coverts barred rufous and black. Underwing rufous or cinnamon-rufous, barred black. Undertail much as uppertail.

Adult female As male, but lacks red on sides of head.

Juvenile As adults, but often rather less heavily barred; can, however, show heavier barring, extending to breast.

Bare parts Bill black or dark brown, with paler, greyish, lower mandible (sometimes becoming whitish at tip). Legs and feet brownish to blue-grey or bluish-green. Eyes reddish to brown. Orbital skin grey.

GEOGRAPHICAL VARIATION Individual variation is considerable, rendering racial delimitations less straightforward.
> *C. b. humei* (NW India, possibly to W Nepal) Large and pale, with greyish head; has streaked throat.
> *C. b. jerdonii* (Bombay and south in western India, to Sri Lanka) Smaller and darker, more rufous, than *humei*, with scaly throat markings.
> *C. b. phaioceps* (N India and C Nepal east to Burma and Thailand) Large and rather dark rufous, with brownish head.
> *C. b. squamigularis* (southern peninsular Thailand south to Sumatra, including Bangka, Belitung and Nias Islands) Fairly small, and paler than northern races. Has obviously barred belly (barring less extensive in Sumatran population).
> *C. b. brachyurus* (Java) Much as *squamigularis*, but less barred on underparts and with slightly longer tail.
> *C. b. badiosus* (Borneo and northern Natuna Islands) Longer-billed than *squamigularis* and nominate. Also has very dark, black, tail narrowly barred rufous, less barring above, and little or no barring on belly; throat feathers black at base, tipped chestnut and edged buff, producing scaly pattern.
> *C. b. fokiensis* (S China and N Vietnam) Sooty below, with greyish-tinged breast; throat broadly streaked black and pale. Both this and the following race have proportionately the longest tail of all races.
> *C. b. holroydi* (Hainan Island) Much smaller than

fokiensis. Very dark, with underparts more chestnut (less grey) than *fokiensis*; throat streaked brown (not black), and crown lightly streaked.

C. b. annamensis (Laos, Cambodia, S Vietnam) Slightly smaller than *fokiensis*. As latter, very dark-plumaged.

MEASUREMENTS Wing 111-122 (*jerdonii, squamigularis*), 129-145 (*humei*), 119-133 (*phaioceps*); tail 51-58 (*squamigularis*), 60-63 (*jerdonii*), 66-73 (*humei*), 58-68 (*phaioceps*); bill (from skull) 25-30 (*jerdonii*), 31-33 (*humei*), 26-31 (*phaioceps*); tarsus 20.9-25.5. Weight: 55-84 (*squamigularis, badiosus*), 82-107 (*jerdonii*), 92-114 (*phaioceps*).

VOICE Highly vocal. Short series of three nasal notes, *kweep-kweep-kweep* or *keenk, keenk, keenk,* delivered in less than 1 sec (sometimes with pause before final note), are given by single birds, and are reminiscent of the calls of Common Myna *Acridotheres tristis*. In encounters, series of four or five *kweek* notes may be heard, some of them perhaps similar to the variable *whi-chi, wi-chee* notes given in the same context. A long, slightly descending and accelerating series of up to 16 notes (of 2 secs duration) may be repeated several times, and probably serves as territorial announcement and helps pair members to keep in contact. Drumming is diagnostic, and unlike that of any other woodpecker in its range: a single roll may be 1.5-5 secs long, and slows gradually to a halt like a stalling motorbike engine, *bdddd-d-d---dt.* Rolls are 2-3 minutes apart. This acoustical signal is delivered commonly, often on bamboo, and may be given by both sexes.

HABITS Often met with in pairs and in close vicinity of nests of tree ants. Forages in practically all strata of the forest, sometimes with mixed-species flocks, preferring somewhat darker, densely vegetated sites though not shunning open sites completely. Searches vines, tree trunks, branches, twigs and even bamboo, at all heights, including the high canopy of tall forest. Has been observed on the ground, where it seeks food in small termite mounds or anthills or even in cow-pats; also searches rotting logs. The chief feeding techniques are gleaning and probing, with an occasional weak and hardly audible blow. Pecks at *Crematogaster* nests from a perch close by; or clings at the nest, tears it apart and gleans the ants swarming out, picking them off its plumage and feet as well. Has been observed to puncture banana stems to feed on the sap oozing out. This woodpecker is almost constantly on the move, remaining at one site only if a good source of food, e.g. ants, can be exploited. May perch crosswise on twigs. Flight bounding, with deep dips. The significance of the resin-like and sticky substance found on the head, abdomen and tail remains to be clarified. Encounters trigger many displays and vocalisations, especially when two pairs are involved simultaneously; tail-spreading and head- and body-swinging with intermittent periods of immobility are much like the behaviour of other woodpeckers. Long rattle calls are uttered mostly by the male and answered by another pair.

FOOD Chiefly ants and their brood, particularly *Crematogaster* species, but also *Pheidole* and *Oecophylla*; also termites and other insects. Vegetable matter, which is taken occasionally, includes fruits (e.g. *Ficus*), nectar and sap.

BREEDING Breeding records from February to June in Sri Lanka and southern India, from April to June in Nepal, Sikkim and Burma, from January to April in Thailand and Malaya, and from April and September in Java. This species is renowned for digging its nest holes (both sexes share this duty) into the football-sized nests of tree-ants of the genus *Crematogaster* situated high up on tree trunks or built lower down (c. 3m) around a fork in a sapling. The nests, when cut out, are still occupied by the ants and their

brood. Relationships with these stinging ants during nesting and roosting seem not to have been studied well, and how the woodpeckers protect themselves is still open to speculation: one possibility is that they acquire the appropriate odour during their regular visits. The ants may, however, destroy the brood if the delicate balance between woodpeckers and ants is disturbed by external events. The nests of other ants (e.g. *Plagiolepis*) may be used in the same way. Nests are also hollowed out in trees and stubs. Clutch comprises 2-3(7) eggs, clutch size increasing northwards. The eggs are translucent and may become stained during incubation. Both sexes incubate for 12-14 days, and feed the young by regurgitation.

REFERENCES Ali 1962; Ali & Ripley 1970; Henry 1971; Herbert 1926; Inskipp & Inskipp 1991; King & Dickinson 1975; Lekagul & Round 1991; MacKinnon 1990; MacKinnon & Phillipps 1993; Medway & Wells 1976; Phillips 1978; Proud 1958; Short 1973a, 1978; Smythies 1953, 1981; Stresemann & Heinrich 1940.

153 CINNAMON WOODPECKER
Celeus loricatus   Plate 45

IDENTIFICATION Length c. 19-23cm. Small, with rather short, almost pointed bill with slightly curved culmen and narrow across nostrils. Very variable, but generally rufous above with some barring, and paler cinnamon below with barring heavy to virtually absent; bushy-crested head is plain rufous or with dark crown streaks. Tail strongly barred. Male has red chin and throat.

Similar species In C America, Chestnut-coloured Woodpecker (156) is distinguished by the lack of contrast in ground colour between its upperparts and underparts and by its head and larger crest being distinctly paler than the body; male Chestnut-coloured also has red from bill base back through eye, but not on throat. Note also the distinct differences in calls and details of habitat use.

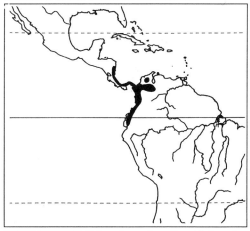

DISTRIBUTION C America and northeast S America, from Nicaragua, through Costa Rica and Panama on both slopes, N and W Colombia, to NW Ecuador. Generally uncommon, but locally fairly common.

HABITAT A bird of humid and wet forest, and rare to absent in drier areas; occasionally visits forest edge, nearby semi-open, old second growth, and clearings. A species of the lowlands and foothills, found from sea level to 760m in Costa Rica and Panama and at up to 1500m in Colombia.

DESCRIPTION

C. l. diversus Adult male Entire head rufous-cinnamon, with forehead to crown/hindcrown broadly streaked black, apart from red-tipped black chin, throat and moustachial area (often also slightly reddish above and behind eyes). Upperparts, including upperwing-coverts and tertials, chestnut-rufous, paler on rump, all narrowly barred black. Flight feathers blackish, with very broad rufous bars. Uppertail black, with very broad cinnamon-buff to whitish bars. Underparts below throat rufous-cinnamon, becoming paler lower down, with conspicuous bold black scaly markings on breast (feathers pale in centre, black submarginally), becoming arrowhead bars on flanks and belly. Underwing rufous, barred black on flight feathers. Undertail as above, but paler.

Adult female As male, but lacks red on throat, having entire head rufous-cinnamon.

Juvenile Much as adults, but dusky-mottled on throat and less regularly marked below; young males redder around the face.

Bare parts Bill greenish-yellow, with horn-coloured culmen. Legs and feet brownish-grey. Eyes red; possibly brown in juveniles.

GEOGRAPHICAL VARIATION Four races, differing mainly in amount of barring. All populations, however, are highly variable individually, especially *innotatus*.
> **C. l. diversus** (Nicaragua into W Panama) Described above. The largest race.
> **C. l. mentalis** (Panama and NW Colombia) Smaller than *diversus*, paler below, and with less barring above and below.
> **C. l. loricatus** (W Colombia and W Ecuador) Closer to *diversus*, but somewhat more barred above and darker and more densely marked below.
> **C. l. innotatus** (N Colombia) Resembles *mentalis*, but even less marked: upperparts very weakly barred or even unbarred, and may lack crown streaks; underparts with merely a few breast spots. Includes form '*degener*' of upper Magdalena valley, which is virtually unmarked.

MEASUREMENTS Wing 106-127, 114-122 (*mentalis*), 119-127 (*diversus*); tail 59-71; bill 20-26.8; tarsus 19-23.7. Weight: 74-83.

VOICE A ringing, somewhat whistled, penetrating series of three to five fast notes, accelerating and descending in pitch and amplitude, described as *peee-peew-peu-pu*, *phet-phet-phet-phet*, or *wheeeét, wheet, wheetit*, sometimes with an introductory *chuweéoo* (also likened to calls of Common Black Hawk *Buteogallus anthracinus*). When agitated, gives a sharp, descending, rolling, parrot-like chatter. Other vocalisations rendered as a hard *chikikikirik*, a squeaky *titititoò*, and a tanager-like *chweé-titit*. Drums in rolls which are slightly slower and shorter than those of Black-cheeked Woodpecker (39), which overlaps in range.

HABITS Usually forages singly or in pairs and away from mixed-species flocks, although may join such flocks now and then. Active at lower levels, particularly in open areas, but near or in the canopy in the interior of forests. Often clings to seedlings and bushes in the undergrowth and regularly visits thin trunks, twigs and branchlets. Pecks frequently, and gleans to some extent. Has, for instance, been observed to peck into swollen nodes of laurel (*Cordia alliodra*) twigs and *Cecropia* trunks for ants, and into tunnels for termites.

FOOD Ants and termites; also fruit (e.g. ripening bananas).

BREEDING Breeding season in Costa Rica from March to May, and from January to April in Colombia. Hole excavated by both sexes, 6-9m up in soft wood of living or recently dead tree. Eggs have apparently not been described.

REFERENCES Hilty & Brown 1984; Ridgely & Gwynne 1989; Skutch 1985; Slud 1964; Stiles & Skutch 1989; Wetmore 1968.

---

154 SCALY-BREASTED WOODPECKER
Celeus grammicus   Plate 45

Other name: Scale-breasted Woodpecker
Forms a superspecies with *undatus*.

IDENTIFICATION Length c. 23-24cm. Small, with shortish, slightly chisel-tipped bill with curved culmen and narrow across nostrils. Head, with rather long crest, and upperparts are rufous and barred black, but rump plain pale yellowish; rufous below, with buff flanks, breast heavily barred. Tail and flight feathers are unbarred. Male has large red moustache reaching onto ear-coverts. Populations south of the Amazon have somewhat darker rump and flanks, lacking yellow tone, while southernmost birds are much paler overall and have pale feather bases showing through.

Similar species Waved Woodpecker (155) is similar, but barring extends over rump and flanks, tail is barred, and the head is paler than the body.

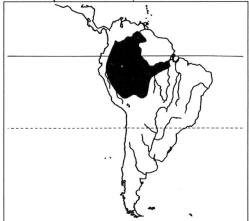

DISTRIBUTION North and north-central S America, in the Amazonian basin from SC Venezuela and NW Brazil (Rio Negro area) to Santarem, Rio Tapajós and N Mato Grosso in the east, and in the west from SW Venezuela, through SE Colombia, E Ecuador and E and SE Peru to Bolivia (Beni). Rather uncommon to common.

HABITAT This woodpecker inhabits rain forest, humid *terra firme* and *várzea* forests, forest edge, second growth, and savannas with scattered trees. It is distributed at altitudes from 100 to 900 (1140)m.

DESCRIPTION

C. g. grammicus Adult male Forehead to crest rufous-chestnut, usually streaked black (streaking variable). Lores and ear-coverts rufous-chestnut. Cheeks and moustachial area broadly red, this colour extending onto front part of ear-coverts. Chin, throat and neck sides chestnut, barred black. Hindneck, mantle, back, scapulars, upperwing-coverts and tertials rufous-chestnut, narrowly barred black; rump pale greenish-yellow to pale yellow-buff, unmarked but very occasionally with some red-tipped feathers; uppertail-coverts plain rufous-chestnut, occasionally somewhat barred. Primaries and secondaries blackish, paler greenish-yellow at bases and narrowly edged/tipped rufous. Uppertail brown-black, feathers edged chestnut (sometimes wholly chestnut at base). Underparts rufous-chestnut, with flanks a much paler yellowish-buff; breast has broad black bars or arrowhead marks, these becoming narrower on lower breast, with sparse spots on belly. Underwing dull brown, with paler yellowish coverts and bases of flight feathers. Undertail brown or yellowish-brown, with cinnamon base.

Adult female As male, but has red of moustachial region replaced by rufous-chestnut.

Juvenile As adults, but with darker head showing some blackish areas; upperparts usually paler, but more broadly barred. Young males have some red in moustachial region.

Bare parts Bill greenish to yellow-green or ivory. Legs and feet dark greenish-grey to grey. Eyes red.

GEOGRAPHICAL VARIATION Four races.
    C. g. grammicus (Venezuela south to NE Peru and W Brazil) Described above.
    C. g. verreauxi (E Ecuador and adjoining NE Peru) As nominate, but much less barred below.
    C. g. subcervinus (south of Amazon river to Mato Grosso) As nominate, but rump and flanks more cinnamon to buff (lacking yellow tone).
    C. g. latifasciatus (SE Peru, N Bolivia, and upper Madeira river in Brazil) Distinctive. Upperparts very pale cinnamon-coloured, with yellow or buffish feather bases visible, and very pale rump; mantle broadly barred; paler ground colour below.

MEASUREMENTS Wing 117-140, 111-131 (*grammicus*), 133-140 (*subcervinus*); tail 68-81 (*grammicus*), 82-83 (*subcervinus*); bill 20-23 (*grammicus*), 22-23 (*subcervinus*); tarsus 20. Weight: 63-75 (*grammicus*), 77-82 (*verreauxi*), 75-87 (*latifasciatus*).

VOICE The common call is a loud, whistling, somewhat nasal *curry-kuuu*, or *doit-gua*. In addition, very loud and metallic *Pring-Pring!* notes, up to four in a series, can be heard.

HABITS Sometimes lives in groups of three to four birds, probably family parties, and frequently associates with mixed-species groups. Forages inconspicuously in middle to upper levels of the canopy on trunks and larger limbs, but also on vines. Pecks rapidly, and probes and gleans the bark surface.

FOOD Feeds on ants and fruit.

BREEDING Breeding season in Venezuela seems to be February to April; this is probably also the nesting season for western populations. Possibly breeds somewhat later in Brazil.

REFERENCES Hilty & Brown 1984; Meyer de Schauensee & Phelps 1978; Parker *et al.* 1982; Sick 1993; Willard *et al.* 1991.

155 WAVED WOODPECKER
Celeus undatus
Plate 45

Forms a superspecies with *grammicus*.

IDENTIFICATION Length c. 23-24cm. Small, with shortish, almost pointed bill with curved culmen and fairly narrow across nostrils. A pale-billed, mainly rufous or chestnut woodpecker with paler bushy-crested head and heavily and completely barred body. Male has broad red moustache reaching onto ear-coverts. Dark-billed southern race is paler, with less heavy markings below.

Similar species Female is similar to female Cinnamon Woodpecker (153), but the two do not meet. See also Scaly-breasted Woodpecker (154).

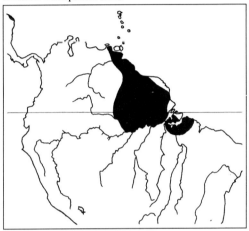

DISTRIBUTION Northeastern S America, from E Venezuela (E Bolívar, Paria, Delta Amacuro) through the Guianas, south to the middle and lower Rio Negro in Brazil and, south of the Amazon, to the lower Tocantins river and E Pará province. Uncommon.

HABITAT Occurs most frequently in dense rain forests, at up to 500m, and occasionally in more open terrain of savanna regions at forest edge, and near rivers.

DESCRIPTION
C. u. undatus **Adult male** Entire head, apart from moustachial area and cheeks, light chestnut-rufous (often paler on crown and crest), barred or unbarred on crown and finely spotted/barred on rear ear-coverts and neck sides. Cheeks and moustachial region red, this colour extending just onto front of ear-coverts. Chin and throat cinnamon-buff, spotted/barred black. Entire upperparts, including upperwing-coverts and tertials, rufous-chestnut, usually paler or yellower on rump, and broadly barred black. Primaries and secondaries black, with cinnamon-rufous bars. Uppertail black, with rufous bars extending variable distance from base towards tip. Underparts rufous, paling to yellow-buff in lower regions, with very broad, irregular wavy bars on breast (breast feathers sometimes black with narrow pale edges, all black with abrasion), bars becoming narrower and more regular on belly and flanks. Underwing cinnamon, barred at bases of flight feathers. Undertail as uppertail but duller, sometimes tinged yellowish.

Adult female As male, but lacks red on head.

Juvenile As adults but duller, with less barring above.

Bare parts Bill dull yellow to yellow-green. Legs and feet green-grey. Eyes red-brown to red.

GEOGRAPHICAL VARIATION Three races.

C. u. undatus (E Venezuela, Guianas and NE Brazil) Described above.

C. u. amacurensis (Delta Amacuro of NE Venezuela) Darker, more chestnut, than nominate, and with head coloured as upperparts (not paler) and rump more cinnamon-rufous (lacking yellow); crown unmarked.

C. u. multifasciatus (Brazil, in Pará east to Tocantins river) Somewhat bigger than above two races, but proportionately shorter-tailed. Plumage paler, more buffy, and streaked (not barred) on crown, ear-coverts and throat; tail often unbarred; paler below, with breast markings generally less heavy. Bill blackish, with paler lower mandible.

MEASUREMENTS Wing 107-120; tail 68. Weight: male 61-73, female 58-68.

VOICE The loud *wit-koa* is very similar to the corresponding call of Scaly-breasted Woodpecker. A soft, husky, whispered *kowahair*, rising in pitch, has also been described. Both sexes drum.

HABITS Forages inconspicuously in the treetops.

FOOD Ants and termites; occasionally seeds.

BREEDING Breeds from end of May to August in the Guianas; possibly in the earlier half of this period in southeast of range. Nest in dead or live tree at 4-30m.

REFERENCES Haverschmidt 1968; Meyer de Schauensee & Phelps 1978; Sick 1993; Snyder 1966; Tostain *et al.* 1992.

---

156 CHESTNUT-COLOURED WOODPECKER
Celeus castaneus   Plate 45

Forms a superspecies with *elegans*, *lugubris* and *flavescens*.

IDENTIFICATION Length c. 23-25cm. Small, with rather short, slightly chisel-tipped bill with curved culmen and fairly narrow across nostrils. An uncommon C American species, dark chestnut in colour with contrasting paler buffish head, latter with long, ragged crest, and with relatively light barring on back and stronger barring below. Male has prominent broad red moustache, and both sexes have a pale bill.

Similar species Overlaps in range with Cinnamon Woodpecker (153), but latter has shorter crest, darker head, a barred tail, and paler and more obviously barred underparts, while male Cinnamon has entire chin and throat red.

DISTRIBUTION C America, from Mexico (S Veracruz, Oaxaca) south through Honduras, Nicaragua and NW Costa Rica to W Panama. Fairly common to common in Mexico, less common further south.

MOVEMENTS Some seasonal movements; wanders into coastal scrub and mangroves in winter.

HABITAT Prefers dense humid evergreen and semi-deciduous forest and tall second growth; resorts to forest edge, and trees with dense foliage and epiphytes, and occasionally found in mangroves. Basically, a woodpecker of the lowlands, which also enters the foothills up to 500m, locally to 750 (1000)m.

DESCRIPTION

Adult male Entire head and crest ochraceous-buff to cinnamon-buff (more golden-tinged on crest), apart from broad area of red on lores, cheeks, moustachial region (and

often on feathers surrounding bill base) and around top of eye, sometimes extending as a line back along crown sides. Upperparts, including upperwing-coverts and tertials, chestnut or rufous-chestnut, paler (yellower) on rump; mantle, back and wing-coverts with variable number of widely spaced broken black bars, and uppertail-coverts unmarked or (more usually) spotted/barred black. Primaries and secondaries dark rufous-brown, blacker at tips, rarely with sparse spots or bars on secondaries. Uppertail dark rufous-chestnut, broadly tipped blackish. Underparts dark rufous-chestnut, with pale feather bases creating a golden-buff area on flanks (not visible on perched bird), all with black U-shaped or V-shaped vermiculations or more regular bars, markings becoming narrower on belly. Underwing with yellowish coverts and with cinnamon bases to dark-tipped flight feathers. Undertail as uppertail, but paler.

Adult female Has head entirely ochraceous-buff, lacking red of male.

Juvenile Duller than adults, often with dark bars on face, and less barred on belly.

Bare parts Bill pale greenish or greenish-white to pale ivory-yellow, tinged blue-green at base. Legs and feet dark olive to grey. Eyes chestnut to brown. Orbital ring grey or blackish.

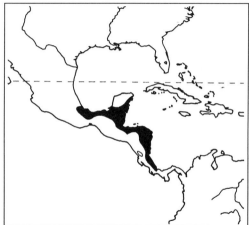

GEOGRAPHICAL VARIATION None. Monotypic.

MEASUREMENTS Wing 120-135; tail 72-90; bill 23-29; tarsus 21-26.6. Weight: 80-105.

VOICE A sibilant, thick, descending whistle, *peew* or *kheeu*, often followed by 2-10 sharp nasal notes, *kheeu, wet-wet-wet...*; rather similar to one call of Red-headed Woodpecker (37). Another vocalisation consists of regular series of trogon-like *howp* notes, which is often followed by a snickering *r'rrp*. Also single, low *kwar*. When excited, a series of sharp double-notes, *wik-kew wik-kew wik-kew*. Drumming rolls last about 1.5 secs, and are shorter and softer than those of Black-cheeked Woodpecker (39).

HABITS Less conspicuous and quieter than Cinnamon Woodpecker, and usually found singly or in pairs, which may feed at very close distance; occasionally with mixed-species flocks. Forages in trees with dense foliage and epiphytes in semi-open, mainly in canopy and subcanopy, down to middle levels along edges. More often on trunks and larger limbs than Cinnamon Woodpecker. Is also able to obtain fruits hanging from distal ends of branches. Pecks into tunnels and hard nests of arboreal termites, and in *Cecropia* trunks; also prises off bark flakes, eating what is uncovered. Pecking and probing are the most frequently seen foraging techniques, followed by hammering and, rarely, gleaning. Moves like a typical woodpecker, but may cling to foliage and may move sideways along a twig.

FOOD Mainly ants and termites, and other insects. Seems to take fruit and arillate seeds (e.g. *Stemmadenia*), and is said to cause damage to cacao.

BREEDING In northern parts of its range breeds from March to June (August), and in Costa Rica and Panama from February to July. The nest is carved, by both sexes, into the soft wood of a living or recently dead tree; 4-21m up, sometimes much lower (e.g. 0.9m in a palm). The clutch contains 3 or 4 eggs (Belize).

REFERENCES Askins 1983; Coates-Estrada *et al.* 1993; Kilham 1979; Land 1970; Ridgely & Gwynne 1989; Russel 1964; Slud 1964; Stiles & Skutch 1989; Wetmore 1968.

---

157 CHESTNUT WOODPECKER
Celeus elegans   Plate 46

Other names: Elegant Woodpecker, Pale-crowned Crested Woodpecker; Chestnut-crested Woodpecker (*jumana* group); Russet-/Rufous-crested Woodpecker (*elegans* group); Yellow-crested Woodpecker (race *leotaudi*)
Forms a superspecies with *castaneus*, *lugubris* and *flavescens*.

IDENTIFICATION Length c. 26-32cm. Small to medium-sized, with short, slightly chisel-tipped bill with curved culmen and fairly narrow across nostrils. A distinctive crested woodpecker, with dark plumage relieved by paler rump (contrasting with black tail), lower underparts and underwing; barring rarely obvious and usually more or less invisible or absent. Males have a red moustache. Populations in northeast corner of range have a longer crest, and entire top of head is paler than rest of head; they also show some white spots on the wing-coverts. This is often a noisy bird, one of the better-known of a generally poorly known genus; it often occurs in small parties, foraging among the lower branches around nests of tree ants. If seen well, unlikely to be confused with other woodpeckers in its range.

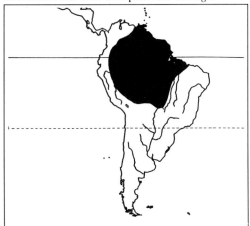

DISTRIBUTION Northern S America, from E Colombia, south through Ecuador and SE Peru to N Bolivia and east through Venezuela to the Guianas, Trinidad, south to N Brazil south of the Amazon (Maranhão, N Mato Grosso, Rondonia). Relatively common.

HABITAT This fairly common woodpecker is found in a variety of tall dense and light forests, including humid *terra*

firme, gallery and *várzea* forests. It also occupies secondary habitats, such as cocoa plantations. Lowlands, between sea level and 1000m in Venezuela and at up to 500m in Colombia and Peru.

DESCRIPTION
C. e. elegans **Adult male** Forehead, crown and long crest buffish-cream. Broad moustachial stripe red. Rest of head, including hindneck, chin and throat, deep chestnut-brown. Mantle, scapulars and back deep rufous-chestnut, usually unmarked but occasionally with faint black bars (rarely, may have yellow feather bases showing through); rump creamy-buff (occasionally some red-tipped feathers); uppertail-coverts usually as rump, sometimes with rufous tips/edges. Upperwing-coverts, tertials, secondaries and inner primaries as back, secondaries barred brown on inner (and sometimes outer) webs, coverts with small white spots or thin shaft streaks, and with creamy area on alula; outer primaries blackish-brown, usually with rufous bars at base of inner webs. Uppertail blackish, with rufous on outermost (concealed) feather. Dark chestnut-brown of throat continues onto breast and underparts (sometimes paler on belly/vent), but with flanks a distinctly paler creamy cinnamon-buff and often obscurely barred. Underwing mainly creamy-buff or pale cinnamon, with browner flight feathers, usually with some barring. Undertail as above, but duller and paler.

Adult female As male, but lacks red moustache.

Juvenile Pattern much as that of adults, but with dull blackish on face and usually mottled darker below. Young males quickly acquire red feathers in moustache and sometimes also in forehead and around eyes.

Bare parts Bill ivory to yellow or greenish-yellow, with darker base, bluish on lower mandible. Legs and feet olive to dark grey. Eyes red-brown to red. Orbital ring blue.

GEOGRAPHICAL VARIATION Occurs in two racial groups, sometimes treated as separate species.

(a) Long-crested, pale-crowned *elegans* group:
   C. e. elegans (French Guiana, adjacent Surinam, and NE Brazil north of Amazon) Described above.
   C. e. hellmayri (E Venezuela, Guyana and most of Surinam) As nominate, but crown darker.
   C. e. deltanus (Delta Amacuro in NE Venezuela) Even darker on crown, but still with long crest.
   C. e. leotaudi (Trinidad) Much smaller than nominate, and paler and brighter, with tawny crown and yellower rump.

(b) Shorter-crested, dark-crowned *jumana* group:
   C. e. jumana (SW Venezuela, E Colombia, NW Brazil, N Bolivia, and Amazonian Brazil south of Amazon) Darker overall than *elegans* group, and with more rufous tertials and secondaries and rufous tips to back and wing-coverts, latter without white spots.
   C. e. citreopygius (E Ecuador and E Peru) Blacker, less rufous, with less yellow in rump and on flanks and less barring in wings.

MEASUREMENTS Wing 132-173, 132-154 (*leotaudi*), 144-167 (*jumana*), 156-166 (*hellmayri*); tail 87-107 (*jumana*), 88-102 (*leotaudi*), 96-99 (*hellmayri*); bill 27-30 (*leotaudi*), 28-32 (*jumana*); tarsus 21-23 (*leotaudi*), 22.9-26.7 (*jumana*). Weight: 93-172; 138-168 (*hellmayri*), 112-146 (*jumana*), 93-139 (*leotaudi*).

VOICE A melodious descending series, *wewa ew-ew-ew-ew-ew-ew*, and rattling screechy (parrot-like) calls, among them a *whick-frrr* or a grating *wháa-jer* or *keeaa*, occasionally rapidly repeated several times; also a *wick-wick-wick...* and a mellow *gwarrr*. Drums (both sexes) frequently and loudly in breeding season: a double rap, *dop-dop*.

HABITS Alone or in pairs or loose groups of up to five birds, frequently associated with mixed-species flocks. Forages inconspicuously mainly at low to medium heights, from the understorey to the subcanopy; moves along larger limbs and trunks. Feeding techniques include gleaning from bark and hammering into arboreal-termite nests.

FOOD Feeds on ants and termites; also dipteran larvae. Also takes fruits (e.g. *Cecropia*, citrus) and berries.

BREEDING Drumming activity has been noted in February in Colombia and in November-February in Trinidad. Enlarged gonads indicate breeding in January-February in S Venezuela and NW Brazil; breeds April-May in French Guiana and Trinidad. The nest, in a dead tree or stub, contains a clutch of 3 eggs.

REFERENCES ffrench 1973; Haverschmidt 1968; Hilty & Brown 1984; Meyer de Schauensee & Phelps 1978; Parker *et al.* 1982; Short 1972b; Sick 1993; Snyder 1966; Willard *et al.* 1991.

---

158 PALE-CRESTED WOODPECKER
Celeus lugubris   Plate 46

Forms a superspecies with *castaneus*, *elegans* and *flavescens*.

IDENTIFICATION Length c. 23-24cm. Smallish, with fairly long, slightly chisel-tipped bill curved on culmen and rather narrow across nostrils. Very distinctive, with long-crested blond-coloured head (male with red moustache), heavily barred back, plain blond rump contrasting with black tail, and all-dark underparts. Flight feathers, including tertials, are characteristically barred with rufous, this feature distinguishing it from very similar Blond-crested Woodpecker (159). Pale-crested has interbred with Chestnut Woodpecker (157) and probably also with Blond-crested, but such events appear to be very infrequent.

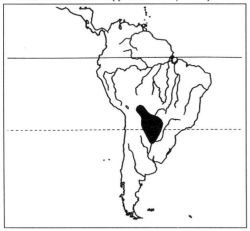

DISTRIBUTION Central S America, in the chaco from NC Bolivia (Beni), through C Mato Grosso, south to Paraguay (not in extreme east) and to NE Argentina (Chaco, Tucumán, Corrientes). Fairly common.

HABITAT This is a woodpecker of dry chaco woodland, semi-deciduous forests and cerrado woodlands. It is frequently seen in areas with palms.

DESCRIPTION
C. l. lugubris **Adult male** Lores, feathering next to nostrils and some feather bases below and behind eye dark brown. Broad moustachial stripe red, this colour occasionally continuing onto forehead and around eyes. Rest of head and crest, plus chin and throat, pale blond to buffish, sometimes tinged cinnamon, and often with some brown feathering joining rear moustache with breast. Hindneck, mantle, upper back and scapulars dark rufous-black, all but hindneck with narrow whitish to pale cinnamon-buff bars; lower back and rump blond to creamy-buff, sometimes with cinnamon tinge; longest uppertail-coverts rufous, with black subterminally. Upperwing-coverts blackish, barred/edged whitish to pale buff; flight feathers blackish-brown, barred rufous on basal half, with tertials fully barred rufous. Uppertail black, with outer (concealed) feathers black-spotted rufous. Underparts dark sooty-rufous, usually with a few brighter rufous feather edges, and becoming more creamy and rufous where flanks meet rump; thighs creamy, variably barred dark; undertail-coverts black, with rufous bars/spots. Underwing brown, barred pale buff or cinnamon, with creamy axillaries and coverts. Undertail as uppertail, but duller.

Adult female Lacks red on face, having moustachial area barred or scaly brown.

Juvenile Much as adults, but with large blackish areas on head and with barring above irregular.

Bare parts Bill greyish to horn-coloured, with paler or ivory-coloured lower mandible. Legs and feet grey. Eyes dark red to red-brown. Orbital ring bluish-grey.

GEOGRAPHICAL VARIATION Two races.
    C. l. lugubris (E Bolivia and western Mato Grosso) Described above.
    C. l. kerri (Paraguay and southern Mato Grosso southwards) Slightly larger and darker than nominate.

MEASUREMENTS Wing 138-148 (*lugubris*), 142-150 (*kerri*); tail 80-92 (*lugubris*), 82-86 (*kerri*); bill 26.3-27.3 (*lugubris*), 21.2-23 (*lugubris*, from nostril) 22-23.2 (*kerri*, from nostril); tarsus 24.1-26 (*lugubris*), 25.3-26.7 (*kerri*). Weight: 115-130 (*lugubris*), (97)134-157 (*kerri*).

VOICE Call *wee-wee-week*. Drums weakly.

HABITS Utilises the middle stratum of its arboreal habitats. Forages by probing, gleaning and pecking. Dead wood is excavated to gain access to tunnels of ants, which are obtained with the sticky tongue.

FOOD *Camponotus, Crematogaster, Dolichoderus* and other ants and their brood.

BREEDING Nesting season spans September-November, or later in the south. Nest hole is excavated in trees or dug into the nests of arboreal ants or termites, at 4-10m.

REFERENCES Dubs 1992; Olrog 1984; Short 1970a, 1972b, 1975.

159 BLOND-CRESTED WOODPECKER
Celeus flavescens   Plate 46

Forms a superspecies with *castaneus*, *elegans* and *lugubris*.

IDENTIFICATION Length c. 25-30cm. Smallish to medium-sized, with medium-long, almost pointed bill with curved culmen and fairly narrow across nostrils. Another striking but very little-known woodpecker of S America. As Pale-crested Woodpecker (158), has long-crested pale creamy head (male with red moustache), barred back, and pale creamy rump with contrasting black tail; underparts are all blackish. The flight feathers and tertials are boldly barred white (not rufous as on Pale-crested). The lower Amazon race has back and wing-coverts mostly buffish with black heart-shaped markings, while those breeding in the area between the two forms (in EC Brazil) are more or less intermediate.

Similar species Pale-crested Woodpecker, whose range just overlaps that of Blond-crested in Paraguay, is similar, but has rusty barring on the flight feathers.

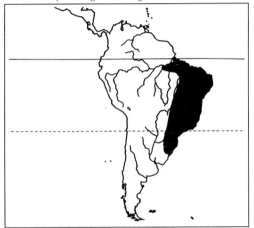

DISTRIBUTION Eastern S America, in Brazil south of the lower Amazon and Rio Tocantins from Maranhão and Pará to SE Mato Grosso and Rio Grande do Sul, west to E Paraguay and Argentina (Misiones). Not uncommon.

HABITAT This woodpecker lives in humid forests, also in savannas and caatinga. It is found at forest edge, and in gallery forest and orchards.

DESCRIPTION
C. f. flavescens **Adult male** Broad moustachial stripe red, this colour sometimes spreading beneath eye, and occasionally lower forehead also red. Rest of head and crest, together with hindneck, chin and throat, pale creamy-buff to yellowish-white, sometimes with a few dark spots on lores and often black streaks (or feather centres) joining rear moustache with breast. Mantle, upper back and scapulars black, narrowly barred white; lower back, rump and uppertail-coverts buffish-white to pale yellow, tail-coverts sometimes with black barring. Upperwing-coverts black, tipped/edged and barred white; flight feathers black, narrowly barred white, but tertials with broad white tips and diagonal bars. Uppertail black, outer (concealed) feather edged/barred whitish. Underparts below throat black, often with hint of paler or even rufous barring on flanks and undertail-coverts; thighs pale yellow or buffish, streaked/spotted black. Underwing as upperwing, but with buffish coverts. Undertail as uppertail, but duller.

Adult female As male, but with red of moustache replaced by black streaks.

Juvenile Duller than adults, with more black around face.

Bare parts Bill horn-coloured or bluish-grey to black, paler (ivory) on lower mandible. Legs and feet blue-grey. Eyes red or red-brown. Orbital ring blue-grey.

GEOGRAPHICAL VARIATION Two distinctive races and one intermediate.
C. f. flavescens (E Paraguay to Rio de Janeiro and southwards) Described above. The largest race.
C. f. ochraceus (lower Amazon and E Brazil south to E Bahia) Smaller and less bulky than nominate, with less black. Head is more buffy or cinnamon-tinged, sometimes with much black around eyes; mantle, back and upperwing-coverts more cinnamon-buff, with variable black spots and heart-shaped markings; rump darker, sometimes cinnamon, with black marks; bars in flight feathers broader and more cinnamon-buff; underparts more sooty, often with buffy-cinnamon feather edges, flanks usually with much cinnamon-buff. Juveniles may have most of head brownish-black. Apparently intergrades with nominate in E Brazil (between SW Bahia and Espírito Santo), where the following, intermediate, race seems to be absent.
C. f. intercedens (W Bahia south to Minas Gerais) Intermediate in size and plumage between above two races, but rather stable. Pale areas whitish to buffy-white, with narrow, irregular black barring above, and black below; may show some rufous in flight feathers.

MEASUREMENTS Wing 133-165, 141-148 (*ochraceus*), 152-162 (*flavescens*); tail 80-88 (*ochraceus*), 88-98 (*flavescens*); bill (from nostril) 20.1-22.7 (*ochraceus*), 23.4-27.9 (*flavescens*); tarsus 22.7-25.9 (*ochraceus*), 26.3-28.8 (*flavescens*). Weight: 110-165 (*flavescens*).

VOICE A resonant *tsew tsew tsew-tsew*, *wee-wee-week*, or *wheep wheep...*, with notes well separated. Also an aggressive *tttrrr* and raucous *wicket wicket*. Drums weakly.

HABITS This little-known woodpecker is seen in pairs or small family groups. Mainly an arboreal species, which may, however, descend to the ground to search for insects. Forages on slender branches with gleaning, probing, and also pecking and hammering, particularly on dead branches. Crest frequently raised and lowered.

FOOD Arboreal ants (*Dolichoderus*, *Crematogaster*), *Camponotus*, and termites are an important part of the diet. Also eats fruits and berries regularly.

BREEDING October-November in Argentina and April-June in E Brazil. Nest hole is excavated into the nest of arboreal ants.

REFERENCES Belton 1984; Olrog 1984; Short 1970a, 1972b; Sick 1993.

160 CREAM-COLOURED WOODPECKER
Celeus flavus   Plate 47

IDENTIFICATION Length c. 24-26cm. Medium-sized, with fairly long, slightly chisel-tipped bill with curved culmen and rather narrow across nostrils. Quite unmistakable: plumage, including long crest, almost entirely pale creamy-buff or yellowish (or even sulphur-yellow), apart from black tail, dark wings and, on male, a red moustache. Easternmost population is browner on breast and mantle. Plumage becomes less bright with wear and soiling. Voice includes a distinctive high-pitched laugh.

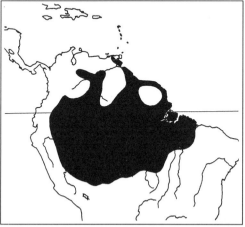

DISTRIBUTION Northern S America, from E Colombia, Venezuela and the Guianas in the north, south to Brazil (Mato Grosso, Espírito Santo) in the east, and through E Ecuador and E Peru to N Bolivia (Beni). Seems to be not uncommon.

HABITAT Often found near water and frequents rain forest, such as *várzea* and swamp forests, occasionally gallery forest, mangroves, deciduous woodland, open woodland and second growth; may also be encountered in other secondary habitats, such as cacao plantations. Essentially a bird of the lowlands, this woodpecker ranges up to 700m.

DESCRIPTION
C. f. flavus **Adult male** Moustachial stripe bright red, sometimes pale-streaked. Apart from wings and tail, entire rest of plumage pale creamy-yellow, buffish, sulphur-yellow or occasionally cinnamon-white, not infrequently with a few brown feathers or feather bases visible (especially on head, mantle and back). Upperwing-coverts variable, but usually with brown bases and sometimes all brown or rufous-brown. Flight feathers variable, usually brown with rufous-chestnut inner webs and edges to outer webs; tertials usually as back and unmarked, but sometimes darker and rarely with one or more dark bars. Uppertail blackish-brown, outer (concealed) feather occasionally with pale bars. Underwing brownish, with creamy-buff coverts and axillaries. (Plumage frequently becomes soiled and discoloured, especially around head and underparts, and with wear may acquire browner tone as darker feather bases start to show.)

Adult female As male, but lacks red moustache.

Juvenile As adults, but usually somewhat more buff or cinnamon-buff and often with some barring on tertials. Young males soon acquire red tips to moustachial feathers.

Bare parts Bill yellowish. Legs and feet dark grey to green-grey. Eyes red or reddish-brown.

GEOGRAPHICAL VARIATION Appears to vary greatly individually, with many intermediates between the four races described below. Delimiting the ranges of the latter is therefore problematic, and in some cases perhaps rather arbitrary, but the ranges given represent areas where more 'typical' examples of the subspecies may be expected. Nominate intergrades with *peruvianus* from NW Brazil to E Ecuador, and with *tectricialis* in E Brazil south of Amazon, while all of the first three races below intergrade in W Brazil south of the Amazon.

  C. f. flavus (north part of range) Described above. Shows the greatest amount of rufous or chestnut colouring in wing.

  C. f. peruvianus (E Peru) Slightly bigger than nominate. Rufous in wings replaced mostly or entirely by brown.

  C. f. tectricialis (Maranhão in NE Brazil) Size much as nominate, but wings more as *peruvianus* (coverts with much brown and flight feathers with much less rufous).

  C. f. subflavus (Bahia and Espírito Santo in E Brazil) Larger than other races. No rufous in wings; feathers of mantle and breast show broad brown bases and centres.

MEASUREMENTS Wing 132-151; tail 83-92; bill 25-28.7; tarsus 23.6-26.6. Weight: 95-131 (*flavus*).

VOICE The most notable call is a high, clear, laughing *wutchuk...kee-hoo-hoo-hoo, pueer, pueer, purr, paw*, or *glew glew glew glew glew*, with the last note lower in pitch. Also a *kiu-kiu-kiu-kiu*, or *whéejah*, which may be repeated and is heard during encounters involving several birds. Generally, calls are higher-pitched and not so rasping as those of Chestnut Woodpecker (157).

HABITS Not shy, and is observed singly, but mostly in pairs or in groups of three or four. It forages in the lower and middle parts of trees, where it specialises in breaking into the nests of arboreal ants. Descends to the ground sometimes.

FOOD Ants (*Crematogaster*) and termites; also eats fruit and seeds.

BREEDING Breeding season extends from April to June in Colombia, possibly somewhat earlier in Venezuela.

REFERENCES Haverschmidt 1968; Hilty & Brown 1984; Meyer de Schauensee & Phelps 1978; Parker & Parker 1982; Sick 1993; Snyder 1966.

161 RUFOUS-HEADED WOODPECKER
Celeus spectabilis   Plate 47

IDENTIFICATION Length c. 26-28cm. Medium-sized, with fairly short, chisel-tipped bill slightly curved on culmen and relatively broad across nostrils. A very little-known woodpecker. Has rufous-chestnut head with long bushy crest (male with red moustache and much red in crest), black-barred buff back and wing-coverts, plain buff rump contrasting with black tail, black breast patch, and heavy to lighter barring below; flight feathers are rufous-chestnut. A virtually unknown and isolated race in E Brazil is very different and much paler-looking, with hardly any barring above or below (see Geographical Variation).

DISTRIBUTION Rare and restricted to central S America, from E Ecuador (Sucumbíos, Napo, Pastaza) and E Peru to

N Bolivia (Cochabamba, Beni); also in E Brazil (W Piauí) in the east.

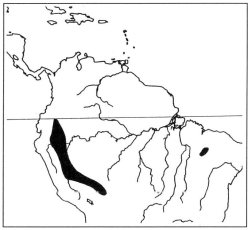

HABITAT Frequents humid tropical forests, especially along rivers and on river islands, often with bamboo or *Gynerium* understorey. Lowlands to about 300m.

DESCRIPTION

***C. s. spectabilis* Adult male** Entire head and crest rufous-chestnut, apart from red moustache, yellow to creamy-buff patch on lower neck side (extending down side of breast), and large area of dull red from above ear-coverts and into crest; lower throat to breast black. Hindneck, mantle, upper back and scapulars creamy-buff to pale cinnamon-yellow, very broadly barred black; lower back, rump and uppertail-coverts yellow-buff or cinnamon-buff, occasionally with a few black streaks. Upperwing-coverts black, edged and narrowly barred creamy-buff; primaries brownish-black with rufous at base, becoming more rufous on inner primaries and wholly rufous-chestnut with black tips on secondaries and tertials, shorter tertials usually barred black. Uppertail black, outer (concealed) feather sometimes pale-barred. Black of lower throat extends as large patch onto breast; breast sides and rest of underparts creamy-buff to pale cinnamon-buff, with black of breast breaking up into heavy bars, which become more like arrowhead markings on flanks and lower underparts. Underwing rufous-cinnamon, with black-barred cinnamon-buff coverts. Undertail as uppertail, but paler or duller.

Adult female Lacks red on head, but may show some hint of red in crest.

Juvenile As adults, but with much blackish colour around front of head and with more red in crown area.

Bare parts Bill pale yellowish or greyish-ivory, with greyer base; darker generally in juveniles. Legs and feet olive-green to greyish. Eyes deep brown.

GEOGRAPHICAL VARIATION Three well-differentiated races.

C. s. spectabilis (E Ecuador and NE Peru) Described above.

C. s. exsul (SE Peru and N Bolivia) As nominate, but less barred above and much less barred below, with heart-shaped or arrowhead markings below black breast patch and just a few spots on belly and bars on flanks.

C. s. obrieni (E Brazil) Virtually unknown. Smaller than above two races. Differs in being almost unmarked on back and lower underparts (has a few bars on mantle and one or two beneath black breast patch); wing-coverts are creamy-buff with only small heart-shaped central marks, and tertials creamy-buff with irregular black spots/streaks; underwing-coverts unbarred, and small outer tail feather pale buffish with black markings. Appears to have a yellower bill.

MEASUREMENTS Wing 136-153; tail 91-100 (*spectabilis*); bill (from skull) 29-30 (*spectabilis*). Weight: 111 (*exsul*).

VOICE Not described.

HABITS Forages singly or in pairs from dense undergrowth to the middle and upper levels of the forest. Also descends to the ground to work over fallen logs. Pecks rather forcefully and more frequently than most of its congeners, except possibly Ringed Woodpecker (162).

FOOD Not known.

BREEDING Breeding season probably June-November.

REFERENCES Parker *et al.* 1982.

162 RINGED WOODPECKER
Celeus torquatus   Plate 47

IDENTIFICATION Length c. 26-28cm. Medium-sized, with long, almost straight, chisel-tipped bill relatively broad across nostrils. A very poorly known yet distinctive species. Large, crested head is contrastingly paler than rufous upperparts, breast is fully black, and tail is barred rufous and black. Males have a red moustache. Those in northeast of range have black upper mantle joining the black breast (black thus encircles body), virtually unmarked upperparts, and plain cinnamon-buff lower underparts. All other populations are black-barred above and from lower breast to undertail-coverts. If seen reasonably well, neither form should present any identification difficulties.

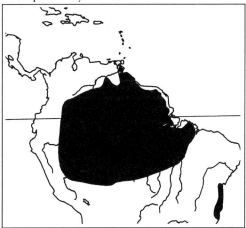

DISTRIBUTION S America, from E Colombia, Venezuela and the Guianas, in the east south to Amazonian Brazil, to Mato Grosso and Maranhão, and in the west south through Ecuador and E Peru to N Bolivia. Uncommon to rare. The isolated subspecies *tinnunculus*, endemic to forest remnants of E Brazil (Bahia, Espírito Santo), is regarded as endangered.

HABITAT Ringed Woodpeckers are fond of tall and humid forests, and therefore frequent rain and gallery forests and also tall second growth and clearings. The altitudinal range extends from 100 to 500m.

DESCRIPTION

***C. t. torquatus* Adult male** Most of head and crest, including hindneck, chin and upper throat, pale rufous-tinged cinnamon, occasionally with tinge of reddish on forehead and sides of crest. Moustachial stripe red, reaching to lower edge of ear-coverts. Black lower throat and line from rear moustache join with black of breast and upper mantle. Entire upperparts from lower mantle to uppertail-coverts, including wing-coverts and tertials, rufous-brown, sometimes with one or two black feathers invading lower mantle and usually with black subterminal bars or V-shaped marks on coverts and one or two (or more) bars on tertials. Flight feathers barred black and rufous, rufous more extensive on secondaries. Uppertail rufous, narrowly barred black and with broader black tip. Black of breast sharply demarcated from unmarked cinnamon-buff of rest of underparts. Underwing cinnamon-buff, with faint barring on primaries. Undertail much as uppertail.

Adult female Lacks red on head.

Juvenile As adults, but with much black on front of head and more barred.

Bare parts Bill grey to yellowish-grey or dull olive-yellow/brown, with paler lower mandible. Legs and feet dark grey. Eyes red to red-brown or brown.

GEOGRAPHICAL VARIATION Three races.

C. t. torquatus (E Venezuela and the Guianas to Pará in NE Brazil) Described above. Intergrades with *occidentalis* in NE Brazil and presumably elsewhere.

C. t. occidentalis (S Venezuela, W and C Amazonian Brazil, E Peru and N Bolivia) Upperparts and wings more barred (but barring variable, sometimes rather weak), and lower breast to undertail-coverts much whiter and moderately to heavily barred; upper mantle black or, more usually, barred rufous and black. Head somewhat darker, more cinnamon-tinged.

C. t. tinnunculus (isolated in E Brazil) As *occidentalis*, but with paler head and more heavily barred above and below (bars on wing much broader); outer tail feathers mostly black, and underwing more strongly barred. Rufous coloration above tends to be somewhat brighter.

MEASUREMENTS Wing 145-161; 151-153 (*torquatus*), 156-157 (*occidentalis*); tail 100-107; bill 31.6-33.1 (*torquatus*), 30.4-34.3 (*occidentalis*); tarsus 21-25. Weight: 107-124 (*torquatus*), c. 134 (*occidentalis*).

VOICE The only call so far described for Ringed Woodpecker is a loud, whistled *kuu kuu kuu kuu* or *peeee peeee peeee...*, recalling the vocalisations of Least Pygmy Owl *Glaucidium minutissimum.*

HABITS Foraging behaviour, and habits in general, are little known. Seems to prefer trunks, and is therefore commonly seen at lower and middle levels of trees; appears, however, to favour the higher sections of the trunk, and some observers have noted this species high up in the canopy. Probably pecks relatively frequently and strongly.

FOOD Ants and seeds have been recorded.

BREEDING No details known.

REFERENCES Haverschmidt 1968; Hilty & Brown 1984; Meyer de Schauensee & Phelps 1978; Parker *et al.* 1982; Sick 1993; Willard *et al.* 1991.

163 HELMETED WOODPECKER
Dryocopus galeatus   Plate 48

IDENTIFICATION Length c. 27-28cm. Medium-sized, with fairly long, slightly chisel-tipped bill with curved culmen and rather broad across nostrils. A very little-known and endangered species of eastern S America. Mainly black and white, with a long red crest, white neck stripe, white rump and entirely barred underparts; the face is buffish, barred dark, and the chin and throat plain buffy-cinnamon. Male has red moustache. The head pattern, fully barred underparts and white rump should render this woodpecker unmistakable for the observer fortunate enough to come across it.

Similar species Note that Lineated Woodpecker (165) may, in poor views, appear superficially similar, especially in Iguazú region of N Misiones (where Lineated shows much rufous on its underparts).

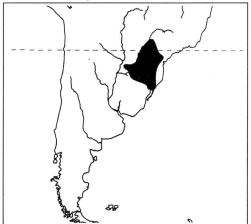

DISTRIBUTION Range small, covering the SE Brazil provinces of São Paulo, Paraná and Santa Catarina (probably extinct in Rio Grande do Sul, where it was restricted to the coastal northwest) on the Atlantic coast, inland to adjacent E Paraguay and N Misiones, Argentina. Although sightings more numerous since mid 1980s, habitat loss and degradation justify its being listed as endangered by Birdlife International.

HABITAT Generally, a woodpecker of tall forests. It has been recorded in primary forest, disturbed and even logged (primary) forest, so long as it is not severely affected. Association with bamboo probably accidental. In lowland valleys, and in cloud forest to 725-900m.

DESCRIPTION
Adult male Forehead cinnamon, becoming red from crown to crest and nape (sometimes with buff/black feather bases showing through). Lores rusty-cinnamon. Ear-coverts and area beneath eye rusty-cinnamon, narrowly vermiculated black. Moustachial stripe with feather bases barred cinnamon and black and tips red, the red often extending beneath eye, onto fore ear-coverts, onto throat and even sometimes around rear ear-coverts to meet red of crest. White stripe from lower rear edge of ear-coverts down neck side to upper breast side. Chin and throat rusty-cinnamon, lower throat usually barred dark. Hindneck, mantle, scapulars and upper back brownish-black to black; lower back, rump and uppertail-coverts (latter very long) creamy-buff, often tinged pale cinnamon, sometimes with a few darker bars on middle back and occasionally on rump.

Upperwing and its coverts brownish-black, inner flight feathers with cinnamon bases. Uppertail black. Lower throat and upper breast blackish, barred cinnamon; central breast to undertail-coverts whitish-buff to cinnamon-buff and entirely barred black. Underwing greyish-brown, with cinnamon coverts and inner wing, coverts variably barred black. Undertail dull blackish.

Adult female Slightly smaller-billed than male, but with somewhat longer wings and tail. Lacks red in moustache and face.

Juvenile Little known, but browner, less black, than adults and with less red on crown; also, ear-coverts grey and more extensively barred.

Bare parts Bill grey to blue-grey, with paler, ivory-coloured, tip. Legs and feet dark grey. Eyes brown.

GEOGRAPHICAL VARIATION None. Monotypic.

MEASUREMENTS Wing 161-174; tail 92-114; bill 31.5-35, tarsus 22.8-24.4. Weight. 124.

VOICE The most common call, probably associated with territorial behaviour, is a loud ringing series of 2-6 notes, *keer-keer-keer-keer-keer-keer* (similar calls of Lineated Woodpecker are longer, faster and less ringing). The pair contact is maintained with less loud, mournful *tu-hu-u-u-u-u* series, of which another call, *kee-doo-doo-doo-doo-doo*, is probably a variant. Startled birds utter soft *chic* notes. Intimate calls between the pair are rendered *che-che-che*. Drumming pattern has been likened to that of *Celeus* species, with further details apparently not described.

HABITS Found mostly singly or in pairs. Forages at 14-15m in the forest interior and lower, down to 2-5m, at forest edge, on branches of a broad range of sizes (2-30cm in diameter), which may also be covered with mosses and lichens. Obtains its prey by removing bark, often combined with pecking, probing under bark, and some gleaning. Hammers only occasionally, with little persistence and without creating large cavities.

FOOD Takes (beetle) larvae living under bark.

BREEDING Present evidence suggests a breeding season from September through to February. Nest seems to be low down (2-3m), which, considering the foraging habits of this species, is somewhat surprising. No further details on the reproduction of this interesting woodpecker are known.

REFERENCES Belton 1984; Collar *et al.* 1992, 1994; Brooks *et al.* 1993; Olrog 1984; Sick 1993.

---

164 PILEATED WOODPECKER
Dryocopus pileatus   Plate 48

Forms a superspecies with *lineatus* and *schulzi*.

IDENTIFICATION Length c. 40-48cm. Very big, with long, broad, chisel-tipped bill slightly curved on culmen. When perched, appears almost entirely black with conspicuous bright red crown and crest, white supercilium and throat, and white band running back from lores and down neck side to upper flanks. Male has a red moustache. In flight, which is only slightly undulating, both sexes reveal very prominent white area on front half of underwing and some white at bases of upper primaries and outer secondaries. Plumage coloration and very large size preclude confusion with any other species within its range, where it has more recently adapted to areas of human habitation. Drums and taps frequently and loudly.

Similar species The even bigger Ivory-billed Woodpecker (180), with pale bill, black throat and crown and more white in wings, is now presumed extinct.

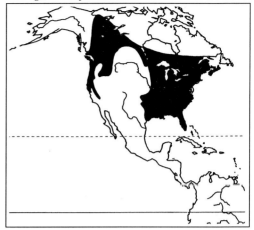

DISTRIBUTION Ranges from S British Columbia east across S Canada to Nova Scotia. In the east, found in the forested parts east of the Plains from E North Dakota to E Oklahoma and E Texas throughout to the Atlantic coast south to Florida. In the west, south through Washington and Oregon to NC California and east to Idaho and Montana. Like its European congener (169), this species was forced to retreat during the period of extensive land clearance, but has regained much of its former range from about 1920 onwards. Generally rather local and not common, but numbers appear to be increasing in eastern parts of range.

HABITAT Inhabits various kinds of forest, deciduous and mixed deciduous and coniferous. These habitats include rather open deciduous to dense mature coniferous stands. Mature, tall and extensive stands are favoured. Found also in second growth, so long as some large trees are present and it is at least 5 years old. Also enters suburbs and parks. Data from Oregon and elsewhere suggest that, for foraging, Pileated Woodpeckers prefer riparian woodland and stands older than 40 years. Nesting habitats are of even greater age, over 70 years old, and often close to water. Juniper woodland and pure pine monocultures are avoided. From sea level to above 1500m in eastern mountains and to about 2300m in the West.

DESCRIPTION
D. p. abieticola **Adult male** Lower forehead/nasal tufts buffish; rest of forehead, crown and long crest bright red. Narrow white supercilium from above eye to side of nape. Black band from upper rear lores through and slightly below eye and upper ear-coverts, becoming narrow at rear and meeting upper hindneck. White stripe from base of upper mandible back to rear neck side, expanding and continuing broadly down side of neck to upper flanks. Moustachial stripe dark red, becoming black at rear and joining with black of foreneck. Chin and upper throat white, sometimes with greyish central streaks. Hindneck and entire upperparts slaty-black to black. Upperwing black, with small white tips to outer primaries and larger area of white at bases of primaries and outer secondaries; alula and primary coverts variably edged white. Uppertail black, initially with small white tips. Lower throat to undertail-coverts greyish-black to blackish, narrowly barred grey on flanks and sometimes also on belly. Underwing white on coverts, axillaries and bases of flight feathers

337

(white joining with white of neck stripe), primary coverts barred blackish, and with broad black tip and trailing edge. Undertail dark greyish. (In worn plumage, black areas become browner, brownish or buff feather bases become visible on crown and in moustache, and narrow white tips to primaries and tail are lost.)

Adult female Somewhat smaller and shorter-billed than male. Has forehead and forecrown black, or black with some brown-buff feather tips, often also with some red tips, and moustache is fully black.

Juvenile Duller than adults, greyer or more sooty, with throat greyish or grey-streaked/barred. Young male has orange-red tips and grey-brown bases to feathers of forehead, crown and small crest, and only vague red tips in moustache; female similar, but has grey-brown forehead, forecrown and crown sides and lacks all red in moustache.

Bare parts Bill slate-grey, with pale bluish-white base to lower mandible and blackish tip. Legs and feet dark blue-grey to brownish-black or grey-black. Eyes pale yellow; blue-grey or slaty in juveniles. Orbital skin greyish-olive; paler in juveniles.

GEOGRAPHICAL VARIATION Varies only a little geographically and mostly clinally. Two races are recognised here.

> **D. p. abieticola** (northern and western part of species' range) Described above. Varies somewhat individually, some westernmost birds having throat all grey or greyish and little or no grey barring below.
> **D. p. pileatus** (southern part of range) Slightly smaller and noticeably shorter-billed than northern abieticola. Florida population averages blacker than others, but matched by some individuals from other areas. A melanistic individual, lacking white markings, has been recorded from Georgia.

MEASUREMENTS Wing 220-253 (abieticola), 214-235 (pileatus); tail 148-174 (abieticola), 140-161 (pileatus); bill 50-60 (abieticola), 41-53 (pileatus); tarsus 33-37.8 (abieticola), 31-35 (pileatus). Weight: 250-340 (abieticola).

VOICE The most general call of this species is single or repeated wuk, cuk or cac notes, particularly on the wing; these are used, among other things, for contact between the pair members; they may be given when approaching the roosting area, and are delivered in series by alarmed birds. Fast, accelerating series of wuk notes also occur. Higher-pitched calls are given upon landing. Mewing calls are associated with sexual activities. During encounters and associated with visual displays, various repeated waak, woick woick and wok notes are uttered. The intimate call (close contact of the pair preceding copulation; during changeovers) is low in pitch, waaa, sometimes repeated in irregular series. Young give squeaking to churring calls. Drum rolls are distinctive in their loudness and full timbre and because they accelerate at the end; they are usually 1-2 secs long and delivered at a rate of 1-2 rolls per minute. Adults in the nest may give loud taps when the partner approaches; double raps may be delivered in the context of copulatory behaviour and hole demonstration.

HABITS Mostly seen singly; paired birds keep loose contact and 'pairs' may roost relatively close together in the non-breeding season. Not very shy. Feeds at all levels, including the ground, where it descends to work over fallen logs or to rob anthills. Dead wood is preferred for foraging. This is a typical excavating woodpecker which often hammers for long periods at one spot. Pecking and hammering comprise 60-95% of the foraging activities in winter. Scaling of bark is also very important. Probing and, even less so, gleaning are minor foraging techniques; they are most important in the breeding season, comprising almost 20% of the foraging activities. Plucks fruit from very thin branches. Seasonal trends in habitat use are not obvious. Flight direct and crow-like, sometimes with an upward swoop or bounding for brief periods (at approaches to a hole). Displays include crest-raising and wing-spreading. Head-swinging displays (bill-waving threat dance) may contain a strong bobbing component and in such displays, which are accompanied by wok-type notes, the head may be raised very high. When the struggle escalates the birds stab at each other. An exaggerated flight, flashing the white parts of the wing, occurs in the mating season, as well as a flutter-aerial-display, or glide. Both sexes defend the territory at its boundaries by calling and drumming; nevertheless, the large (about 480ha, post-breeding) home ranges may overlap by up to 30%. Roosts are used by single birds only. Interspecific interactions involve mainly hole competitors, e.g. squirrels, bluebirds, starlings, flickers and Wood Ducks Aix sponsa.

FOOD The staple is carpenter ants (Camponotus), complemented by larvae of wood-boring beetles, termites and caterpillars. The importance of fruits (cherries, dogwood, wild grapes and the like), berries (e.g. holly, poison ivy, hackberry) and nuts (e.g. acorn, pecan) varies locally; they may comprise almost a third of the diet. Fruits and suet are accepted at feeders.

BREEDING Courtship activities commence as early as winter; eggs are laid in April-May (June). A new nest is usually excavated each year, by both sexes, in the main trunk of old living (in about two-thirds of cases) or long-dead trees with breast-height diameter of 33-91cm, usually exceeding 40cm. Often nests away from clearings, but also on edge, and even in power poles. Nest height varies from 6 to 12 (4-30)m. Nest is completed in about 25 days. Clutch size ranges from 2-4 (5) eggs, average 3.8, and is subject to some latitudinal variation, being larger in northern populations. Incubation, by both sexes, takes about 18 days, with the male incubating at night. Both parents feed the young by regurgitation, brood the young chicks and participate in nest sanitation. Some old records aside, the male seems to take the greater share in nest excavation and brood care. The young fledge after 26-28 days; the parents each feed part of the fledged brood. Family groups may stay together until the time of juvenile dispersal in autumn.

REFERENCES Askins 1983; Bent 1939; Conner 1979, 1980; Conner & Adkisson 1977; Conner & Crawford 1974; Conner et al. 1975; Hoyt 1957; Kilham 1959e, 1973b, 1974a; Koenig 1986; Mellen et al. 1992.

---

165 LINEATED WOODPECKER
Dryocopus lineatus   Plate 48

Other name: Black-mantled Woodpecker (race erythrops)
Forms a superspecies with pileatus and schulzi.

IDENTIFICATION Length c. 30-36cm. Medium-sized to largish, with long, chisel-tipped bill slightly curved on culmen and broad across nostrils. When perched, appears largely black, with red crown and prominent crest, white neck stripe and (except in W Mexico) white band across lower face; usually has a white line on the scapulars, but this is absent in southeast of range (and may also be much reduced when plumage is worn). Male has red moustache. Underparts are barred black and pale from belly to undertail-coverts, with dark breast and dark-streaked throat. Southwestern population is much browner, both above and below, with underpart markings more obscure. Has small amount of pale colour in carpal area, white bases to primaries and white underwing-coverts. Northern birds have a pale bill, and all have pale eyes.

Similar species Black-bodied Woodpecker (166), which meets race *erythrops* of Lineated in parts of Paraguay, Argentina and Bolivia, has a similar face pattern but with paler (grey) ear-coverts and yellowish area at base of bill, and unbarred dark underparts with plain pale throat; it also has a much paler bill and dark eyes, and shows white shafts in rectrices as opposed to Lineated's dark tail shafts (note, incidentally, that Black-bodied can also have white scapular line present or lacking, as in *erythrops*). The two are known to interbreed, at least to some extent (see Black-bodied). A number of *Campephilus* woodpeckers occur within the range of Lineated, but all have more red on the head (females of some with black crowns) and lack red or black moustaches, as well as differing in other ways.

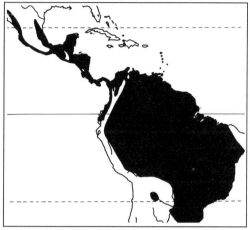

DISTRIBUTION Widely distributed from Mexico (from Tamaulipas and Sonora) south through C America, Colombia, Peru and Paraguay to NE Argentina (Misiones, Chaco, Corrientes), extending east to the Guianas and Trinidad and S Brazil (Rio Grande do Sul). Fairly common to common throughout most of its range.

HABITAT This woodpecker is a bird of humid, transitional and moderately dry areas, but avoids xerophytic areas or marshes (but frequents mangroves). Although it may occasionally be found in dense forests or tall rain forest, more open areas are preferred generally; may therefore be especially numerous around new clearings and at forest edge. It enters pinelands and gallery forest in drier areas, and can also be seen in shaded gardens, moriche groves (Venezuela), on trees in pastures and cultivations, and particularly in second growth with sufficiently large trees (e.g. fast-growing *Cecropia*). Lineated Woodpeckers occur in lowlands, foothills, and even higher, to 1200-2100m.

DESCRIPTION

D. l. lineatus **Adult male** Forehead, crown and crest bright red, often with some dark grey feather bases visible. Area from upper lores, above and below eye and across ear-coverts to hindneck blackish (rarely with very thin white line behind eye), bordered below by white stripe from lores (where usually tinged yellowish) to lower rear border of ear-coverts and down neck side. Moustachial stripe black, with much red in fore part, expanding at rear and joining with black of breast. Chin and throat white, with variable (often heavy) black streaking. Hindneck and upperparts black,

outer scapulars with white outer webs forming line (exceptionally, scapulars may be all black). Upperwing and its coverts black, with white area on bases of inner webs of flight feathers, and (when fresh) white tips to primaries, and usually small whitish area on carpal. Uppertail black (shafts dark). Breast black, this colour occasionally extending onto belly; belly, flanks and undertail-coverts greyish-buff to whitish, variably barred brownish-black (barring varies in depth of colour and in width and evenness). Underwing blackish, with white or pale buff coverts and bases of flight feathers, primary coverts sometimes with small black patch. Undertail brownish-black. (In worn plumage, black areas become browner and feather bases more visible generally.)

Adult female Somewhat smaller than male. Lacks red on forehead, forecrown and moustache, these areas being all black.

Juvenile Duller than adults, with black areas browner; breast more extensively dark, and barring below more obscure and less regular. Flight feathers with more obvious white tips. Head pattern as that of respective adult (rarely, crown may be more yellow than red), but males have much-reduced red in moustache.

Bare parts Bill grey to grey-black, with paler lower mandible and usually dark tip. Legs and feet grey, tinged green, blue or yellow, sometimes olive. Eyes white to pale orange; brown in juveniles. Orbital skin brown.

GEOGRAPHICAL VARIATION Five races, all showing a good deal of individual variation.

   D. l. lineatus (Costa Rica south to W Colombia and E Peru in west and to N Paraguay and São Paulo in east; also Trinidad) Described above. Decreases slightly in size in southeast of range and in north. Northernmost populations tend to be more buff and more irregularly barred below, with somewhat paler bill (thus closer to *similis*).

   D. l. scapularis (W Mexico) Smaller than nominate and adjacent *similis*, but with slight size increase clinally northwards. Differs from all other races in lacking (or almost so) white stripe from lores to neck side. Pale-billed.

   D. l. similis (E and S Mexico south to Costa Rica) Larger than *scapularis*. Ground colour of underparts distinctly buff. Pale-billed.

   D. l. erythrops (Espírito Santo and São Paulo to Rio Grande do Sol and west to E Paraguay and NE Argentina) Larger than southern (adjacent) *lineatus*. Occurs in two forms: those in south lack the white scapular lines of other races, while northern birds may or may not have these markings (proportion of individuals with scapular lines increases towards range of nominate *lineatus*). Exceptionally, may show only partial white on scapulars. Population inhabiting Iguazú area of N Misiones, Argentina, tends to show much rufous in ground coloration of underparts. Dark-billed.

   D. l. fuscipennis (W Ecuador and NW Peru) Smaller than nominate, and with distinctly brown plumage. Upperparts deep brown, breast sooty, and belly to undertail-coverts buffish with obscure, irregular brown barring. Wing and tail shafts pale; undertail glossed yellowish-brown on outer feathers. Dark-billed.

MEASUREMENTS Wing 161-206; tail 101-143; bill 29-44; tarsus 23.5-32. Weight: 136-264; 150-164 (*similis*); male 204-217, female 186-213 (nominate, Surinam); male 182-264 (*erythrops*).

VOICE The call note is a loud sharp *pik*. The rattle commences with such a note, and is rendered by various authors as *kip-whurr, pik-urrr-r-r, ik-rrrr, cuchrrrrrrr, ch'whirrr* or *k'rroo*. The common call of this woodpecker is a loud and explosive, ringing, far-carrying *wicwic-wicwicwic..., wuk wuk wuk, ak-ak-ak-ak..., kyah-yik-yik-yik*, or *weep weep weep weep...* of about 30 notes (falling off at the end). Also delivers an unwoodpecker-like *wer wer wer*. Calls rendered as *wicka, wicka, wicka* have also been described. Both sexes drum loudly with 5-8 slow taps, followed by a long accelerating tattoo.

HABITS Often met with in pairs, which keep frequent vocal contact; also in family groups of 4-6 birds. Single individuals may also join mixed (antwren) flocks. Easily alarmed. Active and noisy, foraging at all heights on limbs and trunk. Readily visits isolated trees in open areas, flying with strong undulations. Forages on trunks and large limbs, occasionally also on isolated trees or even telephone poles. Males prefer larger branches than females. Visits the well-foliated parts of the crown in search of fruits on even very thin twigs. Hammering and pecking deeply and persistently into both live and rotting wood for beetles and their larvae predominate among the feeding techniques, with probing into the excavations also common. Particularly adept in securing ants and their brood associated with *Cecropia*. Frequently prises up and scales pieces of bark from dead trunks and branches. May feed at one spot for 10-15 minutes; after spending some time on one tree, flies a long distance to another, and hence is easily lost to observation in its relatively large territory. May also descend to the ground, where it tosses aside leaves in search of food. Only display described is crest-raising. Remains paired throughout year, but sleeps singly in hole; roost may be dug into arboreal-termite nest. Important hole competitors are toucans. Inferior to Crimson-crested Woodpecker (175), but interactions with *Campephilus* species pass without much hostility in general.

FOOD Beetles and their wood-boring larvae, ants (*Crematogaster, Camponotus, Azteca*) and their brood, caterpillars, orthopteran egg cases; also takes fruit and seeds (*Heliconia*).

BREEDING In Colombia, individuals in breeding condition found from January to February; breeds in the last period of the dry season, March-April, in Panama, April-May in Belize, and in February-April in Trinidad and Surinam. In the southern parts of the range, the nesting season spans July to November. Nests optimally in stubs or tops of stubs of small girth (18-23cm), sometimes high up (27m) in a very tall tree, but also rather low (about 2m). The clutch contains 2-3 eggs. The chicks are fed by regurgitation. The participation of the sexes in all these activities follows the usual pattern.

REFERENCES Askins 1983; Belton 1984; Blake 1965; Haverschmidt 1968; Hilty & Brown 1984; Kilham 1972b; Meyer de Schauensee & Phelps 1978; Olrog 1984; Parker *et al.* 1982; Peterson & Chalif 1973; Russel 1964; Short 1970a, 1975; Sick 1993; Skutch 1969a; Slud 1980; Snyder 1966; Stiles & Skutch 1989; Sutton & Pettingill 1942.

166 BLACK-BODIED WOODPECKER
Dryocopus schulzi   Plate 48

Forms a superspecies with *pileatus* and *lineatus*.

IDENTIFICATION Length c. 29-30cm. Medium-sized to large, with long, straight, slightly chisel-tipped bill broad across nostrils. When perched, appears mostly black apart from red crown and long crest, red moustache (males), white throat, grey ear-coverts, and white band running back from lores and down neck side; white scapular lines are present on most of those breeding in north of range and on some southern ones, while a few show partial/broken white lines. White tail shafts are frequently visible in the field. Has pale bill but dark eyes. In flight, reveals some white at bases of flight feathers and whitish underwing-coverts with a (usually large) dark patch near carpal region. A very poorly known species.

Similar species Lineated Woodpecker (165) is very closely related, but that species differs principally in having dark-barred pale lower underparts (though Black-bodied often shows trace of pale barring), darker ear-coverts, a darker-looking throat (streaked), dark tail shafts, a dark bill and pale eyes. Black-bodied and race *erythrops* of Lineated interbreed where they meet in S Bolivia and in the chaco woodlands of SW Paraguay and NE Argentina; hybrids recorded from these regions appear intermediate between the two in most respects, and may either possess or lack white scapular lines.

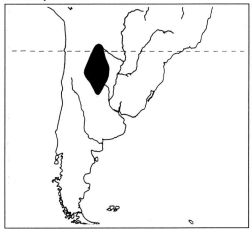

DISTRIBUTION Restricted to a small area in the central and southern chaco of W Paraguay (Nueva Asunción, Boquerón, Presidente Hayes), NC Argentina and S Bolivia (Santa Cruz, Tarija). Rare, and seemingly threatened through, among other things, timber extraction and firewood logging, exotic plantations and expansion of agriculture and cattle-raising.

HABITAT The xeric woodland and savannas of the chaco with *Lithrea, Celtis*, acacias, carob (*Prosopis*) and cacti, and transitional habitats to mesic montane forests with alder and *Tipuana*. Frequent hybridisation with Lineated Woodpecker in more humid chaco areas indicates possible marginal importance of such habitats.

DESCRIPTION
Adult male Nasal tufts conspicuously yellowish-buff. Forehead, crown, nape and long crest bright red, sometimes with some white feather bases showing through. Ear-coverts pale grey, often spotted white, usually bordered

above by very thin white supercilium behind eye (generally more or less invisible in the field). White stripe from lores (where tinged yellowish) backwards through ear-coverts, expanding somewhat just before nape and continuing down neck side. Moustachial stripe red, becoming black at rear and joining with black of breast. Chin and upper throat white to greyish-white, occasionally with very fine brown to blackish streaks (latter rarely visible in the field). Nape sides, hindneck and entire upperparts black; scapulars either all black (most of southern population), or with white on outer webs forming continuous line meeting white of neck stripe (most of northern population, some southern individuals), or with partial white forming broken line (a few throughout range). Upperwing and its coverts black, with white at bases of flight feathers and sometimes whitish area at margin of carpal region. Uppertail black, with fairly prominent white shafts, sometimes with white feather tips when fresh. Underparts from lower throat black to brownish-black, many individuals having very narrow, obscure yellowish barring on lower flanks and belly (rarely, barring somewhat more extensive, reaching upper flanks and even across entire belly). Underwing blackish, with whitish axillaries and coverts, primary coverts with irregular large black patch (latter variable, however, and can be almost absent). Undertail blackish. (As commonly occurs with black-plumaged species, the black areas become browner when worn, and pale/dark feather bases become more obvious on head and other areas.)

Adult female Slightly shorter-billed than male. Has moustache all black, lacking red, and lower forehead generally blackish and sometimes with white specks on forecrown (but red often extends well down forehead, almost to bill).

Juvenile Duller and browner than adults, with more (but obscure) flank barring; forecrown often with white spots. Head pattern as for respective adult.

Bare parts Bill pale ivory-white, with darker culmen and base. Legs and feet dark grey. Eyes deep brown to red-brown. Orbital skin grey to blackish.

GEOGRAPHICAL VARIATION White scapular line occurs throughout species' range, but is more prevalent among northern birds. Southern population averages minimally smaller than others, but differences are clearly insufficient to justify subspecific separation.

MEASUREMENTS Wing 167-186; tail 105-142; bill 30.5-42; tarsus 26-32.

VOICE The common call is a loud *wic wic wic wic wic*, similar to that of Lineated Woodpecker in sound quality, but slower and generally shorter. Much less commonly heard is the harsh rattle (the equivalent call occurs more frequently in Lineated), *ti-chrr*. Drums like Lineated, but possibly with slightly shorter rolls.

HABITS Observed as single individuals, in pairs and, occasionally, in family groups of 5-6 birds. Details of its ecology barely known; forages apparently on trunks and main limbs, with pecking, hammering and probing.

FOOD Unknown.

BREEDING The breeding season extends from October to November (possibly March). Details of its nesting are seemingly unknown; holes (nests and/or roosts) in dead trees or utility poles.

REFERENCES Nieto & Pearman 1992; Olrog 1984; Short 1975.

167 WHITE-BELLIED WOODPECKER
Dryocopus javensis   Plate 49

Other name: Great Black Woodpecker
Forms a superspecies with *hodgei*.

IDENTIFICATION Length 40-48cm. Large to very large, with long, broad-based and chisel-tipped bill with curved culmen. Mostly black, with white belly, males having entire top of head, crest and moustache bright red or orange-red and females having red hindcrown and nape (except female of race *richardsi*, which has wholly black head). Most races show some white on rump, sometimes extensively, and conspicuous in flight when present, variable white in wings and on throat, and black barring on flanks and lower belly.

A powerful-looking woodpecker, usually found solitarily or in pairs and often conspicuously noisy. Unlikely to be confused with any other species.

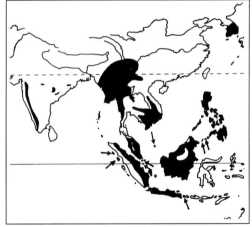

DISTRIBUTION Inhabits mostly primary and secondary forest and forest edges from SW Sichuan and NW and S Yunnan in SW China, south through Burma, most of Thailand, Indochina and Malaysia to the Greater Sundas (including Simeulue Island, Nias Island, Riau and Lingga archipelagos, Bangka, North Natunas and islands off N Borneo), and also Palawan and the Philippines (probably extinct on Cebu), including Sulu archipelago. Isolated populations occur in India, in the west from about 21°N south through the Western Ghats to S Kerala and in the east in the southernmost part of eastern Madhya Pradesh (odd records elsewhere suggest a possible wider distribution in the peninsula); and (a rare and endangered race) in central and southern Korea (and formerly also Tsushima, Japan). This species is everywhere local and uncommon, and in many parts of its range scarce or rare (as in Java, Bali, peninsular Thailand etc.); considered extinct in Singapore, but singles observed at two different sites in August and September 1993 (the first Singapore records since 1988).

HABITAT In its large range this woodpecker inhabits various types of evergreen and deciduous forests, locally also pine forests. It frequents closed primary forest, forest edge, mixed bamboo stands, light secondary forest with large trees, and also appears near cultivation, gardens and in tall mangroves. Wet primary forests with many dead and rotting trees are its favourite haunts, but this species readily populates (selectively) logged and degraded forests. In Japan, before its extinction, it occurred in dense mature coniferous forests mixed with oaks and camphors. Resident below 1000m in most parts of SE Asia and in the Greater Sundas, generally below 600m in Thailand, above 1400m and to 3600m in NE Burma, NW Tonkin and Yunnan; found at 140-1200m in the Philippines (up to 2500m in N Luzon).

DESCRIPTION
D. j. javensis **Adult male** Forehead to crest and nape dark, deep red; fairly broad, deep red moustachial stripe. Rest of head, entire upperparts including tail and wings, and chin to lower breast black, with white flecks/streaks on ear-coverts (especially at rear), sides of neck and chin to throat, and with primaries (tipped white when fresh) with small patch of creamy-white at bases of inner webs. Belly creamy-white, this colour occasionally extending as narrow bars onto lower breast sides; flanks and ventral area normally barred black; undertail-coverts black. Underwing grey-black, with creamy-white coverts and black carpal patch. Undertail greyish.

Adult female Slightly less bulky than male. Has forehead and crown black (but retains red crest) and lacks red in malar area, which is black with white streaking.

Juvenile Duller and browner than adults, with paler throat and often with a trace of white on rump. Juvenile male has red of forehead and crown mottled with black and/or white (feather bases show through), and red of malar area much reduced or visible only as a slight trace.

Bare parts Bill black to greyish-black, with grey (or sometimes pale horn/greenish-yellow) lower mandible. Legs and feet dark grey or blue-grey. Eyes yellow; grey in juvenile. Orbital skin grey.

GEOGRAPHICAL VARIATION A good number of races have been described, of which we recognise 14. These include two isolated races, and eight mostly small races scattered around the Philippines.

D. j. javensis (southern Thailand and peninsular Malaysia to Sumatra and Nias Island, Java, Bali and Borneo and associated islands) Described above. A large race, with very deep red on head, black rump and restricted white in wings. Nias Island population tends to show less barring on flanks.

D. j. parvus (Simeulue Island) Much smaller than nominate and the smallest of all the races. Has black rump and very dark red on crown; hint of buff barring on ear-coverts, throat and breast. Bill all dark.

D. j. feddeni (most of Thailand and Burma and Indochina) Somewhat smaller than nominate *javensis*, with white rump and orange-red head colour and with much white in wings (primary bases); most have white-tipped primaries. Bill colour as *javensis*.

D. j. forresti (montane northern Burma and adjacent SW China) Similar to *feddeni* but much larger, and with proportionately shorter tail; has less white at primary bases, and throat is mainly black, with only few white spots.

D. j. hodgsonii (India) As *javensis*, but distinguished by white rump and much larger all-blackish bill; wings and tail shorter.

D. j. richardsi (Korea; extinct Tsushima) Resembles *forresti*, but even larger and with much longer bill; has more white at primary bases, but male's moustache is somewhat narrower. Female is unique in having head entirely black, with no red. An endangered race.

D. j. hargitti (Palawan) Resembles *javensis*, but has large white rump, crown colour more orange-red, moustache more extensive, and flanks and lower underparts black (with pale thighs). Lower mandible pale greenish-yellow or horn at base.

D. j. mindorensis (Mindoro) As *hargitti* but much smaller, with smaller white rump patch; most have white-tipped primaries. Bill wholly blackish.

D. j. suluensis (Sulu Islands) Small. Most lack white on rump (a few have very small white patch). Lower mandible normally pale.

D. j. confusus (Luzon) As *mindorensis*, but longer-billed and with no (or very little) white on rump; male has more extensive moustache (and some can show darker red on crown). Some have black throat with few white spots, and some have pale lower mandible. Birds from N Luzon are sometimes separated as '*esthloterus*'.

D. j. philippinensis (Panay, Negros, Masbate, Guimaras) Slightly larger than last three races. Has narrow white rump and pale lower mandible; some have black throat with sparse white spots. Male has red of moustache invading throat and face (sometimes including ear-coverts).

D. j. multilunatus (Basilan, Mindanao) Similar to *philippinensis*, but (usually) lacks white on rump (but has much white streaking on neck sides and ear-coverts) and shows buffish barring on breast; most have white-tipped primaries.

D. j. cebuensis (Cebu, extinct) Similar to *multilunatus* but smaller and shorter-billed; bill mostly black. Has concealed white patch on lower back, but less conspicuous throat and breast markings than *pectoralis*.

D. j. pectoralis (Leyte, Samar, Panaon, Calicoan, Bohol) A well-marked race. Similar to *multilunatus*, but has black-streaked white throat and rear ear-coverts, irregular pale bars/streaks on entire breast and more heavily barred flanks; some have a few spots on belly, and occasionally shows hint of white on rump.

Note that *D. (j.) hodgei* is here treated as a separate species, Andaman Woodpecker (168).

MEASUREMENTS Wing 205-208 (*confusus*), 209-222 (*feddeni*), 210-225 (*hodgsonii*), 246-252 (*forresti*); tail 150-165 (*confusus*), 143-154 (*feddeni*), 170-189 (*forresti*); bill 48-52 (*confusus*), 46-55 (*feddeni*), 56-60 (*forresti*); tarsus 32-36, 36-43 (*hodgsonii*). Weight: 197-347.

VOICE A loud single, somewhat variable call note, *kiyow*, *kyah*, *kiauk* or *keer*, is slightly lower-pitched than similar call of Black Woodpecker (169) and more explosive, and is uttered in similar contexts. Racial differences in this vocalisation may exist. Long calls (some are over 5 secs), *kek-ek-ek-ek* or *kiau kiau kiau...*, are given both in flight and when perched. Pair members exchange low *ch-wi*, *ch-wi* notes. Both sexes drum. Rolls are loud and accelerating and, at least at the beginning, slower than those of Black Woodpecker, and possibly a little shorter (less than 2 secs); about three rolls are delivered per minute. At the nest, a low fast tapping may occur.

HABITS Where present, is noisy and conspicuous and usually solitary, although pairs may maintain loose contact and, at times, parties of 4-6 can be observed. Forages from low to upper strata, sometimes 50-200m away from forest in tall trees, on small dead stubs, on fallen timber, and on the ground, searching among litter. It prefers dead trees or dead parts of trees. Pecks and hammers to excavate, and commonly strips bark; these activities are more common than in any other species in its range (except Black Woodpecker, which it meets in Korea and SW China). Also probes and prises off pieces of bark and wood; large pieces of bark are removed before good-sized pits, up to 20cm long and 8cm deep, are worked into the wood. Like its northern congener, it may spend an hour at a single feeding site. Flight crow-like and with powerful wingbeats. Males and females use separate roosts. Displays, apart from a moderate raising of the crest, are virtually undescribed. Males demonstrate at the intended nest with a long series of regular taps. Radius of home range is about 2km. Interspecific interactions with other woodpeckers not well known, but seems to be subordinate to *Mulleripicus*.

FOOD Its diet comprises large ants and their brood, termites, beetles and their (large) wood-boring larvae, and other insects, e.g. bees and Myriapoda. Also takes fruits (*Cornus*).

BREEDING Nesting reported from India in January to March, from Burma between February and May, from N Korea late March to early May, from Malaysia in December to March, and from the Greater Sundas in April and May, as well as August and September. The nest hole is excavated by both sexes, 8-16m up in tall stumps or tall old or half-dead trees. Clutch size is 2, sometimes (northern populations) 3 or 4 eggs. Both parents incubate for 14 days and feed the young by regurgitation. Nestlings fledge after 26 days.

REFERENCES Ali & Ripley 1970; Brazil 1991; Dickinson *et al.* 1991; Gyldenstolpe 1916; Kennedy 1987; King & Dickinson 1975; Kyu-Hwang & Pyong-Oh 1982; Lekagul & Round 1991; MacKinnon 1990; MacKinnon & Phillipps 1993; Medway & Wells 1976; Short 1973a, 1978; Smythies 1953, 1981; Stanford & Mayr 1941.

---

168 ANDAMAN WOODPECKER
Dryocopus hodgei   Plate 49

Other names: Andaman Black Woodpecker
Forms a superspecies with *javensis*.

IDENTIFICATION Length c. 38cm. An unmistakable species within its range, which is restricted to the Andaman Islands. Plumage entirely dull sooty-black. Male has crimson forehead, crown and crest and crimson moustache; female has red confined to rear crown and crest.

DISTRIBUTION Confined to Andaman Islands in NE Indian Ocean, where fairly common in high evergreen forest, preferring tall trees.

HABITAT Tall evergreen forests, often rather open, and mangroves.

DESCRIPTION
Adult male Entire head and upperparts, including wings and tail, greyish-black to sooty-black, apart from crimson forehead, crown and crest and moustachial area. Entire underparts sooty-black.

Adult female As male, but has red only on hindcrown and crest.

Juvenile As adults but duller, browner. Juvenile male has black and white admixed in red crown feathers and much less red in malar area.

Bare parts Bill blackish. Legs and feet slaty-grey. Eyes grey in juvenile, becoming pale yellow in adults. Orbital skin greyish.

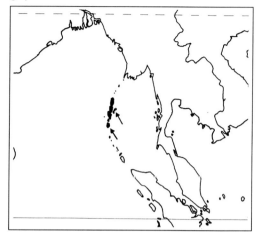

GEOGRAPHICAL VARIATION None. Monotypic.

MEASUREMENTS Wing 180-190; tail of male 130-147; bill (from feathers) 41-47; tarsus 32-33. Weight: 156-225.

VOICE Calls quite different from those of White-bellied Woodpecker (167): a loud chattering *kuk kuk kuk*, terminating with a whistling *kui*; a loud sharp *kik, kik, kik* has also been heard. Drumming is loud and far-carrying.

HABITS Lives in pairs or may be met with in loose family parties. Forages mainly on the trunks of large trees or their main (dead) branches, with powerful hammering. Descends to the ground to hunt for ants.

FOOD Ants.

BREEDING Breeding season extends from January to March. Lays 2 eggs in a nest 6-14m up in the trunk of a dead tree or in a large branch.

REFERENCES Abdulali 1964; Ali & Ripley 1970; Osmaston 1906; Tikader 1984.

---

169 BLACK WOODPECKER
Dryocopus martius   Plate 49

IDENTIFICATION Length c. 45-55cm. Very large, with long, chisel-tipped and very broad-based bill with slightly curved culmen. Within most of its Palearctic range, this is the largest woodpecker (crow-sized) and is unmistakable. Plumage wholly black or blackish, apart from a patch of red from forehead to rear crown (males) or on hindcrown only (females), the nape feathers sometimes raised to form a crest. Juveniles basically similar to adults, though duller. Prominent features include very pale bill and whitish eye. Flies rather unsteadily. Has loud call and drums frequently, in long, loud bursts.

DISTRIBUTION Range covers the cool-temperate zone of the Palearctic. From W Europe (France, Spain), Denmark and Scandinavia (north to Arctic Circle), east between 62° and 69°N to Kamchatka and the Sea of Japan, including islands, and Japan (Hokkaido and extreme N Honshu); southern limits of range include Sierra de Somosierra (Spain), Calabria (Italy), N Greece, N Anatolia, N Iran, Altai, N Mongolia, Korea. Occurs also in SW China, from

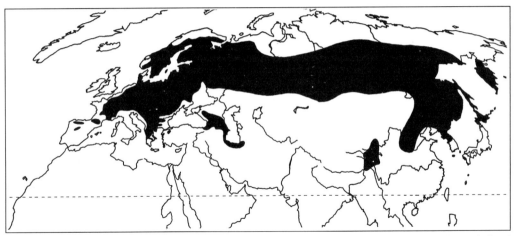

NW Yunnan, through Sichuan, Qinghai and SE Gansu. In first half of twentieth century has extended its range in W Europe and EC European lowlands, and has recently spread from Hokkaido to other parts of Japan. Locally common in some western parts of range, but more uncommon in the east.

MOVEMENTS Resident in most areas, even northern populations being only partially migratory; juvenile dispersal more pronounced. Scandinavian populations migrate in September, early migrants or dispersing birds being recorded somewhat earlier, in August and early September, in C Europe. Some movements even in winter. Farthest distances recorded are between 500 and 1000km. Vertical winter movements take place in some mountainous regions.

HABITAT Within its range this species is found in all types of mature, but not extremely dense and gloomy, forest, and also at forest edge. Scandinavian and Siberian spruce and pine forests with larch, birch, aspen and alder are occupied, as well as all habitat types in primeval Polish forests. In C Europe, occurs in all types of not over-dense deciduous, mixed or coniferous forests, from riparian woodland to subalpine forests. Habitat prerequisites are decaying trees and stumps for foraging, and tall timber for nests and roosts. In Japan, it occurs in open boreal mixed or coniferous forest at elevations from 100 to 1000m, rarely in the lowlands. Asian populations ascend to 1700-2000m. Caucasian and Alpine Black Woodpeckers are found up to the timberline, although they usually prefer sites below 1200m in NE Anatolia found at 750-1900m. Reported in Yunnan and Tibet at up to 4100m.

DESCRIPTION

D. m. martius Adult male Central forehead to rear of crown dark crimson-red to scarlet (a few grey feather bases sometimes showing through). Rest of plumage black, glossed dark blue on upperparts (especially head, neck and upperwing-coverts), and with primaries tinged dark brown; slightly duller below, often with tinge of grey. (In worn plumage, duller, with underparts distinctly grey-tinged, and with red on head admixed with dark grey.)

Adult female As male, except forehead and forecrown glossy black, with red only on hindcrown (red can be almost lost when worn). Bill shorter than male's.

Juvenile Duller than adults, more sooty-black, lacking gloss, and often with paler (dark grey) throat. Red-tipped head feathers duller/paler and with larger dark bases: extent of red as on adults (on male usually absent on lower

forehead), becoming patchy with wear; rarely, may lack red altogether.

Bare parts Bill very pale ivory-white to pale horn, with dark bluish-horn to blackish culmen and tip; mostly whitish on juveniles. Legs and feet dark greyish to bluish-grey; generally blue-grey on juveniles. Eyes whitish or yellowish-white, sometimes pale cream-grey.

GEOGRAPHICAL VARIATION Two races.

> *D. m. martius* (entire range, except SW China) Described above. Varies in size clinally, those from S Europe to Transcaucasia ('*pinetorum*') being slightly smaller than northern breeders, and those from E Asia ('*reichenowi*') averaging larger than western populations, but a fair degree of overlap exists.
>
> *D. m. khamensis* (SW China and Tibet) Has plumage blacker and more glossy than nominate. Bill averages shorter (by some 10%) than that of largest nominate populations in E Asia, but bill length little different from that of southern nominate breeders.

MEASUREMENTS Wing 227-254 (*martius*), 246-260 (*khamensis*); tail 159-173; bill 50-67; tarsus 36-39. Weight: (201)260-340(383).

VOICE The most distinctive calls to be heard at all seasons are a loud *krry-krry-krry...* in flight and an equally distinctive *ke-yaa* upon landing and when perched. Before and during breeding season, gives long series of 10-20 more melodious notes in flight or from a perch: *kwee kweekweekweekwek-wikwik*. Alarm/aggressive notes recall Eurasian Jackdaw *Corvus monedula*: *kiyák*. Intimate calls shorter *kyah* or, rather different, *rirrirrrirr*. Nestlings chatter rhythmically. Drumming consists of long (sometimes over 3 secs) rolls of about 14 (female) to 17 (male) strokes, delivered at a rate of about 4 rolls per minute; males drum more frequently. A loud rhythmic tapping is part of the courtship activities and of changeovers at the nest; both the approaching bird and the one in the hole deliver this signal. In C Europe, Black Woodpeckers are acoustically most active in March and April.

HABITS This is the most conspicuous of all woodpeckers occurring in Europe. Most of the time lives solitarily, the pair staying in loose contact only. Foraging activities are concentrated on the lower levels on tree trunks, mostly below 3m, and the bases of trees, and on the ground. Live and dead trees alike are visited. Seems to be well aware of the location of ant nests in its territory, since it is able to find them even under deep snow cover. Chisels deep elongated rectangular holes (which follow the texture of the tree fibres) into the trunks of trees to reach insects and their brood in burrows deep inside. Bark is removed by tangential blows or prised off in large pieces. Drinking from sap wells has been recorded, as well as the drilling of them. On ground, moves with a few clumsy hops. Climbs straight on tree trunks and larger branches; very rarely perches crosswise. Flight recalls that of of small corvid (jay); lands with an upward swoop. In agonistic interactions, bill-pointing and head-swinging (bill raised well above/behind body axis) are commonly employed. There seems to be competition with Grey-faced (194) or Eurasian Green (191) Woodpeckers, which also prefer similar nest sites. Other hole competitors are European Jackdaw, Eurasian Roller *Coracias garrulus*, Stock Dove *Columba oenas*, Tengmalm's Owl *Aegolius funereus* and Common Starling *Sturnus vulgaris*. A larger number of other animals, from hornets to bats, profit from Black Woodpecker holes. Roosts in old nests or, rarely, in holes made for the purpose. Leaves roost after sunrise and enters it before sunset.

FOOD Mainly ants (*Camponotus, Formica, Lasius*) and their brood; at least locally, seasonal switch from *Camponotus* in winter to *Lasius* in spring has been documented. Wood-boring and bark beetles and their larvae (e.g. cerambycids, elaterids), and various other arthropods, and even occasional snails, are also taken. Also reported to break into beehives. Spruce seeds and beech mast are eaten, but fruits and berries are taken only rarely.

BREEDING Sexual activities may begin in winter (copulation attempts mid January), weeks before the breeding season. After a long period of pair-formation, during which the final location of the nest is decided upon, with the male leading, egg-laying takes place between mid March and mid May. About three-quarters of nests are excavated into living trees, the work taking 10-15 days. Nest is usually well up in a tall tree at heights between (3)5 and 10(27)m; large-sample (n = 102) mean, Norway, 8.0m. Nest entrance vertically oval in shape, measuring 13x 8.5cm. These woodpeckers usually prefer to raise their young in newly constructed holes, but between 20% and 50% of nesting attempts may be made in old holes. Active nests are at least 900m apart. The clutch consists of (2)3-5(6) eggs; average clutch size from 4.74-4.8 eggs (with mean of 3.7 chicks hatching) in Sweden to 3.3 eggs in S Germany. Earlier clutches tend to be larger. Martens are the most important cause of losses through predation. Eggs are incubated for 12(14) days, by both sexes, the male sitting during the night. The sex ratio among chicks may vary greatly among different broods, but the 1:1 relation is maintained on average. In the nestling period, which lasts (24)27-28(31) days, both parents provide for the young. They brood them for about eight days and feed them by regurgitation. The nest is kept clean, save for the last few days before fledging. Young may be fed by a parent (male) for up to a month after fledging. Suggestions of occasional second broods need corroboration.

REFERENCES Bezzel 1985; Blume 1973; Brazil 1991; Cuisin 1973; Dement'ev & Gladkov 1966; Gatter 1981; Glutz von Blotzheim & Bauer 1980; Haila & Järvinen 1977; Hågvar et al. 1990; Klima 1959; Kojima & Arisawa 1983; Kojima & Matsuoka 1985; Miech 1986; Nilsson et al. 1991; Pynnönen 1939; Rost et al. 1992; Serez 1983; Spitznagel 1993; Turcek 1954; Wesolowski & Tomialojc 1986.

170 POWERFUL WOODPECKER
Campephilus pollens   Plate 50

IDENTIFICATION Length c. 32cm. Large, with long, chisel-tipped bill slightly curved on culmen and broad across nostrils. Tail has only 10 feathers (not 12). Face and upperparts black, with pale eyes, and with white stripes across cheeks, down neck and along mantle sides to meet on back, and with white rump (dark-barred cinnamon in Peru). Male has red from forehead to crest and hindneck, whereas female has head, neck and breast entirely black apart from the contrasting white stripe. Lower breast to undertail-coverts barred cinnamon and black. Long and dark (as against pale) bill is a useful field mark, but species is generally unmistakable once seen well. In flight, shows pale rump, broken white bars across flight feathers and white underwing-coverts.

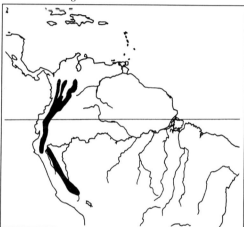

DISTRIBUTION S America, in the Andes from Táchira (Venezuela), through Colombia and Ecuador to Peru, south to Pasco. Fairly common.

HABITAT Mature montane forest, humid and wet forest, cloud forest and forest borders. Often also inhabits secondary forest, open forest and forest edge. Found at altitudes between 900 and 3600m, mainly between (1300) 1800 and 2500m.

DESCRIPTION
C. p. pollens **Adult male** Forehead to crest and hindneck bright red, sometimes with some black and white of feather bases visible. White band from lores to rear edge of ear-coverts, continuing down neck side and to upper breast side. Rest of head, chin and throat black. Lowermost hindneck, mantle, scapulars and upper back black, with narrow white stripes on mantle sides (where often some cinnamon markings) more or less meeting at top of lower back and often joining with neck stripes; lower back and rump white, extremities with a few dark-barred cinnamon-buff feathers; uppertail-coverts black. Upperwing and its coverts black, primaries narrowly tipped white, and with white spots/bars on inner webs of secondaries and all but outermost primaries. Uppertail black, very occasionally with white spots towards tips of outer feathers. Black of throat continues to central breast; lower breast to undertail-coverts cinnamon-buff, with black bars or arrowhead markings, the latter less pronounced on belly. Underwing blackish, barred white and with white coverts. Undertail blackish.

Adult female As male, but red areas of head replaced with black.

Juvenile Duller and browner than adults, with more barring on back, and underparts duller and greyer with broader barring; crest feathers longer. Head pattern as respective adult.

Bare parts Bill black. Legs and feet dark grey. Eyes white to pinkish-white.

GEOGRAPHICAL VARIATION Two races.
    C. p. pollens (Venezuela to Ecuador) Described above.
    C. p. peruviana (Peru) Differs from nominate in having strong cinnamon-buff tone to lower back and rump, which are also normally strongly barred; often has narrow cinnamon-buff bars on uppertail-coverts.

MEASUREMENTS Wing 164-190; tail 106-131; bill 43.5-47.6; tarsus 28.5-35.

VOICE Commonest call *pee-yáw, pee-yáw,* sometimes *pee-yaw-yaw*. A loud *udd'daa-da-da*, described as reedy and strained, apparently distinct among the members of the genus *Campephilus*. The instrumental signal is loud and brief and rendered as a double rap.

HABITS This sturdily built woodpecker is often encountered in pairs. It forages ordinarily in the interior of forests, where it visits predominantly trunks and large limbs at all levels.

FOOD Not known.

BREEDING The breeding season appears to extend from April to August. Nest high up (e.g. 7m) in a tree or telegraph pole.

REFERENCES Fjeldså & Krabbe 1990; Hilty & Brown 1984; Meyer de Schauensee & Phelps 1978; Parker *et al.* 1982.

---

171 CRIMSON-BELLIED WOODPECKER
Campephilus haematogaster Plate 50

Other name: Splendid Woodpecker (race *splendens*)

IDENTIFICATION Length c. 33-34cm. Large, with long, almost straight, chisel-tipped bill broad across nostrils. A rather bulky bird, heftier than sympatric Powerful Woodpecker (170), and, like the latter, very poorly known. Plumage pattern renders it unmistakable. Red crown (with short nape crest), hindneck, sides of neck and rump (latter barred, except in east of range) and deep red underparts with variable dark barring contrast with black/blackish back, wings and tail, and throat, and with buffy-white bands above and below black ear-coverts; female also has broad buffy band down side of neck. In worn plumage, however, the red areas become noticeably duller, with strong element of buff or black admixed. In flight, reveals prominent whitish barring across flight feathers, with pale underwing-coverts.

DISTRIBUTION Along mountains of C America and northern S America, from Panama through Colombia and W Ecuador to Peru. Apparently not uncommon.

HABITAT Humid and wet forest and forest edges; most often inside tall forest, such as semi-open *várzea* forest. Ranges from lowlands to 1600m in Panama, above 900m in Peru, to middle altitudes, locally to 1500-2000m.

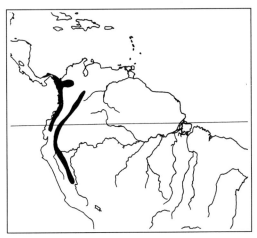

DESCRIPTION
C. h. splendens **Adult male** Nasal tufts buffish. Forehead, crown and small crest, hindneck and sides of neck to uppermost mantle red, bordered with black from bill to mid crown and usually with some black feather bases visible. Central ear-coverts black, this colour sometimes extending back narrowly to meet red of nape. Rest of face, including thin supercilium behind eye, buffish-white to pale cinnamon-buff. Chin, throat and foreneck black, lower throat/foreneck with extensive red feather tips. Most of mantle plus scapulars and upper back black to brownish-black; lower back and rump deep red, with feather bases barred black and cinnamon-buff; uppertail-coverts black. Upperwing and its coverts black or brownish-black, primaries narrowly tipped pale (when fresh), and with large white or buffish-white bars/spots on inner webs of secondaries and all but outermost primaries. Uppertail black. Red of neck sides continues over feather tips of entire underparts, but with bases black and central part of feathers barred black and buff, producing variably barred pattern; undertail-coverts black. Underwing blackish, barred pale, and with white coverts. Undertail blackish. (In worn plumage, the red areas become much duller, with tips wearing away to reveal black bases on crown, throat and foreneck, pale and blackish bars on feathers of rump, and more obvious black and buff barring on underparts; black areas of plumage also become browner.)

Adult female Differs from male in having the buffish-white band across cheeks continuing broadly down side of neck to upper breast side and in lacking red tips to throat and foreneck feathers.

Juvenile Duller than adults, with black areas browner, less red below, and with less obvious barring; has forehead/forecrown more sooty-coloured. Sexes differ as for adults.

Bare parts Bill black to grey-black. Legs and feet brownish-black. Eyes red-brown. Orbital skin black.

GEOGRAPHICAL VARIATION Two races.
    C. h. splendens (Panama to W Ecuador) Described above.
    C. h. haematogaster (E Colombia to Peru) Less barred below and on rump (feathers with more extensive red on tips) and lacks red tips to throat and foreneck; crown generally redder, with smaller black bases.

MEASUREMENTS Wing 176-187; tail 89-104; bill 44.1-50.1; tarsus 34-39. Weight: 225-250.

VOICE The presumed rattle call of this species is low.

Trapped birds squeal loudly. Loud double raps, with more or less clear emphasis on the first stroke.

HABITS This very shy woodpecker is usually encountered in pairs or families. Forages at low levels in dense forest, especially on trunks of large trees, and visits slightly higher levels in more open habitats. Separated from Guayaquil Woodpecker (176), where the ranges of the two overlap, by this preference for lower levels.

FOOD Large adult beetles and very large larvae of wood-boring beetles.

BREEDING Nesting season varies with latitude, from March to May in Panama and from September to April in Colombia and Ecuador.

REFERENCES Hilty & Brown 1984; Parker *et al.* 1982; Ridgely & Gwynne 1989; Wetmore 1968.

172 RED-NECKED WOODPECKER
Campephilus rubricollis   Plate 50

IDENTIFICATION Length c. 30-32cm. Large, with long, almost straight, chisel-tipped bill broad across nostrils. A distinctive species, with entirely red head, long crest and neck, apart from black-bordered white moustache (female) or small black and white mark on lower rear ear-coverts (male), all-black upperparts and plain rufous-chestnut underparts. Has pale bill and pale eyes. In flight, reveals a dark rufous panel on primaries and rufous underwings (darker on coverts) with black trailing edge, but generally appears rather dark.

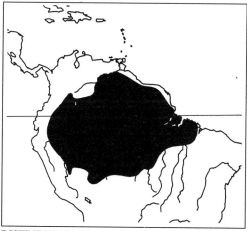

DISTRIBUTION Northern S America, from Venezuela and the Guianas through the Amazonian basin to N Bolivia and E Peru. Within its range, the commonest large woodpecker.

HABITAT Inhabits rain forest, *terra firme* and *várzea* forests and cloud forest, forest edge, light second growth, semi-open woodland on sand, and riverine woodland in savanna regions. Mainly a woodpecker of the lowlands, ranging usually up to 600m only, but locally (S Venezuela, NW Brazil) to 1800m and even 2400m (La Paz, Bolivia).

DESCRIPTION
C. r. rubricollis **Adult male** Small oval-shaped spot of black and white on lower rear ear-coverts. Rest of head, crest and entire neck to uppermost mantle bright red, feathers of

neck and sides of head being black based and with a cinnamon bar below red tip (some barring usually visible, particularly when worn). Upperparts entirely black to brownish-black. Upperwing and its coverts black, bases of primaries with extensive rufous on inner webs and shafts and very occasionally (when fresh) with very small pale rufous to whitish tips to primaries. Uppertail black. Underparts from breast all unbarred rufous to rufous-cinnamon, feathers of upper (and occasionally lower) breast with red tips. Underwing rufous, with darker coverts and blackish tip and trailing edge. Undertail brownish-black.

Adult female Differs from male in lacking oval ear-covert spot; instead has a broad whitish moustachial stripe from base of lower mandible to lower rear edge of ear-coverts, this bordered by a black line above and by black chin and malar stripe below.

Juvenile Duller than adults, more brownish-black and orange-red. Young males have whitish moustache, usually with some red feather tips (but without black borders), and some black feathering on throat/foreneck; females have adult's face pattern, but with more black (extending to forehead and forecrown).

Bare parts Bill pale ivory to greyish-white or pale yellow. Legs and feet blackish-grey or olive. Eyes yellowish-white.

GEOGRAPHICAL VARIATION Three races.
   C. r. rubricollis (northern part of range, south to Amazon river and Ecuador) Described above. The smallest race. Intergrades with *trachelopyrus* in southwest of range.
   C. r. trachelopyrus (NE Peru to La Paz in Bolivia) Large. Darker, more chestnut, below than nominate, and with red feather tips extending to lower breast or to flanks/belly; rufous in wing extends to both webs.
   C. r. olallae (south of Amazon, from Madeira river to Pará and Maranhão in Brazil and south to Cochabamba in Bolivia) Intermediate in size between above two races. Resembles *trachelopyrus*, but brighter.

MEASUREMENTS Wing 169-206; tail 115-121 (*trachelopyrus*); bill 42-47 (*trachelopyrus*). Weight: 178-236.

VOICE The explosive and nasal call can be rendered as *ngkah-ngkah*, *kikka*, and *querra-querra*. It is similar to calls of Crimson-crested Woodpecker (175). Drumming is a loud double tap as in other *Campephilus* species, *to-ró*.

HABITS Found in pairs or small family parties; conspicuous. Actively forages from middle to upper heights on trunks and limbs of tall trees, also visiting lower storey and canopy.

FOOD (Large) larvae of beetles and moths (Pyralidae).

BREEDING Breeds from January to May in the northern part of its range, in November in Ecuador, and in September in Peru. Nest has an oval-shaped entrance.

REFERENCES Haverschmidt 1968; Hilty & Brown 1984; Meyer de Schauensee & Phelps 1978; Parker *et al.* 1982; Sick 1993; Snyder 1966; Willard *et al.* 1991.

173 ROBUST WOODPECKER
Campephilus robustus   Plate 51

IDENTIFICATION Length 32-37cm. Large, with long, almost straight, chisel-tipped bill broad across nostrils. Immediately distinguished by its red head and neck, pale upperparts with contrasting black wings and tail, and heavily barred underparts. Female has a black-bordered whitish moustache. In flight, apart from striking pale upperparts, also shows pale chestnut spots/bars across flight feathers.

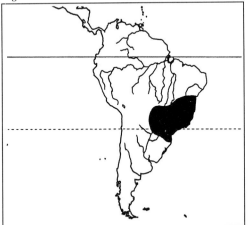

DISTRIBUTION Eastern central S America, in Brazil (Goiás, S Bahia, Espírito Santo, Minas Gerais, to Rio Grande do Sul, W Paraná), Argentina (Misiones) and E Paraguay. Not uncommon in south of range.

HABITAT Humid forests, araucaria forests. Frequents disturbed forests only if large trees are present. Found in lowlands to 1000m, as well as in hills to 2200m.

DESCRIPTION
Adult male Small oval-shaped black and white spot on lower rear ear-coverts. Entire rest of head, small crest, and neck to uppermost breast bright red, often with some black and buff of feather bases visible, especially on neck and ·sides of head (more obvious when plumage worn). Upperparts whitish, tinged pale buff or cinnamon, with a few blackish bars on uppermost mantle and often at sides. Upperwing and its coverts black, with small rusty-buff spots on inner webs of flight feathers. Uppertail black. Underparts from breast buff to whitish-buff, barred black, bars broadest on breast and becoming narrower on belly (where occasionally absent or virtually so). Underwing blackish-brown, with rufous-buff coverts and spots on flight feathers. Undertail blackish-brown.
Adult female Lacks male's oval ear-covert spot, but has whitish moustachial stripe, bordered with black above, and blackish chin.
Juvenile Duller than adults, with black even browner and with less contrasting barring below (bars usually absent on undertail-coverts); upperparts generally whiter. Both sexes have head pattern as adult female, male with red feather tips in moustachial area.
Bare parts Bill horn-coloured, with ivory-yellow at tip and on distal half of lower mandible. Legs and feet dark grey. Eyes white to yellowish-white.

GEOGRAPHICAL VARIATION Monotypic. Slight increase in size clinally southwards.

MEASUREMENTS Wing 175-204; tail 110-131; bill 43.6-50.5; tarsus 32.7-37.9. Weight: 230-294.

VOICE Call note *kee* or *kew*, given both when perched and on the wing. A series of notes, *psó-ko po-po-po-po-rrat.* Drumming is a double tap, *to-plóp* or *thump-ump,* delivered at a rate of 1-3 per minute.

HABITS Rarely joins mixed-species flocks. Forages at all levels, with a slight preference for the middle storey; apparently never or only rarely on the ground. Prefers larger, dead or living trees, where it visits mainly trunks and the base of branches. This species pecks and hammers vigorously, and probes and removes bark. Rarely, its hammering results in appreciable excavations. The only known display is wing-spreading.

FOOD Insects (beetles) and apparently wood-boring larvae. Sometimes takes berries.

BREEDING Breeding season September - October in Argentina.

REFERENCES Brooks *et al.* 1993; Olrog 1984; Short 1970a; Sick 1993.

174 PALE-BILLED WOODPECKER
Campephilus guatemalensis Plate 51

Other name: Flint-billed Woodpecker
Forms a superspecies with *melanoleucos* and *gayaquilensis.*

IDENTIFICATION Length c. 31-38cm. Large, with long, straight, chisel-tipped bill broad across nostrils. Combination of large size, red head and bushy crest (female with black crown and throat), black neck and upperparts with white stripes down neck and mantle sides meeting on back, and barred underparts renders this species fairly unmistakable within its C American range. Has pale yellowish underwing.

Similar species Overlaps in range with Lineated Woodpecker (165), but latter is smaller and less hefty, has blackish sides of head, white cheek stripe and black-streaked pale throat, and also differs in voice and behaviour.

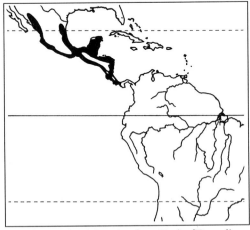

DISTRIBUTION C America, from Mexico (Tamaulipas, S Sonora) through Guatemala to W Panama. Fairly common to common.

MOVEMENTS Possibly some local movements.

HABITAT Locally common in wholly or partly forested

areas, but infrequent in extensively deforested regions. Tall rain forest is inhabited (where sympatric Lineated Woodpecker is absent), as well as humid and dry forest and edge, gaps and clearings with scattered trees; also occurs in tall second growth, and in the lower parts of the pine-oak woodland belt (northern C America), plantations and mangroves. Altitudinal range extends from lowlands and foothills up to 2000m in Mexico and Guatemala, up to 1200 (1500)m in Panama and on the southern Pacific slope of Costa Rica, and to 1000m in the north of Costa Rica.

DESCRIPTION

C. g. guatemalensis **Adult male** Entire head and short bushy crest red, usually a trifle darker on rear ear-coverts and often with some black and white of feather bases showing through (especially when worn). Neck, upper breast and upperparts black, with white stripes from upper neck side continuing down and along sides of mantle to meet in centre of back; lower back, rump and uppertail-coverts occasionally with some paler barring. Upperwing and its coverts black to brownish-black, with whitish bases to flight feathers and (when fresh) white tips to primaries. Uppertail black. Underparts from lower breast buffish-white, tinged pale greenish on flanks/belly, and barred blackish-brown (barring generally broadest on breast, but variable both in width and in depth of colour). Underwing whitish or pale yellowish, with blacker tip and trailing edge. Undertail brown to yellow-brown, paler at base.

Adult female Differs from male in having black on forehead, crown and centre of crest and on chin and throat (chin with some red-tipped feathers).

Juvenile Duller and browner above than adults, and browner below with more obscure barring. Both sexes resemble adult female in head pattern, though red more orangey and side of head more red-tinged brownish-black, but males soon acquire red feathering of adult.

Bare parts Bill ivory-coloured, tinged blue-grey at base; all dark in juveniles. Legs and feet greenish-grey to grey-brown. Eyes pale yellow; grey to brown in juveniles. Orbital skin greyish.

GEOGRAPHICAL VARIATION Three races.

C. g. guatemalensis (Veracruz to Panama) Described above.

C. g. regius (NE Mexico to Veracruz) Larger and longer-billed than nominate.

C. g. nelsoni (NW Mexico, from Sonora to Oaxaca) Averages slightly smaller than nominate. Appears paler, browner, above and less buff-tinged below; shows greater tendency towards brown and black barring on lower back and rump, especially in north of range.

MEASUREMENTS Wing 172-203 (*guatemalensis*), 183-209 (*regius*); tail 87-113 (*guatemalensis*), 93-124 (*regius*); bill 41-50.2 (*guatemalensis*), 43-56.5 (*regius*); tarsus 31-39.4 (*guatemalensis*), 33.5-38 (*regius*). Weight: 205-244 (*guatemalensis*), 263-282 (*regius*).

VOICE A loud bleating note, *kint*, similar to that of Ivory-billed Woodpecker (180). Loud, staggered nasal rattles and sputters, *Ka ka ka ka ka kay, nyuck, nyuck*, suggesting a nuthatch *Sitta*. At intimate contacts, these birds utter whining or moaning sounds or a low *keeu keeu keeu keeu*. The voice of the similar Lineated Woodpecker is more flicker-like. The resounding double rap of Pale-billed is diagnostic (compare, however, Crimson-bellied Woodpecker 171): this instrumental signal consists of two powerful taps in quick succession, the second stroke not so loud. Also reported to produce a roll of about 7 strokes. Wing noise is noticeable when two individuals meet in flight.

HABITS Found singly or in pairs. Paired throughout year, but sleeps singly in holes. Although basically a forest bird, it often forages in cleared areas. Forages at all heights, but prefers middle to fairly high levels, coming lower at edges, clearings or in second growth. Trunks and larger branches are favoured, but also negotiates small twigs. Digs with hammering and pecking deep into decaying trunks, removing large flakes and splinters; also probes into these excavations. Removes bark from dead wood. Other feeding techniques are uncommon. Flies with strong undulations. Raises crest at encounters.

FOOD Insects, mostly larvae of wood-boring beetles (frequently cerambycids), scarabaeid larvae and ant larvae, comprise more than 70% of the diet. Takes some fruit.

BREEDING Breeding season in Mexico and northern C America January to May; August to December further south. Nest is a deep cavity 4-15m up in a large trunk, excavated by both sexes. Only 2 eggs are laid, from which either one or two chicks hatch. Incubation by both sexes in long bouts. Both parents feed the young directly, not by regurgitation.

REFERENCES Askins 1983; Blake 1965; Howell & Webb in press; Land 1970; Otvos 1967; Peterson & Chalif 1973; Ridgely & Gwynne 1989; Russel 1964; Sick 1993; Slud 1964, 1980; Stiles & Skutch 1989; Sutton & Pettingill 1942.

175 CRIMSON-CRESTED WOODPECKER
Campephilus melanoleucos   Plate 51

Other names: Black-and-white Woodpecker; Malherbe's Woodpecker
Forms a superspecies with *guatemalensis* and *gayaquilensis*.

IDENTIFICATION Length c. 33-38cm. Large, with long, chisel-tipped bill slightly curved on culmen and broad across nostrils. A typical red-headed black and white woodpecker, with white neck and mantle stripes meeting on back, and barred underparts. Both sexes show pale area around bill base. Male has small black and white oval patch at lower rear ear-coverts; female has black forehead to centre of crest, and a broad white moustache joining with white neck stripe. In flight, shows white underwing-coverts and some white at bases of primaries. East of the Andes, the distinctive race *malherbii* is much more buff below and has a dark bill (pale in other populations).

Similar species Overlaps widely with Red-necked Woodpecker (172), but latter is easily distinguished by its all-red neck, lack of white neck and mantle stripes and unbarred underparts. Pale-billed Woodpecker (174) may possibly occur near race *malherbii* of Crimson-crested in Panama, but latter's dark bill, somewhat different head pattern (both sexes) and black-barred underparts should separate it fairly easily. In the south of its range, Crimson-crested could possibly approach range of Robust (173) and Cream-backed (177) Woodpeckers, but both have obviously pale mantle and also differ in other ways. In SW Colombia, appears not to meet the very similar and closely related Guayaquil Woodpecker (176), which differs in having lower back and rump barred black and pale buff and in certain details of head pattern. Compare also Lineated Woodpecker (165), whose range overlaps widely with that of Crimson-crested.

DISTRIBUTION Neotropics, from Panama through Colombia and Ecuador to Peru, Bolivia and Argentina

(Corrientes) and C Paraguay, in the east extending from Venezuela, the Guianas and Trinidad to Brazil (Paraná, Bahia). Fairly common in much of range, but uncommon in some regions (e.g. Trinidad).

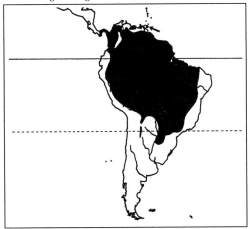

HABITAT This woodpecker is found in a remarkably wide range of habitats, frequenting cloud, rain, gallery and deciduous forests, and also rather open woodland in savannas. Generally, it is more of a savanna bird than Lineated Woodpecker, although the latter occasionally occurs in same area. Crimson-crested Woodpeckers may be met with in second growth, clearings, forest edge, semi-open country, plantations, palm groves, pastures, and in swampy areas; sometimes seen on single trees away from forest. Presence of big dead trees may be an important element of this large woodpecker's habitat. Reaches 900m in C America, and in Venezuela occurs at up to 2000m in the northern parts and to 950m in the south; ranges to 2500 (3100)m in the Andes.

DESCRIPTION
C. m. melanoleucos **Adult male** Feathering around base of bill and front part of moustachial area pale creamy-buff; narrow black line across lower forehead; small oval area of black and white at lower rear edge of ear-coverts. Rest of head and crest red. Throat black. Neck to upper breast and upperparts black, with white stripes down neck and sides of mantle meeting in centre of back (where often a few black spots/bars). Upperwing and its coverts black, primaries with small white tips (when fresh) and with small area of white at bases of inner webs. Uppertail black. Lower breast to undertail-coverts pale buffish-white, sometimes tinged green, and barred blackish-brown (bars broadest on breast). Underwing white, with blackish tip and trailing edge. Undertail blackish.

Adult female Differs from male in having area through central forehead and crown to centre of crest (which is slightly longer than male's) and from rear lores narrowly along lower ear-coverts black, with a broad white moustachial band joining with white neck stripe.

Juvenile Browner above than adults, and usually somewhat darker below, with heavier barring. Both sexes initially have a pinky-red head with pattern similar to adult female's, but with a broader black area across lower ear-coverts and with a whitish supercilium; males soon acquire more red feathering.

Bare parts Bill greyish-ivory to almost white, darker at base. Legs and feet grey or green-grey. Eyes white to pale yellowish. Orbital skin greyish.

GEOGRAPHICAL VARIATION Three races.

C. m. melanoleucos (S America east of Andes, south to Argentina and Brazil) Described above. Intergrades with *malherbii* in E Colombia and widely with *cearae* from Bolivia and NW Argentina across southern Brazil.
C. m. malherbii (W Panama to N and W Colombia) Has dark grey to brown-grey bill. Ground colour of underparts distinctly darker, more cinnamon-buff. Both sexes also have more extensive red in area of eyes.
C. m. cearae (E Brazil) Noticeably smaller, with shorter wings and proportionately shorter tail.

MEASUREMENTS Wing 161-181 (*cearae*), 171-205 (*melanoleucos*, *malherbii*); tail 100-127; bill 38.5-52; tarsus 30-39. Weight: 181-284.

VOICE Although this large woodpecker appears to be relatively silent, a great variety of calls has been described. The main call for keeping contact is a tree-frog-like or oboe-like *kwirr kwirr-ah, squeer squeer-ah-hah*, or *kiarhh rai-ai-ai-ai* uttered when perched or upon landing. When moderately agitated, *ca* and *ca-wa-rr-r* calls can be heard. Shrill, piping *put put puttas*, which may be kept up for minutes, indicates great excitement. Also *chiz-ik* in displays. Low intimate notes before copulation and at changeovers at the nest sound like *wuk wuk, wrr wrr, wun wun*, and *uh uh*. Drumming is typically a strong blow followed by a short, weak vibrating roll, *da-drrr*, consisting of 2-4 strokes (may be inaudible at greater distances); such bursts are usually delivered at a rate of 1-2 per minute, 3 per minute being a fast rate. Single monotonous rolls, *torrrrr*, may be given throughout the day, presumably used by pair members to keep in touch when travelling through the forest together. Males drum more, especially during the nesting season.

HABITS An active, conspicuous and relatively tame woodpecker, which is observed in pairs or small groups; pair members usually keep within 15m, and often much less, of each other. Forages at heights varying from 6 to 25m, most feeding being at intermediate levels, on tall, dead tree trunks in the forest or on isolated trees a considerable distance from actual forest or woodland. A versatile feeder, with a strong preference for wood-boring feeding techniques. Uncovers prey with relatively few powerful blows against bark or surface layers of wood; light taps seem to be more exploratory. Excavates well-rotted stubs for deeper-lying prey; may dig cavities 10cm or more deep, but never as large as the deep troughs dug by Pileated Woodpeckers (164) in N America. Trees are scaled by combining pecking with sideways blows to dislodge pieces of loose bark. Also probes natural cavities or clumps of epiphytes. Frequently hangs upside-down on relatively thin branches and moves along underside of dead limbs high up in the crown. Has deeply undulating flight with deep wingbeats. Moves from one tree to the next rather than making long flights from one 'good' tree to another, and explores many parts of a tree in quick succession; territories consequently are relatively small. Agonistic disputes between males may last over 50 minutes and are almost silent; attacks are met with spread wings. Otherwise, displays with crest-raising and with head-swinging and simultaneous calls. Crimson-crested Woodpeckers are usually tolerant towards sympatric Lineated Woodpeckers, and suffer from hole competition with aracaris (*Pteroglossus*).

FOOD Larvae of large (e.g. 4cm) wood-boring beetles, hard-shelled insects, ants and termites. Also takes pyralid caterpillars, small insects, and berries (*Loranthaceae*).

BREEDING The main breeding season (Panama) covers the end of the rainy season and beginning of the dry season, i.e. November-January; breeding season in Colombia extends from December to May, in the Guianas from December to March, in N Venezuela from April to July, in N and NW Brazil occurs in July, and in Ecuador in April. Farther south, breeding seasons vary: May-August in Bolivia, August-October in Peru, September-November in Argentina. *C. m. cearae* nests November-December. Other Brazilian populations, besides those mentioned, breed May to December. Stubs of large diameter (45-50cm) are optimal for nesting. The nest is high up and has an oval entrance, and is excavated by both sexes. Male and female incubate a clutch of 2-3(4) eggs, incubation stints lasting over half an hour. Both sexes care for the young, which stay with their parents almost to the next breeding season.

REFERENCES ffrench 1990; Haverschmidt 1968; Hilty & Brown 1984; Kilham 1972b; Meyer de Schauensee & Phelps 1978; Olrog 1984; Parker *et al.* 1982; Ridgeley 1981; Ridgely & Gwynne 1989; Short 1970a, 1975; Sick 1993; Snyder 1966; Wetmore 1968.

176 GUAYAQUIL WOODPECKER
Campephilus gayaquilensis   Plate 51

Forms a superspecies with *guatemalensis* and *melanoleucos.*

IDENTIFICATION Length c. 32-34cm. Large, with long, chisel-tipped bill slightly curved on culmen and broad across nostrils. A red-headed, crested, black and white species very closely related to and sometimes considered conspecific with Crimson-crested Woodpecker (175). Differs from the latter mainly in lacking large pale area around base of bill, in having lower back to uppertail-coverts variably barred buffish and black, and in the female having entire forehead to crest red (as male); dark areas generally somewhat browner.

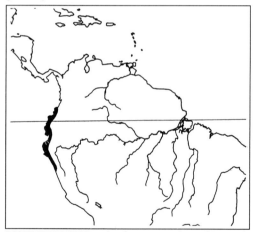

DISTRIBUTION Restricted to western slope of S American Andes and adjacent lowlands, from SW Colombia (SW Cauca) south to NW Peru (south to Cajamarca).

HABITAT This woodpecker replaces Crimson-crested in part of its range. It occurs in humid to dry deciduous forests, at forest edge, in tall second growth, and in mangroves. Reaches to 800m, and occasionally higher, to 1500m (Ecuador, Peru).

DESCRIPTION
Adult male Small black and white oval spot on rear lower ear-coverts. Rest of head and crest red, sometimes with black and buff of feather bases showing through. Chin and

throat black, sometimes with red feather tips at sides. Neck to upper breast, mantle, scapulars and upper back black, with white stripes down sides of neck and mantle meeting in centre of back; lower back to uppertail-coverts variably barred white-buff and blackish, sometimes all blackish in central part of back and rump. Upperwing and its coverts brownish-black to black, browner on flight feathers, with small area of cinnamon or buff on inner webs. Uppertail dark brown to blackish-brown. Lower breast to undertail-coverts whitish-buff to pale cinnamon-buff, barred brownish-black, bars narrower on lower underparts. Underwing white, becoming pale cinnamon at bases of primaries, with brown tip and trailing edge. Undertail brown.

Adult female Differs from male in having broad white moustachial stripe joining with white neck stripe, with black patch at lower rear corner of ear-coverts; fully black chin and throat.

Juvenile As adults, but normally less (or more obscurely) barred on rump and underparts. Young male has head pattern much as adult female, but with some red feather tips in white moustache. Young female differs from adult in having black on forehead and in front of eyes extending as two dark bands back, respectively, through centre of crown and crest and through lower ear-coverts to hindneck, with a patch of white on rear side of head.

Bare parts Bill greyish, paler on lower mandible. Legs and feet greyish-brown to greenish-grey. Eyes pale yellow.

GEOGRAPHICAL VARIATION None. Monotypic.

MEASUREMENTS Wing 175-190. Weight: 230-253.

VOICE Drumming is a loud double rap.

HABITS Probably rather similar to those of Crimson-crested Woodpecker. Often met with in pairs, which are easily detected by their loud hammering. Forages on dead branches in the canopy and in emergent trees.

FOOD Larvae of wood-boring beetles.

BREEDING Recorded in October and May.

REFERENCES Hilty & Brown 1984; Parker *et al.* 1982.

177 CREAM-BACKED WOODPECKER
Campephilus leucopogon   Plate 52

IDENTIFICATION Length c. 28-30cm. Large, with long, straight, chisel-tipped bill very broad across nostrils. Distinctive black-bodied and relatively short-tailed woodpecker with conspicuous pale creamy mantle. Male has red head and crest, with small black and white mark on ear-coverts; female has black on front part of face and through central crown to crest, with contrasting white moustache. In flight, shows pale cinnamon-buff wing patch.

DISTRIBUTION Southern-central parts of S America: from Uruguay, S Brazil (Rio Grande do Sul, Rio Negro), Argentina (La Rioja, Córdoba, Entre Ríos, Corrientes) and W and C Paraguay to NC Bolivia (Santa Cruz, Cochabamba).

HABITAT A species of the xeric woodlands of the chaco; occurs in savannas, pastures with copses, groves, woodland and transitional forests, up to 2500m.

DESCRIPTION
Adult male Small oval spot of black and white at lower rear edge of ear-coverts. Rest of head and crest red, with red feather tips extending a variable distance down foreneck

(latter all black when worn). Hindneck and mantle white, feathers tipped pale cinnamon-buff, becoming black on lower back to uppertail-coverts, sometimes with a few black-barred buff feathers in centre of back. Upperwing and its coverts black, flight feathers with large area of pale cinnamon towards bases of inner webs. Uppertail black. Entire underparts black. Underwing black, with pale cinnamon at bases of flight feathers, and with narrow whitish to pale cinnamon-buff on leading coverts. Undertail black.

Adult female Has less red on head, being black from forehead through crown to central area of crest (which is longer than male's), on lores, around eyes and along lower ear-coverts, with white moustachial stripe bordered by black submoustachial stripe and black upper chin; foreneck and sides of neck all black.

Juvenile Very like respective adult, but with red of head more orangey and somewhat less widespread. Young males similar to adult female, but with red crown to crest and red feathers in white moustache, though has more black on chin/throat; young females have red restricted to rear crown sides and underside of crest.

Bare parts Bill ivory-coloured. Legs and feet grey. Eyes pale yellow.

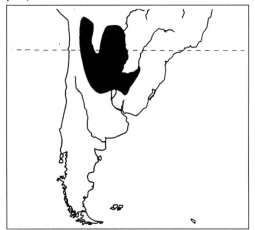

GEOGRAPHICAL VARIATION None. Monotypic.

MEASUREMENTS Wing 170-190; tail 92-107. Weight: 203-281.

VOICE Call a *pi-ow* or *kwee-yaw*, sometimes repeated. Melodious whirring notes are heard during close encounters between pair members. Drumming a double rap.

HABITS Apparently solitary outside the breeding season. Not shy. Visits tall trees, isolated trees in open areas, and descends to fallen logs. Forages mainly by powerful hammering, and less frequently by pecking and probing.

FOOD Larvae of beetles.

BREEDING Breeds mainly in September, to October and November. Nests high up (6-8m) in a tree or palm; entrance 'droplet-shaped'. Both adults feed the nestlings.

REFERENCES Dubs 1983; Gore & Gepp 1978; Hoy 1968; Olrog 1984; Short 1970a, 1975; Sick 1961, 1993.

178 MAGELLANIC WOODPECKER
Campephilus magellanicus   Plate 52

IDENTIFICATION Length c. 36-38cm. Very large, with long, chisel-tipped bill slightly curved on culmen and broad across nostrils. Unmistakable: the only big and black woodpecker within its range, and the largest woodpecker in S America. Virtually all black, male with red head and long crest and female with small amount of red around bill base, both having white on inner webs of tertials. Female's black crest is particularly long and pointed. In flight, also shows some white at base of primaries and in carpal area, forming a single wing patch. White shafts of uppertail-covert feathers sometimes quite pronounced. In worn plumage, can show more extensive white in plumage as white bases of feathers become more visible.

DISTRIBUTION Along the Andes of S South America in S Chile, from Curico to Isla Grande (Tierra del Fuego), and in forested parts of adjacent SW Argentina. Seems to be not uncommon, and perhaps locally even common.

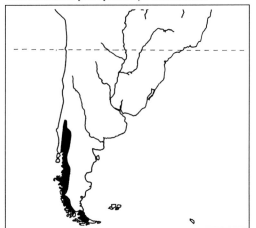

HABITAT Mature *Nothofagus* and *Nothofagus-Cupressus* forest, often with bamboo undergrowth. Also visits disturbed forest and more open woodland. From sea level to the timberline at about 2000m.

DESCRIPTION
Adult male Entire head and long crest red, normally with variable number of black and white bars of feather bases visible (particularly around ear-coverts, on crown and on throat). Rest of plumage glossy black to brown-black (browner on underparts), with white on bases of inner webs of primaries and more broadly on inner webs of tertials, primaries also with small white tips; uppertail-coverts and exceptionally also rump with white shaft streaks (rarely, white extends onto webs), and usually a narrow area of white in alula region. (In worn plumage, black and white bases of head feathers become more obvious, white-based feathers of flanks and belly often show as faint barring, white primary tips are lost, while whole plumage becomes duller and less glossy.)

Adult female As male, but somewhat smaller and shorter-billed, and with red restricted to lower forehead, lores, chin and front part of moustachial area. Crest narrow, and longer than male's.

Juvenile Much as adult female but browner overall, without gloss, and with smaller crest. Young male shows scattered pale red feather tips on head, especially in moustachial region.

Bare parts Bill blue-grey to blackish-grey. Legs and feet dark grey. Eyes yellow, with more golden outer ring.

GEOGRAPHICAL VARIATION None. Monotypic.

MEASUREMENTS Wing 205-228; tail 139-163; bill of male 47.7-60.2, of female 43.5-54.5; tarsus 33-39. Weight: male 312-363, female 276-312.

VOICE Most common calls are explosive, nasal, variable, and of two notes, *pi-caá* to *keé-yew*, also a more gargling *weerr-weeeerrr*. Also rather common are 1-3 *toot* notes, not so nasal in quality as the calls of the two following species (179, 180). In addition, a loud and long *cray-cra-cra-cra-cra-cra*. Loud single or double blows are its instrumental signal.

HABITS Met with singly, in pairs or in groups of 3-4. Forages at all heights, from fallen logs to main trunks and the outer twigs of the crown. Both dead and live trees or parts of trees are visited. Pecks and probes, with sustained powerful hammering less common. Bark is removed now and then, and this species also produces deep excavations. Possible strong ecological dimorphism needs to be studied. Moves swiftly within a tree, may cling in tit-like fashion, and changes trees frequently with audible wing noise. Crest-raising is a common form of display. Distance between pairs about 2km. The only potentially competing woodpecker is the much smaller and apparently less common Striped Woodpecker (109).

FOOD Grubs and adult beetles.

BREEDING Breeds October-January. Holes are 5-15m above the ground in large trees with dead parts, and the entrance is circular to drop-shaped. Clutch comprises 1-4 eggs.

REFERENCES Fjeldså & Krabbe 1990; Hackenberg 1989; Johnson 1967; Olrog 1984; Short 1970b.

---

179 IMPERIAL WOODPECKER
Campephilus imperialis   Plate 52

Forms a superspecies with *principalis*.

IDENTIFICATION Length c. 56-60cm; the world's largest woodpecker. Huge, with very long, chisel-tipped bill slightly curved on culmen and broad across nostrils. Massive size coupled with powerful ivory-coloured bill, black plumage with black and white wings and white mantle stripes and prominent crest highly distinctive. Male with red crown sides, nape and lower part of crest; female with all-black head and extraordinarily long, strongly upcurled crest quite unmistakable. A magnificent woodpecker, once widely distributed in Mexico, but now almost certainly extinct.

Similar species The allopatric Ivory-billed Woodpecker (180), probably also extinct, is similar but somewhat smaller (although still very large), and has prominent white neck stripes.

DISTRIBUTION A Mexican endemic which, though formerly not uncommon, is probably extinct; historical distribution covers the Sierra Madre Occidental in Sonora, Chihuahua, Durango, Jalisco, and Michoacán. A number of recent claimed sightings have not been substantiated.

HABITAT Its haunts are/were extensive park-like stands of large pines, containing many dead trees, in the oak-pine forest belt in mountains at (1670)1900-3050m.

DESCRIPTION
Adult male Side of forecrown back to underside of crest

and nape red, with white feather bases. Rest of head, neck, upperparts and underparts, and tail black, glossed blue on head, neck and upperparts, with narrow white line down each side of mantle. Upperwing black, glossed blue on coverts, with inner primaries tipped white, and secondaries and tertials all white apart from black bases. Underwing similar, but with lesser and median coverts and primary coverts also white (with a few black spots/bars).

Adult female As male, but with no red on head, and with even longer crest curving strongly upwards and forwards.

Juvenile Duller, browner, than adults, unglossed, and with white feathers to all flight feathers, but somewhat less white in secondaries. Both sexes initially without red in head and with very long crest, but red soon appearing on rear of head of male.

Bare parts Bill ivory-white to ivory-yellow. Legs and feet grey. Eyes pale yellow; greyish in juveniles.

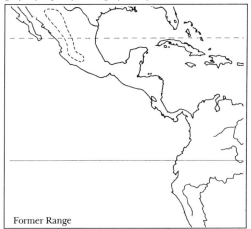

Former Range

GEOGRAPHICAL VARIATION None. Monotypic.

MEASUREMENTS Wing 292-320; tail 183-211; bill of male 78.5-85.5, of female 72.5-84.7; tarsus 45.5-51.

VOICE Toy-trumpet-like calls, apparently similar to those of its close relatives.

HABITS This species lives in pairs and in family groups of 3-5 (10?) birds. The main foraging technique is scaling bark from dead trees and deep excavation. The same tree may be revisited over a prolonged period of time. May cling upside-down and forage on the underside of branches. Groups seem to roost in neighbouring holes. Apparent nest competitors are large parrots.

FOOD Presumably large beetle larvae (Cerambycidae).

BREEDING The egg-laying season is February to June. The nest is excavated high up in the trunk of a dead tree. Clutch of 2 eggs.

REFERENCES Collar *et al.* 1992, 1994; Nelson 1898; Tanner 1964.

180 IVORY-BILLED WOODPECKER
Campephilus principalis   **Plate 52**

Forms a superspecies with *imperialis*.

Ivory-billed (above) and Pileated (below): note differences in distribution of white on both wing surfaces.

IDENTIFICATION Length c. 48-53cm. Very large, with long, chisel-tipped bill slightly curved on culmen and broad across nostrils. A little smaller than the presumably extinct Imperial Woodpecker (179) but similar in plumage, though with a white stripe on side of neck; male also with slightly more red on rear of head, and female with much shorter black crest than female Imperial. Apparently extinct in N America, and probably now also in Cuba.

Similar species Recent reports of this species in southeast N America have usually been shown to have involved misidentified Pileated Woodpeckers (164). Latter, although very big, is smaller than Ivory-billed, has complete white cheek stripe, short white supercilium, white throat and dark bill, and lacks white mantle stripes. When perched, Pileated shows little, if any, white in wings; in flight, it also has less white in upperwing (at bases of primaries only, whereas Ivory-billed has entire inner flight feathers white) and a black underwing with white coverts (Ivory-billed has white underwing with black wingtip and central band). Ivory-bills also fly without undulations and thus give more an impression of a duck than of a woodpecker.

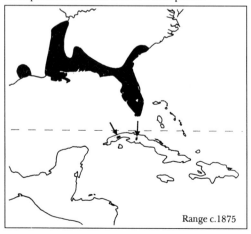

Range c.1875

DISTRIBUTION Most likely extinct in both of its former disjunct areas of occurrence, the SE USA and Cuba, through habitat destruction and direct persecution. Formerly ranged from SE North Carolina, S Kentucky, Illinois, Missouri, Arkansas, Oklahoma through Texas and Louisiana to Florida. In Cuba, this species was found in the east and the west of the island. The last observations on the continent relate to Louisiana, where the last known population was sacrificed for planting soybeans, and other sites between Florida and Texas; recent reports and efforts to find this species in Louisiana, South Carolina, Georgia, Mississippi or Florida (e.g. Jackson 1989; see also literature cited in Collar *et al.* 1992) are probably far too optimistic. The fate of the Cuban population is not much better: although sightings indicate that a few individuals may have survived at least to 1992, the chances of recovery of this beautiful woodpecker are virtually nil; its last stronghold was the eastern mountains (Sierra de Moa, Sierra del Cristal to 1920, Sierra de Nipe), and the last definite sightings were made in 1987.

HABITAT The species' continental habitats consisted of heavy forests in often inaccessible hardwood and cypress swamps; originally, probably associated mainly with pine forests with many dead trees. In Cuba, in forests of the lowlands and the mountains. In the latter, pine forests (*Pinus cubensis*) form(ed) the last haunts. Lowland habitats were probably more diverse and included tropical hardwood and mixed pine forests. The presence of many dead trees, particularly also after fires, is important. At least 16km² of suitable habitat are needed to hold one pair.

DESCRIPTION
C. p. principalis **Adult male** Side of forecrown back to underside of crest, rear head and nape red, with paler feather bases. Rest of head, neck, upperparts and underparts, and tail black, glossed blue above and browner below, but with white stripes from lower edge of rear ear-coverts extending backwards and down neck sides and broadly along mantle sides to meet in centre of back; some indication of vague pale barring on flanks not infrequent, and occasionally some white spots in outer tail. Upperwing black, glossed blue on coverts, with inner primaries tipped white and secondaries and tertials all white apart from black bases. Underwing similar, but with lesser and median coverts and primary coverts also white, usually with a few black spots/bars on primary coverts.

Adult female Slightly smaller than male and lacking red on head, but with somewhat longer crest (sometimes slightly upcurved).

Juvenile Browner and less glossy than adults, with shorter crest; white tips to all primaries, but less white on underwing. Head pattern of both sexes initially as adult female, young male acquiring red of adult gradually over first three months.

Bare parts Bill ivory-white to creamy. Legs and feet medium to pale grey. Eyes white to creamy-white; brown in juveniles.

GEOGRAPHICAL VARIATION Two very similar races.
    C. p. principalis (formerly SE USA; now extinct) Described above.
    C. p. bairdii (Cuba, but probably now extinct) Differs from nominate only in having slightly shorter and narrower bill and in white neck stripe extending a little further forwards along lower edge of ear-coverts.

MEASUREMENTS Wing 240-263 (*principalis*), 236-255 (*bairdii*); tail 147-166 (*principalis*), 137-165 (*bairdii*); bill of male 63-73 (*principalis*), 59-61 (*bairdii*), of female 60.5-67.5 (*principalis*), 58-60 (*bairdii*); tarsus 40.4-46 (*principalis*), 40-42 (*bairdii*). Weight: c. 450-570.

VOICE The common note when alarmed is *kent* or *hant*,

often repeated sometimes in fast series, and like a clarinet or toy-trumpet in timbre; this call is also uttered as double-note, with emphasis on first note and second being lower-pitched. Pair members exchange low conversational notes. Nestlings initially utter a weak buzz, later a louder chirp. Instrumental signal consists of single or double raps and tapping at or, respectively, in the nest.

HABITS Forages at low to upper levels, rarely, if at all, descending to the ground. Dead trees, for instance pines killed by fire, or dead parts of live trees are the favoured feeding sites. Removing bark from dead trees with blows of the bill is a very common feeding mode, and scaled trees may give away this species' presence. Also produces deep pits similar in size to those made by Pileated Woodpecker, but in the case of Ivory-billed they lead to the tunnels of beetle larvae rather than ants. Stops at one feeding site for a few minutes to half an hour. Flight is direct and not undulating, but before landing this huge woodpecker makes an upward swoop. Displays with crest-raising and possibly with head-swinging. Home ranges are huge; maximum density in USA was 0.006 pairs/10ha. Interactions with Pileated Woodpeckers may have been detrimental to the declining Ivory-billed populations.

FOOD The main components of its diet are (large) larvae of wood-boring beetles (Cerambycidae, Buprestidae, Scolytidae, Elateridae and Eucnemidae), which are also fed to the young. Also takes fruits, berries and nuts.

BREEDING In N America, this species bred in January-April; nesting season in Cuba March-June, with a peak in April. The nest is excavated in large dead or dying trees, occasionally palms in Cuba, at 8-15m. Entrance more or less vertically oval or drop-shaped, measuring a minimum of 8.9cm in diameter to a maximum height of 14.6 (17)cm and a maximum width of 12cm (average Pileated Woodpecker nest measures 8.9-11.5cm in diameter). Clutch 2-3 eggs, usually 3-4. Incubation by both sexes, the male incubating at night. Both parents feed the young directly. Brooding and nest sanitation apparently mainly the male's chore. The young are regularly fed by the parents for at least two more months after fledging, which takes place about five weeks after hatching, and they remain much longer still in the parents' territory.

REFERENCES Allen & Kellogg 1937; Bent 1939; Bond 1985; Dennis 1948; Short & Horne 1990; Tanner 1942.

181 BANDED WOODPECKER
Picus miniaceus   Plate 53

Other name: Banded Red Woodpecker

IDENTIFICATION Length c. 23-26cm. Small, with shortish, slightly chisel-tipped bill curved on culmen, fairly broad across nostrils and very broad at base. Has dull red crown and wings and yellow tips to crest feathers. Back is generally dull olive with paler barring (bars indistinct in worn plumage), with somewhat brighter, unbarred rump, while underparts are barred pale and dark; throat and breast dull brownish. Female has white-speckled face.

Similar species Crimson-winged Woodpecker (183) is similar, but is brighter overall, with greener and unbarred upperparts, all-green underparts with bars confined to flanks, and male has red moustache.

DISTRIBUTION Found from peninsular Thailand and Burma south of 12°30'N, south to Sumatra, including Bangka, Belitung and Nias Islands, W and C Java and Borneo. Rather uncommon in north of range, becoming

more frequent southwards (e.g. the commonest forest woodpecker in Singapore), but rare in Java.

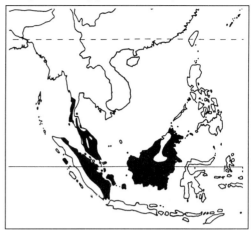

HABITAT Frequents mainly dense primary (dipterocarp) evergreen forest, but also occurs in secondary growth, forest edge and open woods, including rubber plantations, gardens and mangroves at lower altitudes. Its altitudinal range extends from the lowlands to montane habitats, usually below 900m in SE Asia, although found up to 1200m. In Java up to 1500m and in Borneo to 1400m, possibly to 1700m.

DESCRIPTION
P. m. perlutus **Adult male** Forehead reddish-brown; crown to nape dull red, with thin, elongated crest feathers extensively yellow at tips. Sides of head and neck dark brown, with reddish feather tips. Chin and throat brown, usually tipped rufous. Upperparts dull greenish-olive, becoming yellow on rump, with mantle and back barred dull buffish; uppertail-coverts olive-brown, often with some dull buff barring. Upperwing-coverts dull red (this colour usually extending partly onto scapulars), frequently with an element of olive tinging; flight feathers brown, outer webs of primary bases, secondaries and tertials extensively dull olive-tinged red, and barred buffish on outer webs and bases of inner webs of primaries and on inner webs of secondaries. Uppertail blackish. Upper breast rufous-brown, occasionally with faint barring; lower breast to undertail-coverts whitish-buff to pale rufous, narrowly barred dark brown, bars strongest on flanks. Underwing brown, barred buff. Undertail brownish to buff-brown. (In worn plumage, red areas become browner and pale barring on upperparts less obvious.)

Adult female Slightly smaller than male, but with proportionately longer tail. Has face and throat browner, lacking most of red feather tips, and with pale buffish speckling.

Juvenile Duller than adults, with more obscure barring below. Males have some red on crown and nape, females only on hindcrown/nape area.

Bare parts Bill blackish-grey, paler on lower mandible. Legs and feet green-grey to dull greenish. Eyes dark rufous-chestnut to red.

GEOGRAPHICAL VARIATION Four races.
　　P. m. perlutus (S Burma and peninsular Thailand) Described above.
　　P. m. malaccensis (Malaysia, Sumatra and Borneo) Very like *perlutus*, but dark bars below broader.
　　P. m. niasensis (Nias Island) A little smaller than *malaccensis* and brighter overall, with stronger red on

crown and red-tinged mantle feathers, red extending to upper breast; yellower above.

P. m. miniaceus (Java) Averages longer-billed. Breast more clearly barred than in other races and often with pale speckling; mantle feathers red-tipped.

MEASUREMENTS Wing 113-132; tail 73-91; bill 25-29; tarsus 22.8-24.1. Weight: 79-102.

VOICE Single *keek* call notes. A screaming *kwee*, jay-like, singly or in series of up to seven notes on the same pitch, *chewerk-chewerk-chewerk*. A shorter call, described as a mournful, descending *peew*, is sometimes uttered at intervals or is interspersed in *kwi-wi-ta-wi-kwi* series during encounters. Not known to drum.

HABITS An unobtrusive woodpecker, met with singly or in pairs, which may feed close together. Forages at all levels of the forest, but is most easily observed at lower heights, where it searches for food among vines and dense branches, on large-diameter trunks, particularly of dead trees, and on fallen logs. In the canopy, visits branches, decayed stubs and the bases of epiphytes. Tapping with light blows, probing and gleaning are the main foraging modes. Movements are slow and deliberate; may pause for some time to scan the surroundings, and a single site is exploited for a considerable period. Visual displays include crest-raising, and swinging movements of head and body. In addition, a gliding and floating flight, interspersed with weak fluttering, is given by the male in the presence of the female.

FOOD Ants and their eggs and larvae.

BREEDING Breeding records from Malaysia and the Greater Sundas span January to August; excavation of an apparent nest was observed in Borneo in August. Both sexes excavate the breeding hole, in decayed trees or dead and rotten parts of live trees. The male roosts in the nest. Lays 2 or 3 eggs.

REFERENCES King & Dickinson 1975; Lekagul & Round 1991; MacKinnon 1990; MacKinnon & Phillipps 1993; Medway & Wells 1976; Robinson 1928; Short 1973a, 1978; Smythies 1981.

---

182 LESSER YELLOWNAPE
Picus chlorolophus   Plate 53

Other name: Lesser Yellow-naped Woodpecker
Forms a superspecies with *puniceus*.

IDENTIFICATION Length c. 25-28cm. Small to medium-sized, with fairly long, almost straight, chisel-tipped bill broad across nostrils. A highly variable species, both individually and geographically, but always with prominent yellow crest and green or greenish upperparts, and with dull red in flight feathers (but red generally not visible at rest). In most of range, underparts are dark green on breast and paler and dark-barred below this, but southernmost and easternmost populations are generally all dark on underparts with reduced amount of (pale) barring. Males have red on crown sides (entire crown/hindcrown red in southern half of India and in Sri Lanka) and a short red moustache (except in east of range), while females usually have small amount of red at sides of hindcrown; one or two pale stripes running backwards from the bill are present in all populations apart from those from C India to Sri Lanka. This is a common woodpecker in most of its range, sometimes fairly tame, and rather noisy.

Similar species Greater Yellownape (184) is larger and more uniformly dull green, with a more prominent and generally upturned bright yellow crest (head looks triangu-

lar in shape), and has a yellow throat or moustache (rufous on female) and unbarred underparts (note that Greater Yellownape lacks all red in plumage). Crimson-winged (183) and Checker-throated (185) Woodpeckers have a yellow crest, but both have much red or chestnut in the wings and also differ in too many other ways to cause any confusion.

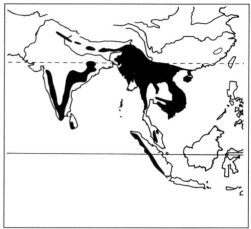

DISTRIBUTION This species occurs from the western foothills of the Himalayas at around 76°E, south to Sri Lanka and east to Guangxi and Hainan in S China, and then south through SE Asia to southern Vietnam, with isolated populations in Fujian in SE China and in the W Malaysian and Sumatran highlands. Common to fairly common throughout most of its range, but rather rare in China.

MOVEMENTS Recorded as a rare vagrant to NE Pakistan.

HABITAT Inhabits evergreen and moist deciduous forests, dry forests, teak forest, woodland, bamboo, scrub, plantations and well-wooded village gardens. Habitats are most diverse in India, especially where no other congeners occur. Ranges from foothills (800m) to 1400m in Sumatra. In SE Asia (Malaysia, Thailand and Vietnam), from lowlands (above 900m in Malaysia) to 1800m, an elevation also reached in Sri Lanka; and to about 2100m in Sikkim and Nepal, where common only to 1750m.

DESCRIPTION
P. c. chlorolophus Adult male Forehead and crown green, bordered at sides and rear with red feather tips, becoming golden-yellow or orange on crest and hindneck. Ear-coverts and neck sides olive-green, usually with small area of white just behind upper corner of eye. Upper lores black. Lower lores to eye and below lower edge of ear-coverts white, streaked/mottled olive. Moustachial stripe red, with some olive-green feather bases usually showing. Chin and throat olive to greyish, variably marked with white streaks/bars, the latter often forming vague border to red moustache (but throat pattern very variable; on some mainly whitish but on a few all dark). Upperparts, upperwing-coverts and tertials green, tinged golden-yellow, with rump often brighter. Flight feathers with outer webs of secondaries and of inner primaries rufous, edged green (rufous more prominent when wings worn); rest of primaries and inner webs of secondaries dark brown, with white bar-like spots. Uppertail blackish, outer feathers washed green. Lower throat and breast greyish-green to dark green; belly to undertail-coverts off-white, with slightly diffuse olive to olive-grey or brownish-olive arrowhead bars. Underwing brownish with olive coverts, barred whitish. Undertail as uppertail, but generally duller.

Adult female A little smaller than male. Lacks red in moustache and has red of crown confined to a small patch at rear sides.

Juvenile Much as adults, but duller above, more barred on breast, and with less red on crown than respective adult.

Bare parts Bill blackish-grey, paler (often yellow-green) at base of lower mandible. Legs and feet greyish-green. Eyes red-brown to dark red. Orbital skin slaty-grey.

GEOGRAPHICAL VARIATION Varies considerably individually and geographically; of many races described, nine are recognised here, all being highly variable.

P. c. chlorolophus (E Nepal east to N Vietnam) Described above. The most brightly coloured above (yellow-tinged) of all races, and with the most golden or orange colour on crest. Population in Laos ('*laotianus*') appears to intergrade with *annamensis* in south and with *citrinocristatus* in north.

P. c. simlae (Himachal Pradesh to W Nepal) The largest race, with longer wings and longer tail than nominate. Upperparts greener, less yellow, and nape less golden.

P. c. annamensis (SE Thailand to S Vietnam) Smaller than nominate, and darker green above. Crown with more extensive red; lower underparts whiter, with barring reaching onto lower breast but rather more obscure on belly/flanks.

The following six races all have dark underparts with variable pale markings.

P. c. chlorigaster (C and S India) Smaller than above three races. Distinctly darker green on upperparts; underparts dull olive-green, with light pale bar-like spotting on flanks and belly and pale spots on breast. Face lacks white markings, and crown shows more red and less extensive yellow in crest.

P. c. wellsi (Sri Lanka) As *chlorigaster* but somewhat darker, with pale markings below reduced and with even more red on crown (obscuring much of yellow crest); wings with slightly more rufous.

P. c. citrinocristatus (Tonkin part of N Vietnam, and Fujian) Upperparts only slightly yellow-tinged; underparts sooty-grey, with bare tinge of green (strongest on breast), and with some paler bars on flanks. Has pale cheek stripe, but red moustache of male more or less lacking.

P. c. longipennis (Hainan) As *citrinocristatus* but slightly smaller, with stronger green tinge below and with flanks more barred.

P. c. rodgersi (W Malaysian highlands) As *chlorigaster* in plumage, but more barred (less spotted) below, with prominent pale cheek stripe, less red on crown and slight golden tinge to crest.

P. c. vanheysti (Sumatran highlands) As *rodgersi*, but somewhat yellower above and greener (less grey) below.

MEASUREMENTS Wing 115-146; tail 74-104; bill (from skull) 24-33; tarsus 19-24. Weight: 57-74 (*chlorigaster*), 74-83 (*simlae*).

VOICE A loud, mournful, bulbul-like *pee-a* or *peee-ui*, with emphasis on first syllable, is the most common call; also a short *chak*. (Usual calls of Greater Yellownape are more disyllabic.) Also utters slow series of up to ten notes, *kwee-kwee-kwee-kwee-kwee*. Low chuckling noises are heard in close intersexual confrontations. Drums only occasionally.

HABITS Noisy and conspicuous. Forages singly, in pairs or in small groups comprising an adult pair and their young. Regularly joins mixed-species flocks, particularly with babblers, drongos and other insectivores, jays and magpies, or other woodpeckers. Forages in smaller trees, in the undergrowth, often on fallen logs and dead trees in windthrow areas. Seems usually to prefer tree trunks and larger branches, but also manages to move along thin pendent branches to get at nests of *Crematogaster* ants, or to probe at flowers. Forages commonly on the ground, and even goes after insects living in dung pats. Except in the company of other species, movements are slow, and much time may be spent at one feeding site. Gleaning and probing are the main foraging techniques, excavating by pecking and hammering being infrequent. The crest is raised when other individuals are close or during flights between foraging sites. Calls are delivered with crest raised and the bill pointing upwards.

FOOD Ants including *Crematogaster*, beetles and their larvae (including dung beetles); other insect larvae. Also takes berries and nectar.

BREEDING Breeds from February to July, but mainly March-April, in Sri Lanka; from April to May in Sikkim; from March to May in Burma; and from February to May in Malaysia. Nests, excavated by both sexes, may be lower than 2m from the ground, mostly below 5m, or as high as 20m. Various species of trees are used, which may be dead or provide a dead branch as nest site. The clutch contains 3 or 4 (5) eggs, 1-2 in the south. Both sexes incubate, and feed the young by regurgitation.

REFERENCES Ali 1962; Ali & Ripley 1970; Diesselhorst 1968; Gyldenstolpe 1916; Henry 1971; Inskipp & Inskipp 1991; Lekagul & Round 1991; MacKinnon & Phillipps 1993; Medway & Wells 1976; Phillips 1978; Proud 1958; Roberts 1991; Robinson 1928; Short 1973a; Smythies 1953; Stanford & Mayr 1941.

---

183 CRIMSON-WINGED WOODPECKER
Picus puniceus   Plate 53

Forms a superspecies with *chlorophus*.

IDENTIFICATION Length c. 25cm. Small, with longish, almost straight, chisel-tipped bill broad across nostrils. Green body with contrasting red wings, red crown and 'untidy' yellow crest make this a fairly distinctive woodpecker. Male has a red moustache, female's face being all green, and both have a bicoloured bill and a fairly prominent area of bluish to grey bare skin around the eye. Fairly common throughout its range.

Similar species Banded Woodpecker (181) is much less brightly coloured and less green, with wings a duller red, and is barred below (and, less obviously, above).

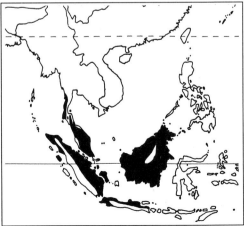

DISTRIBUTION Resident from S Burma (Tenasserim) and peninsular Thailand south through W Malaysia (extinct Singapore) to Sumatra, including Nias and Bangka Islands, Java and Borneo. Common to fairly common throughout its range, and one of the most frequently encountered woodpeckers in the Malaysian rainforest.

HABITAT Evergreen primary and secondary forest with scattered tall trees, forest edge and plantations. May also visit coastal scrub and gardens in Sumatra and Java (though still very much a forest bird). A lowland species which ranges up to 600m, locally to 900m, but also up to 1300m (Fraser's Hill, Malaysia) and 1500m, especially where the similar Lesser Yellownape (182) is absent. The latter replaces it at higher altitudes. Is said to occur at up to 1500m in Borneo.

DESCRIPTION
P. p. observandus **Adult male** Forehead to hindcrown dark red, often with dark olive feather bases showing through; elongated nape feathers forming yellow crest, yellow continuing down hindneck (and even at times onto uppermost mantle). Lores black. Short red moustachial stripe. Rest of head, chin and throat olive-green, generally unmarked. Upperparts, including scapulars, yellowish-green (yellowest when fresh), with brighter, yellower rump. Upperwing-coverts crimson-red (this often extending partly onto scapulars), inner webs sometimes with some green; tertials green, with crimson-red on outer webs extending variable distance towards tip; primaries and secondaries blackish-brown, outer webs of secondaries and basal edges of primaries crimson-red, and with well-spaced pale yellowish spots on inner webs of all feathers and on outer webs of most primaries. Uppertail brownish-black. Underparts dark olive to olive-green, with pale buffish spots or arrowhead marks on flanks (sometimes very diffuse and obscure). Underwing brown, barred pale yellowish on coverts and bases of flight feathers. Undertail brownish, suffused olive.

Adult female Lacks male's red moustache.

Juvenile Duller than adults, often greyer above and below, with more extensive markings on underparts; red of head less extensive, normally confined to rear and sides of crown. Young males have at least some red tips in moustache, often almost as adult.

Bare parts Bill dark brown or grey-brown, with contrasting yellow to greenish-yellow lower mandible. Legs and feet dark greenish to olive. Eyes red to red-brown. Orbital skin blue to blue-grey.

GEOGRAPHICAL VARIATION Three races.
  P. p. observandus (range of species, except Java and Nias Island) Described above.
  P. p. puniceus (Java) Larger and darker than *observandus*. Rump more or less concolorous with back; throat browner.
  P. p. soligae (Nias Island) Paler than *observandus*, yellower above and greyer below; red of crown extends further onto crest, which thus shows much less yellow.

MEASUREMENTS Wing 117-138; tail 76-104; bill 26-31.5; tarsus 23-24. Weight: 77-96.

VOICE A single *peep*, about half as long as the *pee-a* call of Lesser Yellownape, is heard occasionally. Usually calls with a very distinctive *peé-bee*, the second syllable a little lower-pitched and shorter; may be extended to *peé-dee-dee-dee*. This call may be uttered during short pauses in foraging, or in long calling sessions, e.g. near the roost. Five to seven and more low-pitched *peep* notes, about two per second, are uttered in encounters, particularly when several birds are

involved. Low *wee-eek* series are heard when two woodpeckers meet at close distance. Drums rather weakly, in short bursts of less than 1 sec duration.

HABITS Forages singly, but mainly in pairs which keep in contact at moderate distances. Regularly joins mixed-species flocks. Favours tall trees, particularly emergent forest trees, even when these are in lower second growth or are free-standing. Seen mainly in the canopy on trunks and major branches. It finds its food on the bark, notably where there are lichens, and in crevices, by hammering in short bursts (frequently in hard live wood), probing, gleaning, and removing pieces of bark. Moves rather systematically over the bark, rarely spending much time (to 15 minutes) on a single spot. Appears to be more active than Banded Woodpecker, but less so than Checker-throated (185). Displays with conspicuous crest-raising, particularly when calling; at the same time the bird points its bill up, almost vertically. In close encounters, head- and body-swinging can be seen in addition.

FOOD Mainly ants and termites, including their eggs and grubs.

BREEDING Nests in January and February in W Malaysia, in June in Borneo, and breeds in September in C Java (these data should be taken as rough guidelines only; the breeding season is most likely more spread out and should be investigated). The hole is high up (18m has been reported) in a tree. Clutch 2 or 3 eggs.

REFERENCES King & Dickinson 1975; Lekagul & Round 1991; MacKinnon 1990; MacKinnon & Phillipps 1993; Medway & Wells 1976; Robinson 1928; Short 1973a, 1978; Smythies 1981.

---

184 GREATER YELLOWNAPE
Picus flavinucha   Plate 54

Other name: Greater Yellow-naped Woodpecker
Forms a superspecies with *mentalis*.

IDENTIFICATION Length c. 33-34cm. Rather large, with long, slightly chisel-tipped bill variably curved on culmen and fairly broad across nostrils, but broad at base. Mostly dark green, usually paler or greyer below, with conspicuous erect or somewhat upcurved yellow crest and yellow hindneck, and with flight feathers barred rufous and black; most populations have black and white pattern on throat. Male has prominent yellow throat and/or moustache, the yellow being replaced generally with chestnut on females. The neat crest gives the head a distinct triangular-shaped appearance when viewed from the side. A common woodpecker, often found in pairs or loose family parties which maintain constant vocal contact; active and noisy.

Similar species The somewhat smaller Checker-throated Woodpecker (185) is similar in shape and plumage, but has obvious reddish-brown on wings (including coverts) and chestnut neck sides and breast, lacks yellow throat/moustache, and appears not to overlap in range (occurs at lower levels where the two species approach each other). Lesser Yellownape (182) overlaps widely, but is smaller, with a different shape to head and crest, has at least some barring below, and has a different head plumage which always shows some red (Greater Yellownape lacks obvious red in all plumages).

DISTRIBUTION Ranges from the lower Himalayan slopes in Garhwal and Kumaon southeast in India to Orissa and NE Andhra Pradesh, and east to SE Tibet and in China to

S Yunnan, SE Sichuan, Guangxi and Hainan, with isolated population in C Fujian, and south through Burma and Indochina, with further isolated populations in the montane forests of W Malaysia and Sumatra. Common or fairly common throughout its range, but rare in China.

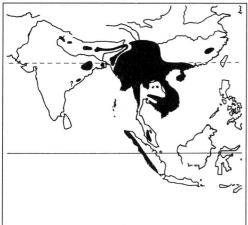

HABITAT Lives in various types of forest, in teak forests, open evergreen and in deciduous forests with tall trees, in oak and sal (*Shorea*) forests, in mixed and in pine forests, and in secondary growth; now and then near edges or on single dead trees in clearings. Retreats to forest patches in cultivated areas. Lowlands, in Sumatra above 800m, in W Malaysia above 900m and up to 2000m; elsewhere in SE Asia and India up to 2750m; in Nepal, most common between 300 and 1500m.

DESCRIPTION
P. f. flavinucha **Adult male** Forehead and crown olive-green, feathers tipped rufous-brown when fresh (rufous tips sometimes restricted to forehead and crown sides); tips of elongated hindcrown feathers and nape bright golden-yellow, this colour continuing down hindneck. Lores and ear-coverts dark olive-green, becoming blacker on rear neck sides. Chin and throat, including moustachial area, bright yellow; lower throat feathers blackish with white edges. Upperparts, including scapulars, plus wing-coverts and tertials, bright yellowish-green, darker on coverts, tertials sometimes with some rufous barring on inner webs. Primaries and secondaries dark green, becoming blackish-brown on outer primaries, all broadly barred rufous on both webs. Uppertail blackish. Olive-black of neck sides extends across upper breast, becoming plain greenish-grey on rest of underparts. Underwing brownish, barred paler. Undertail blackish-brown, washed greenish on outer feathers.

Adult female Somewhat less bulky and shorter-billed than male. Yellow of chin, throat and moustachial area replaced by rufous-brown.

Juvenile Duller than adults, with less golden crest, and with greyer underparts. Young males have buffy-yellow throat, occasionally spotted dark, rufous colour in moustache, and may show some red feather tips on crown; females much as adult, but with less rufous on throat.

Bare parts Bill dark grey, darker at base and paler (sometimes whitish) at tip. Legs and feet green-grey or grey. Eyes brownish-red or reddish; brown in juveniles. Orbital skin grey to greenish or blue-grey.

GEOGRAPHICAL VARIATION Seven races are recognised here, although several others have also been described.

P. f. flavinucha (northern part of range, from NW India to N Vietnam) Described above. Much individual variation. Generally large, with size decreasing clinally from north to south. Northwesternmost birds average longer-winged and generally show less of a yellow tinge to upperparts; separated as '*kumaonensis*', but differences are probably insufficient to warrant subspecific status.
The remaining races are all darker green above, with barring in wings redder and crest generally more yellow (less golden), and males lack or have much-reduced yellow on throat.
P. f. styani (Hainan) Crest pale yellow; reddish bars extend to wingtips.
P. f. ricketti (Tonkin area of N Vietnam, east to Fujian) As *styani*, but slightly longer-winged and darker-billed; reddish primary bars more extensive. Intergrades with *pierrei*.
P. f. pierrei (SE Thailand to southernmost Vietnam) Slightly yellower above than previous two races, and with less extensive barring on primaries.
P. f. mystacalis (N Sumatra) Breast more extensively dark green; wing barring reduced; lacks black and white markings on lower throat.
P. f. korinchi (SW Sumatra) As *mystacalis*, but darker green above, paler on belly, and with wing barring duller and browner.
P. f. wrayi (Malaysian highlands) Similar to *pierrei*, but smaller and darker. Male has brighter yellow moustache and yellowish/rufous-yellow patch on upper throat.

MEASUREMENTS Wing 132-185; tail 113-135; bill (from skull) 37-45; tarsus 27-32. Weight: 153-198.

VOICE The usual calls are a variety of *keep* notes, including disyllabic *chup-chup* or *ke-eep*. Others include rather variable (often loud) *kiyaep*, *kyew* or *kyaa* calls, some with a distinctly wavering quality, all of which may be delivered as call-series. These may be confused with vocalisations of Checker-throated and Laced (187) Woodpeckers, and bear resemblance to those of Scaly-bellied (189) and Rufous (152) Woodpeckers. An especially long and accelerating series, *kwee-kwee-kwee-kwee-kwee-kwee-kwee-kwee-kwi-kwi-kwi-wi-wi-w i-wik*, similar to that of Eurasian Green Woodpecker (191), is exchanged between pair members and may also serve as territorial announcement. During intimate contacts between the sexes, low vocalisations can be heard. Drums infrequently, with weak and rapid rolls.

HABITS A shy and restless woodpecker, met with in pairs and in family groups of four to five; commonly associates loosely with various species of drongo, babbler or bulbul. Prefers to forage on the trunks and branches of small to large trees, although it may be observed at all levels of the forest, but seldom, if ever, visits the ground. All foraging techniques directed to the surface, such as gleaning, reaching, sweeping away debris, and probing, are common; excavating or even single pecks are rare. Moves rapidly when on smaller branches, and perches crosswise. Raising of the crest is the most common display when two individuals come into closer contact. More intense display involves not only erected crest, but also lifting the head with bill pointed upwards.

FOOD Animal food consists mainly of ants and termites, and large insect larvae, particularly of wood-boring beetles (Cerambycidae); unusual items are centipedes and frogs, and may take nestlings of other hole-nesting species. Berries and seeds are among the vegetable matter consumed.

BREEDING Breeding season extends from March to June in India, and probably about two months earlier in Thailand and Malaysia; nests April to May in Sumatra. The nest, between 3 and 6 (15)m up in a tree, is excavated by both sexes. The clutch of 3 or 4 eggs is incubated by both parents, which also share brood-feeding. The fledglings remain with the parents for a while.

REFERENCES Ali 1962; Ali & Ripley 1970; Inskipp & Inskipp 1991; Lekagul & Round 1991; MacKinnon & Phillipps 1993; Medway & Wells 1976; Robinson 1928; Short 1973a; Smythies 1953; Stresemann & Heinrich 1940.

185 CHECKER-THROATED WOODPECKER
Picus mentalis   **Plate 54**

Forms a superspecies with *flavinucha*.

IDENTIFICATION Length c. 26-28cm. Smallish to medium-sized, with fairly long, chisel-tipped bill curved on culmen and rather broad across nostrils. Reasonably distinctive, being mostly dark green with reddish/rufous wings, chestnut neck sides and breast, a yellow crest, and black and white throat pattern.

Similar species See Greater Yellownape (184).

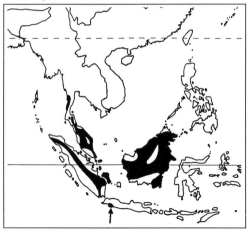

DISTRIBUTION An uncommon to locally common species, occurring from southernmost Burma (Tenasserim, from Mergui south) and south peninsular Thailand southwards to Sumatra, including Bangka Island, Java and Borneo, but rare in Java (where it survives only in the west, in very small numbers).

HABITAT Inhabits primary evergreen or moss forests in lowlands and mountains, especially wetter parts, preferring areas with dense understorey and large trees, such as dipterocarps. Also frequents densely overgrown clearings, dense forest edge, and occasionally the landward edge of mangroves; rarely ventures into dense and tall secondary growth, or to scrub or cultivated land. Keeps below 1000m in Thailand, ranges up to 1200m in Malaysia, and occurs up to 1600m and 1700m in the Greater Sunda Islands.

DESCRIPTION
P. m. humii **Adult male** Forehead and crown dark green to olive-green, sometimes with rufous feather tips at sides, becoming yellow on elongated nape feathers and on hindneck (crest often tinged rufous just behind the yellow).

Ear-coverts dark green, feathers tipped rufous when fresh. Moustachial area dark olive-green, spotted/streaked whitish. Chin and throat white, streaked olive-green (can be more barred on lower throat). Sides of neck rufous-chestnut, this colour extending across breast. Upperparts, including scapulars and tertials, and lesser coverts, green, slightly tinged yellow (brighter yellow on rump). Greater and median upperwing-coverts bright reddish-chestnut, narrowly margined green when fresh; flight feathers blackish-brown, with outer webs of secondaries and of inner primaries reddish-chestnut, all with rufous bar-like spots on both webs (spots obscured by reddish parts of feathers). Uppertail blackish. Underparts below breast green, tinged bronzy. Underwing brown, greener on coverts, and barred cinnamon-rufous. Undertail much as uppertail.

Adult female Somewhat shorter-billed than male. Has chestnut of neck extending forwards along moustachial region to lower bill base and often onto chin.

Juvenile As adults, but with less red in wings and with rufous-chestnut from breast over entire underparts; may show trace of red on nape. Young males soon acquire adult's moustachial pattern.

Bare parts Bill dark grey, paler on lower mandible. Legs and feet olive to grey. Eyes red to red-brown or brown. Orbital skin olive to olive-grey.

GEOGRAPHICAL VARIATION Two fairly distinct races.

> *P. m. humii* (range of species, except Java) Described above. In southern Borneo, some individuals are noticeably small, but most are little different from those in N Borneo.
> *P. m. mentalis* (W Java) Clearly bigger than *humii*, though proportionately shorter-billed. Duller and darker above, and with chestnut of neck more extensive and partly concealing yellow of crest and nape. Male has chin, throat and moustachial area blackish, spotted with white; female has chestnut spreading over virtually whole of chin and throat.

MEASUREMENTS (*humii*) Wing 118-147; tail 90-94; bill 32-33; tarsus 22-23. Weight: (88) 97-109 (113).

VOICE Single *kyick* calls are heard from mildly agitated individuals. They may be followed by series of longer *kwee* or *kyew* notes, which can also be given as single calls. Long series of *wi* notes are similar to, but lower than, corresponding calls of Greater Yellownape, higher-pitched than those of Laced Woodpecker (187), and more rapid than either. Drums in rather short bursts, and with a strike rate slightly faster than that of Grey-faced (194) and significantly faster than that of Crimson-winged (183) Woodpecker.

HABITS Mostly observed singly, occasionally in pairs, and not infrequently may be seen together with warblers, babblers, flycatchers etc. in mixed-species flocks. Forages in lower and middle storeys (3-15m); is thus most frequently seen in the lower canopy and in higher parts of the understorey, where it visits the trunks of smaller trees, low branches, decaying stubs with epiphytes, and vines. The most frequent feeding techniques are gleaning and probing; may prise off obstacles, and occasionally peck, but only rather infrequently excavates with intense hammering. In the course of feeding activities, may cling upside-down to the substrate and employs a good deal of fluttering to reach prey items. Moves very rapidly and in a lively manner through its habitat on a rather erratic path. When flying between foraging sites, the crest is raised, particularly by males.

FOOD Ants, termites, larvae, beetles, grasshoppers, cockroaches and other insects, with occasional berries, comprise the diet.

BREEDING Breeding recorded in March and April in Malaysia, March in W Java, and in February to June in Borneo. Nest excavated in dead stubs. Clutch 2 or 3 eggs.

REFERENCES King & Dickinson 1975; Lekagul & Round 1991; MacKinnon 1990; MacKinnon & Phillipps 1993; Medway & Wells 1976; Short 1973a; Smythies 1981.

---

186 STREAK-BREASTED WOODPECKER
Picus viridanus   Plate 55

Other name: Burmese Scaly-bellied (Green) Woodpecker
Forms a superspecies with *vittatus*.

IDENTIFICATION Length 30-33cm. Small to medium-sized, with longish, fairly broad-based and slightly chisel-tipped bill. Mainly bronzy-green above with yellowish rump, and with red (male) or black (female) crown; entire underparts heavily marked with dark and light scalloping, appearing markedly scaly. Moustache black with some white streaking, but reasonably distinct. Has a peculiar '*kirr*' call apparently not given by other, similar woodpeckers.

Similar species Main confusion species within small range is Streak-throated Woodpecker (188), both sexes of which are very similarly patterned above and below. Streak-throated is best distinguished by its much less prominent (sometimes virtually invisible) moustache, its pale eye, and its generally paler, less greenish underparts with resultant bolder-looking scaly markings (but beware effects of soiling from tree trunks); it also has a brighter yellow rump, but this difficult to discern at rest. Laced Woodpecker (187) is also similar (and is often considered conspecific with Streak-breasted); note Laced's unmarked yellow-green or buffish-yellow throat and upper breast (but juvenile Laced can be more extensively streaked below) and its normally much better-defined and less streaked moustache. In all cases, good views are essential for correct identification.

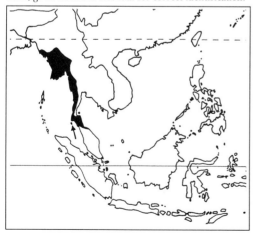

DISTRIBUTION Distribution not clearly understood. Seems to be resident in Burma from about 22°N south to SW Thailand and south in peninsular Thailand to about 7°S. Throughout this very small range this is an uncommon bird, though possibly overlooked.

HABITAT This species is at home in forests, as well as coastal scrub. In W and SW Thailand, where it overlaps with Laced, it is restricted to moist evergreen hill forests; elsewhere, inhabits both inland forests and secondary growth, together with mangroves and coastal scrub.

DESCRIPTION
Adult male Forehead to nape and slight crest red; base of forehead, upper lores and narrow line bordering crown black. Very narrow white line from front edge of eye, extending around eye and back along lower border of black line to nape; lower lores and ear-coverts off-white to greyish or buff, ear-coverts faintly streaked dark. Variable buffish moustachial stripe, bordered below by distinct white-streaked black malar stripe. Chin and throat pale brown, throat usually with distinct green/olive tinge and variably streaked white. Hindneck and sides of neck bronzy yellow-green; mantle, back and scapulars bronzy-green, rump dull yellow-green, uppertail-coverts olive-green. Upperwing-coverts and tertials dark bronze-green, darker than back; flight feathers blackish-brown, bronze-green on outer webs of secondaries, with narrow pale buffy-white bars on inner webs of all feathers and also on outer webs of primaries. Uppertail blackish, with poorly defined brownish bars on most/all feathers. Underparts below throat olive-green, paler towards rear, feathers having whitish or buff edges, tip and central streak, producing bold scaly pattern; undertail-coverts whitish, streaked dark olive. Underwing brownish, barred whitish, coverts white with olive barring. Undertail as uppertail, but paler.

Adult female Slightly shorter-billed than male. Lacks male's red on head, entire forehead to nape being black.

Juvenile As adults, but duller above and below, with underpart scaling more diffuse and often with stronger tail barring. Juvenile male has orange-red on crown.

Bare parts Bill dirty yellowish, lower mandible paler, with blackish culmen and tip. Legs and feet grey-green. Eyes reddish-brown, more red in some (most?) individuals.

GEOGRAPHICAL VARIATION None clearly documented, but situation complicated by existence of closely related Laced Woodpecker; some Streak-breasted in west of range approach (and are possibly indistinguishable from) the latter. Further research is required.

MEASUREMENTS Wing 128-143; tail 89-115; bill 31-36.5; tarsus 25. Weight: c. 90-120.

VOICE Gives at least one note, an explosive *kirr* (recalling Banded Pitta *Pitta guajana*), which is not known for Laced Woodpecker, although other vocalisations are similar. These include *tcheu-tcheu-tcheu-tcheu-...* series.

HABITS Forages much on the ground and on moss-covered trees and boulders.

FOOD Ants.

BREEDING Known to breed from February to April in Burma.

REFERENCES Deignan 1955; King & Dickinson 1975; Lekagul & Round 1991; Smythies 1953.

187 LACED WOODPECKER
Picus vittatus   Plate 55

Other name: Laced Green Woodpecker
Forms a superspecies with *viridanus*.

IDENTIFICATION Length 30-33cm. Medium-sized, with relatively short, fairly broad-based and somewhat chisel-tipped bill with curved culmen. A green woodpecker with black tail and yellow rump, plain buffy-yellow throat and upper breast and boldly streaked (scaly or scalloped) lower underparts. Sides of head grey, often slightly tinged bluish, with pale moustachial stripe and prominent black malar stripe; thin white supercilium from above eye extends to nape, bordered above by narrow black margin to bright red crown (male) or by wholly black crown (female).

Similar species Two very similar species occur within same range. Most likely to be confused with closely related and possibly conspecific Streak-breasted Woodpecker (186), which overlaps in parts of Burma and Thailand. Laced is best distinguished by its paler throat (usually unstreaked) and unmarked yellowish upper breast, its more distinct black (sometimes with a few white specks or streaks) malar stripe, and its somewhat less bronzy upperparts. Where the two overlap in S and W Thailand, Laced frequents mangroves, tall coastal scrub and drier deciduous woodland, whereas Streak-breasted is restricted to moist evergreen forests of the lower hills. Streak-throated Woodpecker (188) is slightly smaller, has a much less distinct moustache (sometimes virtually absent) and a pale eye, and has entire underparts boldly scalloped. Juvenile Laced with streaks extending onto throat can be very difficult to separate unless good views obtained.

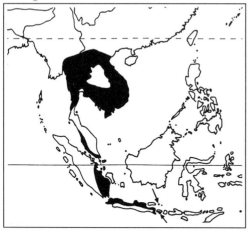

DISTRIBUTION Occurs from about 20°N in eastern Burma east to about 102°E in SW China (Yunnan), south through the western half of Thailand (absent from most of peninsular Thailand); along its northeastern border, and throughout Laos, Cambodia and Vietnam (except Tonkin in N Vietnam); also further south in Langkawi Islands and western Malaysia, Singapore, Lingga Islands, eastern Sumatra, Java, Bali and Kangean Islands. Locally common, though very rare in northeast (Yunnan); numbers in Sumatra severely reduced through loss of habitat.

HABITAT Bamboo, deciduous and evergreen forests, secondary growth, coconut groves, and village and suburban gardens. Inhabits rather open coastal forest and scrub, including casuarinas, mangroves and coconut plantations. In W and SW Thailand, where it overlaps with Streak-

breasted, mainly restricted to mangroves, drier deciduous woodlands and coastal scrub, rarely in gardens. Resident from sea level to 200m in the Greater Sundas, and to 1500m in SE Asia.

DESCRIPTION
Adult male Forehead to crown and short crest red, bordered by thin black line which extends to upper lores and bill base. Narrow white eye-ring extends as short supercilium to nape. Ear-coverts pale greyish to buffish, often tinged bluish, and faintly streaked brown. Lower lores buffy or whitish, extending into diffuse pale moustachial stripe; malar area prominently black, usually with a few small white streaks or spots. Chin and throat plain whitish-buff to pale yellowish-green or yellow, becoming buffish-yellow or olive-buff on breast. Hindneck, sides of neck and upperparts, including scapulars, yellowish-green, with rump more obviously yellowish. Upperwing as on Streak-breasted. Uppertail blackish, outer feathers usually (also central feathers sometimes) with a few narrow whitish bars. Lower breast to vent buffy to greenish-white, all feathers with olive-green submarginal markings on both webs, creating scaly pattern; undertail-coverts similar, but with colours more olive and white. Underwing-coverts yellowish-white, barred brown, flight feathers brownish with whitish bars. Undertail as uppertail but paler, outer feathers often showing dull yellow tinge.

Adult female Slightly shorter-billed than male and lacks latter's red on crown, having forehead to nape black.

Juvenile Duller above and below, with underpart markings more diffuse, and usually has at least some streaking extending upwards onto throat; tail generally more clearly barred than on adults. Juvenile male has orangey-red crown.

Bare parts Bill has dirty yellow upper mandible with blackish culmen and tip, lower mandible dull yellow with darker tip. Legs and feet grey-green. Eyes reddish-brown or red.

GEOGRAPHICAL VARIATION Southern and eastern populations tend to have more of a bronzy tinge to upperparts (as Streak-throated) and rump colour tends more towards orange in the east, but these differences are subject to individual variation and are not sufficient to warrant any racial separation. In the west, the situation is complicated by the presence of Streak-throated Woodpecker. Further study of these two forms is required.

MEASUREMENTS Wing 125-148; tail 110-135; bill 30.2-34.3; tarsus 26-27.5. Weight: c. 105-132.

VOICE Utters *keep* notes or double *kee-ip* calls singly. Fledglings vary these calls and may even produce trill-like notes. A variable call, singly or in short series, is given in flight. Laced Woodpeckers announce their presence with long series of notes. In comparison with Grey-faced Woodpecker (194), the notes are lower-pitched, shorter, and delivered in faster succession. In close encounters, loud or low variations of *wick, a-wick, a-wick* series are uttered. Drums in steady rolls, very like those of Checker-throated Woodpecker (185), which see.

HABITS This species is met with singly or in pairs, which keep in close contact. Forages on the ground, but less so than sympatric Grey-faced Woodpecker, on fallen trees, as well as in bamboo and trees. In the latter case, it prefers the trunks or larger branches, staying low in mangroves, and, in palms, the bases of the fronds; on bamboo, pays particular attention to the nodes. Feeding techniques include vertical and lateral pecking, probing, and, when on the ground, sweeps away debris and probes into the ground or mud (mangroves). As with its congeners, crest-raising is a common display; swinging head-body movements occur also.

FOOD Beetles and flies.

BREEDING Nests can be found from February to June in Malaysia and Thailand, and in January, April and September in Java. The clutch comprises 3 or 4 eggs.

REFERENCES Deignan 1955; King & Dickinson 1975; Lekagul & Round 1991; MacKinnon 1990; MacKinnon & Phillipps 1993; Medway & Wells 1976; Short 1973a.

---

188 STREAK-THROATED WOODPECKER
Picus xanthopygaeus   Plate 55

Other name: Little Scaly-bellied (Green) Woodpecker

IDENTIFICATION Length 30cm. Small to medium-sized, with rather long, broad-based and slightly chisel-tipped bill with slightly curved culmen. Green above, with yellow rump and red (male) or pale-streaked black (female) crown; underparts rather pale, but covered with very heavy dark arrowhead markings. Moustache poorly defined. Has pale eye.

Similar species In west of range overlaps with Scaly-bellied Woodpecker (189), which is bigger, with a pale bill, and has plain throat and upper breast, more distinct moustache and heavier and blacker scalloping on lower underparts. In SE Asia, two very similar woodpeckers, Streak-breasted (186) and Laced (187), occur. Laced is best distinguished by its unmarked yellowish or buffish throat, upper breast and neck sides and its much more obvious moustache; Streak-breasted is even closer in appearance to Streak-throated, but is darker below with rather less prominent scaling, has a somewhat more clear-cut moustache and its rump is a duller yellowish. Both species have a dark eye (pale in Streak-throated).

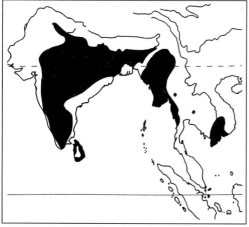

DISTRIBUTION Resident from about 77°E in NW India and the lower foothills of the Himalayas in southern Nepal eastwards through Sikkim, Assam, Bangladesh and Burma to W Yunnan in China, extending south through India to Sri Lanka and east to SW Thailand; also in Cambodia, southern Laos and southern Vietnam. Fairly common in east of range, but uncommon to rare in Burma and Thailand and very rare in Yunnan; few recent records from Indochina, where current status uncertain.

HABITAT Avoids dense forests, instead frequenting more open deciduous, dry dipterocarp, semi-evergreen, sal and mixed bamboo forests. Habitats also include secondary growth, sparsely wooded park-like country, teak and particularly rubber plantations and tea estates. A woodpecker of the lowlands and lower hills from about 300 to 1500m in Sri Lanka, and up to 465m, rarely to over 900m, in Nepal, although reported from the Himalayan foothills up to 1700m.

DESCRIPTION
Adult male Forehead to hindcrown and crest red, with variable amount of black across nape and continuing along border of crown to upper lores and bill base. Ear-coverts greyish, streaked brown-black or brownish, bordered by thin white supercilium above and by narrow white moustachial stripe below which continues to lower lores; malar stripe dusky blackish, greatly obscured by pale whitish tips and edges (can appear to merge with throat). Chin and throat off-white, with variable (often extensive?) fine dark brown or olive streaks. Hindneck and upperparts, including scapulars, yellow-tinged green, with rump and most of uppertail-coverts bright yellow (sometimes with some orange feathers admixed). Upperwing-coverts and tertials dark green, tertials darker at bases (where they may have a few white bars); flight feathers brownish-black, outer webs of secondaries dark green, with white bars on inner webs of secondaries and both webs of primaries. Uppertail blackish, most/all feathers narrowly barred brown. Breast to belly whitish to pale buffy-white, tinged green on breast, all feathers having broad olive edges and tips (and occasionally shaft streaks) forming distinct scaly or scalloped pattern or arrowhead markings; these are sometimes more diffuse and less conspicuous on lower belly. Undertail-coverts whitish, with dark arrowheads. Underwing brownish, paler on coverts, all barred white. Undertail dark brown, washed dull yellow, with variable narrow dull yellow-brown bars.

Adult female As male, but lacks red on head, forehead to nape being black with greyish streaking.

Juvenile Less yellow-tinged above, and with grey feather bases creating more variegated appearance; appears less scaly below owing to arrowhead marks being broader. Juvenile males have less extensive red on head than adult.

Bare parts Bill dark brown or grey-brown, with dull yellow base to lower mandible. Legs and feet greyish-green (to yellowish-brown?). Eyes white or pale pinkish, darker at periphery.

GEOGRAPHICAL VARIATION None known, despite fairly large range.

MEASUREMENTS Wing 121-138 (142); tail 76-97; bill (from skull) of male 25-38; tarsus 21-26. Weight: 83-111.

VOICE Seems to be a rather quiet woodpecker. A sharp, single *queemp* and drumming are the only acoustic signals reported.

HABITS Generally solitary. Forages very frequently on the ground, and may climb on boulders.

FOOD Ants and termites, and other small insect larvae. Feeds also on flower nectar and on seeds.

BREEDING Breeding season spans March to May on the Indian subcontinent, and coincides with the southwest monsoon, (April) May to September, in Sri Lanka. The nest, about 30cm deep, is excavated by both sexes in a tree trunk or large branch, sometimes very low (0.6m), but usually from about 4 to 8m. Lays 3-5 eggs. Both parents feed the young.

REFERENCES Ali & Ripley 1970; Diesselhorst 1968;

Henry 1971; Inskipp & Inskipp 1991; Lekagul & Round 1991; Phillips 1978.

189 SCALY-BELLIED WOODPECKER
Picus squamatus   Plate 55

Other names: Scaly-bellied Green Woodpecker, Common Scaly-bellied Woodpecker

IDENTIFICATION Length c. 35cm. Medium-sized to large, with long, almost straight, slightly chisel-tipped bill fairly broad across nostrils. A pale-billed woodpecker of mountain regions. Green above, with yellower rump, and pale below with heavy scale-like pattern from lower breast downwards; wings and tail barred. Male has red forehead to nape bordered at sides with black, female has top of head all black, and both have a white supercilium and black moustache. Western race *flavirostris* is much paler overall. Juveniles resemble adult female, but with more diffuse and more extensive scaling below. Rather noisy, frequently uttering loud calls; often descends to the ground.

Similar species Streak-throated Woodpecker (188) has similar pattern, but is much smaller, dark-billed, and has less striking underpart markings; although their ranges overlap, the two do not normally occur in same habitat or at same elevation.

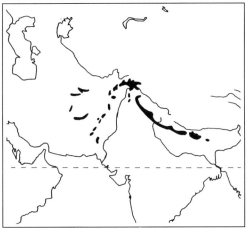

DISTRIBUTION Found discontinuously from W and E Afghanistan and W and N Pakistan (including Chitral and Gilgit) through Kashmir and the lower Himalayas to eastern Nepal, and in Sikkim and Darjeeling area; also in S Tibet, north of Nepal border. Formerly extended west into Transcaspia, but apparently now extinct west of Afghanistan. Common to fairly common in places, but local.

MOVEMENTS Himalayan populations partly move to lower altitudes in winter.

HABITAT Frequents coniferous and mixed coniferous forest, and forests of temperate deciduous trees, such as oaks and ash. This species is adaptable and is found in juniper scrub forest, coniferous forest (*Abies spectabilis*, *Picea smithiana*), pine forests, subtropical dry deciduous forest, and arid areas wherever tamarisk scrub, groves, orchards or plantations provide foraging and nest sites; also inhabits large clearings of burned forests with plenty of dead and decaying trees. In the northwest of its range, restricted to riparian woodland dominated by poplars. Frequently in orchards in winter. This woodpecker is found on Himalayan slopes from 1500 to 3700m, locally

down to 600m; ventures above the timber line outside the breeding season.

DESCRIPTION
P. s. squamatus **Adult male** Forehead, crown and nape red (usually with some black/grey feather bases showing through), becoming more orangey in a narrow wedge down hindneck. Upper lores and narrow line along crown side black, bordered below by white supercilium from above eye (where thin) to side of nape, with narrow black eye stripe below this. Lower lores yellowish-white. Cheeks and ear-coverts olive-grey, becoming greener/yellower on neck sides. Moustachial stripe black, streaked whitish. Chin, throat and breast olive, variably grey-tinged. Upperparts and upperwing-coverts green, becoming yellow on rump and uppertail-coverts, the latter with obvious green bases. Flight feathers and primary coverts blackish-brown, secondaries and tertials with green outer (and part of inner) webs, all barred white/whitish. Uppertail dark brown, barred buff-white, with strong green suffusion on outer feathers. Underparts below breast greyish-white, tinged greenish, all feathers having broad, complete, black submarginal lines (producing markedly scaly appearance) and usually also thin black shaft streaks. Underwing barred brown and white, coverts with yellowish cast. Undertail as uppertail but paler, with yellowish barring. (In worn plumage, upperparts much greyer, sometimes irregularly grey-mottled, with duller yellow rump, breast greyer, and underpart markings even more contrasting; black and grey feather bases of crown very obvious.)

Adult female Somewhat shorter-billed than male, and perhaps a duller green. Lacks red on head, having forehead to nape black with grey streaks.

Juvenile Greyer than adults, especially above (where appears blotchy grey and dull green), and with black hindneck; entire underparts, including (greyer) breast, with scaly pattern (though markings duller and less contrasting than on adults). Male has much black in red of crown.

Bare parts Bill pale horn-yellow to pale yellowish-grey, usually darker at tip. Legs and feet greenish-grey to olive-green. Eyes pinkish-red, with paler outer ring; brownish in juveniles.

GEOGRAPHICAL VARIATION Two fairly well-differentiated races.
  P. s. squamatus (NE Afghanistan east to Sikkim) Described above.
  P. s. flavirostris (Afghanistan, excluding northeast, and W Pakistan) Much paler than nominate, with yellow tinge to upperparts, whiter throat, pale olive-buff breast and yellowish belly to vent; scaling narrower, brownish (not black) and less contrasting.

MEASUREMENTS Wing 149-172; tail 114-136; bill 27-33; tarsus 27-28. Weight: 156-194.

VOICE Characteristic for this species, but variable. Rather rarely, a single, nasal, drawn-out call note, *cheenk* or *peer*, similar to the *keep* call of Laced (187) and other *Picus* woodpeckers. Also a short and high-pitched *kik*. The main call, also given in flight, is a melodious disyllabic, vibrating *klee-guh kleeguh*, *Klee-wi*, *Klee-wi* or *kuik-kuik-kuik*, rapidly repeated three to eight times; it is used for advertising, and is often associated with drumming. Gives laughing calls similar to those of Eurasian Green Woodpecker (191). Soft notes are heard in close encounters between two individuals. In greater excitement, utters squeaky *chissuh-chissuh* calls. Nestlings give a loud wheezing *chuff-chuff*. Drums regularly in the breeding season.

HABITS Its noisy flight and frequent calls reveal this woodpecker's presence. Forages singly or in pairs, the family staying together for a while after the young have fledged. Forages by pecking and hammering on trees; descends to the ground regularly and may also visit rocks. Moves on the ground by hopping. Flight deeply undulating.

FOOD Ants and termites dominate the diet, which also includes larvae of wood-boring insects; also takes berries in winter.

BREEDING Courtship activities start in March. Both sexes participate in nest-hole construction; many holes may be started before a final hole, which may also be one from a previous year, is accepted. Nests are excavated in all kinds of trees and may be rather low, even close to the ground (30cm) or in exposed roots in a river bank, in a wide range of tree species, including holm oaks, pistachios, apricots and tamarisks. The circular entrance is 6cm wide, the nest itself extending 30cm downwards. Main egg-laying season is early to late May, extremes appearing to be late April and early June. The voluminous nest chamber contains 4-6 eggs. Both sexes incubate, the young hatching after 17 days. They are fed by regurgitation, come fully feathered to the hole entrance after two weeks, and accompany their parents after fledging.

REFERENCES Ali & Ripley 1970; Christison & Ticehurst 1943; Dement'ev & Gladkov 1966; Diesselhorst 1968; Inskipp & Inskipp 1991; Löhrl & Thielcke 1969; Martens & Eek In press; Roberts 1991; Short 1973; Whistler 1930.

---

190 JAPANESE WOODPECKER
Picus awokera   Plate 56

Other names: Wavy-bellied Woodpecker, Japanese Green Woodpecker

IDENTIFICATION Length c. 29-30cm. Medium-sized, with fairly long, broad-based and pointed bill with slightly curved culmen. Endemic in Japan. Green above, with grey face, male with red crown (female grey and black on crown), and heavily barred from breast to undertail-coverts. Has red and black moustache.

Similar species Unlikely to be confused with any other woodpecker within its restricted range in Japan south of Hokkaido. Grey-faced (194) occurs on Hokkaido and, although highly sedentary, could possibly straggle south, but is easily distinguished by its lack of barring below.

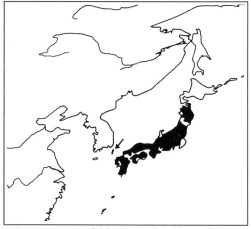

DISTRIBUTION A fairly common inhabitant of hill areas and low mountains of Japan, from northernmost Honshu

south to Shikoku, Kyushu, Yakushima and Tanegashima and including the offshore islands of Tobishima, Awashima, Sado and Tsushima.

MOVEMENTS Moves to lower habitats in severe winters.

HABITAT In the north it frequents fairly open mixed forest and in the south warm-temperate evergreen forest; rarely in mature conifer plantations. Has recently become more common in parks and gardens. Occurs most commonly at 300-1400m, but also occasionally extending somewhat higher in the mountains (to about 2000m), particularly in the primitive *Cryptomeris* forest on Yakushima, and also descending to lowlands.

DESCRIPTION
Adult male Lower forehead and lores to below eye blackish; mid forehead to nape red, broadening at rear and with variable amount of admixed black and grey feathers (especially in nape area). Supercilium, ear-coverts and sides of nape grey, often tinged greenish when fresh. Moustachial stripe black, with extensive red in centre. Chin white to greyish-white. Hindneck greyish-green; mantle, scapulars and back grey-green to olive-green, feathers becoming broadly tipped yellow on rump and central uppertail-coverts, outer coverts being green. Upperwing-coverts and tertials green, edged and tipped bronzy-yellow; flight feathers blackish-brown, outer webs of secondaries and inner primaries greenish, and with white bars on inner webs of all feathers and also on outer webs of outer primaries. Uppertail mid to dark brown, central feathers edged green, with indistinct paler broad yellow-brown bars. Throat white, often tinged greyish (can also show some blackish in throat centre), becoming greyish-white or pale buffish-green on breast and paler on belly; lower breast to flanks and belly boldly marked with broad dark brown vermiculated barring, bars tinged greenish-olive on flanks; undertail-coverts buffish, barred dark. Underwing off-white, barred brown, bars blackish on coverts. Undertail as uppertail, but paler.

Adult female As male but slightly smaller, with shorter bill. Crown lacks red, being grey with black streaks/bars in centre (sometimes forming more solid black patch), but usually shows small patch of red on nape. Has less red than male in centre of moustache.

Juvenile Much as adults but duller overall, with grey tone above; barring below coarser, especially on breast.

Bare parts Bill yellowish, with blackish culmen and tip, or with tip and most of upper mandible blackish. Legs and feet pale grey, tinged green or bluish. Eyes red.

GEOGRAPHICAL VARIATION Three races often recognised: large and pale 'awokera' (Honshu, Tobishima, Awashima, Sado), smaller and darker 'horii' (Shikoku, Kyushu, Tsushima), and smallest and darkest 'takatsukasae' (Tanegashima, Yakushima). These, however, simply reflect a natural cline of decreasing size (slight) and increasing darkness of plumage from north to south, and subspecific separation hardly seems justified.

MEASUREMENTS Wing 133-149; tail 82-99; bill 28.3-35.2; tarsus 21.5-27.5. Weight: 120-138.

VOICE Quite vocal before and during breeding season. A loud call note, *piyo*, distinguished from that of Grey-faced Woodpecker by its more whiplash-like character. Also *ket*, *ket*. Drums in rolls which are slightly faster, and also longer, than those of Japanese Great Spotted Woodpecker (104).

HABITS Forages mainly at middle levels at 2-10m on larger branches to slender twigs. As with many other species, seasonal shifts in foraging preferences occur;

lower levels are visited in January-May. Compared with Grey-faced, seems to forage little on the ground (about 20% in winter). Gleaning and pecking are the most common feeding techniques, followed by probing and sapsucking (winter, early spring). Enters the roost at about sunset: earlier in adverse weather conditions, otherwise slightly after sunset.

FOOD The main component of the diet is ants (*Lasius, Formica, Camponotus, Crematogaster*); other arthropods taken are Hemiptera, beetles and their larvae, and spiders. Also eats fruits, berries, seeds (*Sorbus, Rhus, Ilex*) and nectar.

BREEDING Breeding season extends from April to June. Nests in trees at 2-4m; holes (possibly only roosts) are also dug in telephone poles. Clutch comprises 7 or 8 eggs.

REFERENCES Brazil 1991; Chiba 1969; Fujii 1993; Ishida 1990a, 1990b; Kazama 1980.

191 EURASIAN GREEN WOODPECKER
Picus viridis   Plate 56

Other names: Green/European Green Woodpecker; Levaillant's/Algerian Woodpecker, North African Green Woodpecker (race *vaillantii*)

IDENTIFICATION Length c. 31-33cm. Medium-sized to large, with long, slightly chisel-tipped bill slightly curved on culmen and broad across nostrils. Distinctive and fairly unmistakable within its almost solely W Palearctic range. Appears predominantly bright green or yellowish-green, greyer and paler below and with light barring on flanks (except in Iberia), with bright red crown and nape and (except in southwest) a large area of black around eye. Both sexes also have a broad dark moustache (contiguous with eye patch in those races which possess the latter): on males this is mostly red or black-bordered red, on females fully black, but both races of N African race *vaillantii* (often treated as a separate species) have wholly black moustache. In flight, which is remarkably undulating, brilliant yellow rump is the most striking and attention-catching feature; wings are barred. Juveniles differ noticeably from adults: strongly spotted above and barred below, with a much-subdued version of adult head pattern. Often noisy and intrusive, with loud laughing call, but can be shy; spends much time on the ground.

Similar species Likely to be confused only with Grey-faced Woodpecker (194), which overlaps in much of Eurasian Green's range. Grey-faced, however, is somewhat smaller and less powerful, with smaller bill (looks less 'nose-heavy'), less bright overall, with less yellow appearance (rump is yellow, but not so bright as on the larger species), and is greyer below; it also has a largely grey head with thinner moustache (black in both sexes), and only male has red on head (confined to front part of crown).

DISTRIBUTION Restricted almost entirely to the W Palearctic, where widespread from about 66°N in coastal C Norway and around 46°N in E Sweden south to the Mediterranean, with a distinctive race inhabiting NW Africa (northern parts of Morocco, Algeria and Tunisia), and east to about 50°E in W Russia; extends through much of Turkey, and from the Caucasus to N Iran and just into SW Turkmenia, with a further population in Zagros mountains of SW Iran. Absent from most islands, including Ireland. Common to very common throughout much of its range, but local in parts (e.g. Turkey); it has spread northwards into Scotland since the 1950s, but a decline is evident in several European countries in recent decades.

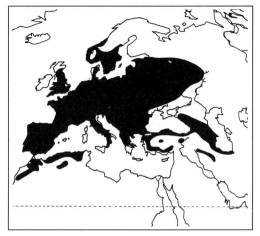

MOVEMENTS Essentially non-migratory, with some local winter movements. Continental European populations disperse on average less than Grey-faced Woodpecker, although extreme distances of up to 170km have been recorded.

HABITAT This woodpecker is found in a great variety of semi-open habitats; in extensively wooded areas, it is confined to larger open sections or clearings. A usually common bird of forest edge, copses, parks, orchards and residential areas, usually near mature deciduous trees, but may be associated with conifers in mountains and in the north. However, requires a higher proportion of deciduous trees than Grey-faced Woodpecker. In N Africa, *vaillantii* occurs in openings and clearings of holm-oak and cedar forests. This species' habitats span a wide altitudinal range, from coastal areas and lowlands up to subalpine forests, where nests may be found at up to 2100m in the western and up to 1500m in the eastern Alps, at 1500-1700m in NE Anatolia, at 950-2600m in N Africa, while Caucasian populations reach 3000m.

DESCRIPTION
P. v. viridis **Adult male** Forehead to nape bright red, usually with some grey feather bases visible (especially on crown). Nasal tufts, lores, cheeks and broad area around eye (reaching back to central crown side) black, this continuing over moustachial/malar region, the latter with broad red stripe in centre. Rear ear-coverts pale green, with paler feather bases showing through, becoming darker on neck side. Chin and upper throat greyish-white, often tinged light green. Hindneck and upperparts bright yellow-green, becoming bright yellow on rump and uppertail-coverts, the latter with green bases usually well visible. Upperwing-coverts and tertials as back, sometimes tinged golden/bronzy; primaries and their coverts blackish, inner feathers edged green, and with white spots on both webs forming bars; secondaries green (tinged golden) on outer webs and blackish with white half-bars on inner webs. Uppertail blackish, feathers edged green, faintly barred pale on central feather pair and sometimes also very indistinctly on others. Underparts from throat yellow-green, becoming paler and more yellowish in lower regions, with fairly indistinct olive-grey to greenish arrow-head marks or bars from lower flanks to undertail-coverts. Underwing barred grey and white, coverts tinged yellow or green. Undertail as uppertail, but outer feathers paler and more clearly barred. (In worn plumage, appears greener and less yellow above and greyer below, with flank barring more obvious; grey bases to crown feathers more extensive/widespread.)

Adult female Much as male, but lacks red in moustache; flank bars may reach further up.

Juvenile Distinctive, with profuse but somewhat obscure bars and spots. Upperparts dull olive with whitish spots/bars, rump duller yellow and barred; underparts pale greenish/yellowish with dark spotting on upper breast and barred from lower breast downwards; head spotted and

Juvenile

streaked, with prominent grey feather bases showing throughout the red forehead to nape, black areas duller and less well defined; wings and tail more barred. Male usually shows a few narrow red feather tips in moustache. Plumage much as adult by autumn.

Bare parts Bill dark grey or brownish-black, with paler, greenish, base to lower mandible. Legs and feet olive-grey. Eyes white or whitish, tinged pink or with pinkish outer ring; duller or greyer in juveniles.

GEOGRAPHICAL VARIATION Five races, two of which are fairly distinct.

P. v. viridis (range of species, excluding areas occupied by the following four races) Described above. Shows slight increase in size clinally eastwards.

P. v. karelini (Italy east to Bulgaria, Asia Minor, N Iran and SW Turkmenistan) Close to nominate, but slightly smaller and duller, less yellow (more grey). Intergrades with nominate in northwest of range.

P. v. innominatus (Zagros mountains, SW Iran) Resembles *karelini*, but sides of head and underparts very pale, almost whitish; upperparts somewhat greyer, less green, often with small paler spots on mantle and scapulars; bars on wings and tail more prominent. Juveniles even more strongly spotted and barred than in other races. A putative form *bampurensis*, known only from the type locality in Bampur river basin in SE Iran, is said to show particularly well-marked tail bars and wing spots and heavy barring over entire lower underparts, but the validity and/or survival of this isolated population requires further investigation (note that strong underpart barring may occur in some *karelini*).

P. v. sharpei (Pyrenees and Iberia) Rather short-billed and distinctive. Resembles *karelini* apart from facial pattern: lores blackish, but area around eye dusky greenish-grey and ear-coverts similarly greyish, with thin whitish line above moustache (white more obvious on female); male has moustache virtually all red, with minimal black border. Underparts show little or no barring. Juveniles less heavily patterned.

P. v. vaillantii (N Africa, from NW Morocco to NW Tunisia) Distinctive and often treated as a full species. Closest to *sharpei*, but slightly shorter-billed and somewhat paler below, with fairly strong barring in lower region. Both sexes have all-black moustache, bordered above by rather well-marked white line, and area around eyes and back through ear-coverts grey-green

(male thus very like female *sharpei*); female differs from all other races in having red restricted to nape and sides of hindcrown, with crown blackish-grey. Juveniles less heavily barred and spotted than those of other races.

MEASUREMENTS Wing 155-172 (*viridis*), 155-169 (*karelini*), 154-170 (*vaillantii*); tail 95-104 (*viridis*), 98-114 (*vaillantii*); bill (from skull) 42-48 (*viridis*); tarsus 28-33 (*viridis*). Weight: 138-250 (*viridis*).

VOICE Most calls are variations of *kyack* or *kewk* notes, which are delivered singly or as regular or loose series. The calling bird may be perched or on the wing. Some of the calls are very similar to those of Grey-faced Woodpecker. In agonistic contexts, calls become more explosive, *kyik* or *kyik, kyik, kyik....* The most distinctive call is heard in the breeding season: a laughing, somewhat accelerating *klew-klew-klew..*, decreasing more or less in loudness and with the notes closely strung together. Nestlings are noisier than those of Grey-faced and respond to the presence of feeding adults with *rak-ak-ak*. The calls of N African *vaillantii* are thinner and more whistling, and the series less regular. Nestlings chatter more readily than those of Grey-faced Woodpecker, from day seven on. Only rarely drums, and then in weak, irregular and decelerating bouts in vicinity of the nest. In C Europe, acoustically most active in March and April.

HABITS This is a rather conspicuous woodpecker. It lives solitarily, in pairs which keep contact with calling, and in family groups. Forages mostly on the ground. Pecks funnel-shaped holes up to 12cm deep in the ground, after having swept away moss, dead leaves, debris or snow with the bill, and procures its prey with the action of its very long tongue. Such holes, which may be exploited in lengthy and repeated visits, expose the tunnel systems of ants, which appear en masse when disturbed by the woodpecker. When snow cover is heavy, may dig tunnels almost 1m long to reach its prey. Forages also on trunks and branches, buildings and rocks by gleaning and probing. Takes sap on ringed trees, but has not been recorded drilling sap wells. Moves only short distances on the ground. Flight low and heavily undulating. Displays in agonistic encounters are interspersed with sharp calls, and consist of jerky upward movements of the bill, head-swinging with crown feathers raised, and wing-flicking. Most intense display in agonistic encounters consists of wing-spreading and opening the bill. Opponents are circled on the wing with extremely spread tail. Males feed the female during courtship, e.g. prior to copulation. Roosts in holes, including those of other species, rarely in nestboxes and on buildings. Enters roost earlier when weather conditions are adverse; otherwise, may roost somewhat earlier than Great Spotted Woodpecker (104).

FOOD Ants are the major food, with meadow-dwelling species of the genera *Formica* (winter) and *Lasius* (spring to autumn) the dominant groups; generally, larger species are preferred. Also takes various other insects, earthworms and snails, and occasionally catches reptiles. Sometimes eats fruits (apples, pears, cherries, grapes), berries and, rarely, seeds.

BREEDING Courtship activities start in March, although calling commences much earlier, in December. The egg-laying season spans early April (locally March) to June. Nests in trees, commonly between 2 and 10(12)m. The hole is excavated in dead or soft living wood in unbroken trees (poplars are favoured in Norway) in two to four weeks. The entrance, circular or vertically oval, measures about (75)64 x 64(50)mm. Both sexes incubate the 5-8 (4-11) eggs, the male sitting during the night. The young hatch after 14-17 days, and are fed by regurgitation by both parents; feeding decreases just before the young fledge, which takes place after 23-27 days in the nest. The fledglings are divided between the parents, with which they stay for three to seven weeks.

REFERENCES Bezzel 1985; Blume 1961, 1973; deBruyn *et al*. 1972; Dement'ev & Gladkov 1966; Dvorak *et al*. 1993; Glutz von Blotzheim & Bauer 1980; Hågvar *et al*. 1990; Heim de Balsac & Mayaud 1962; Klima 1959; Löhrl 1977; Miech 1986; Serez 1983; Spitznagel 1993; Turcek 1954.

192 RED-COLLARED WOODPECKER
Picus rabieri   Plate 56

IDENTIFICATION Length c. 30cm. Medium-sized, with fairly long and broad-based, slightly chisel-tipped bill with curved culmen. An Indochinese endemic, very little known. Dark green above and rather paler green below, with lower underparts mottled/streaked dark and pale. Both sexes have characteristic and diagnostic red collar (less marked on female), and male also has entire crown and (usually) moustachial area red.

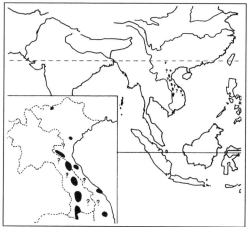

DISTRIBUTON A very poorly known resident throughout the forests of Laos (except northwest) and in Vietnam from Tonkin to C Annam, also in SW China in extreme S Yunnan (at Hekou, on Tonkin border); in 1980s found in Annam at Kon Cha Rang, farther south than its previous known range in Vietnam. Was considered to be a threatened species, but recent observations indicate that it may be commoner than formerly realised; appears locally common in Laos and scarce to locally common in Vietnam.

HABITAT Incompletely known and requires further investigation. Apparently locally common in primary and secondary semi-evergreen forest, at up to 700m in Vietnam.

DESCRIPTION
Adult male Forehead to nape red, with some blackish streaks on crown, red extending forwards below ear-coverts to join red moustachial area and continuing across upper breast. Lores and ear-coverts dull pale green, often with some red feather tips or a red suffusion; indistinct short, narrow whitish or whitish-green supercilium from above eye to just behind it. Chin and throat pale greenish-buff, often streaked white, and sometimes with red of lower throat extending slightly up onto throat centre. Hindneck green, sometimes with a few red feather tips; rest of

upperparts, including scapulars, dark bright green, slightly paler on rump; uppertail-coverts green, with dark shaft streaks. Upperwing-coverts and tertials green with bronze tinge (sometimes also tinged red); flight feathers blackish-brown, outer webs of secondaries bronzy-green or tinged reddish, with broad white bars on inner webs of all feathers and narrower white spots/bars on outer webs of primaries. Uppertail blackish, central feathers edged green. Lower breast and upper belly green, somewhat paler than upperparts; feathers of flanks and lower belly olive-green, with off-white shaft streaks and rather diffuse paler green edges and tips, producing scaly or streaky pattern; undertail-coverts olive-grey, edged and tipped olive-green. Underwing whitish, barred greyish-brown. Undertail blackish, clearly tinged green-yellow, especially on outer feathers, central feathers sometimes with narrow paler bars.

Adult female As male, but has green (not red) forehead and crown, latter streaked blackish, and also lacks red coloration in facial area, with moustachial region generally less red (or even blackish); may also show less obvious red collar on sides and front of neck.

Juvenile Juvenile male differs from adult in being duller above and greyer below, and has red of collar extensively admixed with orange or yellow. Juvenile female apparently unknown.

Bare parts Bill black or blackish-grey, with base of lower mandible a paler greenish or yellowish-green. Legs and feet yellowish-green or greenish-grey. Eyes reddish-brown or pinkish-brown.

GEOGRAPHICAL VARIATION None known, but seems unlikely to show any major variation within its restricted range.

MEASUREMENTS Wing 125-141; tail 116-120; bill (culmen) 34-36; tarsus 29-30.

VOICE Not described. Drums in fast irregular rolls of medium length.

HABITS Found singly, in pairs or in family parties. Regularly accompanies mixed-species flocks, e.g. with babblers, laughingthrushes and other woodpeckers. Often forages low down on trees and, like many of its congeners, this species seems to forage frequently on the ground.

FOOD Ants probably form the main bulk of the diet.

BREEDING Evidence from museum specimens suggests January to March as the breeding period. Juveniles observed in northern Vietnam in early July.

REFERENCES Delacour & Jabouille 1931; King & Dickinson 1975; Robson *et al*. 1989; Short 1982; Wildash 1968.

193 BLACK-HEADED WOODPECKER
Picus erythropygius   Plate 57

IDENTIFICATION Length 33cm. A medium-sized, fairly slim, predominantly green woodpecker, with rather narrow pointed bill with slightly curved culmen. Mainly black head with striking yellow throat, breast and neck diagnostic. Male has red in centre of crown. In flight, both sexes show bright red rump (often just about visible also at rest) and white bars on flight feathers. Normally encountered in small parties of up to six birds, often very noisy and restless. Unmistakable.

DISTRIBUTION Uncommon to locally common from about 22-23˚N in Burma south through central and eastern

Burma to Tenasserim and east through parts of N, W and C Thailand, southern half of Laos and Cambodia to Vietnam (north to S Annam). Generally uncommon, but locally common.

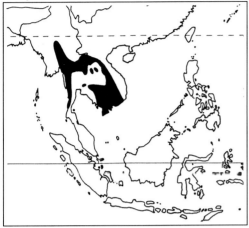

HABITAT Deciduous forests, especially dry dipterocarp, and open scrub country. Occurs at up to 900m in N Thailand and Vietnam, but more common below 600m.

DESCRIPTION

P. e. erythropygius **Adult male** Forehead, lores and cheeks to nape black, with red patch in centre of crown (extending sometimes down to eye); a few individuals have a thin whitish line extending from eye and over ear-coverts. Side of neck, chin, throat and upper breast bright yellow, brightest on side of neck and throat and often tinged olive on upper breast. Hindneck black, becoming yellow-green on mantle and back; rump quite extensively bright red, extending onto central uppertail-coverts; uppertail-coverts otherwise olive-green with indistinct black shaft streaks. Upperwing-coverts darker green (less yellow-tinged) than upperparts; tertials blackish-green; primary coverts and flight feathers blackish, latter with five or six fairly broad white bars (narrower on outer webs of primaries). Uppertail blackish, central feathers edged green (indistinctly) and with obscure pale barring towards base. Lower breast brownish-white, with faint arrowhead markings, becoming paler and whitish with heavier brown or blackish arrow-heads or bars on flanks and belly; undertail-coverts white, heavily barred dark brown. Underwing white or off-white, with blackish bars across flight feathers. Undertail as uppertail, but paler.

Adult female As male, but lacks red on crown, which is entirely black.

Juvenile Upperparts less yellow than on adults, throat paler, and upper breast buff rather than yellow, with markings below more diffuse. Juvenile male has central crown black with some admixed red feather tips.

Bare parts Bill greyish-horn to olive-yellow, darker at tip. Legs and feet pale grey to grey-green. Eyes very pale, whitish to lemon-yellow. Narrow orbital skin slate-grey.

GEOGRAPHICAL VARIATION Two very similar races, which intergrade in central part of species' range.

    P. e. erythropygius (eastern part of range, west into Thailand) Described above.

    P. e. nigrigenis (Burma and W Thailand) Very like nominate, but has dark, blackish, bill; male may show more red in crown.

MEASUREMENTS Wing 144-160. Weight: 100-135.

VOICE Common call a loud double-note. Also a distinctive, undulating, yelping laughter: *ka-tek-a-tek-a-tek-a-tek......* or *cha-cha-cha, cha-cha-cha*, rapidly repeated, with the stress on the first note in each series.

HABITS This shy woodpecker is usually met with in small, noisy groups of 2-6 birds, often associated with jays or treepies. Forages in the canopy and in the understorey, but also seems to descend to lower levels, e.g. to stumps and to the ground. Active and restless, constantly on the move through its forest habitat. Flight appears to be less undulating than that of Eurasian Green Woodpecker (191).

FOOD Appears to be fond of termites; also takes ants and other invertebrates.

BREEDING Nesting season apparently February to June.

REFERENCES King & Dickinson 1975; Lekagul & Round 1991; Smythies 1953.

---

194 GREY-FACED WOODPECKER
Picus canus   Plate 57

Other names: Grey-headed Woodpecker, Grey-headed Green Woodpecker; Black-naped (Green) Woodpecker (for some races)

IDENTIFICATION Length 26-33cm. Small to medium-sized, with fairly long, slightly chisel-tipped and rather broad-based bill with moderately curved culmen. Highly variable, but most races are green or greenish above with bright yellow-green rump and paler below, and have no obvious barring except on wings. Grey sides to head, with black malar stripe. Many races have black crown and nape, males always with red forehead patch. The rare aberrant Sumatran race *dedemi* is highly distinctive, being largely dull red above, with bright red rump and (males) forehead, and is unlikely to be misidentified within its very restricted range.

Similar species In the W Palearctic, main confusion species is Eurasian Green Woodpecker (191), and hybridisation between latter and Grey-faced has in fact been recorded in C Europe: Eurasian Green is somewhat bigger, with brighter yellow-green or grass-green upperparts and brighter yellow rump, and has different head pattern (black face, and red extending to hindneck); on the wing, Grey-faced

Grey-faced (above; European race) and Eurasian Green (below) in flight; note the former's less heavy appearance and less bared belly/flanks.

369

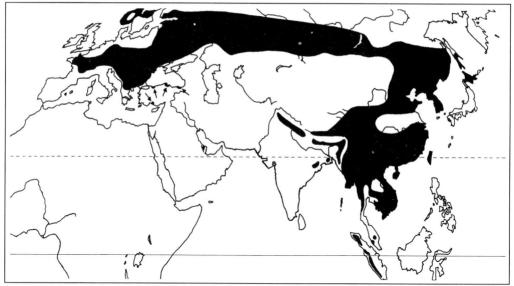

appears less 'nose-heavy' than Eurasian Green, and abdomen exhibits less barring. In SE Asia, Laced (187), Streak-breasted (186) and Streak-throated (188) Woodpeckers are all slightly smaller and have scaly or scalloped pattern on underparts, while males of all three differ from Grey-faced in having scarlet-red on head extending to nape/hindneck. Japanese Woodpecker (190) has heavily barred flanks and lower underparts and more red on head, though is unlikely to occur within range of Grey-faced (possibility of stragglers of either species occurring within the range of the other is very slight).

DISTRIBUTION Widely distributed over northern Eurasia, in the north largely not beyond the 64° latitude, from S Norway east through C Russia to the Amur basin (50-45°N), Sakhalin and Hokkaido. Southern border of range comprises C France, N Italy through the Balkans (not on Mediterranean coasts), N Greece, N Turkey, the northern foothills of the Altai, south of Lake Baikal, China, Burma, Thailand and Indochina; also from the western Himalayas to C Nepal, SE Tibet, Sikkim, Bhutan, Bangladesh and NE India. In addition occurs on Taiwan, Hainan, Sumatra, and in Malaysia (Gunung Tahan and Cameron Highlands). Common, if rather local, throughout most of its range, including in SE China, but rare to very rare in W Malaysia and Sumatra.

MOVEMENTS Essentially non-migratory. Local movements comprise changes from breeding habitats to more favourable (lower) winter grounds (riparian woodlands, human habitations). Normally disperses farther than Eurasian Green Woodpecker, and some nomadic winter movements occur among northern Asian populations and in connection with the irregular movements of Scandinavian Great Spotted Woodpeckers (104).

HABITAT Its wide range implies that this species occupies a great diversity of habitats. It is found in various types of temperate and moist subtropical forests, woodland, and second growth with evergreen, deciduous and coniferous trees; trees can be dense, but some open ground is required as well. Visits open country only when woodland is close by. In Europe, open country with many copses, in not-too-dense forests, floodplain forest, parks, orchards, and gardens. Associated mostly with deciduous trees, but locally in pine-oak woodland or more open coniferous montane forests with larch (*Larix*). Broadly overlaps with Eurasian Green Woodpecker, but more often in forest interior. Avoids pure coniferous taiga in C Siberia, preferring broadleaf forests. Open alder or oak forest are its habitats in Nepal and northern Burma, and populations of Tibet and W China inhabit open deciduous and coniferous country. Race *hessei*, in Burma and Thailand, prefers deciduous forests and drier and more open parts of teak forest over evergreen jungle; in the highlands of S Annam, Vietnam, it shows a liking for native pine forests. Other habitats in Asia include bamboo groves mixed with second growth. Generally, this species occupies a considerable altitudinal range, from lowlands to montane forests. In C Europe it is a hill bird. The lower altitudinal limit is at about 900m in Malaysia, and 1000m in Sumatra. It is found up to 1300m in the Alps (non-breeding birds considerably higher), to 2100m in NW India, to 2600m in Nepal (more common below 2000m, however), to 2300m in northern Burma, to 1830m elsewhere in mainland SE Asia, and to 2000m in Sumatra.

DESCRIPTION
P. c. canus **Adult male** Head and neck mostly ashy-grey, slightly tinged greenish when fresh, darker on nape and neck, with scarlet-red upper forehead and forecrown (often yellowish at rear edge), crown usually with very fine black streaks. Black upper lores and narrow black malar stripe, latter broadening slightly and often mottled grey at rear. Chin and throat pale grey-white, tinged buff or olive. Mantle, scapulars and back olive-green, merging into yellowish or greenish-yellow on rump and uppertail-coverts, latter mottled olive-green (feather bases). Upperwing-coverts olive-green, occasionally with slight bronze or yellowish tinge; primaries and their coverts greyish-black to brownish-black, with small whitish spots on outer (and sometimes some inner) webs forming broken bars across entire primaries; secondaries greyish-black with dull olive-green outer webs, outer feathers often with some paler spots. Uppertail green-tinged brown, with obscure paler bars. Underparts pale grey, with slight tinge of pale olive-green (especially on lower flanks and belly) when fresh, and occasionally with obscure darker arrowhead markings in lowermost regions. Underwing and its coverts greyish, heavily barred across entire surface. Undertail blackish, tipped greenish-grey, with a few obscure paler bars.

Adult female Averages slightly smaller than male, with proportionately slightly shorter bill. Head much plainer, lacking red on forehead/forecrown, which instead is pale grey with narrow black shaft streaks (often faint when fresh), though occasional individuals show a few scattered red feather tips on forehead; black malar stripe usually weaker and often incomplete.

Juvenile Duller than adults, greyer above with slight scaly appearance and with rump more greenish-yellow; some wing-coverts, tertials and secondaries often show indistinct barring; malar stripe narrow and more diffuse and mottled. Initially has inconspicuous darker barring on lower underparts. Juvenile male has crown patch smaller than adult's and orange-red (less scarlet), with grey feather bases often visible.

Bare parts Bill blackish-brown to grey-brown or grey-black, usually with olive tinge, with most of lower mandible and basal cutting edges of upper pale greyish or olive-yellow. Legs and feet olive-grey to yellowish-olive. Eyes white (tinged pinkish or bluish), or deep carmine-red with admixed white; red-brown or with admixed white in juveniles.

GEOGRAPHICAL VARIATION Many races have been described throughout the species' vast range, but some of these are differentiated on only very minor, insignificant characters and barely warrant separation. Here, we follow Short (1982) in recognising 11 races; these can be divided into two main groups, with two isolated races.

(a) Northern *canus* group (greyish, with grey crown):
    P. c. canus (Europe east to western Siberia) Described above.
    P. c. jessoensis (eastern Siberia, NE China, Manchuria, Korea, Sakhalin and Hokkaido) Variable, generally slightly paler and greyer, less green, than nominate, but much overlap and many (especially when fresh) are indistinguishable from the latter. Intergrades with *kogo* in C China and with *guerini* in eastern China.

(b) Southern and eastern *guerini* group (greener, with black crown, latter often streaked grey):
    P. c. guerini (eastern Yangtze river west to C Sichuan) Greenish above and below, with black nape; females have pale-streaked black crown. Intergrades with *sordidior* in Sichuan.
    P. c. sobrinus (Fujian, Guangdong, Guangxi and NE Vietnam) Has golden tint above and is greener, less grey below.
    P. c. tancolo (Hainan and Taiwan) Smaller than *sobrinus*. Deep green upperparts, very green underparts and an obviously greyer face.
    P. c. kogo (China, from Shanxi west to Qinghai and south to Sichuan) Larger than *guerini* and paler green; female has black nape and pale-streaked black crown (some are greyish-green on head top).
    P. c. sordidior (south of *kogo*, in W Sichuan, SE Tibet, Yunnan and NE Burma) Larger than *guerini* (as *kogo*) and dark (as eastern *guerini*).
    P. c. hessei (Nepal and N India east through Burma and most of Thailand to Vietnam) Even darker than *sordidior*: dark golden-green above and deeper green below (even less grey than others in this group), with tail darker and less barred; crown and nape deep black, and males show more extensive red from forehead to mid crown. Size diminishes clinally from northeast to southwest. Intergrades with *sanguiniceps* in Nepal.
    P. c. sanguiniceps (westernmost Nepal, NW India and Pakistan) The largest race of all. Plumage as *hessei*, but less golden or bronzy above; male has even more extensive red on crown.

(c) Isolated races:
    P. c. robinsoni (Malaysian mountains: Gunung Tahan and Cameron Highlands) Small. Whole plumage above and below very dark green but for paler throat and yellow-green rump; crown and nape black, crown slightly streaked on female, and forehead and forecrown red on male.
    P. c. dedemi (Sumatran highlands) The smallest and darkest race of all. Highly distinctive: deep brownish-red above, with brighter red rump and unbarred blackish tail; reddish-brown with admixed grey and greenish below, with blackish undertail-coverts; crown and nape unstreaked black, male with small red forehead patch. Juveniles are less red, more blackish, above and below.

Note that hybridisation with Eurasian Green Woodpecker has been recorded in C Europe.

MEASUREMENTS Wing 137-155 (*canus*), 138-157 (*jessoensis*), 130-140 (*tancolo*), 149-156 (*kogo*), 136-156 (*hessei*), 145-165 (*sanguiniceps*), 132-140 (*robinsoni*); tail 92-104 (*canus*), 90-118 (*jessoensis*), 99-116 (*hessei*), 98-116 (*sanguiniceps*), 99-109 (*robinsoni*); bill (from skull) 36-44 (*canus*), 40-45 (*jessoensis*), 42-44 (*kogo*), 36-42 (*hessei*), 38-49 (*sanguiniceps*), 33-43 (*robinsoni*); tarsus 25-29 (*canus*), 24-27.8 (*jessoensis*), 28-30.5 (*robinsoni*). Weight: 125-165 (*canus*), 110-206 (*jessoensis*), 137 (female of *hessei*), 143-165 (*sanguiniceps*).

VOICE Single *kik* calls are very similar to those of Laced Woodpecker, but higher-pitched. The most characteristic call constitutes a descending sequence of 5-20 clearly separated mournful notes: *kiu, kiu, kiu.....*, *pew, pew, pew...*, easy to imitate by whistling (the female's series usually shorter and more raucous; there may also be racial differences in the number of syllables). Call-series of Himalayan birds is softer and less descending than equivalent series of C European birds. At close distances, the pair exchanges low *dyook dyook...* series. Low to moderately loud *kyak kyak kyak...* mark agonistic situations; in body-swinging displays, *wite-wite..* calls are uttered. Outside the breeding season, *keek, kak kak kak...* calls are common. Nestlings chatter when a parent is at the hole or feeding them. Drums regularly at acoustically most active time, which in Europe is in March and April, before breeding. Rolls are longer than those of Laced Woodpecker, but the rhythm is slightly slower; in Europe, rolls consist of 19-40 strokes, delivered at a steady rate of about 20/secs.

HABITS Although not very shy, this species is less conspicuous than Eurasian Green or Laced Woodpeckers. Usually observed singly outside the breeding season, otherwise in pairs or small family parties. In tropical areas (e.g. Thailand), it may feed with mixed bird flocks of other terrestrial foragers. Regularly feeds on the ground, probing into the soil, pushing and digging with the bill and using the tongue to lick up prey. Arboreal foraging comprises single pecks, some excavation in decaying wood at low levels, and intensive use of the tongue at crevices and sites of decayed wood. Funnel-shaped holes dug into the ground serve as repeatedly used sources of ants, which appear when disturbed. Grey-faced Woodpecker licks from sap wells, but seems not to ring trees itself. Uses simple anvils now and then. On the ground, it moves with heavy hops. Otherwise, appears to be more lively and agile than Eurasian Green, and readily flies even short distances within a tree. Displays in agonistic contexts consist of variations of jerky bowing movements, often associated with calling; at low intensities forward movements and stiff-necked postures prevail, but at other times displaying birds swing their body and head laterally, keeping the bill in line with the body axis, at the same time bowing. In the courtship period, birds land with fluttering wingbeats, a display associated with the presence of a partner and a hole. Other, more aggressive displays include erecting the nape feathers ('bullnecked' posture) or the crest, wing-flicking and wing- and tail-spreading. Both partners call extensively prior to and during copulations, which also may take place on the ground. Feeding of female by the male seems to occur occasionally. Territories are maintained with calling and are established about a month before egg-laying. Usually loses out to Eurasian Green Woodpecker in interspecific encounters. Some indirect evidence also exists that Grey-faced Woodpeckers outcompete Black Woodpeckers (169), although at roosts they are generally inferior to other species. Roosts in holes, including those made by other species, rarely in nestboxes and in buildings. Females enter the roost later than males.

FOOD The diet appears to be more varied than that of Eurasian Green, though ants (*Myrmica*, *Lasius*), termites and their brood still prevail and often comprise more than 90% of stomach contents. Also takes other insects (e.g. coleopterous larvae) and spiders, and known to rob bird nests. Fruits (e.g. apple, pear, cherries, camphor), berries, seeds (e.g. *Rhus*), nuts and acorns, and nectar are also consumed. Regularly visits feeders.

BREEDING The egg-laying season commences somewhat later than that of Eurasian Green Woodpecker and extends from end of April to early June in C Europe, Russia and NW India; breeds from April to June in Sikkim and northern Burma. Nest hole, commonly between (0.2) 1.5 and 8 (24)m up, is excavated in dead or soft living wood or in fungus-afflicted hard wood. Construction accomplished in 9-20 and more days; the entrance, a vertical oval, measures about 60 x 55mm. Clutch size varies geographically and generally comprises (4)5-8(10) eggs; 4-5 in the Himalayas, 7-9 in C Europe. Both sexes incubate; the male sits during the night, and seems to incubate more even during the day. The young hatch after 14-17 days, and are fed by regurgitation by both parents equally; helping by a second female is known to have occurred. They fledge after 23-27 days and stay with the parents for some time afterwards.

REFERENCES Ali 1962; Ali & Ripley 1970; Bezzel 1985; Blume 1973; Blume & Ogasawara 1980; Conrads 1964; Conrads & Herrmann 1963; Cramp 1985; Dement'ev & Gladkov 1966; Glutz von Blotzheim & Bauer 1980; Greenway 1940; Gyldenstolpe 1916; Haila & Järvinen 1977; Inskipp & Inskipp 1991; King & Dickinson 1975; Klima 1959; Lekagul & Round 1991; Löhrl 1977; MacKinnon & Phillipps 1993; Martens & Eck in press; Matsuoka & Kojima 1985; Medway & Wells 1976; Miech 1986; Proud 1958; Robinson 1928; Short 1973a; Spitznagel 1993; Stanford & Mayr 1941; Südbeck 1993; Südbeck & Meinecke 1992.

---

195 OLIVE-BACKED WOODPECKER
Dinopium rafflesii   Plate 58

Other name: Olive-backed Three-toed Woodpecker

IDENTIFICATION Length c. 26-28cm. Medium-sized, with fairly long, chisel-tipped bill slightly curved on culmen and narrow across nostrils. Has only three toes. Combination of olive-green upperparts and underparts with white-spotted flanks, striped black and white head and neck, and prominent red (male) or black (female) crown and long crest distinguishes this from all other woodpeckers within its range. The throat and malar/moustachial area show a

strong yellow, yellowish-buff or rusty coloration. In fresh plumage, usually shows bronze or yellow tinge to upperparts and yellowish or even orange or crimson tips to rump feathers, but rump is never truly crimson.

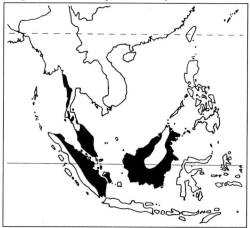

DISTRIBUTION Confined to SE Asia, where it occurs from S Burma (south from Tennaserim) and peninsular Thailand, through W Malaysia to Sumatra, including Bangka Island, and Borneo; recently found at around 13°N in SW Thailand (Kaeng Krachan NP). Uncommon to rare throughout its range, though perhaps somewhat commoner in parts of Borneo.

HABITAT Dense, wet evergreen forests, including swamp forests and mangroves. Normally avoids secondary growth and clearings. Mainly in lowlands and hills, up to 1200m, and, in Borneo, locally even to 1600m.

DESCRIPTION
D. r. rafflesii **Adult male** Forehead, crown and crest red with buff feather bases, and narrowly bordered black. Broad white supercilium from above eye to nape, bordered below by broad black stripe to hindneck. Lores buffy-yellow, merging into white stripe running backwards beneath ear-coverts and extending as very broad white band down neck side to upper breast side. Moustachial stripe cinnamon to yellowish or rusty (sometimes with red feather tips), becoming black at rear and continuing as black border to white neck stripe. Chin and upper throat cinnamon, yellowish or rusty-yellow. Hindneck and uppermost mantle black; rest of upperparts dark olive-green with bronzy or yellowish feather tips, rump and uppertail-coverts occasionally with orange tips (rarely, tips dull reddish). Upperwing-coverts bronzy or yellowish olive-green; flight feathers brownish-black, with yellow-green outer webs to secondaries, inner webs with white spots. Uppertail black. Lower throat to undertail-coverts olive to greyish-olive, often with rusty staining, flanks usually with prominent white spots (can be lacking). Underwing dark brownish, spotted white. Undertail olive-black.

Adult female Has red on head replaced by black, with forehead generally more olive or buffy; crest slightly smaller than male's.

Juvenile Duller and greyer than adults. Males have crown blackish or dark olive, with red only on crest or perhaps also with a few scattered red spots on forehead. Females resemble adult, but with crown more olive in tone.

Bare parts Bill grey to greyish-black. Legs and feet (three toes) blue-grey or grey. Eyes dark red-brown.

GEOGRAPHICAL VARIATION Individual variation considerable, but only two races recognisable, differing merely in size.

D. r. rafflesii (range of species, apart from Borneo) Described above.

D. r. dulitense (Borneo) Smaller than nominate in all measurements.

MEASUREMENTS Wing 137-149 (*rafflesii*), 119-139 (*dulitense*); tail 104-109 (*rafflesii*); bill 31-36 (*rafflesii*); tarsus 24-27 (*rafflesii*). Weight: 87-119 (*rafflesii*), 76-84 (*dulitense*).

VOICE The single call note, *chak*, and a rapid series of loud notes are most commonly heard. The call-series occurs in two versions, which may also differ functionally. A slow *chakchakchak-chak*, with 6-34 notes, varies in rate and pitch, and sometimes single notes are appended; it is heard when pair members interact. The other is one-and-a-half times faster and more regular, with 10-50 notes, and territorial proclamation seems to be its main function. These calls are more rapid and higher-pitched than the corresponding vocalisations of Laced Woodpecker (187) and are rather like those of Eurasian Green Woodpecker (191). During encounters, and sometimes associated with head-swinging, low *ch-wee, ch-wee, ch-wee* calls may be heard. A soft, even trilling *ti-i-i-i* and a squeaky *tiririt* have also been described. Not known to drum, but incubating birds may tap in soft regular bursts of 10-12 strokes.

HABITS Single birds and pairs, which keep vocal contact, forage at low and middle heights (below 10m), on fallen logs, at the bases of trees and saplings, and to the tops of lower saplings and snags and on branches of the lower crown. Rarely, ventures out of the forest to visit dead stumps. Its main foraging mode is gleaning, but pecks now and then, more frequently than Common Flameback (197). Moves slowly and continuously, with only brief pauses. Displays include raising of the crest, bowing movements, and head-swinging. The male feeds the female as part of the courtship.

FOOD Ants, termites and especially ant pupae.

BREEDING Nesting season in Borneo appears to be October; April and May in W Malaysia. Nest excavated even in live wood, by both sexes, which also share incubation duties. The male roosts in the nest.

REFERENCES King & Dickinson 1975; Lekagul & Round 1991; MacKinnon & Phillipps 1993; Medway & Wells 1976; Robinson 1928; Short 1973a; Smythies 1981.

---

196 HIMALAYAN FLAMEBACK
Dinopium shorii   Plate 58

Other name: Himalayan/Three-toed Golden-backed Woodpecker

Forms a superspecies with *javanense*.

IDENTIFICATION Length c. 30-32cm. Medium-sized, with fairly long, almost pointed bill curved on culmen and narrow across nostrils. Normally has three toes (fourth vestigial or lacking). A striking species, with black and white face and neck, golden-olive upperparts strongly suffused red, and with bright red rump contrasting with black tail. (Note that apparent colour of upperparts can change according to light, distance and optical aids used, this being applicable to all *Dinopium* and *Chrysocolaptes* species.) Male has red crown and bushy crest, these being white-streaked black on female, and two thin black lines enclose reddish (male) or white (female) moustache. Has buffish-brown area on throat and breast, rest of underparts being whitish with dark scallop markings.

Similar species Very similar to western forms of Common Flameback (197), and distinguishable only with difficulty, but the two are likely to overlap only in Burma. Common Flameback is best told by the black line down the centre of its throat, its darker (blacker-looking or more black-and-white) breast and by its single, black moustachial stripe, while female Common may also show heavier white crown streaking than female Himalayan, but these differences are detectable only with good and reasonably prolonged views. In addition, Himalayan appears to prefer denser primary forest, whereas Common Flameback is more at home in open woodland and woodland edge (also gardens and parks etc.).

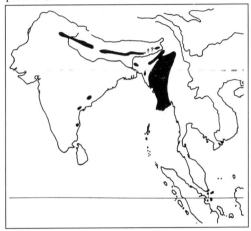

DISTRIBUTION Fairly common locally from NW India (Haryana province and S Himachal Pradesh) eastwards through lowlands and southern foothills of Himalayas to N Bangladesh and Burma. An isolated population also occurs in a few places in the Eastern Ghats of peninsular India.

HABITAT Mature deciduous and semi-evergreen forest, negatively affected by deforestation. In Nepal, restricted to deciduous-forest zone, preferring primary lowland forests with *Ficus* and *Bombax*. Lowlands and foothills to about 700m, but below 300m in Nepal.

DESCRIPTION

D. s. shorii Adult male Forehead yellowish-red, becoming red on crown and crest, narrowly bordered black from forecrown to nape. Supercilium from above eye to nape side white. Black stripe from eye to hindneck, bordered below by white band from lores to lower neck side which continues broadly down side of neck to breast side. Moustachial stripe pale reddish with black outline, becoming all black at rear and continuing down onto breast side. Chin whitish with thin buff-brown central line, latter broadening through centre of throat and expanding over most of upper breast, where bordered with black spots. Hindneck and upper mantle black; lower mantle, scapulars and upper back olive-green with yellower or golden feather tips, and with strong element of red on edges and tips; lower back, rump and some uppertail-coverts bright red, uppertail-coverts otherwise blackish olive-brown. Upperwing-coverts and tertials as scapulars, coverts with a hint of red; flight feathers blackish-brown, with yellow-olive outer webs of secondaries, and with inner webs spotted white. Uppertail black. Underpart feathers white with brownish-black edges and black tips, creating somewhat scaly pattern. Underwing brown, spotted white. Undertail brownish-black, tinged yellow-olive on outer feathers.

Adult female Lacks red on head. Has olive to buff forehead, becoming blackish-brown to black with narrow white streaks on crown and crest; moustache white with black outline.

Juvenile Dingier and browner than adults, with markings below more obscure. Young males have red only on crest, with forehead and crown brownish-buff and streaked paler; female has brown crown and crest with broad pale streaks.

Bare parts Bill blackish. Legs and feet green-grey or brownish-green. Eyes red, red-brown or (presumably immatures) dark brown; also reported as gold or crimson.

GEOGRAPHICAL VARIATION Two races are recognised, though they differ only insignificantly.

D. s. shorii (range of species, apart from eastern fringe) Described above.

D. s. anguste (Burma and possibly also adjacent areas to west) Bill, wing and tail a little smaller than in nominate. Perhaps tends to have slightly less red on back than nominate, but this feature inconstant and much overlap. Females, however, have crown streaking much finer than nominate females, and virtually unstreaked hindcrown.

MEASUREMENTS Wing 147-166; tail 95-104; bill (from skull) 37-44; tarsus 23-24. Weight: 101.

VOICE Utters a rapid, tinny *klak-klak-klak-klak-klak*, this call apparently being slower than and not so loud as similar vocalisation of Greater Flameback (199).

HABITS Poorly known. May associate with Greater Flameback where the two occur together.

FOOD Not known.

BREEDING Not well known. Breeds in April, when (2) 3 eggs are laid.

REFERENCES Ali & Ripley 1970; Diesselhorst 1968; Fleming *et al.* 1984; Inskipp & Inskipp 1991.

---

197 COMMON FLAMEBACK
Dinopium javanense   Plate 58

Other names: Common Golden-backed Woodpecker, Golden-backed Three-toed Woodpecker
Forms a superspecies with *shorii*.

IDENTIFICATION Length c. 28-30cm. Medium-sized, with rather short, pointed bill curved on culmen and narrow across nostrils. Has only three toes. A conspicuously patterned crested woodpecker, widely distributed and generally common. Most races have black and white head and neck (male with red crown and crest), golden to olive upperparts with bright red rump, and black and white underparts; female has white-streaked black crown and crest. Western Philippines male has red invading face, a distinct reddish tinge to neck and breast, and female lacks white crown spots but has red nape crest. As with many woodpeckers, pale areas of face and underparts are often stained brownish. Frequently occurs in pairs, with much calling, and regularly enters gardens. Flight quick and darting.

Similar species Very like Himalayan Flameback (196), whose range overlaps that of Common in Burma, but has different colour/pattern on throat and breast and a single black moustachial line. Best distinguished from superficially similar Greater Flameback (199) by its smaller size, much shorter, less powerful bill, neater (less shaggy, more

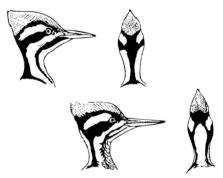

Head patterns of Common (above) and Greater (below) Flamebacks: note differences in bill length, moustache and hindneck pattern.

pointed) crest, black (not white) hindneck and upper mantle, single black moustachial line, usually darker eyes, and the fact that it has only three toes (Greater has four). Note that, with all flamebacks, the apparent colour of the upperparts can change from red to olive or gold depending on light, distance and optical aids used.

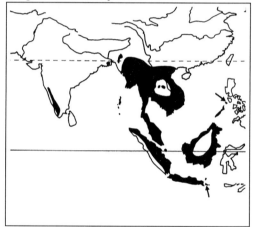

DISTRIBUTION A locally common species which occurs in SW India, from about 16°N south to Kerala, from Bangladesh and C and S Assam east to SW Yunnan and south throughout SE Asia (except N Burma), and to Sumatra (including Riau archipelago), Java, Bali, Borneo (mainly coastal and including islands off northeast coast), and the western Philippines.

HABITAT Common in moist secondary and open forests, open deciduous woodland, scrub and mangroves; also found in teak forests and, at higher elevations, in pine forests. Particularly favours penang and coconut groves, cultivations, gardens, parkland, and golf courses. Mainly a bird of the lowlands, it can also be found at up to 1000m in the Greater Sundas, to 1530m in continental SE Asia and to 1700m in India.

DESCRIPTION

D. j. intermedium **Adult male** Forehead and upper lores brownish-red, becoming red on crown and crest (crown narrowly edged black). Supercilium from above eye to nape side white. Black stripe from eye to hindneck, bordered below by broad white stripe from lores which continues as expanded white band down side of neck onto breast side. Thin black moustachial stripe, broader at rear, continuing down onto upper breast. Chin and throat whitish, with central line of (usually narrow) black spots from bill base, spots generally becoming somewhat broader and more numerous on lower throat. Hindneck and upper mantle black; rest of mantle, scapulars and upper back olive, strongly suffused golden and with yellow feather tips/edges (sometimes also with hint of orange or red); lower back and rump bright red; uppertail-coverts blackish-brown, occasionally tinged olive. Upperwing-coverts much as scapulars; outer webs of secondaries and tertials olive-yellow, rest of flight feathers blackish-brown with white spots on inner webs. Uppertail black. Breast to undertail-coverts white, all feathers irregularly edged and tipped black, black markings being heaviest on breast and becoming less prominent and more bar-like on lower underparts. Underwing brown, spotted white. Undertail brownish-black, tinged yellowish on outer feathers.

Adult female Crown and crest black, with white streaks.

Juvenile Very like adults, but with breast more blackish-brown and with white spots, and more obscurely barred on lower underparts. Young males have mainly black forehead and crown, with red crest; females have pale crown streaks more spot-like.

Bare parts Bill blackish to dark grey-brown, with paler base and lower mandible. Legs and feet (three toes) grey or brown, usually tinged greenish. Eyes red-brown or brown; greyer in juveniles. Orbital skin black.

GEOGRAPHICAL VARIATION Six races, only one of which is distinctive.

  D. j. intermedium (Bangladesh and Assam east through Burma and SW Yunnan/C China and south to Indochina) Described above.

  D. j. malabaricum (W India) Very like *intermedium*, but averages slightly smaller. Back and wings less golden-yellow and more olive.

  D. j. javanense (W Malaysia, Sumatra, W Java and Borneo) Smaller than above two races, but otherwise very similar; can show buffish tinge to face/throat. Bornean population tends to be slightly less orangey on back and slightly more barred below, but these traits insignificant bearing in mind individual variation.

  D. j. exsul (E Java and Bali) As *javanense*, but has underparts strongly (but irregularly) barred and females have narrow orange to red nape band.

  D. j. raveni (NE Borneo and Eraban Island) Very like nominate *javanense*, but perhaps more buff and less black below and throat more broadly spotted; females tend to have crown streaks very narrow.

  D. j. everetti (Philippines: Balabac, Palawan and Calamian Islands) Distinctive. Both sexes show obvious pale reddish or buffy-brown tone to throat, neck and upper breast, with throat spots more extensive (and spreading to otherwise unmarked upper breast), and more barred pattern below. Males have red of crown extending onto sides of head, where dark eye-stripe broader, and with a variable amount of red feather tips in moustache (which can appear virtually all red); females have large area of red on nape and crest, much narrower pale supercilium (as on male), and crown lacks white streaks or has very small streaks mainly on forecrown.

MEASUREMENTS Wing 124-140 (*javanense*), 135-143 (*malabaricum*), 136-165 (*intermedium*); tail 101-107 (*javanense*), 83-95 (*malabaricum*); bill 23-28 (*malabaricum*), 27-30 (*intermedium*); tarsus 22-24. Weight: 67-90 (*javanense*), 85-98 (*everetti*), 79-100 (*intermedium*).

VOICE In flight, a variable series of notes is uttered, *kowp-owp-owp-owp*. Perched birds give single or double *kow* calls.

Wicha like calls accompany displays during encounters. The rattle is a harsh prolonged *churrrrrrr*, or *ka-di-di-di-di-di-di*, generally more rapid than that of Olive-backed Woodpecker (195). Drums more softly than Greater Flameback.

HABITS Lives in pairs, which keep frequent vocal contact, and also joins mixed-species flocks. Found at all heights, but seems to prefer lower parts of large as well as young trees. On palms, inspects frond scars on the trunk and all parts of the crown. The main foraging modes are gleaning, with reaching sidewards, and probing, with some occasional pecking, for instance to remove loose pieces of bark; sometimes hawks for passing insects. Climbing movements are rapid and erratic, with only short stops made at any one site. Foraging activities may, however, be broken by periods of motionless perching. May cover long distances when changing feeding sites. Crest-raising and swinging head and body movements, during close encounters, are the common displays.

FOOD Ants, insect larvae, small scorpions, cockroaches and other insects.

BREEDING Breeding recorded in India from (January) February to April (June), in Thailand in June, in Malaysia from January to July, and in Borneo in April, May, July, November and December; in Palawan, a female was heard calling to her mate from a nest hole about 10m up in a dead tree on 20 March. Nest is excavated low down (2m or less) or high up (10m), mostly below 5m, in a tree or stump in open areas; usually in a fruit tree or coconut palm. Clutch of 2 or 3 eggs.

REFERENCES Ali & Ripley 1970; King & Dickinson 1975; Lekagul & Round 1991; MacKinnon 1990; Medway & Wells 1976; Robinson 1927; Short 1973a; Smythies 1953, 1981.

---

198 BLACK-RUMPED FLAMEBACK
Dinopium benghalense   Plate 58

Other names: Lesser Flameback, Lesser/Black-rumped Golden-backed Woodpecker

IDENTIFICATION Length c. 26-29cm. Small to medium-sized, with rather long, almost pointed bill curved on culmen and fairly narrow across nostrils. Has four toes. Superficially similar to others of its genus, but differs in having black (not red) lower back and rump (though these areas are washed olive in southwestern populations). Back and wings are a rich golden or golden-olive, contrasting with black upper mantle and rump, and the wing-coverts usually have at least some white spots, as do the flight feathers. Chin and throat show much black. Some black feather bases are normally visible in red of male's crown, and in worn plumage forehead and crown can appear largely black; female has red crest, but forehead and forecrown are black with white spots. Sri Lankan race *psarodes* differs markedly in having back and wings deep red, with more black on head and underparts and usually fewer pale spots on wing-coverts, and male also has more black in crown. Pale areas of face and underparts frequently become stained. This is often rather a tame species, and one of the commonest and most widespread in the Indian subcontinent.

DISTRIBUTION Ranges from Pakistan eastwards through S Nepal to Assam and W Burma and south throughout India to Sri Lanka. Common.

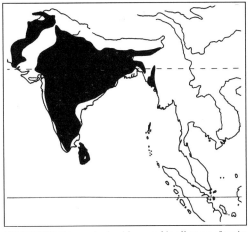

HABITAT This species is widespread in all types of moist to dry woodland, but avoids heavy forest and arid regions. Found in coconut and palmyra palm (*Borassus*) plantations, well-wooded gardens, roadside avenues, urban areas, open types of jungle, etc. In Sri Lanka, the northern golden-backed form ('*tehminae*') is found in coastal areas, frequenting palmyra and coconut plantations, and scrub jungle; red-backed form (*psarodes*) is common in lowland areas, both wet and dry, up to 1500m, but probably breeds not above 900m. On the continent this is also a bird of open woodland, sal forest, groves around villages, old gardens, and tree plantations along roads and canals. It reaches elevations of 1700m in India and about 915m in W Burma.

DESCRIPTION

D. b. benghalense **Adult male** Forehead and crown feathers black with red tips; crest red. White-streaked black band from eye through ear-coverts, enclosed by white supercilium from eye and white stripe from lores which meet at rear and continue as broad band down side of neck to upper breast side. Chin and throat black, broadly streaked white. Hindneck and upper mantle black; lower mantle, scapulars and upper back rich golden-yellow; lower back to uppertail-coverts black. Upperwing-coverts golden-olive, but outer medians (and most of lessers) black with triangular white subterminal spots, and inner greater coverts often with white central streak; flight feathers brownish-black, with outer webs of tertials and secondaries golden-olive, primaries and inner webs of secondaries and tertials bearing well-spaced white spots. Uppertail black. Underparts below throat white to buffish-white, feathers broadly edged and tipped black on breast, black markings becoming narrower and/or much reduced on lower underparts and sometimes more bar-like on belly and undertail-coverts. Underwing brown, coverts largely white with black barring. Undertail brownish-black. (In worn plumage, forehead and crown become mostly black, and olive feather bases may be visible on back.)

Adult female Has red hindcrown and crest, but forehead and forecrown are black with small white spots.

Juvenile Duller than adults, with black areas browner and with underparts greyer and more obscurely marked. Males have narrower red tips to crown feathers and sometimes white crown spots; females lack or have much-reduced spotting in crown.

Bare parts Bill blackish or grey-black, sometimes horn-tinged. Legs and feet greyish-green. Eyes red-brown to crimson. Orbital skin green.

GEOGRAPHICAL VARIATION Individual variation considerable, which, together with presence of intergrading populations, blurs racial divisions. Here, we recognise four races.

D. b. benghalense (N India east to Assam) Described above.

D. b. dilutum (Pakistan) Back and wings generally a paler golden-yellow, and underparts whiter.

D. b. puncticolle (C India south to about 8°N in Sri Lanka) Back and wings more orange-yellow, and throat spotted rather than streaked white; lower underparts often more creamy-buff. Western and south-western populations (often separated as '*tehminae*') have a distinct olive wash to the rump and wing-coverts, and wing-covert spots are often smaller or even lacking. Shows clinal decrease in size southwards, and intergrades with *benghalense* in north and with following race in N Sri Lanka.

D. b. psarodes (= *D. b. erithronothos*; most of Sri Lanka) Distinct from other races in having deep crimson-red back and wings, and often red tips to feathers of rump/uppertail-coverts. Also has more black in crown (especially at sides) and on side of head (black eye-stripe usually extends to hindneck), and often more black on throat and underparts. Tail is proportionately longer than in other races. Intergrades with previous race in north of range.

MEASUREMENTS Wing 136-156 (Sri Lanka, 128-141); tail 80-95 (Sri Lanka, 75-90); bill (from skull) 31-43; tarsus 23-28. Weight: 86-133.

VOICE Vocalisations include a call-scream (in flight) and a rattling scream (contact between pair members). Call note a single strident *kierk*. A rattle consisting of repeated *kyi-kyi-kyi*, reminiscent of White-breasted Kingfisher *Halcyon smyrnensis*, is given from a perch or in flight. High-pitched squeaks are uttered by excited birds in encounters. Nestlings supposedly hiss when threatened. Drums in weak bouts of 2-3 secs duration.

HABITS Less shy than most woodpeckers, and often seen in pairs and with mixed-species flocks. Arboreal foraging takes place at all levels. Breaks into the leaf-nests of the fierce red ant *Oecophylla smaragdina*, but also descends to the ground to feed at ant nests. Clings to underside of horizontal branches, and may move backwards occasionally. Jerky movements in close contact between sexes, and crest-raising by males, are the known displays of this woodpecker. Male has also been observed feeding insects to the female. Aggressive interactions with White-naped Woodpecker (200) have been recorded.

FOOD The main food is ants, such as *Camponotus* and *Meranoplus*, and the diet even includes larvae and pupae of the red ant *Oecophylla smaragdina*. Spiders, caterpillars, weevils, and other beetles are taken occasionally. Fruits (e.g. mango) and nectar are other not uncommon constituents of the diet.

BREEDING Breeds chiefly from March to April, southern populations again in July and August; in Sri Lanka, from December to September, whenever conditions are favourable. Nests are built, by both sexes, into trees with soft or hard wood (acacias, tamarisks, mangos, palms etc.) at heights between 3 and 6m and higher; entrance hole about 8cm in diameter. The clutch, comprising 2 or 3 eggs, is incubated by both parents for 17-19 days. Both feed the chicks, by regurgitation. The young take about three weeks to fledge. Sometimes a second brood is reared in one season.

REFERENCES Ali & Ripley 1970; Ganguli 1975; Henry 1971; Inskipp & Inskipp 1991; Mason & Lefroy 1912; Phillips 1978; Roberts 1991.

199 GREATER FLAMEBACK
Chrysocolaptes lucidus   Plate 59

Other names: Greater/Large Golden-backed Woodpecker

IDENTIFICATION Length c. 28-34cm. Medium-sized to large, with long, chisel-tipped bill barely curved on culmen and broad across nostrils. A widely distributed woodpecker with an extraordinary range of geographical plumage variation (greater than in any other species) and also wide size variation. All races are long-billed and have red lower back and rump, and most have the lower hindneck and upper mantle partly white or pale coloured. In general terms, populations from India to Indonesia have golden-green to olive or bronzy back and wings, a white face with broad black band from eye to hindneck and two thin black moustachial lines, and white underparts boldly scalloped with black; males have red crown and crest, while females have these parts white-spotted black or (in E Java) golden-yellow or orange. Sri Lankan population, however, has back and wings dark red (darker than rump) and a notice-ably pale bill. In the Philippines, westernmost breeders have mainly golden-green back and wings, a white neck striped black, and the entire head is red with a dark spot on ear-coverts; all other Philippine races have dark red back and wings with a variable head pattern (in both sexes). Most distinctive is the race on Negros and nearby islands: the entire face (on female entire head), neck and underparts are a beautiful bright golden-yellow. The differences between westernmost (NW Indian) and easternmost (E Philippines) populations of this woodpecker are so great that the observer familiar only with one would take the other to be a totally separate species. See also Geographical Variation. Greater Flameback is a locally fairly common woodpecker, usually found in pairs or family parties; active and noisy, it drums loudly and frequently.

Similar species In India, White-naped Woodpecker (200) is immediately distinguished by its all-white hindneck and white triangle on mantle, and its black rump. Those *Dinopium* species with a red rump are similar to Greater Flameback, but they all have the bill shorter than the head (equally long on Greater), a fully black hindneck and upper mantle, and dark eyes. See also Common Flameback (197), whose range overlaps in many areas. In Sri Lanka, the respective races of Greater and Common Flamebacks both have red back and wings, but Common is smaller, with a darker rump and a much shorter, dark bill and dark eyes.

DISTRIBUTION Occurs mainly below about 1200m, from Garhwal and Kumaon southwards through much of the Indian subcontinent, including Sri Lanka, east through southern Nepal to S Yunnan in SW China and south through Burma and Indochina to Indonesia east to Bali, including Riau, Lingga, Bangka and Kangean Islands, and also in NE Borneo (E Sabah) and the Philippines. Through-out much of its range it is common or locally common, but in some areas (e.g. Yunnan) decidedly rare, and only few recent records from Java (in east) and Bali.

HABITAT A forest-loving species of rather open decidu-ous and evergreen forest. Can therefore be observed in secondary forest, at the edge of primary forest, in riparian woodland in open country, in old plantations and, occa-sionally, close to and in mangroves, although coastal

districts are rarely inhabited on the Indian subcontinent; by contrast, it is virtually restricted to mangroves in the Malaysian peninsula, Sumatra and Borneo. More humid areas are preferred. Mature lowland forests with big trees, and mixed *Bombax-Ficus* are its main habitats in Nepal. At the other end of its vast range, in the Philippines, it is found in primary forest, mature secondary forest to lighter sec-ondary forest with dense understorey, dense riparian vegetation, also near cultivation, in mango groves and close to human settlements. Found at all elevations, to over 2100m, in Sri Lanka, at up to 920m in Nepal, and to 1600m in northern India and to 1800m in the south; keeps below 1200m in SE Asia, and occurs from lowlands to (600)-1500m, to the upper fringe of the dipterocarp zone, in the Philippines.

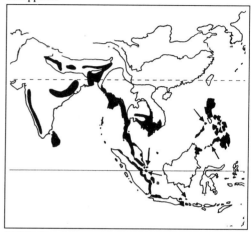

DESCRIPTION

C. l. guttacristatus **Adult male** Lower forehead olive-brown; upper forehead, crown and crest red, narrowly bordered black. Broad white band from eye to side of nape, with contrasting black band from eye through ear-coverts to hindneck. White stripe extends backwards from lores and down side of neck. White moustachial area is bordered above and below by two thin black lines which meet at rear and continue as single line irregularly down side of foreneck. Chin and throat white with a dark central line, becoming more heavily black-marked (barred/streaked) on lower throat. Upper hindneck black; lower hindneck and upper-most mantle white/whitish, the latter variably marked with black; rest of mantle, scapulars, upper back, upperwing-coverts and tertials golden-olive or golden-green; lower back and rump bright crimson-red; uppertail-coverts black. Flight feathers blackish with outer webs of secondaries olive-gold, all with white spots on inner webs. Uppertail black. Underparts white or buffish-white (often stained brownish), with feathers edged and tipped black, black markings strongest on throat and breast (which appear more as black with white spots), becoming narrower and browner on belly to undertail-coverts (which appear much paler). Underwing brown, spotted/barred white. Undertail brownish-black.

Adult female As male, but has forehead, crown and crest black with rounded white spots (not streaks).

Juvenile Duller than adults, with back and wings more olive (but often with reddish tinge) and usually with some paler spots/bars on mantle or back, and greyer with more obscure markings below. Young males have less red on head than adults and show variable amount of pale spotting on forehead and crown.

Bare parts Bill blackish, blackish-brown or dark grey. Legs and feet greenish-brown. Eyes creamy-white to yellowish, with more orangey outer ring; brown to red in juveniles (of all races).

GEOGRAPHICAL VARIATION As well as considerable individual variation, shows extreme geographical variation in plumage, especially in east of range. Size also varies appreciably, being largest in the north and west. Of the many races described, the following, listed from west to east, are considered acceptable. Further research may reveal that some of these (especially where isolated on islands) have evolved into distinct, full species.

C. l. guttacristatus (NW India and Nepal east to Yunnan and south to Indochina) Described above. The largest race, with size decreasing clinally southwards. Includes northwestern '*sultaneus*'.

C. l. socialis (western coast of India) Slightly smaller than *guttacristatus*. Back and wings somewhat darker (more olive, less golden), with red of rump extending farther up back.

C. l. stricklandi (Sri Lanka) Smaller than mainland populations. Back and wing-coverts entirely dark red; more black on head and side of neck, with much narrower white supercilium (especially on female). Bill and eyes very pale.

C. l. chersonesus (Malaysia, Singapore, Sumatra, and W and C Java) As *socialis* but smaller, and with broader black markings below and broader white supercilium.

C. l. andrewsi (NE Borneo, from around Sandakan to Sebatik Island) Larger than *chersonesus*, with dark markings below distinctly browner, less black, and with flanks more barred.

C. l. strictus (E Java) Small. Back and wings yellow-green; red of rump duller and with indication of spots/bars; pale areas of head and breast distinctly buffish. Female has crown and crest golden-yellow to orange-gold, occasionally with dark barring. Eyes darker than in other races.

C. l. kangeanensis (coastal E Java, Bali and Kangean Islands) Smaller than *strictus*, with redder rump, reduced black facial markings, and dark markings below narrower and browner. Female has crown and crest golden-yellow.

The following six races are endemic in the Philippines; all have bright red eyes and are relatively small in size:

C. l. erythrocephalus (Balabac, Palawan and Calamian group) Back and wings golden-green with traces of red (all other Philippine races are red-backed); red of rump extends well up back and shows hint of dark barring; dark markings below very narrow. Neck with narrow longitudinal black and white stripes. Male has entire head and crest red (paler on throat), with black spot on lower rear ear-coverts and thin dark moustache; female's head is similar in pattern but darker, with pale golden crown spots. Red of head reduced on juveniles. Both sexes have pale bill and legs.

C. l. lucidus (Basilan and nearby Zamboanga peninsula of W Mindanao) Back and wings red, sometimes with gold admixed; underparts with heavy, broad black markings. Ground colour of face, neck and upper breast reddish-buff. Female has crown and crest dark olive-brown to reddish-black with dark golden spots.

C. l. montanus (most of Mindanao) As *lucidus* but slightly smaller, and with more gold or yellow in upperparts; dark markings below browner, less black. Female similar to female *lucidus*.

C. l. rufopunctatus (Bohol, Leyte, Samar and Panaon) Back and wings entirely dark red; reddish-buff ground colour to face, neck and breast; belly strongly patterned dark. Male usually has black-bordered pale red

moustache; female has crown and crest dark brown with reddish-buff spots.

C. l. xanthocephalus (Negros, Guimaras, Panay, Masbate and Ticao) Small, but highly distinctive. Apart from red crown and crest, male has head, neck and entire underparts golden-yellow, with dark markings restricted to foreneck and upper breast; usually shows thin blackish moustache (sometimes with some reddish below it). Female has entire head yellow, often tinged orange on crest. Dark red back and wings may show hint of golden colour, and uppertail-coverts are tipped red. Bill and legs pale.

C. l. haematribon (Luzon, Polillo and Marinduque) Dark red back and wings often tinged olive; hindneck and upper mantle show much black; lower underparts tinged buffy and with grey-brown barring obscure. Male has ground colour of face and neck whitish, lacking red tones, and with much black spotting; female has dark head, with prominent white spots from forehead to crest. Birds from Polillo are sometimes separated as '*grandis*'.

MEASUREMENTS Wing 128-188: 144-180 (*guttacristatus*), 142-150 (*stricklandi*), 135-155 (*haematribon*), 136-141 (*lucidus*); tail 92-102 (*guttacristatus*), 79-95 (*stricklandi*), 75-102 (*haematribon*); bill 50-64 (*guttacristatus*), 42-45 (*stricklandi*), 32.6-42.4 (*haematribon*), 38-46 (*rufopunctatus*); tarsus 28-31 (*guttacristatus*), 27-31 (*stricklandi*), 27 (*haematribon*). Weight: 150-233 (*guttacristatus*), 110-145 (*haematribon*), 125-164 (*rufopunctatus*), 127 (*lucidus*).

VOICE Single *kik* calls are heard occasionally. Short or longer series, especially in flight, of highly variable *kowk-kowk..*, *ke-dew-kow* or single *kow* notes are heard more commonly. These calls bear some resemblance to those of Eurasian Green (191) or Black (169) Woodpeckers. Variable, rapid and sometimes rather long metallic or insect-like series, monotonous or varying in speed and pitch, *di-di-di-di-di-di-di...*, *tibittititititit...* or *kilkilkitkitkit...*, constitute this species' 'rattle call', which is delivered both on the wing and when perched; this call may also involve some variation at the subspecies level, and in view of the extensive plumage variation in this species will merit closer study. During close encounters, *t-wuit-wuit* series are uttered. Drums loudly and, presumably at onset of the breeding season, frequently; rolls are about 2 secs long and clearly accelerating and weakening.

HABITS This confiding woodpecker lives in pairs and can also be met with in family parties, which roost at night in close proximity. Will associate with other woodpecker species, e.g. White-bellied (167). Almost exclusively visits big trees and snags, even when these are somewhat isolated in rather open surroundings; much dead wood is required. Sometimes descends to the ground. In trees, it prefers trunks and larger branches. Gleans rarely, pecking and hammering to excavate wood for wood-boring larvae being the most conspicuous foraging modes; after large pieces of bark have been removed with powerful lateral blows, probing for prey follows. Pecking and probing are also used to uncover subsurface prey among epiphytes. Some flycatching may occur if the occasion (e.g. swarming termites) arises. Movements are rapid, and a tree is searched from the base of the trunk to the canopy, though much time is spent at a single site when the substrate is excavated. Long distances may be covered (including over open areas) when moving from one tree to the next. The pair maintains regular vocal contact. As with so many other woodpecker species, crest-raising is a common display when Greater Flamebacks meet; at closer distance, head-swinging may be observed. Prolonged conspicuous interactions may occur when three (or more) individuals are involved.

FOOD Large moth caterpillars, larvae of wood-boring beetles, which are also fed to the young, pupae, ants and other insects. Also takes nectar.

BREEDING The breeding season in northern India spans March to May, in the south December to March, and in Sri Lanka it extends from (August) October to April, but mainly December to January; breeding also commences in December in mainland SE Asia. In the Greater Sundas, nesting takes place July to November, while Philippine populations breed between February and August. The nest is excavated in trees of all kinds, at heights between 2 and 20m, often in soft live wood (although the heart of the trunk may be rotten); nest construction, carried out by both sexes, may take four weeks. The entrance is vertically oval in shape. The clutch, of 2 eggs in southern areas and 4-5 in the north, is incubated for 14-15 days by both parents. The young, which fledge after 24-26 days, are fed by both parents, which carry the food in the tip of their bill. After fledging, they stay with their parents for some weeks, possibly until the onset of the next breeding season.

REFERENCES Ali 1962; Ali & Ripley 1970; Henry 1971; Inskipp & Inskipp 1991; King & Dickinson 1975; Lekagul & Round 1991; MacKinnon 1990; Medway & Wells 1976; Noske 1991; Phillips 1978; Rabor 1977; Rand & Rabor 1960; Short 1973a; Smythies 1953, 1981; Winkler *et al.* 1994.

---

200 WHITE-NAPED WOODPECKER
Chrysocolaptes festivus   Plate 59

Other names: Black-rumped Woodpecker, Black-backed Woodpecker

IDENTIFICATION Length c. 29cm. Medium-sized, with very long, almost straight, chisel-tipped bill broad across nostrils. A distinctive woodpecker with black and white face and golden-green wing-coverts, instantly identified by its white hindneck and mantle with contrasting black scapulars and rump. Male has red crown and crest, these being yellow on the female. Juveniles are duller but with similar characteristic pattern, and may show a hint of red on the rump.

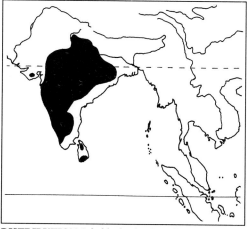

DISTRIBUTION Inhabits lowlands and hills of the Indian subcontinent. Occurs from Gujarat in the west, north to around 30˚N in N Uttar Pradesh and east to West Bengal, and southwards in the lowlands to Sri Lanka,

where found locally in northern and southern parts. Rather sparsely distributed and nowhere common.

HABITAT In the northern parts of its range, it occurs in open broadleaf forest. In most areas found in open deciduous woodland and scrub; also enters cultivations with scattered trees. In Sri Lanka confined to a few places in the dry zone, where it may be concentrated in the coconut groves surrounding villages. Basically, a woodpecker of the lowlands and foothills (up to about 1000m).

DESCRIPTION
C. f. festivus **Adult male** Forehead white, spotted brown; crown and crest red, narrowly bordered black. Broad white supercilium from rear of eye to side of nape, sometimes meeting white of hindneck. Broad black band from eye through ear-coverts, extending down neck side to upper breast side (and sometimes also continuing upwards behind supercilium to nape), bordered below by white stripe from lores. Two thin black lines enclose white malar area. Chin and throat white, with narrow black central line. Hindneck and mantle unmarked white, contrasting with black scapulars and innermost upperwing-coverts, back, rump and uppertail-coverts (rump occasionally with some yellowish feather edges). Upperwing-coverts mostly olive-green, with strong golden-yellow suffusion and golden tips/edges (occasionally tinged red); flight feathers brownish-black, with olive-yellow outer webs to secondaries and tertials, and with white spots on (usually) both webs. Uppertail black. Underparts white, with black gular stripe breaking up into streaks on foreneck and breast, the streaking becoming narrower on lower underparts; undertail-coverts often more barred. Underwing dark grey, spotted white. Undertail brownish-black.

Adult female Has crown and crest deep yellow, usually with some brown at front and sides.

Juvenile Pattern as that of adults, but duller, with black areas browner; may show a trace of red on rump. Males have yellow/golden crown with orange-red feather tips laterally and on crest; female's crown much as adult, but with some orange in nape/crest area.

Bare parts Bill blackish. Legs and feet green-grey. Eyes red to pale orange; brown in juveniles.

GEOGRAPHICAL VARIATION Two races.
    C. f. festivus (mainland range of species) Described above.
    C. f. tantus (Sri Lanka) Slightly smaller than nominate. Has blackish forehead, broader black gular stripe and broader black streaks below, thus appearing somewhat darker overall.

MEASUREMENTS Wing 142-162; tail 72-85; bill 38-48; tarsus 26-31. Weight: 213.

VOICE The laughing rattle of this species, *kwirri-rr-rr-rr-rr*, has been likened both to the rattle of Yellow-crowned Woodpecker (97) and to the corresponding call of Greater Flameback (199), although it differs from the latter's in being weaker and in sound quality. Generally, this species should have a similar set of calls to that of its congener, and like that species is also known to drum.

HABITS Individuals of this active but shy woodpecker feed alone, or in pairs which maintain vocal contact at intervals; adults may also be accompanied by their offspring. Forages in lower strata, on tree trunks, and occasionally descends to the ground, especially on bare patches. Pecking and hammering seem to be major feeding techniques. Roosts are occupied by single birds. Seems to be subordinate to the smaller but more aggressive Black-rumped Flameback (198) in interspecific conflicts.

FOOD Both ants and larvae of wood-boring insects have been reported in the diet, as well as seeds, the latter seemingly indicating the ingestion of fruits.

BREEDING Breeding season varies regionally, but seems generally to span November to March; in Sri Lanka, nesting White-naped Woodpeckers may be found also in August and September. A new nest hole is excavated each year, at heights between 2 and 7 m in a tree or palm stump; entrance not circular, instead being pear-shaped. The clutch contains usually only 1, rarely 2 (3), eggs. As with other woodpeckers, both sexes share nest construction, incubation and caring for the young, which stay with the parents for a long time after fledging.

REFERENCES Ali & Ripley 1970; Henry 1971; Inskipp & Inskipp 1991; Phillips 1978.

201 PALE-HEADED WOODPECKER
Gecinulus grantia　　　　Plate 60

Forms a superspecies with *viridis*.

IDENTIFICATION Length c. 25-27 cm. Small and stocky, with rather short to fairly long, chisel-tipped bill slightly curved on culmen and broad across nostrils. Has only three toes. Rather plain and dark in appearance, with short crest; found mostly in bamboo areas. Dull red above (but can appear brighter red, depending on lighting) and dark olive below, with paler head and noticeably pale bill; fairly broad but rather indistinct bars on wings and tail. Male has pink to reddish crown patch, while female's crown is greenish. Juveniles are duller and darker, with plain crown. Eastern populations are more olive, less red, above, darker-headed, and less olive below, males having more strongly pink crown patch.

Similar species Unlikely to be confused. Bamboo Woodpecker (202), which is very closely related and sometimes treated as conspecific with Pale-headed, is similar in appearance and habits, but seems not to overlap in range (the two may, however, approach each other in Laos); Bamboo has bronzy-greenish upperparts and an unbarred tail, and the male has a much redder (less pink) and larger crown patch that extends to the nape.

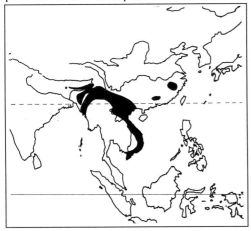

DISTRIBUTION Ranges from easternmost Nepal east through Assam and N Bangladesh, Mizoram and Manipur and across W, N and C Burma (and possibly extreme N Thailand, on Mekong river) to S China east to Fujian,

extending south through Laos and Vietnam. Widespread and locally common in Vietnam; elsewhere local, possibly not uncommon in places where sufficient habitat remains, but rare (or even extinct) in Bangladesh, extremely rare (probably extinct) in Thailand and rare in China; only a few records from E Nepal, where not discovered for certain until 1974.

HABITAT Frequents moist zones with evergreen forest, secondary mixed bamboo forest, secondary forest and scrub; the presence of bamboo is highly favoured. It may be found up to 1200m, but usually keeps below 1000m.

DESCRIPTION
G. g. grantia **Adult male** Crown to nape and crest greenish-yellow, with central patch of red-tipped pinkish feathers (reaching to upper nape). Rest of head and neck buffy-green to pale olive-brown, tinged yellow, becoming darker and more olive on chin and throat. Upper mantle dark olive; rest of upperparts, including upperwing-coverts plus secondaries and tertials, dull brownish-crimson. Primaries brown, narrowly edged dull red on outer webs, with broad buff bars. Uppertail blackish-brown, edged reddish, with variable broad buff barring. Underparts uniformly dark olive or brownish-olive, sometimes browner in lower ventral region. Underwing brownish with faint barring, coverts mottled grey and whitish. Undertail as uppertail, with dull yellow-green cast.

Adult female Lacks pink/red on head, having forehead to nape yellow-green, becoming yellower at rear.

Juvenile Both sexes resemble adult female but are darker, with dark brown upperparts (little red) and very dark brown to grey-brown underparts.

Bare parts Bill pale horn-yellow to whitish or pale bluish-ivory, somewhat darker (grey or greenish) at base. Legs and feet (three toes) olive-green. Eyes red or reddish-brown.

GEOGRAPHICAL VARIATION Three seemingly disjunct populations, varying mainly in colour of upperparts (reddest in west) and crown pattern.
G. g. grantia (western part of range, east to W Yunnan, China) Described above.
G. g. indochinensis (SW Yunnan, Laos and Vietnam) Duller red above than nominate, greyer and less yellow on sides of head, and with more sooty-brown (less olive) underparts; dull buffish wingbars more extensive, continuing over secondaries. Crown patch of male more pinkish, with less crimson.
G. g. viridanus (SE China, in Fujian and N Guangdong) Bigger than above races, with proportionately longer tail but shorter bill. Even less red than *indochinensis*, with more olive upperparts (red more obvious on greater coverts), and grey-brown below. Male's crown patch dull pink and rather restricted.

MEASUREMENTS Wing 125-134; tail 79-87; bill (from skull) 25-27; tarsus 23-24.

VOICE Suprisingly like that of Middle Spotted Woodpecker (102) in quality. The usual contact call is a nasal *chaik-chaik-chaik-chaik* or *kwéek kwek-kwek*, four to five times in succession, accelerating and becoming lower towards the end. When agitated or disturbed, utters loud, corvid- or castanet-like rattles, *kereki kereki kereki kereki*. Also a series of *kwee-kwee*... notes. Drums in fast and steady rolls (like those of Lesser Spotted Woodpecker, 93) of medium length.

HABITS Often met with in pairs and small family parties. This quiet and shy woodpecker forages mainly in the lower levels of its habitat on the trunks of smaller trees, or, particularly, large bamboo. Rarely visits the canopy, fallen logs or the ground.

FOOD Mainly ants, larvae of beetles, and other insects.

BREEDING Breeds from (March) April to May. Nest is excavated 1-6m up in a dead tree or rotten stump, and 3 eggs are laid.

REFERENCES Ali 1962; Ali & Ripley 1970; Inskipp & Inskipp 1991; King & Dickinson 1975; Lekagul & Round 1991; Smythies 1953.

202 BAMBOO WOODPECKER
Gecinulus viridis   Plate 60

Forms a superspecies with *grantia*.

IDENTIFICATION Length c. 25-26cm. Small, with fairly long, chisel-tipped bill straight or slightly curved on culmen and broad across nostrils. Has only three toes. A modest-looking species, found almost exclusively in areas of bamboo. Rather dark-plumaged, with bronzy yellowish-green tinge to upperparts and paler head and bill, the buffish wingbars being rather inconspicuous; male has bright red crown and small crest, these being dark straw-yellow on female.

Similar species Distinguished from other mainly green or greenish woodpeckers in its range by its very dark and uniform underparts, paler and uniform face and pale bill, as well as by its habitat preferences. See also Pale-headed Woodpecker (201).

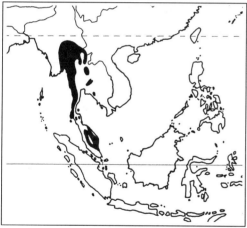

DISTRIBUTION Found discontinuously in S and SE Burma and adjacent NW and W Thailand, N Laos, parts of C and S Thailand and peninsular Malaysia. Generally uncommon and local, depending on habitat availability.

HABITAT Frequents evergreen and deciduous forest with extensive bamboo, and almost exclusively clusters of large bamboo. More in the lowlands in the northern parts of its range, between 600 and 1400m farther south.

DESCRIPTION
Adult male Crown to nape red. Rest of head buffy-brown, tinged yellow, becoming more golden-green on rear crown sides and neck sides and darker and browner on chin. Upperparts, including upperwing-coverts and tertials, dull yellowish-green with rather strong bronzy cast, rump and uppertail-coverts having dark crimson feather tips. Primaries and secondaries dark brown, narrowly edged greenish on outer webs, with rather ill-defined pale bars (may be stronger on primaries). Uppertail blackish-brown, edged

greenish. Underparts uniformly dark olive brown, perhaps just slightly paler in lowermost regions. Underwing brownish with faint barring, coverts mottled grey and whitish. Undertail brown, with dull yellowish cast.

Adult female Lacks red on head, having dull greenish-yellow crown becoming yellower (more ochre or straw-coloured) on nape and crest.

Juvenile Both sexes resemble adult female, but darker and browner above and very dark and often grey-tinged below.

Bare parts Bill pale yellow to whitish, somewhat darker (grey or greenish) at base. Legs and feet (three toes) olive-green. Eyes dark red or reddish-brown.

GEOGRAPHICAL VARIATION Malaysian birds tend to be a shade darker, with narrower wingbars and (female) more uniform crown and nape, but some northern individuals show similar variation and separation of Malaysian population as '*robinsoni*' seems unwarranted. Treated as monotypic.

MEASUREMENTS Wing 119-139; tail 86-91; bill 25-26; tarsus 24-28.

VOICE Single *bik* calls are heard occasionally. Most commonly, however, utters dry rattles, the undulating quality of which is due to changes in loudness and pitch, but not in speed of delivery; this call resembles similar calls of the Bay Woodpecker (205), but is slower. Another loud call is a clear *Keép-kee-kee-kee-kee-kee-kee*, delivered at the rate of about three notes per second. During encounters, variations of *Kweek-week-week-week-week*, *wee-a-wee-a-wee* or *Kwi-kwi-week-week-kweek-kweek* can be heard. Drums in loud bursts of about 1 sec duration.

HABITS Usually an unobtrusive bird, which is met with either singly or in pairs. Descends to the ground only occasionally. Most easily detected by its light pecking when foraging. The main foraging substrate is live or dead bamboo, where it gleans and probes into fractures, crevices, cracks and various holes. Pecking is light and not sustained for very long, resulting in very small round holes just above the nodes of bamboo stalks (only at the nodes can this specialised woodpecker exert a strong enough grip for more forceful actions). It moves between nodes in a peculiar way, gliding along the smooth surface while clasping right around the stalk. Movements are slow and deliberate, and the substrate is searched carefully for prey. The crest is rather commonly held slightly raised.

FOOD Much as that of Pale-headed Woodpecker.

BREEDING The nest, about 25cm deep, is excavated into bamboo above a node.

REFERENCES Gyldenstolpe 1916; King & Dickinson 1975; Lekagul & Round 1991; Medway & Wells 1976; Robinson 1928; Short 1973a.

203 OKINAWA WOODPECKER
Sapheopipo noguchii   Plate 60

Other name: Pryer's Woodpecker

IDENTIFICATION Length c. 31-35cm. Medium-sized, with long, strongly chisel-tipped bill slightly curved on culmen and broad across nostrils. A rare and endangered endemic of Japan, restricted to northern Okinawa, where the only other woodpecker is the very small and very different Pygmy Woodpecker (92). Noticeably long-tailed and very dark, in the field usually appearing uniformly dull brown and inconspicuous in its gloomy forest habitat. If closer views are obtained, it reveals a deep red tone to the underparts and rump, with a paler face, throat and bill. Male has red-tipped crown feathers and female has black crown. Juveniles duller and greyer, less red.

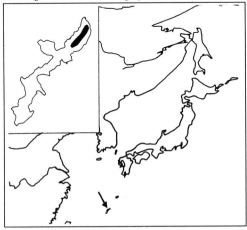

DISTRIBUTION Found only in the Yambaru mountain chain, extending a little south of Tanodake, in the northern third of Okinawa in the southern Ryukyus. Very local, rare and endangered; probably fewer than 100 individuals survive.

HABITAT Restricted to undisturbed, mature subtropical evergreen broadleaf forest in the central mountain range of Yambaru; occasionally encountered also in secondary forest outside its main range. On hilltops with large trees, down to forest edge along clearings or roads. Locations with soft, decaying wood are preferred, and places with conifers appear to be avoided.

DESCRIPTION
Adult male Forehead to nape red, with blackish feather bases visible (especially on forehead). Nasal tufts, lores and line above eye pale buffish-brown, becoming darker and browner with deep brown streaking on ear-coverts and side of neck, and with indication of a darker stripe in malar region. Chin and throat to upper breast paler grey-brown with a hint of whitish coloration. Hindneck and upperparts rich dark brown with dull, deep red red feather tips, red being most obvious on rump and uppertail-coverts. Upperwing and its coverts very dark brown, flight feathers edged reddish and with small white bar-like spots on outer primaries and on inner webs of inner primaries and secondaries (bars often very narrow and inconspicuous on closed wing). Uppertail noticeably long, blackish-brown. Central breast and breast sides (rather well demarcated but not sharply so from throat/upper breast) and rest of underparts dark brown, feathers tipped dull red, becoming more extensively reddish (larger tips) on belly and flanks

and almost entirely deep red on undertail-coverts. Underwing brown, barred whitish on flight feathers. Undertail brown, paler at sides.

Adult female Slightly shorter-winged and shorter-billed than male. Lacks red on head, having forehead to nape black, sometimes with some paler feather bases showing through.

Juvenile Duller and greyer than adults, with red of feather tips absent or much reduced/subdued. Males have less red on head top than adult.

Bare parts Bill pale yellow, greener at base and darker (browner) at base of upper mandible. Legs and feet dark slaty-grey. Eyes deep red-brown or brown.

GEOGRAPHICAL VARIATION None. Monotypic.

MEASUREMENTS Wing 148-158.

VOICE Calls can be heard the year round, with a peak in the breeding season. The most prominent are long irregular series of clear, whistled notes, *kwe kwe kwe* or *pwip pwip*, somewhat similar to calls of Eurasian Green (191), Grey-faced (194) or Japanese (190) Woodpeckers. Also commonly heard are several *kup* notes, *kyu-kyu*, or *kyu-kyu-kup* calls. When disturbed, utters single *whit* notes. Nestlings seem to have two distinct types of note, rendered respectively as *kyaa* and *pip*. Drums at a rate of about three rolls per minute. Rolls vary greatly in length, from about 0.5 sec to more than 1 sec, are accelerating and slightly slower in rhythm than those of Grey-faced.

HABITS Most likely to be seen when active at forest edge. Forages in the canopy, especially when feeding on fruits, on larger branches, trunks, snags, fallen trees and in leaf litter. The main foraging stratum is near the ground (mostly below 5m), where this woodpecker searches tree trunks, bamboo and fallen logs. Pecking and hammering appear to be very important techniques, and numerous signs of these activities can be found in the habitat; such signs comprise deep excavations measuring about 4cm in length on larger trunks, branches and stumps, while smaller fallen branches are hacked to pieces. As with other species which prefer very soft and rotten wood, some of the forceful foraging methods are more like digging than excavating. Harder live wood and bamboo bear smaller holes after this woodpecker has worked them over. Probing and sweeping aside litter are also frequent foraging activities. Displays are not well known, but wing-flicking is shown by agitated birds.

FOOD Large arthropods, beetle larvae (e.g. Cerambycids), spiders. Feeding of a gecko to nestlings has also been observed. Fruits, berries and seeds (*Rhus, Rubus*) also play an important role.

BREEDING Egg-laying takes place from late February to May, typically in March and April, with nestlings being found up to June. Nest holes are excavated in large old trees, at heights between 3 and 9m, often on the underside of a large sloping branch; the entrance is ovate. One or two chicks are raised per brood.

REFERENCES Brazil 1991; Chiba 1969; Ishida 1989; Short 1973b.

204 MAROON WOODPECKER
Blythipicus rubiginosus   Plate 61

IDENTIFICATION Length 23cm. Small, with long, straight, chisel-tipped, bright pale yellow bill broad across nostrils. Plumage very dark, with upperparts distinctly maroon-chestnut, and generally unbarred except on flight feathers. Male has variable patch of crimson on sides of nape and neck.

Similar species Within its range, unlikely to be confused with any other species given good views. Bay Woodpecker (205) is much bigger and is barred rufous and black on entire wings and upperparts. The red race *dedemi* of Grey-faced Woodpecker (194) inhabiting the Sumatran highlands (where rare) is also much bigger and has a grey, red and black head with a dark bill, and flight feathers more obviously barred (black and white).

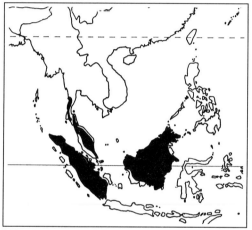

DISTRIBUTION Inhabits evergreen forests from about 12°30'N in southern Burma and southern peninsular Thailand south through the Malay peninsula to Sumatra and Borneo. Common in Thailand, uncommon in W Malaysia, and common in Sumatra and Borneo.

HABITAT Maroon Woodpeckers are birds of the understorey of primary and secondary evergreen forest, second growth, bamboo, and rubber plantations, though favouring primary forest with dense undergrowth, as found, for instance, along small watercourses. Mainly a bird of lowland forest and rainforest, it ranges up to 900m in Thailand, to 1800m elsewhere in SE Asia, and to 2200m in Sumatra and Borneo.

DESCRIPTION
Adult male Head dull olive-brown, with paler feather tips to forehead; feathers of sides of nape, often also of hindcrown (and occasionally also in malar region), tipped crimson. Mantle, back, rump and uppertail-coverts brown with dull reddish-chestnut suffusion, unbarred apart from one or two obscure bars near bases of feathers (bars more numerous on rump and uppertail-coverts). Upperwing-coverts dull brownish-red, often with a few indistinct pale arrow-shaped marks towards tips; flight feathers dark brown, edged and tipped dull reddish, and with narrow, indistinct, paler (buffish) bars. Uppertail dark brown, inconspicuously and narrowly barred slightly paler. Throat dull brown, becoming contrastingly darker sooty-brown to blackish on breast and remaining underparts, breast sometimes with a few reddish-tipped feathers. Underwing dull brown. Undertail as uppertail, but somewhat paler.

Adult female Very like male, but with shorter bill and lacks crimson on head/neck, instead often having dull reddish tinge to feather tips of hindcrown and nape. Barring on flight feathers may be somewhat more prominent.

Juvenile Much as adults, but upperparts generally have a dull orangey tinge rather than dull red. Shows more extensive red on crown, that of juvenile male being more intense in nape area than on adult male.

Bare parts Bill pale yellow or yellowish-white (ivory-coloured) to deeper yellow, with dark greenish (on female often blackish) base. Legs and feet grey or grey-brown to blackish. Eyes deep red or brownish-red; brown in juveniles.

GEOGRAPHICAL VARIATION Populations of Sumatra and Borneo average slightly smaller than northern ones, but overlap is considerable. Minor variations in plumage are insufficient to warrant racial separation.

MEASUREMENTS Wing 110-132; tail 62-86; bill 30-36; tarsus 22.6-25.5. Weight: 64-92.

VOICE Usual calls are metallic *pit, pyick* or *kyuk* notes accompanied by flicks of the wing and given repeatedly. Sometimes double-note *kik....kik..* or *chikick* is heard, the second syllable markedly higher in pitch. Also, a wavering sequence of 6-14 higher-pitched call-note elements, *kik-kik-kik-kik-kik-kik*, slowing down a little. Loud, descending series of 7-11 or more longer notes, *chai-chai-chai-chai...*, are specific vocalisations of the Maroon Woodpecker and are higher-pitched than similar utterances of Bay Woodpecker. Drumming has not yet been described.

HABITS Met with singly or in pairs, which keep loose vocal contact. A woodpecker of the very low strata (usually below 6m), moving along the ground and, unless alarmed, climbing only a few metres up trees. Forages on live trees, rotten snags, and fallen decaying logs of all sizes. Procures prey by hammering rotten wood into pieces with the strong, chisel-tipped bill. Moss or other debris is removed from the trunk, and within minutes medium-sized pits (2-3cm deep, to 7cm long) are excavated. The only displays described are crest-raising and wing-flicking accompanied by calls.

FOOD Beetle and other insect larvae form the bulk of its diet.

BREEDING Breeding records span December to May in Malaysia, and in the uplands of Borneo nests have been found in January, but the breeding season probably extends to August. Nest site may be at edge of dense forest.

REFERENCES King & Dickinson 1975; Lekagul & Round 1991; MacKinnon & Phillipps 1993; Medway & Wells 1976; Robinson 1928; Short 1973a; Smythies 1981.

205 BAY WOODPECKER
Blythipicus pyrrhotis   Plate 61

Other names: Red-eared Bay/Red-reared Rufous Woodpecker

IDENTIFICATION Length 30cm. Medium-sized, with long, pale, chisel-tipped and very broad-based bill. Upperparts dark rufous with prominent broad black barring. Male has bright scarlet patch on side of hindneck. Often forages at low levels or on ground in dense undergrowth, usually in pairs, when difficult to observe; calls may reveal presence (and look for pale bill and throat).

Similar species Female could be mistaken for Rufous

Woodpecker (152), but is larger, with longer and pale bill, and has different habits.

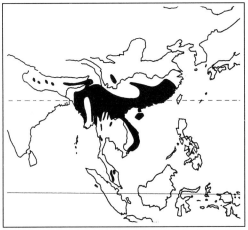

DISTRIBUTION S and SE Asia, from Himalayan foot-hills of C Nepal (recorded several times in W Nepal, where possibly regular) eastwards through uplands of Bangla-desh and S Assam, Burma, N, W and SW Thailand and northern Indochina (not recorded Cambodia), to SE China north to about 27°N in Fujian; isolated mountain populations also occur in western Sichuan at around 30°N, in Malaysia, in southern Vietnam and on Hainan Island. Because of its skulking habits and the fact that it frequents thick under-growth it is probably overlooked in many areas, and its range may well be greater than that currently realised. Generally uncommon, but locally common in Vietnam and parts of Thailand.

MOVEMENTS Records outside the breeding season down to 75m indicate some vertical movements.

HABITAT Found always in dense growth. This condition is met in dark evergreen and in mixed deciduous forest, and in mixed bamboo forest, as found, for instance, in heavily wooded ravines. This upland woodpecker, whose habitats are well separated from those of the congeneric Maroon Woodpecker (204), usually occurs from 600 to 2200m, but occasionally down to the foothills, in Thailand; in N Annam, Vietnam, it is even found down to 50m above sea level. In Nepal it is most common between 1500 and 2500m, but may be encountered at the valley bottoms as well. Ranges up to 2750m in Burma, and is found above 1000m in Malaya.

DESCRIPTION
B. p. pyrrhotis **Adult male** Forehead, lores, chin and throat pale brownish-buff, generally unmarked; ear-coverts slightly darker and with pale streaks. Crown, short crest and nape dark brown, with variable rufous or buff streaking. Sides of neck bright crimson, this extending variably to a few feathers of nape (crest). Mantle and scapulars to uppertail-coverts dark brown to blackish, with fairly narrow dark rufous bars and very fine pale shaft streaks, pattern often obscured when fresh but becoming prominent in worn plumage; rufous and blackish bars on uppertail-coverts about equal in width. Upperwing and its coverts barred rufous and black, bars about equal in width on coverts but black bars becoming much narrower on flight feathers, the latter often with a reddish tinge to rufous coloration. Uppertail medium rufous, with narrow, widely spaced black bars (bars occasionally lacking). Underparts from breast and below dark brown, with fairly obvious tinge of rusty, usually with inconspicuous narrow rusty bars on

lower belly and lower flanks; undertail-coverts deep ru-fous, barred black. Underwing and undertail as above, but colours paler.

Adult female Has shorter bill than male. Lacks red mark-ings on head, which appears paler than rest of plumage.

Juvenile Generally duller and darker below than adults, faintly barred rufous, and more prominently barred above; head darker, with prominent pale streaks. Juvenile male has dull red on nape.

Bare parts Bill pale yellow or pale greenish-yellow, with greyish-green base. Legs and feet greyish-black with faint yellowish tinge. Eyes red-brown.

GEOGRAPHICAL VARIATION Five races are currently recognised.
    B. p. pyrrhotis (western part of range, east to Laos, Yunnan and Sichuan) Described above. Variable in plumage, but generally with rusty tone to breast and wings (lacking or much reduced in other races). Sichuan population is little known, but possibly larger than nominate and may be a separate race (but insufficient data as yet to establish racial affinities). Those in northern Vietnam are intermediate between nominate and *annamensis*.
    B. p. sinensis (SE China, from Guizhou and Guangxi east to Fujian) Paler overall than nominate, often with narrow pale buff streaks on breast; bars on upperparts tend towards cinnamon-rufous.
    B. p. annamensis (southern Vietnam highlands) Much darker below than *sinensis*, almost blackish, and usually without any bars, and much more rufous (less cinna-mon) above. Male has restricted amount of red on head.
    B. p. hainanus (Hainan mountains) Small and short-billed. Browner, less sooty-black, below than *annamensis*.
    B. p. cameroni (Malaysian highlands) Very dark, as *annamensis*, but male has even less red on head.

MEASUREMENTS Wing 130-157 (*pyrrhotis*); tail 82-98 (*pyrrhotis*); bill 39-48 (*pyrrhotis*); tarsus 29-30 (*pyrrhotis*). Weight: 126-170 (*pyrrhotis*), 100-102 (*cameroni*).

VOICE Single call notes are rare (mostly, they are associ-ated with rattle calls); they are longer than the *pit* calls of its congener, and lower-pitched. Long, dry rattles of up to 30 *pit* elements are more commonly heard, especially when the woodpeckers are disturbed: they are faster than rattles of Maroon Woodpecker and change in tempo and pitch, giving this call an undulating quality, *dit-d-d-di-di-di--di-dit-d-d-di-di-di...*, likened by some to a steam-engine starting up (or to human laughter). Another type of call-series of up to 24 notes comprises long *kwaa* elements delivered at a rate of about four notes per second (slower than in the similar call of Maroon Woodpecker), dropping down the scale and with elements and the intervals betwwen them becoming shorter at the end. A somewhat slower version of this series, and linked with it through intermediate calls, consists of 9-13 notes and is the call with which the pair maintains contact and probably also functions as territorial announcement; this descending and accelerating call, *pee--pee--pee--pee--pee--pee-pee-pee-pee-pee-a*, can be heard over great distances. Dis-turbed birds utter magpie-like calls, *kecker-rák kecker-rák....* Not known to drum.

HABITS A wary woodpecker, and very difficult to observe in the shadows of its habitat. Normally seen singly, mainly because the pair maintains only loose acoustic contact, but the birds do not forage close to each other. In this and other behaviour this species is rather similar to Maroon Wood-pecker, though it is less confined to the lower strata of the forest and extends its foraging into the middle storeys.

Nevertheless, most of the time it concentrates more than half of its activities within 3-4m of the ground on trunks, rotting snags, logs on the ground, on saplings, vines and bamboo, hardly ever venturing into the periphery of a tree crown. Rapidly and without much noise it digs big holes into soft, rotten wood, probes into crevices, removes moss and other epiphytes to glean prey hidden beneath, and even sallies forth to capture prey in the air. The only displays so far described are crest-raising and wing-flicking when calling.

FOOD Termites, ants, large larvae of wood-boring beetles, various other insects, and occasional berries form the diet.

BREEDING Breeds in (January?) May and June. The nest is low, between 1 and 4m up, excavated by both members of the pair in live or dead wood. Lays 2 or 3, occasionally 4, eggs. The parents share incubation and brood-feeding.

REFERENCES Ali 1962; Ali & Ripley 1970; Deignan 1945; Inskipp & Inskipp 1991; King & Dickinson 1975; Lekagul & Round 1991; Martens & Eek in press; Medway & Wells 1976; Robinson 1928; Short 1973a; Smythies 1953; Stresemann & Heinrich 1940.

---

206 ORANGE-BACKED WOODPECKER
Reinwardtipicus validus   Plate 64

IDENTIFICATION Length 30cm. A medium-sized to rather large woodpecker with a short tail and a long, slightly curved, broad-based bill with distinct chisel tip. Male is red on crown and short crest, with dark wings barred rufous on flight feathers, and has a contrasting broad, very pale band from hindneck to rump, which is variably tinged orange (darkest on rump); underparts fairly deep reddish. Female is similar in pattern, but has crown dark brown, hindneck to rump whitish, and underparts dull greyish-brown. Rather noisy, calling frequently and tapping loudly (but drums infrequently, in short weak bursts). Unlikely to be confused with any other species.

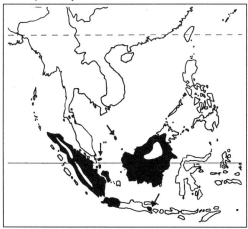

DISTRIBUTION Inhabits lowland forests of SE Asia, from southern Burma (south Tenasserim) and southernmost Thailand through Malaysia to Sumatra, Java (where restricted mainly to western half of the island), and Borneo, including Riau, Bangka and Natuna islands. Uncommon or scarce in most of its range, and rare in Java, but commoner in Sumatra and Borneo.

HABITAT Inhabits primary or secondary evergreen rainforest, coastal vegetation, mature plantations, and can also be observed along forest edge and in clearcut areas with single dead trees. A woodpecker of the lowlands, extending uncommonly to hilly country throughout range. Keeps below 1000m in peninsular Thailand and Malaysia, where it is most common below 700m. In Java, in lowlands and occasionally in montane habitats up to 2200m. Common in lowland forests of Borneo, where it has also been found up to 2000m.

DESCRIPTION
R. v. xanthopygius **Adult male** Forehead, crown and short crest red, bordered pale orange. Sides of head orange-brown, becoming darker/browner towards rear. Chin and malar area golden-brown. Lower nape and hindneck white, narrowly bordered brownish-grey; mantle and back feathers extensively tipped yellow to orange, becoming deeper orange to red on rump; uppertail-coverts dark brown to dark dull orange. Scapulars and upperwing-coverts black-brown, very occasionally narrowly edged paler or yellowish; flight feathers blackish, with three to five broad rufous-chestnut bars across all feathers, extending as spots onto primary coverts. Uppertail very dark brown. Foreneck and sides of neck and most of remaining underbody brown, but with broad deep red feather tips creating largely red appearance, narrowly edged yellowish on flanks and lower breast to belly; ventral region grey-brown, becoming dark brown on undertail-coverts and undertail. Underwing barred brownish or cinnamon, with coverts sometimes a paler buffish and barred brown.

Adult female Differs from male in lacking all red and yellow tones. Forehead to nape and crest dark brown; sides of head grey-brown, streaked darker; hindneck to rump entirely white or off-white. Narrow band on sides of neck faintly tinged rufous, otherwise foreneck to ventral region all dark greyish-brown with obscure paler barring on flanks and belly. Tail and wings as male.

Juvenile Much as adult female, but young males usually show some indication of red in crown and often a hint of yellow-orange on rump.

Bare parts Bill light brown, with yellowish lower mandible. Legs and feet brownish to grey. Eyes brownish to orange-red.

GEOGRAPHICAL VARIATION Two poorly differentiated races.
   R. v. xanthopygius (range of species, apart from Java) Described above.
   R. v. validus (Java) Normally differs from *xanthopygius* in showing more red on rump/lower back of male (but much overlap between races), and in having variable brown barring on back and rump (sometimes fairly well defined on upper back) and a yellow-olive (male) or brownish (female) suffusion on rump.

MEASUREMENTS Wing 146-160; tail 85-86; bill 44-45; tarsus 30. Weight: 155-185.

VOICE Various loud, ringing, typical woodpecker calls, which generally resemble those of Maroon Woodpecker (204). *Pit* call notes occur singly or are repeated in loose irregular series; they are lower-pitched than similar calls of *Picoides* or *Picus* woodpeckers, but higher than the calls of Greater Flameback (199). Similar notes may form slow regular *kit kit kit kit kit-it* series of about nine elements terminating with a double-call, which rises sharply on the last note. Other, higher-pitched and more irregular series may commence with a lower-pitched note. Much faster series of *pit* notes form the rattle of this species. Loud rapid *wicka*-calls, *wheet-wheet-wheet-wheet-wheow* or *polleet, polleet,* and excited *toweetit-toweetit, cha-cha* have also been described. Calls of fledglings represent softer versions of the *pit* call, and resemble irregular adult rattles. Drums weakly in very short bursts.

HABITS Lives in pairs and family parties. Forages in very low (rarely) and middle strata, and in the canopy as well. Attacks rotting logs on the ground, dead stumps, tree trunks and larger branches, but even visits thin vines. Rather easy to detect, for it pecks and hammers with loud blows to excavate the foraging substrate, sometimes spending minutes to excavate at a single site. Often it removes bark with lateral strokes, or within a short time opens holes in the bark. Between these conspicuous activities moves rapidly along trunks and branches. Trees, stumps and logs are searched systematically, i.e. without moving great distances between foraging locations. Displays include crest-raising, bill-directing, wing-flicking, wing-spreading and swinging head movements, which may be intensified into mechanical jerks; these displays are associated with many vocalisations.

FOOD Beetle larvae, termites, caterpillars, ants and other insects.

BREEDING Breeding extends from January to September; regional differences need to be substantiated with more data, as do all other aspects of reproduction. Nest, excavated in dead tree, contains 1-2 eggs. Fledglings, at least, are fed directly and not by regurgitation.

REFERENCES King & Dickinson 1975; Lekagul & Round 1991; MacKinnon 1990; MacKinnon & Phillipps 1993; Medway & Wells 1976; Robinson 1928; Short 1973a, 1978; Smythies 1981.

---

207 BUFF-RUMPED WOODPECKER
Meiglyptes tristis   Plate 62

Other name: Fulvous-rumped Woodpecker

IDENTIFICATION Length 17-18cm. Small and short-tailed, with fairly long, narrow-based and rather pointed bill with curved culmen. Heavily barred buff and black, with pale buffish-white rump; head and short crest (often raised) very thinly barred, and usually shows buffish eye-ring, and buffy area surrounding base of bill. Male has inconspicuous deep red moustache. Active but rather unobtrusive, frequenting middle and upper levels of forest.

Similar species Distinctive when seen well. Buff-necked Woodpecker (209) is longer-tailed and appears darker overall, with much narrower barring, has unbarred head with buff neck patch, and lacks pale rump.

DISTRIBUTION Resident from around 14°N in S Burma (Tenasserim) and peninsular Thailand, through Malaysia to Sumatra (including islands of Nias and Bangka), W Java, North Natunas and Borneo (including Banggi and northeast islands). Common to fairly common throughout most of range, but rare in Java (no recent records) and extinct in Singapore.

HABITAT Occurs in both primary and secondary forests, and may be found in rather open coastal habitats as well as in inland forests. Most common at forest edges, around clearings, areas of second growth within forests, and in second growth. Also frequents mature rubber stands, and orchards. From lowlands to 600m in Thailand, to 800m in Malaysia, and up to 1100m in other parts of its range in mainland SE Asia.

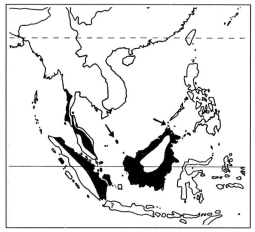

DESCRIPTION
M. t. grammithorax **Adult male** Head, neck and short crest buff, with narrow black vermiculated barring (bars usually less pronounced or lacking in frontal area), and with pale buff eye-ring, lores and area around base of bill. Short, dark red moustachial stripe. Mantle, upper back and uppertail-coverts barred black and buffish-white; lower back and rump plain buffish-white. Upperwing and its coverts black, with buffish-white bars, the latter broadest on covert tips and on inner webs of flight feathers. Uppertail black, with thin buffish barring. Underparts entirely barred black and buffish-white, more narrowly on upper breast and broadly on lower flanks, and with dark bars usually coalescing to form more solid dark (brownish to blackish) patch around upper belly. Underwing blackish-brown, with buffish-white coverts. Undertail brown, narrowly barred buff.

Adult female As male but lacks red in moustachial region, which is barred black and buff.

Juvenile As adults, but dark areas duller, more brownish, and dark barring usually broader; often only obscurely barred below, appearing mostly dark.

Bare parts Bill black. Legs and feet grey to greenish. Eyes deep brown.

GEOGRAPHICAL VARIATION Two fairly distinctive races.

    M. t. grammithorax (entire range of species, except Java) Described above. Populations from Sumatra and Borneo average somewhat smaller in wing and tail than mainland birds, but individual variation causes considerable overlap and subspecific status is not justified.

    M. t. tristis (Java) Shows narrower and whiter barring above and much more black below, and can also have some white on upper flanks.

MEASUREMENTS Wing 84-100; tail 46-47; bill 18-19; tarsus 18.6-18.8. Weight: 31-50.

VOICE A single *pit* or *chit*, also given as a double click or in loose series, may be heard from mildly excited birds and from those in flight. Can easily be confused with calls of Grey-and-buff Woodpecker (210). Another call, *pee*, is about five times longer and appears to be a sign of alarm. The *wicka*-calls in encounters between sexes recall similar vocalisations of American flickers. A soft rattle, *drrrrrr...*, announces presence over longer distances; this trill, which is higher-pitched than the corresponding vocalisation of Buff-necked Woodpecker, can last over 2 secs and has a wavering quality, since it rises in pitch around the middle of the signal. Drumming is weak; 18 to over 40 beats are delivered at a rate of 15/secs, faster at the beginning and slower later, and rolls last for 1.5-3 secs.

HABITS A quiet woodpecker which is often met with in pairs, which keep more or less close contact; may join mixed-species flocks of other small insectivorous birds. Forages in the canopy of tall trees on twigs and the distal ends of branches, and in saplings and smaller trees. Feeding sites are usually several trees apart. Gleaning and occasional probing are the most common feeding techniques, whereby the food is gathered from the bark and from tips and leaves of tiny twigs; rarely pecks, with weak blows. Movement is rapid, and it frequently perches crosswise or hangs upside-down like a tit. Flight direct, like a songbird's, and readily employed. In encounters, both sexes display with head-swinging and *wicka*-calls. Excited birds sometimes raise their crown feathers to form a crest.

FOOD Ants and other insects.

BREEDING The breeding season is not well known; it probably extends from March to July. The nest can be rather low (below 2m) or high up (8-15m), and may be excavated, by both sexes, in a live tree or in a dead stump. Lays 2 eggs.

REFERENCES King & Dickinson 1975; Lekagul & Round 1991; MacKinnon 1990; MacKinnon & Phillipps 1993; Medway & Wells 1976; Short 1973a, 1978; Smythies 1981.

208 BLACK-AND-BUFF WOODPECKER
Meiglyptes jugularis   Plate 62

IDENTIFICATION Length c. 22cm. Small and short-tailed, with fairly long, rather narrow-based and slightly chisel-tipped bill with strongly curved culmen. Plumage mostly black, with white on rump, hindneck and sides of neck and also on scapulars and tertials, and barred face; has prominent black crest. Male has some inconspicuous red in moustachial area. Unobtrusive, tending to keep to upper levels of trees, often hanging upside-down from branches.

Similar species Likely to be confused only with Heart-spotted Woodpecker (211), but differs from latter in having white hindneck (as well as neck sides), black throat with pale barring/streaking, and barred head, as well as narrow pale bars on flight feathers; also has longer tail (extends beyond wings when perched). Note also that female Heart-spotted has white forehead and forecrown and male lacks red moustache.

DISTRIBUTION Resident from W, E and S Burma, including Tenasserim, east through parts of Thailand, and in Indochina except Tonkin in northern Vietnam. Uncommon to rare throughout its range.

HABITAT A species of evergreen forest which in many parts of its range shows a distinct preference for more open areas, such as forest edges and clearings, and also bamboo growth, and often seems to avoid dense forest. A lowland species which occurs in forested areas up to 900m (1000m).

DESCRIPTION
Adult male Forehead to mid crown and entire ear-coverts black, narrowly barred pale buff; hindcrown and nape feathers plain black and elongated to form long crest. Lores mainly buff, often with some black barring. Short moustachial stripe formed by dark red feather tips (often appears barred red and black). Hindneck and sides of neck

creamy-white, this extending as buffish-white onto sides of breast; mantle, upper back and uppertail-coverts black (mantle may have a few pale bars); rump white to buffish-white. Inner scapulars black, outers mainly white to pale creamy-buff. Upperwing and its coverts mostly black, coverts tipped creamy and flight feathers with thin white to buff bars (broader on inner webs); tertials white to pale creamy-buff, with prominent broad dark bars on distal parts (pattern variable). Uppertail black. Throat black, variably barred buff (can appear checkered); rest of underparts (apart from buffy-white breast sides) black or brown-black, sometimes with two or three whitish bars on lower flanks and rarely also on belly. Underwing dusky, with black tip and whitish bars, coverts creamy-white. Undertail brownish-black.

Adult female As male but lacks red in moustachial region, which is barred black and buff.

Juvenile As adults, but duller, with head more clearly barred.

Bare parts Bill black, often with slightly paler base to lower mandible. Legs and feet grey-green or grey-blue. Eyes brown.

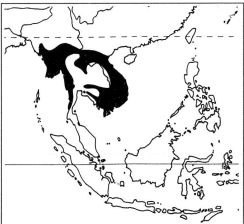

GEOGRAPHICAL VARIATION None. Monotypic.

MEASUREMENTS Wing 95-107. Weight: 50-57.

VOICE Calls similar to those of Heart-spotted Woodpecker. A nasal *ki-yew* and a call-series, *...tititit-wéek week week.*

HABITS Found singly or in pairs, and not noted in association with other species. Behaviour not well known, but habits appear to be similar to those of Buff-rumped (207) and Heart-spotted Woodpeckers. Often hangs upside-down on small leafy twigs and branches in understorey and middle storey.

FOOD Ants and other insects.

BREEDING Breeding season March-June.

REFERENCES King & Dickinson 1975; Lekagul & Round 1991.

209 BUFF-NECKED WOODPECKER
Meiglyptes tukki   **Plate 62**

IDENTIFICATION Length c. 21cm. Small, with moderate-length, fairly narrow-based and pointed bill with strongly curved culmen. Mostly dark brown, narrowly barred buff apart from plain head, and with black upper breast and distinctive buff patch on side of neck. Male has red moustache. Dark plumage, lack of pale rump and absence of obvious crest distinguish this from all other woodpeckers within its range.

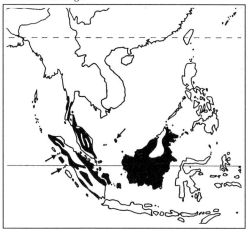

DISTRIBUTION Inhabits forested areas from southeasternmost Burma (from about 12˚30'N in Tenasserim) and peninsular Thailand, south through Malaysia to Sumatra and most of its islands, Bangka Island, North Natunas and Borneo (including Banggi Island off N Sabah). Uncommon on the continental mainland, but commoner elsewhere.

HABITAT Frequents primary and tall secondary evergreen forests with dense undergrowth and rotting stumps; less often at edges and clearings than Buff-rumped Woodpecker (207). Restricted to the lowlands generally below 600m (occasionally to 1200m) in mainland SE Asia, and reaches 1000m in the Greater Sundas.

DESCRIPTION
M. t. tukki **Adult male** Head, including forehead to short crest, hindneck and ear-coverts, dark grey-brown or olive-brown (forehead often slightly paler or, rarely, with hint of red); may show somewhat darker indistinct eye-stripe. Moustachial region red, barred black and buffy at rear. Side of neck with large buff, buffish-white or yellowish-buff patch extending from lower edge of rear ear-coverts to rear throat sides. Chin and throat barred blackish-brown and buff. Entire upperparts, upperwing-coverts and uppertail dull dark olive-brown, all narrowly barred buff, wing-coverts occasionally also edged dull red. Flight feathers dark brown, narrowly barred buff, bars becoming broader and paler (whitish) on inner webs. Lower throat and upper breast blackish-brown (in latter area sometimes obscured by barring); rest of underparts brown, all narrowly barred buff, bars slightly broader on flanks but often only vaguely defined on centre of belly. Underwing brown, with pale coverts and bases of flight feathers. Undertail as uppertail.

Adult female As male, but lacks red in malar region.

Juvenile Pale bars broader than on adults, and dark throat/breast patch is less well defined. Juvenile male has reddish

moustache and sometimes also red tips to forehead and (less often) crown feathers.

Bare parts Bill black, with much paler, greyish or whitish, lower mandible. Legs and feet greyish-green to grey-brown. Eyes deep crimson, reddish-brown or brown.

GEOGRAPHICAL VARIATION Five rather poorly differentiated races are recognised.

M. t. tukki (continental mainland, Natuna Islands and N Borneo, Sumatra, Banyak Islands and Bangka) Described above. Natuna population (sometimes separated as 'azaleus') may show more obscure barring.

M. t. percnerpes (S Borneo) Strongly barred. Brown, generally lacking olive tinges, but often shows more rusty or reddish tone than *tukki*.

M. t. batu (Batu Islands) Blackish crown and more contrasting blackish breast patch.

M. t. pulonis (Banggi Island, off N Borneo) Much longer-billed than other races. Browner, less olive, and with paler throat.

M. t. infuscatus (Nias Island) Slightly shorter-winged than other races. Barring weak, pale bars tending to be obscured; dark crown.

MEASUREMENTS Wing 86-110; tail 64-65; bill 22-23; tarsus 20.9-21.2. Weight: 43-64.

VOICE Single *pee* calls similar to those of Buff-rumped Woodpecker, and series of *dwit* or *ki-ti-ki-ti-ki-ti-ki-ti* notes and *wick-wick-wick-wick…* calls during encounters are heard occasionally. The most common vocalisation is a monotone high-pitched trill, *kirr-r-r*, which is lower in pitch, longer and slower than the trill of Buff-rumped; as with the latter, it may slow down towards the end, although not so distinctly, and in some trills the pitch may rise in the terminal phase. Both sexes drum. Single rolls may last less than 1 sec and over 3 secs and contain from about a dozen to almost 60 beats. The initial section of longer bouts and shorter bouts is delivered at a faster rate than the final one, the rhythm being on average similar to the drumming of Downy Woodpecker (113).

HABITS Occurs singly or in pairs, which sometimes stay in close contact and feed side by side; regularly joins mixed-species flocks. Forages in middle and lower strata of the forest, and often comes down into low bushes, saplings, overgrown gulleys and the like, and, altogether, uses more diverse sites than Buff-rumped Woodpecker. Higher strata are visited mainly when with other birds. Forages on branch tips and leaf buds in the crowns of tall trees, but also visits larger branches and trunks and decayed logs of the understorey. The dominant foraging mode is gleaning, with some probing, pecking and working at dead wood. Movements are rapid, and in most cases only a short time is spent at a single spot or tree. The pair uses trills to keep vocal contact over greater distances. During encounters, head-swinging displays are given, accompanied by vocalisations.

FOOD Ants and termites.

BREEDING Nesting occurs in May and June in Malaysia; young have been found in early June in Borneo. Nest is built in rotten wood in a live tree, or low in a tree stump at 1.5-5m. Clutch of 2 eggs is laid. The young are fed by both parents, apparently by regurgitation.

REFERENCES King & Dickinson 1975; Lekagul & Round 1991; MacKinnon & Phillipps 1993; Medway & Wells 1976; Robinson 1928; Short 1973a, 1978; Smythies 1981.

210 GREY-AND-BUFF WOODPECKER
Hemicircus concretus   Plate 63

Other name: Grey-breasted Woodpecker

IDENTIFICATION Length 13-14cm. Very small and compact, with longish, straight, chisel-tipped bill with rather broad base. A distinctive species, with slender neck, large head and markedly short, rounded tail. Mainly dark grey with prominent long crest, whitish hindneck and rump, thin white neck stripe, upperparts boldly edged and tipped pale (scaly pattern) and lower underparts barred; male has red forehead, crown and top of (or entire) crest; as the prominent crest is partly raised much of the time, sexes may be distinguished readily. Juveniles have much broader pale edges to upperparts and stronger barring below, both sexes showing dull cinnamon crown and crest with variable amount of red in centre of crest (less on female). Owing to big-headed appearance, short tail and the characteristic coloration of the head and underside, unlikely to be confused with Buff-rumped Woodpecker (207).

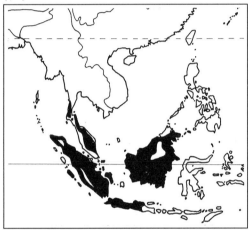

DISTRIBUTION Range extends from about 11°N in peninsular Thailand and S Tenasserim, Burma, south through Malaysia to Sumatra (including N Mentawai and Bangka Island), Java (except in east) and coastal Borneo. Uncommon throughout most of its range, but locally common in Sumatra and possibly Borneo.

HABITAT Occurs in primary evergreen forest, but prefers open country, evergreen secondary forest, forest edge, gardens and plantations; seems to favour the presence of bamboo in its habitat. In SE Asia below 900 to 1000m, in Borneo up to 1500m.

DESCRIPTION
H. c. sordidus **Adult male** Forehead, crown and fore part of crest red. Rest of head (including rear crest) and neck dark grey, apart from whitish hindneck and uppermost mantle and thin pale line running from rear moustachial region down neck side. Lower mantle, back and upperwing-coverts dark brownish-black, all feathers broadly edged and tipped buffish-white to white; rump whitish, normally stained buff by peculiar sticky, resin-like substance (origin of which is unclear); uppertail-coverts black, tipped white. Tertials black, edged and tipped pale buff, or pale buff with large black heart-shaped spots; flight feathers black, inner webs of primaries edged buffish-white, secondaries with a few buffy-white bars. Uppertail black, sometimes barred paler (especially on outer feathers). Grey of head/

neck extends to chin, throat, breast and belly, where normally tinged olive or buff (belly occasionally buffish or faintly barred buff); flanks and undertail-coverts barred black and buff/white. Underwing blackish, with buff patch at base of primaries, coverts buffish or barred black and white. Undertail as uppertail.

Adult female Shorter-billed than male. Lacks red on head (may rarely show trace of red or cinnamon-rufous).

Juvenile Upperparts much more broadly edged and tipped pale (light rufous-buff rather than whitish) than on adults, and underparts are more heavily barred with pale rufous-buff; top of head cinnamon-rufous with narrow black feather tips, male with variable red in centre of crest (red area reduced on female). Some juveniles with very heavy rufous barring on underparts also have narrow whitish stripe from rear malar region to hindneck.

Bare parts Bill greyish-black. Legs and feet dark brown. Eyes red-brown.

GEOGRAPHICAL VARIATION Two well-differentiated races.
> *H. c. sordidus* (entire range, except Java) Described above. Varies somewhat individually. Sumatra and Borneo populations ('*coccometopus*') are considered insufficiently different to warrant separation, and are included within this race.
> *H. c. concretus* (W and C Java) Slightly larger and darker than *sordidus*, with darker hindneck and darker, blackish-grey, on lower underparts; males (including many juvenile males) have entire crest red.

MEASUREMENTS Wing 78-90; tail 27-29; bill 20.2 (male longer-billed than female); tarsus 15.7-15.9. Weight: 27-32.

VOICE Various typical woodpecker calls. The call note is a sharp *chick*, *pit* or *tsip*, rather similar to the calls of Buff-rumped Woodpecker, only slightly higher-pitched and louder. Similar but longer drawn out are *peew*, *ki-oo*, *ki-yow*, or *kee-yew* notes, uttered during encounters and also associated with crest-raising; they are practically identical with the corresponding calls of Heart-spotted Woodpecker (211). A vibrating *chitterr*, even more wavering than the rather similar trill of Buff-rumped Woodpecker, is delivered in agonistic situations and during aerial chases. Drums weakly.

HABITS Most easily detected through familiarisation with its calls. This tiny woodpecker is a bird of the treetops, where it forages among twigs and leaves as well as on trunks and branches; trees projecting above the rest of the vegetation seem to be especially attractive, even when isolated in an open area. Occasionally seen in bushes. The main foraging technique is gleaning, but frequently pecks, more so and more loudly, at least, than Buff-rumped or Buff-necked Woodpeckers (209); also prises off bark and probes. Usually moves rapidly in the dense foliage of the canopy, flitting between twigs, branches and leaf clusters. Hops, twists, peeks under leaves, and clings tit-like to twigs and fruits. When moving along trunks, darts in all directions and is able to move almost straight downwards, head first. Sexual differences in foraging with respect to micro-habitat selection and relative use of foraging techniques may exist, but they are insufficiently documented. Flies long distances over the forest or open areas to commute between feeding sites. The most common display is crest-raising. This woodpecker appears to be rather aggressive even in encounters between the sexes, in which the male usually is dominant; despite this, groups of up to ten may be observed, and this species also joins mixed-species flocks.

FOOD Diet includes fruits such as lime and *Loranthus.*

BREEDING Almost nothing is known about the reproductive behaviour. Breeding season in Malaysia appears to span April to July; in Java, May and June. Apparently, nest cavities and (several) roosts may be close to each other, and are constructed at heights between 9 and 30m.

REFERENCES King & Dickinson 1975; Lekagul & Round 1991; MacKinnon 1990; MacKinnon & Phillipps 1993; Medway & Wells 1976; Robinson 1928; Short 1973a, 1978; Smythies 1981.

---

211 HEART-SPOTTED WOODPECKER
Hemicircus canente   **Plate 63**

IDENTIFICATION Length 15-16cm. Very small, with long, relatively slender but broad-based bill with chisel tip. Appears 'dumpy', with thin neck, large head with prominent crest, and strikingly short and rounded tail. Has black, white and greyish plumage with white rump, throat and wing patch, and with bold heart-shaped markings on tertials and some wing-coverts; female has white forehead and forecrown. Juvenile often has blackish underparts, including throat, thus isolating white stripe down side of neck. A very active bird, usually in the upper parts of trees, often revealing its presence by its squeaky calls.

Similar species Confusable with Black-and-buff Woodpecker (208), but lacks the latter's white hindneck, barred head and throat and barring on flight feathers, and has shorter tail. Note female Heart-spotted's diagnostic white forehead.

DISTRIBUTION Occurs from SW India north along the coast to about 21°N and then east to the Himalayan foothills in Assam; formerly stated to occur in Bangladesh, but only one recent record from that country, in the northeast in 1984. Present also from Burma south of 20°N, through parts of Thailand south to around 9°N and locally east into Cambodia, throughout Laos and in southern Vietnam (S Annam and Cochinchina). Rather local and scattered, but fairly common in some parts of range.

HABITAT Found in moist and dense deciduous and evergreen forests, at forest edge, in secondary forest, bamboo, and open deciduous forest; in west of range also has a liking for bamboo and coffee plantations (and teak), and in Cochinchina shows a similar predilection for bamboo. A mainly lowland species, ranging from the plains up to 1000m in SE Asia and to 1300m in India.

DESCRIPTION

Adult male Forehead and forecrown black, with very small, indistinct white spots or speckles (can form more obvious white bars, though generally invisible in the field); rest of upper part of head, from lores back to crest and hindneck,

plain black. Throat, moustachial region and sides of neck white, tinged buff or cream, becoming olive-grey or buffish-grey on lower throat and breast. Upperparts except rump black, sometimes with some white bars on back and/or uppertail-coverts; rump white or off-white (as with previous species, a sweet-smelling sticky substance causes buff staining of rump). Inner scapulars black; outer scapulars, tertials, lesser and median coverts and a variable number of inner greater coverts white or buffish-white with large, bold black heart-shaped marks subterminally, remaining coverts black with very narrow white edges and tips; flight feathers black, narrowly edged white on inner webs. Uppertail black. Olive/grey of breast becomes black on belly and undertail-coverts (black areas sometimes very narrowly barred); a rare dark phase has entire underparts black. Underwing blackish, with white on coverts and at base of primaries. Undertail blackish.

Adult female Shorter-billed and shorter-winged than male, and differs in having forehead and forecrown unmarked white or buffish-white.

Juvenile Similar to adult female, but all pale areas generally more buffy, less white, and forehead often partly barred black; usually darker below, dark brownish to black, including on throat, but always with at least some white down sides of neck.

Bare parts Bill dark brown to brownish-black. Legs and feet brown, sometimes tinged greenish. Eyes brown to dull red-brown.

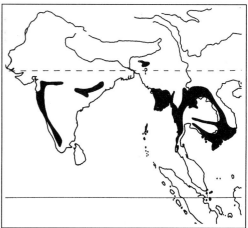

GEOGRAPHICAL VARIATION Individual variation fairly marked, but with no significant geographical pattern. Very slight increase in size in India from southwest to northeast, but this is negligible (and much overlap exists). No races are recognised.

MEASUREMENTS Wing of male 92-103, of female 85-98; tail of male 28-37, of female 28-38; bill of male 20-25, of female 17-21; tarsus of male 17-20, of female 16-19. Weight: 37-50.

VOICE Frequently gives a squeaky and nasal *ki-yew*, *chirrick* or *ch-yew*, with emphasis on the second syllable, repeated several times and very similar to the corresponding call of Grey-and-buff Woodpecker (210). An uninflected high-pitched *kee-kee-kee-kee* and a long-drawn grating *chur-r* have also been described. Displays with *su-sie* notes. Drums weakly and infrequently.

HABITS Usually met with singly or in pairs, or in mixed-species groups. Forages on twigs in the canopy, but also on trunks and higher dead branches, where it gleans, pecks and hammers. No quantitative data exist which relate the significant morphological differences between the sexes with differences in foraging behaviour. Often seen perched crosswise on a twig. Moves rapidly along twigs and branches. Flight is deeply undulating. Displays associated with vocalisations consist of bowing or bobbing movements. The significance and origin of the resin-like substance found in the middle of the back of this and the previous species remain obscure.

FOOD Ants, termites, larvae, and other insects comprise the bulk of its diet.

BREEDING Breeds mainly from November to April. The tiny nest hole is excavated into a dead branch or even a fence post at rather low heights, 1-4m, but occasionally much higher. Clutch comprises 2 or, more commonly, 3 eggs.

REFERENCES Ali & Ripley 1970; Bock & Short 1971; Lekagul & Round 1991; Menon 1985; Short 1973a.

212 ASHY WOODPECKER
Mulleripicus fulvus Plate 64

Other names: Fulvous Woodpecker, Celebes Woodpecker

IDENTIFICATION Length c. 40cm. Large, with long, slightly chisel-tipped bill curved on culmen and narrow across nostrils. A long-tailed Sulawesi endemic and unmistakable; the only other woodpecker on the island is the diminutive and totally different Sulawesi Woodpecker (88). In flight, however, it may at first glance give the impression of a hornbill. Plain dark slaty-brown above, including on wings and tail, and uniformly buff below (often stained reddish or yellowish); head and neck dark grey, finely speckled whitish. Males have a deep red face, more extensive (reaching to hindcrown) in southern population, while females have the head concolorous with the neck and similarly speckled; both sexes have pale eyes. Juveniles are more spotted.

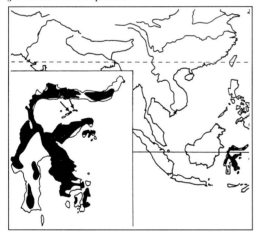

DISTRIBUTION Confined to Sulawesi, including the islands of Muna, Buton (Butung), Mantehase (Manterawu), Bangka and Lembeh, and the archipelagos of Banggai and Togian.

HABITAT Prefers closed, gloomy forests; rarely close to human habitation. Occurs from the lowlands to the mountains up to 2200m.

DESCRIPTION
M. f. fulvus **Adult male** Forehead, lores, cheeks and moustachial area dark red, this colour extending back usually to central crown and front part of ear-coverts (but often more restricted at rear); a few dark feather bases may be visible, forming a dark line on lores. Rear head and hindneck dark grey, becoming paler grey-buff on chin, throat and foreneck, all with very small whitish spots. Upperparts and upperwing dark grey-brown to blackish-slate, somewhat paler on uppertail-coverts and a shade darker on wings (may occasionally show some pale spots and/or shaft streaks, especially on tail-coverts). Uppertail dark grey-brown to blackish-grey, unmarked. Underparts below throat rich buff to creamy yellowish-brown, rather greyer on breast and often washed a soft yellow-grey on flanks (underparts frequently stained dark reddish or yellow-brown through foraging activities). Underwing pale brownish-grey to rather dark grey. Undertail pale brown to grey, washed yellow.

Adult female As male, but with red of head replaced by dark grey with very fine pale spots (except on forehead).

Juvenile Much as adults, but duller and more spotted. Both sexes have red on face, less than on adult male and even more restricted on young female.

Bare parts Bill black. Legs and feet greenish-grey, tinged bluish on some. Eyes pale yellow. Orbital skin grey.

GEOGRAPHICAL VARIATION Two races.
 M. f. fulvus (northern part of Sulawesi) Described above.
 M. f. wallacei (southern Sulawesi) Slightly longer-winged and longer-tailed than nominate, blacker tail, but with shorter bill and perhaps a shade paler in plumage. Red coloration of male is somewhat brighter and more widespread, reaching to upper nape and rear ear-coverts.

MEASUREMENTS Wing 176-192; tail 145-172; bill 28-45; tarsus 30-33.

VOICE Voice not very loud, and muffled. A laughing, rapid *hew-hew-hew-hew-hew-hew*. Drums ardently in the breeding season.

HABITS Met with in pairs or family groups of up to five birds. Indirect evidence indicates at least occasional ground foraging, probably breaking into termite mounds, but may also suggest foraging in dead, rotted stumps and stubs.

FOOD Termites and caterpillars.

BREEDING Drumming activity and evidence from specimens indicate that nesting takes place in March-August. Nest in hole of a dead tree. Clutch size 2-3 eggs.

REFERENCES Meyer & Wigglesworth 1898; Stresemann 1940; White & Bruce 1986.

213 SOOTY WOODPECKER
Mulleripicus funebris Plate 64

Other name: Tweeddale's Woodpecker (race *fuliginosus*)

IDENTIFICATION Length c. 30cm. Medium-sized, with longish, almost pointed bill curved on culmen and narrow across nostrils. A Philippine endemic. Entire plumage very dark, blackish or (in south) grey, except for red on face (in south, only on moustache) of male; very fine pale speckles on head and neck visible at closer ranges. Has pale eyes and pale or darkish bill. Juveniles are similar to adults, but more heavily spotted.

Similar species White-bellied Woodpecker (167) is much bigger and has a white belly.

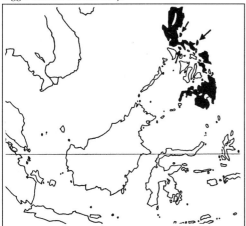

DISTRIBUTION Found only in the Philippines, where present on Luzon, the Polillo islands, Catanduanes and Marinduque and, in the south, Samar, Leyte and Mindanao. Uncommon to locally numerous.

HABITAT Occupies all types of forest with the exception of mossy forests; usually seen in evergreen forest, secondary forest, forest edge, and near cultivations. Found also in montane oak and pine forest above 300m, to altitudes of about 1350m.

DESCRIPTION

M. f. funebris **Adult male** Forehead and forecrown, lores, cheeks, moustachial region and front of ear-coverts dark red, usually with at least some black feather bases showing (on some, red does not extend far onto forecrown); rest of head and neck black, sometimes slightly greyish on throat, and finely spotted with white (spots sometimes lacking). Entire upperparts, including upperwing and tail, blue-glossed black and unmarked. Underparts also blackish, but appearing slightly paler, more sooty-black, and unglossed; may rarely show a few small pale spots on breast. (In worn plumage, becomes browner and less glossy, with fewer/no spots and with black feather bases more visible on face).

Adult female Lacks red, having entire head blackish with fine white spots (latter may be few or absent).

Juvenile As adults, but duller and browner and without gloss; pale spots bigger but less sharply defined. Males have red on face, as adult.

Bare parts Bill blackish, with pale horn-yellow centre to lower mandible. Legs and feet brownish-grey. Eyes pale yellow.

GEOGRAPHICAL VARIATION Four races, three very poorly differentiated and one rather distinct.

    M. f. funebris (C and S Luzon, Catanduanes and Marinduque) Described above. Intergrades with *mayri* in C Luzon.

    M. f. mayri (N Luzon) Tends to have longer bill and longer tail than nominate, though considerable overlap exists. Bill yellowish-grey or ivory-yellow, with grey base.

    M. f. parkesi (Polillo islands) Very like nominate, but perhaps slightly larger on average. Extent of red on male's head similar, but not reaching to forecrown.

    M. f. fuliginosus (Samar, Leyte and Mindanao) Differs from above races in shorter tail and shorter, deeper bill, paler coloration overall, and less extensive red on

head of male. Upperparts, wings and tail more slaty-grey than black, and underparts greyer; male has red restricted to a broad moustache (occasionally with faint traces of red elsewhere on face) and rest of head tends to be greyer; female's head also generally paler than in northern races. Bill relatively short and deep, pale ivory-yellow with a darker base.

MEASUREMENTS Wing 147-171; tail 125-145; bill 35.5-39; tarsus 28-30.5. Weight: 139-183.

VOICE Although calling is reported by many observers, more detailed descriptions seem to be lacking.

HABITS Usually met with singly or in pairs, which maintain frequent vocal contact. Forages in the upper storeys (above 20m) of tall trees which may be live or partly or fully dead.

FOOD We have been unable to find any pertinent records.

BREEDING The breeding season is not well corroborated; it seems to extend from March to May (Luzon, Polillo) and April to August (Samar and Leyte).

REFERENCES Danielsen *et al.* 1993; Dickinson *et al.* 1991; Goodman & Gonzales 1990.

214 GREAT SLATY WOODPECKER
Mulleripicus pulverulentus   Plate 64

IDENTIFICATION Length c. 50cm. Very large (the biggest Old World woodpecker), with very long, strong chisel-tipped bill, long neck and long tail; a slight crest is often evident. Plumage almost wholly dark grey or blackish slate-grey with small white spots, but with pale throat; males have small red moustache. Although generally uncommon or rare throughout its range, can be conspicuously noisy where present, often in small parties of up to six birds. Has distinctive whinnying call. Unmistakable (at first glance, however, flying birds may be mistaken for hornbills).

DISTRIBUTION A mainly lowland resident from about 77°E in NW India east through Nepal, Sikkim, Bhutan and Assam to SW China (S Yunnan), extending south through N Bangladesh, Burma, Thailand and Indochina (from N Annam) to the Greater Sundas (including the Riau archipelago and North Natunas, but not Bali) and Palawan. Very scarce in much of range; found locally throughout the Burmese foothills, uncommon or rare from Indochina to Indonesia, though locally common in southern Vietnam; very rare in northeast of range, but more common in Borneo, where it also occurs in uplands.

HABITAT Primary semi-open moist deciduous and tropical evergreen forests, adjacent secondary forests, clearings with scattered tall trees, and similar almost park-like woodland. Locally, prefers dipterocarp and teak forests. Found also in mature sal forests, swamp forest and tall mangroves.

Most frequent in lowlands and lower hills below 600m, but also in montane habitats up to 1100m (foothills of Himalayas) and occasionally to 2000m.

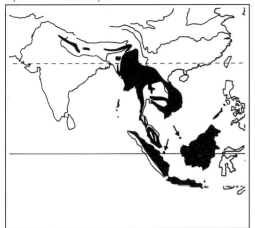

DESCRIPTION

M. p. harterti **Adult male** Rear of moustachial area (cheeks) scarlet-red with a few paler streaks; rest of head and upperparts slate-tinged grey, somewhat darker on lores, ear-coverts and sides of chin, and with variable amount of whitish feather tips forming small spots (often most prominent on ear-coverts and hindneck). Chin and throat creamy to yellow-buff, feathers of lower throat tipped pale red. Tail and entire wings darker slate-grey, feathers very narrowly edged/tipped blue-grey. Underparts below throat slate-grey, slightly paler than upperparts, with small pale streak-like spots (can be extensive on upper breast), becoming paler grey or even whitish on lower belly.

Adult female Lacks red moustache, entire malar area being slate-grey, and lacks red tips to lower-throat feathers.

Juvenile General plumage duller, with obvious brown tinge, particularly above, and chin and throat whiter rather than cream or buff; underparts generally more spotted than on adults. Juvenile male has red moustache, larger than on adult, and can also show some red on crown.

Bare parts Bill yellowish-grey to grey-white on lower mandible and base of upper mandible, which is blackish on culmen and tip. Legs and feet blue-grey or greenish-grey. Eyes brown. Orbital skin pale grey.

GEOGRAPHICAL VARIATION Rather slight, but individual variation makes racial delimitation difficult. Varies only slightly and inconstantly in size throughout range, though Palawan population is shorter-winged. Westernmost populations (Nepal to N Assam) are darker grey, especially below, and male's red moustache is a deeper crimson: it was formerly described as *M. p. mohun*, but some birds from Burma and Thailand appear identical. Only two races seem currently acceptable.

> *M. p. harterti* (India and Nepal east to SW China and Indochina) Described above. Intermediates between this and the following race occur in peninsular Thailand.
>
> *M. p. pulverulentus* (Malaysia, south through Greater Sundas and east to Palawan) Darker overall, more greyish-black.

MEASUREMENTS Wing 215-250; tail 134-162; bill 60-65; tarsus 36-41. Weight: 360-563.

VOICE For a bird of its size, the vocalisations appear to be not loud. The farthest-reaching and most frequently heard call is a loud whinnying cackle of two to five, most commonly four, notes, *woikwoikwoikwoik*, the initial note often slightly higher-pitched and the terminal one distinctly lower in pitch and a bit delayed; in shorter three- or four-note version of the whinny, consecutive notes drop even more in pitch. The whinny is frequently given in flight. Single *dwot* calls, varying somewhat in sound, strength and duration, are heard when the woodpecker is perched or in flight. When members of a pair come into very close contact, they call with low and soft mewing notes. In more agonistic situations and together with head-swinging, *ta-whit* or *dew-it* calls are uttered. Drumming has been reported to be loud, but it seems to be a signal used much less commonly than it is by other large woodpeckers.

HABITS Noisy and conspicuous when present. Found usually in pairs, and regularly roams through the forest in noisy family parties of 4-6 (to 12 and more) birds. When foraging, sometimes associates with other woodpeckers, such as White-bellied (167) and Greater Flameback (199). Forages mainly in tall trees, including solitary ones in open areas; covers large distances to reach these trees, and the species' home range is correspondingly very extensive. Also visits smaller trees and saplings at low levels. When searching for food, climbs up trunks and larger branches slowly, pausing frequently at crevices and other promising depressions and cracks in the bark. In the crown, may perch crosswise, even on small branches. Foraging techniques include gleaning, probing, pecking, prising off bark, and hammering with powerful and loud blows to excavate wood. Gleaning is most important, and the long neck and bill are rather helpful for reaching a long way out. Does not remain long at one spot to peck or hammer. Although relatively nimble in its foraging among branches, it climbs almost in 'slow motion'. The flight, which takes it high above the trees, often over long distances between successive foraging patches, is noisy (the feathers rustle), and is also less dipping than in other woodpeckers and almost crow-like. Although the pair forages together and stays in permanent vocal contact, the sexes roost in separate cavities, as with most other woodpeckers. Displays include a curious head-swinging, in which the head appears to lag behind the body in its swinging movement. Associated with this display are short whinny calls, and, especially during chases, the wings are extended widely, with the tail also spread. Interspecific interactions are seemingly associated with holes and involve White-bellied Woodpecker (167) and hornbills. Arboreal mammals also represent an important group of competitors.

FOOD Ants dominate the diet, which also, however, includes other insects, such as the larvae of wood-boring beetles. May possibly also eat small fruits.

BREEDING Nesting season in W Malaysia appears to be March-August. Both sexes take part in the excavation of the nest, although the male does most of the work. Old nests are probably used only when the pair is forced to leave its new one by unrelenting competitors. The nest is very high up (9-45m) in a tree and dug into large trunks or branches, with an entrance of about 10cm in diameter. Clutch contains 2-4 eggs. Both sexes incubate and feed the young. The fledged young stay with the breeding pair probably until the next breeding cycle commences.

REFERENCES Ali 1962; Ali & Ripley 1970; King & Dickinson 1975; Lekagul & Round 1991; MacKinnon 1990; MacKinnon & Phillipps 1993; Medway & Wells 1976; Robinson 1928; Robson *et al.* 1989; Short 1973a, 1978; Smythies 1953, 1981; Stresemann & Heinrich 1940.

BIBLIOGRAPHY

Abdulali, H. 1964. The birds of the Andaman and Nicobar Islands. *J. Bombay Nat. Hist. Soc.* 61: 483-571.

— 1968. Sap sucking by Indian woodpeckers. *J. Bombay Nat. Hist. Soc.* 65: 219-221.

Ahlén, I., Andersson, Å., Aulén, G., & Pettersson, B. 1978. Vitryggig hackspett och mellanspett - två hotade arters ekologi. *Anser*, Suppl. 3: 5-11.

Ali, S. 1962. *Birds of Sikkim.* Oxford Univ. Press, London.

— & Ripley, S. D. 1970. *Handbook of the birds of India and Pakistan.* Vol. 4. Oxford Univ. Press, Bombay.

Allen, A. A., & Kellogg, P. P. 1937. Recent observations on the Ivory-billed Woodpecker. *Auk* 54: 164-184.

Andersson, Å., & Hamilton, G. 1972. Vitryggiga hackspetten *Dendrocopos leucotos* i Östergötland. *Vår Fågelvärld* 31: 257-262.

Antevs, A. 1948. Behavior of the Gila Woodpecker, Ruby-crowned Kinglet, and Broad-tailed Hummingbird. *Condor* 50: 91-92.

Aravena, R. 1928. Notas sobre la alimentación de la aves. *Hornero* 4: 153-166.

Askins, R. A. 1983. Foraging ecology of temperate-zone and tropical woodpeckers. *Ecology* 64: 945-956.

Atwell, G. D. 1952. The breeding of the Cardinal Woodpecker at Gatooma, Southern Rhodesia. *Ostrich* 23: 88-91.

Aulén, G., & Lundberg, A. 1991. Sexual dimorphism and patterns of territory use by the White-backed Woodpecker *Dendrocopos leucotos. Ornis Scand.* 22: 60-64.

Austin, G. T. 1976. Sexual and seasonal differences in foraging of Ladder-backed Woodpeckers. *Condor* 78: 317-323.

Balát, F., & González, H. 1982. Concrete data on the breeding of Cuban birds. *Acta Sc. Nat. Brno* 16: 1-46.

Bannerman, D. A. 1933. *The birds of tropical West Africa.* Vol. 3. Oliver & Boyd, Edinburgh.

Baptista, L. F. 1978. A revision of the Mexican *Piculus* (Picidae) complex. *Wilson Bull.* 90: 159-181.

Barbour, T. 1923. Birds of Cuba. *Mem. Nuttall. Orn. Club.*

Bardin, A. V. 1986. The effect of Great Spotted Woodpecker predation on breeding success of Willow Tit and Crested Tit. *Ekologiya* (6): 77-79.

Bates, G. L. 1930. *Handbook of the birds of West Africa.* J. Bale, sons, and Danielson, London.

Beals, E. W. 1970. Birds of a *Euphorbia-Acacia* woodland in Ethiopia: habitat and seasonal changes. *J. Anim. Ecol.* 39: 277-297.

Belcher, C. F. 1930. *The birds of Nyasaland.* The Technical Press, London.

— & Smooker, G. D. 1936. Birds of the colony of Trinidad and Tobago. Part IV. *Ibis* 13/6: 792-813.

Belton, W. 1984. Birds of Rio Grande do Sul, Brazil. Part 1. Rheidae through Furnariidae. *Bull. Am. Mus. Nat. Hist.* 178: 371-631.

Benítez-Díaz, H. 1993. Geographic variation in coloration and morphology of the Acorn Woodpecker. *Condor* 95: 63-71.

Bennun, L. A., & Read, A. F. 1988. Joint nesting in the Acorn Woodpecker. *Trends Ecol. Evol.* 3: 319.

Bent, A. C. 1939. Life histories of North American Woodpeckers. *Smiths. Inst. US Nat Mus. Bull.* 174.

Berger, B., Föger, M., Büchele, S., & Dallinger, R. 1994. Der embryonale Sauerstoffverbrauch des Buntspechts (*Dendrocopos major*): Einfluß von Entwicklungsmodus und Bebrütungszeit. *J. Ornithol.* 135: 101-105.

Bernstein, H. A. 1861. Ueber Nester und Eier javascher Vögel. *J. Ornithol.* 9: 113-128.

Bezzel, E. 1985. *Kompendium der Vögel Mitteleuropas. Nonpasseriformes.* Aula-Verlag, Wiesbaden.

Birkhead, T. R., & Møller A. P. 1992. *Sperm competition in birds.* Academic Press, London.

Blackford, J.L. 1955. Woodpecker concentration in burned forest. *Condor* 57: 28-30.

Blake, E. R. 1965. *Birds of Mexico. A guide for field identification.* Univ. Chicago Press, Chicago & London.

Block, W. M. 1991. Foraging ecology of Nuttall's Woodpecker. *Auk* 108: 303-317.

Blume, D. 1961. Über die Lebensweise einiger Spechtarten (*Dendrocopos major, Picus viridis, Dryocopus martius*). *J. Ornithol.* (Suppl.) 102: 1-115.

— 1968. *Die Buntspechte (Gattung* Dendrocopos*).* A. Ziemsen Verlag, Wittenberg Lutherstadt.

— 1973. *Schwarzspecht, Grünspecht, Grauspecht.* 3rd ed. A. Ziemsen Verlag, Wittenberg Lutherstadt.

— & Jeide, K. 1965. Trinkende und badende Spechte. *Orn. Mitt.* 17: 154-156.

— & Ogasawara, K. 1980. Zur Brutbiologie des Grauspechts (*Picus canus*). *Orn. Mitt.* 32: 209-212.

Bock, C. E. 1970. The ecology and behavior of the Lewis Woodpecker (*Asyndesmus lewis*). *Univ. California Publ. Zool.* 92: 1-100.

— 1971. Pairing in hybrid flicker populations in eastern Colorado. *Auk* 88: 921-924.

— & Bock, J. H. 1974a. Geographical ecology of the Acorn Woodpecker: diversity versus abundance of resources. *Amer. Nat.* 108: 694-698.

— & — 1974b. On the geographical ecology and evolution of the Three-toed Woodpeckers, *Picoides tridactylus* and *P. arcticus. Am. Midl. Natur.* 92: 397-405.

— , Hadow, H. H., & Somers, P. 1971. Relations between Lewis' and Red-headed Woodpeckers in southeastern Colorado. *Wilson Bull.* 83: 237-248.

— & Larson, D. L. 1986. Winter habitats of sapsuckers in southeastern Arizona. *Condor* 88: 246-247.

Bock, W. J. 1959. The scansorial foot of woodpeckers, with comments on the evolution of perching and climbing feet in birds. *Amer. Mus. Novitates* No. 1931: 1-45.

— 1963. Evolution and phylogeny in morphologically similar groups. *Amer. Nat.* 97: 265-285.

— 1964. Kinetics of the avian skull. *J. Morph.* 114: 1-41.

— 1966. An approach to the functional analysis of bill shape. *Auk* 83: 10-51.

— & Short, L. L. 1971. 'Resin secretion' in *Hemicircus* (Picidae). *Ibis* 113: 234-236.

Bond, J. 1985. *Birds of the West Indies.* 5th edition. Collins, London.

Brackbill, H. 1969a. Reversed mounting by the Red-headed Woodpecker. *Bird-Banding* 40: 255-256.

— 1969b. Red-bellied Woodpecker taking bird's eggs. *Bird-Banding* 40: 323-324.

Bradley, P. 1985. *Birds of the Cayman Islands.* P. E. Bradley, Georgetown.

Brazil, M. A. 1991. *The birds of Japan.* Christopher Helm, London, and Smithsonian Institution Press, Washington, D.C.

Brenowitz, G. L. 1977. An analysis of Gila Woodpecker vocalizations. *Wilson Bull.* 90: 451-455.

— 1978. Gila Woodpecker agonistic behavior. *Auk* 95: 49-58.

Britton, P. L. (ed.) 1980. *Birds of East Africa.* EANHS, Nairobi.

Brooks, T. M., Barnes R., Batrina L., Butchart S. H. M., Clay R. P., Esquivel E. Z., Etcheverry N. I., Lowen J. C., & Vincent J. 1993. Bird surveys and conservation in the Paraguayan Atlantic forest. Birdlife Intl. Study Rep. No. 57, Cambridge.

Brugger, C., & Taborsky, M. 1994. Male incubation and its effects on reproductive success in the Black Swan. *Ethology*, 38: 138-146.

Burt, W. H. 1930. Adaptive modifications in the woodpeckers. *Univ. Calif. Publ. Zool.* 32: 455-524.

Campbell, R. W., Dawe, N. K., McTaggart-Cowan, I., Cooper, J. M., Kaiser, G. W., & McNall, M. C. E. 1989. *The birds of British Columbia.* vol. 2. Royal Br. Col. Mus., Victoria, B.C.

Chapin, 1939. The birds of the Belgian Congo, II. *Bull. Amer. Mus. Nat. Hist.* 75: 1-632.

Chauvin, B. 1987. Association spontanée d'un signal appris et de la représentation pictographique d'un objet chez le pic épeiche (*Dendrocopos major*). *Cah. Ethol. appl.* 7: 39-48.

Chauvin-Muckensturm, B. 1980. Une manipulation complexe chez le Pic Epeiche (*Dendrocopos major*). C.R. Acad. Sc. Paris, Série D 291: 489-492.

Cheng, Tso-Hsin. 1964. *China's economic fauna: birds.* Translation: U.S. Dept Commerce, Washington, D.C.

— 1987. *A synopsis of the avifauna of China.* Science Press, Beijing, and Paul Parey Scientific Publ., Hamburg.

Chiba, S. 1969. [Stomach analysis of Japanese woodpeckers]. *Misc. Rep. Yamashina Inst. Ornith.* 5: 487-510.

Christie, D. A. 1990. Mystery photographs. 158. Middle Spotted Woodpecker. *Brit. Birds* 83: 395-396.

— & Winkler, H. 1994. White-backed and Middle Spotted Woodpeckers. *Birding World* 7: 283-285.

Christison, A. F. P., & Ticehurst, C. B. 1943. Some additional notes on the distribution of the avifauna of northern Baluchistan. *J. Bombay Nat. Hist. Soc.* 43: 478-487.

Clancey, P. A. 1964. *The birds of Natal and Zululand.* Oliver & Boyd, Edinburgh & London.

— 1988. Relationships in the *Campethera notata, C. abingoni* and *C. (a.) mombassica* complex of the Afrotropics. *Bull. Brit. Orn. Club* 108: 169-172.

Clayton, D. H., & Cotgreave, P. 1994. Relationship of bill morphology to grooming behaviour in birds. *Anim. Behav.* 47: 195-201.

Coates-Estrada, R., Estrada, A., & Meritt, D., Jr. 1993. Foraging by parrots (*Amazona autumnalis*) on fruits of *Stemmadenia donnell-smithii* (Apocynaceae) in the tropical rain forest of Los Tuxtlas, Mexico. *J. Trop. Ecol.* 9: 121-124.

Cody, M. L. 1969. Convergent characteristics in sympatric species: a possible relation to interspecific competition and aggression. *Condor* 71: 222-239.

Collar, N. J., Gonzaga, L. P., Krabbe, N., Nieto, A. M., Naranjo, L. G., Parker, T. A., III, & Wege, D. C. 1992. *Threatened birds of the Americas.* International Council for Bird Preservation, Cambridge, UK.

— , Crosby, M. J., & Stattersfield, A. J. 1994. *Birds to Watch 2: the world list of threatened birds.* Birdlife International. Cambridge, UK.

Collins, N. M., Sayer, J. A., & Whitmore, T. C. (eds.) 1991. *The conservation atlas of tropical forests: Asia and the Pacific.* Macmillan Press Ltd, London and Basingstoke.

Colston, P. R., Curry-Lindahl, K., & Coe, M. 1986. *The birds of Mount Nimba, Liberia.* Brit. Mus. Nat. Hist., London.

Conner, R. N. 1976. Nesting habitat for Red-headed Woodpeckers in southwestern Virginia. *Bird-Banding* 47: 40-43.

— 1979. Seasonal changes in woodpecker foraging methods: strategies for winter survival. Pp. 95-105 in J. G. Dickson, R. N. Conner, R. R. Fleet, J. C. Kroll & J. A. Jackson (eds.), *The role of insectivorous birds in forest ecosystems.* Academic Press, New York.

— 1980. Foraging habitats of woodpeckers in southwestern Virginia. *J. Field Ornithol.* 51: 119-127.

— & Adkisson, C. S. 1977. Principal component analysis of woodpecker nesting habitat. *Wilson Bull.* 89: 122-129.

— & Crawford, H. S. 1974. Woodpecker foraging in Appalachian clearcuts. *J. Forestry* 72: 564-566.

— , Hooper, R. G., Crawford, H. S., & Mosby, H. S. 1975. Woodpecker nesting habitat in cut and uncut woodlands in Virginia. *J. Wildl. Manage.* 39: 144-150.

— & Kroll, J. C. 1979. Food-storing by Yellow-bellied Sapsuckers. *Auk* 96: 195.

— & Locke, B. A. 1982. Fungi and Red-cockaded Woodpecker cavity trees. *Wilson Bull.* 94: 64-70.

— , Snow, A. E., & O'Halloran, K. A. 1991. Red-cockaded Woodpecker use of seed-tree/shelterwood cuts in eastern Texas. *Wildl. Soc. Bull.* 19: 67-73.

Conrads, K. 1964. Über das 'Drohschwenken' und einige Rufe beim Grauspecht (*Picus canus*). *J. Ornithol.* 105: 182-185.

— & Herrmann, A. 1963. Beobachtungen beim Grauspecht (*Picus canus* Gmelin) in der Brutzeit. *J. Ornithol.* 104: 205-248.

— & Mensendiek, H. 1980. Zum Konsum von Fichtensamen durch den Buntspecht (*Dendrocopos major*) im Winterhalbjahr. *Orn. Mitt.* 32: 204-207.

Conway, C. J., & Martin, T. E. 1993. Habitat suitability for Williamson's Sapsuckers in mixed-conifer forests. *J. Wildl. Manage.* 57: 322-328.

Cramp, S. (ed.) 1985. *Handbook of the birds of Europe, the Middle East and North Africa: the birds of the Western Palearctic.* Vol. 5. Oxford Univ. Press, Oxford.

Crockett, A. B., & Hadow, H. H. 1975. Nest site selection by Williamson's and Red-naped Sapsuckers. *Condor* 77: 365-368.
— & Hansley, P. L. 1977. Coition, nesting and postfledging behavior of Williamson's sapsuckers in Colorado. *Living Bird* 16: 7-19.
Cruz, A. 1977. Ecology and behavior of the Jamaican Woodpecker. *Bull. Florida State Mus., Biol. Sciences* 32: 149-204.
Cuisin, M. 1973. Note sur la repartition du Pic noir. *L'Oiseaux et RFO* 43: 305-313.
Cyrus, D., & Robson, N. 1980. *Bird atlas of Natal.* Univ. Natal Press, Pietermaritzburg.
Danielsen, F., Balete, D. S., Christensen, T. D., Heegaard, M., Jacobsen, O. F., Jensen, A., Lund, T., & Poulsen, M. K. 1993. *Conservation of biological diversity in the Sierra Madre Mountains of Isabela and southern Cagayan Province, The Philippines.* DENR-ICBP, Manila, and DOF, Copenhagen.
Davis, D. E. 1955. Determinate laying in Barn Swallows and Black-billed Magpies. *Condor* 57: 81-87.
Davis, J. 1965. Natural history, variation, and distribution of the Strickland's Woodpecker. *Auk* 82: 537-590.
deBruyn, G. J., Goosen-deRoo, L., Hubregtse-van den Berg, A. I. M., & Feijen, H. R. 1972. Predation of ants by woodpeckers. *Ekologia Polska* 20: 83-91.
Deignan, H. G. 1945. The birds of northern Thailand. *Bull. U.S. Natl Mus.* no. 186: 1-616.
— 1955. Remarks on *Picus vittatus* Vieillot and some of its allies. *Ibis* 97: 18-24.
Delacour, J., & Jabouille, P. 1931. *Les Oiseaux de l'Indochine Française.* Exposition Coloniale Internationale, Paris.
Dement'ev, G. P., & Gladkov, N. A. 1966. *Birds of the Soviet Union.* Vol. 6. Israel Programme for Scientific Translation, Jerusalem.
Dennis, J. V. 1948. A last remnant of the Ivory-billed Woodpeckers in Cuba. *Auk* 65: 497-507.
Desfayes, M, & Praz, J. C. 1978. Notes on habitat and distribution of montane birds in southern Iran. *Bonn. zool. Beitr.* 29: 18-37.
Diamond, J. 1990. Alone in a crowded universe. Woodpeckers can teach us about the probability of visits by flying saucers. *Natural History* 99: 30-34.
Dickey, D. R., & van Rossem, A. J. 1938. The birds of El Salvador. *Zool. Ser. Field Mus. Nat. Hist.* 23: 1-609.
Dickinson, E. C., Kennedy, R. S., & Parkes, K. C. 1991. *The birds of the Philippines.* BOU Check-list no. 12. BOU, Tring, Herts.
Diesselhorst, G. 1968. Beiträge zur Ökologie der Vögel Zentral- und Ost-Nepals. Pp. 1-420 in W. Hellmich (ed.), *Khumbu Himal*, vol. 2. Universitätsverlag Wagner, Innsbruck & München.
Dorst, J. 1956. Notes sur la biologie des Colaptès, *Colaptes rupicola*, des hauts plateaux Péruviens. *L'Oiseau et RFO* 26: 118-125.
Downer, A., & Sutton, R. 1990. *Birds of Jamaica.* Cambridge Univ. Press, Cambridge.
Dowsett-Lemaire, F. 1983. Studies of a breeding population of Olive Woodpeckers, *Dendropicos griseocephalus* in montane forests of south-central Africa. *Gerfaut* 73: 221-237.
— 1989. Ecological and biogeographical aspects of forest bird communities in Malawi. *Scopus* 13: 1-80.
Dubs, B. 1983. *Phloeoceastes leucopogon* - Brutvogel im Pantanal, Mato Grosso do Sul, Brasilien. *J. Ornith.* 124: 294.
— 1983. *Die Vögel des südlichen Mato Grosso.* Verbandsdruckerei-Betadruck, Bern.
— 1992. *Birds of southwestern Brazil.* Betrona Verlag, Küsnacht.
Dunning, J. B. 1992. *CRC handbook of avian body masses.* CRC Press, Boca Raton, Florida.
duPont, J. E. 1971. *Philippine birds.* Delaware Mus. Nat. Hist., Greenville, Delaware.
Earlé, R. A. 1986. Reappraisal of variation in the Ground Woodpecker *Geocolaptes olivaceus* (Gmelin) (Aves: Picidae) with notes on its moult. *Navors. nas. Mus., Bloemfontein* 5: 72-92.
Eates, K. R. 1937. A note on the distribution and nidification of the Northern Yellow-fronted Pied Woodpecker [*Leiopicus mahrattensis blanfordi* (Blyth)] in Sind. *J. Bombay Nat. Hist. Soc.* 39: 628-631.
Everett, M. J. 1987. The Arabian Woodpecker in North Yemen. *Sandgrouse* 9: 74-77.
Faaborg, J. 1985. Ecological constraints in West Indian Bird distributions. *Orn. Monogr.* 36: 621-653.
Feindt, P. 1956. Zur Psychologie und Stimme des Mittelspechts. Pp. 99-113 in *Weigold-Festschrift, Natur und Jagd in Niedersachsen.*
—, & Reblin, K. 1959. Die Brutbiologie des Mittelspechts. *Beitr. Naturkde Niedersachsen* 12: 36-48.
ffrench, R. 1973 (2nd ed. 1990). *A guide to the birds of Trinidad and Tobago.* Livingston, Wynnewood, Penn.
Fiora, A. 1933. El peso de las aves. *Hornero* 5: 174-188.
Fjeldså, J. 1991. Biogeographic patterns in birds of high Andean relict woodlands. *Acta XX Congr. Int. Orn.*: 342-353.
— & Krabbe, N. 1990. *Birds of the high Andes.* Apollo Books, Svendborg.
Fleming, R. L., Sr, Fleming, R. L., Jr, & Bangdel, L. S. 1984 (3rd ed.). *Birds of Nepal.* Nature Himalayas, Kathmandu.
Fletcher, S. D., & Moore, W. S. 1992. Further analysis of allozyme variation in the Northern Flicker, in comparison with mitochondrial DNA variation. *Condor* 94: 988-991.
Franke, I. 1991. Disjunct bird distributions along the west slope of the Peruvian Andes. *Acta XX Congr. Int. Orn.*: 317-326.
Franz, J. 1937. Beobachtungen über das Brutleben des Weißrückenspechts. *Beitr. Fortpflbiol. Vögel* 13: 165-174.
Fretwell, S. 1978. Competition for discrete versus continuous resources: tests for predictions from the MacArthur-Levins models. *Amer. Nat.* 112: 73-81.
Fritsch, R. H. 1952. Speicher und Schmieden der Spechte. *Naturw. Rundsch.* 5: 108-112.
Frugis, S., Malaguzzi, G., Vicini, G., & Cristina, P. 1988. *Guida ai Picchi del mondo.* Museo Regionale di Scienze Naturali, Torino.
Fujii, T. 1993. Initial roosting time of the Japanese Green Woodpecker *Picus awokera. Strix* 12: 222-223.
Gamboa, G. J., & Brown, K. M. 1976. Comparative foraging behavior of six sympatric woodpecker species. *Proc. Iowa Acad. Sci.* 82: 179-181.

Ganguli, U. 1975. *A guide to the birds of the Delhi area.* Indian Council of Agricultural Research, New Delhi.
Gatter, W. 1981. Der Schwarzspecht-ein Zugvogel? *Beih. Veröff. Naturschutz Landschaftspflege Bad.-Württ.* 20: 75-82.
Gebauer, A. 1982. Komfortverhalten und Rekelbewegungen beim Buntspecht *Dendrocopos major. Zool. Anz.* 208: 283-288.
— 1984. Die Lautentwicklung beim Buntspecht, *Dendrocopos major* (L.). *Mitt. zool. Mus. Berl.* 60, Suppl.: *Ann. Orn.* 8: 107-127.
—, Kaiser, M., & Wallschläger, D. 1984. Beobachtungen zum Verhalten und zur Lautgebung des Mittelspechts (*Dendrocopos medius*) während der Nestlingszeit. Teil I: Brutbiologische Daten und Verhalten. *Beitr. Vogelkd.* 30: 115-137.
—, — & — 1992. Beobachtungen zum Verhalten und zur Lautgebung des Mittelspechts (*Dendrocopos medius*) während der Nestlingszeit. Teil II: Das Lautinventar. *Beitr. Vogelkd.* 38: 175-199.
Gibbs, J. N. 1983. 'Sap-sucking' by woodpeckers in Britain. *Brit. Birds* 76: 109-117.
Glutz von Blotzheim, U. N., & Bauer, K. 1980. *Handbuch der Vögel Mitteleuropas.* Vol. 9. Akademische Verlagsgesellschaft, Wiesbaden.
Godfrey, W. E. 1986. *The birds of Canada.* Natl. Mus. Canada, Ottawa.
Gonzales, P. C., & Rees, C. P. 1988. *Birds of the Philippines.* Haribon Foundation for the Conservation of Natural Resources, Manila.
Goodge, W. R. 1972. Anatomical evidence for phylogenetic relationships among woodpeckers. *Auk* 89: 65-85.
Goodman, S. M., & Gonzales, P. C. 1990. The birds of Mt. Isarog National Park, southern Luzon, Philippines, with particular reference to altitudinal distribution. *Fieldiana: Zoology* 60: 1-39.
Goodwin, D. 1968. Notes on woodpeckers (Picidae). *Bull. Brit. Mus. (Nat. Hist.), Zool.* 17: 1-44.
Gore, M. E. J., & Pyong-Oh, W. 1971. *The birds of Korea.* Royal Asiatic Soc., Seoul.
— & Gepp, A. R. M. 1978. *Las aves del Uruguay.* Mosca Hnos., Montevideo. 283pp.
Gowaty, P. A., & Lennartz, M. R. 1985. Sex ratios of nestling and fledgling Red-cockaded Woodpeckers (*Picoides borealis*) favor males. *Amer. Nat.* 126: 347-353
Greenway, J. C., Jr. 1940. Oriental forms of *Picus canus. Auk* 57: 550-560.
— 1943. Oriental forms of the Pygmy Woodpecker. *Auk* 60: 564-575.
Grimes, L. G. 1976. The occurrence of cooperative breeding behaviour in African birds. *Ostrich* 47: 1-15.
Günther, E. 1993. 'Umgekehrte Begattung' beim Mittelspecht (*Dendrocopos medius*). *Orn. Jber. Mus. Heineanum* 11: 107-108.
Gwynne, D. T. 1991. Sexual competition among females: what causes courtship-role reversal? *Trends Ecol. Evol.* 6: 118-121.
Gyldenstolpe, N. 1916. Zoological results of the Swedish Zoological Expeditions to Siam 1911-1912 & 1914-1915. IV. Birds II. *Kungl. Svenska Vetenskapsakademiens Handlingar* 56 (2): 1-160.
— 1951. The ornithology of the Rio Purús region in Western Brazil. *Arkiv f. Zool.* Ser 2, vol. 2, no. 1: 1-320.
Hackenberg, C. 1989. Ornithologische Notizen zum borealen Teil Patagoniens. *Trochilus* 10: 113-148.
Hadow, H. H. 1973. Winter ecology of migrant and resident Lewis' Woodpeckers in Southeastern Colorado. *Condor* 75: 210-224.
Haffer, J. 1961. A new subspecies of woodpecker from northern Colombia: *Picumnus cinnamomeus persaturatus, subsp. nova. Novedades Colombianas* 1: 397-400.
Hagen, J. M., & Reed, J. M. 1988. Red color bands reduce fledging success in Red-cockaded Woodpeckers. *Auk* 105: 498-503.
Hågvar, S., Hågvar, G., & Mønness, E. 1990. Nest site selection in Norwegian woodpeckers. *Holarct. Ecol.* 13: 156-165.
Haig, S. M., Belthoff, J. R., & Allen, D. H. 1993. Examination of population structure in Red-cockaded Woodpeckers using DNA profiles. *Evolution* 47: 185-194.
—, Walters, J. R., & Plissner, J. H. 1994. Genetic evidence for monogamy in the cooperatively breeding Red-cockaded Woodpeckers. *Behav. Ecol. Sociobiol.* 34: 295-303.
Haila, Y., & Järvinen, O. 1977. Competition and habitat selection in two large woodpeckers. *Ornis Fenn.* 54: 73-78.
Håland, A., & Toft, G. O. 1983. Hvitryggspettens forekomst og habitatvalg på Vestlandet. *Vår Fuglef.* 6: 3-14.
Harwin, R. M. 1972. Aggressive behaviour of *Campethera bennetti. Ostrich* 43: 183-184.
Hauser, D. C. 1959. Reverse mounting in the Red-bellied Woodpeckers. *Auk* 76: 361.
Haverschmidt, F. 1951. Notes on the life history of *Picumnus minutissimus* in Surinam. *Ibis* 93: 196-200.
— 1953. Notes on the life history of the Blood-colored Woodpecker in Surinam. *Auk* 70: 21-25.
— 1968. *Birds of Surinam.* Oliver & Boyd Ltd, Edinburgh & London.
Heim de Balsac, H., & Mayaud, N. 1962. *Les oiseaux du Nord-ouest de l'Afrique.* Éd. P. Lechevalier, Paris.
Hendricks, P., McAuliffe J. R., & Valiente-Banuet A. 1990. On communal roosting and associated winter social behaviour of Grey-breasted Woodpeckers. *Condor* 92: 254-255.
Henry, G. M. 1971 (2nd ed.). *A guide to the birds of Ceylon.* Oxford Univ. Press, Oxford
Herbert, E. G. 1926. Nests and eggs of birds in central Siam. *J. Siam Soc. Nat. Hist.* Suppl. 6: 323-3??
Hilty, S. L., & Brown, W. L. 1984. *A guide to the birds of Colombia.* Princeton Univ. Press, Princeton.
Hindwood, K. A. 1959. The nesting of birds in the nests of social insects. *Emu* 59: 1-36.
Hochebner, T. 1993. Siedlungsdichte und Lebensraum einer randalpinen Population des Mittelspechts (*Picoides medius*) im niederösterreichischen Alpenvorland. *Egretta* 36: 25-37.
Hogstad, O. 1970. On the ecology of the Three-toed Woodpecker *Picoides tridactylus* (L.) outside the breeding season. *Nytt Mag. Zool.* 18: 221-227.
— 1971a. Stratification in winter feeding of the Great Spotted Woodpecker

Dendrocopos major and the Three-toed Woodpecker *Picoides tridactylus*. *Ornis Scand.* 2: 143-146.
— 1971b. Trekker fra flagspettens (*Dendrocopos major*) vinternaering. *Sterna* 10: 233-241.
— 1976. Sexual dimorphism and divergence in winter foraging behaviour of Three-toed Woodpeckers *Picoides tridactylus*. *Ibis* 118: 41-50.
— 1977. Seasonal change in intersexual niche differentiation of the Three-toed Woodpecker *Picoides tridactylus*. *Ornis Scand.* 8: 101-111.
— 1991. The effect of social dominance on foraging by the Three-toed Woodpecker *Picoides tridactylus*. *Ibis* 133: 271-276.
Hollom, P. A. D., Porter, R. F., Christensen, S., & Willis, I. 1988. *Birds of the Middle East and North Africa*. Poyser, Calton.
Hölzinger, J. 1990. Weißbrückenspecht *Dendrocopos leucotos* (Bechstein, 1803) Brutvogel auf dem Peloponnes. *Kartierung mediterr. Brutvögel* 4: 19-22.
Hooper, R. G., & Lennartz, M. R. 1981. Foraging behavior of the Red-cockaded Woodpecker in South Carolina. *Auk* 98: 321-334.
Hostos, R. A., & Chinchilla, L. P. 1989. Tres nuevas subspecies de aves (Picidae, Parulidae, Thraupidae) de la Sierra de Perija, Venezuela y lista hypotetica para la avifauna Colombiana de Perija. *Boletín no. 146 tom. 43 de la Sociedad Venezolana de Ciencias Naturales*: 7-24.
Howell, S. N. G., & Webb, S. In press (1995). *A guide to the birds of Mexico and northern Central America*. Oxford Univ. Press, Oxford.
Howell, T. R. 1952. Natural history and differentiation in the Yellow-bellied Sapsucker. *Condor* 54: 237-282.
— 1953. Racial and sexual difference in migration in *Sphyrapicus varius*. *Auk* 70: 118-126.
Hoy, G. 1968. Über Brutbiologie und Eier einiger Vögel aus Nordwest-Argentinien. *J. Ornithol.* 109: 425-433.
Hoyt, S. 1957. The ecology of the Pileated Woodpecker. *Ecology* 38: 246-256.
Huber, J. 1965. Großer Buntspecht bearbeitet Teichmuscheln. *Orn. Beob.* 62: 120-121.
Inouye, R. S., Huntley, N. J., & Inouye, D. W. 1981. Non-random orientation of Gila Woodpeckers' nest entrances in saguaro cacti. *Condor* 83: 88-89.
Inskipp, C., & Inskipp, T. 1991 (2nd ed.). *A guide to the birds of Nepal*. Christopher Helm, London.
Irwin, M. P. S. 1978. Distribution, overlap and ecological replacement in Bennett's Woodpecker *Campethera bennettii* and the Golden-tailed Woodpecker *Campethera abingoni* in Rhodesia. *Honeyguide* 93: 21-28.
— 1981. *The birds of Zimbabwe*. Quest Publishing, Salisbury.
Ishida, K. 1989. The protection of and research strategy for the populations of *Dendrocopos leucotos owstoni* and *Sapheopipo noguchii*. *Strix* 8: 249-260.
— 1990a. The status of woodpeckers in Japan. Pp. 13-20 in A. Carlson & G. Aulén (eds.), *Conservation and management of woodpecker populations*. Swedish Univ. Agric. Sci., Dept Wildlf. Ecol., Report 17, Uppsala.
— 1990b. Woodpecker activities and forest structure, with regard to recording techniques for conservation research. Pp. 103-115 in A. Carlson & G. Aulén (eds.), *Conservation and management of woodpecker populations*. Swedish Univ. Agric. Sci., Dept. Wildlf. Ecol., Report 17, Uppsala.
— & Ueta, M. 1992. Great Spotted Woodpecker *Dendrocopos major* and Japanese Pygmy Woodpecker *D. kizuki* foraged on lizards in Japan. *Jap. J. Ornithol.* 40: 75.
Jackson, J. A. 1970a. Character variation in the Hairy Woodpecker (*Dendrocopos villosus*). PhD dissertation, Univ. Kansas.
— 1970b. A quantitative study of the foraging ecology of Downy Woodpeckers. *Ecology* 51: 318-323.
— 1974. Gray rat snakes versus Red-cockaded Woodpeckers: predator-prey adaptations. *Auk* 91: 342-347.
— 1976. A comparison of some aspects of the breeding ecology of Red-headed and Red-bellied Woodpeckers in Kansas. *Condor* 78: 67-76.
— 1977. Red-cockaded Woodpeckers and pine red heart disease. *Auk* 94: 160-163.
— 1989. Past history, habits, and present status of the Ivory-billed Woodpecker (*Campephilus principalis*) in North America. Report to to the U.S. Fish and Wildlife Service.
— 1994. Red-cockaded Woodpecker (*Picoides borealis*). Pp. 1-19 in A. Poole & F. Gill (eds.), *The Birds of North America*, No. 85. The Academy of Natural Sciences, Washington, D. C.: The American Ornithologists' Union.
James, F. C. 1970. Geographic size variation in birds and its relationships to climate. *Ecology* 51: 365-390.
— 1991. Signs of trouble in the largest remaining population of Red-cockaded Woodpeckers. *Auk* 108: 419-423.
Jenkins, J. M. 1979. Foraging behavior of male and female Nuttall Woodpeckers. *Auk* 96: 418-420.
Jenni, L. 1983. Habitatnutzung, Nahrungserwerb und Nahrung von Mittel- und Buntspecht (*Dendrocopos medius* und *D. major*) sowie Bemerkungen zur Verbreitungsgeschichte des Mittelspechts. *Orn. Beob.* 80: 29-57.
Johnson, A. W. 1967. *The birds of Chile and adjacent regions of Argentina, Bolivia, and Peru*. Vol. 2. Platt, Buenos Aires.
Johnson, N. K., & Johnson, C. B. 1985. Speciation in sapsuckers (*Sphyrapicus*): II. Sympatry, hybridization, and mate preference in *S. ruber daggetti* and *S. nuchalis*. *Auk* 102: 1-15.
— & Zink, R. M. 1983. Speciation in sapsuckers (*Sphyrapicus*): I. Genetic differentiation. *Auk* 100: 871-884.
Johnston, D. W. 1975. Ecological analysis of the Cayman Island avifauna. *Bull. Florida State Mus.* 19: 235-300.
Judson, O. P., & Bennett, A. T. D. 1992. 'Anting' as food preparation: formic acid is worse on an empty stomach. *Behav. Ecol. Sociobiol.* 31: 437-439.
Junge, G. C. A., & Mees, G. F. 1958. The avifauna of Trinidad and Tobago. *Zool. Verh.* 37: 1-172.
Kaiser, M. 1990. Untersuchungen zur Biomechanik des Balztrommelns der Spechte (*Picidae*). *Beitr. Vogelkd.* 36: 129-159.
Kalisz, P. J., & Boettcher, S. E. 1991. Active and abandoned Red-cockaded Woodpecker habitat in Kentucky. *J. Wildl. Manage.* 55: 146-154.
Kazama, T. 1980. Telephone pole breakage caused by Green Woodpeckers *Picus awokera*. *J. Yamashina Inst. Ornithol.* 12: 225-226.
Kelly, J. F., Pletschet, S. M., & Leslie, D. M., Jr. 1993. Habitat associations of Red-cockaded Woodpecker cavity trees in an old-growth forest of Oklahoma. *J. Wildl. Manage.* 57: 122-128.

Kilham, L. 1958. Sealed-in winter stores of Red-headed Woodpeckers. *Wilson Bull.* 70: 107-113.
— 1959a. Mutual tapping of the Red-headed Woodpecker. *Auk* 76: 235-236.
— 1959b. Bark-eating of Red-headed Woodpeckers. *Condor* 61: 371-373.
— 1959c. Territorial behavior of wintering Red-headed Woodpeckers. *Wilson Bull.* 70: 347-358.
— 1959d. Head-scratching and wing-stretching of woodpeckers. *Auk* 76: 527-528.
— 1959e. Behavior and methods of communication of Pileated Woodpeckers. *Condor* 61: 377-387.
— 1961. Downy Woodpeckers scaling bark on diseased elms. *Wilson Bull.* 73: 89.
— 1962a. Nest sanitation of Yellow-bellied Sapsucker. *Wilson Bull.* 74: 96-97.
— 1962b. Reproductive behavior of Downy Woodpeckers. *Condor* 64: 126-133.
— 1965. Differences in feeding behavior of male and female Hairy Woodpeckers. *Wilson Bull.* 77: 134-145.
— 1966. Reproductive behavior of Hairy Woodpeckers. I. Pair formation and courtship. *Wilson Bull.* 78: 251-265.
— 1968. Reproductive behavior of Hairy Woodpeckers. II. Nesting and habitat. *Wilson Bull.* 80: 286-305.
— 1970. Feeding behavior of Downy Woodpeckers. I. Preference for paper birches and sexual differences. *Auk* 87: 544-556.
— 1971. Reproductive behavior of Yellow-bellied Sapsuckers I. Preference for nesting in *Fomes*-infected aspens and nest hole interrelations with flying squirrels, racoons, and other animals. *Wilson Bull.* 83: 159-171.
— 1972a. Shortness of tail in Red-crowned Woodpeckers and their habit of entering roost holes backward. *Condor* 74: 202-204.
— 1972b. Habits of the Crimson-crested Woodpecker in Panama. *Wilson Bull.* 84: 28-47.
— 1973a. Colonial-type nesting in Yellow-shafted Flickers as related to staggering of nesting times. *Bird-Banding* 44: 317-318.
— 1973b. Unusual attack of intruding male on a nesting pair of Pileated Woodpeckers. *Condor* 75: 349-350.
— 1974a. Loud vocalizations by Pileated Woodpeckers on approach to roosts or nest holes. *Auk* 91: 634-636.
— 1974b. Copulatory behavior of Downy Woodpeckers. *Wilson Bull.* 86: 23-34.
— 1974c. Early breeding season behavior of Downy Woodpeckers. *Wilson Bull.* 86: 407-418.
— 1977. Nesting behavior of Yellow-bellied Sapsuckers. *Wilson Bull.* 89: 310-324.
— 1979. Chestnut-colored Woodpeckers feeding as a pair on ants. *Wilson Bull.* 91: 149-150.
King, B. 1978. April bird observations in Saudi Arabia. *J. Saudi Arabian Nat. Hist. Soc.* No. 21: 3-24.
—, & Dickinson, E. C. 1975. *A field guide to the birds of South-East Asia*. Collins, London.
King, Bernard, 1974. Anting-like behaviour and food of Wryneck. *Brit. Birds* 67: 388.
Kipp, F. A. 1956. Progressive Merkmale des Jugendkleides bei den Spechten. *J. Ornithol.* 97: 403-410.
Kirby, V. C. 1980. An adaptive modification in the ribs of woodpeckers and piculets (Picidae). *Auk* 97: 521-532.
Klima, M. 1959. Einige Beobachtungen über das Spechtringeln an Bäumen. *Zool. Listy* 8: 33-36.
Knystautas, A. J. V., & Sibnev, J. B. 1987. *Die Vogelwelt Ussuriens: Avifaunistisches zwischen Amur und Japanischem Meer*. Ziemsen, Wittenberg Lutherstadt.
Koch, R. F., Courchesne, A. E., & Collins, C. T. 1970. Sexual differences in foraging behavior of White-headed Woodpeckers. *Bull. Soc. Calif. Acad. Sci.* 69: 60-64.
Koen, J. H. 1988. Stratal distribution and resource partitioning of birds in the Knysna forest, South Africa. *Afr. J. Ecol.* 26: 229-238.
Koenig, W. D. 1984. Geographic variation in the clutch size in the Northern Flicker (*Colaptes auratus*): Support for Ashmole's hypothesis. *Auk* 101: 698-706.
— 1986. Geographical ecology of clutch size variation in North American woodpeckers. *Condor* 88: 499-504.
— & Mumme, R. L. 1987. *Population ecology of the cooperatively breeding Acorn Woodpecker*. Princeton Univ. Press, Princeton, N.J.
—, — & Pitelka, F. A. 1983. Pp. 235-261 in S. K. Waser (ed.), *Social behaviour of female vertebrates*. Academic Press, New York.
—, — & —1984. The breeding system of the Acorn Woodpecker in central coastal California. *Z. Tierpsychol.* 65: 289-308.
—, Stanback, M. T., & Hooge, P. N. 1991. Distress calls in the Acorn Woodpecker. *Condor* 93: 637-643.
Koepcke, M. 1983 (2nd ed.). *The birds of the department of Lima, Peru*. Harrowood books, Newton Square, Penn.
Kojima, K., & Arisawa, H. 1983. Habitat and food habit of the Black Woodpecker *Dryocopus martius* in Hokkaido. *Tori* 32: 109-111.
— & Matsuoka, S. 1985. Studies on the food habits of four sympatric species of woodpeckers. I. Grey-headed Green Woodpecker *Picus canus* in winter. *Tori* 33: 103-111.
-- & — 1985. Studies on the food habits of four sympatric species of woodpeckers. II. Black Woodpecker *Dryocopus martius* from winter to early spring. *Tori* 34: 1-6.
Koplin, J. R. 1969. The numerical response of woodpeckers to insect prey in a subalpine forest in Colorado. *Condor* 71: 436-438.
Kyu-Hwang, H., & Pyong-Oh, W. 1982. Ecology and conservation of the Tristram's Woodpecker, *Dryocopus javensis richardsi* Tristram in Korea. *J. Yamashina Inst. Ornithol.* 14: 254-269.
Labranche, M. S., & Walters, J. R. 1994. Double brooding in Red-cockaded Woodpeckers. *Wilson Bull.* 106: 403-407.
Land, H. C. 1963. A tropical feeding tree. *Wilson Bull.* 75: 199-200.
— 1970. *Birds of Guatemala*. Livingston, Wynnewood, Penn.
László, V. 1988. The study of bird species foraging on the bark. *Aquila* 95: 83-92.
Lawrence, L. de K. 1967. A comparative life-history study of four species of woodpeckers. *Ornithol. Monogr.* no. 5: 1-156.

Leck, C. F. 1969. Observations of birds exploiting a Central American fruit tree. *Wilson Bull.* 81: 264-269.

Lekagul, B., & Round, P. D. 1991. *A guide to the birds of Thailand.* Saha Karn Bhaet, Bangkok.

Lennartz, M. R., & Harlow, R. F. 1979. The role of parent and helper Red-cockaded Woodpeckers at the nest. *Wilson Bull.* 91: 331-335.

—, Hooper, R. G., & Harlow, R. F. 1987. Sociality and cooperative breeding of Red-cockaded Woodpeckers, *Picoides borealis. Behav. Ecol. Sociobiol.* 20: 77-88.

Ligon, J. D. 1968a. Observations on Strickland's Woodpecker, *Dendrocopos stricklandi. Condor* 70: 83-84.

— 1968b. Sexual differences in foraging behavior in two species of *Dendrocopos* woodpeckers. *Auk* 85: 203-215.

— 1970. Behavior and breeding biology of the Red-cockaded Woodpecker. *Auk* 87: 255-278.

— 1973. Foraging behavior of the White-headed Wodpecker in Idaho. *Auk* 90: 862-869.

Lima, S. L. 1983. Downy Woodpecker foraging behavior: foraging by expectation and energy intake rate. *Oecologia* 58: 232-237.

— 1984. Downy Woodpecker foraging behavior: efficient sampling in simple stochastic environments. *Ecology* 65: 166-174.

Löhrl, H. 1977. Zur Nahrungssuche von Grau- und Grünspecht *(Picus canus, P. viridis)* im Winterhalbjahr. *Vogelwelt* 98: 15-22.

— & Thielcke, G. 1969. Zur Brutbiologie, Ökologie und Systematik einiger Waldvögel Afghanistans. *Bonn. zool. Beitr.* 20: 85-98.

Lüdicke, M. 1933. Wachstum und Abnutzung des Vogelschnabels. *Zool. Jb., Abt. Anat. Ontog. Tiere* 57: 465-534.

Lundquist, R. W., & Manuwal, D. A. 1990. Seasonal differences in foraging habitat of cavity-nesting birds in the southern Washington Cascades. *Studies in Avian Biology* 13: 218-225.

Macdonald, D. W., & Henderson, D. G. 1977. Aspects of the behaviour and ecology of mixed-species bird flocks in Kashmir. *Ibis* 119: 481-493.

MacDonald, J. D. 1957. *Contribution to the ornithology of western South Africa.* Trustees Brit. Mus., London.

McFarlane, R. W. 1992. *A stillness in the pines. The ecology of the Red-cockaded Woodpecker.* W. W. Norton & Co., New York.

MacKinnon, J. 1990. *Field guide to the birds of Java and Bali.* Gadjah Mada Univ. Press, Yogyakarta.

— & Phillips, K. 1993. *The birds of Borneo, Sumatra, Java, and Bali.* Oxford Univ. Press, Oxford.

Maclean, G. L. 1985. *Roberts' Birds of South Africa.* 5th ed. Cape Town, J. Voelcker Bird Book Fund.

MacRoberts, M. H. 1970. Notes on the food habits and food defense of the Acorn Woodpecker. *Condor* 72: 196-204.

— & MacRoberts, B. R. 1976. Social organization and behavior of the acorn woodpecker in central coastal California. *Ornithol. Monogr.* 21: 1-115.

Majumdar, N. 1978. On the occurrence of the Black-naped Green Woodpecker, *Picus canus hessei* Gyldenstolpe (Piciformes: Picidae) in Orissa. *J. Bombay Nat. Hist. Soc.* 75: 924.

Malacarne, G., Cucco, M., & Camanni, S. 1991. Coordinated visual displays and vocal duetting in different ecological situations among Western Palearctic non-passerine birds. *Ethology, Ecology & Evolution* 3: 207-219.

Malherbe, A. 1861. *Monographie des Picidés.* Vols. 1-3. Metz.

Marelli, C. A. 1919. Sobre el contenido del estómago de algunas aves. *Hornero* 1: 221-228.

Marin, A. M., & Carrion B, J. M. 1991. Nests and eggs of some Ecuadorian birds. *Ornitologia Neotropical* 2: 44-46.

Marshall, D. B. In press. *Threatened and sensitive wildlife of Oregon's forests and woodlands.* Audubon Soc., Portland, Oregon.

Martens, J., & Eck, S. In press. Towards an ornithology of the Himalayas. Systematics, ecology and vocalizations of Nepal birds. *Bonn. zool. Monogr.*

Martin, J. W., & Kroll, J. C. 1975. Hoarding of corn by Golden-fronted Woodpeckers. *Wilson Bull.* 87: 553.

Martin, T. E. 1993. Evolutionary determinants of clutch size in cavity-nesting birds: Nest predation or limited breeding opportunities? *Amer. Nat.* 142: 937-946.

— & Li, P. 1992. Life history traits of open- vs. cavity-nesting birds. *Ecology* 73: 579-592.

Martins, R. 1988. April bird observations in the Yemen Arab Republic (North Yemen), 1987. *OSME Bull.* 21: 1-9.

Matsuoka, S. 1979. Ecological significance of the early breeding in White-backed woodpeckers *Dendrocopos leucotos. Tori* 28: 63-75.

Matthysen, E. 1990. Upward and downward movements by bark-foraging birds: the importance of habitat structure. *Ibis* 132: 128-129.

—, Grubb, T. C., & Cimprich, D. 1991. Social control of sex-specific foraging behaviour in Downy Woodpeckers, *Picoides pubescens. Anim. Behav.* 42: 515-517.

May, P. R. A., Fuster, J. M., Newman, P. A., & Hirschman, A. 1976. Woodpeckers and head injury. *Lancet* 1: 454-455.

—, —, Haber, J., & Hirschman, A. 1979. Woodpecker drilling behavior. An endorsement of the rotational theory of impact brain injury. *Arch. Neurol.* 36: 370-373.

Mayfield, H. 1958. Nesting of Black-backed Three-toed Woodpecker in Michigan. *Wilson Bull.* 70: 195-196.

Medway, Lord, & Wells, D. R. 1976. *The birds of the Malay Peninsula.* Vol. 5. Witherby, London.

Meijering, M. P. D. 1967. Werkzeuge der Spechte. *Ardea* 55: 91-111.

Meinertzhagen, R. 1954. *Birds of Arabia.* Oliver & Boyd, Edinburgh.

Mellen, T. K., Meslow, E. C., & Mannan, R. W. 1992. Summertime home range and habitat use of Pileated Woodpeckers in western Oregon. *J. Wildl. Manage.* 56: 96-103.

Menon, G. K. 1985. On the source of 'resin' in the plumage of Heart Spotted Woodpecker, *Hemicircus canente. Pavo* 23: 107-109.

Meyer, A. B., & Wigglesworth, L. W. 1898. *The birds of Celebes and the neighbouring islands.* Vol. 1. R. Friedländer, Berlin.

Meyer de Schauensee, R., & Phelps, W. H., Jr. 1978. *A guide to the birds of Venezuela.* Princeton Univ. Press, Princeton N.J.

Miech, P. 1986. Zum Ringeln einiger Spechtarten (Picinae) in Flachland.

Orn. Ber. Berlin (West) 11: 39-76.

Miller, A. H. 1955. The avifauna of the Sierra del Carmen of Coahuila, Mexico. *Condor* 57: 154-178.

— 1963. Seasonal activity and ecology of the avifauna of an American equatorial cloud forest. *Univ. Cal. Publ. Zool.* 66: 1-73.

— & Bock, C. E. 1972. Natural history of the Nuttall Woodpecker at the Hastings reservation. *Condor* 74: 284-294.

Milne, K. A., & Hejl, S. J. 1989. Nest-site characteristics of White-headed Woodpeckers. *J. Wildl. Manage.* 53: 50-55.

Moore, W. S. A., & Koenig, W. D. 1986. Comparative reproductive success of Yellow-shafted, Red-shafted and hybrid Flickers across a hybrid zone. *Auk* 103: 42-51.

Moran, S. 1977. Distribution and characteristics of the damage of the Syrian Woodpecker, *Dendrocopos syriacus* (Hemp. & Ehr.) (Aves: Picidae), in polyethylene irrigation pipes in fruit orchards. *Phytoparasitica* 5: 127-139.

Morrison, M. L., & With, K. A. 1987. Interseasonal and intersexual resource partitioning in Hairy and White-headed Woodpeckers. *Auk* 104: 225-233.

Morse, D. H. 1972. Habitat utilization of the Red-cockaded Woodpecker during the winter. *Auk* 89: 429-435.

Moskovits, D. 1978. Winter territorial and foraging behavior of Red-headed Woodpeckers in Florida. *Wilson Bull.* 90: 521-535.

Mumme, R. L., Koenig, W. D., & Pitelka, F. A. 1988. Costs and benefits of joint nesting in the Acorn Woodpecker. *Amer. Nat.* 131: 654-677.

Neill, A. J., & Harper, R. G. 1990. Red-bellied Woodpecker predation on nestling House Wrens. *Condor* 92: 789.

Nelson, E. W. 1898. The Imperial Ivory-billed Woodpecker, *Campephilus imperialis* (Gould). *Auk* 15: 217-223.

Nesbitt, S. A., Gilbert, D. T., & Barbour, D. B. 1978. Red-cockaded Woodpecker fall movements in a Florida flatwoods community. *Auk* 95: 145-151.

Newman, K. 1989. *Newman's Birds of Botswana.* Southern Book Publishers.

Nieto, A. M., & Pearman, M. 1992. Distribution, status and taxonomy of the near-threatened Black-bodied Woodpecker *Dryocopus schulzi. Bird Conserv. Interntl* 2: 253-271.

Nilsson, S. G., Johnsson, K., & Tjernberg, M. 1991. Is avoidance by Black Woodpeckers of old nest holes due to predators? *Anim. Behav.* 41: 439-441.

Noble, G. K. 1936. Courtship and sexual selection of the Flicker (*Colaptes auratus luteus*). *Auk* 53: 269-282.

Norberg, R. Å. 1981. Why foraging birds in trees should climb and hop upwards rather than downwards. *Ibis* 123: 281-288.

— 1986. Treecreeper climbing; mechanics, energetics and structural adaptations. *Ornis Scand.* 17: 191-209.

Noske, R. A. 1991. Field identification and ecology of the Greater Goldenback *Chrysocolaptes lucidus* in Malaysia. *Forktail* 6: 72-74.

Nuorteva, M., Patomäki, J., & Saari, L. 1981. Large poplar longhorn, *Saperda carcharias* (L.), as food for White-backed Woodpecker, *Dendrocopos leucotos* (Bechst.). *Silva Fennica* 15: 208-221.

Oatley, T. B., Earlé, R. A., & Prins, A. J. 1989. The diet and foraging behaviour of the Ground Woodpecker. *Ostrich* 60: 75-84.

Oberholser, H. C. 1974. *The bird life of Texas.* Univ. Texas Press, Austin & London.

Olrog, C. C. 1984. *Las aves Argentinas.* Administración de Parques Nacionales, Buenos Aires.

Olson, S. L. 1983. Evidence for a polyphyletic origin of the Piciformes. *Auk* 100: 126-133.

— 1985. The fossil record of birds. Pp. 79-238 in D. S. Farner, J. R. King & K. C. Parkes (eds.), *Avian Biology*, vol. 8. Academic Press, Orlando.

Olsson, O., Nilsson, I. N., Nilsson, S. G., Pettersson, B., Stagen, A., & Wiktander, U. 1992. Habitat preferences of the Lesser Spotted Woodpecker *Dendrocopos minor. Ornis Fennica* 69: 119-125.

Osmaston, B. B. 1906. Notes on Andaman birds with accounts of the nidification of several species whose nests and eggs have not been hitherto described. *J. Bombay Nat. Hist. Soc.* 17: 156-163.

— 1916. Curious habits of woodpeckers in the Kumaon hills. *J. Bombay Nat. Hist. Soc.* 24: 363-366.

Otvos, I. S. 1967. Observations on the feeding habits of some woodpeckers and woodcreepers. *Condor* 69: 522-525.

Ouellet, H. 1977. Relationships of woodpecker genera *Dendrocopos* Koch and *Picoides* Lacépède (Aves: Picidae). *Ardea* 65: 165-183.

Parker, T. A., & Parker, S. A. 1982. Behavioral and distributional notes on some unusual birds of a lower montane cloud forest in Peru. *Bull. Br. Orn. Club* 102: 63-70.

—, —, & Plenge, M. A. 1982. *An annotated checklist of Peruvian birds.* Buteo Books, Vermillion, S. Dakota.

—, Schulenberg, T. S., Graves, G. R., & Braun, M. J. 1985. The avifauna of the Huancabamba region, northern Peru. *Ornithol. Monogr.* 36: 169-197.

Pasinelli, G. 1993. Nachweis eines Helfers bei einer Brut des Mittelspechts *Dendrocopos medius. Orn. Beob.* 90: 303-304.

Payne, R. B. 1989. Egg size of African honeyguides (Indicatoridae): specialization for brood parasitism? *Tauraco* 1: 201-210.

Paz, U. 1987. *The birds of Israel.* Christopher Helm, London.

Peña, M. R. 1994. *Guia de aves Argentinas.* 2nd ed. Vol 3. L.O.L.A., Buenos Aires C.F.

Peterson, A. W., & Grubb, T. C., Jr. 1983. Artificial trees as a cavity substrate for woodpeckers. *J. Wildl. Manage.* 47: 790-798.

Peterson, R. T., & Chalif, E. L. 1973. *A field guide to Mexican birds.* Houghton Mifflin, Boston.

Pettersson, B. 1983. Foraging behaviour of the Middle Spotted Woodpecker *Dendrocopos medius* in Sweden. *Holarctic Ecol.* 6: 263-269.

— 1985. Extinction of an isolated population of the Middle Spotted Woodpecker *Dendrocopos medius* (L.) in Sweden and its relation to general theories on extinction. *Biol. Conserv.* 32: 335-353.

Pflumm, W. 1979. Beobachtungen zum Bearbeiten von Lärchenzapfen (*Larix decidua*) in einer Schmiede des Buntspechts (*Dendrocopos major*). *J. Ornithol.* 120: 64-72.

Phillips, A., Marshall, J., & Monson, G. 1964. *The birds of Arizona.* Univ. Arizona Press, Tucson.

Phillips, N. R. 1982. Observations on the birds of North Yemen in 1979. *Sandgrouse* 4: 37-59.

Phillips, W. W. A. 1978. *Annotated checklist of the birds of Ceylon (Sri Lanka).* Wildlife & Nature Protection Society of Sri Lanka & Ceylon Bird Club, Colombo.

Pierce, V., & Grubb, T. C. Jr. 1981. Laboratory studies of foraging in four bird species of deciduous woodland. *Auk* 98: 307-320.

Poliwanowa, N. N., Schibnew, J. B., & Poliwanow, W. M. 1974. Zur Biologie des Spitzflügelspechtes. *Falke* 21: 369-375.

Popp, J., & Ficken, M. S. 1991. Comparative analysis of acoustic structure of passerine and woodpecker nestling calls. *Bioacoustics* 3: 255-274.

Porter, M. L., Collopy, M. W., Labisky, R. F., & Littell, R. C. 1985. Foraging behavior of Red-cockaded Woodpeckers: an evaluation of research methodologies. *J. Wildl. Manage.* 49: 505-507.

Portmann, A. 1962. Zerebralisation und Ontogenese. *Medizin. Grundlagenfschg* 4: 1-62.

Prigogine, A., & Louette, M. 1983. Contacts secondaires entre les taxons appartenant à la superespèce *Dendropicos goertae*. *Gerfaut* 73: 9-83.

Proud, D. 1958. Woodpeckers drumming. *J. Bombay Nat. Hist. Soc.* 55: 350-351.

Pynnönen, A. 1939. Beiträge zur Kenntnis der Biologie finnischer Spechte. *Ann. Zool. Soc. Zool.-Bot.-Fenn. Vanamo* 7 (2): 1-166.

— 1943. Beiträge zur Kenntnis der Biologie finnischer Spechte. II. *Ann. Zool. Soc. Zool.-Bot.-Fenn. Vanamo* 9 (4): 1-60.

Rabor, D. S. 1977. *Philippine birds and mammals.* Univ. Philipp. Press, Quezon City.

Raffaele, H. A. 1989. *Birds of Puerto Rico and the Virgin Islands.* Princeton Univ. Press, Princeton, N.J.

Rand, A. L. 1951. Birds from Liberia. *Fieldiana: Zoology* 32: 558-653.

—, Friedmann, H., & Traylor, M. A., Jr. 1959. Birds from Gabon and Moyen Congo. *Fieldiana: Zoology* 41: 219-411.

— & Rabor, D. S. 1960. Birds of the Philippine Islands: Siquijor, Mount Malindac, Bohol, and Samar. *Fieldiana: Zoology* 35: 223-441.

Reed, J. M., Doerr, P. D., & Walters, J. R. 1988. Minimum viable population size of the Red-cockaded Woodpecker. *J. Wildl. Manage.* 52: 385-391.

Reiser, O. 1929. Naturwissenschaftlicher Beitrag über den Verlauf der von der k. Akademie der Wissenschaften in Wien 1903 unter Leitung von weiland Hofrat Dr. F. Steindachner nach Nordost-Brasilien entsendeten Sammelexpedition. *Ann. Nat. Hist. Mus. Wien* 43: 1-73.

Reller, A. W. 1972. Aspects of behavioral ecology of Red-headed and Red-bellied Woodpeckers. *Amer. Midl. Natur.* 88: 270-290.

Remsen, J. V. 1977. Five bird species new to Colombia. *Auk* 94: 363.

Rensch, B. 1931. Die Vogelwelt von Lombok, Sumbawa und Flores. *Mitt. Zool. Mus. Berlin* 17: 451-637.

Repasky, R. R., Blue, R. J., & Doerr, P. D. 1991. Laying Red-cockaded Woodpeckers cache bone fragments. *Condor* 93: 458-461.

Rice, J., Anderson, B. W., & Ohmart, R. D. 1980. Seasonal habitat selection by birds in the lower Colorado River valley. *Ecology* 61: 1402-1411.

Richardson, D. M., & Smith, D. L. 1992. Hardwood removal in Red-cockaded Woodpecker colonies using a shear V-blade. *Wildl. Soc. Bull.* 20: 428-433.

Ridgely, R. S., & Gwynne, J. A. 1989 (2nd ed.). *A guide to the birds of Panama.* Princeton Univ. Press, Princeton.

Ridgeway, R. 1914. The birds of North and Middle America. Part 6. *Bull. U. S. Natl. Mus.* No. 50: 1-882.

Ritter, W. E. 1938. *The California Woodpecker and I.* Univ. Calif. Press, Berkeley.

Roberts, G. R., McLachlan, G. R., & Liversidge, R. 1985. *Roberts' Birds of South Africa.* 4th ed. Cape Town, J. Voelcker Bird Book Fund.

Roberts, T. J. 1991. *The birds of Pakistan.* Vol. 1. Oxford Univ. Press, Karachi.

Robinson, H. C. 1927. *The birds of the Malay Peninsula.* Vol. I. H.F. & G. Witherby Ltd, London.

— 1928. *The birds of the Malay Peninsula.* Vol. II. H.F. & G. Witherby Ltd, London.

Robson, C.R., Eames, J.C., Wolstencroft, J.A., Cu, N. & Van La, T.1989. Recent records of birds from Viet Nam. *Forktail* 5: 71-97.

Robson, C.R., Eames, J.C., Cu, N. & Van La, T.1993. Further recent records of birds from Viet Nam. *Forktail* 8: 25-52.

Rogacheva, H. 1992. *The birds of Central Siberia.* Husum Druck- und Verlagsgesellschaft, Husum, Germany.

Rost, R., Lang, E., & Ley, H.-W. 1992. Männchen-Überschuß bei Schwarzspechtnestlingen (*Dryocopus martius*)? *J. Ornithol.* 133: 203-208.

Roth, R. R. 1978. Attacks on Red-headed Woodpeckers by flycatchers. *Wilson Bull.* 90: 450-451.

Rudolph, D. C., Kyle, H., & Conner, R. N. 1990. Red-cockaded Woodpeckers vs rat snakes: the effectiveness of the resin barrier. *Wilson Bull.* 102: 14-22.

Ruge, K. 1968. Zur Biologie des Dreizehenspechts *Picoides tridactylus* L. 1. Beobachtungsgebiet, Aktionsgebiet, Nahrungserwerb, Trommeln, Pendelbewegungen. *Orn. Beob.* 65: 109-124.

— 1969. Beobachtungen am Blutspecht *Dendrocopos syriacus* im Burgenland. *Vogelwelt* 90: 201-223.

— 1970a. Die Lautäußerungen des Blutspechts, *Dendrocopos syriacus. J. Ornithol.* 111: 412-419.

— 1970b. Zum Ringeln der Spechte. *J. Ornithol.* 111: 496.

— 1971. Zur Biologie des Dreizehenspechts *Picoides tridactylus* L. 3. Beobachtungen während der Brutzeit. *Orn. Beob.* 68: 256-271.

— 1973. Über das Ringeln der Spechte ausserhalb der subalpinen Nadelwälder. *Orn. Beob.* 70: 173-179.

Russel, S. M. 1964. A distributional study of the birds of British Honduras. *Orn. Monogr.* 1: 1-195.

Sassi, M. 1939. Die Vögel der Österreichischen Costa-Rica-Expedition. II. *Temminckia* 4: 135-222.

Sauer, F. 1957. Ein Beitrag zur Frage des 'Einemsens' von Vögeln. *J. Ornithol.* 98: 313-317.

Scherzinger, W. 1972. Beobachtungen am Dreizehenspecht (*Picoides tridactylus*) im Gebiet des Nationalparks Bayerischer Wald. *Orn. Mitt.* 24: 207-210.

— 1990. Is competition by the Great Spotted Woodpecker the cause for White-backed Woodpeckers rarity in Bavarian forest national park? Pp. 81-91 in A. Carlson & G. Aulén (eds.), *Conservation and management of woodpecker populations.* Swedish Univ. Agric. Sci., Dept. Wildlf. Ecol., Report 17, Uppsala.

Selander, R. K. 1966. Sexual dimorphism and differential niche utilization in birds. *Condor* 68: 113-151.

— & Giller, D. R. 1959. Interspecific relationships of woodpeckers in Texas. *Wilson Bull.* 71: 107-124.

— & — 1963. Species limits in the woodpecker genus *Centurus* (Aves). *Bull. Amer. Mus. Nat. Hist.* 124: 213-274.

Serez, M. 1983. Über die Spechte in Nordostanatolien (Türkei). *Orn. Mitt.* 35: 287-289.

Shaw, T. 1936. The birds of Hopei province. *Zoologica Sinica* 15: 1-974.

Sherrill D. M., & Case, V. M. 1980. Winter home ranges of 4 clans of Red-cockaded Woodpeckers in the Carolina Sandhills. *Wilson Bull.* 92: 369-375.

Short, L. L. 1965a. Hybridization in the flickers (*Colaptes*) of North America. *Bull. Amer. Mus. Nat. Hist.* 129: 307-428.

— 1965b. Variation in West Indian flickers (Aves, *Colaptes*). *Bull. Florida State Mus.* 10: 1-42.

— 1967. Variation in Central American flickers. *Wilson Bull.* 79: 5-21.

— 1969. The foraging association of Green-barred Flickers and Campo Flickers in Argentina. *Wilson Bull.* 81: 468-470.

— 1970a. Notes on the habits of some Argentine and Peruvian woodpeckers (Aves, Picidae). *Amer. Mus. Novitates* No. 2413: 1-37.

— 1970b. The habits and relationships of the Magellanic Woodpecker. *Wilson Bull.* 82: 115-129.

— 1971a. Woodpeckers without wood. *Nat. Hist. Mag.* 80: 66-74.

— 1971b. The systematics and behavior of some North American Woodpeckers, genus *Picoides* (Aves). *Bull. Amer. Mus. Nat. Hist.* 145: 1-118.

— 1971c. Notes on the habits of Bennett's Woodpeckers in Kruger Park. *Ostrich* 42: 71-72.

— 1971d. The affinity of African with Neotropical woodpeckers. *Ostrich* 8 (Suppl.): 35-40.

— 1971e. The evolution of terrestrial woodpeckers. *Amer. Mus. Novitates* No. 2467: 1-23.

— 1971f. Notes on South African woodpeckers. *Ostrich* 42: 89-98.

— 1972a. Systematics and behavior of South American Flickers (Aves, *Colaptes*). *Bull. Amer. Mus. Nat. Hist.* 149: 1-110.

— 1972b. Relationships among the four species of the superspecies *Celeus elegans* (Aves, Picidae). *Amer. Mus. Novitates* No. 2487: 1-26.

— 1973a. Habits of some Asian woodpeckers (Aves, Picidae). *Bull. Amer. Mus. Nat. Hist.* 152: 253-364.

— 1973b. Habits, relationships, and conservation of the Okinawa Woodpecker. *Wilson Bull.* 85: 5-20.

— 1974a. Habits of three endemic West Indian woodpeckers (Aves, Picidae). *Amer. Mus. Novitates* No. 2549: 1-44.

— 1974b. Relationship of *Veniliornis 'cassini' chocoensis* and V. *'cassini' caquetanus* with *V. affinis. Auk* 91: 631-634.

— 1974c. Habits and interactions of North American Three-toed Woodpeckers (*Picoides arcticus* and *Picoides tridactylus*). *Amer. Mus. Novitates* No. 2547: 1-42.

— 1975. A zoogeographic analysis of the South American Chaco avifauna. *Bull. Amer. Mus. Nat. Hist.* 154: 163-352.

— 1978. Sympatry in woodpeckers of lowland Malayan forest. *Biotropica* 10: 122-133.

— 1982. *Woodpeckers of the world.* Delaware Museum of Natural History, Greenville, Del.

— 1988. Woodpeckers. Pp. 512-566 in C. H. Fry, E. K. Urban & S. Keith (eds.), *The birds of Africa,* vol. 3. Academic Press, London.

— & Horne, J. F. M. 1981. Vocal and other behaviour of Stierling's Woodpecker. *Scopus* 5: 5-11.

— & — 1988. Current speciation problems in Afrotropical Piciformes. *Acta XIX Congr. Inter. Ornithol.*: 2519-2527.

— & — 1990. The Ivory-billed Woodpecker - The costs of specialization. Pp. 93-98 in A. Carlson & G. Aulén (eds.), *Conservation and management of woodpecker populations.* Swedish Univ. Agric. Sci., Dept. Wildlf. Ecol., Report 17, Uppsala.

—, & Muringo-Gichuki, C. 1990. Annotated Check-list of the Birds of East Africa. *Proc. Western Found. Vertebr. Zool.* 4: 61-246.

Sibley, C. G., Ahlquist, J. E., & Monroe, B. L., Jr. 1988. A classification of the living birds of the world based on DNA-DNA hybridization studies. *Auk* 105: 409-423.

— & Monroe, B. L., Jr. 1990. *Distribution and taxonomy of birds of the world.* Yale Univ. Press, New Haven & London.

Sick, H. 1961. Die Spechte *Trichopicus cactorum* und *Scapaneus leucopogon* in Brasilien. *J. Ornithol.* 102: 401-403.

— 1993. *Birds in Brazil.* Princeton Univ. Press, Princeton.

Sinclair, I., Hockey, P., & Tarboton, W. 1993. *Illustrated guide to the birds of Southern Africa.* New Holland, London.

Simpson, S. F., & Cracraft, J. 1981. The phylogenetic relationship of the Piciformes (class Aves). *Auk* 98: 481-494.

Skutch, A. F. 1948a. The life history of the Golden-naped Woodpecker. *Auk* 65: 225-260.

— 1948b. Life history of the Olivaceous Piculet and related forms. *Ibis* 90: 433-449.

— 1955. The Hairy Woodpecker in Central America. *Wilson Bull.* 67: 25-32.

— 1956. Roosting and nesting of the Golden-olive Woodpecker. *Wilson Bull.* 68: 118-128.

— 1969. Life histories of Central American birds III. *Cooper Ornith. Soc., Pacific Coast Avifauna,* no. 5: 1-580.

— 1985. *Life of the woodpecker.* Ibis, Santa Monica.

Slud, P. 1964. The birds of Costa Rica. Distribution and ecology. *Bull. Amer. Mus. Nat. Hist.* 128: 1-430.

— 1980. The birds of Hacienda Palo Verde, Guanacaste, Costa Rica. *Smiths. Contr. Zool.* no. 292. Smithsonian Institution Press, Washington, D.C.

Smith, C. F. 1941. Lewis, Woodpecker migration. *Condor* 43: 76.

Smythies, B. E. 1953. *The birds of Burma.* 2nd ed. Oliver & Boyd, London.

— 1981. (3rd ed.) .*The birds of Borneo.* Malayan Nature Soc, Kuala Lumpur.

Snyder, D. E. 1966. *The birds of Guyana.* Peabody Museum, Salem, Mass.

Southern, W. E. 1960. Copulatory behavior of the Red-headed Woodpecker. *Auk* 77: 218-219.

Spitznagel, A. 1993. Warum sind Spechte schwierig zu erfassende Arten? *Beih. Veröff. Naturschutz Landschaftspflege Bad.-Württ.* 67: 59-70.

Spring, L. W. 1965. Climbing and pecking in some North American wood-peckers. *Condor* 67: 457-488.

Stacey, P. B., & Bock, C. E. 1978. Social plasticity in the Acorn Woodpecker. *Science* 202: 1298-1300.

Stacey, P. B., & Ligon, J. D. 1987. Territory quality and dispersal options in the Acorn Woodpecker, and a challenge to the habitat-saturation model of cooperative breeding. *Am. Natur.* 130: 654-676.

Stager, K. E. 1961. A new bird of the genus *Picumnus* from eastern Brazil. *Los Angeles County Mus. Contr. Sci.* no. 46: 1-4.

— 1968a. A new piculet from Amazonian Bolivia. *Los Angeles County Mus. Contr. Sci.* no. 143: 1-2.

— 1968b. A new piculet from southeastern Peru. *Los Angeles County Mus. Contr. Sci.* no. 153: 1-4.

Stagg, A. J. 1985. *The Birds of S. W. Saudi Arabia, an annotated check-list.* 2nd ed. Stagg, Riyadh.

Stanback, M. T. 1994. Dominance within broods of the cooperatively breed-ing Acorn Woodpecker. *Anim. Behav.* 47: 1121-1126.

Stanford, J. K., & Mayr, E. 1941. The Vernay-Cutting expedition to northern Burma. Part V. *Ibis* 5, 14th series: 479-518.

Steinbacher, J. 1934. Untersuchungen über den Zungenapparat indischer Spechte. *J. Ornithol.* 82: 399-408.

— 1957. Über den Zungenapparat einiger neotropischer Spechte. *Senckenbergiana Biologica* 38: 259-270.

Stenberg, I. 1990. Preliminary results of a study on woodpeckers in Møre and Romsdal county, western Norway. Pp. 67-79 in A. Carlson & G. Aulén (eds.), *Conservation and management of woodpecker populations.* Swedish Univ. Agric. Sci. Dept. Wildl. Ecol., Report 17, Uppsala.

Stickel, D. W. 1965a. Territorial and breeding habits of Red-bellied Wood-peckers. *Amer. Midl. Natur.* 74: 110-118.

— 1965b. Wing-stretching of Red-bellied Woodpeckers (*Centurus carolinus*). *Auk* 82: 503.

Stiles, G. F., & Skutch, A. F. 1989. *A guide to the birds of Costa Rica.* Cornell Univ. Press, Ithaca, NY.

Stresemann, E. (G. Heinrich) 1940. Die Vögel von Celebes. Teil III. Systematik und Biologie. *J. Ornithol.* 87: 389-487

— & Heinrich, G. 1940. Die Vögel aus Mount Victoria. *Mitt. Zool. Mus. Berlin* 24: 151-264.

— & Stresemann, V. 1966. Die Mauser der Vögel. *J. Ornithol.* 107 (Suppl.): 1-445.

Südbeck, P. 1993. Zur Territorialität beim Grauspecht (*Picus canus*). *Beih. Veröff. Naturschutz Landschaftspflege Bad.-Württ.* 67: 143-156.

— & Meinecke, H. 1992. Grauspecht-Weibchen *Picus canus* als Helfer an der Bruthöhle. *J. Ornithol.* 133: 443-446.

Sullivan, K. A. 1984a. The advantages of social foraging in Downy Wood-peckers. *Anim. Behav.* 32: 16-22.

— 1984b. Information exploitation by Downy Woodpeckers in mixed-species flocks. *Behaviour* 91: 294-310.

— 1985a. Selective alarm calling by Downy Woodpeckers in mixed-species flocks. *Auk* 102: 184-187.

— 1985b. Vigilance patterns in Downy Woodpeckers. *Anim. Behav.* 33: 328-330.

Sutton, G. M. 1953. Bronzed Woodpecker. *Wilson Bull.* 55: 65-67.

— & Pettingill, O. S., Jr. 1942. Birds of the Gomez Farias region, southwestern Tamaulipas. *Auk* 59: 1-34.

Swierczewski, E. V. & Raikow R. J. 1981. Hindlimb morphology and, phylogeny, and classification of the Piciformes. *Auk* 98: 466-480.

Tanner, J. T. 1942. The Ivory-billed Woodpecker. *Natl Audubon Soc., Res. Rep.* No. 1: 1-111. (Reprinted by Dover Public. Inc., New York, 1966).

— 1964. The decline and present status of the Imperial Woodpecker of Mexico. *Auk* 81: 74-81.

Tarboton, W. R. 1970. Notes on the Bearded Woodpecker. *Bokmakierie* 22: 81-84.

— 1976. Aspects of the biology of *Jynx ruficollis*. *Ostrich* 47: 99-112.

— 1990. Identifying woodpeckers. *Birding in SA* 42: 15-17.

Tate, J., Jr. 1973. Methods and annual sequence of foraging by the sapsucker. *Auk* 90: 840-856.

Taylor, B., & Taylor, C. A. 1988. The status, movements and breeding of some birds in the Kikuyu Escarpment Forest, central Kenya highlands. *Tauraco* 1: 72-89.

Thompson, P. M., *et al.* 1994. Recent notable bird records from Bangladesh. *Forktail* 9: 13-44.

Tikader, B. K. 1984. *Birds of Andaman and Nicobar Islands.* Zool. Survey India, Calcutta. 167 pp.

Tobalske, B. T. 1992. Evaluating habitat suitability using relative abundance and fledging success of Red-naped Sapsuckers. *Condor* 94: 550-553.

Tostain, O., Dujardin, J.-L., Érard, C., & Thiollay, J.-M. 1992. *Oiseaux de Guyane.* Soc. Étud. Orn., Brunoy.

Trail, P. W. 1980. Ecological correlates of social organization in a communally breeding bird, the Acorn Woodpecker, *Melanerpes formicivorus*. *Behav. Ecol. Sociobiol.* 7: 83-92.

Travis, J. 1977. Seasonal foraging in a Downy Woodpecker population. *Condor* 79: 371-375.

Turcek, F. 1954. The ringing of trees by some European woodpeckers. *Ornis Fennica* 31: 33-41.

van den Berk, V. 1990. The rapid movement of a Turkish-ringed Wryneck to Beirut, Lebanon. *OSME Bull.* 24: 15-17.

van Marle, J. G., & Voous K. H. 1988. *The birds of Sumatra.* BOU check-list No. 10. BOU, Tring, Herts.

van Tyne, J. 1926. An unusual flight of Arctic Three-toed Woodpeckers. *Auk* 43: 469-474.

Vaurie, C. 1959a. Systematic notes on Palearctic birds. No. 35 Picidae: The genus *Dendrocopos* (Part 1). *Amer. Mus. Novitates* No. 1946: 1-29.

— 1959b. Systematic notes on Palearctic birds. No. 36 Picidae: The genera *Dendrocopos* (Part 2) and *Picoides*. *Amer. Mus. Novitates* No. 1951: 1-24.

— 1959c. Systematic notes on Palearctic birds. No. 37 Picidae: The subfamilies Jynginae and Picumninae. *Amer. Mus. Novitates* No. 1963: 1-16.

— 1965. *The birds of the Palearctic fauna: Non-passeriformes.* H. F. & G. Witherby, London.

Verheyen, R. 1957. Bijzonderheden over het jongkleed der speckten (Picidae). *Gerfaut* 47: 177-182.

Villard, P., & Beninger, C. W. 1993. Foraging behavior of male Black-backed and Hairy Woodpeckers in a forest burn. *J. Field Ornithol.* 64. 71-76.

Voous, K. H. 1947. On the history of the distribution of the genus *Dendrocopos*. *Limosa* 20: 1-142.

Vuilleumier, F. 1967. Mixed species flocks in Patagonian forests, with re-marks on interspecies flock formation. *Condor* 69: 400-404.

Walker, G. R. 1939. Notes on the birds of Sierra Leone. *Ibis* 81: 401-450.

Wallace, R. A. 1974. Ecological and social implications of sexual dimorphism in five melanerpine woodpeckers. *Condor* 76: 238-248.

Wallschläger, D. 1980. Über das Trommeln des Mittelspechts. *Falke* 27: 310-312.

Walters, J. R. 1990. Red-cockaded Woodpeckers: a 'primitive' cooperative breeder. Pp. 69-101 in P. B. Stacey & W. D. Koenig (eds.), *Cooperative breeding in birds.* Cambridge Univ. Press, Cambridge.

— 1991. Application of ecological principles to the management of endan-gered species: the case of the Red-cockaded Woodpecker. *Ann. Rev. Ecol. Syst.* 22: 505-523.

—, Doerr, P. D., & Carter, J. H., III. 1988. The cooperative breeding system of the Red-cockaded Woodpecker. *Ethology* 78: 275-305.

—, — & — 1992a. Delayed dispersal and reproduction as a life-history tactic in cooperative breeders: fitness calculations from Red-cockaded Wood-peckers. *Amer. Nat.* 139: 623-643.

—, Copeyon, C. K., & Carter, J. H., III. 1992b. Test of the ecological basis of cooperative breeding in Red-cockaded Woodpeckers. *Auk* 109: 90-97.

Wareman, H. W. 1988. Die Zucht des Schläfenfleckspechts (*Melanerpes pucherani*). *Trochilus* 9: 31.

Wesolowski, T., & Tomialojc', L. 1986. The breeding ecology of woodpeckers in a temperate primaeval forest - preliminary data. *Acta Orn.* 22: 1-21.

West, J. D., & Speirs, J. M. 1959. The 1956-57 invasion of Three-toed Woodpeckers. *Wilson Bull.* 71: 348-352.

Wetmore, A. 1968. The birds of the republic of Panamá. Part 2. Columbidae (Pigeons) to Picidae (Woodpeckers). *Smithsonian Misc. Coll.* 150 (2): 1-605.

— 1926. Observations on the birds of Argentina, Paraguay, Uraquay and Chile. *Bull. U.S. Natl. Mus.* 133: 1-448.

Whistler, H. 1930. The birds of the Rawal Pindi District, N. W. India. *Ibis* 12/6: 247-279.

— & Kinnear, N. B. 1949. *Popular handbook of Indian birds.* 4th ed. Gurney & Jackson, London.

White, C.M.N., & Bruce, M.D. 1986. *The birds of Wallacea.* BOU checklist No.7. BOU, Tring, Herts.

Wickler, W. 1978. A special constraint on the evolution of composite signals. *Z. Tierpsychol.* 48: 345-348.

Wiedenfeld, D. A., Schulenberg, T. S., & Robbins, M. B. 1985. Birds of a tropical deciduous forest in extreme northwestern Peru. *Ornithol. Monogr.* 36: 305-316.

Wiktander, U., Nilsson, I. N., Nilsson, S. G., Olsson, O., Pettersson, S., & Stagen, A. 1992. Occurrence of the Lesser Spotted Woodpecker *Dendrocopos minor* in relation to area of deciduous forest. *Ornis Fennica* 69: 113-118.

Willard, D. E., Foster, M.S., Barrowclough, G. F., Dickerman, R. W., Cannell, P. F., Coats, S. L., Cracraft, J. L., & O'Neill, J. P. 1991. The birds of Cerro de la Neblina, Territorio Federal Amazonas, Venezuela. *Fieldiana: Zoology* 65: 1-80.

Williams, J. B. 1975. Habitat utilization by four species of woodpeckers in a central Illinois woodland. *Am. Midl. Natur.* 93: 354-367.

— 1980. Foraging by Yellow-bellied Sapsucker in Central Illinois during spring migration. *Wilson Bull.* 92: 519-523.

— & Batzli, G. O. 1979a. Interference competition and niche shifts in the bark-foraging guild in central Illinois. *Wilson Bull.* 91: 400-411.

— & — 1979b. Competition among bark-foraging birds in central Illinois: Experimental evidence. *Condor* 81: 122-132.

Willimont, L. A., Jackson J. A, & Jackson B. J. S. 1991. Classical polyandry in the West Indian Woodpecker on Abaco, Bahamas. *Wilson Bull.* 103: 124-125.

Willson, M. F. 1970. Foraging behavior of some winter birds of deciduous woods. *Condor* 72: 169-174.

Winkler, H. 1968. Das Schmiedeverhalten des Blutspechtes (*Dendrocopos syriacus*). *Egretta* 10 (2): 1-8.

— 1971. Die artliche Isolation des Blutspechts *Picoides (Dendrocopos) syriacus*. *Egretta* 14: 1-10.

— 1972a. Beobachtungen an Kleinspechten. *Egretta* 14: 21-24.

— 1972b. Beiträge zur Biologie des Blutspechtes. Das nicht-reproduktive Verhalten. *Z. Tierpsychol.* 31: 300-325.

— 1973. Nahrungserwerb und Konkurrenz des Blutspechts, *Picoides (Dendrocopos) syriacus*. *Oecologia* 12: 193-208.

— 1979a. Foraging ecology of Strickland's Woodpecker in Arizona. *Wilson Bull.* 91: 244-254.

— 1979b. Bemerkungen zum Maurenspecht, *Picoides major numidus*. *J. Ornithol.* 120: 290-298.

—, Christie, D. A., & Nurney, D. 1994. The colourful world of woodpeckers: an Oriental perspective. *OBC Bull.* No. 19: 30-33.

— & Leisler, B. 1985. Morphological aspects of habitat selection in birds. Pp. 415-434 in M. L. Cody (ed.), *Habitat selection in birds.* Academic Press, New York.

—, Newton, A., & Newton, S. in press. On the ecology and behaviour of the Arabian Woodpecker *Picoides dorae*. *Sandgrouse*.

— & Short, L. L. 1978. A comparative analysis of acoustical signals in Pied Woodpeckers (Aves, Picoides). *Bull. Amer. Mus. Nat. Hist.* 160: 1-109.

Witt, K. 1988. Anhaltend extreme Brutdichte des Buntspechts (*Dendrocopos major*) und bevorzugte Brutbaumwahl in einem Berliner Mischwaldpark. *Vogelwelt* 109: 114-118.

Wood, B. 1989. Biometrics, iris, and bill coloration, and moult of Somali forest birds. *Bull. Br. Ornithol. Club* 109: 11-22.

Yamagami, N. 1992. An observation of the Japanese Pygmy Woodpecker *Dendrocopos kizuki* and their helper. *Strix* 11: 336-338.

Yom-Tov, Y., & Ar, A. 1993. Incubation and fledging durations of woodpeck-ers. *Condor* 95: 282-287.

Zimmer, J. T. 1942. Studies of Peruvian birds. No. XL. Notes on the genus *Veniliornis*. *Amer. Mus. Novitates*. No. 1159: 1-12.

Zusi, R. L., & Marshall, J. T. 1970. A comparison of Asiatic and North American Sapsuckers. *Nat. Hist. Bull. Siam Soc.* 23: 395-407.

INDEX OF SCIENTIFIC AND ENGLISH NAMES

Species are listed by their English vernacular name (e.g. Acorn Woodpecker), together with alternative names where relevant, and by their scientific specific name, followed by the generic name as used in this book (e.g. *formicivorus, Melanerpes*); in addition, subspecies are listed by their scientific name, followed by the species name (e.g. *albeolus, Melanerpes formicivorus*). Genera are given separately; since, for certain species, a number of authorities use different generic names (e.g. '*Centurus*'), these are also listed with a reference to the genus where they have been placed in this work.

Numbers in italic type refer to the main systematic entry and those in bold type to plate numbers.